RESEARCH
for
MARKETING
DECISIONS

PRENTICE-HALL INTERNATIONAL SERIES IN MANAGEMENT

4th edition

RESEARCH
for
MARKETING
DECISIONS

PAUL E. GREEN

University of Pennsylvania

DONALD S. TULL

University of Oregon

PRENTICE-HALL, INC., ENGLEWOOD CLIFFS, NEW JERSEY 07632

Library of Congress Cataloging in Publication Data

GREEN, PAUL E (date)
  Research for marketing decisions.

  (Prentice-Hall international series in management)
  Includes bibliographical references and index.
  1. Marketing research. I. Tull, Donald S.,
joint author. II. Title.
HF5415.2.G68 1978   658.8′3   77–24414
ISBN   0–13–774158–8

Printed in the United States of America

10   9   8

Prentice-Hall International, Inc., *London*
Prentice-Hall of Australia Pty. Limited, *Sydney*
Prentice-Hall of Canada, Ltd., *Toronto*
Prentice-Hall of India Private Limited, *New Delhi*
Prentice-Hall of Japan, Inc., *Tokyo*
Prentice-Hall of Southeast Asia Pte. Ltd., *Singapore*
Whitehall Books Limited, *Wellington, New Zealand*

Contents

3

II

4

5

6

7

Nonprobability sampling procedures. Probability-sampling designs.
The decision concerning what size sample to take.
Estimating sample size by traditional methods.
The Bayesian approach to sample-size determination.
Evaluation of the traditional and Bayesian approaches.
Summary. Assignment material.

8

Introduction. General comments on data tabulation.
A case study. The management problem. The research design.
Marginal tabulations. Cross tabulations.
Analysis of remaining responses. Recapitulation.
Implications of study. Summary. Assignment material.

III

9

Introduction. More on cross tabulation. Chi-square tests.
Indexes of agreement. An overview of multivariate procedures.
Summary. Assignment material.

10

Introduction. Some basic concepts. Multiple and partial regression.
Computerized regression. Multicollinearity and related problems.
Summary. Assignment material.

11

Introduction. The nature of experimentation. Multiple classifications.
Computer routines for the analysis of variance and covariance.
Interpreting experimental results.
Field experimentation in marketing.
Summary. Assignment material.

IV

ADVANCED TECHNIQUES IN ANALYZING
ASSOCIATIVE DATA

12

**Other Techniques
for Analyzing Criterion-Predictor Association**

Introduction. Two-group discriminant analysis.
Computerized two-group analysis. Multiple discriminant analysis.
Automatic interaction detection.
Other techniques for criterion-predictor association.
Summary. Assignment material.

13

Factor Analysis and Clustering Methods

Introduction. Basic concepts of factor analysis.
Principal components analysis. Computerized factor analysis.
Other topics in factor analysis. Basic concepts of cluster analysis.
Applications of cluster analysis. Summary. Assignment material.

14

Multidimensional Scaling and Conjoint Analysis

Introduction. MDS fundamentals. The development of MDS.
Types of MDS models. Marketing applications of MDS.
Potential applications. Fundamentals of conjoint analysis.
Analyzing the data. Other aspects of conjoint analysis.
Applications of conjoint analysis. Summary. Assignment material.

V

SELECTED ACTIVITIES IN MARKETING RESEARCH

15

Forecasting Procedures in Marketing Research

Introduction.
The nature of forecasting. Approaches to forecasting sales.
Forecasting techniques. Forecasting market share.
Probability forecasting and cost versus value of information.
Summary. Assignment material.

16

Introduction. Market strategy formulation.
Brand and service positioning. Market segmentation.
Positioning and segmentation combinations—a beer company
  example.
Segment-congruence analysis. Summary. Assignment material.

17

Introduction. New-product development and testing.
Testing components of the marketing mix.
Large-scale market simulators. Summary. Assignment material.

Appendix A

Table A-1 Cumulative normal distribution—values of probability
Table A-2 Upper percentiles of the t distribution
Table A-3 Percentiles of the χ^2 distribution
Table A-4 Percentiles of the F distribution
Table A-5 Short table of random numbers
Table A-6 Short table of random normal deviates

Appendix B

Appendix C

Preface

In the original (1966) edition of this book, our Preface contained the following comments:

Any field which is subject to systematic inquiry can be characterized by: (a) *content*—what the researcher attempts to study; (b) *method*—the conceptual basis or strategy of inquiry; and (c) *techniques*—the procedures or tactics by which the strategy is implemented.

The motivation for this book has arisen from our feeling that marketing research has now reached a stage of development where traditional methods and techniques require synthesis and extension. We believe this book is novel in two major respects.

With respect to method, the unifying concept of this book is that *marketing research is a cost-incurring activity whose output is information of potential value for management decision.* With the advent of modern statistical decision theory—the so-called Bayesian approach—a framework now exists for making this general concept operational. . . .

With respect to technique, this book again departs from tradition in terms of the relatively large coverage given to newer research procedures. . . . We hope that discussion of these techniques— which are either omitted entirely or given more limited description in most current marketing research texts—will help close the gap between textbook coverage and the content of contemporary professional journals devoted to the advancement of research technique in marketing.

This, the fourth edition of the book, may be appropriately called the *pedagogical* edition. While we have updated the content of the preceding edition, the most marked changes have entailed a reduction in the book's methodological scope and technical level. In brief, we have tried to respond to the wishes of users of previous editions by providing a considerably simpler and more streamlined version.

The book still emphasizes the place of modern analytical tools, such as decision theory and multivariate analysis, in the design and conduct of marketing research. Moreover, various packaged computer programs for analyzing data are described and their results interpreted in the context of illustrative marketing problems. However, the current edition presents this material from a more pragmatic and user-oriented (rather than practitioner-oriented) viewpoint.

Part I of the book is mainly concerned with problem formulation and marketing decision making. Here we discuss the basic concepts of decision models, including the role of Bayesian analysis in assessing the value versus cost of marketing research information. We look at marketing problems first from the standpoint of the marketing executive and then from the perspective of the researcher. Next we show how the researcher's view of the problem is translated into a research design.

Part II is directed toward implementation of the research design through the collection of data. We discuss the preparation of questionnaires, procedures for gathering marketing information, the fundamentals of scaling techniques, and respondent sampling methods.

Part III is devoted to the analysis of collected data via the better-known techniques of cross tabulation, chi square, regression, and the analysis of variance and covariance. Each procedure, as it is introduced, is described conceptually and applied numerically to a data set that is small enough to enable the reader to work through the calculations easily and quickly.

Part IV is concerned with the more advanced tools of data analysis—discriminant analysis, automatic interaction detection, factor analysis, clustering methods, multidimensional scaling techniques, and conjoint analysis. However, again we try to present this material as simply as possible, consistent with its higher technical level.

Part V discusses selected activities in marketing research—sales and cost forecasting, market segmentation studies, and tools for designing new marketing strategies. A number of actual case studies, drawn from various consulting experiences, are used to show how the multivariate methods of Parts III and IV can be applied to marketing problems.

Appendix A provides the basic statistical tables used in the text. Appendix B includes a selection of cases, of varying length and technical level, for classroom use at the discretion of the instructor. Appendix C presents a rather extensive bibliography on marketing applications of scaling and multivariate techniques.

In conclusion, the fourth edition maintains our interest in providing the student with a modern discussion of marketing research. Moreover, we feel that the present edition does this without undue concentration on the more esoteric aspects of research methodology.

Many people helped shape the content and style of the present edition. Thorough critiques of the third edition were provided by Professors David L. Appel, University of Notre Dame; Gert Assmus, Dartmouth College; Gary T. Ford, University of Maryland; Thomas A. Klein, University of Toledo; Donald G. Morrison, Columbia University; and Venkataraman Srinivasan, Stanford University. Dr. Seymour Banks, Vice President of Leo Burnett U.S.A., also gave us some helpful comments on the preceding edition.

Extensive and insightful reviews of the present edition were provided by Professors Ford and Morrison and, in addition, by Professor Gerald S. Albaum, University of Oregon. Professor Ronald E. Frank, University of Pennsylvania, also provided useful comments on selected chapters of the manuscript.

Manuscript typing was expertly carried out by Lynda Kenny, Joan Leary, and Frances Pickett. Michael Devita handled the computer runs with his customary skill and aplomb. The marketing and production staff of Prentice-Hall cooperated in ways too numerous to catalog.

To all of these benefactors we extend our sincere thanks and appreciation. We hope that the final product reflects well on the efforts of the many talented people who helped us produce it.

PAUL E. GREEN

DONALD S. TULL

Problem
Formulation

Marketing Research— 1
Content and Strategy

INTRODUCTION

Marketing is a restless, changing, dynamic field. Since 1920 many important and dramatic changes have taken place in marketing. Thousands of new products, including those of entire new industries such as plastics and electronics, have appeared on the market. Two completely new national communication media have been introduced and supported entirely by marketing expenditures. The corporate chain form of organization, the widespread application of the self-service principle, automatic vending, and computerized checkout systems are but a few of the developments that have brought about sweeping changes in marketing methods. During this same period the proportion of the labor force engaged in marketing has increased substantially, rising from slightly less than 10% in 1920 to over 22% in 1975.[1]

Concomitant with these changes has been the gradual but pronounced shift in orientation of firms from production to marketing. The marketing executive has assumed a wider range of responsibilities that have grown in complexity. An ever-increasing premium has been placed on making sound marketing decisions.

In response to this requirement a formalized means of acquiring information to assist in the making of marketing decisions has emerged. This means is *marketing research*, the subject of this book.

In this chapter we describe the nature of marketing research and its relation to decision making. Emphasis is placed throughout on the general

---

[1]The percentage of the labor force engaged in distribution for each decade from 1870 through 1950 is given in Harold Barger, *Distribution's Place in the American Economy Since 1869* (Princeton, N.J.: Princeton University Press, 1955), p. 8. A comparable percentage for 1975 has been developed from Bureau of Labor Statistics data.

problem of rational decision making under conditions of uncertainty and on the informational needs of the marketing executive. Special attention is given to the concept of the value of information in reducing the costs of uncertainty associated with managerial decision making.

In the first section we deal with the nature and content of marketing research. We then examine the characteristics of marketing management from the standpoints of the components of decisions and the generic types of decisions that have to be made. Problem-situation models are introduced and the meaning of the term "information" is examined.

The formulation of problems in terms of the objectives desired, the environment in which the problem exists, and the alternative actions under study can be viewed from the standpoint of either the manager or the researcher. Although both groups have the common goal of ensuring that sound decisions are made, organization and communication constraints cast each in a different role. Problem formulation is examined in turn from the viewpoint of each group.

In order to develop satisfactorily the concept of the value of information, we introduce the reader to some of the formal notions of decision theory. We cover the more common choice-criterion models and such topics as personalistic probability, expected value, and introductory comments on the Bayesian approach to decision making under uncertainty.

THE CONTENT OF MARKETING RESEARCH

What Is Marketing Research?

Research connotes a systematic and objective investigation of a subject or problem in order to discover relevant information or principles. It can be considered to be primarily "fundamental" or primarily "applied" in nature. *Fundamental research*, frequently called *basic* or *pure research*, seeks to extend the boundaries of knowledge in a given area with no necessary immediate application to existing problems; an example is the development of an algebra of logic by George Boole and others. *Applied research* attempts to use existing knowledge as an aid to the solution of some given problem or set of problems: for example, the use of Boolean algebra, some one hundred years after it was developed, as the foundation for the logical design of electronic digital computers.

In a problem-solving context the emphasis is on applied research. For the purposes of this book, therefore, the following definition is a useful one:

> *Marketing research* is the systematic and objective search for and analysis of information relevant to the identification and solution of any problem in the field of marketing.

Some comments are in order concerning this definition. Marketing research is a *systematic* search for and analysis of information. Careful planning through all stages of the research is a necessity. Starting with a clear and concise statement of the problem to be researched, good research practice requires that the information sought, the methods to be used in obtaining it, and the analytical techniques to be employed be systematically and carefully laid out in advance if at all possible.

Objectivity in research is all-important. Marketing research has sometimes been defined as "the application of scientific method to marketing." The heart of scientific method is the objective gathering and analysis of information. Research projects that are carried out for the purpose of "proving" that a prior opinion is correct are, at best, a waste of time and resources; if research is intentionally slanted to arrive at predetermined results, a serious breach of professional ethics is involved.

It will be noted that the definition adopted contains no reference to a "thorough" search for and analysis of information. When the nature of the problem requires it, thoroughness is, of course, desirable. For many marketing problems, however, the time and money spent to obtain and analyze thoroughly the information relevant to their solutions would be completely out of proportion to the benefits gained. The thoroughness with which the research is conducted, therefore, depends upon the nature of the problem.

Although the definition given above is useful, it is by no means the only definition of marketing research, nor is it necessarily the most useful one for other purposes. The management of a company, for example, would be well advised to choose a less general and more detailed statement to define the specific functions of its marketing research department.

Historical Development of Marketing Research

An inevitable result of the specialization of production and the growth of companies has been the separation of management and the markets that their companies serve. Paul Revere, as a highly skilled silversmith, dealt directly with his customers. Most of the tankards, platters, teapots, and other silver items he produced were custom-made. He was immediately and directly aware of his customers' needs and desires and their reactions to his products and the prices that he charged.

By contrast, the president of Revere Copper and Brass, Inc., the directly descendant company of Paul Revere's original business, is isolated to a large extent from the thousands of customers his company serves. Instead of being able to obtain information directly as to market requirements and the adequacy of his company's products and marketing programs to meet these requirements, he must rely on other sources.

Marketing research was developed as a specialized function to obtain and analyze information about the market and the company's activities in serving it. In one sense it completes a communication "loop" between the seller and the market. Through advertising and personal selling, an elaborate and formally organized system of communication is established between the seller and the market. Marketing research is a formally organized system of communication from the market back to the seller; in engineering parlance, one of the functions it serves is to act as a "feedback" loop.

MARKETING RESEARCH IN PRACTICE

Marketing research projects are conducted on a broad array of topics by a variety of types and sizes of organizations. They are performed by companies for internal use, by commercial marketing research firms, and by government and nonprofit institutions.

We know a great deal about the nature of marketing research projects conducted and who conducts them as a result of research carried out in this area. As shown in Table 1-1, a sizable amount of research is done to *identify* marketing problems. About two-thirds of the 1,322 respondent companies conduct studies of market potential, market share, and market characteristics, and carry out market analyses to help determine if their sales performance is at the level it should be. More than 60% of all companies also have short-

**Table 1-1   Problem identification research
conducted by and for respondent companies***

	PERCENTAGE OF COMPANIES DOING	PERCENTAGE OF STUDIES DONE BY:		
		Marketing Research Department	*Other Departments*	*Outside Firms*
Market potential	68	81	11	8
Market share	67	81	12	7
Market characteristics	68	84	8	8
Market analysis	65	65	32	3
Short-range forecasting	63	65	33	2
Long-range forecasting	61	64	33	3
Studies of business trends	61	71	25	4

*1,322 companies responded.

Source: Adapted from D. W. Twedt, *A Survey of Marketing Research* (Chicago: American Marketing Association, 1973), p. 41.

and long-range forecasts and studies of business trends prepared to help identify future problems as opportunities in the marketing of their products.

As indicated by Table 1-1, the marketing research department conducts most (about 82%) of the studies of market potential, market share, and market characteristics. The remaining percentage of these types of projects is carried out by other departments within the company (approximately 10%) and outside firms (about 8%). (The outside firms who conduct such studies are commercial marketing research firms, management consultants, and advertising agencies.)

The marketing research department is responsible for about two-thirds of the market analyses, short- and long-range forecasts, and studies of business trends that are performed. Close to one-third of such projects are carried out by other departments inside the company—primarily accounting and finance departments—and a small percentage is conducted by outside firms

Table 1-2 shows the types of research projects carried out to help *solve* marketing problems and by whom they are done. Over one-half of the responding companies do studies in one or more aspects of product, pricing, and advertising and sales research. Nearly one-half the companies do distribution research as well.

The extent to which the marketing research department is responsible for conducting problem-solving research projects varies considerably by problem area. As shown in Table 1-2, whereas three-fourths of all new product-acceptance and competitive-product studies are done by the company's marketing research department, the department is involved in only about one-fourth of sales-compensation studies. There are some areas of problem-solving research in marketing that seem naturally to fall to other departments or outside agencies—for example, certain types of advertising research (often done by the company's advertising department or its advertising agency) and research involving costs and quotas (frequently conducted by the accounting department).

Government agencies, trade associations, trade periodicals, and colleges and universities are other organizations that do marketing research. Such agencies of the federal government as the Federal Trade Commission, the Anti-Trust Division of the Department of Justice, the Food and Drug Administration, and the Interstate Commerce Commission carry out studies in specific marketing problems from time to time. Trade associations and trade periodicals often collect and disseminate marketing research data on the industries with which they are concerned. Bureaus of business and economic research at universities also regularly conduct research projects of interest to marketers, as do chambers of commerce, brokerage houses, railroads, airlines, and such reporting services as Standard and Poor's, Moody's, and Dun and Bradstreet.

Table 1-2   **Problem-solving research**
              conducted by and for respondent companies*

	PERCENTAGE OF COMPANIES DOING	PERCENTAGE OF STUDIES DONE BY:		
		Marketing Research Department	Other Departments	Outside Firms
Product research				
Competitive-product studies	63	75	13	12
New-product acceptance and potential	64	75	16	9
Testing existing products	57	57	32	11
Product-mix studies	44	47	35	18
Packaging research	51	67	30	3
Pricing research	56	55	42	3
Advertising and sales research				
Establishment of order, quotas, territories	57	39	59	2
Studies of advertising effectiveness	49	48	13	39
Sales-compensation studies	45	24	72	4
Promotional studies of premiums, deals, etc.	39	56	30	14
Copy research	37	41	15	44
Media research	44	34	21	45
Distribution research				
Distribution-channel studies	48	57	37	6
Plant and warehouse location studies	47	37	57	6

*1,322 companies responded.

Source: Adapted from D. W. Twedt, *A Survey of Marketing Research* (Chicago: American Marketing Association, 1973), p. 41.

The largest supplier of secondary data for use in marketing studies is, of course, the federal government. This and other sources of secondary data are discussed in Chapter 3.

THE CHARACTERISTICS OF MARKETING MANAGEMENT

A primary characteristic of management is *decision making*. Decisions and decision making underlie and permeate the management process. Since the terms "decision making" and "managing" are so closely interwoven, we shall use them as though they were synonymous.

In considering the characteristics of marketing management, it is appropriate that we examine the decision-making process. We shall first be concerned with the types of decisions to be made. We shall then consider the role of problem-situation models in decision making and the meaning of the term "information."

Types of Management Decisions

Six types of management decisions may be usefully distinguished:

1. *Deciding what the problems are:* recognizing and defining the problems currently faced by the organization.
2. *Selecting the immediate problem for solution:* determining priorities according to the importance of the problems and the timing of their solution.
3. *Solving the problem selected:* finding alternative solutions, evaluating the consequences of each, and selecting the most favorable one.
4. *Implementing the solution:* making the decisions necessary to carry out the solution decided upon.
5. *Modifying the original solution based upon observation of results:* deciding whether, when, and how original solutions should be modified after experiencing results.
6. *Establishing policy:* deciding which problems occur often enough and are sufficiently similar to warrant a policy decision; making the policy decision.

The primary activity of marketing management is making such decisions with regard to marketing problems. Problems in the areas of product design, price, distribution, and promotion must be identified; the more important and pressing ones selected for solution; the best possible solution reached, based on the information available; the solution implemented; the solution modified when additional information obtained from experiencing results so dictates; and, where required, policy established to act as a ready-made solution for a recurrence of the problem.

Problem-Situation Models and Decision Making

Suppose that a marketing manager is considering increasing the advertising appropriation for one of the company's products. As long as one of the company's objectives is to increase profits, the decision to increase the appropriation will be at least partially dependent upon the amount of net additional sales generated. Net additional sales will in turn depend upon such factors as the nature of the campaign, the advertising–sales response relationship, and the actions of competitors.

A necessary part of the process of this decision—or of any one of the generalized types of decisions discussed in the preceding section—is the formulation of a problem-situation model. The model may take many forms, ranging from implicit models that the decision maker may not even be aware of using to elaborate mathematical models solved with the aid of a computer. Regardless of form, one or more models *must* be used each time a decision is made.

What, then, is a *model*? Although the word has many connotations, some of which are taken up in Chapter 2, we shall use it here to refer to a conceptual scheme that specifies a measure of the outcome(s) to be achieved, the relevant variables, and their functional relationship to the outcome(s).

We may define a problem-situation model in symbolic form as follows[2]:

$$U = f(A_i, S_j)$$

where U = the measure of the outcomes, the payoff, of each alternative course of action

A_i = the variables that are under the control of the decision maker—i.e., the variables that define the alternative courses of action

S_j = the environmental factors, either variables or constants, over which the decision maker has no control (alternative descriptions of the environmental factors comprise the *states of nature* of the problem)

f = the functional relationship between the dependent variable U and the independent variables (and constants) A_i and S_j

To return to our example of the decision concerning increasing the advertising appropriation, what kind of a problem-situation model might be appropriate? We have already indicated that the nature of the decision-making process requires that some model or models be used. In this case the executive may have a set of intuitive, nonformalized judgments, which might be expressed somewhat as follows: "Assuming that nothing else changes, as advertising for this product is increased, sales will increase in the form of a 'flat S' curve. I think we are on the lower end of the curve."

If pressed further, the executive might agree that his conception of the sales–advertising relationship could be represented by a graph. Some specification of the level of the other controllable variables and of the environmental variables would have to be made; let us assume that they are all held at their present levels. The graph would be of the general nature of Figure 1-1, with present sales and advertising designated as s and a, respectively.

[2]This definition of a problem-situation model is based on that given in R. L. Ackoff, Shiv Gupta, and J. S. Minas, *Scientific Method: Optimizing Applied Research Decisions* (New York: John Wiley & Sons, Inc., 1962).

Figure 1-1   Model of sales-advertising relationship

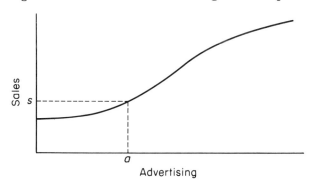

Or, an analysis of the sales–advertising relationship in the past might indicate that it takes the form of a Gompertz-type (S-shaped) curve such that the equation

$$\log Y = \log k + (\log G)B^p$$

where Y is sales response, p is amount of advertising, and k, G, and B are constants, provides a reasonably good predictive equation over the range of advertising of interest to the decision maker.

Several points concerning this example are worth noting. First, we have been dealing with *explicit* forms of a model. It should be clearly understood, however, that if the conceptualization of a specific problem by the decision maker remains *implicit*, it is no less a model. It may be, in fact, that an explicit model is not worth the cost of formulation.

The second point concerns the form in which explicit models may be expressed. In our example, the same basic explicit model was described by a verbal statement, a graph, and an equation. Models described verbally are known simply as *verbal models*. Those that are expressed as a graph or diagram are known as *diagrammatic models*. Models represented in equational form are called *symbolic models*. All explicit models may be described in one or more of these forms.

A third point relates to the degree of simplification of models. Models are necessarily simplifications and abstractions to some degree of the reality of the problem situation. It is not possible to consider either all the variables or all their possible interactions in the illustrative problem just considered— or, for that matter, in any marketing problem. Rather, the decision maker attempts to abstract the important elements of the problem situation and represent them so that they are simple enough to be understood and manipulated, yet realistic enough to portray the *essentials* of the situation.

This point leads in turn to an examination of the manner in which problem-situation models are used. The general form of the model, $U = f(A_i, S_j)$, in theory permits predictions of U for continuous values (within appropriate limits) for each of the variables in the A and S subsets. As a practical matter, however, neither the nature of the functional relationships nor the value of some of the environmental variables can usually be determined well enough to make such predictions worthwhile. Often, a more realistic and viable way of using a problem-situation model is to structure the problem into a relatively small number of discrete *courses of action* and *states of nature*. That is, we designate the courses of action we want to consider by specifying two or more levels of one or more of the controllable subset of variables (A) while holding the others constant. Similarly, we designate the states of nature under which outcomes are to be predicted by specifying two or more levels of one or more of the environmental (S) subset of variables. The problem-situation model is then applied to predict the outcome for each action–state pair.

A simplified application to an advertising problem, similar to the one described above, will help to illustrate this procedure. Suppose that a change in the promotional program for a product is being considered which would allocate a part of the present media expenditures to the distribution of samples of the product to consumers. To make such an action worthwhile a net increase in sales would have to result. Whether or not additional sales *will* result will depend upon how well the consumers who receive the samples like the product, the possible loss of sales from the reduction in media expenditures, competitor actions, and other factors.

Assume that the problem has been structured into the two courses of action and two states of nature shown in Table 1-3. Note that the two courses of action—adopting the new promotional program or retaining the present one—are concerned with two controllable variables: amount of advertising expenditure and adding a new promotional medium. No change is contemplated in any of the other controllable variables.

Table 1-3   Promotional-program illustration

Action	S_1: *New Promotional Program Superior*	S_2: *Old Promotional Program Superior*
A_1: adopt new	$U_{11} = f(A_1, S_1) = 15$	$U_{12} = f(A_1, S_2) = -7$
A_2: retain old	$U_{21} = f(A_2, S_1) = -2$	$U_{22} = f(A_2, S_2) = 4$

The two states of nature shown in Table 1-3 reflect different environmental conditions. In state S_1 the environment is such that consumer purchases will increase more as a result of the sampling than they decrease as a result of the reduction in advertising expenditures. The reverse is true in state S_2. Other environmental variables may be assumed to be the same between the two states.

Although Table 1-3 illustrates the application of the problem-situation model, it immediately raises another question: How does one go about selecting a course of action without knowing which state of nature is the true state? If the new promotional program in our example is adopted, there is a potential gain of 15 units *if* S_1 is the true state and a loss of 7 units if it is not. Similarly, if the old program is retained, a loss of 2 units will result *if* S_1 is the true state and a gain of 4 units if it is not.

The answer to the question of which alternative to choose, given the conditional payoffs of each, lies in the choice criterion adopted. *Choice-criterion models* have been developed by decision theorists to illustrate this problem. We consider several such models in a later section of this chapter.

A further comment about models is in order. We have already noted that they may be either implicit or explicit. We have also observed that sometimes the cost of explicating an implicit model is greater than the benefit received. When the cost of formulation is justifiable, however, explicit models are preferable for several reasons. The most important of these are the following:

1. *Clarification.* Explication usually results in the clarification of relationships and interactions. The need for more rigorous definitions of key variables often becomes apparent.
2. *Objectivity.* As a correlative of clarification, the process of explicating the model often discloses rationalizations and unfounded opinions that had not been recognized as such before.
3. *Communication.* When alternative implicit models of the same problem situation are held by different people, discussion frequently results without common points of reference, and communication problems arise. Explication reduces these problems.
4. *Improvement of models.* Explicit models can be tested by different persons and in differing situations to see if the results are reproducible. The degree of adaptability and range of applicability can thus be extended.

Having considered problem-situation models and introduced the concept of choice-criterion models, we will now specify more completely what is meant by the term "information."

Information and Decision Making

Information as used here refers to *recorded experience that is useful for decision making.* In other words, it consists of that recorded experience which will reduce the level of uncertainty in making a decision.

This definition clearly makes the existence of information dependent upon the decision maker and the context of the decision. For example, the half-life of carbon 14 may be information to the archeologist who is attempting to date some recently unearthed artifacts; to the executive who is concerned with introducing a new consumer product it can hardly be classified as such.

The model that is being used for a specific problem situation defines both the information required for solution and the way in which it will be interpreted. An example will help to illustrate this point.

Consider the advertising-effects model diagrammed in Figure 1-2.[3]

**Figure 1-2   Hierarchy of effects of advertising model
and related research**

This model represents a view that has been widely held in advertising circles for many years. It conceptualizes the psychological processes the typical consumer is believed to undergo after exposure to advertising. The research techniques related to each step in the progression indicate the kinds of information that can be obtained to provide a measure of advertising "effectiveness."

If this model is correct, at least two important implications result. First, measures at any one of the intermediate stages should show a high

[3] Adapted from K. S. Palda, "The Hypothesis of Hierarchy of Effects: A Partial Evaluation," *Journal of Marketing Research*, 2 (February, 1966), 13–24, and R. C. Lavidge and G. A. Steiner, "A Model for Predictive Measurements of Advertising Effectiveness," *Journal of Marketing*, 25 (October, 1961), 59–62.

correlation with sales. This permits dispensing with the difficult and costly research that attempts to measure directly the sales effects of advertising. Second, a time lapse is implied, suggesting that there is a lagged effect of advertising on sales. Both of these implications are of obvious importance in decisions as to what kinds of data to obtain and how to interpret them.

This example makes clear that models and information for problem solving are closely interrelated. It also illustrates some of the informational needs that arise in formulating and using decision models.

It is apparent that information can never be available to the extent that the decision maker would desire if no costs were involved. Since obtaining information is a cost-incurring activity, rational decision making necessarily involves consideration of the *value* of information. The *amount* of information is important only as it affects the value. The notion of the value of information is introduced later in this chapter and discussed more fully in Chapter 2.

DECISIONS UNDER UNCERTAINTY— PROBLEM FORMULATION FROM THE MANAGER'S VIEWPOINT

We now turn to informational needs as viewed by the marketing executive. These needs will arise in connection with a variety of marketing problems:

1. What media should be employed in next year's advertising campaign?
2. Should the new product, now undergoing test marketing, be commercialized?
3. If I reduce the price of the larger package size, will my total profits be increased?
4. Should my distributors be given exclusive territories in the Southwest?

Questions such as these presuppose opportunities for choice. But the consequences attached to the choices are not known with certainty. As a matter of fact, the marketing executive frequently faces problems in areas where little or no directly related information is available. He often deals with more or less unique events, and the experience gained in dealing with earlier problems must somehow be searched and analyzed for relevance to his current problem situation.

Components of a Problem

As implied earlier, a problem consists of a set of specific components. These components are: (1) the decision maker(s) and his (their) objectives;

(2) the environment or context of the problem; (3) alternative courses of action; (4) a set of consequences that relate to courses of action and the occurrence of events not under the control of the decision maker; and (5) a state of doubt as to which course of action is best.

The Decision Maker and His Objectives

The decision maker may not always be represented by a single individual; marketing decisions may be made by a marketing group of two or more people. Moreover, some members of the group may not agree with the choice made because of differences either in objectives (i.e., valued outcomes) or in their appraisal of the effectiveness of means chosen to achieve the objectives. In other situations an individual may be performing the role of agent for some superior or group of superiors.

In later chapters we shall be describing decision theory and its applications as though only a *single* individual represented the decision maker, knowing full well that a gross simplification is being made. Not that the theory cannot be extended to deal with group decision making; but such an extension would require knowledge of the group's objectives and a means of combining conflicting objectives or conflicting viewpoints as to the preferable course of action. These extensions would carry us far beyond the scope of this book.

The objectives of the decision maker provide motivation for the decision. These objectives, or goals, may range from a desire to maintain or increase company profits and market share to personal goals concerned with maintaining prestige and a desire to advance in the corporation. However, most of the objectives with which we shall deal involve only monetary considerations (e.g., net profits, cash flow, return on investment) and, hence, represent another simplification of the real world.

The decision maker's objectives may also be characterized by their hierarchical nature at any given moment and their evolution over time. For example, an increase in the firm's profits may come about through an increase in the firm's sales, which, in turn, may be accomplished by the firm's sales personnel contacting a greater number of new accounts per month. The goal for the salesperson may be to increase sales contacts 10% over those made in some base period, but this represents a subgoal, consistent, it is hoped, with a higher-level objective. The decision theorist also faces the problem of estimating changes in objectives over time. Current value theory generally assumes that objectives remain stable over the relevant decision period, again a simplifying assumption.

Finally, we shall be assuming that the decision maker really knows what his objectives are and that he can communicate these thoughts to the market researcher. In practice, such is often not the case. One of the major jobs of the research practitioner is to attempt to draw out these objectives and to ascertain the relevance of the proposed research to the decision maker's goals and state of information.

Environment of the Problem

Every problem exists within a context of the characteristics of the company and of the market—consumer tastes and preferences, level of income and rate of growth in the market areas, the degree of competition and competitor action and reaction, and the type and extent of governmental regulation. These environmental factors may individually and collectively affect the outcome of the decision made. The researcher must assist the manager in identifying these relevant environmental factors.

Consider the problem of deciding whether to introduce a new consumer product. Some of the environmental factors that could affect the decision are as follows:

- The types of consumers that comprise the potential market.
- The size and location of the market.
- The prospects for growth or contraction of the market over the planning period.
- The buying habits of consumers.
- The current competition for the product.
- The likelihood and timing of entry of new competitive products.
- The current and prospective competitive position with respect to price, quality, and reputation.
- The marketing and manufacturing capabilities of the company.
- The situation with respect to patents, trademarks, and royalties.
- The situation with respect to codes, trade agreements, taxes, and tariffs.

Although this listing is by no means exhaustive, it illustrates some of the more important environmental factors that could influence the outcome of the decision and so must be considered in the problem statement. Each problem has a comparable set of environmental factors to be considered.

Alternative Courses of Action

A *course of action* is a specification of some behavioral sequence, such as the construction of a new warehouse, the adoption of a new package design, or the introduction of a new product. All courses of action involve, either implicitly or explicitly, the element of time. For example, "Construct a warehouse, starting next week" is a different course of action from "Construct a warehouse, starting next year." A course of action that indicates

"Do nothing new" is just as much a course of action as one denoting a change from the status quo.

Actions, of course, can be taken only in the present. A decision to *stipulate* a program of action becomes a commitment, made in the present, to follow some behavioral pattern in the future. The implementation of this course of action may well extend over time as, for example, a program involving the construction of a new plant. Courses of action may thus range in complexity from a single act to be implemented immediately to a large set of related acts proceeding either in parallel or sequentially over time. The time interval, which becomes a part of the course of action, may be highly important since both the costs of implementation and the probabilities of alternative outcomes will typically vary as a function of time. Forecast error usually increases as a function of time. Frequently, however, implementation of some action may be delayed pending the receipt of better information with relatively little cost associated with this delay.

Two additional points about courses of action will be mentioned briefly here and then developed more fully in later chapters. First, courses of action can be spelled out in greater or lesser degree, depending upon the problem under consideration. For some purposes it may be sufficient merely to state the course of action: "Add two new salespeople in the Chicago district starting next month." In other instances a more detailed specification (regarding the type of salespeople to be hired in terms of previous experience, education, product familiarity, etc.) may be required. Second, courses of action may include *decision rules*, that is, various conditional statements in the program of action. For example, a course of action may be: "Start designing a new plant; if sales from the existing plant exceed 100,000 units by the end of next year, start new plant construction; if not, reconsider the decision to build a new plant." We shall call this type of course of action a *contingency plan*, since its implementation is dependent upon some unknown event at the time of stipulation. Although we have a *recipe* for reacting to each possible event, we do not know *which* act will be implemented until one of the possible events occurs.

The Consequences of Alternative Courses of Action

The world of uncertainty is a common world for the marketer. When a marketer chooses a course of action, he can rarely be certain of the consequences since the choice is usually based on incomplete information about the various factors that influence the decision's outcome. A primary job is thus to list the possible outcomes of various courses of action. But these outcomes will depend upon various environmental factors. For example, suppose that a manufacturer of industrial belting is interested in increasing the tensile strength of this product. Presumably, higher production costs will be incurred in effecting this increase in strength. The decision to modify the product will be dependent upon additional sales anticipated through marketing a stronger product. The additional sales will obviously depend upon how customers react to the modification, the actions that competitors take, and so on.

As discussed earlier, the phrase "state of nature" is frequently used to refer to alternative descriptions of the decision maker's environment. Moreover, as was shown in Table 1-3, each action–state pair leads to a set of consequences that can ultimately be expressed as a payoff.

As before, the term "consequence" is relative. In the promotional-program example, the immediate consequence or outcome may represent sales of so many physical units. The final payoff of the decision maker, however, may represent the cash flow generated by these additional sales. As such, it would include assumptions about price, production costs, and the time span and pattern of cash inflows and outflows. If the decision maker were also to treat these assumptions as states of nature, it is clear that an expansion of Table 1-3 would be required.

It should now be apparent that the choice of courses of action, states of nature, and the details of the consequences of combining each course of action with each state of nature depend upon the decision maker's model of the problem. Expansion of each class of variables can take place either *intensively* (specifying each variable in greater detail) or *extensively* (increasing the number of courses of action, states of nature, etc.). The primary notion to keep in mind is that all these entities are *conceptual* and no rules exist about how detailed the problem's structure should be. That is, no one model of the problem can be considered to be the "correct" one.

State of Doubt

To solve a problem is to select the best course of action for attaining the decision maker's objectives. A state of doubt as to which course of action is best can arise under three main classes of conditions:

1. *Certainty* with respect to each course of action leading to a specific outcome. The problem here, however, is that the number of courses of action may be so large (even infinite) that some mathematical means is necessary to identify the best alternative.
2. *Risk* with respect to each action leading to a set of possible outcomes, each outcome occurring with a "known" probability. For example, if a fair coin is tossed, we may assume that over the long run the proportion of heads will approach one-half; however, on any single toss we cannot predict whether a head or a tail will appear.
3. *Uncertainty* with respect to outcomes, given a particular course of action. In this view of decision making we assume that the relative frequencies of the probabilities are *not* known. One version of this

class of models, exemplified in the Bayesian approach to decision making (to be described later), assumes that the decision maker can express various "degrees of belief" as to the occurrence of alternative outcomes. Moreover, he may be able, in many cases, to collect more information regarding the "true" state of nature.

Other versions of the uncertainty class (called total ignorance models) assume that the probabilities to be attached to alternative outcomes are either not applicable to begin with, or if they are, must be equal for each outcome that can occur.

Most marketing problems are characterized by a situation of *uncertainty*. The decision maker is usually dealing with a set of more or less unique conditions. His experience in dealing with broadly similar—if not identical—problems may permit him to assign various "degrees of belief" to the occurrence of various possible outcomes, given specific courses of action. We shall emphasize the Bayesian approach in the latter part of this chapter and in Chapter 2, as well.

DECISIONS UNDER UNCERTAINTY—
PROBLEM FORMULATION
FROM THE RESEARCHER'S VIEWPOINT

Having discussed problem formulation from the eyes of the decision maker—the recipient of the research, we next take the viewpoint of the researcher—the information supplier.

A carefully formulated problem is a necessary point of departure for competently conducted research. There should be as clear and thorough an understanding as possible on the part of both the researcher and the decision maker as to the precise purposes of the research. In effect, this statement of purpose involves a *translation of the decision maker's problem into a research problem and study design*. The decision maker is faced with a problem for which he must recognize alternative courses of action, choosing among them to accomplish one or more objectives. The research problem is to provide relevant information concerning recognized (or newly generated) alternative solutions to aid in this choice. To determine what information is required, the researcher will try to identify and understand the major elements of the problem faced by the decision maker. As stated earlier, these elements are:

1. The objectives to be accomplished.
2. The recognized alternative courses of action.
3. Aspects of the problem's environment that may affect the outcome of the possible courses of action.

Determining Objectives

Objectives range from the very general, such as profit maximization, to the highly specific, such as obtaining a particular account. They also vary from jointly agreed-upon corporate objectives to the particularized objectives of each employee. In this section we shall be concerned with the objectives of the decision maker, whether general or particular, as they affect the formulation of the problem to be researched.

Suppose that the marketing manager says, "I need to know how effective our last advertising campaign was." Superficially, it may seem that this is an adequate statement of the objective of the research project to be initiated —to determine the effectiveness of the last advertising campaign. However, on reflection it is apparent that this statement does not state an objective at all. Why does he want this information? If his purpose is to evaluate the agency's handling of the campaign, an entirely different kind of research may be appropriate than if the purpose is, say, to use the information to aid in deciding on the level and allocation of the advertising budget for the coming period. Knowledge of the specific objectives may well influence the kind of information desired and the degree of accuracy that is required. The research problem cannot be adequately formulated, therefore, without knowing the objectives of the client.

It is the exceptional project in which the objectives are explained fully to the researcher. The decision maker will seldom have formulated his objectives completely, and, even if he has, may not be willing to disclose all of them. *The researcher will normally need to take the initiative*, therefore, in developing a clear statement of objectives. This can frequently turn out to be a difficult task, but it is nonetheless a necessary and valuable one.

Direct questioning of the executive concerned about his objectives can only be successful in those cases where he is able and willing to disclose them. Since we have already indicated that these conditions are seldom fully met, it is usually necessary to resort to indirect methods of determining objectives. Two techniques are useful in this indirect approach.

The first of these is the "explosion" of the problem through exploring with the decision maker what is meant exactly by the terms in his statement of the problem. For example, in the statement "I need to know how effective our last advertising campaign was," the researcher must know what the marketing manager means by the word "effective" in order to ensure that the problem statement he formulates specifies the kinds of information that the manager needs. Does he mean the extent to which the campaign *informed* the audience of the content of the advertising? If so, the research project will need to be designed to measure such variables as audience level, recall, and level of knowledge. If he means the degree to which the campaign *persuaded* the audience of the merits of the product, then a different kind of research project is needed. In this case, a measurement of changes in attitudes and/or preferences will need to be made and linked with exposure to the advertising. Or, if he means the volume of *sales* resulting from the campaign, still another kind of research project will be required. By raising such questions, noting the answers, and probing where required, the researcher can be much further along toward a clear formulation of the problem in terms of the appropriate measurements required. By this process he may also provide a valuable service to the manager by helping him to understand more fully the possible objectives and to sort out the important ones.

A second approach to clarification of the objectives is to raise questions as to what actions would be taken, given specified outcomes of the study. If the research shows that the last campaign was ineffective, will the advertising budget be increased? Different appeals used? Allocation of the budget among media changed? A new agency given the account? These types of questions can and should be raised with the manager. It is often helpful to raise them with subordinates or other appropriate members of the organization as well, in terms of what actions they think *would* be taken, as a result of the possible outcomes of the research.

It should be apparent at this stage that problem formulation is not and cannot be delayed in its entirety until after the research problem has been selected. In fact, these two activities, and design of the research as well, must be done at least somewhat simultaneously, rather than sequentially. Careful problem formulation may well eliminate some problems as candidates for research.

Alternative Courses of Action and Statement of Hypotheses

As discussed earlier, alternative courses of action are the various possible solutions to the problem. It is usually desirable that as many alternatives as possible be recognized during the problem-formulation stage and stated in the form of research hypotheses to be examined.

A *hypothesis* is an assertion about the "state of nature" and, from a practical standpoint, often implies a possible course of action with a prediction of the outcome if the course of action is followed. The prediction thus becomes an assertion about a state (or states) of nature, frequently stated in terms of the objective (or objectives) to be accomplished. For example, if a decision is to be made concerning whether or not to adopt a new package, and the immediate objective is to obtain a 15% share of the market, a hypothesis may be stated that adoption of the proposed new package *will* result in a market share of at least 15%. It will then become the task of the researcher to obtain information to test this assertion (by developing hypotheses concerning acceptance on a trial-market basis) and thus to assist in the process of deciding whether or not to change to the new package.

How does the researcher recognize relevant alternative courses of action and thus develop hypotheses? It is clear that this process is at least as much an art as it is a science, as it is dependent to a significant extent on the experience, judgment, and creative capabilities of the individuals concerned. It is also apparent that relevant alternative courses of action should be closely related to the objectives to be achieved.

There is perhaps no better illustration of this relationship than the general problem of diversification of products. While there is almost always the general objective of increasing profit through the additon of new products, other objectives are invariably present as well. Utilization of excess capacity in one or more of the functional areas of the business (manufacturing, marketing, etc.), reducing seasonal or cyclical fluctuations in sales, and rounding out the product line are a few of the possible objectives for diversification. If one of the major objectives is to utilize excess manufacturing capacity, this may greatly limit the number of possible products that should be considered. The relevant possible courses of action are therefore closely tied to the objectives of diversifying.

The identification of possible courses of action is closely related to the problem-situation model. Once the objectives have been agreed upon, the formulation of the model consists of:

1. Determining which variables *affect* the solution to the problem.
2. Determining which of these variables are *controllable* and to what extent control can be exercised.
3. Determining the *functional relationship* of the variables. The nature of this relationship will indicate which variables are critical to the solution of the problem.

Examples of failures to follow through these three aspects of the problem-situation model are not difficult to find. The aircraft industry at the end of World War II, for example, was faced with the loss of most of the market for its major product. In looking for new products to generate business to replace this loss, many of the companies failed to identify both the critical and the controllable variables. One company introduced a highly engineered (and highly priced) motorized wheelbarrow. Tolerances in the motor were to aircraft standards. The product was unsuccessful, both because of competition from lower-priced entrants and because of the inability of the company to market and service it adequately. The patents were later sold to a construction equipment manufacturer. High-tolerance engineering was certainly not the critical variable in this problem.

The Environment of the Research Problem

The effects of the environment of the problem—those factors which both *affect* the outcome and are *uncontrollable*—cannot be predicted with

certainty. However, for a given problem it may be sufficient to consider only a few of the many possible outcomes for each of the alternatives. For example, in a decision concerning whether or not to introduce a new product, the executive may be interested only in whether the sales volume is likely to exceed or not exceed some desired level.

We shall find that many ways exist to formulate a problem in terms of the set of mutually exclusive and exhaustive states of the problem environment that are to be considered. In fact, one of the jobs of the market researcher is to assemble information concerning the firm's environmental variables to assist in identifying the states of nature that should be considered. The possible states may range from fairly detailed descriptions to broad, summarizing descriptions in which data are condensed into a relatively small number of potential sales levels over a specific time period.

In summary, the marketing researcher, to be effective as an information supplier, must work closely with his client in effecting a transformation of the client's problem into a research problem. Since the researcher's and client's interests are both concerned with the potential value versus cost of the research findings, the researcher must become aware of, and *assist in*, the identification of objectives, courses of action, and environmental variables, insofar as they affect the design of the research investigation. For that matter, his efforts should be oriented toward helping the manager decide whether or not *any* investigation is justified.

PROBABILITY THEORY AND DECISIONS

Probability theory, the foundation of statistics, is perhaps as controversial a subject as one could find when it comes to the interpretative aspects of its own concepts. Of course, one can study probability theory strictly as an abstract system and hence avoid the problems of interpretation. When it comes to interpreting probabilities in the real world, however, we might ask the reader how he would react to the following statements:

1. I will assign a probability of 1/6 to the appearance of a six on the next throw of a well-balanced die.
2. I have observed, over a long period, a process that produces metal parts. The defective proportion of metal parts produced so far is 0.08. I am willing to assume that the probability of this process's producing a defective part in the immediate future is 0.08.
3. I personally feel that the chance of my going to Mexico this year is 0.05.

Our experience with tossing dice suggests that almost everyone would agree with the first probability statement. Our agreement stems from the large amount of empirical evidence that has been assembled on die tossing and, perhaps, an examination of the way in which the die is constructed (symmetrically). Most of us would feel reasonably comfortable in assigning the same probability (0.08) to the production of a defective part, particularly if additional knowledge suggests that the process can be treated as stable over time and we have no reason to believe that the appearance of a good or bad part changes the probability of the next part's being good or defective. But perhaps many of us would feel uneasy about statement 3; we are not at all sure about the relevancy of the experience underlying this probability assignment and how our personalistic probability would be modified in the light of new information.

Judgment pervades all measurements and interpretations of probability. Two of the major views of probability theory are the relative-frequency view and the personalistic view. The *relative-frequency* view defines probability as the limit of a sequence of relative frequencies as the sequence approaches infinity. Before going further, however, we must agree that in any practical situation we can observe only a finite number of trials; hence, we must *postulate* this limit. Experience with tossing symmetrical dice and coins neither substantiates nor refutes the notion of a limiting frequency. We should be clear on the central point that probability is *not an observed relative frequency*; moreover, the relative-frequency view, strictly speaking, does not tell us what to expect on a *single* toss (the probability of a six would be either 1 or 0 according to this point of view).

Our more limited experience with the metal-part production process may arouse more disagreement about using the observed proportion of defective parts as an estimate of the probability. We might be more inclined, for example, to change this probability assignment as more experience with the process accumulates than we would be to change our probability assignment of 1/6 to the toss of a six as more evidence against this assertion accumulates. Of course, if we had reason to suspect the "trueness" of the die, we might behave in the same manner as we would regarding the production process. But, compared to the production process, the past experience gained in tossing symmetrical dice is overwhelming.

The *personalistic view* of probability is more like the view held by the man on the street. Those who subscribe to the personalistic view find it quite natural to assign probabilities to unique events. Personalistic or subjective probability relates to the degree of belief or confidence one has in the occurrence of a particular state of the world, as expressed in decision-making terms. Several procedures have been described for eliciting this degree of belief. One of these, suggested by Schlaifer,[4] is that the decision maker conceptualize

---

[4]Robert Schlaifer, *Probability and Statistics for Business Decisions* (New York: McGraw-Hill Book Company, 1959), pp. 11–13. Also, see Robert Schlaifer, *Analysis of Decisions under Uncertainty* (New York: McGraw-Hill Book Company, 1969) and Howard Raiffa, *Decision Analysis* (Reading, Mass.: Addison-Wesley Publishing Company, Inc., 1968).

a "standard lottery" of, say, 100 numbered balls in an urn and a corresponding set of numbered lottery tickets. The decision maker has a (conceptual) right to receive some worthwhile prize if he draws a ticket whose number corresponds with the number of a ball drawn from the urn. The personalistic probability assigned, for example, to the occurrence of a trip to Mexico this year is derived by imagining the number of lottery tickets (in this case, five) which he would wish to have in the standard lottery in order to be indifferent to receiving the prize provided by winning the lottery or receiving the same prize if the event "trip to Mexico this year" occurred.

The personalistic approach admits the assignment of probabilities to unique as well as repetitive events. In some cases the probability assignments will be based on more or less "public" experience in the sense that most people would assign the same or nearly the same probability to the event. In most marketing problems, however, the particular experience involved will be possessed by one or at most a few individuals. If such is the case—*and no additional information can be gathered*—the approach recommends action consistent with these beliefs. When additional data can be collected, these initial judgments may be modified according to procedures to be introduced in Chapter 2. As we shall see, the incorporation of new information, if economically justified, tends to bring into much closer correspondence opinions that initially may be at wide variance, a comforting thought to the reader who is uneasy about the subjective aspect of this view of probability.

DECISIONS UNDER UNCERTAINTY— CHOICE-CRITERION MODELS

We have now considered problem-situation models and problem formulation from the viewpoints of the manager and the researcher. It is appropriate to turn our attention to *choice-criterion* models—the models concerned with choosing a course of action, given the outcomes for each alternative action under the various states of nature.

In recent years several theories have been proposed for dealing with the problem of making rational decisions under uncertainty. By *rational* is meant choice behavior consistent with the assumptions underlying the model—nothing more. The fact that several different theories exist for making decisions under uncertainty is an indication of the many possible models according to which one can choose courses of action. In this context we use the term "model" to represent an ideal of how one should behave if he agrees that the assumptions underlying the model are intuitively appealing. No claim is made in any of these theories that people *do* behave as the model implies or that the model represents how one *should* choose for all time;

rather, these *prescriptive models* represent the frameworks currently proposed by people who have taken the notion of decision making under uncertainty as a serious problem for research.

The choice-criterion models with which we shall be concerned are the maximin, the minimax regret, the Laplace, and the Bayesian.

The Maximin Criterion

The *maximin criterion* is so named because it requires the decision maker to choose the action that *max*imizes the *min*imum payoff. That is, the decision maker determines what the worst outcome could be for each action–state of nature pair and chooses the course of action whose worst outcome could be, for each action, better than that of any other action. When using this criterion, it is assumed that the decision maker has no meaningful information on which to base probability assignments to the various states of nature. Application of the maximin model to the previously described promotional-program problem (see Table 1-3) is illustrated in Table 1-4.

**Table 1-4 Application of maximin criterion
(promotional-program illustration)**

Action	S_1: New Promotional Program Superior to Old	S_2: Old Promotional Program Superior to New	Minimum Payoff
A_1: adopt new	15	−7	−7
A_2: retain old	−2	4	−2 (max.)

The new promotional program in this illustration involved the distribution of samples of the product in lieu of a portion of media advertising. Since the worst payoff if the new promotional program is adopted is −7, while if the old program is retained it is only −2, the decision maker who uses the maximin model will choose act A_2: retain the old program.

This model is clearly a conservative one, as it assumes, in effect, that the worst that can happen will happen. It is difficult to imagine any new commercial venture that does not have a negative payoff for some state of nature. Consequently, persistent use of the maximin criterion would prevent such ventures from being initiated. When one considers that this is the case even when the potential loss is small and the gain large, one must question the consistent use of this model for choice among alternative actions.

The Minimax Regret Criterion

The *minimax regret model* is a closely related, if somewhat more sophisticated, version of the maximin model. The name for this model is coined from the decision rule it employs: it requires that the decision maker *minimize* the *maximum regret* that could be incurred.

This decision criterion, formulated by L. J. Savage,[5] uses the maximin criterion but applies it to a choice among outcomes expressed as levels of "regret." The same assumption is made that the worst possible outcome will occur, given each state of nature.

To apply this criterion, therefore, we must first transform the payoff matrix to a regret matrix. We do so by assuming in turn that each state of nature will be the true state, and then determining the resulting conditional regret associated with each action. In our illustration, if state S_1 is the true state we would have incurred *no* regret by choosing action A_1, since 15 units is the maximum outcome we could have realized under that state of nature. However, we would incur 17 units (15 + 2) of regret by having chosen action A_2. Applying the same reasoning to state S_2, we arrive at the regret matrix shown in Table 1-5 for our promotional-program problem.

Table 1-5   Application of minimax regret criterion (promotional-program illustration)

Action	S_1: New Promotional Program Superior to Old	S_2: Old Promotional Program Superior to New	Maximum Regret
A_1: adopt new	0	11	11 (min.)
A_2: retain old	17	0	17

The decision based on this criterion, then, is to choose act A_1: adopt the new program, since this choice minimizes the maximum regret that can be incurred.

The minimax regret criterion is subject to the same criticism as the maximin rule: it assumes a persistently malevolent nature.

The Laplace Criterion

The *Laplace* criterion, unlike the maximin or minimax regret criteria, employs assignments of probabilities to the occurrence of each state of nature.

[5]L. J. Savage, "The Theory of Statistical Decision," *Journal of the American Statistical Association*, 46 (March, 1951), 56–67.

These probabilities are based on the principle of insufficient reason, however, and are restricted to a single type of probability set as a result. The *principle of insufficient reason* states that, if there is no evidence to suggest that any one event from a mutually exclusive and exhaustive set of events is more likely to occur than any other, each event should be considered to have the *same* probability of occurrence. Application of this criterion is shown in Table 1-6.

Table 1-6 Application of the Laplace criterion (promotional-program illustration)

Action	$P(S_1)$	S_1: New Promotional Program Superior to Old	$P(S_2)$	S_2: Old Promotional Program Superior to New	Expected Value
A_1: adopt new	0.5	15	0.5	−7	4.0 (max.)
A_2: retain old	0.5	−2	0.5	4	1.0

As the table shows, assignment of equal probabilities over the states of nature, S_1 and S_2, results in assigning $P = 0.5$ to each state. If one then takes a weighted average of the payoffs assigned to each state of nature for a given act, an expected value is obtained. For act A_1, the expected value or payoff is 4.0 units $[4.0 = 0.5(15) + 0.5(-7)]$; the expected value for act A_2 is found similarly. The Laplace criterion requires that the course of action with the highest expected value be chosen. Thus, in our example the decision would be made to adopt the new promotional program.

The major criticism of this decision rule is that it is not necessarily independent of the number of states of nature specified in the model. Since equal probabilities are assigned to each state of nature, the probability for each state will be $P = 1/n$, where n is the number of states of nature. As n changes, the probabilities attached to each state change, and, except in special cases, the expected values change.

For most real problems there are many possible listings of states of nature. For example, we could easily and reasonably increase the number of states in our promotion illustration by adding a third one, S_3, defined as "new and old promotional programs equally effective." With the addition of the third state the probability of each becomes $P = 0.33$. Similarly, we could expand to four states of nature by dichotomizing the present S_1 and S_2 definitions into "greatly superior" and "moderately superior," respectively. With this structuring of the model, the probability of each state becomes $P = 0.25$.

Each of the three preceding criteria assumed "total ignorance" about the true state of nature. If a research project were being conducted to obtain information for a decision to be made using any one of these choice-criterion models, it would be limited to developing alternative actions, defining states of nature, and estimating the payoffs of the action–state pairs. No consideration would be given to obtaining information to help decide which state of nature is likely to be the true state.

In practice, however, it is a rare situation in which the decision maker does not possess *some* information about the likelihood of the occurrence of each state. The fact that he has included certain states of nature in structuring the problem argues that he has assigned some probability greater than zero to the occurrence of each. It seems even more unusual that a decision maker would not want information that would help him assess more precisely the probability of occurrence of each state.

The Bayesian Approach

The Bayesian approach[6] to decision making under uncertainty embodies several notions that may not be familiar to the student of traditional statistics. As mentioned earlier, in traditional statistics use was made of the relative-frequency view of probability (i.e., the limit of a sequence of relative frequencies over the long run).

In contrast, the Bayesian approach makes use of personal probabilities —for example, the confidence that the decision maker has in the truth of a specific proposition, where this confidence is expressed numerically and where the expressed judgments obey certain rules of consistency. The Bayesian approach, in effect, treats "uncertainty" problems as if they were "risk" problems by using personal probabilities in lieu of relative-frequency probabilities. For introductory purposes, let us apply this approach to the promotional-program illustration and assume that the decision maker's prior probabilities of S_1 and S_2 occurring are 0.6 and 0.4, respectively. The results are shown in Table 1-7.

By employing the same procedure as used in the Laplace criterion— that is, by multiplying each payoff by the appropriate probability and summing the products—one obtains an expected value. For example, if the decision maker chooses act A_1, his expected value is 6.2 units; that of act A_2 is, of course, 0.4 unit. If he wished to adopt the choice criterion of maximizing expected value, he would choose act A_1. He would make this choice even though he believes that there is a 40% chance for S_2 to occur, which would result in a loss of 7 units.

[6]So named for its frequent use of Bayes' theorem, developed by an eighteenth-century clergyman, Thomas Bayes.

Table 1-7 Application of Bayesian approach
(promotional-program illustration)

Action	$P(S_1)$	S_1: New Promotional Program Superior to Old	$P(S_2)$	S_2: Old Promotional Program Superior to New	Expected Value
A_1: adopt new	0.60	15	0.40	−7	6.2 (max.)
A_2: retain old	0.60	−2	0.40	4	0.4

The marketing executive is usually dealing with events that are unique. No two marketing problems are ever precisely the same, and most have substantive differences from the closest analogous situation faced by the executive in the past. There is little opportunity, therefore, to determine relative-frequency, objective-type probabilities.

The Bayesian approach considers both objective probabilities, where applicable, and personalistic probabilities. In a situation where a decision maker possesses partial information about the relevant probabilities, he may elect a strategy of collecting more information before making a final choice among the courses of action. *He will do so only, however, if the value of the additional information is greater than the cost of obtaining it.* The value versus the cost of information is a central issue in marketing research. The Bayesian approach provides a framework for the formal treatment of this problem and operationalizes the measurement of information value. We describe this framework and the Bayesian approach to the determination of information value in Chapter 2.

SUMMARY

In this chapter we examined the nature of marketing research and its relationship to the making of marketing decisions under uncertainty. The strategy of using marketing research to provide information whenever the expected value exceeds the estimated cost was introduced, as were basic concepts to be developed in depth in subsequent chapters.

We next considered the characteristics of marketing problems. We discussed the basic components of a problem situation—objectives, environment, alternatives, and state of doubt—and the generic types of decisions managers must make. We examined problem-situation models and the necessity for using some problem-solving model, whether implicit or explicit, for decision making. The basic requirement of a model became more evident as we considered the meaning of the term "information" and the role of the model in specifying the information needed for decision making. The concept of value of information was stressed in this discussion.

We then described the components of a problem under uncertainty, first as viewed by the recipient of the research, the marketing manager. We discussed each problem component in some detail and then showed, by means of a simplified example, how a problem could be structured for application of the Bayesian approach.

We next viewed the decision problem from the eyes of one specific information provider, the marketing researcher, and then discussed the type of dialogue that can be fruitfully undertaken between manager and researcher. This dialogue can encompass objectives, courses of action, and environmental variables affecting decision outcomes.

The chapter concluded with a discussion of various choice-criterion models. The maximin, minimax regret, Laplace, and Bayesian models were considered.

ASSIGNMENT MATERIAL

1. Assume that you are faced with the alternative of changing a package design for a firm marketing frozen peas. Describe the major environmental conditions that could affect sales and cost considerations associated with changing over to the new design.

2. A manufacturer of bowling equipment introduced a new line of bowling balls in the territory in which the company had been the least successful with allied lines of products. The line was introduced with the price, promotional support, and distribution channels that were planned for use if the product was introduced nationally. The rationale of selecting this territory was explained by the statement, "If the new line is successful in this territory, it should be even more successful in all of the others."

   a. What choice-criterion model is (or models are) implicit in the selection of this territory to test the new line of bowling balls?

   b. Assuming that you could use only one sales territory for test marketing the new line, is this the one you would choose? Why?

3. Using the operation of a household thermostat as a model, construct a theory for modeling call frequency of salespeople on key accounts.

   a. What is your measure of effectiveness?

   b. What are the control variables?

   c. What functional relationship appears plausible?

   d. Criticize the thermostat model as an appropriate "analogy" in this context.

4. Suppose that you have the following conditional payoff table for establishing a franchising operation in the restaurant field.

ALTERNATIVE	S_1 Probability	S_1 Payoff	S_2 Probability	S_2 Payoff	S_3 Probability	S_3 Payoff
A_1: establish franchises in 20 states	0.2	+$250	0.5	+$100	0.3	−$400
A_2: establish franchises in 10 states	0.2	+$100	0.5	+$ 40	0.3	−$100
A_3: do not establish franchises	0.2	0	0.5	0	0.3	0

What decision would you make if you used a:
a. Maximin decision rule?
b. Minimax regret decision rule?
c. Laplace decision rule?
d. Bayesian decision rule?

5. Of what value is it to the marketing researcher to explore with his client the actions that would be taken, given alternative survey outcomes, *before* the survey is undertaken?

Marketing Research—   2
the Value and Cost of
Decision-Making Information

INTRODUCTION

In Chapter 1 we described several models for making decisions under uncertainty—maximin, minimax regret, the Laplace criterion, and Bayesian decision theory. Of these, only the last one is designed to evaluate the addition of *new information* to the decision process. Indeed, the Bayesian approach provides a formal way for evaluating marketing research as an information supplying and cost-incurring activity.

This chapter discusses the fundamentals of Bayesian decision theory in terms of the problems it is designed to solve and the kinds of marketing research applications for which it is useful.

To set the stage, we first present a very simple example of Bayesian decision theory—an example that nevertheless demonstrates all the basic principles. We then proceed to a more realistic illustration that deals with the potential use of marketing research in determining whether or not a new product should be introduced.

The next section discusses the nature of the payoff entries that figure so prominently in Bayesian calculations. We discuss such topics as net present value and attitudes toward risk, as formally incorporated into utility functions.

The chapter concludes with a discussion of the practical aspects of Bayesian decision theory and its application to actual business problems.

THE ESSENTIALS OF BAYESIAN DECISION THEORY

As already indicated in Chapter 1, today's marketing manager is being faced with both a growing number of specialized procedures for performing marketing research and an increased need for obtaining relevant information about the consequences of alternative marketing courses of action. What would appear to be needed is some framework for measuring the effectiveness of alternative marketing research studies. Fortunately, such a framework has recently become available from the field of applied statistics.

Statistical methodology is no stranger to the marketing researcher. The computation of averages and measures of dispersion as well as the use of probability sampling have been commonplace in marketing research, almost since its inception. What *is* new to marketing research, however, is the increasing emphasis being placed on *analytical*—as opposed to descriptive—statistics. In particular, the Bayesian decision model, briefly described in Chapter 1, has provided a way to deal analytically with many types of marketing problems. For the practical business person, the books by Schlaifer[1] and Chernoff and Moses[2] stand out as key references on Bayesian theory.[3]

Ironically, one of the foundations of Bayesian decision theory was built more than 200 years ago. At that time an English clergyman, Thomas Bayes, proposed a procedure for combining new information about the likelihood of alternative *states of nature* being the true state with judgments existing *before* receipt of the new information. Although modern Bayesian theory bears little relationship to Thomas Bayes' pioneering work, the name has stuck.

Virtually all decision making—marketing or otherwise—takes place under conditions of uncertainty about the variables that will influence the consequences of the decision. Will the new product, now undergoing test marketing, fail or succeed if introduced nationally? Will ad *A* or ad *B* pull more reader attention? If we raise the price of our product's economy package by 5 cents, what will happen to unit sales volume and profits? The illustrations are endless.

Like it or not, the marketing manager is usually forced to *take chances* and consequently runs the risk of making wrong decisions. Of course, the more certain he is of the outcomes, the lower his risk. Moreover, the better some course of action is over competing options, under a wide variety of possible environmental conditions, the less is the risk of incurring sizable costs if he *is* wrong.

Frequently the marketing manager can avail himself of additional information related to the consequences of the alternatives being considered.

[1]Robert Schlaifer, *Probability and Statistics for Business Decisions* (New York: McGraw-Hill Book Company, 1959).

[2]H. Chernoff and L. E. Moses, *Elementary Decision Theory* (New York: John Wiley & Sons, Inc., 1959).

[3]It is interesting to note that the principles of Bayesian decision theory now appear in virtually all introductory statistics texts. As examples, see Morris Hamburg, *Statistical Analysis for Decision Making* (New York: Harcourt, Brace & World, Inc., 1970) and L. H. Smith and D. R. Williams, *Statistical Analysis for Business: A Conceptual Approach*, 2nd ed. (Belmont, Calif.: Wadsworth Publishing Company, Inc., 1976).

Usually the information is not perfectly accurate and costs something to collect and analyze. Moreover, the manager frequently has available several information-gathering options of varying cost and accuracy. The questions which Bayesian decision theory is designed to answer are basically two:

1. How should the manager choose among alternative information-gathering options, including the option of gathering no additional information at all?
2. Having made this choice, what action should he finally take?

Behind these commonsense questions there exists a large body of detailed and technical theory. Our purpose here is to discuss only the barest outlines of the Bayesian approach, by means of a simple gambling example. We shall then step from this artificial world to the real environment of managerial decision making and marketing research.

A Simplified Example

One nice thing about gambling illustrations is that they have almost universal appeal even if the context seems artificial. The following "game" contains all the essential concepts of Bayesian decision theory; that is, its *structure* is similar to many real-world marketing problems, although its content is rather trivial.[4]

Assume that we have three small boxes which we shall call *A*, *B*, and *C*. Outwardly the boxes look alike. We are told that box *A* contains two gold coins, box *B* contains a gold and a silver coin, and box *C* contains two silver coins. The boxes are put in random order on a table and we are allowed to perform a simple experiment, to choose a box at random and, without observing the contents of the box, draw a single coin. Suppose that the coin drawn happens to be gold. Based on this experimental evidence we are asked to state the probability that the remaining coin is also gold or, in other words, that box *A* was chosen.

We can reason as follows. Before we were given the datum that the first coin drawn was gold, our prior probability of drawing box *A* was 1/3. This assumes that our state of knowledge with respect to the characteristics of each box led to the assignment of an equally likely measure over all states of nature: *A*, *B*, and *C*. (A person who thinks that he possesses extrasensory perception might not wish to make an equiprobable assignment at all; Bayes' theorem handles either case.)

We can next ask ourselves the following question: Given the choice of each box, *A*, *B*, and *C*, respectively, how likely is it that we would have observed a gold coin? Had we chosen box *A*, it is clear that we must observe

[4]See P. E. Green, "Bayesian Decision Theory in Advertising," *Journal of Advertising Research*, 2 (December, 1962), 33–41.

a gold coin on a single draw from the box since *both* coins in *A* are gold; thus, a probability of one is correct. Given that box *B* was chosen, the probability is 1/2 that our first draw would have produced a gold coin, since box *B* contained one gold and one silver coin. Given that we chose box *C*, it is clear that the chances of drawing a gold coin are zero, since both coins in *C* are silver. These probabilities are *conditional* probabilities. For example, the probability of drawing a gold coin, conditional upon having picked up box *B*, is 1/2.

From here it is but a short step to Bayes' theorem. Figure 2-1 shows a diagrammatic representation of the problem. The area of the rectangle is

Figure 2-1 Pictorial presentation of probabilities—box problem

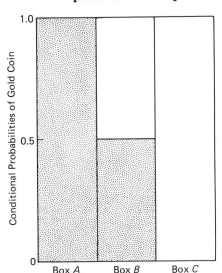

Source: Reprinted, with permission, from P. E. Green, "Bayesian Decision Theory in Advertising," *Journal of Advertising Research*, 2 (December, 1962), 33–41. Copyright © 1962 by the Advertising Research Foundation.

first divided into three vertical strips of equal area, which represent the prior probabilities of drawing box *A*, *B*, or *C*. Next, the relevant probabilities are pictured by shading the area of each strip in proportion to the probability of observing a gold coin. Thus, all of strip *A* is shaded, half of strip *B* is shaded, and none of strip *C* is shaded.

Since, in performing our experiment, we have *observed* a gold coin, we must revise our prior probabilities to reflect this new information; that is, only the shaded area is now relevant. Moreover, the shaded area under each vertical strip represents the combined occurrence of (1) choosing a particular box and (2) getting a gold coin. These are joint events. Now, if we divide the shaded area between the relevant boxes *A* and *B*, it is clear that two-thirds of this total area is contained in the vertical strip *A*; hence, the revised probability of having drawn box *A* is now 2/3 versus a 1/3 probability of having drawn box *B*. Obviously, given our information that the coin is gold, we have *not* drawn box *C*.

Bayes Theorem

Bayes' theorem merely formalizes this approach. Suppose that we wanted to find, for example, the probability that box *A* was drawn, given the observance of a gold coin. We can use the following formula (Bayes' theorem), where $P(g|A)$ stands for the conditional probability of observing a gold coin, given that we have drawn box *A*; $P(A)$ stands for the probability of drawing box *A* in the first place; and $P(A|g)$ stands for the conditional probability of having drawn box *A*, given the information that the coin was gold. Other symbols are defined analogously.

$$
\begin{aligned}
P(A|g) &= \frac{P(g|A) \cdot P(A)}{P(g|A) \cdot P(A) + P(g|B) \cdot P(B) + P(g|C) \cdot P(C)} \\
&= \frac{1 \cdot 1/3}{(1 \cdot 1/3) + (1/2 \cdot 1/3) + (0 \cdot 1/3)} \\
&= 2/3
\end{aligned}
$$

From our previous discussion we already know that this solution, 2/3, agrees with our intuitive analysis of the problem. Notice that the revised or "posterior" probability is conditional upon a *particular* observed event; the appearance of a silver coin would have changed the posterior probability assigned to box *A* from 2/3, in the gold coin case, to zero.

More generally, given some observed sample event *E*, Bayes' theorem states that the conditional probability of a particular state of nature S_i being true is

$$
P(S_i|E) = \frac{P(E|S_i) \cdot P(S_i)}{\sum_{i=1}^{n} P(E|S_i) \cdot P(S_i)}
$$

$P(S_i)$ is the *prior* probability of state of nature S_i and $P(E|S_i)$ is the *conditional* probability of observing the event *E*, given that S_i is true. (In the preceding example, E denotes the gold coin, while the S_i's are boxes A, B, and C.) Finally, the product $P(E|S_i) \cdot P(S_i)$ is the *joint* probability of observing E under state of nature S_i. If E denotes the gold coin and S_i denotes box A, then $P(E|S_i) \cdot P(S_i)$ is the joint probability of drawing a gold coin from box A; as we know, it is $1 \cdot 1/3$ or $1/3$.

So much for probability revision. We must now determine how the approach is used in evaluating courses of action. As we recall from Chapter 1, the criterion for choosing among courses of action under the Bayesian approach is: choose the act that leads to the highest expected or weighted average payoff. We can modify our example to illustrate this criterion.

Assume that we have the option to bet or not bet that we will choose box A from the three boxes on the table. Suppose that we would win $1.00 if A were drawn, but would lose $0.60 if box B were drawn and would lose $0.50 were we to draw box C. Suppose further that we are not allowed to run an experiment before betting; that is, not allowed to observe one of the two coins in each box.

A pictorial representation of these initial ground rules appears in the upper branch of the *tree diagram* shown in Figure 2-2. Looking at the extreme right of the upper branch, we note the conditional payoffs, $1.00, −$0.60, and −$0.50, associated with drawing box A, B, or C, respectively. To find the *expected* payoff associated with "bet," we merely multiply these payoffs by our prior probabilities, $1/3$, $1/3$, and $1/3$, and sum the products, leading to a negative expected payoff of −$0.03: that is, we would lose 3 cents per bet on the average. Obviously, if maximizing expected monetary value is our criterion, we would select the "no bet" action with an expected payoff of zero. Therefore, we put a double slash through the "bet" branch to indicate that this act is not taken.

Consider another modification of the problem. Assume that *before* we decide whether to bet or not we are allowed to observe one coin from the box chosen. To conduct this experiment we are charged $0.10. Conditional payoffs are the same as before. The major difference is that we can delay our choice of whether to bet or not until *after* we have observed the results of our experiment and it will cost us $0.10 to run the experiment.

The lower branch of the tree diagram of Figure 2-2 summarizes the features of this strategy. If we look at the extreme right portion of the lower branch, following the subbranch labeled "gold coin," we note the probabilities: 0.67, 0.33, and 0. These represent the *posterior probabilities* derived from applying Bayes' theorem on the assumption that a gold coin is observed. Notice that the expected payoff associated with "bet" is $0.47, clearly higher than that associated with "don't bet." Therefore, the double slash through the "no bet" subbranch indicates that, if we observed a gold coin, we would choose the "bet" rather than "no bet" act.

Before the fact, however, it is possible that we may observe a silver rather than a gold coin. If we follow this branch and look at the posterior

Figure 2-2   Decision tree—box betting problem

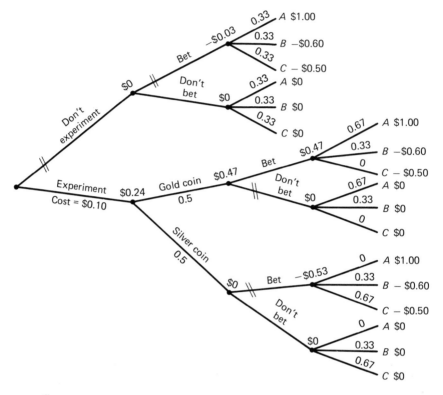

probabilities—0, 0.33, and 0.67 for *A*, *B*, and *C*, respectively—the expected payoff associated with "betting" is very poor, −$0.53. It is clearly to our advantage *not* to bet if we observe a silver coin—hence, the double slash through the "bet" subbranch. But we must still compute the probabilities of getting a gold versus silver coin. These are known as *marginal probabilities*, and they represent the sum of a set of joint probabilities involving mutually exclusive events. Their calculation, along with the calculation of the joint probabilities, is shown in Table 2-1.

Now we may obtain the expected payoff of $0.24 by again averaging over the payoffs associated with the *best* act taken after the observance of each possible result of the experiment, that is, $0.24 = (0.5 × $0.47) + (0.5 × $0). The expected payoff must then be reduced by $0.10, the cost incurred in using this strategy, leading to a *net* expected payoff of $0.14. This figure is still higher than the $0 associated with the best act under

Table 2-1 Calculation of joint and marginal probabilities for box problem

	Box A	*Box B*	*Box C*	*Marginal*
Gold coin	1/3	1/6	0	1/2
Silver coin	0	1/6	1/3	1/2
Marginal	1/3	1/3	1/3	1

"don't experiment"; hence, we double-slash the upper main branch of the tree.

To summarize, our best strategy is: (1) to conduct our experiment and (2) to take the best act after observing the experimental results; this means that we bet if a gold coin appears and do not bet if a silver coin appears. If we do this, our average payoff per play, after deducting the cost of the experiment, is $0.14.

Before leaving this example, let us introduce one additional complication. Suppose that we could enlist the services of a shill who, for a payment of $0.25, could secretly give us a signal that would indicate *without error* the nature of the box we picked up before we had to decide whether or not to bet. What is the net value of this *perfect* information?

Inasmuch as the shill cannot influence our choice process (but only tell us *after* we have picked up a box which box it is), about one-third of the time we pick up box *A* and, being given its identification, will decide to bet. We will make $1.00. Two-thirds of the time we will pick up box *B* or box *C* and, upon being told this, will not bet. On these occasions we will make $0. Thus, our average *gross* payoff per play will be

$$1/3 \times \$1.00 + 2/3 \times \$0 = \$0.33$$

Since our shill charges $0.25 per play for his service, our expected net payoff is only $0.33 − $0.25, or $0.08. We note that this is less than the $0.14 payoff of the second option. Here is a case in which the net value of even *perfect* information is *less* than the net value of less reliable (but cheaper) information.

The *expected value of perfect information* (EVPI) is an important concept in Bayesian analysis. In general, to compute EVPI we can reason as follows: if we had perfect information about which state of nature prevails, we would always take the best action available to us. In the preceding example we would bet under box *A* conditions and would not bet under box *B* or box *C* conditions. However, *before* the fact we do not know which event will occur. Hence, we must multiply each of the best payoffs under *A*, *B*, or *C* conditions by the prior probability that further inquiry (e.g., use of the shill's services) will reveal the true state. This reasoning leads to the $0.33 gross payoff noted above.

The *difference* between $0.33 and the best expected payoff under the *prior* probabilities case (in the sample problem it is *not* to bet, carrying an expected payoff of zero) is defined as EVPI and represents an upper bound on what we should pay for even perfect information.

From Gambling Game to the Real World

As simple as the preceding example appears, it nonetheless demonstrates some significant points about the economics of decision making. Consider the situation of a marketing manager faced with the problem of whether or not to increase the level of product advertising in a particular marketing area. Like the gambler, the manager has alternative courses of action. We also assume that he wants to achieve certain objectives, such as earning a maximum return on his advertising investment.

As our manager reflects on his problem, however, he realizes that, under some levels of response to increased advertising effort, the additional advertising would more than pay for itself in terms of the profits from increased sales volume. Under other levels of response—certainly under no increase in sales at all—payoffs would be higher if he did not increase his advertising expenditures. Presumably his deliberations include the possible effects of competitors' options for changing *their* levels of advertising and the resultant impact on total industry sales and his firm's market share. The trouble is that our decision maker does not know for certain what *will* happen, and must deal with payoffs that are conditional upon one of *several* possible events.

In most situations, however, the decision maker has had experience in facing at least broadly analogous situations and has been exposed to the events preceding his particular problem situation. For example, he may well feel that some of the possible events are more likely to occur than others. Bayesian decision theory formalizes this notion by assuming that it is possible to assign numerical weights, in the nature of betting odds, such that they obey certain requirements for consistency. These numerical weights, called *prior probabilities*, may be based on long-run, "objective" experience with very similar problems; in other instances they may be more "subjective."

But, like our mythical gambler, the manager can often attempt to improve his view regarding the likelihood that each state of nature is the "true" underlying event *before* having to take final action. That is, he may elect to "experiment" before making a final choice among alternatives. The marketing manager might conduct a test campaign before deciding whether to increase the total level of promotion.

Gathering additional data usually involves a cost, however, and rarely are data so accurate as to foretell perfectly the true state of nature. Decision makers usually must cope with both experimental (sampling) and systematic error. Thus, the manager is forced to weigh the cost of the test campaign against its potential value in supplying information.

THE COST AND VALUE OF RESEARCH INFORMATION

Let us now take a more realistic example in which Bayesian decision theory can be used to assess the value versus cost of marketing information. Moreover, our approach will be more formal and detailed than the simple gambling illustration. We shall describe three types of analyses:

1. *Prior analysis*, which concerns which act should be chosen under conditions involving the decision maker's prior (before receipt of any new information) probabilities only.
2. *Posterior analysis*, which deals with which act should be chosen after the receipt of new information bearing on the states of nature.
3. *Preposterior analysis*, which deals with the strategic question of whether new information should be purchased (and, if so, how much) before making a final, or terminal, decision.

Suppose that the research and development phase of a new-product candidate is nearing completion and a decision must be made concerning whether the product should be commercialized. The alternative strategies are:

- *Strategy 1:* Make the decision concerning whether to introduce the new product on the basis of prior probabilities only.
- *Strategy 2:* Conduct the test marketing operation and make the decision of whether or not to introduce the new product on the basis of both prior and additional information.

Expected Payoff before Research— Evaluation of Strategy 1

In evaluating strategy 1, suppose that the prior analysis is as shown in Table 2-2. As shown there, three payoff levels have been judged to be relevant if the product is introduced; that is, a 15% market share, for which the payoff is estimated at $20 million; a 5% market share, with an estimated payoff of $5 million; and a 1% market share, with a payoff estimated at −$10 million. The prior probabilities attached to each of these possible states of nature are 0.3 for the 15% market share, 0.5 for the 5% market

Table 2-2 Prior analysis—new-product introduction

| | STATE OF NATURE | | | | | | |
| | S_1 | | S_2 | | S_3 | | |
ALTERNATIVE	$P(S_1)$	15% Market Share (millions of dollars)	$P(S_2)$	5% Market Share (millions of dollars)	$P(S_3)$	1% Market Share (millions of dollars)	Expected Payoff (millions of dollars)
A_1: introduce the product	0.3	20	0.5	5	0.2	−10	6.5
A_2: do not introduce the product	0.3	0	0.5	0	0.2	0	0.0

share, and 0.2 for the 1% market share. The expected payoff of introducing the product (in the light of current information only) is

$$0.3(\$20 \text{ million}) + 0.5(\$5 \text{ million}) + 0.2(-\$10 \text{ million}) = \$6.5 \text{ million}$$

The payoff of not introducing the product is, of course, 0. Thus, the *prior* analysis suggests that the new product be introduced.

Expected Payoff after Research—
Evaluation of Strategy 2

In evaluating strategy 2, our task would be simplified if we could assume that the additional information we obtain from the market test is perfect— that is, that we could identify with certainty the optimal act under strategy 2. If, after collection of the market test data, we could conclude with certainty which act, A_1 or A_2, is the better act, then the expected payoff would be equal to

$$0.3(\$20 \text{ million}) + 0.5(\$5 \text{ million}) + 0.2(0) = \$8.5 \text{ million}$$

Since we have already calculated the best expected payoff without additional information and found it to be $6.5 million, the *expected value of perfect information* would be

$$\$8.5 \text{ million} - \$6.5 \text{ million} = \$2.0 \text{ million}$$

Even if we were assured of getting perfect information, we would be well advised not to spend more than $2 million to obtain it.

Realistically, however, we know that the information obtained will not be perfect; there will almost always be some uncertainty present as to which is the preferable act after collecting additional information. How, then, can we determine the expected payoff after collecting the information when we recognize that the information we obtain will be imperfect?

To do this, it is necessary that a *preposterior analysis* be made. Before we proceed with an example, it may be helpful to set down the procedural steps that we will have to take to determine the expected payoff *after* receiving the research information from the test market. These steps are as follows:

1. For each of the possible relevant outcomes that the market test could yield, determine the marginal probability of getting each specific outcome. (In our example, the marginal probabilities are calculated and shown in Table 2-4.)
2. For each specific outcome of the market test, calculate the posterior probabilities. (The posterior probabilities in our example are calculated in Table 2-5.)
3. Calculate the expected payoff of each possible act under the strategy involving additional data collection (via the market test) and select the act that leads to the highest expected payoff on the basis of the information then available. Multiply the expected payoff, conditional upon which outcome occurs, by its marginal probability of occurrence. Sum the products to obtain an expected payoff after the market test. (These calculations are made in Figure 2-3.)

As noted in the prior analysis, it was decided that three possible states of nature were relevant: S_1, a market share of 15%; S_2, a market share of 5%; and S_3, a market share of 1%. Let us assume that the following possible outcomes of the market test are the relevant ones with respect to drawing inferences concerning the true state of nature: Z_1, a test market share of 10% or more; Z_2, a test market share between 3 and 10%; and Z_3, a test market share of 3% or less. Let us suppose that we assign the probabilities shown in Table 2-3 to each of these outcomes, conditional upon the given state of nature being the true state. For example, the conditional probability assigned to getting outcome Z_1, given state of nature S_1, is $P(Z_1|S_1) = 0.6$. Conditional probabilities associated with S_2 and S_3, respectively, are $P(Z_1|S_2) = 0.3$ and $P(Z_1|S_3) = 0.1$.

Having made this assignment of conditional probabilities, we are now in a position to calculate the *joint probability* of a given state of nature's being the true state *and* its being identified as such by a given test market outcome. The joint probability for each of the states of nature and each of the test-

Table 2-3 Assignment of conditional probabilities to possible outcomes of market test operations—new-product introduction

	POSSIBLE OUTCOME		
STATE OF NATURE	Z_1: Market Share in Test $10\% \le M.S.$	Z_2: Market Share in Test $3\% < M.S.$ $< 10\%$	Z_3: Market Share in Test $M.S. \le 3\%$
S_1: 15% market share	0.6	0.3	0.1
S_2: 5% market share	0.3	0.5	0.2
S_3: 1% market share	0.1	0.2	0.7
Total	1.0	1.0	1.0

market outcomes is calculated and shown in Table 2-4. For example, the joint probability of S_2's being the true state of nature *and* being identified correctly by outcome Z_2 is

$$P(S_2 \text{ and } Z_2) = P(S_2) \cdot P(Z_2 \mid S_2) = 0.5 \times 0.5 = 0.25$$

Table 2-4 Calculation of joint and marginal probabilities of states of nature and market test outcomes—new-product introduction

STATE OF NATURE	MARKET-TEST OUTCOME			TOTAL $P(S_i)$
	Z_1	Z_2	Z_3	
S_1	0.3(0.6) = 0.18	0.3(0.3) = 0.09	0.3(0.1) = 0.03	0.30
S_2	0.5(0.3) = 0.15	0.5(0.5) = 0.25	0.5(0.2) = 0.10	0.50
S_3	0.2(0.1) = 0.02	0.2(0.2) = 0.04	0.2(0.7) = 0.14	0.20
Total—$P(Z_j)$	0.35	0.38	0.27	1.00

Note that the sum of each row is the marginal probability of that state of nature's being the true state and is equal to the prior probability assigned initially (Table 2-2). Note also that sum of each column is the *marginal probability* of getting each specific outcome from the market test. The probability of getting outcome Z_1, a test market share of 10% or more, for example, is 0.35. The marginal probabilities $P(Z_j)$ are required to implement the first step in the procedure outlined above.

We may now calculate the posterior probabilities of each state of nature's being the true state, given a specific outcome of the market test. These calculations are made in Table 2-5. For example, it may be seen that the (conditional) probability of state S_1, given outcome Z_1 is 0.5143; $P(S_1 | Z_1)$ $= 0.5143$. These probabilities are central to our analysis, as they are the revised probabilities incorporating the additional information that would be obtained from the market test. As illustrated in the coin example, they are computed from Bayes' theorem.

Table 2-5   Calculation of posterior probabilities of states of nature and market test outcomes—new-product introduction

	MARKET-TEST RESULTS		
STATE OF NATURE	$P(S_i | Z_1)$	$P(S_i | Z_2)$	$P(S_i | Z_3)$
S_1	0.18/0.35 = 0.5143	0.09/0.38 = 0.2368	0.03/0.27 = 0.1111
S_2	0.15/0.35 = 0.4286	0.25/0.38 = 0.6579	0.10/0.27 = 0.3704
S_3	0.02/0.35 = 0.0571	0.04/0.38 = 0.1053	0.14/0.27 = 0.5185
	1.0000	1.0000	1.0000

Now that the *posterior probabilities* $P(S_i | Z_j)$ have been determined, we may apply them to determine the expected payoff of each act, conditional upon the outcome of the market test. As shown in Figure 2-3, the optimal act for outcomes Z_1 and Z_2 is A_1 (introduce the product), as the payoffs are $11.858 and $6.972 million, respectively. The optimal act for outcome Z_3 is A_2 (not to introduce the product) as the payoff of introduction is negative in this case.

A final step (see Figure 2-3) is needed to find the expected payoff *after* research. We may calculate this value by multiplying each of the conditional payoffs by its marginal probability of occurrence. The *unconditional payoff* is, therefore,

$$0.35(\$11.858) + 0.38(\$6.972) + 0.27(0) = \$6.800 \text{ million}$$

By conducting the market test, therefore, we obtain a gross expected payoff of $6.800 million. It should be kept in mind that this payoff does *not* take into account the cost of the research—in this case, the market test.

**Figure 2-3   Determination of expected payoff after market test—
new-product introduction (payoffs in millions of dollars)**

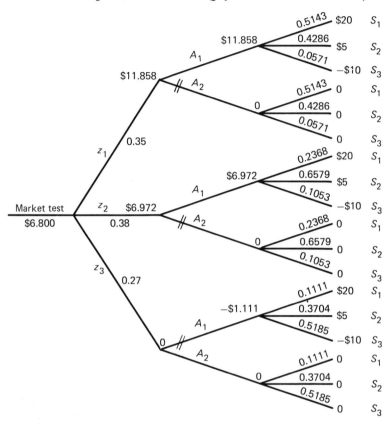

Net Expected Payoff of Research

The *net expected payoff of research* is defined as the expected value of additional information minus the expected cost of acquiring it.

The *expected value of additional information* is the difference between the expected payoff of the best act *before* research and that of the best strategy *after* research. We found that the best act before research was to introduce the product and that the expected payoff *before* research was $6.500 million. The best strategy, given the research, is to introduce the product under survey outcomes Z_1 and Z_2, but not under outcome Z_3. The expected payoff *after* research was $6.800 million. The expected value of additional information is therefore $300,000.

Let us suppose that the expected cost of conducting the market test is $150,000. The net expected payoff of research is then $300,000 − $150,000 = $150,000. Since the net expected payoff of research is positive, it is clear that the market test should be carried out before deciding whether to introduce the new product.[5]

MEASURING CONDITIONAL PAYOFFS

So far, the examples in this chapter and in Chapter 1 have assumed that the conditional payoffs associated with each act and state of nature were given. In practice, however, these payoffs might be quite difficult to obtain. Our concern now is with the following types of questions:

1. What classes of revenues and costs are relevant for decision making?
2. What is the influence of the time period over which the payoffs are anticipated?
3. What are the various ways in which payoffs can be expressed?
4. How can the problem of risk be handled within the payoff framework?

Future Outlays and Opportunity Costs

In the usual business situation, the payoffs will be expressed in monetary terms. In determining what revenues and costs are relevant for deriving conditional payoffs, a guiding principle is to *include only those revenues and costs that are affected by the alternatives being evaluated.* For many problems a useful way to view the payoff figures is in terms of cash flow. For this purpose the firm can be viewed as a giant cash register in which cash outflows and cash inflows are anticipated. Concern with future revenues and outlays implies that we are not interested in "sunk" costs but only in those costs that would be changed by changes in the course of action presently pursued.

In some cases relevant costs will be of an *opportunity loss* nature, that is, the cash inflow that could be generated in the most productive alternative use of the firm's resources. For example, if the outlay required to increase promotional expenditures precluded the opportunity to use this cash in a research program aimed at product improvement, the opportunity foregone under this course of action may represent the relevant alternative payoff for the firm to consider.

---

[5] If *other* research options were available, we would, of course, choose that option that carried the *highest* net expected payoff.

The Time Horizon and Net Present Value

So far we have been rather vague with respect to how far in the future we wished to compute the conditional payoffs associated with various courses of action. In some problems, the *time horizon* may correspond to the time period of promotional expenditure budgeting—for example, one year. In capital budgeting problems, however, where sizable outlays for new plant and equipment or executive manpower are involved, the planning horizon may be much longer, and consideration should be given to discounting future cash flows to present value.

As a simple illustration of *present-value analysis,* assume that a firm is faced with the problem of determining whether it should set up production facilities for printing a promotional catalog or have the catalog printed by an outside firm. Assume that the necessary printing machinery costs $30,000 and has an anticipated life of five years. In addition, working capital (recoverable at the end of five years) of $5,000 would be required. Salvage value of the machinery at the end of five years is assumed to be zero.

We assume that the firm projects the cash savings (from using its own machinery rather than outside printing) anticipated at the end of each year as shown in Table 2-6. We assume that all cash savings (over the cost to have

**Table 2-6 Catalog printing investment proposal,
10% interest rate**

Year	Year-end Cash Savings ($)	Outlays ($)	Discount Function	Net Present Value ($)
0		(−)35,000	1.000	−35,000
1	10,000	—	0.909	9,090
2	12,000	—	0.826	9,912
3	12,000	—	0.751	9,012
4	12,000	—	0.683	8,196
5	17,000	—	0.621	10,557
				11,767

the catalogs printed by an outside firm) occur at year's end and that the recovery of working capital is included at the end of five years as a "cash saving." Discounting each cash inflow or outflow to present value (annual interest rate equal to 10%) yields a figure of $11,767. This figure is interpreted as the cash generated beyond that required to pay back all outlays and yield an average annual return of 10% on the present value of those outlays. Since the net present value is positive, the investment would be undertaken. This calculation represents a numerical illustration of the formula

$$\text{NPV} = \sum_{i=0}^{n} \frac{R_i - O_i}{(1 + r)^i}$$

where   NPV = net present value
   R_i = cash inflow at the end of time period i
   O_i = cash outflow at the end of time period i
   r = firm's cost of capital, expressed in decimal form

In computing present values the marginal cost of capital[6] is often used, since it is relatively easily determined and incorporates an allowance for risk. However, in dealing with decision problems via the Bayesian approach *several* conditional net present values may have to be calculated, depending upon the alternative states of nature that are postulated. Once calculated, the resultant conditional payoffs could then be handled in a manner similar to any other problem in Bayesian analysis.

Expected Monetary Value versus Utility Considerations

So far we have been assuming that the decision maker desires only to maximize expected monetary value (or expected payoff). This criterion assumes a rather *special set of risk attitudes* on the part of the decision maker.

To illustrate the nature of this assumption, suppose that a decision maker were faced with the alternatives shown in Table 2-7. If we calculate

Table 2-7   Two investment alternatives with different expected (monetary) values and dispersions

A_1: receive O_1 = $50,000 with $P(O_1) = 0.5$
receive O_2 = −$10,000 with $P(O_2) = 0.5$
A_2: receive O_3 = $10,000 with $P(O_3) = 0.5$
receive O_4 = −$2,000 with $P(O_4) = 0.5$

---

[6]This is the rate that would have to be paid to obtain financing of a project with its anticipated level of risk.

the expected values of the alternatives A_1 and A_2, we find that

$$
\begin{aligned}
\text{EV}(A_1) &= 0.5(50,000) + 0.5(-10,000) \\
&= \$20,000 \\
\text{EV}(A_2) &= 0.5(\$10,000) + 0.5(-2,000) \\
&= \$4,000
\end{aligned}
$$

If the decision maker were to follow the criterion of maximizing expected monetary value, he would choose act A_1. It is quite possible, however, that in some situations the decision maker could not afford to risk a possible loss of $10,000, even though this alternative carries a higher expected value. If this situation does prevail, some other set of values would have to be substituted for monetary payoffs in order to reflect the decision maker's attitudes toward risk.

Decision theorists have been concerned with this problem, and several procedures have been proposed for dealing with it. We shall discuss briefly only one such procedure: von Neumann–Morgenstern utility.[7]

Von Neumann–Morgenstern utility is a scale used in a rather special way to make predictions concerning a decision maker's preference for gambles involving specific payoffs whose attainment is subject to risk. To return to the data of Table 2-7, suppose that we were to ask our decision maker to rank in order of preference the following set of conditional outcomes:

$$
\begin{aligned}
O_1 &= \$50,000 \\
O_2 &= -\$10,000 \\
O_3 &= \$10,000 \\
O_4 &= -\$2,000
\end{aligned}
$$

The decision maker replies that he would prefer the receipt of O_1 to O_3 to O_4 to O_2. Suppose that we arbitrarily assign "utilities" (index numbers) to outcomes O_1 and O_2, the highest and lowest outcomes in the decision maker's array of preferences, as follows:

$$
\begin{aligned}
U(O_1) &= 1 \\
U(O_2) &= 0
\end{aligned}
$$

We would then ask the decision maker to visualize a choice between receiving outcome O_3 versus a one-time gamble involving the receipt of O_1 with prob-

---

[7]A lucid discussion of utility theory can be found in W. J. Baumol, *Economic Theory and Operations Analysis*, 4th ed. (Englewood Cliffs, N.J.: Prentice-Hall, Inc., 1977).

ability P and the receipt of O_2 with probability $1 - P$. What probability would have to be associated with the outcome O_1 such that he would be just indifferent toward receiving O_3 for certain and participating in the gamble with O_1 and O_2 as the only possible outcomes?

Suppose that the decision maker replies that this "indifference" probability is 0.8. Then we define the decision maker's utility for outcome O_3 by the equation

$$U(O_3) = P(O_1) \cdot U(O_1) + [1 - P(O_1)] \cdot U(O_2)$$
$$= 0.8(1) + 0.2(0)$$
$$= 0.8$$

Similarly, we could determine the "indifference" probabilities for other outcomes O_4, and so on, so as to arrive at the decision maker's utility as a function of monetary payoff. Suppose that the utility function (indicated by the solid line) shown in Figure 2-4 results from this set of hypothetical gambles. A linear function (dashed line) is also drawn, for comparison, on

Figure 2-4   Hypothetical utility functions

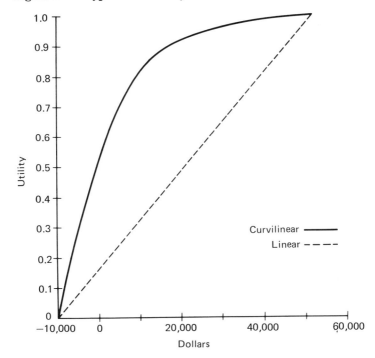

the same chart. In practice, we would determine both lines from a limited set of gambles and interpolate between points.

We are now ready to discuss an important assumption that underlies the use of the following criterion: "Choose that course of action that maximizes expected (monetary) value."

Use of expected (monetary) value assumes that the decision maker's utility function is linear with respect to money.

To illustrate, suppose that we now return to the two investment alternatives of Table 2-7 and translate the conditional monetary outcomes into utilities by reading off the utility value (ordinate scale) for each monetary value (abscissa scale) and then determining the expected utility for each gamble under the curvilinear utility function and the linear utility function, respectively. The expected utility under the *curvilinear utility function* is

$$EU(A_1) = 0.5(1) + 0.5(0)$$
$$= 0.50$$
$$EU(A_2) = 0.5(0.8) + 0.5(0.44)$$
$$= 0.62$$

and under the *linear utility function,*

$$EU(A_1) = 0.5(1) + 0.5(0)$$
$$= 0.5$$
$$EU(A_2) = 0.5(0.33) + 0.5(0.13)$$
$$= 0.23$$

Notice first that the curvilinear utility function is concave downward; that is, marginal utility declines with increasing quantities of money. We can say that this individual is *risk averse*. Using this function, the second alternative [with expected utility $EU(A_2) = 0.62$] would be chosen. As can be noted, this choice is the opposite of that which would be made if the decision maker were attempting to maximize expected (monetary) value.[8] In the case of the linear utility function, however, the choice is *not* reversed. It can be shown mathematically that the adoption of the criterion "Maximize expected (monetary) value" implies that the decision maker's utility function is *linear* with respect to money (at least over the monetary range in question).

---

[8]It should also be pointed out that utility functions for "risk-seeking" persons—where marginal utility increases with increasing quantities of money—could occur in some cases. This curvilinear function would be concave *upward*.

The Practical Use of Utility Functions

The theoretical aspects and mathematical assumptions that underlie utility functions go well beyond the scope of this book. By this brief exposition we have intended merely to acquaint the reader with the notion and show the mechanics of eliciting utility functions by means of interrogating the decision maker regarding a set of hypothetical gambles.

We shall continue to use the criterion of maximizing expected (monetary) value while realizing that in some situations this criterion may not be applicable. But work in the *empirical* derivation of utility functions has been quite meager to date. To the authors' knowledge, no industrial firm is employing utility calculations routinely as a basis for decision making. The theoretical and practical problems in employing these procedures still present major difficulties. Our purpose in presenting even this brief discussion is to show not only that expected (monetary) value is of importance to the decision maker, but that the *dispersion* and, perhaps, the *whole shape of the distribution of conditional payoffs* may be important as well. For the present, if the marketing research analyst believes the maximization of expected (monetary) value to be inappropriate, he should attempt to present the whole distribution of conditional payoffs to the decision maker in cases where the dispersion and/or shape of these distributions differ markedly among the alternatives under consideration.

THE MANAGER—RESEARCHER DIALOGUE

We can now observe that the Bayesian approach emphasizes the key role of *managerial judgment* in the whole decision process that involves the relationship of marketing research to managerial action. Indeed, the manager is placed in the position of "make or buy" with regard to information. The manager can elect to *make*—use his prior experience and other less formal means of information—or to *buy* additional information through the utilization of marketing research (which frequently can be supplied by either internal groups or outside consulting firms).

Second, this kind of orientation also suggests that the marketing researcher must work closely with the user of the information to be able to bring his own particular type of expertise to bear on the problem. The marketing researcher's skills can be utilized in a variety of ways within the theoretical decision format. These functions include: (1) problem identification, (2) the search for and identification of relevant courses of action, (3) the estimation of alternative consequences of a given course of action and the probabilities associated therewith, and (4) the estimation of the accuracy and cost of alternative investigations.

Third, the data inputs required in the application of the Bayesian approach are usually best assembled through the *interaction of manager and researcher*. Each can contribute his specific type of knowledge and experience to the formulation and solution of the problem. Although this may sound commonplace, the truth of the matter is that all too frequently the marketing researcher is not asked—even permitted—to assist in the structuring of a managerial problem. Rather, he may be given the type of directive "Find out all you can about the market for tranquilizers." If the researcher can implement this type of request, he must serve principally as a "fact finder," unaware of the use to which the findings are to be put, the scale of effort to be devoted to the inquiry, and the accuracy required in his findings.

Like many models, the value of the Bayesian framework would seem to lie more in the types of *questions* that its utilization generates than the kinds of answers it provides. Although applying the model to actual business problems may often require fairly sophisticated procedures—for example, computer simulation or mathematical statistics—the basic logic agrees with common sense. Its major impact is to force the manager and the researcher to look at marketing research in terms of its value in reducing the costs of wrong decisions. Dogmatic statements such as "Take a 10% sample of all households," "Get the most accurate data available," and so on thus become suspect within a framework that attempts to compare the value of the information with the cost of acquiring it.

The implications of the Bayesian approach suggest that marketing research studies should be geared to the costs incurred in making decisions in the absence of additional information; that is, the breadth and cost of marketing research studies should relate to *other* components of the decision situation. For example, if prior uncertainty and the costs of wrong decisions are both low, a small-scale investigation (or no investigation at all) may be indicated. If the potential information is so inaccurate as to produce little reduction in prior uncertainty, again the study may not justify its cost. In other instances, of course, the stakes, the initial uncertainty, and the anticipated accuracy of the market study may justify large expenditures for additional information.

INDUSTRIAL APPLICATIONS
OF THE BAYESIAN APPROACH

Now that we have discussed the conceptual basis of the Bayesian model, illustrated its application, and discussed its implications from the standpoint of marketing manager and researcher interaction, some comments should be given on the present stage of its application in industry.

As with any new approach, the time lag between methodological innovation and routine use is frequently long. Reported applications of the Bayesian approach are still sparse, owing no doubt to corporate security as well as to the relative newness of the methodology. We comment briefly on the nature of some of these applications.

Introduction of New Products

One of the earliest applications of Bayesian analysis involved a new-product study. The management of a large chemical firm was faced with the question of whether to introduce a new product (a packaging material designed for further processing by industrial fabricators) on the basis of the data then available regarding its chances of commercial success.[9] There were two questions:

1. Should the decision as to whether the product should be introduced be made "now" or one year later?
2. Given the answer regarding proper timing of the decision, what size of plant and what pricing policy should be followed?

The product in question was designed to compete in some 20 end-use markets. Estimates of sales were prepared for three sets of environmental conditions—most probable, optimistic, and pessimistic. Three pricing strategies and two plant sizes were considered, in all combinations, as tactical alternatives.

The venture was "run on paper" (actually in an electronic computer) under a variety of environmental conditions. It turned out that the choice of plant size and pricing policy was insensitive to variations in the environment; that is, given commercialization (now or one year hence) a particular pricing strategy–plant size combination was best. Under the pessimistic set of conditions, however, even this "best" alternative would not yield a satisfactory return.

The second part of the analysis was concerned with the wisdom of delaying commercialization of the new product until one year hence, when, presumably, more reliable data could be obtained regarding the chances of the new product's commercial success. Delaying the decision would defer the start of revenues—if the product were successful—and hence the opportunity to earn a return on these cash flows. Moreover, an additional out-of-pocket expense (of $2.6 million) would be involved in keeping the development going and obtaining further commercial data on acceptance of the product by fabricators who were cooperating in end-use tests.

What was not known was the *accuracy* that had to be associated with the new data to justify delay of the venture, but the analyst did have enough

[9]This example is drawn from Wroe Alderson and P. E. Green, *Planning and Problem Solving in Marketing* (Homewood, Ill.: Richard D. Irwin, Inc., 1964), p. 229.

information to solve for this accuracy level. The answer turned out to be 90%; that is, management would need *almost perfect information* regarding the occurrence of the appropriate state of nature to justify delay.

Figure 2-5 shows the structure of the analysis. As can be seen from the tree diagram, given "no delay," the best present decision was to build the (already determined best-sized) plant. If so, an expected cash flow of $7.8 million was indicated. Given a one-year delay, *with perfect information*, the payoff could only be increased to $9.4 million. It was hardly surprising that management did not feel that information of anywhere near the high accuracy required to justify the delay could be obtained over the next year. Thus, the expected costs of delay exceeded the expected value of delay.

Risk Analysis

Hertz has described a topic related to Bayesian analysis—*risk analysis*—which can also be applied to marketing and financial planning problems.[10] The author suggests first that most of the variables in capital budgeting forecasts (for example, market size, selling prices, market share, required investment) are not known with certainty, particularly the marketing variables. Hertz discusses the development of subjective probability distributions for each key variable to be obtained from experienced executives in the firm. The next step involves simulating the impact of possible variations in each of the variables on the venture's overall financial return. The simulation is performed by a computer.

Figure 2-6 shows a schematic of the method that Hertz describes. Using a Monte Carlo technique (in which the various probability distributions are empirically sampled via random-number draws), Hertz is able to calculate the cash flow associated with a large number of combinations of marketing and cost factors. The output of the program is a *distribution* of possible rates of return—each with an associated probability. If management is willing to select an option according to the arithmetic mean of this distribution (or if the distribution is first transformed to utility values that reflect management's attitude toward risk), the procedure is similar to Bayesian prior analysis, as already described.

Decision Trees

Decision-tree analysis—with or without probability revisions—has many users in marketing research. As an illustration, Villani and Morrison show how a decision tree can be constructed to estimate demand for a new

---

[10]D. B. Hertz, "Risk Analysis in Capital Investment," *Harvard Business Review*, 42 (January–February 1964), 95–106.

Figure 2-5 Influence of delay on decision to build plant

Legend

Opt. = optimistic forecast
M.P. = most probable forecast
Pess. = pessimistic forecast
R.&D. = additional research and
          development expenditures

Payoffs expressed in millions
of dollars

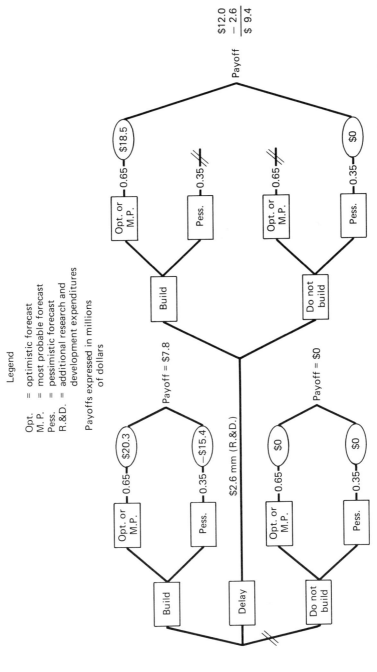

Payoff
$12.0
− 2.6
$ 9.4

Source: Reprinted, with permission, from W. Alderson and P. E. Green, *Planning and Problem Solving in Marketing* (Homewood, Ill.: Richard D. Irwin, Inc., 1964), Chap. 8, p. 229.

Figure 2-6   Risk simulation for investment planning

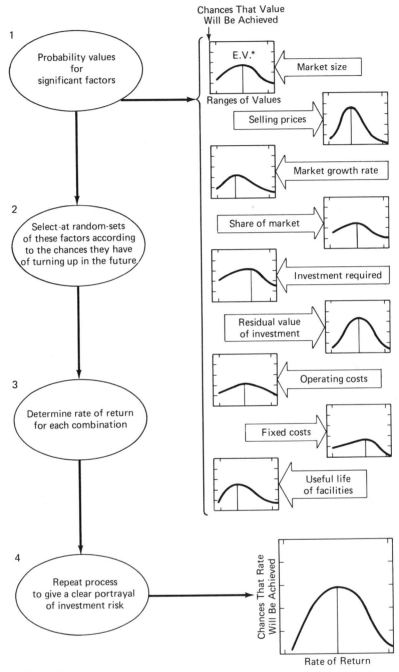

Source: Reprinted, with permission, from D. B. Hertz, "Risk Analysis in Capital Investment," *Harvard Business Review*, 42 (January–February, 1964), 95–106.

product formulation, such as a different type of chocolate in a candy bar or a different type of coffee blend.[11]

As Villani and Morrison point out, potential customers for the new brand are drawn from two categories—users and nonusers of the current formulation. A consumer selected from each category has some probability of trying the new formulation and, having tried it, some probability of liking it. Since the two pools of potential customers (users versus nonusers) are likely to vary in initial size and in their trying and liking probabilities as well, the authors propose that the category sizes and probabilities be estimated separately for each group.

Figure 2-7, adapted from Villani and Morrison's article, shows how the decision tree provides a useful tool for portraying the needed inputs to their model. For example, the expected number of customers for the new formulation, as obtained from the users category, is found by multiplying the number of people in that category by the probability of trying the new formulation, which, in turn, is multiplied by the conditional probability of liking, given that one has tried the new formulation.

Figure 2-7   Decision tree for demand estimation

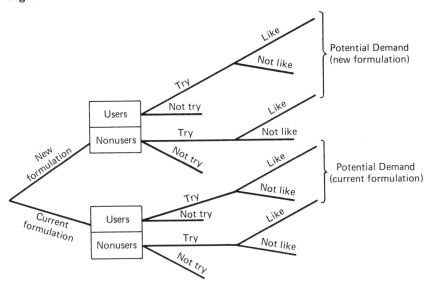

Source: Adapted, with permission, from K. E. A. Villani and D. G. Morrison, "A Method for Analyzing New Formulation Decisions," *Journal of Marketing Research*, 13 (August, 1976), 284–88, published by the American Marketing Association.

---

[11]K. E. A. Villani and D. G. Morrison, "A Method for Analyzing New Formulation Decisions," *Journal of Marketing Research*, 13 (August, 1976), 284–88.

Note that the decision tree of Figure 2-7 provides a simple way of showing the steps needed to develop the demand estimates. One can easily see, for example, how demand for the new formulation depends upon consumers drawn initially from users and nonusers of the current formulation.

SUMMARY

This chapter has presented the fundamentals of the Bayesian approach to decision making under uncertainty. Our motivation was to use this model as a means for assessing the value versus cost of information that can be provided by marketing research. Two numerical examples—one highly simplified and the other more detailed—were used to illustrate the following basic ideas:

1. Prior analysis.
2. Posterior analysis.
3. Preposterior analysis, including the computation of the expected value of perfect information.

We showed how various information-gathering options could be evaluated in terms of their net expected payoffs.[12]

We next discussed the related topics of determining the payoff entries and the role that utility functions could play in quantifying attitudes toward risk. This led to a discussion of the potential value of Bayesian analysis in the general manager–researcher dialogue that is useful in the design and implementation of marketing research studies. We concluded the chapter with brief descriptions of industry applications of Bayesian decision analysis and related methods.

ASSIGNMENT MATERIAL

1. Bernard B. Bayes, a sophisticated marketing research analyst, is charged with the assignment of recommending whether his firm should produce a new Christmas toy, the Mechanical Frump. His boss feels that a 60–40 chance exists that the toy will be successful.

---

[12]More extensive discussion of Bayesian methods can be found in the introductory text, Howard Raiffa, *Decision Analysis, Introductory Lectures on Choices under Uncertainty* (Reading, Mass: Addison-Wesley Publishing Company, Inc., 1968) and in the more technical book by John Pratt, Howard Raiffa, and Robert Schlaifer, *Introduction to Statistical Decision Theory* (New York: McGraw-Hill Book Company, 1965).

The payoff table (entries in thousands of dollars) is as follows:

Action	$P(S_1)$	S_1	$P(S_2)$	S_2
A_1: produce	0.6	150	0.4	−100
A_2: do not produce	0.6	0	0.4	0

Two market survey firms have submitted bids for doing the field work of interviewing toy store owners. The Alpha Company is known to conduct highly accurate surveys (at rather high cost), whereas the Beta Company's accuracy is somewhat lower but so is its cost. Pertinent conditional probabilities of survey results Z_1 (indicating S_1) and Z_2 (indicating S_2) are as follows:

Firm	Conditional Probabilities	Cost ($)
Alpha Company	$P(Z_1 \mid S_1) = P(Z_2 \mid S_2) = 0.9$ $P(Z_1 \mid S_2) = P(Z_2 \mid S_1) = 0.1$	50,000
Beta Company	$P(Z_1 \mid S_1) = P(Z_2 \mid S_2) = 0.7$ $P(Z_1 \mid S_2) = P(Z_2 \mid S_1) = 0.3$	30,000

Mr. Bayes has the following options: conduct no survey; buy Alpha's survey; buy Beta's survey.
a. Evaluate the expected payoff of each option. Prepare appropriate decision trees.
b. What is the expected value of perfect information?
c. Would your answer to part (a) change if the prior probability assignment over S_1 and S_2 were 0.9 and 0.1, respectively? If so, how?

2. The Bronstein Abacus Corporation is considering a proposal to develop a new calculator. The initial cash outlay would be $1 million. Development time is one year. If successful, the firm anticipates revenues (over the life cycle of the product) as follows:

end of year 2: $200,000
end of year 3:   300,000
end of year 4:   400,000
end of year 5:   500,000

If the new calculator is unsuccessful, the firm anticipates cash inflows of zero. The firm feels that a 90–10 chance exists for success of the product. Given a 10% annual cost of capital, should the venture be undertaken?

3. The Kiefer Oil Corporation is faced with the decision of whether or not to delay a decision regarding a new venture, pending the receipt of additional information on its success, given commercialization. The payoff matrix (entries in millions of dollars) is as follows:

Action	S_1	S_2
A_1: commercialize	20	-10
A_2: do not commercialize	0	0

The firm would incur a $3 million cost if the decision regarding the project were delayed. The conditional probabilities of Z_1 (indicating S_1) and Z_2 (indicating S_2), given the information anticipated to be developed in the delay period are

$$P(Z_1 | S_1) = P(Z_2 | S_2) = 0.8$$
$$P(Z_1 | S_2) = P(Z_2 | S_1) = 0.2$$

Management elected to delay the venture. What can we infer from this action about the prior probabilities $P(S_1)$ and $P(S_2)$, assuming that in the *absence* of the survey management would have chosen act A_1?

4. Describe how one could structure the decision of which college to choose for graduate work in business administration as a problem in Bayesian analysis.

5. How might the Bayesian model be used to examine actual decision makers' reactions to the receipt of new information in a decision problem under uncertainty?

The Tactics
of Marketing Research—
Research Design

INTRODUCTION

In Chapter 1 we described marketing research as an activity concerned with acquiring and analyzing information related to the identification and solution of marketing problems. The strategy of research—utilizing the Bayesian framework of cost versus value of information—was discussed in Chapter 2.

In this chapter we turn to the problem of research *tactics* as considered from the viewpoint of the marketing researcher. More specifically, we are concerned with the sources and means available for acquiring marketing information and the types of research designs appropriate for organizing and analyzing this information.

We first consider the characteristics of research design and the role it plays in information collection. Exploratory, descriptive, and causal studies are defined and discussed. We then turn to an introductory treatment of the general sources of information, in which we consider in turn: (1) secondary information, (2) respondents, (3) natural experiments, (4) controlled experiments, and (5) simulation. Continuous panels are discussed in the context of natural experiments and controlled experiments. The treatment in this chapter of these five sources of marketing information is descriptive in nature and is for the purpose of giving a broad overview of alternative sources. We examine surveys of respondents and controlled experiments—two of the major sources of information—in detail in subsequent chapters.

We conclude the chapter by returning to the problem of the economics of research design and examining it within the context of the cost and value of information.

RESEARCH DESIGN

A *research design* is the specification of methods and procedures for acquiring the information needed to structure or to solve problems. It is the overall operational pattern or framework of the project that stipulates what information is to be collected, from which sources, and by what procedures. If it is a good design, it will ensure that the information obtained is relevant to the research problem and that it was collected by objective and economical procedures.

Although research designs may be classified by many criteria, the most useful one concerns the major purpose of the investigation. On this basis we may identify the broad classes of designs as exploratory, descriptive, and causal.

Exploratory Studies

The major purposes of *exploratory studies* are the identification of problems, the more precise formulation of problems (including the identification of relevant variables), and the formulation of new alternative courses of action. An exploratory study is often the first in a series of projects that culminate in one concerned with the drawing of inferences that are used as the basis of management action.

The design of exploratory studies is characterized by a great amount of flexibility and ad hoc versatility. By definition, the researcher is involved in investigating an area or subject in which he is not sufficiently knowledgeable to have formulated detailed research questions. No clear hypotheses have been developed about the problem. He is seeking information that will enable him to formulate specific research questions and/or to state hypotheses about the problem.

An example of an exploratory study is one conducted by a major manufacturer of kitchen ranges. The purpose of the research was to "investigate the design of our ranges to see if it can be improved functionally." One part of the project design involved setting up a booth in department stores handling the brand and inviting women to simulate the cooking of a meal calling for one menu item to be boiled, another fried, another simmered, and so on. It was discovered that the women almost invariably used the same burners for the same type of cooking: for example, the left front burner for frying, the left back burner for boiling, and the right back burner for simmering. These exploratory research findings led to a prototype redesign of the burners and additional research on them along with research on preferences and usage patterns of ranges with respect to baking and the storage of cooking utensils.

Despite the necessity for flexibility in exploratory study design, we can distinguish three separate stages that are usually included in exploratory studies and typically conducted in the sequence listed. These are: (1) a search of secondary information sources, (2) interviews with persons who are knowledgeable about the subject area being explored, and (3) the examination of analogous situations.

Search of Secondary Sources

Secondary sources of information, as used in this section, are the rough equivalent of the "literature" on the subject. (We shall use this term in an expanded sense later in this chapter.)

It is the rare research problem for which there is no relevant information to be found by a relatively quick and inexpensive search of the literature. If the question to be answered by the research project referred to above is "How might we improve the functional design of our ranges?" it is likely that information bearing on this question will have been published. Studies performed on this subject by home economists at universities, by governmental agencies, or by women's magazines will probably have been made and published.

A later section of this chapter deals with secondary sources of information in more detail.

Obtaining Information from Knowledgeable Persons

This stage of the exploratory investigation is a natural complement to the use of secondary information. After having searched secondary sources, it will usually be desirable to talk with persons who are well informed in the area being investigated.

This survey is sometimes called an *experience survey* or a *pilot survey.* Rarely is it structured in the sense of a formal questionnaire being prepared, a probability sample selected, or the sample size specified in advance. Rather, the usual procedure is to look for competent, articulate individuals and talk with them about the problem. They will often suggest others who should be reached; a "referral" sample frequently results. The investigator continues these interviews until he feels that the marginal return in information becomes less than the costs involved.

With respect to the redesign of ranges, knowledgeable persons—housewives—were asked to provide information. A convenience sample was taken of housewives who were shopping in the department stores where booths were installed. Observations were made until it was established that there was a consistent behavior pattern with respect to the use of each burner. Once this finding was established, this phase of the exploratory study was terminated.

Examination of Analogous Situations

It is also logical that one will want to examine analogous situations to determine what can be learned about the nature of the problem and its variables. Analogous situations consist of case histories and simulations. Examination of case histories is one of the older methods of marketing research, whereas the use of simulations is one of the newer methods.

Case histories that are similar in content are generally available and provide a fruitful area of investigation for the exploratory study. They are well suited for use in exploratory studies in that the examination of another actual case problem will often help clarify the nature of the problem at hand, suggest which variables are relevant, and give indications of the nature of the relationship of the variables. This method of investigation is widely used in the behavioral sciences, where it is called the "case study."

However, the results of the investigation of case histories are always to be considered as suggestive rather than conclusive. Since the examination is being conducted on an after-the-fact basis, it is not possible to manipulate the independent variables or to randomize treatments and the selection of groups concerned. For these reasons the interpretations reached concerning the relevancy and relationships of variables are judgmental and always subject to error.

In the case of the problems concerning redesign of kitchen ranges, ready-made case histories may well be available in the form of previous design changes made by competitors. One might be able to observe what happened to the sales of one or more competitors' ranges following design changes. As always in case studies, one would have to examine the situation(s) carefully to try to identify and assess the effect of any other independent variable changes (price, advertising, changes in income, etc.) on sales. Tentative conclusions can be reached, however, and a hypothesis stated. This hypothesis can be tested in a subsequent causal study designed for that purpose if it is desired to do so.

Simulation of the general problem situation (discussed later in the chapter) may also be useful for providing a better understanding of the problem and its components. Simulation involves the construction of a model representing the situation and, in effect, experimenting with it rather than the actual situation.

Descriptive Studies

Much research is concerned with *describing* market characteristics or functions. A market-potential study is made that describes the number, distribution, and socioeconomic characteristics of potential customers of a product; a market-share study is conducted to find out the share of the market received by both the company and its competitors; or a sales analysis is made, that states sales by territory, type of account, size or model of product, and the like. Descriptive studies are also made in product research (a listing and comparison of the functional features and specifications of competitive products, for example), promotion research (the demographic characteristics of the audience being reached by the current advertising program), distribution research (the number and location of retailers handling the company's products that are supplied by wholesalers versus those supplied by the company's distribution centers), and pricing research (competitors' prices by geographic area). It is obvious that the examples of descriptive research given thus far cover only a few of the possibilities.

These studies often involve the description of the extent of the association between two or more variables. A frequency distribution of sales by the income levels of consumers is an example. This type of information may be used to draw inferences concerning the relationship between the variables involved. It may also be used for purposes of prediction.

Although associations can be used only to infer, and not to establish, a causal relationship, they are often useful for predictive purposes. It is not always necessary to understand causal relations in order to make accurate predictive statements. The striking of a match is a simple illustration. Based on past experience and an examination of associated conditions (whether the match is dry, if the surface on which it is to be struck is the right kind, etc.), a statement can be made with a high probability of success as to whether or not a given match will ignite. This assertion can be made with no knowledge of the chemical reaction that takes place when the match is struck; that is, it can be based solely on descriptive information. In fact, the average user of matches can probably make as accurate a predictive statement as can a chemist in this situation.

Descriptive information often provides a sound basis for the solution of marketing problems, even though it does not "explain" the nature of the relationship involved. The basic principle involved is to find correlates of the behavior it is desired to predict that are measurable at the time the predictive statement is made.

Descriptive research, in contrast to exploratory research, is marked by the *prior formulation of specific research questions*. The investigator already knows a substantial amount about the research problem, perhaps as a result of an exploratory study, before the project is initiated. He should be able to define clearly what it is that he wants to measure and to set up appropriate and specific means for measuring it.

An example of a descriptive study is one performed by a company that was considering entering the greeting card industry. A previous exploratory study had revealed that only 2% of the sales of greeting cards was made through supermarkets. Since the potential of this type of outlet is large, and other outlets were heavily franchised or otherwise dominated by well-entrenched companies in the field, a descriptive study was performed to answer the specific question, "What are the major problems of selling greeting cards in volume through supermarkets?" The answers obtained resulted in the company's developing a greeting card vending machine that is being used successfully in supermarkets.

Descriptive research is also characterized by a preplanned and structured design. As contrasted with the flexibility of the exploratory study, the descriptive study should be planned carefully with respect to the sources of information to be consulted and the procedures to be used in collecting information. Since the intent of the study is to provide answers to specific questions, more care is normally exercised against the possibility of systematic (nonrandom) errors than is the case with the exploratory study.

The designs used in descriptive research can employ one or more of the following sources of information: (1) secondary sources, (2) respondents, (3) natural experiments, (4) controlled experiments, and (5) simulation.

Causal Studies

Causal Relationships

Although descriptive information is often useful for predictive purposes, where possible we would like to know the *causes* of what we are predicting —the "reasons why." Further, we would like to know the relationships of these causal factors to the effects that we are predicting. In part, this is, no doubt, because we each have an innate desire to understand. Of a more direct and practical consequence, however, is the fact that, if the causes of the effects we want to predict are understood, our ability both to predict and to control these effects is almost invariably improved.

Causation as a subject of discussion and systematic inquiry (the science of etiology) dates back to the time of the early Greeks. Plato, Aristotle, St. Thomas Aquinas, Kant, Hume, Newton, Locke, Mill, and Freud are but a few of those who have contributed to this inquiry. No attempt will be made to summarize each of these contributions, but it is important that an understanding of what is meant by "cause" be reached before we proceed.

Suppose that a particular manufacturer of color television sets reduces the wholesale price of his sets by 10% and that this reduction is passed on to the consumer. Further, assume that sales to the consumer rose by 15% during the succeeding three months as compared with a like period prior to the price reduction. Did the price cut *cause* the increase in sales?

Deterministic Causation

Real-world events occur in and are affected by a real-world environment. The nature of this environment determines the "rules" that describe the relationship between events. The nature of the relationship between price and quantity of television sets sold by the state-owned monopoly in the Soviet Union is quite different from that for an individual producer in the United States.

Suppose that we establish a functional relationship between two events, X and Y, such that "Y is some function of X." This statement may be written

$$Y = F(X)$$

Further, suppose that we know the environment of these two events well enough to determine the "rule" that relates them, and thus specify F. Once we specify X, we have completely determined Y. In this case we may say that X is both a *necessary* and a *sufficient* condition for Y. We must specify X, but only X, to determine Y. We may, therefore, say that X is a *deterministic cause* of Y. We may define a deterministic cause as any event that is necessary and sufficient for the subsequent occurrence of another event.[1]

Returning to our example, would it be realistic to conclude that the price cut was a deterministic cause of the sales increase? Clearly, it would not. Many factors other than price affect the level of sales; a change in price is, therefore, not a sufficient condition for determining the level of sales.

Probabilistic Causation

Our discussion of problem-situation models in Chapter 1 permits us to generalize beyond the last example: relationships in marketing usually involve several variables. As further complications, these relationships are almost invariably complex, subject to change, and difficult to measure.

Consider now a multivariable relationship of the form

$$Y = F(X_1, X_2)$$

where X_1 and X_2 are independent. Assuming that we are able to specify F, the variables X_1 and X_2 become *jointly* necessary and sufficient to determine Y.

Suppose that we know the value of X_1 but do not know the value of X_2. Since X_1 and X_2 are assumed to be independent, no inferences can be drawn about the value of X_2 from the known value of X_1. Note that, in this situation, the only statements we can make about the value of Y must be conditional upon the unknown value of X_2. The effect on Y of a known change in

[1]This definition, and the definition of probabilistic cause in the next section, follow that in R. L. Ackoff, Shiv Gupta, and J. S. Minas, *Scientific Method: Optimizing Applied Research Decisions* (New York: John Wiley & Sons, Inc., 1962), Chap. 1.

X_1 may be reinforced, counteracted, or left the same, depending upon what happens to X_2. X_1 is not sufficient to determine Y.

Where multivariable relationships exist, we may say that any one of the independent variables X_j is a *probabilistic cause* of the effect Y. The term *producer* is sometimes used, and will be used here, as being synonymous with probabilistic cause. When the term "producer" is used, the resulting effect is referred to as a *product*.

In the more general case, we may define a probabilistic cause, or producer, as any event (e.g., X_1 or X_2) that is necessary but not sufficient for the subsequent occurrence of another event, Y.

Are we to conclude that the price reduction was a producer of the sales increase (product) in our example? Given that we believe that the price level and amount of sales of television sets are inversely and functionally related, we are, in fact, drawing that conclusion.

The reader should be careful not to read more into the last statement than is actually there. Note that it does *not* say that the price reduction determined the amount of the sales increase, or that it was even a major factor in bringing about any increase in sales. It may have been that a newly redesigned model series prompted a concomitant change in advertising and in price, and the other changes were more important producers of the sales increase than the price change.

Bases for Inferring Causal Relationships

What kinds of evidence can be used for drawing inferences about causal relationships? There are three types of such evidence: (1) associative variation, (2) sequence of events, and (3) absence of other possible causal factors.

Associative Variation. Associative variation, or "concomitant variation," as it is often termed, is a measure of the extent to which occurrences of two variables are associated. Two types of associative variation may be distinguished:

1. *Association between two variables*—a measure of the extent to which the presence of one variable is associated with the presence of the other.
2. *Association between the changes of two variables*—a measure of the extent to which a change in the level of one variable is associated with a change in the level of the other.

As an example, suppose that the brand manager of a particular brand of detergent notices that sales have shown an unusually large increase in the third quarter, and suppose that he is also aware that a number of detergent sales personnel took a retraining course during the second quarter. How may he determine if the retraining was a producer of the sales increase?

Two basic approaches, with variations on each, can be followed to obtain evidence concerning this relationship. The first is to start with the hypothesized producer (salesperson retraining) and see if there is an associated variation with the product ("large" territorial sales increase). This could be done by determining which salespeople had been retrained during the second quarter and comparing the net changes in sales between the second and third quarters in their territories with the corresponding net changes in sales of those salespeople who were not retrained during the second quarter.

The second approach is to start with the product ("large" territorial sales increase) and work back to the producer (salesperson retraining). If this approach were used, all territories with "large" sales increases would be examined to determine whether they were predominantly those of salespeople who had been retrained during the second quarter.

Suppose that one of these approaches was used to collect information that showed a high degree of association between "large" territorial sales increases and salesperson retraining. Would this information constitute experimental "proof" of a causal relationship?

The answer to this question is, unfortunately, "No, it would not." The reasons why this is the case are discussed in detail in later chapters. It is sufficient to state here that this associated variation might be the result of random variation or the result of both variables being associated with some extraneous variable (a change in the point-of-sale displays provided to the salespeople who took the retraining course, for example). If we have no basis for believing that either of these situations exists, then we may use the associated variation as a basis for inferring—but not scientifically testing—that there is a causal relationship.

Sequence of Events. A second characteristic of a causal relationship is the requirement that the causal factor occur first; the producer must precede the product. In order for the salesperson retraining to have resulted in an increase in sales, the retraining must have taken place prior to the sales increase.

The fact that a possible producer precedes a product does not establish that a causal relationship exists between the two, however. It might be that it was simply a coincidence that the retraining took place prior to the sales increase. It might also be that sales training and sales increases are associated but not causally related. (A salesman may shave every day before going to work, but shaving is not a cause of his going to work.)

It is not always easy to determine the sequence of events. In such cases where an actual causal relationship does exist, it is difficult to determine which is the producer and which is the product. The relationship between shelf space and sales is an example. Other factors being equal, those brands having the larger relative amounts of shelf space tend to have higher sales. Other factors being equal, those brands having the higher sales tend to be allotted the larger relative amounts of shelf space.

Absence of Other Possible Causal Factors.   A final basis for inferring causation is the absence of any possible causal factors (producers) other than the one or ones being investigated. If it could be demonstrated, for example, that no other factors present could have caused the sales increase in the third quarter, we could then logically conclude that the salesperson training must have been responsible.

Obviously, in an after-the-fact examination of a situation such as the detergent sales increase, it is impossible ever to clearly rule out all other factors. One could never be completely sure that there were no competitor, customer, or company-initiated causal factors that would account for the sales increase.

In experimental designs in which control groups are used, it is possible that some of the variables that might otherwise obscure or lead to a misinterpretation of the relationship(s) under study can be controlled. In addition, a soundly designed experiment will include an attempt to balance the effects of the uncontrolled variables on the experimental results in such a way that only random variations resulting from the uncontrolled variables will be measured.

For example, an experiment might be designed in which salespeople who have not yet undergone retraining are matched in pairs with respect to age, past sales history, type of territory, and other variables believed to be possible determinants of sales performance. A control group could then be chosen by selecting one salesperson from each pair at random who would not be retrained during the period of the experiment. The experimental group would then consist of the other salesperson from each of the pairs, who would be retrained. An analysis of the differences in sales results for the two groups during the period of the experiment could then be made to test the hypothesis that salesperson retraining does result in a significant increase in sales.

Conclusions Concerning Types of Evidence

No one of the three types of evidence, nor, indeed, all three types combined, can ever demonstrate conclusively that a causal relationship exists. However, we *can* obtain evidence that makes it highly reasonable to conclude that a particular relationship exists.

The accumulation of evidence from various investigations will, if all findings point to the same conclusion, increase our confidence that a causal relationship exists. A diversity of types of evidence is also convincing in this respect. If evidence of all three of the types discussed above can be obtained, the resulting inference is more convincing than if the evidence is of only one type.

Causal Inference Studies

Over the last few pages we have considered the nature and meaning of causation and the types of evidence that can be useful for drawing inferences about causal relationships. We now turn to a consideration of the design of causal studies.

There are two broad classes of designs for causal inference research: (1) natural experiments and (2) controlled experiments. The distinguishing feature between the two is the extent of intervention by the investigator in the situation under study. As the name implies, a *natural experiment* may not require investigator intervention in the situation at all and, at most, will involve intervention only to the extent required for measurement. A *controlled experiment* will require investigator intervention to control and to manipulate variables of interest as well as to measure the response.

The salesperson-retraining example (as originally described) is an illustration of a natural experiment. In this case no intervention was involved in the situation; the measurements made were conducted as a normal part of doing business. Had the investigator wanted to measure results other than those normally measured—the amount of shelf space in retail stores the company's detergents had in the affected territories before and after the retraining of salespeople, for example—there would necesssarily have been investigator intervention to the extent required to perform such measurements.

One possible controlled experiment for assessing the effect of sales retraining on the level of sales has already been described. Investigator intervention was involved in matching the salespeople in pairs and randomly selecting one from each pair for inclusion in the test group. The experimental procedures were, therefore, the determinant of which salespeople were to be retrained. Clearly, intervention of this kind is not always practical or even possible.

It is apparent from the discussion thus far that causal studies presuppose a considerable amount of knowledge by the investigator about the variables being studied. The design of causal inference studies is also highly formalized. The experiment just described uses a form of "before–after with control group" design. We shall describe some specific designs of both natural and controlled experiments later in the chapter.

Since we have now considered the three general classes of marketing research designs (exploratory, descriptive, and causal), it is appropriate that we turn to a consideration of the sources from which studies using one or more of these designs obtain marketing information.

THE SOURCES OF MARKETING INFORMATION

There are five major sources of marketing information. These are: (1) secondary sources, (2) respondents, (3) natural experiments, (4) controlled experiments, and (5) simulation. In this section we shall introduce and briefly describe each so that the reader will have an overview and an introduction to subsequent chapters that describe some of these sources in more detail.

Secondary Sources of Information

Secondary information is information that has been collected by persons or agencies for purposes other than the solution of the problem at hand. A furniture manufacturer, for example, who needs information on the potential market for furniture in the Middle Atlantic states has many secondary sources of information available to him. The federal government collects and publishes information on the numbers of families, family formation, income, and the number and sales volume of retail stores, all by geographic area. It also publishes special reports on the furniture industry. Many state and local governments collect similar information for their respective areas. The trade associations in the furniture field collect and publish an extensive amount of information about the industry. Trade journals are a valuable source of secondary information, as are special studies done by other advertising media. These and other sources will yield much information of value to the researcher concerned with this problem.

Reasons for Obtaining Secondary Information

As a general rule, no research project should be conducted without a search of secondary-information sources. This search should be conducted early in the problem investigation and prior to any organized collection of information from primary sources. There are several reasons for this.

1. *Secondary information may solve the problem.* If adequate data are available from secondary sources, primary data collection will not be required.

2. *Search costs are substantially lower than primary collection costs.* A comprehensive search of secondary sources can almost always be made in a fraction of the time and cost required for the collection of primary information. Although many marketing problems do not warrant the expenditures involved for primary information collection, it is a rare situation in which obtaining secondary data is not worth the time and cost invested.

3. *Secondary information has important supplementary uses.* Even when the secondary information obtained is not adequate for solving the problem involved, it often has valuable supplemental uses. These include:

    a. Helping to define the problem and formulate hypotheses about its solution. The assembling and analyzing of available secondary data will almost always provide a better understanding of the problem and its context and will frequently suggest solutions not considered previously.

    b. Helping to plan the collection of primary data. An examination of the methods and techniques employed by other investigators in similar studies may be useful in planning the present one. It may also be of value in establishing classifications that are compatible with past studies so that trends may be more readily analyzed.

    c. Use in defining the population and selecting the sample in primary information collection.

Secondary information falls into two categories, the distinguishing feature being whether it is available within the company or must be obtained from outside sources. We shall call that secondary information which is available within the company, *internal secondary information*, and refer to that from outside the company as *external secondary information*.

Internal Secondary Information

All companies collect information in the everyday course of conducting business. Orders are received and filled, costs are recorded, salespeople's reports are submitted, engineering reports are made—these are but a few of the many sources of information, collected by companies for other purposes, that are often useful to the researcher.

A basic source of information, one that is all too often overlooked, is the sales invoice. By simple analyses of the information available on the company's sales invoice, one can determine the level and trend of sales quite easily by such characteristics as the following:

1. Model and size of product by territory.
2. Model and size of product by type of account.
3. Model and size of product by industry.
4. Average size of sale by territory.
5. Average size of sale by type of account.
6. Average size of sale by industry.
7. Average size of sale by salesperson.

8. Proportion of sales volume by model and size of product.
9. Proportion of sales volume by territory.
10. Proportion of sales volume by type of account.
11. Proportion of sales volume by size of account.
12. Proportion of sales volume by industry.

External Secondary Information

External secondary information is available in a staggering array and amount. It also is applicable to all of the major types of marketing research projects and is mainly concerned with the noncontrollable aspects of the problem: the total market size, market characteristics, and competitor products, prices, promotional efforts, and distribution methods.

The major sources of external secondary information are: (1) governmental (federal, state, and local), (2) trade associations and trade press, (3) periodicals, (4) institutions, and (5) commercial services. The federal government is by far the largest single source. Both governmental and trade sources are so important that the experienced and competent researcher will be thoroughly familiar with them in his field of specialization. Periodicals and the publications of research projects conducted by universities and research institutes frequently provide valuable information. Commercial services of many types are available that are highly useful for specific research problems.

Market performance studies on consumer products, for example, will normally require such demographic information as the number of consumers (or consuming units) by age group, income class, sex, and geographic area. Such data are usually available on a reasonably recent basis from censuses conducted by federal, state, and local governments. The *Census of Population* and the *Census of Housing* taken by the U.S. Department of Commerce every ten years are the most comprehensive of such censuses.

Information on new products and processes are available from such sources as patent disclosures, trade journals, competitors' catalogs, testing agencies, and the reports of such governmental agencies as the Food and Drug Administration, the Department of Agriculture, and the Bureau of Standards.

An extensive amount of information is available concerning advertising. Through the *Publishers Information Bureau*, for example, one can obtain a compilation of expenditures by medium for each competitor. The *Audit Bureau of Circulation* provides data on the numbers of magazine copies sold under specified conditions. The reports of the *Standard Rate and Data Service* provide complete information on the rates and specifications for buying advertising space and time. A number of commercial services, such as the *Nielsen Radio–Television Index*, the *Hooperating, Trendex*, the *Starch Advertis-*

ing Readership Service, and *AdTel* supply measures of audience exposure to specific advertisements or programs.

There are also a substantial number of sources and amounts of data available for distribution research. The *Census of Business* provides information on retail and wholesale sales by type of outlet and geographic area. The *Census of Manufacturers* lists geographical and industry data on manufacturers including costs of materials and quantities of products produced. *County Business Patterns* gives the locations of businesses by a large number of classifications.

An unfailing earmark of the experienced researcher is his knowledge of specific sources and efficient search procedures for other published sources of relevant information. This personal knowledge is indispensable in finding, evaluating, and using information from secondary sources. With the mass of secondary information currently being published, however, even the experienced researcher will often need to refer to general reference works, bibliographies, indexes, and other guides to ensure that he has obtained all the secondary information relevant to the particular problem on which he is working.

Information from Respondents

A second major source of information is that obtained from respondents. Asking questions and observing behavior are primary means of obtaining information whenever people's actions are being investigated or predicted. The term *respondent* literally means "one who responds; answers." For our purposes it will be useful to include both verbal and behavioral response in the usage of the term. That is, we shall consider both the information obtained from asking people questions and that provided by observing behavior or the results of past behavior as comprising information from respondents.

Information from Communication with Respondents

The *survey*, in its many forms, is a widely used and well-known method of acquiring marketing information through communicating with a group of respondents. Information is obtained from consumers, industrial users, dealers, and others who are knowledgeable about the problem at hand. People are asked questions through personal interviews, telephone interviews, and mail questionnaires. They are asked for information as either part of a self-contained, "one-time" survey or repetitively as part of a continuing panel.

Questioning of respondents is virtually a necessity if one wants to obtain information about level of knowledge, attitudes, opinions, and motivations, or intended behavior. If, for example, a bank were considering providing for its depositors a service of direct payment of utility and credit card bills, the only practical way of determining how much the depositors knew about this type of service, their attitudes and opinions about it, and whether or not they intended to use it would be to ask them.

Although questioning of respondents is often the most efficient and economical way to obtain information, it requires considerable skill and care in application if the information is to be of maximum value. At best, people will respond with information that they are *able* to provide. At worst, misleading and highly biased information may result.

The kinds of information that may be obtained from respondents and the errors it is subject to are discussed in detail in Chapter 4. The different means of communicating with respondents are discussed in Chapter 5.

Information from Observation of Respondents

Relevant information for many marketing problems may be obtained by observing either present behavior or the results of past behavior. The researcher who requires information on the color and style preferences for men's shoes may well find this method ideally suited to his purpose.

Observational methods make it possible to record behavior as it occurs and thus to eliminate errors arising from the reporting of the behavior. For example, the researcher who observes the number of units and brands of a product class actually bought in supermarkets by a sample of housewives rather than questioning the housewives later will have avoided the errors inherent in relying on respondents' memories.

For reasons that are apparent, observing people's behavior cannot be used effectively to obtain information about the level of knowledge, opinions, and motivations, or the intended behavior of respondents. In some instances, where the behavior is private or impossible to observe, it cannot be used at all.

Observation of respondents is discussed in detail in Chapter 5.

Information from Natural and Controlled Experiments

The subject of natural and controlled experimental designs was briefly treated earlier in this chapter. In this section we shall describe and evaluate some specific types of designs in each category.

Three types of evidence were described as providing the bases for drawing inferences about causal relationships: associative variation, sequence of events, and absence of other possible causal factors (producers). Either natural or controlled experimental designs are capable of providing the first two, but only controlled experiments can provide reasonably conclusive evidence concerning the third, the absence of other possible producers.

The kind of evidence that is required to support the inference that other producers could not have been the causative ones varies, depending upon the producer being investigated. However, there are some general classes of variables affecting designs that deserve mention. These are: (1) history, (2) maturation, (3) testing effect, (4) instrument effect, and (5) selection.

History deals with events outside the design that affect the dependent variable. History is therefore comprised of the producers that are extraneous to the design. In the salesperson-retraining example, the level of competitive promotion and advertising, the overall level of demand, or any one of many other producers may have changed substantially in some of the territories. Clearly, the longer the time period involved, the greater the probability that history will significantly affect the results.

Maturation is concerned with the changes that occur with the passage of time in the people involved in the design. For example, as time passes, salespeople gain more experience in selling and hence know their customers better, and the customers become better acquainted with the product. Again, the effect of maturation on the results is a direct function of the time period involved.

Testing effect has to do with the learning or conditioning of the persons involved in the design as a result of knowing that their behavior is being observed and/or that the results are being measured. If the salesperson knows that he is being retrained as a part of a study to determine how effective retraining is, he may act differently than he would have otherwise. A frequent problem in research design is that a "before" measurement is desired, but it is recognized that making such a measurement may alert the subjects that they are participating in a study. If they surmise that an "after" measurement will be taken, they may become sensitized to the variables involved and behave differently as a result.

Instrument effect refers to the changes in the measuring instrument or process that may affect the measurements obtained. If total dollar sales volume per territory on a "before" and "after" basis were being used to determine the effect of retraining, a price change in the interim could clearly make a substantial difference. This is an obvious change in the measuring instrument, but many other and more subtle changes can occur. The learning process on the part of the investigators, a change in investigators, or simply boredom or fatigue may affect the measurements and thus the interpretation of results.

Selection is concerned with the effect of the selection procedure for the test and control groups on the results of the study. If the selection procedure is randomized, the effect will be a measurable random variation. However, if the selection is by the investigator, self-selection, or some other nonrandom (purposive) procedure, the results will be affected in a nonmeasurable manner. Sizable systematic errors may well result.

The following notational system will be used in the discussion of natural and controlled experimental designs:

- *X* represents the exposure of test groups to an experimental treatment of a producer or event whose effect is to be observed and/or measured.
- *O* refers to the measurement or observation taken.
- *R* indicates that individuals have been selected at random for groups to receive differing treatments or that the groups have been assigned at random to differing treatments.
- Movement from left to right indicates a sequence of events. When *O*'s and *X*'s are found in a given row, they are to be interpreted as having occurred in sequence and to the same specific individual or group. Vertical arrangement of symbols is to be interpreted as the simultaneous occurrence of the events that they denote.

Natural Experiments

A *natural experiment* is one in which the investigator intervenes only to the extent required for measurement. There are three classes of designs for natural experiments: (1) time series and trend designs, (2) cross-sectional designs, and (3) combinations of the two.

Time Series and Trend Designs

Time series and trend designs are similar in concept, yet their differences in implementation and analytic procedures warrant a brief discussion. A *time series design* involves obtaining data from the same sample (or population) for successive points in time. The common method of gathering primary data of this kind is to collect current data at successive intervals through the use of a continuous panel. One may, however, collect current and retrospective data from respondents during a single interview. If the latter technique is used, respondent recall must be depended upon to reconstruct quasi-historical data. An alternative method of obtaining data for past periods, when available, is to use secondary sources.

Trend data differ from time series data in that they are obtained from statistically matched samples drawn from the same population over time. Current data are gathered from each successive sample.

Both time series and trend data are used to investigate the existence and nature of causal relationships based on associative-variation and sequence-of-events types of evidence. While individuals or households are the most commonly used sample units, data are also obtained from retail stores, wholesalers, manufacturers, and other units.

Since trend designs provide no continuity in the sample units from whom data are obtained, there is no opportunity to observe changes over time in individual sample units. Trend data, therefore, can only be analyzed in the aggregated form in which they are collected. Time series data generated from continuous panels and, to a lesser extent, from retrospective interviews permit analysis of effects by individual sample units. Microanalyses of this type can provide valuable information on buyer behavior including purchase rates, brand switching, and brand loyalty. The analysis of microeffects is called *longitudinal analysis.*

Time series and trend designs involve, at a minimum, one treatment and a subsequent measurement. At the other extreme they may involve a large number of measurements with several interspersed treatments. We now describe and discuss four types of time series and trend designs.

After-Only without Control Group. This design is often termed a "tryout" or a "one-shot case study." It is the simplest of all designs, as it involves only one nonrandomly selected group, one treatment, and one measurement. Symbolically, it may be diagrammed as follows:

$$X \quad O \tag{1}$$

If not already apparent, the many weaknesses of this design may be illustrated by applying it to the salesperson-retraining problem. Assume that no prior measurement of sales volume of the salespeople to be retrained had been made. A group of salespeople are selected by a nonrandom method and retrained (X); a measurement (O) is made after the retraining.

Since no prior measurement of sales volume of each of the retrained salespeople was made, there is no method, short of making assumptions as to what would have happened in the absence of retraining, of estimating what the effect of the retraining was. The effects of history, maturation, and selection are all potentially substantial and nonmeasurable.

It is hardly necessary to add that the use of this design is to be avoided if at all possible.

Before–After without Control Group. This design, as the name implies, is the same as (1) with the addition of a "before" measurement. In its simplest form it is shown as

$$O_1 \quad X \quad O_2 \tag{2}$$

and in an extended form as

$$O_1 \quad O_2 \quad O_3 \quad O_4 \quad X \quad O_5 \quad O_6 \quad O_7 \quad O_8 \tag{3}$$

Although design (2) is relatively weak, it is frequently used. It is a decided improvement over (1) in that the apparent effect of the treatment, $O_2 - O_1$, is measured. In terms of the salesperson-retraining illustration, a measurement (O_2) of sales volume of the retrained salesperson is made for the quarter after the sales retraining (X) and compared with a similar measurement (O_1) for the same quarter of the preceding year.

Design (3) is an improvement over design (2) in that data for a larger number of periods are available. The apparent results of the treatment (X) can be analyzed either as the difference of averages

$$\left(\frac{O_1 + O_2 + O_3 + O_4}{4} - \frac{O_5 + O_6 + O_7 + O_8}{4} \right)$$

or the difference in trends of the "before" and "after" measurements. It is this type of design that is implicit in many of the aggregate analyses made of consumer-panel data.

The weaknesses of both designs (2) and (3) include neglect of the effects of history, maturation, testing effect, instrument effect, and selection. History clearly can play a large role in determining the level of difference in the before and after measurements, as can maturation. Since measurements are made both before and after the treatment, both testing effect and instrument effect can be present. The testing effect can be particularly important in design (3). The effect of nonrandom selection is also potentially present in both designs. Careful investigation and close scrutiny are necessary to estimate the effect of each of these uncontrolled and unmeasured sources of variation.

   Multiple Time Series. In using a time series design the possibility of establishing a control group should always be investigated. It may be possible to find a comparable, if not equivalent, group to serve as a control against which to compare the results of the group that underwent the treatment involved. This design may be diagrammed as

O_1	O_2	O_3	O_4	X	O_5	O_6	O_7	O_8	
O_1'	O_2'	O_3'	O_4'		O_5'	O_6'	O_7'	O_8'	(4)

where the primed O's represent measurement of the control group. Note that the individuals comprising the groups were not selected at random. It may be possible, however, to select at random the group that will receive the treatment.

This design can be easily adapted to the sales-retraining evaluation problem. If it is assumed that the sales volume of each of the salespeople is measured during each period as a matter of course anyway, a group could be selected for retraining after period 4. Either a comparable group or all the rest of the salespeople could be selected as the control group. After the sales of both groups in the periods after the training had been measured, the apparent effect of the retraining would be shown by comparing the differences in average sales volume for the two groups before and after treatment.

This design is a substantial improvement over design (3) in that the control group, even though purposively selected, provides a basis for allowing for history, maturation, and testing effect. To the extent that the groups are similar, the effects of each of these factors will *tend* to affect both groups in the same manner. The nonrandom selection of the test and control groups, although less than ideal, may provide a practical and workable substitute for situations where random selection is not possible.[2]

Cross-Sectional Designs

Cross-sectional designs involve measuring the product of interest for several groups at the same time, the groups having been exposed to differing levels of treatments of the producer whose effect is being studied. Cross-sectional designs may be viewed diagrammatically as follows:

$$
\begin{array}{cc}
X_1 & O_1 \\
X_2 & O_2 \\
X_3 & O_3 \\
\cdot & \cdot \\
\cdot & \cdot \\
\cdot & \cdot \\
X_n & O_n
\end{array}
\qquad (5)
$$

Examples of frequent applications of this design are studies of the effect of such variables as price or level of advertising in different geographic areas. This design can be used when direct manipulation of the producer involved is not possible or practical. The effect of the different levels of treatment is measured by determining the degree of association between producer and product. The techniques that can be employed are discussed in later chapters.

History may play a critically important role in cross-sectional designs. There may be a sizable differential effect of extraneous producers between the groups being measured. The effects of maturation and testing tend to be reduced to a minimal level, and the instrumentation effect is certainly no greater than in any other design.

Combination Cross Sectional, Time Series Designs

A number of designs employing a combination of time series and cross-sectional treatment and measurement may be used in observational studies.

---

[2]We discuss in Chapter 11 an alternative form of dealing with test-object differences, called *covariance analysis.*

The multiple-time-series design [design (4)] could be considered a combination of the two, as it involves measurements of a product for different groups at the same time as well as for the same group over time.

Combination designs are well adapted for use with consumer-panel data. One commonly used design is the *ex post facto* test-control group. In this design the test and control groups are not known until *after* the treatment has been administered. This design is illustrated as follows:

$$\begin{matrix} O_1 & X & O_3 \\ O_2 & & O_4 \end{matrix} \qquad (6)$$

This design is widely used in connection with testing the sales effectiveness of price changes, "deals," and advertising. Data on the sales of the brand of interest are reported regularly by the members of the continuous consumer panel. After a given advertisement is run (X), panel members may be questioned to determine whether or not they saw it. Those who saw it are a part of the test group, since they have had exposure to the treatment involved. Those who did not see the advertisement become a part of the control group. The apparent effect is determined by comparing the difference in test and control-group purchases before with that after the advertising was run.

The *ex post facto* determination of test and control-group members is another selection method used as a substitute for random selection. Self-selection is involved; the individuals determine by their actions whether or not they will be included in the test or the control group. The self-selection feature of this design can be an important source of systematic error. It has been demonstrated in many studies of advertising, for example, that the individual who has seen the advertising for a particular brand is more likely to have purchased the brand *before* he saw the advertising than is the person who did not see it.

A variation of the same general design is the *nonequivalent control group*. There is purposive selection in advance of the treatment, and measurements are made on the test and control groups. The selection of the two groups must of necessity be determined entirely by the problem environment.

An example of the use of this type of design occurred in the early stages of the development of network television. Advertising of a hand soap on network television was initiated at a time when only about one-half of the present number of cities were covered by stations. An analysis was made of sales to network versus nonnetwork cities and compared with sales to the same cities for a comparable period before television advertising was initiated. In this case it was evident that the test and control cities were not equivalent, since a larger amount was spent on advertising in other media in nonnetwork cities than in network cities.

In addition to the error induced by the method of selection, testing effect may be a substantial contributor of error in this design. Despite these error sources, the design is a useful one. It can be adapted to a variety of situations to provide information relatively quickly and inexpensively, particularly when panel data are already available.

Controlled Experimental Designs

In *controlled experiments*, investigator intervention is required beyond that for measurement purposes. Specifically, two kinds of intervention are required:

1. Manipulation of at least one assumed causal variable.
2. Random assignment of subjects to experimental and control groups.

Manipulation of at least one variable is required in order to administer the treatment or treatments whose effects it is desired to measure. In this section we shall describe some common single-variable designs. Multivariable designs are treated in Chapter 11.

Randomized assignment of subjects to experimental and control groups is for the purpose of controlling differences arising from extraneous variables. Through use of a random selection procedure, systematic errors due to selection are eliminated, and the effects of the many extraneous variables tend to be equalized between the experimental and the control groups as the size of these groups increases. Random selection permits the use of inferential statistical techniques for analyzing the experimental results. The most fundamental technique for this purpose is analysis of variance. The rationale and some applications of analysis of variance are treated in Chapter 11.

Three single-variable experimental designs are described below.

After-Only with Control Group

The simplest of all experimental designs is the *after-only with control group*. It requires only one treatment and an "after" measurement of both the experimental and the control group. Yet it has the essential requirements of the true experiment: manipulation of at least one variable and randomly selected test and control group. It may be illustrated as follows:

$$R \quad X \quad O_1$$
$$R \qquad\;\; O_2$$

(7)

The absence of a "before" measurement is a feature that concerns many researchers about this design. Banks has described this concern and some possible explanations for it:

The pre-test is a concept deeply imbedded in the thinking of research workers in the social sciences but it is not actually essential to true experimental designs. Almost all the agricultural experiments are run without pre-tests. In the social sciences, however, it seems difficult to give up the notion that the experimental and the control groups might have been unequal before differential experimental treatment and rely upon randomization to reassure us that there will be a lack of initial biases between groups. Perhaps this belief comes from the fact that we have not run many experiments in the social sciences and marketing.[3]

This design, by avoiding the "before" measurement, provides control over the testing and instrument effects. It is of major interest, therefore, when "before" measurements are impractical or impossible to obtain and/or when the testing and instrument effects are likely to be serious.

A common application of this design is in the testing of direct-mail advertising. Random-sampling procedures are used to select an experimental and a control group. Direct-mail pieces are sent to the experimental group and withheld from the control group. "After" measurements of sales to each group are made, and the differential is determined $(O_1 - O_2)$.

Before-After with One Control Group

If "before" measurements are added to design (7), we arrive at the following configuration:

$$
\begin{array}{lccc}
R & O_1 & X & O_2 \\
R & O_3 &   & O_4
\end{array}
\tag{8}
$$

This design is very similar to that of (6) but with an important difference: the experimental and control groups are randomly selected, rather than self-selected. Most of the sources of systematic error are controlled in this design. Maturation is controlled in the sense that it is present in both the experimental and control groups. The same observation applies to the testing effect, although it should be noted that no measurement of the testing effect is possible in this design. (Such a measurement is possible in the next design to be discussed.) History is controlled so long as the two "before" measurements (O_1 and O_3) and the two "after" measurements (O_2 and O_4) are made at the same time. A potential instrumentation effect is established, as is always the case when sequential measurements are made on the same subjects and the same measuring instruments are used.

---

[3]Seymour Banks, *Experimentation in Marketing* (New York: McGraw-Hill Book Company, 1965), p. 35.

This design offers three ways to evaluate the effect of the treatments: $O_2 - O_1$, $O_2 - O_4$, and $(O_2 - O_1) - (O_4 - O_3)$. If the results of each of these evaluations are consistent, the strength of our inferences about the effect of the experimental treatment is substantially increased.

An example of the use of this design is in advertising tests that use a dual cable television system with two consumer purchase panels (one from the subscribers to each cable). "Before" measurements can be made on the test and control panels, an experimental advertising treatment introduced on the test cable, and "after" measurements made for both panels.

Four-Group, Six-Study Design

Suppose that we combine (7) and (8) and arrive at the following design:

$$
\begin{array}{cccc}
R & O_1 & X & O_2 \\
R & O_3 & & O_4 \\
R & & X & O_5 \\
R & & & O_6
\end{array}
\tag{9}
$$

This design provides not only the opportunity of testing the effect of the experimental variable, but also that of testing the effect of testing and the combined effects of maturation and history.

The effect of the treatment can be evaluated in a number of ways, the usual ones being to determine the differentials $O_2 - O_1$, $O_2 - O_4$, $O_5 - O_6$, $O_4 - O_3$, and $(O_2 - O_1) - (O_4 - O_3)$.

The "after" measurements provide a useful basis for drawing inferences about the testing effect as well as that of the treatment. They can be placed into a 2×2 table as follows:

	No X	*X*
"Before" measurements taken	O_4	O_2
No "before" measurements taken	O_6	O_5

The effect of the treatment can be estimated from the difference in the column means. The difference in row means provides the basis for estimating testing effect. The differences in the individual cell means can be used for testing the *interaction* of testing and treatment. Analysis-of-variance procedures are useful for analyzing these results. This procedure and the nature of interaction in experiments are described in Chapter 11.

We now consider continuous panels, which may be used for data collection in either a natural or a controlled experimental design.

Continuous Panels and Experimental Designs

The term *panel* has been widely used in two different senses. It often refers to a consumer jury—a sample of people who are interviewed or whose reactions are measured concerning some actual or contemplated action. Consumer juries are used to evaluate new product ideas, proposed changes in present products, and prospective advertising themes and copy and to conduct taste tests. The conditions under which responses are obtained range from observation in a laboratory to interviews in the respondents' homes.

The other common use of the term "panel," and the one on which we shall focus here, refers to a sample of individuals, households, or firms from whom information is obtained at successive time intervals. The term *continuous panel* clearly connotes the process of collection of data from the same sample units over successive reporting periods. When we refer to a "panel" hereafter, it will be a continuous panel unless otherwise specified.

Panels are most commonly used for the following purposes:

1. As *consumer purchase panels*, which record purchases in a consumer "diary" and submit them periodically.
2. As *advertising audience panels*, which record programs viewed, listened to, and/or publications read.
3. As *dealer panels*, which are used to provide information on levels of inventory, sales, and prices.

Of these types of panels, the consumer purchase panel is the most often used and has the widest range of applications. Consumer purchase panels were initiated during the thirties. Since then, such panels have been established by many different organizations, including the federal government, various universities, newspapers, manufacturers, and marketing research firms. The largest of the consumer panels is maintained by NPD Research, Inc. This panel is comprised of 13,000 families and is national in coverage. Another large and well known national consumer panel is the one maintained by the Market Research Corporation of America.

The typical consumer purchase panel furnishes information at regular intervals on continuing purchases of the products covered. The type of product, brand, weight or quantity of unit, number of units, kind of package or container, price per unit, whether special promotion was in effect, store name, and date and day of week are reported for each product bought. In the NPD and MRCA panels these data are recorded in "diaries," which are mailed in each month.

Advertising audience panels are undoubtedly more widely publicized than other panels. It is from these panels that television and radio program ratings are derived. These panels are operated by independent research agencies rather than the media—both for reasons of economy and to avoid any question of partisanship. Dealer panels are sponsored by both individual firms and independent research agencies. The Nielsen Retail Index is prepared from audits conducted every 60 days on a fixed national sample of food and drug stores. Each store in the sample is audited to obtain information on purchases, inventories, sales, special promotions, and prices of each brand of each product class of interest. The resulting data are compiled, analyses made, and reports distributed to clients.

The information obtained from panels has many applications. The changes in *level of sales to consumers* may be analyzed directly without the problem of determining changes in inventory levels in the distribution channel. Trends and *shifts in market composition* may be analyzed, both by type of consumer and by geographic areas. A continuing *analysis of brand position* may be made for all brands of the product class. Analyses of trends of sales by *package* or *container* types may be made. The relative importance of types of *retail outlets* may be determined. Trends in *competitor pricing* and *special promotions* and their effects can be analyzed along with the effects of the manufacturer's own price and promotional changes. *Heavy purchasers* may be identified and their associated characteristics determined. Similarly, *innovative buyers* may be identified for new products and an analysis of their characteristics made to aid in the prediction of the growth of sales. *Brand-switching* and brand-loyalty studies may be made on a continuing basis.

It is apparent that panels established for advertising audience measurement and dealer panels have similar advantages that accrue from the collection of data at regular intervals. Audience-measurement panels provide a continuous record of the size and composition of the audience for the medium measured. If television viewing is being measured, for example, a week-by-week measurement of the audience for each program is provided, permitting trends to be spotted quickly. Similarly, in the case of dealer panels, inventory buildups or depletions may be determined and corrective measures taken long before this requirement would have been recognized from factory sales data.

The Panel as a Natural Experimental Design

The normal course of operation of a consumer panel generates a continuing set of natural experimental data. Buyer responses to changes in any of the controllable or environmental variables affecting purchase decisions are recorded in the normal process of conducting the panel. Audience and dealer panels provide similar response measurements.

Time-series, cross-sectional, and combination cross-sectional, time series designs are all inherent in panel data. To illustrate their application, suppose that we have increased the price of our product in selected territories. We can analyze the price-increase effect, either at the aggregated or individual household level, using the data from those territories in which price was increased with either the after-only without control group or before–after without control group designs [designs (1) through (3) above]. A cross-sectional analysis may be made by comparing, for a given period after the increase, the purchase data for the territories in which the price was raised with those in which no change was made [design (5) above]. A preferable approach here would be to use a combination cross-sectional, time series design and compare the change in purchases before and after the price increase in the territories in which price was increased (test group) with the change for those territories in which price was not changed (control group). Such a study could employ either design (4) or (6) above.

The limitations of each of these designs discussed earlier apply when they are used with panel data as well. A major difficulty, of course, is in sorting out the effect of the price increase from the extraneous producers affecting purchases over time and among territories. In this illustration selective price increases by territory would only have been made in response to differing conditions among the sales territories (a price increase by competitors, higher levels of demand, etc.). *History* variables must therefore be analyzed carefully in using panel data.

Controlled Experimental Designs Using Panels

The controlled experimental design in conjunction with a panel is most often applied to market tests of prospective new products, different levels of promotion, new campaign themes, price changes, and combinations of two or more of these variables. Consider, for example, a market test of a general price increase. The requirement of random selection of test and control groups can be met by selecting territories at random in which to raise prices. The remaining territories automatically comprise the control group. Depending upon the kinds of information desired, an after-only with control group [design (7) above], a before–after with one control group [design (8)], or a four-group, six-study [design (9)] may be used.

The general advantages and limitations of these designs were discussed earlier. We must, however, consider the limitations that arise from the use of the panel for measurement, applicable to both natural and controlled experimental designs.

The Limitations of Continuous Panels

Although panels can provide highly useful marketing information that is difficult to obtain by alternative research methods, there are some important limitations. The first of these limitations involves *selection* and stems from the difficulty of obtaining cooperation of the families or firms selected in the sample and the resulting effect on the degree of representativeness of the panel. To be most useful for drawing inferences about the population being studied, the sample should be drawn by a random process. The sample of families to comprise a consumer purchase panel may be chosen randomly, but the typical panel has experienced a high refusal rate during the period of establishment and a high attrition rate, once in operation. It has recently been reported (privately) for two of the major consumer panels that approximately 85% of sample families are retained through one year of operation.

There is evidence to indicate that the characteristics of both those families who refuse to participate and those who later drop from the panel are different from those who agree to participate and remain. In the MRCA panel, it was found that a significantly higher percentage of nonurban households agreed to participate than did urban households. In another consumer panel, it was found that a larger proportion of nonusers than users of the products about which purchase data were being reported dropped out after the first interview. To reduce the bias introduced by such nonrandom attrition, replacements are typically chosen from families with the same demographic and usage characteristics as those lost from refusals and dropouts.

An additional source of bias is the *testing effect* arising from continued participation in the panel. Since the individual is undoubtedly conditioned to some extent by the fact that data on purchases are reported, panel members may become atypical in their purchase behavior as a result of being a part of a panel.

Panel data may also be systematically biased through *instrument effects*. The majority of panels use *diaries* for reporting. These are self-administered, structured questionnaires. An attempt is made to have panelists record each purchase in the diary at the time it is made to avoid having to rely on the memory of the purchaser. To the extent that this is not done the accuracy of the data suffers. If properly filled out and submitted on schedule, the information is relatively inexpensive to obtain. However, in those cases where there are omissions or the diary is not mailed on time, either a followup personal or telephone interview must be made or else the data must be omitted from the tabulation. If the followup interview is made, the cost of obtaining the data is increased considerably. If it is not made, possible biases are introduced and the total amount of data is decreased.

Despite these limitations, the use of data from panels has become widespread. If the panel is administered carefully, the resulting data are important additions to the information required for making sound marketing decisions.

We now turn to a brief consideration of simulation as a source of marketing information.

Simulation

The expense, time involved, or other problems associated with field experimentation may preclude it as a source of information for a particular operational situation. In such cases it may be desirable to construct a model of the operational situation and "experiment" with it instead of the real-world situation. The manipulation of such models is called *simulation*.

This approach to obtaining information has a long history in, and is borrowed from, the physical sciences. An example of using physical analogs for simulative purposes is the use of scaled replicas of aircraft in a wind tunnel. The model can be tested under widely varying simulated conditions of wind velocity, altitude, and speeds, and its performance can be observed. It is far less expensive and time-consuming to use such simulation procedures than to construct and test actual prototype aircraft on test flights.

Physical analogs are not often used in marketing, but conceptual models are constructed and manipulated to obtain information on the effect of varying combinations of the variables involved in specified ways. The information obtained consists of numerical outputs from the simulation models. As such, it differs from that provided by secondary sources, respondents, and field experimentation. The latter sources provide information directly from the situation being investigated. Simulation provides information from an *imitation* of this situation.

Simulation can be defined as a *set of techniques for manipulating a model of some real-world process for the purpose of finding numerical solutions that are useful in the real process that is being modeled.* Models that are environmentally "rich" (that is, that may contain complex interactions and nonlinear relationships among the variables, probabilistic components, time dependencies, etc.) are usually too difficult to solve by standard analytical methods such as the calculus or various mathematical programming techniques. Rather, the analyst views a simulation model as an *imitation* of the process or system under study and attempts to run the system on paper (or by means of a computer) to see "what would happen if" a particular policy were put into effect.

Simulations may be used for research, instruction, decision making, or some combination of these applications. Their use as an aid in decision making is our primary concern here. As a historical illustration of a market simulation developed for that purpose, the Simulmatics Corporation[4] reported on the development of a "marketing microcosm" consisting of almost 3,000 (hypothetical) persons who purportedly were representative of the U.S. population. The analyst could then study the impact of various

[4]*Simulmatics Media-Mix: Technical Description* (New York: The Simulmatics Corporation, 1962).

media schedules on the reading characteristics of this "toy" population, and attempt to extrapolate these findings to the total universe. The microcosm was stratified by such characteristics as age, sex, educational level, race, political affiliation, and so forth. By means of the computer model, alternative media schedules could be "tested" on the microcosm and summary figures prepared on the type of audience and projected size and frequency with which the population is exposed to each media schedule.

Kotler and Schultz[5] describe 15 selected simulations developed during the 1960s for marketing decision-making applications. Seven of these were simulations of marketing systems (including the one by Simulmatics just described), seven were simulations to help make decisions concerning marketing mix elements (new product, price, advertising, and sales-force decisions), and one was a simulation of interviewing costs in marketing surveys. Since 1970 the reports of marketing simulations include three dealing with marketing systems[6-8] and three concerned with one or more of the mix elements.[9-11]

For the marketing researcher, the import of the various research studies being conducted in computer simulation should not be ignored. It is becoming increasingly apparent that the marketing researcher's role will be expanded to deal not only with the traditional tasks of data gathering, but also with the manipulation and extensive analysis of the data as well. The authors speculate that the marketing researcher of the future will be as well at home in designing computer simulation models (and using other management science tools) as he currently is in designing questionnaires, forecasting company sales, and estimating market potential for new products.

CHOOSING A RESEARCH DESIGN

The overview of research designs and sources of marketing information just presented should make it apparent that, given a specified problem, many

[5]Philip Kotler and R. L. Schultz, "Marketing Simulations: Review and Prospects," *The Journal of Business*, 43 (July, 1970), 237–95.

[6]M. R. Lavington, "A Practical Microsimulation Model for Consumer Marketing," *Operational Research Quarterly*, 21 (March, 1970), 25–45.

[7]A. Kitchener and D. Rowland, "Models of a Consumer Product Market," *Operational Research Quarterly*, 22 (March, 1971), 67–84.

[8]J. W. Bryant, "A Simulation Model of Retailer Behaviour," *Operational Research Quarterly*, 26 (April, 1975), 133–49.

[9]D. H. Gensch, "Different Approaches to Advertising Media Selection," *Operational Research Quarterly*, 21 (June, 1970), 193–217.

[10]J. J. Lambin, "A Computer On-Line Marketing Mix Model," *Journal of Marketing Research*, 9 (May, 1972), 119–26.

[11]R. L. Schultz and J. A. Dodson, Jr., "A Normative Model for Marketing Planning," *Simulation & Games*, 5 (December, 1974), 363–81.

competing designs can provide relevant information. Each design will have an associated expected value of information and incurred cost.

Suppose, for example, that a researcher is assigned the task of determining the market share of the ten leading brands of cigarettes. There are many possible ways of measuring market share of cigarette brands, including questioning a sample of respondents, observing purchases at a sample of retail outlets, obtaining sales figures from a sample of wholesalers, obtaining sales figures from a sample of retailers and vending machine operators, obtaining tax data, subscribing to a national consumer panel, subscribing to a national panel of retail stores, and, possibly, obtaining data directly from trade association reports or a recent study by some other investigative agency.

That this listing is not exhaustive is illustrated by the approach to this problem taken by one imaginative, if somewhat naive, researcher, who hired a group of small boys to pick up empty cigarette packages beneath the stands at John F. Kennedy Stadium in Philadelphia during an Army–Navy football game. He had a sample of 100,000 persons and concluded that, with this large a sample, a counting of the empty packs of each brand should provide a very good estimate of market share. He neglected to consider that he had a self-selected sample from a universe of sports enthusiasts, a highly disproportionate representation of military personnel, and that only a few brands of cigarettes were sold at the concession booths.

The selection of the "best" design from among the alternative designs is no different in principle from choosing among the alternatives in making any decision. The associated expected value and cost of information must be determined for each contending design. If the design is such that the project will yield information for solving more than one problem, the expected value should be determined for all applicable problems and summed. The design with the highest, positive, net expected payoff of research should be selected.

SUMMARY

In this chapter we have dealt with a subject of central importance to the research project—the research design. We have described what a research design is, discussed the classes of designs, and examined the major sources of marketing information that the various designs employ. Finally, we considered the cost and value of alternative designs.

Treating these topics has provided the opportunity to present an introduction and an overview of the next several chapters. These chapters deal with major sources of marketing information—respondents, experimentation—and the means of obtaining and analyzing information from them.

ASSIGNMENT MATERIAL

1. President Kennedy's assassination occurred on November 22, 1963, and the Dow Jones Index of Industrial Stock Prices fell 21 points on that day.
   a. What kind of evidence is necessary to *prove* that the assassination caused the decline in stock prices?
   b. Is such evidence available?

2. You are a senior analyst in the marketing research department of a major steel producer. You have been requested to make a forecast of domestic automobile production for the forthcoming calendar year and, from this forecast, to make a forecast of the total tonnage of steel that will be used by the automobile manufacturers.
   a. Is this an exploratory, descriptive, or causal study?
   b. What data would be useful for making the forecast of steel tonnage to be used by domestic automobile manufacturers next year?
   c. How would you design the study to obtain these data?
   d. How would you go about locating sources of secondary data useful for the forecast?
   e. What external secondary data are, in fact, available that would be useful for this purpose? From what sources can they be obtained?

3. You are product manager for brand M margarine, a nationally distributed brand. Brand M has been declining in absolute level of sales for the last four consecutive months. You ask the marketing research department to do a study to determine why sales have declined.
   a. Is this an exploratory, descriptive, or causal study?
   b. What data would be useful for determining why sales have declined?
   c. How would you design the study to obtain these data?
   d. How would you go about locating sources of secondary data useful for determining why sales have declined?
   e. What external secondary data are, in fact, available that would be useful for this purpose? From what sources can they be obtained?

4. You are the manager of product planning and marketing research for the personal appliances department of a large and widely diversified corporation. You have under consideration a proposal to produce and market a hearing aid, an appliance line in which your

company currently does not have a product. You have assigned one of the analysts to work on this project.

a. Is this an exploratory, descriptive, or causal study?

b. What data would be useful for making the decision concerning whether or not to develop and introduce a hearing aid?

c. How would you design a study to obtain these data?

d. How would you go about locating sources of secondary data useful for this purpose?

e. What external secondary data are, in fact, available that would be useful to you? From what sources can they be obtained?

5. Suppose that you are the manager of a supermarket and want to determine the sales effectiveness of the announcement of items over the public address system in the store. Describe how you would design an experiment to test the sales effectiveness of an announcement of frozen orange juice, using the before–after with one control group design.

Obtaining
and Organizing
Respondent Data

Information
from Respondents

4

Respondents are a major source of marketing information. It will be recalled from Chapter 3 that we defined the term "respondent" to include a person who provides information passively through observation of his behavior as well as actively through verbal response. We shall therefore be concerned with both information obtained by asking questions of people and that provided by observing behavior or the results of past behavior.

In this chapter we shall first examine the types of information that can be obtained from respondents. Our concern will be with those types of information that can be used for predicting what actions marketing participants would take, given that a particular course of action is chosen in solving a specific marketing problem. The types of information relevant to predicting behavior are as follows:

- Behavioral correlates
    Past behavior
    Intended behavior
- Nonbehavioral correlates
    Socioeconomic characteristics
    Level of knowledge
    Attitudes—opinions

These types of information are considered in turn in the first section of this chapter.

We shall then consider the types of errors that can arise in obtaining such information. These are sampling error, nonresponse error, and response error.

TYPES OF INFORMATION THAT CAN BE OBTAINED FROM RESPONDENTS

As we have already seen, all marketing decisions involve recognizing alternatives and making predictions In this respect there is nothing unique about marketing decisions, as all decisions involve these elements. Marketing decisions are distinguished from others simply by the fact that they always involve to some extent the prediction of the behavior of *market participants*. Choose any marketing problem, and the decisions made to solve it will ultimately turn, in whole or in part, on a prediction of the behavior of consumers, industrial users, middlemen, or competitors.

Consider such marketing problems as deciding whether to introduce a particular new product, to raise the price of an existing product, to change distribution channels, or the determination of the advertising budget. The solution to each of these problems involves forecasting the behavior of one or more groups of market participants.

We now consider the types of information that can be obtained from these market participants for use in forecasting behavior.

Behavioral Correlates

Past Behavior

Past behavior is a type of information that has wide usage as a predictor of future behavior. Each of us relies heavily upon this method of prediction in our everyday relationships with our family, friends, and associates. When we state that we "know" someone well, we are implicitly saying that we believe we are able to predict his behavior over a wide range of social situations. This ability to predict stems to a considerable extent from observations of past behavior. In more formal applications, the use of trend, seasonal, and cyclical data for forecasting (*persistence model methods*) is an example of the use of recorded information of past behavior to predict future behavior.

Regardless of the nature of the variable or variables to be forecasted, a basic premise involved in the use of information on past behavior in the prediction of future behavior is that there is a relationship between the two that to some extent is stable. This relationship may or may not be understood, in the sense that the underlying causal factors relating the two are identified and measured. Recognizing that the degree of stability is sometimes difficult to determine and that the extent of our understanding of the relationship is always imperfect, we nonetheless must believe that there is some continuity and stability in the behavior patterns of people. To believe otherwise would require us to abandon predictions concerning behavior and to preclude our making decisions in which such predictions play an essential part.

The record of past behavior may have been obtained from a natural situation or a controlled experiment. The assumption that there is a continuing and relatively stable relationship between past and future behavior is basic to and explicitly recognized in the use of controlled experiments in marketing. Test marketing operations are carried out involving such variables as product variations, differing prices, and varying levels of advertising for one basic purpose—to obtain information on customer and/or competitor response to the differing levels of the variables involved. This recorded response is used to predict future responses, even though in many cases allowances must be made for expected changes in conditions.

Information on the past behavior of respondents, whether obtained via experimental or nonexperimental methods, is frequently sought. The typical consumer study, for example, concerns itself in part with determining such "facts" as what brands have been used, the last brand bought, where and with what frequency purchases are made, what the exposure to company advertising has been, and similar aspects of past behavior. A formal classification of types of information with respect to past behavior toward products is concerned with three categories—*acquisition, use,* and *possession.* Within each of these behavioral areas information on what, how much, how, where, when, in what situation, and who becomes useful for understanding consumption patterns for the product. The requirements of the particular study will dictate which of these types of information will be required. Table 4-1 shows the requirements for a study on tomato juice to determine, among other things, whether a new type of container should be developed.

Intended Behavior

Intentions may be defined as presently planned actions to be taken in a specified future period. What more logical method of predicting the future behavior of respondents could be used, it might be asked, than to determine what their intentions are? After all, intentions are self-predictions of behavior, and thus, if obtained from the people whose behavior we want to predict, they would seemingly be the most direct and reliable method of prediction.

Intentions are a relevant and commonly sought type of information. However, consideration of our own experiences in terms of what we have planned to do vis-à-vis what we have actually done later should serve to raise some questions concerning the reliability of intentions as a predictive tool. The question "What will you do?" must always be answered conditionally. The degree of assurance that can be given that planned actions will be translated into actual actions varies widely, depending upon circumstances

Table 4-1 Information on past behavior exploratory study of tomato juice usage patterns

	Acquisition	*Use*	*Possession*
What	What brand of tomato juice did you buy last time? What is your regular brand?	What dishes do you cook, or prepare with tomato juice?	What brands of tomato juice do you now have on hand?
How much	What size can of tomato juice do you usually buy? About how often do you buy tomato juice? About how many cans do you buy at a time?	About how much juice does your family drink in a week? For which purpose, drinking or cooking, does your family use more juice?	Do you now have any unopened cans of tomato juice on hand? (If "Yes") About how many cans do you now have?
How		How does your family use tomato juice? Beverage _____ Cooking _____ Both _____	How do you store tomato juice after it is opened? Can _____ Bottle _____ Plastic container _____ Other _____
Where	Do you usually do your food shopping at a particular store or supermarket? (If "Yes") What is the name of the store?		
When	About how long has it been since you last bought tomato juice?		
In what situation		Do you ever serve tomato juice as a beverage to friends?	
Who	Who in your family usually does the shopping?	Who in your family drinks tomato juice?	

and future happenings, many of which are outside the control of the respondent.

The results of one study of expected and actual purchase rates of a number of products and services are shown in Table 4-2.[1] Intentions data were collected from a panel of respondents using a 0-to-10 scale to measure purchase probabilities. Verbal definitions were assigned to each point on the scale. A 10 was defined as "absolutely certain of buying" and a 0 as "absolutely no chance of buying." The definition of a 5 was given as "five chances out of ten of buying" and the other points between 1 and 9 inclusively were similarly defined.

Table 4-2   Expected versus actual purchase rates during a 90-day period

Product or Service	Expected Purchase Rate (%)	Actual Purchase Rate (%)	Difference
Ride local bus	29.1	28.4	−0.7
Trip in camper, motor home, or trailer	14.7	10.2	−4.5
Buy common stock, preferred stock, or mutual fund	15.2	9.1	−6.1
Buy or lease automobile, new or used	12.6	12.5	−0.1
Buy TV set	8.7	7.4	−1.3

Expected purchase rates were calculated as the average purchase probability for each item. The actual rate was determined by reinterviewing the panel members 90 days later to find out what purchases had actually been made.

Many judgments and expectations are bound up in a concurrently valid statement of intentions to buy. Such variables as expected change in financial status, price expectations, general business forecasts, and predictions of need all contribute to the final intention decision. Since each of these is (to some extent, at least) a random variable, it seems plausible to suppose that the intender views them as such and that his stated intention is based upon a subjective probability of purchase. This supposition is supported by the fact that intentions data with assigned probabilities have generally proven to be more accurate than those expressed in "either/or" form. Verbal attitude

[1]Adapted from a table given in C. J. Clawson, "How Useful Are 90-Day Purchase Probabilities?" *Journal of Marketing*, 35 (October, 1971), 45.

scales and variously calibrated probability scales (such as the one used in collecting the data for Table 4-2) have been used. A commonly used verbal attitude scale consists of five categories: (1) definitely will buy, (2) probably will buy, (3) might buy, (4) will not buy, and (5) don't know. Numerical scales of up to 101 (including 0) points have also been used.

A major use of intentions data has been in forecasting sales. In general, forecasts of sales of industrial products using intentions data have been better than those for consumer products. The survey of intended new plant and equipment expenditures that is conducted annually by the Department of Commerce had, for the period 1948 through 1969,[2] an average error of less than 3%. By contrast, the difference between expected and actual purchase rates of the items in Table 4-2 in terms of forecast error range from a low of 0.8% for automobiles [(12.6 − 12.5)100/12.5] to a high of 67.0% for securities [(15.2 − 9.1)100/9.1] for a forecast period of 90 days. Given this degree of variability in forecast accuracies it is understandable why the Bureau of the Census discontinued the Consumer Buying Expectations Survey in 1973 because it was concluded that the data it provided were only "marginally" useful.[3]

Nonbehavioral Correlates

So far we have discussed what people have done and what they intend to do as correlates of what they will do. We now need to examine the non-behavioral correlates that are useful for predicting what they will do.

Socioeconomic Characteristics

Why is information on the social and economic characteristics of respondents often useful for forecasting what they will do? The answer to this question, if not already obvious, can be readily suggested by an illustration. The Radio Corporation of America, in introducing color television in the fifties, was very much interested in the age, income, educational, and occupational composition of the market. They judged that the initial market for color television sets would be comprised of families that were proportionally higher in income and educational levels and that were older on the average than either the black-and-white set owners or the population as a whole. These judgments were subsequently confirmed by a study of the early purchasers of color sets. This information was useful for both pricing and promotional decisions, since certain characteristics were found to be cor-

[2]As reported in G. B. Nimsatt and J. T. Woodward, "Revised Estimates of New Plant and Equipment in the United States, 1947–1969: Part II," *Survey of Current Business*, 50 (February, 1970), 23.
[3]U.S. Department of Commerce, Bureau of the Census, "Consumer Buying Indicators," *Current Population Reports*, Series P-65, No. 46, p. 5.

relates of purchase behavior. That is, an association was found to exist between families with these characteristics and purchase of color television sets.

In studies of consumers where there is a basis for believing that such an association might exist, information is obtained on one or more socioeconomic characteristics. The ones on which information is most frequently obtained are income, occupation, level of education, age, sex, marital status, and size of family. While socioeconomic characteristics are by far the most widely used bases for classification of consumers, other bases exist and their use is increasing. Among these are preferences, personality traits, perceived risk, and such measures of actual buying behavior as amount purchased and brand loyalty.

In general, the identification of consumer classifications is useful in marketing so long as: (1) there is differential purchase behavior among the segments of the market identified, (2) there are practicable means of differentiating the marketing effort among segments, and (3) it is worthwhile to do so. It may be interesting to know, for example, that owners of vans show different personality traits than owners of standard models; such knowledge will be useful in marketing automobiles, however, only if it can be used in developing and evaluating appeals for each type of buyer.

Two commonly used and widely accepted classifications of consumers are by stage of the life cycle and by life-style. The *life-cycle stages* experienced by most households in the United States consist of the following:

1. Young unmarrieds.
2. Young marrieds, no children.
3. Young marrieds, children, youngest child under six.
4. Older marrieds, children, youngest child six or over.
5. Older marrieds, children maintaining separate households.
6. Solitary survivor, older single people.[4]

The life-cycle stage has obvious implications with respect to purchases associated with family formation (furniture, appliances, household effects, and housing) and addition of children (food, clothing, toys, expanded housing). Other, less obvious relationships exist as well. New-car buying reaches its peak among the older married couples whose children have passed the age of six. A second stage of furniture buying takes place when children begin to date and have parties at home. Dental work, travel, and purchases of insurance are examples of service purchases associated with the life cycle.

---

[4]Of the many good articles dealing with the life-cycle concept, one of the most comprehensive is W. D. Wells and George Gubar, "Life Cycle Concept in Marketing Research," *Journal of Marketing Research*, 3 (November, 1966), 355–363.

Life-style has a close association with membership in a social class. It is a basis for segmenting customers by values, attitudes, opinions, and interests, as well as by income. These differences tend to be expressed through the products bought and the stores patronized as well as the section in which one lives, club membership, religious affiliation, and other means. These media are used, either consciously or subconsciously, as symbolic representations of the class to which the person perceives he belongs (or to which he aspires).

The most common designation of social classes is the one originally used by Warner, or some close variant thereof.[5] These are the by now familiar *upper*, *middle*, and *lower* class designations, each divided into upper and lower segments. Thus, the Warnerian classification results in six classes ranging from the UU (upper upper) down through the LL (lower lower).

Although less direct and more subtle than life-cycle stage in its effect on overt buying behavior, there can be little question but that an upper-middle-class household will show more similarity in purchasing and consumption patterns of food, clothing, furniture, and housing to another upper-middle-class household than it will to a blue-collar, upper-lower-class household. The media to which the managerial–professional, upper-middle-class family is exposed and the appeals to which it responds are also likely to be closer to those of other managerial–professional families than to those of the blue-collar family.

Classification of consumers is vital if we are to learn more of consumer behavior and to utilize this information in developing more efficient marketing techniques. Empirical classification procedures, while by no means commonly employed, are beginning to be more widely used in marketing studies. Such techniques as regression analysis, factor analysis, discriminant analysis, cluster analysis, and canonical analysis are described in later chapters. Examples of the use of the techniques for consumer classification purposes are given in these chapters also.

Although the discussion thus far has focused on consumers, similar classification requirements exist and are used in studies of industrial users and middlemen. Comparable characteristics of these firms include sales volume, number of employees, and the type of products manufactured or handled.

Information on Extent of Knowledge

The assertion that the *extent of knowledge* about a situation is one of the determinants of the behavioral response to it borders on being a tautology. So long as the action taken is at all rational, the amount that is known (or

---

[5]See W. L. Warner et al., *Social Class in America* (New York: Harper & Row, Publishers, 1960), esp. pp. 6–32, and S. J. Levy, "Social Class and Consumer Behavior," in *On Knowing the Consumer*, ed. J. W. Newman (New York: John Wiley & Sons, Inc., 1966), pp. 146–60.

believed to be known) about the situation will influence the action. Translated into terms of the color television example, the extent of the prospective purchasers' knowledge about the quality of picture, reliability, and price undoubtedly influenced their decision to purchase or not purchase. The extent of the purchasers' knowledge concerning the relative levels of these variables among brands also undoubtedly played a major role in their choice of brand.

Prediction of what actions respondents will take, therefore, is often aided by knowing "how much they know." This is especially so in making advertising budget and media allocation decisions, for example, where the decisions are strongly affected by the levels of awareness and the extent of knowledge of potential audiences concerning the product and its attributes.

Information on Attitudes and Opinions

Extensive studies of attitudes and opinions have been made by investigators in the fields of psychology, sociology, and political science over a wide range of subject areas. The most widely known opinion studies are the public opinion polls that have been conducted regularly since the 1930s. Among behavioral scientists, the intensive study of the attitudes of the American soldier in World War II has been a landmark since its publication.[6]

The study of people's behavior in business and economic contexts is also a behavioral science. As such, it has been a natural consequence that many of the techniques employed in these related fields have been adopted, adapted, and applied to business problems. Marketing research has made wide use of opinion–attitude studies to obtain information applicable for the solution of marketing problems.

The terms "attitude" and "opinion" have frequently been differentiated in psychological and sociological investigations. A commonly drawn distinction has been to view an *attitude* as a predisposition to act in a certain way and an *opinion* as a verbalization of the attitude. Thus, a statement by a respondent that he prefers viewing color to black-and-white television programs would be an opinion expressing (one aspect of) the respondent's attitude toward color television.

When used to predict actions that the respondent will take, this distinction between "attitude" and "opinion" rapidly becomes blurred. Since the major purpose of attitude–opinion research in marketing is to predict behavior, this differentiation is, at best, of limited usefulness. We shall therefore use the terms interchangeably.

Attitude research in marketing has been conducted with the use of both

---

[6]Samuel Stouffer et al., *The American Soldier: Adjustment During Army Life, Studies in Social Psychology in World War II* (Princeton, N.J.: Princeton University Press, 1949). Three additional volumes were published during 1949–1950.

qualitative and quantitative techniques. In either form, problems are encountered that are more severe than those involved in obtaining any of the other types of descriptive information discussed. Despite these problems, which we shall discuss in later chapters in some detail, attitude–opinion research has been widely used to provide information for choosing among alternatives. Its greatest use has been in the areas of product design and advertising. Other uses have been in the selection of store locations, developing service policies, and in choosing company and trade names.

The attitudes and opinions of prospective buyers clearly affect purchase decisions. Consequently, the marketing manager should be as well informed as possible about both the nature of the relevant attitudes and opinions and the intensity with which they are held.

THE SOURCES OF ERROR IN INFORMATION FROM RESPONDENTS

Interpersonal communication and observation are activities in which each of us is highly experienced. Much of our time each day is spent in communicating and observing. We ask and respond to questions, usually verbally and in informal face-to-face situations. We observe the actions of others each time we are in visual contact with them.

Casual reflection on our experiences in asking and replying to these everyday-type questions and in making informal observations would suggest to most of us that we are relatively skilled in the roles of both questioner–observer and respondent. To be sure, we are aware that we often receive less information than we need, and that the information we get is not always entirely accurate or clear. We are also aware that on occasion we give out misinformation and misinterpret what we have observed. Evaluating our experiences as a whole, however, most of us feel reasonably competent to obtain and to provide information via communication, and to obtain information by observation.

When viewed against this background of informal experience, it seems almost paradoxical that the asking of seemingly straightforward questions and receiving straightforward answers, or the observing of people's behavior in a formalized information-seeking context, could be attended by serious problems. Yet the subtleties and complexities of obtaining information from respondents are such that they have been the subject of extensive investigation and experimentation for the past forty years.

Any formal effort to obtain information from a sample of respondents is subject to three major sources of error: sampling error, nonresponse error, and response error. We shall introduce here the first two of these, sampling and nonresponse errors, and treat them in detail in a later chapter. The third, response error, we shall consider at length in this chapter.

Sampling Error

Sampling, or *experimental, error* arises in research projects because not everyone in the population of interest is included. For example, prior to deciding on the final design characteristics of its turbine-powered passenger car, the Chrysler Corporation selected a sample of 200 motorists to drive the car under everyday driving conditions for a period of three months. Their purpose was to obtain consumer reactions to the car under conditions of actual use.

In any sampling situation the usual result is that the sample selected is not completely representative with respect to the characteristics of the population from which it is drawn. In the case above, the motorists chosen to "test-drive" the turbine car may have had different reactions, on the average, to its performance characteristics and styling than the entire population of motorists. Since the sample was selected to estimate the reaction of the population of motorists, an exact determination of the *amount* of sampling error could not be made.

In the general case, however, the range of the sampling error can be controlled by changing the characteristics of the sample taken. Further, as we shall see later, if a *probability* sample is taken, we can measure the extent of the sampling error by calculating confidence intervals. These topics and others pertaining to the sampling process are discussed in Chapter 7.

Nonresponse Error

A *nonresponse error* occurs when an individual is included in the sample to be taken but, for any of many possible reasons, is not reached. In the testing of the turbine car the problem of nonresponse was minimal. In most consumer surveys, however, this is a source of a potentially sizable error.

Families who, after several attempts, cannot be reached generally have different characteristics than those who can be reached to provide information. For example, families in which all members are usually away from home during the day differ from those families in which at least one member can usually be found at home with respect to age, number of small children, and the proportion of time in which the wife is employed.

The seriousness of nonresponse error is magnified by the fact that the direction of the error is often unknown, and, while the maximum error due to the nonresponse can be determined (by assuming that the nonrespondents would each have responded in a given way), it is difficult to estimate the actual magnitude of the error.

A method of estimating both the direction and the magnitude of the nonresponse error is that devised by Politz and Simmons.[7] In addition to the regular questions on the questionnaire, each respondent is asked on how many of k similar periods (evenings if the respondent is being interviewed in the evening) he or she would have been home.

For example, one typically sets up seven respondent groups, where the estimated proportion of the time persons in each group are at home is 1/7, 2/7, . . . , 7/7 of the time. Having done this, one estimates a total-sample mean by weighting the separate results of each group by the *reciprocal* of the estimated proportion of the time that the members of that group are at home. In this way respondents who are not often at home receive more weight (than those who are usually at home) in the calculation of the weighted mean.

Response Error

Response error occurs in the collection of information from an individual if the reported value differs from the actual value of the variable concerned.

It will be recalled that a respondent was defined as a person who either provides information actively through communication or passively through his behavior being observed. When we speak of response error, therefore, it should be understood that it is inclusive of errors arising through either communication, observation, or both.

What are the sources of response error? In answering this question it will be helpful to consider the stages involved in providing information. The information must first be *formulated;* that is, it must be assimilated and made accessible for transmission. Once this has been accomplished, it must be *transmitted.* Errors can arise in either stage or in both. We shall use the term *inaccuracy* to denote the errors arising in the formulation stage. The term *ambiguity* will be understood to mean the errors arising in the transmission stage.

Since the purpose of making this distinction in types of response errors is to help understand and thus to control this important source of error, it is appropriate that we examine each type of error in some detail.

Inaccuracy

We have agreed that "inaccuracy" refers to errors that are made in the formulation of information. Suppose that a respondent is asked the question, "Do you intend to buy a new automobile within the next six months?" and

[7]Alfred Politz and Willard Simmons, "An Attempt to Get the 'Not at Homes' into the Sample without Callbacks," *Journal of the American Statistical Association*, 44 (March, 1949), 9–31.

that his answer is limited to "Yes," "No," or "Uncertain." A brief examination of possible answers and subsequent actions indicates that there are two different kinds of inaccuracies. If the respondent answers "Yes," but really has no intention of buying a car within this period or, conversely, answers "No," but does intend to buy a car, then we may say that there is *concurrent inaccuracy* in his statement.

Suppose, however, that his present intention is to buy a new car; he so indicates in his answer, and then he does not, in fact, buy one within six months. Or, alternatively, he does not now intend to buy, he answers "No" to the question, and then buys a car within the six-month period. There is no concurrent inaccuracy in either case; the response has reflected the actual intention of the person. The intention, however, was not followed. In this situation we have what may be termed *predictive inaccuracy.*

Predictive inaccuracy as a source of response error is a special case related to intentions data. In each of the other types of information obtained from respondents (information on past behavior, socioeconomic characteristics, level of knowledge, and opinion–attitude), only concurrent inaccuracies occur as a source of error in formulating the desired information.

With the exception of the information on intentions, therefore, our major concern in understanding and reducing response errors resulting from inaccuracy will be with respect to concurrent inaccuracy.

Sources of Inaccuracy

What are the sources of inaccuracy? Both our everyday experiences and empirical evidence suggest that there are two basic sources. Inaccurate information may result from either the *inability* or the *unwillingness* of the respondent to provide the desired information. In those instances where observation is used, this statement may also be applied to the observer; the observer may be unable or unwilling to provide the desired information.

We can readily understand the inability of people to provide information because of its being inaccessible. Even such a simple and straightforward question as "What is the model year of your family car?" may result in an information-formulation problem, particularly if the car is several years old. If the additional question were asked "What brand or brands of tires do you now have on your car?" most respondents would have even more difficulty in providing an accurate answer without looking at the tires. Finally, if the question were asked, "What reasons did you have for buying brand A tires instead of some other brand?" most respondents would have still more difficulty in providing an accurate answer.

When we move to the problem of *unwillingness* of respondents to provide accurate information, we are faced with a more complex topic. Here we are dealing with the motivations of people: why they are not willing to formulate accurately the information desired. No fully accepted "general theory" of motivation has yet emerged from the behavioral sciences to which we can turn to assist in explaining this type of behavior. However, by again applying everyday experiences to this problem, and adding some research findings and the accumulated experiences of practitioners, several reasons are suggested why people may not be willing to make accurate information accessible.

Except in those instances where the respondent provides information through being observed in a natural situation, there are always costs (negative utilities) attached to his formulating information. The *time* required is one such cost that is always present. Others that are often present include *preceived losses of prestige*, some degree of *invasion of privacy*, and the social cost of formulating information that is perceived to be in *conflict with investigator opinions*.

We may postulate that, when it is possible to do so, the respondent will tend to act in a manner that will reduce these costs. Such behavior will sometimes result in his providing inaccurate information.

Time Costs. Perhaps the most common reason for respondent unwillingness to provide accurate information is the result of the time required to make the information available. He may simply be busy and wish to complete the interview as quickly as possible. In this circumstance it is not unusual for the respondent to decide that abrupt answers are the easiest and quickest way of terminating the interview. Rather than reflecting on or verifying the information he provides, he gives hasty, ill-considered answers and resists probing if attempted. Inaccurate information results.

Perceived Losses of Prestige. When information involving the prestige of the respondent is sought, there is always a tendency toward inaccurate formulation in the direction of the higher-prestige responses. Although this tendency is recognized by all experienced practitioners, two problems remain: (1) recognizing the items of information that the respondent will interpret as having prestige content, and (2) measuring the amount of the inaccuracy resulting therefore.

Some informational items have prestige content associated with them by virtually all respondents. Among these are such socioeconomic characteristics as age, income, and educational level. Other informational items are more difficult to identify as having prestige content, however. Information on the place of birth or residence is an example. People who live in rural areas or in suburbs are prone to give the nearest city in answer to questions concerning where they live. In part, this no doubt reflects a belief that the investigator would not otherwise recognize the location given; in part, it may also reflect a higher level of prestige associated with being born or living in a large and well-known city.

An example of a still more subtle prestige association that resulted in a sizable error in information obtained is illustrated by the experience of a marketing research firm that conducted a study on nationally known brands of beer. One of the questions asked was, "Do you prefer light or regular beer?" The response was overwhelmingly in favor of "light" beer. Since sales data indicated a strong preference for "regular" beer, it was evident that the information was inaccurate. Subsequent investigation revealed that the respondents viewed people who drank light beer as being more discriminating in taste. They had, therefore, given answers that, in their view, were associated with a higher level of prestige.

The problem of measuring the amount of inaccuracy resulting from this source is usually difficult to solve satisfactorily. In the ideal case it requires that information be available on the item from sources that are external to the sample and, further, that these external data be more accurate than those obtained from the respondents. Clearly, in most cases such data are not available; if they were, the information would not have been collected from the respondents.

One approach to the solution to this problem is to ask for the information in two different ways. When one is obtaining information on respondents' ages, for example, it is a common practice to ask early in the interview, "What is your present age?" and later "In what year were you born?" or "In what year did you enter high school?" Another approach is to use indirect questions. In one study, when respondents were asked, "Are you afraid to fly?" very few people indicated any fear of flying. In a followup study when they were asked, "Do you think your neighbor is afraid to fly?" most of the neighbors turned out to have severe anxieties about flying.

A promising method for obtaining information about sensitive matters is the *randomized-responses* technique.[8] When using this technique the investigator presents two questions, either of which can be answered by a "Yes" or a "No," one innocuous (e.g., "Were you born in May?") and the other sensitive (e.g., "Did you shoplift any items from the Downtown Mall during the month of December?"). The respondent is asked to flip a coin or use some other randomizing device to select which question to answer, and then to answer the indicated question. The respondent is instructed *not* to tell or in any way communicate to the interviewer which question was answered.

The proportion of respondents who answered "Yes" to the sensitive question can be estimated from the formula

$$P(\text{yes} \mid \text{sens. quest.}) = \frac{P(\text{yes}) - P(\text{innoc. quest.})P(\text{yes} \mid \text{innoc. quest.})}{P(\text{sens. quest.})}$$

[8]C. Campbell and B. L. Joiner, "How to Get the Answer without Being Sure You've Asked the Question," *The American Statistician*, 27 (December, 1973), 229–31.

In the example, if the proportion of respondents who answered "Yes" is 0.06, the proportion born in May (determined from the Census of Population) is 0.08, and the probability of answering each question is 0.5, the estimated proportion who answered "Yes" to the shoplifting question would be

$$P(\text{yes} | \text{shoplifting question}) = \frac{0.06 - (0.5)(0.08)}{0.5} = 0.04$$

This is a point estimate of the (hypothetical) proportion of the population from which the sample was drawn who shoplifted at the place during the period specified.

Invasion of Privacy. Clearly, some topics on which information is sought are considered to be private matters. When such is the case, both non-response and inaccuracy in the responses that are obtained can be anticipated. Matters about which respondents resent questions include money matters or finance, family life, personal hygiene, political beliefs, religious beliefs, and even job or occupation. Either indirect questions or the randomized-response technique can sometimes be used to avoid intrusion. If direct questions are used concerning such matters, they should be placed as near the end of the questionnaire as other considerations permit.

Conflict with Opinions Imputed to the Investigator. A complex source of inaccuracy stems from the respondents' appraisal of the investigator and the opinions and expectations that are imputed to him. Although much remains to be learned about the nature of the "cues" from which respondents draw inferences about investigators' opinions, there is sufficient evidence to conclude both that such inferences are drawn and that they influence responses.[9]

The investigator's appearance and manner will often influence responses. An example is a cosmetics study that showed an unexpectedly high reported usage of luxury cosmetics among women from low-income families. In this case, one woman interviewer had conducted all of the interviews in the low-income area. She was an exceptionally well-dressed and carefully groomed person who was known to be a very competent interviewer. The director of the study hypothesized that the responding women had reported using more expensive cosmetics than they actually used because they thought that these were the kinds of cosmetics the interviewer used. To test this hypothesis, a matronly woman, dressed similarly to the women to be interviewed, was asked to call on the same respondents and use the same questionnaire on the

[9]An excellent review article with an extensive bibliography on this topic is by H. W. Boyd, Jr., and Richard Westfall, "Interviewer Bias Revisited," *Journal of Marketing Research*, 2 (February, 1965), 58–63.

following day. The reported brands of cosmetics used were much less expensive, on the average, in this series of interviews.[10]

The level of rapport established between the investigator and the respondent is an important factor in reducing inaccuracy of response. There have been instances in which the respondents reported later that they thought they were being interviewed for such purposes as establishing a credit rating, investigating past income tax returns, or determining whether their house met the requirements of the local building code. It is understandable that, under these conditions, the respondent might not be willing to give candid and informative answers to all the questions asked.

Unwillingness of the Investigator. So far we have considered only the unwillingness of the respondent to provide accurate information. The investigator's side of the coin should also be considered. The investigator may be unwilling to obtain accurate information, even if the respondent is willing to provide it.

The most common form of this problem is interviewer cheating. The ways in which the interviewer may obtain inaccurate information deliberately and his motives for doing so are limited only by his ingenuity and personality. It may be, for example, that an interviewer finds that a particular question is embarrassing to ask. As a result, he may decide to supply his own answer or to make an estimate or inference of what the respondent's answer would be if the question were asked. (It is probable that this happens relatively frequently with respect to the age and income of respondents.) At the other extreme, reports of "interviews" are occasionally submitted without the "interviewer" having taken the trouble to contact any respondents. A compromise between these extremes is the interviewing of friends but listing the names of the people that were supposed to be interviewed.

Like embezzling, interviewer cheating can be kept to a low level of incidence but not eliminated completely. Careful selection, training, and supervision of interviewers will eliminate much of the problem. In addition, control procedures can and should be established that will reduce it even more.

The simplest control procedure is the "call-back." If the interviewers are aware that a subsample of respondents will be queried after the interviewing reports have been turned in, the fear of being caught will discourage cheating. If the information on an initial interview is found to disagree significantly with that on the call-back interview, additional call-backs may be made on respondents originally interviewed by the same person.

Other control procedures include the analysis of responses obtained by each investigator and the use of "cheater" questions. In studies where the volume of information obtained makes it worthwhile to use machines for

[10]E. G. Morgan, "The Right Interviewer for the Job," *Journal of Marketing*, 16 (October, 1951), 201–2.

tabulation and analysis, analyses of the patterns of responses obtained by each interviewer can be made at very little additional cost. Significant variations from expected norms can then be investigated.

The use of "cheater" questions in the questionnaire is a less widely used and publicized control device. Questions can be devised that will disclose fabricated answers with a reasonably high probability of success. Understandably, the research directors using this technique have not been interested in publicizing either the fact that they use it or the type of questions they use.

Ambiguity

Ambiguity may be defined as the errors made in interpreting spoken or written words or behavior. Ambiguity, therefore, occurs in the transmission of information, either through communication or observation.

Now suppose we conduct an experiment. Before reading further, and without reading the last paragraph again, write what you understand the word "ambiguity" to mean. After you have finished, compare your definition with the first sentence in the last paragraph.

The experiment has two possible outcomes:

1. Your definition and the one given above have the same meaning. If this is the case, the definition is not ambiguous to you.

2. Your definition and the one given above do not have the same meaning. If this is the case, and you read the definition carefully the first time, the experiment has provided a personal example of ambiguity.

Although the definition given above was not intended to be ambiguous, the careful reader might logically raise some questions about the interpretation intended, particularly if he were inclined to press a point here and there. Consider the following questions and answers:

Question: Did you intend the word "or" in the definition to mean "and/or," the inclusive disjunction, or just "or," the exclusive disjunction?

Answer: We intended it to mean "and/or." The meaning intended was "Ambiguity refers to errors made in interpreting spoken *and/or* written words *and/or* behavior."

Question: Why didn't you write it that way?

Answer: Because we thought it would be clearer to the average reader if we just used "or."

Question: Were you aware that there are other words in your definition that have different usages?

Answer: Yes. Most words have different usages.

Question: Were you aware that "ambiguity" normally is used to refer to the condition that permits errors in interpretation rather than to the errors as such?

Answer: Yes. We used it to mean the errors as such because that was the meaning we wanted the word we used to have. "Ambiguity" was the best word we could think of to help convey that meaning.

Ambiguity is present in all languages and especially so in ours. The short discourse just completed contains examples of but a few of the difficulties encountered in attempting to express an idea clearly.

It is apparent that a single section of one chapter of a book on marketing research will not solve the general problem of ambiguity, or even the problem as it is encountered in research. This section will, however, point out the general areas in which it is encountered in marketing research, and describe methods that have been used successfully to identify and to reduce it.

Ambiguity in Communication

Unambiguous communication in research requires that the question asked and the answers given each mean the same thing to the questioner and the respondent. A two-step process is therefore involved:

1. Question as under- stood by questioner	*is same as*	Question as understood by respondent
2. Answer as under- stood by respondent	*is same as*	Answer as understood by questioner

The first step in this process is the controlling one. If the question is not clearly understood by the respondent, frequently the answer will not be clearly understood by the questioner. To illustrate this point, in an actual research project on tomato juice, the question

Do you like tomato juice?
    Yes ☐   *No* ☐   *Neither like nor dislike* ☐

was changed, after pretesting, to

Do you like the taste of tomato juice?
    Yes ☐   *No* ☐   *Neither like nor dislike* ☐

Even a careful reading of these two questions may not disclose any real difference in their meaning. If this is the case, it is clear that you are making the same assumption about the referent of "like" as did the analyst who drew up the question, that "like" refers to "taste." In pretesting, however, it was discovered that some housewives answered "Yes" with other referents in mind. They "liked" the amount of vitamin C their children get when they drink tomato juice, they "liked" the tenderizing effect that tomato juice has when used in the cooking of meat dishes, and so on. Note that, if the wording of the question had not been changed, there would have been a complete misunderstanding in some cases of the simple, one-word answer "Yes."

The question both initiates and gives direction to the communication process in research. In addition, the form and wording of the question, unlike that of the answer, can be completely controlled by the researcher. It is not surprising, therefore, that a large number of investigations have been carried out on both the form and wording of questions. It is appropriate that we consider both question form and question wording and their relationships to ambiguity.

Forms of Questions.   Three basic forms of questions may be distinguished: the free-answer question, the dichotomous question, and the multiple-choice question. These forms are roughly analogous, respectively, to essay, true–false, and multiple-choice questions on examinations.

The *free-answer,* or *open, question* is, as the name implies, a question that has no fixed alternatives to which the answer must conform. The respondent answers in his own words and at the length he chooses. Interviewers are usually instructed to make a verbatim record of the answer.

An example of a free-answer question in the tomato-juice study already referred to is

What suggestions could you make for improving tomato juice?

The suggestions made included packaging it in glass containers, finding some way to keep it from separating, and improving the flavor through the use of such additives as lemon juice, salt, and vodka.

Free-answer questions are almost invariably shorter than multiple-choice questions and are usually shorter than dichotomous questions. A corollary characteristic is that free-answer questions are also invariably less complex in sentence structure than multiple-choice questions on the same issue, and are usually less complex than dichotomous questions.

Common sense suggests, and reading tests have confirmed, that short and simply structured sentences are more easily understood than long and complex ones. The tendency toward ambiguity of the long and complex sentence is accentuated, if anything, by *listening* to it rather than *reading* it. Further, there would seem to be no reason to believe that the findings would be any different for questions than for declarative statements. Based on these premises, we should be on reasonably sound grounds for drawing inferences about the relative probability of ambiguity in questions and answers based on length and complexity of structure.

Free-answer questions place greater demands on the ability of the respondent to express himself. As such, this form of question provides the opportunity for greater ambiguity in interpreting answers. To illustrate, consider the following verbatim transcript of one respondent's reply to the question:

What suggestions could you make for improving tomato juice?

I really don't know. I never thought much about it. I suppose that it would be nice if you could buy it in bottles because the can turns black where you pour the juice out after it has been opened a day or two. Bottles break, though.

Should the conclusion be drawn that she had "no suggestion," "suggested packaging in a glass container," or "suggested that some way be found to prevent the can from turning black around the opening?" Note that she seems to have made the implicit assumption that the bottle would *not* turn black around the opening.

From the criteria previously stated, we may tentatively conclude that the free-answer question provides the *lowest probability of the question's being ambiguous, but the highest probability of the answer's being ambiguous*, compared with the other two question forms.

The *dichotomous question* has two fixed alternatives of the type "Yes— No," "In favor—Not in favor," "Use—Do not use," and so on. It is the most frequently used form of question in marketing research. The question quoted earlier,

Do you like the taste of tomato juice?
      Yes ☐   *No* ☐   *Neither like nor dislike* ☐

is an example of a dichotomous question.

It will be observed that a third alternative has been added in the question in the example to allow for those people who do not have a definite liking or disliking for tomato juice. It is usually desirable to provide a category of this type to avoid forcing the respondent to take a definite stand when he may really be neutral.

In the example above the implied alternatives are clear and do not have to be stated. For many issues, however, the alternatives must be stated in the body of the question, as they would not otherwise be clear. The following is an example of such a question:

Do you think that next year the price of cars will be higher, lower, or about the same as now?

In terms of length and complexity of structure, the dichotomous question falls between the free-answered question (shortest and least complex) and the multiple-choice question (longest and most complex). The dichotomous question places the least demands on the respondent in terms of formulating and expressing an answer. With respect to ambiguity in dichotomous questions, therefore, we may tentatively conclude that this form of question provides roughly *an average probability of the question's being ambiguous, but the lowest probability of the answer's being ambiguous,* compared with the other two forms.

The *multiple-choice question* provides several set alternatives for the answer to it. In this respect it is in the middle ground between the free-answer and the dichotomous question.

An example of the multiple-choice type of question from the tomato juice study is as follows:

Would you say you use the brand you do because it is the most reasonably priced, or because it is a brand you are used to and can rely on, or because you like the taste, or because of some other reason?

      Reasonably priced ☐   *Like taste* ☐

      Used to and rely on ☐   *Other* ☐

It should be noted that this question could have been asked as a free-answer question. The choice between the free-answer and the multiple-choice forms of asking question must always be made if the same question is not asked in both forms.

The multiple-choice question must be longer and more complex than either the free-answer or dichotomous questions in order to state the several alternatives. The statement of the alternatives is provided to assist the respondent in recalling and in formulating his answer. In giving this assistance, however, added opportunities to misunderstand the question are also provided.

A common source of ambiguity in the multiple-choice question is the difficulty of making the alternatives mutually exclusive. In the above example this requirement was met reasonably well. (It might be argued, however, that one would have to be "used to" and be able to "rely on" the taste's being consistently the same in order to give the "taste" alternative as the answer.)

Another common source of ambiguity in multiple-choice questions is the implied restriction on alternatives. The example strongly implies that the respondent *should have a single, most important reason* for using the brand. This may very well not be the case.

There is a tendency for the alternatives appearing first and last in a multiple-choice question to be used as answers more frequently than those in other positions. This systematic error, often called *position bias or order bias*, may be indicative of ambiguity in the question. One experiment in which several alternatives were presented in different positions to matched samples of respondents resulted in the top position, on the average, outdrawing the middle position by 6 percentage points. The bottom position outdrew the middle position by 2 percentage points. In no instance did the middle position outdraw the top or bottom position.[11]

This problem can be solved satisfactorily in most cases by rotating the order of the alternatives. This may be done by printing cards for each of the desired different orders of alternatives and instructing the interviewers to use the cards in a prescribed sequence.

With respect to ambiguity in multiple-choice questions, we may tentatively conclude that this form of question provides the *highest probability of the question's being ambiguous, and an average probability of the answer's being ambiguous*, compared with the other two forms.

Table 4-3 summarizes our tentative conclusions concerning the form of question and the probability of ambiguity. These conclusions should not be used as the final arbiter on the choice of question form. Some question forms are suited better to eliciting certain kinds of information than others. In "reason why" questions, for example, one would normally use free-answer or multiple-choice questions rather than dichotomous ones.

Table 4-3   Form of question and relative probability of ambiguity

	RELATIVE PROBABILITY OF AMBIGUITY	
FORM OF QUESTION	*Question*	*Answer*
Free-answer	Lowest	Highest
Dichotomous	Average	Lowest
Multiple-choice	Highest	Average

Each question form has its proponents. Each has been used extensively. There is no one "best" form of question for obtaining all types of information from respondents.

Question Wording.   The wording of questions is a critical consideration in obtaining information from respondents. Consider the following three

[11]Reported in S. L. Payne, *The Art of Asking Questions* (Princeton, N.J.: Princeton University Press, 1951), pp. 84–5.

questions and the percentage of affirmative responses to each from three matched samples of respondents:[12]

> *Do you think anything <u>should</u> be done to make it easier for people to pay doctor or hospital bills?*
> (82% replied "Yes.")
>
> *Do you think anything <u>could</u> be done to make it easier for people to pay doctor or hospital bills?*
> (77% replied "Yes.")
>
> *Do you think anything <u>might</u> be done to make it easier for people to pay doctor or hospital bills?*
> (63% replied "Yes.")

These questions differ only in the use of the words *should, could,* and *might.* Although these three words have different connotations, they are sometimes used as synonyms. Yet the responses, at the extreme, are 19 percentage points apart. This difference is the same as the amount by which the *Literary Digest* was in error in predicting the percentage of the popular vote for Landon in 1936, a prediction that is used as a classic illustration of the dire results of improper sampling procedures.

The ability to construct clear, unambiguous questions is an art rather than a science. It has remained so despite the extensive investigations and accumulated experience of practitioners over the past four decades. Although principles of question wording have evolved, they are more indicative than imperative.

In general, we may summarize these principles by asserting that ambiguity in question wording arises from one or more of the following sources: (1) question length, (2) respondent unfamiliarity with one or more words, (3) ambiguity of one or more words in context, (4) two questions combined in one, and (5) lack of specificity. A brief discussion of each of these sources of ambiguity in question wording is in order.

1. *Questions that are too long.* There is a class of questions known as "flabbergasters" that are long, complex, and verge on being incomprehensible. A classic example is a reported 13-line question asking farm managers whether they used mostly inductive or deductive logic.

Each word in a question is a potential source of ambiguity. The greater the number of words, the more complex the structure of the question must become. For both these reasons, brevity in question construction is a virtue. As a general rule of thumb, questions should be held to no more than 20 words if at all possible.

The following question has been paraphrased from one actually used on a survey in a different field:

[12] *Ibid.*, pp. 8, 9.

> *Do you think of new car dealers as being independent businessmen like appliance dealers and furniture merchants who own their own stores, or as being employees of the automobile companies?*

Suppose, if you will, that this question is being read to you rather than your reading it. It refers to three different types of businesses, as well as to owning one's business versus being employed by a manufacturer. The researcher who constructed this question went to the trouble of using at least ten extra words which add opportunities of having the question misunderstood. Do you think that you would be more likely to understand the question above or this revised and shortened version?

> *Do you think of new car dealers as owning their business, or as being employees of the automobile companies?*

2. *Questions that use one or more words that are unfamiliar to the respondent.* The vocabulary used in questions should match that normally used by the respondents as closely as possible. For example, the wording of the question

> *Do you think that the processing of dehydrated soups reduces the caloric content?*

might well be appropriate if it is to be asked of a group of food chemists. It would require a heroically optimistic researcher, however, to consider seriously asking this question of a sample of consumers. There are at least four words that individually, and in some cases collectively, would be unfamiliar to some consumers.

The principle of matching question vocabulary and respondent vocabulary is not always easy to follow. In the case of a group of food chemists, there is a similarity of training and a common usage of terms. It is probable that their individual vocabulary levels are uniformly high. For this group, question vocabulary and respondent vocabulary can be matched reasonably well. In the case of consumers, however, vocabulary levels vary widely.

When the sample of respondents is at all large and nonhomogeneous in background, it is desirable to word the question at the lowest vocabulary level represented in the sample. For consumers, this means that questions must be worded as simply as possible. The researcher must guard against the use of more difficult synonyms for their simpler equivalents such as "observe" instead of "see," "obtain" instead of "get," and "purchase" instead of "buy."

The question should be worded to be understood by the respondent— not to impress him with the researcher's vocabulary. Impressing other people through the use of an extensive vocabulary should be left to pedants.

3. *Questions that use one or more words that are ambiguous in context.*

A common source of ambiguity of words in context is the way in which the question is constructed. Some illustrations of ambiguities arising from poor sentence structure are given below.

> *After receiving the Magnavox stereo set you ordered, did a repre-*
> *sentative of the Sight and Sound Company telephone you promptly?*
> (Did the representative call after *the company* received the set
> or after *you* received it?)
>
> *Did you plan to buy a service policy after the set was one year old?*
> (Were your plans made to buy a policy before the set was one year
> old, or to buy it after the set was one year old? Or were your plans
> made after the set was already one year old?)

A more serious and less easily corrected source of ambiguity of words in context is words that have two or more meanings. Most words have several meanings out of context, and we rely on the topic being discussed to indicate the intended meaning. For example, the word "set" used in the above questions has more than 250 meanings. In these questions the meaning intended should be clear. In many cases, however, the intended meaning of a word is not clear from the context in which it is used. Consider the following question:

> *Have you been satisfied with the service provided by the Sight and*
> *Sound Company?*

In this question, both the words "you" and "service" are subject to mis-interpretation. Does "you" mean the person being addressed only, or does it include his family? Does "service" refer to the assistance and consideration given the customer in making purchases or does it refer to the repair of equipment done by the company?

   4. *Combined questions.* Careless question wording sometimes results in two questions being asked as one. A question asked of commuters is illustrative of such questions.

> *Which would you say is the more convenient and economical way*
> *to commute, by car or by train?*

It is obvious that the respondent who believed that one method was more convenient and the other more economical could not logically answer the question as it was asked.

Combined questions should be avoided. The above question should have been broken into two separate questions, one dealing with "convenience" and the other with "economy."

5. *Questions that lack specificity.* Ambiguity often arises because of the vagueness of questions. A question such as

Do you listen to FM stations regularly?

will involve ambiguity because it is by no means clear whether "regularly" means three times a day, twice a week, once a month, or some other frequency of listening.

If the question is to be understood correctly, the desired information must be clearly specified.

Procedures for Recognizing and Reducing Ambiguity in Communication. Every research design that uses communication to obtain information should have as many safeguards against ambiguity as possible. Procedures should be employed to recognize where ambiguity may be present and to reduce it to the lowest practicable level.

Three procedural steps are useful for these purposes and should be considered in every project. They are: (1) alternative question wordings, (2) pretesting, and (3) verification by observation.

1. *Alternative question wording.* We have already seen that the present state of the art of question formulation cannot guarantee unambiguity. In questions where there is reason to suspect that ambiguity may exist, it is advisable to consider alternative wordings and forms of questions to be asked of subsamples of respondents.

The simplest application of this procedure applies to dichotomous questions. If it is believed that the order in which the alternatives are stated may influence the responses, the question can be asked of half the sample of respondents with the alternatives in one order, and of the other half with the order reversed. For example, the question

Which make of car would you say is more powerful, Ford or Chevrolet?

can be asked of half the respondents, and the question

Which make of car would you say is more powerful, Chevrolet or Ford?

of the other half. If the order of the alternatives does, in fact, affect the responses, this will become apparent and can be allowed for in interpreting the results.

The use of this simple experimental technique costs little more than having an extra set of questionnaires printed. It may reveal no significant differences in response. If so, it will usually be worth the cost involved simply to know that this is the case. Where significant differences in response are discovered, it will be even more worthwhile as a warning in interpreting the information.

2. *Pretesting.* Pretesting of questionnaires is a virtual necessity. The only way to gain real assurance that questions are unambiguous is to try them.

Pretesting is almost always done initially by asking proposed questions of associates. To be truly effective, however, pretesting of questions should be conducted by asking them of a group of respondents who are similar to those to be interviewed in the final sample.

It is the rule, rather than the exception, that questions will be revised as a result of pretesting. Several versions of a question may need to be considered as a result of pretesting before the final version is decided upon.

3. *Verification by observation.* Whenever cost, time, and the type of information desired permits, information obtained through communication should be verified by observation. The housewife may state that the only brand of floor wax she uses is Johnson's. Where possible, it is desirable to verify this statement partially by observing whether this is the only brand of floor wax she now has on hand.

Clearly, verification by observation is not always possible or practical. In the above example, the housewife may object to a pantry audit. Even greater difficulties would be involved in attempting to verify via observation her statement that she waxes the floors once each week.

Ambiguity in Observation

Although it has been suggested that, where practical to do so, information obtained by communciation should be verified by observation, the implication should not be drawn that observation is free of ambiguity. If we conduct a pantry audit and find that Johnson's Wax is the only brand on hand, this in itself does not disclose whether it was purchased or received as a gift, whether it is used or not, or, if used, for what purpose.

In making observations we each select, organize, and interpret visual stimuli into a picture that is as meaningful and as coherent to us as we can make it. Which stimuli are selected and how they are organized and interpreted are highly dependent upon both the backgrounds and frames of reference of the observer. If a customer, a floorwalker, and the department manager are each standing side by side on the mezzanine overlooking the jewelry department, what each "sees" will very likely differ markedly from what the others "see."

The trained observer will invariably "see" more that relates to his specialty in an ambiguous situation than the untrained observer. As an illustration, a few years ago a cereal manufacturer ran a promotional campaign involving a drawing contest for children. Each child who entered was required to submit (along with a box top) a picture he had drawn that depicted brand X cereal being eaten. The contest was run, the prizes awarded on the basis of artistic merit, and the brand manager turned his attention to other matters. A short time later a psychologist who worked for the company happened to see the pictures. He asked to be permitted to study them. He found that a sizable proportion of them showed a child eating cereal alone, often with no other dishes on the table. This suggested to him that cereal is often eaten by children as a between-meal snack. A later study by the company's marketing research department showed that cereals are eaten between meals by children in greater amounts than are eaten for breakfast. The advertising program of the company was subsequently changed to stress the benefits of its cereals as between-meal snacks.

SUMMARY

This chapter has been concerned with a discussion of the information that may be obtained from respondents. We considered two primary aspects of this topic: first, the types of information that could be obtained that would be useful for predicting response to alternate courses of action and, second, the errors that occur in obtaining such information.

Both behavioral correlates and nonbehavioral correlates were discussed as being useful for predicting response to alternate courses of action. Behavioral correlates include past behavior and intended behavior. Nonbehavioral correlates include socioeconomic characteristics, level of knowledge, and attitudes and opinions.

We then turned to an examination of the sources of error in information from respondents. The three major classes of errors, sampling error, nonresponse error, and response error, were identified. We examined in detail inaccuracy and ambiguity as sources of response error.

ASSIGNMENT MATERIAL

1. Indicate whether you agree or disagree with the statement below and state the reasons for your position:

   One of the important reasons for the use of surveys is that they can obtain sound information on what people's actions in the future will be.

2. State the conditions under which you believe information on past behavior can be a reliable predictor of future behavior.

3. State the conditions under which you believe information on intentions can be a reliable predictor of future behavior.

4. The manufacturer of a certain brand of nationally advertised and distributed frozen fruit juices has retained you as a consultant to advise on a questionnaire that is being prepared. The purpose of the survey is to determine consumer opinions and attitudes about frozen versus fresh fruit juices. Personal interviews are to be conducted on a randomly selected sample of families.

   a. The questions listed below are being considered for the questionnaire. Comment on each, indicating whether you would leave the question as it is or would change it. If you think it should be changed, rewrite it as you believe it should be asked.

      (1) Do you or any of your family drink fruit juices?
                        *Yes*_____   *No*_____
      If *Yes*:
      (2) Is the juice drunk at a meal or between meals or both?
         *At meal*_____   *Between meals*_____   *Both*_____
      (3) Do you prefer frozen or fresh juice?
                        *Frozen*_____   *Fresh*_____
      (4) What advantages, if any, do you believe using fresh juice has to using frozen juice?
      (5) What advantages, if any, do you believe using frozen juice has to using fresh juice?
      (6) What brand or brands of juice do you regularly buy?

                        _____
                        _____
                        _____   *Don't know*_____
      (7) On this card is a list of fruit juices. Tell me which are your family's first, second, and third choices.
                        grape   _____
                        tomato   _____
                        lime   _____
                        lemonade   _____
                        orange   _____
                        V-8   _____
                        other   _____
      (8) What is the last brand of juice bought by your family?
                        _____   *Don't know*_____

   b. Classify each of the above questions by type (*free-answer, multiple-choice, or dichotomous*).

5. A consumer organization sponsored a study of retail store managers to determine to what extent unethical practices were followed. As

part of the study a sample of managers were asked to flip a coin and, if the result was heads, to answer the question

"Were you born in April?"

If the coin came up tails, they were asked to answer the question

"Before the last sale held by your store, were some items marked up in price so that they could later be 'reduced' to the original price and shown as being on sale?"

Sixteen percent of the store managers answered "Yes" to the question they answered. What is the estimated proportion of store managers who had merchandise marked up in price before putting it "on sale"?

The Means 5
of Obtaining Information
from Respondents

In the last chapter we discussed the types of information that can be obtained from respondents that are useful in solving marketing problems. We also examined the kinds of errors that can arise in obtaining such information. We now need to consider the *means* of obtaining information from respondents.

How may we obtain information from respondents? The general answer to this question is that the same methods are used that we use in our everyday, informal association with people. If we want to find out something from someone, we either ask them, observe their behavior (or results of their behavior) in the area in which we are interested, or do both. Formal research has simply formalized these methods. To be sure, many techniques, some of them highly ingenious, have been developed and are in use. All of these techniques, however, ultimately reduce to some form of communication and/or observation.

In this chapter we shall consider in turn these processes of communication and observation as means of obtaining information. We preface the examination of these processes, however, with a discussion of research methodology in the behavioral sciences and its relationship to methods in marketing research.

The Behavioral Sciences and Marketing Research—
Some Observations on Method

Marketing research is only one of several fields of activity that are concerned with formalized means of obtaining information from people. The use of the term "behavioral sciences" for the fields of psychology, sociology, social psychology, and social anthropology is in itself indicative of the necessity of observing and communicating with people to develop and extend knowledge in each of these areas.

Each of the behavioral disciplines has made contributions to the body of techniques available for obtaining information from respondents, as has marketing research. An examination of the evolution of research techniques in each of these fields indicates that many parallel and independent developments have taken place along with interchanges and adaptations to fit the requirements of the borrowing field.

Perhaps all behavioral scientists (or nearly all, at any rate) will agree with the following proposition:

> The underlying motivations of most observable human acts have emotional and subconscious content as well as rational and conscious content.

We should, no doubt, have to define and redefine terms before general agreement is reached, but the basic proposition as stated does not seem particularly controversial to the present-day behavioral scientist.

It is just beyond this proposition, however, that controversy does arise. It was observed earlier that it is not unusual for scientists to find the most controversial concepts of their disciplines to be those dealing with the foundations of the field. The behavioral sciences are no exception. There has been a longstanding and deep-rooted controversy in each of the disciplines with regard to the fundamental questions of any science: "What can be known?" and "How can it be known?" Two philosophical views concerning these questions have emerged in the behavioral sciences. The first, the *objectivist* view, holds that we can acquire knowledge of human behavior only through investigatory methods restricted to the study of overt verbal and physical behavior with the minimum necessary interaction between investigator and subject. The research must be replicable and the data from which inferences are drawn publicly available.

The opposing view, the *subjectivist* approach, is that each human act is a unique event that can be understood only within the context of the actor's perception of the situation, his motives, the alternatives available for achieving them, and the choice process he uses. The subjectivist insists that empathetic interaction of investigator and subject (the *verstehen* method) is necessary to ensure meaningful understanding of motives and human behavior. Research data may *not* be replicable nor can they be made publicly available except through the interpretation of the researcher.

Each position has an articulate group of spokespersons. Yet the seemingly opposing positions have actually complemented as well as contradicted each other. The one is properly concerned with the testing of hypotheses concerning human behavior using the rigorous procedures of scientific method, the other with generating hypotheses by obtaining insights into the vagaries and complexities of motives and resultant behavior.

The difference in methodological concept carries through, of course, to technique. The objectivists tend to use direct, undisguised means of obtaining information, including survey research using structured interviews and laboratory and field experimentation. The subjectivists, with their basic inclination toward interpersonal interaction, prefer unstructured to structured interviews, projective techniques to direct questioning, and participant observation to experimentation.

This methodological issue has perhaps been most vigorously debated in psychology. It has centered there on the question of psychometric versus clinical diagnosis. The question at issue is whether standardized psychometric tests have greater predictive validity than personal evaluation by a qualified clinician.

Both the objectivist and the subjectivist views, along with their associated techniques, are represented in marketing research. Before World War II, marketing research and survey research using the structured interview were virtually synonymous. While there had always been concern with determining motivational influences on buyer behavior, the attempts to obtain this information from respondents had consisted mostly of direct questioning. In effect, the burden of assessing and verbalizing the motivational causes of his buying behavior was placed on the buyer—a burden he was not always willing or able to assume.

The introduction and use in marketing research of the depth interview and various projective techniques took place shortly after World War II. These techniques were originally known collectively by the generic term "motivation research." This term is misleading, since the techniques have been used for attitudinal and opinion studies, company and brand image studies, and selection of brand names as well as for studies of buyer motivation. In addition, they are not exhaustive of all techniques available for research on motivation. Fortunately, the term "motivation research" is now properly reverting to use for studies that relate to research on buyer motivation.

Our concern here is with first describing and then evaluating the means of obtaining information from respondents. We first discuss communication with respondents.

COMMUNICATION

Interviews in marketing research are usually classified by two major characteristics. An interview is either _structured_ or _unstructured_, depending upon whether a formal questionnaire has been formulated and the questions asked in a prearranged order. An interview is also either *direct* or *indirect* as a result of whether the purposes of the questions asked are intentionally disguised. Cross-classifying these two characteristics provides four different types of interviews. That is, an interview may be: (1) structured and direct, (2) unstructured and direct, (3) structured and indirect, or (4) unstructured and indirect. Types (1) and (2) are basically objectivist, types (3) and (4), subjectivist.

We discuss each type of interview in turn (although the discussion of the two indirect types of interviews is combined). We then discuss the media through which interviews may be conducted.

Structured–Direct Interviews

The usual type of interview conducted during a consumer survey to obtain descriptive information is one using a formal questionnaire consisting of nondisguised questions, a questionnaire designed to "get the facts." If the marketing research manager of a television set manufacturer wants to find out how many and what kinds of people prefer various styles of television cabinets, for example, he may have a set of questions drawn up that asks for these facts directly. Assuming that personal interviewing is being used, each interviewer will be instructed to ask the questions in the order given on the questionnaire and to ask only those questions. The resulting interviews will be *structured–direct* in nature.

A portion of a questionnaire designed to obtain information on furniture styles owned, television cabinet design preferences, and socioeconomic characteristics follows:

Which of the styles of furniture shown in these pictures is most nearly similar to your furniture?

  (show folder with furniture pictures)

| *Style A* | *Style C* | *Style E* |
| *Style B* | *Style D* | *Style F* |

Which of the styles of television cabinets shown in these pictures do you like best?

  (show folder with cabinet pictures)

| *Style H* | *Style J* | *Style L* |
| *Style I* | *Style K* | *Style M* |

What is (your)(your husband's)(your wife's) occupation?

About how much was the total income of you and (your husband) (your wife) last year from salary and other sources?

Less than $5,000 _____	*$10,000 to $14,999* _____
$5,000 to $7,499 _____	*$15,000 to $24,999* _____
$7,500 to $9,999 _____	*$25,000 and over* _____

For a problem of this type, the structured–direct interview has many desirable features. Since the questions are formulated in advance, all the required information can be asked for in an orderly and systematic fashion. The exact wording of the questions can be worked out carefully to reduce the possibility of misunderstandings and influencing the answer by the phrasing used. Pretests can (and should) be made on the questionnaire to discover any problems in the wording and/or ordering of questions before the questionnaire is in its final form.

The same questions are asked each of the respondents in the same order. This serves to provide maximum control of the interviewing process and to reduce the variability in results caused by differences in interviewer characteristics. This type of interview is less demanding so far as the abilities of the interviewer are concerned, permitting less skilled interviewers to be used and a resulting lower cost per interview. Editing, tabulating, and analyzing the information obtained are also facilitated, since standardized, direct questions are asked and the answers are recorded in a uniform manner.

The major problems associated with this type of interview are those involved with wording questions properly and the difficulties encountered in getting unbiased and complete answers to questions concerning personal and motivational factors. Despite these problems, the structured–direct interview is by far the most commonly used type of interview in marketing research.

Unstructured–Direct Interviews

In the *unstructured–direct* method of interviewing, the interviewer is given only general instructions on the type of information desired. He is left free to ask the necessary direct questions to obtain this information, using the wording and the order that seems most appropriate in the context of each interview.

Unstructured–direct interviews are often used in exploratory studies. Many research projects that use a formal questionnaire for the final interviews go through an exploratory phase in which respondents are contacted and unstructured interviews are held. These interviews are useful in obtaining a clearer understanding of the problem and determining what areas should be investigated. To use again the color television example, the company that is considering entering the field will want to know what consumers' experiences with color television have been, what their attitudes are toward it, suggestions they have for improvement, and so on. Pilot interviews that are unstructured and direct at the beginning of such a project are often helpful in determining which topics should be included on the final questionnaire.

This type of interview is also often useful for obtaining information on motives. If the owner of a color set is asked the free-answer question, "Why did you buy your color television set?" the answer is almost certain to be incomplete and may be worthless. Consider, for example, answers such as "Because we needed a television set," "Our old set wasn't working well," or "Because it was on sale." These answers are expressions of proximate causes rather than motivational causes. When motivations are given, such as "We enjoy color television more than black-and-white television," they are rarely complete. The added enjoyment may be because the picture is more lifelike, because of the aesthetic effect of color, because of the prestige the owner attaches to having a color set, or some combination of these and other factors. In addition, it is probable that there were motives other than "enjoyment" that influenced the purchase.

When used to establish motives the unstructured-direct interview is known as a *depth interview*, the terminology being borrowed from the field of psychology. The interviewer will continue to ask probing questions of the type "What did you mean by that statement?" "Why do you feel this way?" and "What other reasons do you have?" until he is satisfied that he has obtained all the information he can, considering time limitations, problem requirements, and the willingness and ability of the respondents to verbalize motives.

It should again be noted that there is always the danger that people will consciously or unconsciously offer wrong answers to prestige questions or to questions about why they took a particular action. Although the depth interview using direct questions may assist the respondent to recognize and to verbalize motives that otherwise would not have been disclosed, it still does not satisfactorily solve this problem in all cases.

The unstructured interview is free of the restrictions imposed by a formal list of questions. The interview may be conducted in a seemingly casual, informal manner in which the flow of the conversation determines which questions are asked and the order in which they are raised. The level of vocabulary used can be adapted to that of the respondent to ensure that the questions are fully understood and that rapport is developed and maintained. The flexibility inherent in this type of interview, when coupled with the greater informality that results when it is skillfully used, often results in information being disclosed that is not obtained in a structured–direct interview.

In the structured–direct interview, the questionnaire is, in effect, the dominant factor in the interview. The interviewer's role is simply that of a question asker. In the unstructured interview, the interviewer must both formulate and ask questions. The unstructured interview can therefore be only as effective in obtaining complete, objective, and unbiased information as the interviewer is skilled in formulating and asking questions. The major problem in unstructured–direct interviews is accordingly that of ensuring that competent interviewers are used. Higher per-interview costs result, both as a result of this requirement and the fact that unstructured interviews generally are longer than those in which a questionnaire is used. In addition, editing and tabulating problems are more complicated as a result of the varied order of asking questions and recording answers.

Structured– and Unstructured–Indirect Interviews

Psychologists have long recognized that direct questioning of patients is frequently of little value for diagnostic purposes. The patient is usually unable and often unwilling to give accurate answers to direct questions. To solve this problem, a number of techniques have been devised to obtain information by *indirect* means. Most of these techniques employ the principle of *projection*. That, is, the subject is given a nonpersonal, ambiguous situation and asked to describe it. The person giving the description will tend to interpret the situation in terms of his own needs, motives, and values. The description, therefore, involves a projection of characteristics of personality to the situation described. These techniques include *word association, sentence completion tests, interpretation of pictorial representations,* and other devices that have been developed as a means of inducing people to project their feelings. They have been most widely used for studies on those consumer products that are similar in quality, performance, and price—notably for such products as automobiles, soaps and detergents, gasoline, cigarettes, food products, beverages, and drug sundries.

Most indirect interviews are at least *partially structured* in that they are conducted by using a predevised set of words, statements, one or more cartoons, pictures, or other representations to which the subject is asked to respond. However, the interviewer usually is allowed considerable freedom in questioning the respondent in order to ensure a full response. Indirect interviews, therefore, are commonly neither fully structured nor unstructured: ordinarily they utilize both types of questions.

Focus-Group Interviews

Perhaps the best-known and most widely used type of indirect interview is that conducted with a *focus group*. A focus-group interview is one in which a group of people jointly participate in an unstructured–indirect interview. The group, usually consisting of 8 to 12 people, is generally selected purposively to include persons who have a common background or similar buying or use experience that relates to the problem to be researched. The interviewer, or *moderator*, as he or she is more often called, attempts to focus the discussion on the problem areas in a relaxed, nondirected manner. The objective is to foster involvement and interaction among the group members during the interview that will lead to spontaneous discussion and the disclosure of attitudes, opinions, and information on present or prospective buying and use behavior.

Focus groups are used primarily for the definition of problems, to provide background information, and for the generation of hypotheses rather than to provide solutions for problems. Areas of application include the examination of new product concepts, the generation of ideas for improving established products, the development of creative concepts for advertising, and the determination of effective means of merchandising products. Focus-group interviews are often held to help determine the subject areas on which questions should be asked in a later, large-scale, structured–direct interview.

An example of the use of the focus-group technique is in the development of an advertising and merchandising program to dealers of fiber glass radial tires.[1] Just prior to the introduction of the new glass radial tires, Owens-Corning Fiberglas conducted a series of 15 focus-group interviews with mass merchandise, oil company, and private-label dealers to see what the dealers perceived as being the key benefits and merchandising aids that would best help them sell the new type of tires. Previous research had indicated that consumers would buy the glass radials provided they were less expensive than steel radials. Since glass radials were to be 15 to 20% lower in price than steel radials, Owens-Corning expected no problems with dealer acceptance of the new tires. Instead, in the focus interviews, they found that the dealers were afraid that the problems they had had with glass bias belted tires when they were introduced some eight years earlier would be repeated with the glass radial tires. As a result, sales themes and promotional copy were reworked to assure dealers that consumer acceptance of the new tires would be good, performance would be high, and they should have a minimum of problems with the new product.

The Third-Person Technique

The simplest way of obtaining information through indirect questioning of a respondent is to ask for the view of a neighbor, an (unnamed) associate, or some other person whose views on the subject at hand might reasonably be known. This permits the respondent to project his own views with no feeling of social pressure to give an "acceptable" answer.

The study on flying referred to earlier that was performed for a commercial airline is a good example of the use of this technique. It will be recalled that when respondents were asked, "Are you afraid to fly?" very few people gave any indication of fear. The major reasons given for not flying were cost and the inconvenience of getting to and from the airport plus the uncertainty of airline schedules during the winter due to bad weather. When, in a followup study, respondents were asked, "Do you think your neighbor is afraid to fly?" most of the neighbors who traveled by some other method of transportation were said to do so because they were afraid to fly.

[1]"Owens-Corning Listens to Dealers," *Sales Management*, 114 (March 3, 1975), 23.

An early study using a variation of this technique that has come to be regarded as a classic is the study by Haire on instant coffee. This study was conducted when instant coffee was being introduced (1949). The purpose of the study was to determine the motivations of consumers toward instant coffee in general and Nescafé, a brand of instant coffee, in particular.[2]

Interviews of consumers had been conducted using a questionnaire employing direct questions. Among the questions asked were "Do you use instant coffee?" and (if "No") "What do you dislike about it?" The majority of the unfavorable responses were of the general content "I don't like the flavor." This answer was suspected to be a stereotype rather than revealing the true reasons. An indirect approach was therefore decided upon.

Two shopping lists were prepared that were identical in every respect except that one contained "Nescafé instant coffee" and the other "Maxwell House coffee (drip grind)." These shopping lists were shown alternately to a sample of 100 respondents, each being unaware of the other list. Each subject was given the following instructions:

Read the shopping list below. Try to project yourself into the situation as far as possible until you can more or less characterize the woman who bought the groceries. Then write a brief description of her personality and character. Wherever possible indicate what factors influenced your judgment.

The results were quite revealing. The descriptions given are summarized as follows:[3]

1. 48% of the people described the woman who bought Nescafé as lazy; 4% described the woman who bought Maxwell House as lazy.

2. 48% of the people described the woman who bought Nescafé as failing to plan household purchases and schedules well; 12% described the woman who bought Maxwell House this way.

3. 4% described the Nescafé woman as thrifty; 16% described the Maxwell House woman as thrifty; 12% described the Nescafé woman as spendthrift; 0% described the Maxwell House woman this way.

4. 16% described the Nescafé woman as not a good wife; 0% described the Maxwell House woman this way; 4% described the Nescafé woman as a good wife; 16% described the Maxwell House woman as a good wife.

[2]Mason Haire, "Projective Techniques in Marketing Research," *Journal of Marketing*, 14 (April, 1950), 649–56.
[3]*Ibid.*, p. 652.

The implications of these findings seem clear. The woman using the instant coffee was characterized as being lazier, less well organized, more of a spendthrift, and not as good a wife as the one using the conventional coffee. These imputed characteristics must have been the result of the respondents' projecting their own feelings toward instant coffee in their descriptions of the woman using it.

This study has been replicated a number of times. The general acceptance of instant coffee and the change in dietary habits since it was done originally have resulted in different findings in the more recent studies.[4]

Word Association Tests

Word association tests have been used since 1879 by psychologists and are considered to be the forerunner of more recent projective techniques.

The test consists of presenting a series of stimulus words to a respondent who is asked to answer quickly with the first word that comes to mind after hearing each. The respondent, by answering quickly, presumably gives the word that he associates most closely with the stimulus word.

A word association test was used by the American Telephone and Telegraph Company to choose the name that best communicated the service provided by long distance dialing. Seven names were tested, including "Nationwide Dialing," "Customer Toll Dialing," and "Direct Distance Dialing." Responses to "Nationwide Dialing" were (somewhat surprisingly) weighted in the direction of "worldwide," an apparent interpretation that this new system would permit dialing telephone numbers all over the world. "Customer Toll Dialing" received a high response rate of "money" and "charges," indicating an unfavorably high association with the cost of making long distance calls. "Direct Distance Dialing" was chosen by AT&T since it seemed to convey the idea of long distance dialing without the use of an operator and did not have any unfavorable associations.

Sentence Completion Tests

Sentence completion tests are similar to word association tests, both in concept and in use. A sentence stem (the beginning phrase of a sentence) is read to the respondent, who is asked to complete the sentence quickly and with the first thought that occurs to him.

Sentence completion was one of the techniques used in a study of automobile buying. The purpose of the study was to probe the motivations of automobile buyers to provide a sounder basis for advertising. Such sentence stems were used as

[4]See, for example, G. S. Lane and G. L. Watson, "A Canadian Replication of Mason Haire's 'Shopping List' Study," *Journal of the Academy of Marketing Science*, 3 (Winter, 1975), 48–59.

People who drive a convertible . . .
Factory workers usually drive . . .
Most of the new cars . . .
When I drive very fast . . .

Some selected responses of men and women to two of the sentence stems illustrate how inferences of motivational influences can be drawn through the use of this technique.[5]

Sentence stem: When you first get a car . . .
   Women's responses:
      . . . you can't wait till you drive.
      . . . you would go for a ride.
      . . . you would take rides in it, naturally.
      . . . you would put gas in it and go places.
   Men's responses:
      . . . you take good care of it.
      . . . I want to make darn sure it has a good coat of wax.
      . . . check the engine.
      . . . how soon can I start polishing it.
Sentence stem: A car of your own. . .
   Women's responses:
      . . . is a pleasant convenience.
      . . . is fine to have.
      . . . is nice to have.
   Men's responses:
      . . . I would take care of it.
      . . . is a good thing.
      . . . absolutely a necessity.

The interpretation of these results was as follows:

The women's responses indicated that for them a car is something to use and that pride of ownership stresses being seen in the car. For men a car was something for which they should be protective and responsible. Their emphasis was on examining the car and doing things to it. Men appeared to feel closer to their car and regarded it as more of a necessity than did women.[6]

[5] As reported in J. W. Newman, *Motivation Research and Marketing Management* (Cambridge, Mass.: Harvard University Graduate School of Business Administration, 1957), 227–28.
[6] *Ibid.*, p. 228.

Thematic Apperception Tests

The *Thematic* (for themes that are elicited) *Apperception* (for the perceptual–interpretative use of pictures) *Test* (TAT) consists of one or more pictures or cartoons that depict a situation relating to the product or topic being studied. Generally, one or more persons are shown in an ambiguous situation and the respondent is asked to describe or to assume the role of one of these people.

The most common form of the TAT as used in marketing research is the cartoon. The cartoons shown in Figures 5-1 and 5-2 were used to study the price–quality association of a sample of women with respect to a beauty cream. Each woman in the sample was shown one of the cartoons (in random order) and asked to describe first the person in the cartoon and then to indicate what she thought the beauty cream shown would be like.

The general nature of the responses for the cartoon showing the 49-cent beauty cream are well summarized by the answers of one of the women:

"Any female over 18 interested in her appearance who falls for the advertising claims and doesn't have too much money to spend on cosmetics." "It's a poor quality product that is probably greasy and oily."

For the cartoon showing the $5.00 cream, the responses given below are generally representative of those of the sample:

"Someone who cares what she looks like—possibly a business girl interested in her appearance."

"It's a cream that leaves your skin clear and refreshed. It probably would keep your skin young-looking by softening and cleansing the skin."

The reader may draw his own conclusions as to the association of price and quality for this product. (Before a sound conclusion can be reached, however, additional information is needed with respect to the size and nature of the sample used.)

The Depth Interview

There is substantial use of the unstructured, informal interview in marketing research to explore the underlying predispositions, needs, desires, feelings, and emotions of the consumer toward products and services. This method of interviewing was discussed earlier in this chapter and referred to as a "depth interview."

Figure 5-1

49¢

Beauty Cream

Figure 5-2

$5.00

Beauty Cream

Insofar as obtaining information on motivations is concerned, the concept of "depth" refers to the level at which underlying motivations are uncovered. Both the method of interviewing and the term "depth interview" were borrowed from clinical psychology, where the method has been used to probe and assess the sources and nature of the problems of patients. In marketing research, the "depth" of the interviews has been varied but with a general level that is substantially less "deep" than the level used in the field of psychology.

The *depth interview* in marketing research may consist of either direct or indirect questions, or some combination of the two. The skilled interviewer will generally employ both types of questions. A direct, free-answer question such as "What are the major reasons why you bought your CB radio?" might well be followed up, for example, with an indirect question such as "Why do you think people who own CB radios bought them?" By following leads and cues provided by respondents, phrasing questions to continue the flow and pattern of the conversation and to maintain the rapport established, the competent interviewer can explore and probe the underlying motivations of the respondent.

Many examples of the use of depth interviewing in marketing research could be cited. One, which again relates to coffee, is reported by Newman.[7] Depth interviews were the basic research technique used in a study done for the Pan-American Coffee Bureau by the Institute for Motivation Research. Exploratory depth interviews were conducted with 36 respondents, and an additional sample of 96 respondents were depth-interviewed later.

In each depth interview, "a trained interviewer encouraged the respondent to talk freely about his associations and feelings related to coffee. Direct questions seldom were asked. Instead the interviewer attempted by skillful probing to learn what was important to the respondent and to investigate the emotional facets that often determined apparently rational behavior.[8]

Interviewer instructions for the initial set of 36 interviews are given in Figure 5-3. These instructions are worthy of careful reading, since they illustrate both the major strength—adaptability—and the primary weakness—opportunity for subjective biases in interviewing and interpretation—of the depth interview.

Several recommendations were made as a result of the study. One of these was to change coffee, in psychological terms, from a "sinful and escapist" beverage to a positive, life-accepting product. Although many of the respondents showed a liking for coffee, they were afraid of drinking too much of it and reluctant about letting young people drink it. A second recommendation was to provide a greater variety of coffee flavors. Coffee should not just be "coffee"; restaurants should treat it as more of a specialty by listing four

[7]Newman, *Motivation Research*, 156–227.
[8]*Ibid.*, p. 161.

Figure 5-3   Pan-American Coffee Bureau study—interviewer instructions

---

Sample Note: Of your two respondents, please make sure that you have represented one male, one female; one "dark strong" coffee drinker, one "light weak" coffee drinker; one "heavy drinker" (6–8 cups per day), one "light drinker" (2–3 cups per day).

Just for Your Information

There are 5 major practical questions that we want to answer in this study:

1. What is the real role of coffee drinking in people's lives today?
2. Why people drink coffee more frequently, or less?
3. Why people prefer stronger, or weaker coffee brewing?
4. At what age levels and why is coffee drinking morally possible?
5. Any special feelings about coffee on the part of older people.

To answer these questions, we need to probe for the whole range of people's feelings about coffee and its real role in their lives. Encourage maximum spontaneity and feel free to probe any area that seems likely to be significant.

It would be most helpful for these initial interviews if you could just get people talking freely on all their feelings about coffee for an hour or so.

The areas below are to be probed only after fullest possible rambling free association is exhausted.

Some Suggested Research Areas

Among others, try to probe the following areas that we have found helpful in our preliminary field testing:

1. *Spontaneous Associations*—First try to encourage maximum free association with coffee, *everything that comes into people's minds as they think of coffee.* . . . Probe in detail for *all sensory* impressions, smell, taste, appearance, etc.
2. *Kinds of Coffee*—All impressions about different types of coffee—strong, weak, black, etc., difficulties in making coffee, how one brews coffee, etc. . . .
3. *Coffee Drinking Occasions*—When respondent drinks coffee and attitudes to coffee at all these specific occasions—when it is most wanted, best liked. . . .
4. *Best Cup*—The *best* cup of coffee—how it tasted, etc. . . . .
5. *Childhood*—Impressions of coffee in childhood—when first asked for some—parents' attitude—when he and friends first started drinking coffee—all impressions of that first cup, taste, smell, etc.
6. *His Children*—Any comments about or requests for coffee by his children —what he said—at what age allowed, or will be allowed, to drink coffee?
7. *Frequency*—Average number of cups per day— . . . .
8. *Health*—All feelings about coffee and health— . . . .

---

or five varieties of coffee. A third recommendation was that coffee advertising should be more permissive about suggesting how people should make and drink their coffee, since people were proud of having individual tastes and, in some cases, resented authoritarian advertisements that told them the "right" way of making coffee.

Other Techniques

Other variations of projective techniques have been used that are similar in nature but different in form from those already described. The *repertory grid*, for example, is a partially structured technique that requires the respondent to compare objects along dimensions that he or she selects. The usual procedure is to present the interviewee with a pack of cards on which brand names are printed. The respondent is asked to cull unfamiliar brands from the pack, and three cards with familiar brand names are selected at random. Following this, the respondent is asked to describe a way in which any two of the familiar brands are like each other and different from the third. The respondent is then asked to rate all the brands with respect to this dimension. The response may be in the form of a paired comparison, a ranking, or a numerical rating on a scale. This process is repeated using three different brands until the dimensions of the respondent are exhausted. Additional respondents are interviewed until no new dimensions are given. On the average, 40 interviews are required to identify most of the relevant dimensions.[9] An example of the repertory grid technique appears in Chapter 17.

Story completion, a logical extension of the sentence completion technique, consists of presenting the beginning of a situational narrative to a respondent, who is asked to complete it. The general underlying principle is that the person will project his own psychological interpretation of the situation into the response.

Projection through *sketching* by the respondent has been used in a study of supermarket layout and design.[10] A sample of 50 housewives was asked to "draw a supermarket" in conjunction with an interview. Some of the findings, of which the reader may make his own interpretations, were: (1) the meat department was omitted in about 1 out of 10 drawings, produce in 1 out of 5, and dry groceries in 1 out of 4; (2) the produce department was drawn first in about 2 out of 5 drawings, meats in 1 out of 5, dairy in 1 out of 6, and dry groceries in 1 out of 6; (3) the meat department was, on the average, drawn about 50% *larger* than the dry groceries department. Actually it is only about one-third as large as the dry groceries department in a store of the dimensions involved. Produce was drawn 80% as large as dry groceries, though it, too, occupies only about one-third of the space actually allotted to dry groceries.

[9]Reported in G. D. Hughes, "The Measurement of Beliefs and Attitudes," in *Handbook of Marketing Research*, ed. Robert Ferber (New York: McGraw-Hill Book Company, 1974), pp. 3–19.

[10]H. E. Krugman, "The 'Draw a Supermarket' Technique," *Public Opinion Quarterly*, 24 (Spring, 1960), 148–49.

INTERVIEWING MEDIA

Several alternative media are available for obtaining information from respondents through communication. Respondents may be interviewed in person, interviewed by telephone, or they may be mailed a questionnaire to which they are asked to respond.

The Personal Interview

As the name implies, the *personal interview* consists of an interviewer asking questions of one or more respondents in a face-to-face situation. The interviewer's role is to get in touch with the respondent(s), ask the desired questions, and to record the answers obtained. The recording of the information obtained may be done either during or after the interview. In either case, it is a part of the interviewer's responsibility to ensure that the content of the answers is clear and unambiguous and that it has been recorded correctly.

While it is substantially more expensive on a per-completed-interview basis, the personal interview as a collection medium has several advantages relative to telephone interviews and mail questionnaires. It provides the opportunity to *obtain a better sample*, since virtually all the sample units can be reached and, with proper controls and well-trained interviewers, nonresponse can be held to a minimum. It also gives the *opportunity to obtain more information*, as a personal interview can be of substantially greater length than either a telephone interview or mail questionnaire. Finally, it permits *greater flexibility*. More freedom is provided for adapting and interpreting questions as the situation requires, especially in the case of unstructured personal interviews.

The limitations of the personal interview are the cost and the response bias that may be induced by poorly trained or improperly selected interviewers. The reader will recall the discussion of interviewer-induced response bias in the last chapter.

The Telephone Interview

Telephone interviews are sometimes used in lieu of personal interviews, especially when the information must be collected quickly and inexpensively and the amount of information required is limited.

The telephone interview is well suited to such research problems as determining "coincidental" viewing of television or listening to radio programs. In this type of study, calls are placed to a sample of telephone subscribers during the time the program is on the air. The person receiving the call is simply asked "Are you now watching television?" and, if so, "What program you are watching?" Other questions such as "How often do you watch this program?" "Who sponsors this program?" and the like may also be asked. The result is a rapid and inexpensive measurement of audience level.

Either a *structured* or *an unstructured* interview may be held. Since the amount of information sought is usually well defined, nonconfidential in nature, and limited in amount, virtually all telephone interviews are structured in nature. This medium does not lend itself well to *indirect* interviews and has not been used for this purpose.

The telephone interview has advantages in addition to speed and economy. It is frequently easier to get the cooperation of people over the telephone than in a personal interview. This is particularly true in industrial surveys, where an executive may be busy with appointments and unable to see an interviewer when he makes a personal call (if a prior appointment has not been made) but can be reached readily by telephone. Interviews by telephone may also successfully be conducted during evening hours, a time when many people are reluctant to be interviewed personally.

The basic limitations of telephone interviews are the limited amounts of information that can be obtained and the bias that exists in any sample of subscribers. Subscribers have different characteristics from nonsubscribers, particularly with respect to income and location. The inability to include nonsubscribers in the sample may seriously affect the findings. Perhaps even more sample bias is induced in the typical telephone survey by the high proportion of subscribers who are not listed in the directory, either because of having an unlisted number or as a result of moving. One study found that 9% of the subscribers at the beginning and 18% of the subscribers at the end of the directory year were not listed in the Greater Cincinnati area directory.[11]

A technique for including nonlisted telephone numbers in the sampling frame is called *random-digit dialing*. Information can be obtained from the telephone company as to which four-digit blocks of numbers have been assigned for each exchange. Telephone numbers may then be generated by using a table of random numbers. While some unused numbers are generated, the frame error resulting from nonlisted numbers in the telephone directory is eliminated.

The Mail Interview

Mail interviews have been widely used for a variety of purposes. Some indication of the extent of use, both by product or service and by geographic area, is provided by the fact that for several years the Soviet film industry has sponsored mail surveys to evaluate films.

Mail questions provide great versatility at relatively low cost. A questionnaire may be prepared and mailed to people in any location at the same

[11]S. L. Cooper, "Random Sampling by Telephone—An Improved Method," *Journal of Marketing Research*, 1 (November, 1964), 45.

cost per person: the cost of preparing the questionnaire, addressing the letter or card sent, and the postage involved. Unless the name is requested, the respondent remains anonymous and therefore may give confidential information that otherwise would be withheld. He may also answer the questionnaire at his leisure, rather than being forced to reply at the time a personal or telephone call is made.

Serious problems are involved in the use of mail questionnaires, however. Perhaps the most serious is the problem of nonresponse. Typically, those people who are indifferent to the topic being researched will not respond. It is usually found necessary to send additional mailings to increase response. Even with added mailings, response to mail questionnaires is generally a small percentage of those sent; the modal response rate is often only 20 to 40%. Experiments involving preliminary contact by letter or telephone call, cover letters, and monetary inducements have increased response rates dramatically in some cases.

Since the people responding tend to do so because they have stronger feelings about the subject than the nonrespondents, biased results are to be expected. To measure this bias, it is necessary to contact a sample of the nonrespondents by other means, usually by telephone interviews. The low level of response, when combined with the additional mailings and telephone (or personal) interviews of nonrespondents, results in substantial increases in the per-interview cost. The initial low cost per mailing may therefore be illusory.

Additional limitations are the length of time required to complete the study and the inability to ensure that questions are understood fully and answers recorded properly.

Warranty Card

A variation of the mail interview that is frequently used is the *warranty card*. Most consumer durables have a warranty card included in the package or crate. The buyer is instructed to fill out the card and send it to the manufacturer if he wishes to take advantage of the warranty. Information is usually requested on where the item was purchased, what kind of store or outlet sold it, and the date of purchase. If the item is of the type that may be used as a gift (an electric shaver, for example), information on the purpose of the purchase is also sought. Although warranty cards do not provide an extensive amount of information, response rates are substantially higher than for the usual mail questionnaire.

Telegram Interviews

Another variation of the mail questionnaire is the use of *telegrams*. One of the earliest formal marketing research studies recorded, a study to estimate grain production by county in the United States in 1879, involved the use of telegrams. Although this method of requesting information is used infrequently, it has the advantage of rapidity and a relatively high rate of response. Apparently, people who receive telegrams requesting information are impressed and somewhat flattered by the trouble taken to solicit information from them. Offsetting these advantages, however, is the limitation on the amount of information that can be obtained and the obvious higher cost of the medium.

A third variation of the mail questionnaire is the questionnaire that is delivered personally and is either returned via a representative of the research organization or by mail. Dealer surveys are often conducted in this manner, the salesmen calling upon them being used to deliver the questionnaire.

OBSERVATION

The remaining major method of collecting information is through observation. *Observation* is used to obtain information on both current and past behavior of people. Rather than asking respondents about their current behavior, it is often less costly and/or more accurate if the behavior is observed. We clearly cannot observe past behavior, but the *results* of such behavior are often observable. For example, instead of asking such questions as "What brand of television set do you own?" and "Is it equipped to receive programs on UHF channels?" the best and simplest procedure may be simply to look at the set.

Observation may be used as the sole means of collecting data or, as is frequently the case, it may be used in conjunction with other means. It is a method that should always be considered in designing marketing research investigations that call for information on past or current behavior. In some circumstances, observation is the *only* means of collecting the data desired. A department manager in Macy's department store in New York City will need information on the prices of similar products at Gimbel's if he wants to ensure that his prices remain competitive. The observation of Gimbel's prices through "shopping" is the only means of collecting this information. As a matter of practice, both department stores continuously "shop" each other to determine prices.

In other circumstances, alternative methods of collecting information are available, but observation may be the preferable method, either from considerations of *cost*, improved *accuracy*, or both. Respondents often cannot and sometimes will not report information accurately. In the example cited above, the respondent may not remember the brand of the television set and may very well not understand what "UHF" means. Brand usage reports of well-established brands generally show a "halo effect," an upward bias reflecting the prestige the respondent associates with the use of the brand. The Johnson Wax Company, for example, has found that respondent reports of brand purchases of floor wax vary widely from the actual brand of floor wax that the consumer has on hand.

The major applications of observation as an information-collection method may be classified into the categories of the *audit*, coincidental *recording devices*, and a general classification, *direct observation*.

The Audit

Audits are performed in practice on both distributors and consumers. The *distributor audit* is the more widely known of the two.

The commercially available Nielsen Retail Index, and audit of retail stores performed each 60 days, was described in Chapter 3. As indicated there, data from this and audits available through other research agencies provide estimates of *market size, market share, geographic pattern of the market, seasonal purchasing patterns*, and *results of promotional and pricing changes*.

Manufacturers often perform their own audits of distributors through their salespeople. Although the data collected are not as comprehensive as those described above, information on inventories and prices can usually be obtained and reported. These salesperson audits have the additional advantage of ensuring that the salespeople check inventories and prices as a routine part of their sales calls. Improved sales performance is an important co-product of such an auditing program.

Pantry audits of consumer homes is a second type of audit that is sometimes performed. In this type of audit, the field worker takes an inventory of the brands, quantities, and package sizes that the consumer has on hand. When this type of audit is performed on a recurring basis, inconspicuous labels may be attached to the package showing the date the item was first included in the inventory. When the audit is combined with questioning of the consumer, an estimate of usage may be made. The pantry audit is relatively expensive in terms of data obtained, compared with a self-reporting consumer panel, however. Its use has declined as the use of consumer panels has increased.

Recording Devices

A number of electromechanical devices for "observing" the behavior of respondents are in use in marketing research. Some of these devices are used primarily in laboratory-type investigations and others for recording behavior in its natural setting. Illustrative of the types of *recording instruments* used in laboratory studies are the eye camera, the pupilometric camera, and the psychogalvanometer. Two of the devices used in noncontrived situations are the motion-picture camera and the Audimeter.

The "observing" of respondent behavior in a laboratory situation with the aid of recording devices has been largely confined to the pretesting of advertising. *Eye cameras*, for example, are specially designed cameras that record eye movements in relation to the specific location of material on a page. Subjects may be given an advertisement and, through the use of the photographic record provided by the eye camera, analyses can be made of the pattern in which the advertisement is "read." A determination may be made of which parts of it tend to attract attention initially, the relative amounts of time spent in looking at the illustration versus that used for reading the copy, which portions of the copy are actually read, and so on.

The *pupilometric camera* photographs eye movements of an entirely different sort and for a different purpose. The dilation and restriction of the pupil of the eye has been found to correlate with the degree of interest aroused by the visual stimulus. Interest-arousing stimuli result in the dilation of the pupil. An advertisement or a product that has a pleasurably toned interest to the subject will be evidenced by dilation of the pupil. Further, there are indications that the *extent* of pupil dilation will indicate *degree* of interest. While this technique has not yet been fully validated, it shows some promise as a means of measuring consumer interest.

The *psychogalvanometer* is used for measuring the extent of the subject's "response" to the advertisement. The principle involved is that the perspiration rate of the body is increased by excitement. The amount of stimulation provided by an advertisement, therefore, can be measured by recording changes in perspiration rate. This is done by measuring the change in electrical resistance in the palms of the subject's hands.

Other devices are also used for "observing" behavior under laboratory conditions. In general, all such devices have the advantage of permitting careful and detailed observations of behavior that could not be made otherwise. They have the added advantage of providing permanent records of the behavior observed. In using these devices, however, one should always keep in mind two important questions: (1) Is the behavior we are observing a valid predictor of the behavior we want to predict? and (2) Are the subjects behaving as they would in a natural situation?

The answer to the second question can clearly be in the affirmative if the observation is made outside of the laboratory and in the natural situation. Hidden *motion-picture cameras*, for example, are used in many situations to record respondent behavior. One such application was a study performed for a manufacturer of frozen juice concentrates who was considering changing the design and amount of information given on the label. Before this change was made, information was needed on the extent to which consumers actually read information on labels. Hidden cameras were stationed in a sample of supermarkets in front of the frozen food cases, and pictures were taken of consumers selecting frozen juice concentrates. An analysis of these pictures indicated that far more time was spent in the selection and more careful attention given the information on the label than had previously been believed to be the case.

The *Audimeter* is another device for recording respondent behavior under normal conditions. It is, in effect, an electromechanical equivalent of the consumer "diary" so far as obtaining a record of television viewing is concerned. It is used by the A. C. Nielsen Company to record automatically the times the television set is turned on and off and the stations to which it is tuned. It is installed in the television sets of a selected panel of families. The tapes on which the recording is made are collected and the National Nielsen TV Ratings is issued every two weeks. Measurements of *total, average,* and *share* of audience are available to clients.

This method of recording the viewing behavior of set owners has some obvious advantages. It permits a complete and accurate record to be obtained of the programs to which each set included in the panel was tuned. Careful analyses can be made of switching during a program to determine the effect of competing programs and of commercial messages. It has the limitation shared by all fixed-sample collection procedures with respect to the inability of obtaining a completely random sample. It also fails to provide information concerning the number of viewers of the program that are tuned in or, indeed, whether the program is actually being watched at any particular time.

Direct Observation

Direct observation of people and how they behave in situations of interest is a commonly used method of collecting information. Many studies have been made of shopping behavior to determine the relative effects of such variables as displays, availability, and reliance on salesperson advice on the brand selected and the quantity purchased. Supermarket and department store managers continually rely on observation of traffic flows and length of waiting lines to determine the proper location of the various lines of products and the number and location of salespeople and cash registers. An important consideration in the location of banks, retail stores, and entire shopping centers is the amount and pattern of traffic at alternative sites.

Information obtained from direct observation of purchasers can be highly useful in helping to answer such questions as

Who actually buys the products?

Do they appear to be influenced by an accompanying person?

To what extent do brand choices appear to have been made earlier versus at the point of purchase?

What proportion of shoppers appear to check prices?

What proportion of shoppers study the package before purchase?

Direct observation of purchasers has some obvious limitations. Though perhaps more serious to the subjectivist than the objectivist, some of the limitations are important to both. It is apparent that the observers will selectively perceive and record those actions that seem meaningful to them. Thus, the selection of acts to record will depend upon the behavioral model of the observer. Direct observation discloses *what* rather than *why*. Motivation must be inferred. Inferences are often difficult to substantiate as a result of lack of control over important variables.

Participant observation, as the name implies, is a form of observation in which the observer actually participates in the activities of the group he wishes to study. Examples are anthropologists who live with native tribes, labor economists who join a union, and sociologists studying poverty who move to a low-income neighborhood. This form of observation has been rarely used in marketing research, as by their nature marketing activities do not usually lend themselves well to such a technique. Participant observation studies of both industrial and retail salespeople have been made, however.

DIRECT VERSUS INDIRECT RESEARCH TECHNIQUES—AN ASSESSMENT

Opinion has been divided among practitioners about the role and relative merits of indirect research techniques in marketing research. This division reflects in marketing research the objectivist–subjectivist debate in the behavioral sciences in general. The controversy has largely centered on three areas: the applicability of the techniques, sample selection and sizes employed, and the accuracy of utilizing disguised modes of obtaining such information.

Applicability of Indirect Research Techniques

The basic premises leading to the *use* of indirect research techniques are as follows:

1. The criteria employed and the evaluations made in most buying and use decisions have emotional and subconscious content.
2. This emotional and subconscious content is an important determinant of buying and use decisions.
3. Such content is not adequately and/or accurately verbalized by the respondent through direct communicative techniques.

4. Such content is adequately and accurately verbalized by the respondent through indirect communicative techniques.

How valid are these premises? From the earlier discussion of specific cases, we have already seen that they are valid for some problems. Conversely, it is not difficult to cite cases in which one or more of the premises are not valid. The general answer to the question of whether the premises are valid or not must then be that it "depends upon the problem."

As it stands, this is a correct but not a very satisfactory answer. To extend it somewhat and to give it more meaning, it is useful to review the categories of situations in which information might reasonably be sought from respondents and to decide in which of these categories indirect research techniques are the proper ones to apply. Four situational categories can be distinguished in which information might be sought from respondents.

First is the category in which *the information desired is known to the respondent and he will give it if asked.* Direct questioning will therefore provide all of the needed information in this situation. If the reason a consumer does not buy brand X tires is because he believes they do not wear as well as they should, he will willingly say so if given the opportunity.

Second, *the information desired is known to the respondent, but he does not want to divulge it.* Matters that are considered to be private in nature, that are believed to be prestige- or status-bearing, or are perceived as presenting a potential respondent–investigator opinion conflict may not be answered accurately. That many people do not fly because they are afraid to do so; that stout people often do not diet because they are afraid that they will not gain the social acceptance they desire anyway; that otherwise quiet and retiring people sometimes buy powerful cars because it gives them a feeling of superiority on the highway are not reasons that will likely be expressed openly and candidly in response to direct questions. When underlying motivations of this general nature are believed to exist, indirect techniques are well suited to elicit such information.

Third, *the information desired is obtainable from the respondent, but he is unable to verbalize it directly.* When the respondent has reasons he is unaware of, such as the association of the use of instant coffee with lack of planning and spendthrift purchasing, or the refusal to accept a palatable aspirin because of the association of effectiveness of headache remedies with the requirement that they be taken with water, properly designed and administered indirect techniques can be highly useful for uncovering such motivations.

Fourth, *the information desired is obtainable from the respondent only through inference from observation.* In some cases motivations of respondents are so deepseated that neither direct nor indirect methods of questioning will bring them to the surface. An experiment in which the same detergent packaged in three different-colored boxes resulted in the opinion of housewives using them that the detergent in the blue box left clothes dingy, that the one in the yellow box was too harsh, and that the one in the blue-and-yellow box was both gentle and effective in cleaning is an illustration of color association and its effect on assessment of product quality that very likely would not have been discovered through either direct or indirect questioning. In another experiment, orange-scented nylon hose placed on a counter in a department store next to identical, but unscented, hose were bought by approximately 90% of the women making purchases. Questioning of the women who bought the scented hose as to why they preferred the hose they bought resulted in answers such as "of better quality," "sheerer," and the like.

Of these four informational categories, two of them lend themselves to the use of indirect research techniques. It remains, of course, for the analyst to decide in which one or more of these categories the information he requires will fall.

While not the universally applicable methodology nor the panacea that some proponents have claimed, indirect research techniques can provide information on some types of marketing problems that is not presently obtainable by other means.

Sample Selection and Sizes

The subject of sampling is considered in detail in subsequent chapters. However, it is desirable to examine here the typical sampling procedures and practices that have been used in "motivation" research studies, as this has been an area of considerable controversy.

Sample selection in motivation research studies has tended to be done on nonprobabilistic (purposive) bases rather than by probabilistic methods. Typically, selection has been on a judgment or quota basis. As an illustration, the instructions to interviewers in the Pan American Coffee Bureau study asked each interviewer to select two respondents: "one male and one female; one 'dark strong' coffee drinker, one 'light weak' coffee drinker; one 'heavy drinker' (6–8 cups); one 'light drinker' (2–3 cups per day)." Although this sample was selected for exploratory purposes, unfortunately it is not an isolated example.

Serious sampling errors can result from purposive sampling, and, in any case, the extent of the sampling error is unknown. One of the reasons often given for using purposive rather than probability sampling is the high nonresponse rate. To refer again to the coffee study cited above, the statement was made in the instructions to the interviewers, "... it would be most helpful ... if you could just get people talking freely on all their feelings about coffee for an hour or so." One can well imagine that some sample members would be reluctant to spend this much time in an interview.

A second area of controversy over the samples typically taken in motivation research studies relates to their *size*. Generally, samples have been small, often ranging from 20 to 50 in size. The use of a small sample in a motivation research study suggests that the population of psychological attributes and motivations being sampled is sufficiently homogeneous that only a limited sample is required to provide an adequate representation of the population. However, the bulk of the evidence amassed by psychologists suggests that motivations are myriad in number and varied in their effect on behavior. To assume that the motivations of a very small group of people adequately represent those of the population at large is to ignore the high degree of variability that empirical studies have substantiated.

The Validity of the Findings

What about the validity of indirect research findings? How has their performance in these respects compared with that of the more conventional research methods?

The question of validity of findings is, of course, the heart of the issue here, as it is in the general objectivist–subjectivist controversy. Unfortunately, to raise the question is to beg it; no definitive answer can be given. As has already been indicated, the answer is necessarily conditional on the nature of the problem being investigated.

An observation does need to be made, however, about the differences in judging validity by the "clients" of basic research versus those of decisional research projects. The client of the basic research project is the professional in the field. Judgment of the validity of findings of a study is a highly impersonal process and one that is seldom urgent. The purpose of the project is either to make the best estimate of a population parameter or to conduct the best test of a hypothesis within the constraints of available resources. In the absence of data that can be used for direct validation, the basic research project is judged tentatively on the basis of method. The rules of evidence for a basic research study require that the *procedures be public*, the *results investigator-independent*, and the project *replicable*.

Since indirect research methods violate each of these requirements to some extent, there has been a reluctance on the part of some basic researchers to give even tentative acceptance to unvalidated findings of studies that employ indirect methods. They tend to look upon indirect research methods as a means of generating hypotheses for testing by objectivist methods rather than as a source of valid findings.

The client for a decisional research project has a different set of requirements. Rather than wanting to be assured that the best estimate of a parameter or the most definitive test of a hypothesis has been made, he needs information that will assist him in making the *best decision* possible in the circumstances. The procedures of the investigation need not be public, and there is seldom a need for replication. He works directly with the researcher and is able to raise any questions he has about the project. He usually will have had the opportunity to judge the validity of the findings of past research projects conducted by either the researcher or the organization for which he works. An assessment of validity of the findings must be made *now;* to await the outcome to determine if the findings are valid would obviate the very purpose for which the research was conducted. Judgment of degree of validity therefore turns out to be a much more subjective process in decisional than in basic research.

Indirect techniques serve several useful purposes in marketing research. They can be used to obtain information from respondents unwilling or unable to provide it by direct methods, to check the validity of responses to direct techniques, and to provide supplemental information. Included in the supplemental information that is of value is that which suggests hypotheses that can be tested by direct methods.

SUMMARY

In this chapter we first examined the methodological controversy between objectivists and subjectivists in the behavioral sciences and its carryover into marketing research.

We then considered communication as a means of obtaining information from respondents. The types of respondent interviews—structured–direct, unstructured–direct, and structured– and unstructured–indirect—were discussed. In the indirect types of interviews we described the more commonly used projective techniques, including the third-person technique ("What does your neighbor think of . . . ?"), word association, sentence completion, Thematic Apperception Tests, and depth interviews.

The media through which interviews may be conducted were next considered. The personal interview, the telephone interview, and the mail interview were discussed, including the merits and limitations of each.

We then considered the means of obtaining information through observation of respondents. The various forms of audits, recording devices, and direct *observation* were described and their applications discussed.

Finally, an assessment was made of direct versus indirect research techniques from the standpoints of applicability to marketing problems, sample selection and sizes, and validity of findings.

ASSIGNMENT MATERIAL

Situations 1 through 3 are identical in initial statement with some of the problems given at the end of Chapter 3. The concern here is with information that could perhaps be obtained from respondents that is not available from other sources.

1. You are a senior analyst in the Marketing Research Department of a major steel producer. You have been requested to make a forecast of domestic automobile production for the forthcoming calendar year and, from this forecast, make a forecast of the total tonnage of steel that will be used by the automobile manufacturers.

   a. What information, if any, that could be obtained from respondents would be useful for making the forecast of steel tonnage that will be used by the automobile manufacturers? If it is concluded that no useful information could be obtained from respondents, so indicate and do not answer questions (b) through (e).

   b. What techniques are applicable for obtaining each item of information?

   c. Design a survey to obtain the information desired. Prepare all instructions, collection forms, and other materials required to obtain such information.

   d. Estimate the cost of conducting the survey you have designed.

   e. In your judgment, based on the limited data given, would your study provide a positive net expected payoff of research? Explain.

2. You are product manager for brand M margarine, a nationally distributed brand. Brand M has been declining in absolute level of sales for the last four consecutive months. What information, if any, that could be obtained from respondents would be useful for determining the cause or causes of this decline?

3. You are Manager of Product Planning and Marketing Research for the Personal Appliances Department of a large and widely diversified corporation. You have under consideration a proposal to produce and market a hearing aid, an appliance line in which your company currently does not have a product.

   a. What information, if any, that could be obtained from respondents would be useful for deciding whether or not to develop and introduce a hearing aid? If it is concluded that no useful information could be obtained from respondents, so indicate and do not answer questions (b) through (f).

   b. What techniques are applicable for obtaining each type of information?

   c. Design a survey to obtain the information desired. Prepare all instructions, collection forms, and other materials required to obtain such information.

   d. Estimate the cost of conducting the survey you have designed.

　　e. In your judgment, based on the limited data given, would your study provide a positive net expected payoff of research?

　　f. Contrive the necessary data and make the necessary calculations to determine the net expected payoff of research.

4. Comment on the following statement:

> "The proper role of motivation research is to suggest rather than to test hypotheses."

Measurement and Scaling in Marketing Research

6

INTRODUCTION

As indicated in Chapters 4 and 5, survey procedures for obtaining respondent data represent one of the most prevalent sources of marketing research information. In many cases of practical interest—new-product-concept testing, corporate image measurement, ad copy evaluation, and the like—the researcher will be seeking information of a psychological nature—for example, how the new-product concept is evaluated by consumers or what the firm's image is. If useful data are to be obtained, the researcher must exercise care in defining what is to be measured, informed judgment in deciding how to make the measurements, and expertise in conducting the measuring operations and analysis of the resulting data.

Definitions play a significant role in scientific inquiry and especially so in the behavioral sciences. In the first section of this chapter we focus on operational defining and its use in research. Increasingly, behavioral scientists are paying greater attention to the working definitions of their particular disciplines. Operational definitions—that is, specification of the performances that are required to establish a concept—are thought by many to provide the means for making the behavioral sciences more rigorous and objective.

Closely allied to the process of defining is the process of measurement. In the next section we shall discuss various types of measurements and the relationship of measurement scales to the interpretation of statistical techniques. This section serves as useful background for the discussion of psychological scaling methods in this chapter and for multivariate statistical analysis, to be covered in later chapters.

The purpose of the remainder of the chapter is to discuss basic concepts of psychological scaling, as related particularly to the study of consumer perception, preference, and motivation. We discuss various methods for collecting scaling data (paired comparisons, rankings, ratings, etc.) in terms of their mechanics and assumptions regarding their scale properties.

Specific scaling procedures such as Thurstonian Case V scaling, the semantic differential, and the Likert summated scale are then illustrated. We conclude with a discussion of validity and reliability problems associated with scaling methods.

Throughout the chapter we emphasize procedures that typically (but not necessarily) lead to unidimensional scales, in which stimulus objects or people are scaled along a single continuum. Later chapters extend these procedures to analyses in which stimulus objects or people may be represented as points (or vectors) in a multidimensional space.

DEFINITIONS IN RESEARCH

An important part of the practice of research entails the construction, use, and modification of definitions. We cannot measure an "attitude," a "shelf facing," a "market share," or even "sales," without first having defined what is meant by each of these terms.

Two classes of defining can be distinguished. *Constitutive defining* is roughly similar to dictionary defining. Here we convey the meaning of a concept in terms of still other concepts whose meaning is assumed to be more familiar to the inquirer. One constitutive definition of an *attitude*, for example, is "an enduring organization of motivational, emotional, perceptual, and cognitive processes with respect to some aspect of the individual's world."[1]

Operational defining establishes the meaning of a concept through specifying what is to be observed and how the observations are to be made. Generally this involves specifying: (1) the class of persons, objects, events, or states to be observed; (2) the environmental conditions under which the observation takes place; (3) the operations to be performed in making the observations; (4) the instruments to be used to perform the operations; and (5) the observations to be made.[2] An attitude of consumers toward a given brand, for example, can be operationally defined as the results obtained from: (1) consumers of the brand, (2) at a given time and in a given geographic area, who are (3) personally interviewed using a (4) specified attitudinal scale to obtain (5) the response information provided by the attitude scale.

Measurements and operational definitions often go together. Attitudes toward products may be defined operationally as numerical ratings on a

[1]D. Krech and R. S. Crutchfield, *Theory and Problems in Social Psychology* (New York: McGraw-Hill Book Company, 1948), p. 152.

[2]R. L. Ackoff, Shiv Gupta, and J. S. Minas, *Scientific Method: Optimizing Applied Research Decisions* (New York: John Wiley & Sons, Inc., 1962).

like–dislike scale. Various aspects of advertisement recall are often defined by having magazine readers go through an unmarked copy of the magazine and note those ads that they remember seeing and those they remember reading, at least in part. In other recall procedures the respondents are presented with cards showing the names of all products advertised in a particular issue of some magazine. Respondents are then asked to pick out those products for which they remember seeing an advertisement. This is followed by their (unaided) description of the ads, the copy points remembered, what information they got out of the ad, and so on.

In still other situations (e.g., theater tests) the effectiveness of a television commercial is defined in terms of the difference in the proportion of audience members who state a particular brand that they would like to receive (if they should turn out to be winners in a studio lottery) before and after watching a series of commercials about one or more of the brands of interest. The effectiveness of direct-mail ads is often defined operationally in terms of the percentage of recipients who respond to the ad's offer. Many other examples could be mentioned.

MEASUREMENT

Measurement Defined

Consider the following set of incomplete statements: (1) *"The mean amount of shelf facing that our brand is currently receiving is . . ."*; (2) *"The Consumer Price Index for the first quarter of this year was . . ."*; (3) *"The preferred brand of this product class, as determined from a survey of consumers, is . . ."*; (4) *"The number of supermarkets carrying one or more of our brands in April was . . . ."* What process is required to supply the missing information in each?

Most of us will agree that the answer to this question is "measurement." Yet if we reflect on why we gave that answer, it may not be immediately apparent. The first statement requires a determination of lengths to complete it, the second an observation of prices, the third a questioning of consumers, and the fourth an enumeration. Nor is there a common underlying metric for the measurement process. Statement (1) involves a universal standard, statement (2) an arbitrary standard, statement (3) a ranking, and statement (4) a categorization. (As we shall see shortly, these are examples of the use of different *scales* of measurement.)

It is only at a more abstract level that we find the common elements that led us to identify the process involved in completing each of the above statements as "measurement." Conceptually, *measurement* can be defined as a way of obtaining symbols to represent the properties of persons, objects, events, or states, which symbols have the same relevant relationship to each other as do the things represented.[3] In each of the above instances it is necessary that symbols be obtained (numbers for the mean length of shelf facings and the price index, numbers or other symbols for the ranking of preferences and categorization of supermarkets). If they are to be useful as information, the symbols must be interpretable as having the same relevant relationship to each other as do the things represented.

Primary Types of Scales

To many people the term "scale" suggests such devices as yardsticks, pan balances, gasoline gauges, measuring cups, and similar instruments for finding length, weight, volume, and the like. That is, we ordinarily tend to think about measurement in the sense of well-defined scales possessing a natural zero and constant unit of measurement. In the behavioral sciences, however, the researcher must frequently settle for less-informative scales. For example, if a consumer is asked to rank a set of toothpaste brands according to overall desirability, the resulting "scale" does not possess the properties associated with most physical measures; for example, it is not meaningful to add two ranks together in order to get a third rank member.

Scales can be classified into the following major categories: (1) nominal, (2) ordinal, (3) interval, and (4) ratio. Each scale possesses its own set of underlying assumptions regarding the correspondence of numbers with real-world entities. These correspondences can progress from scale to scale as our knowledge about the phenomenon increases. Examples are the measurement of color and temperature.

Nominal scales are the least restrictive of scales. In this type of scale the numbers serve only as labels or tags for identifying objects, properties, or events. For example, we can assign numbers to baseball players or telephone subscribers. In the first case each player receives a different number (any convenient numbers will do) and we have a simple legend for moving from number label to player's name. That is, we have a one-to-one correspondence between number and player and are careful in making sure that no two or more players receive the same number (or that a single player is assigned two or more numbers). Telephone numbers are another illustration of nominal scales, as are classifications into categories. The classification of supermarkets by "carry our brand" versus "do not carry our brand" categories is an illustration of the use of a nominal scale.

It should be clear that nominal scales permit only the most rudimentary of mathematical operations. We can count the number of stores that carry each brand in a product class and find the modal (highest number of men-

---

[3] Adapted from Ackoff, Gupta, and Minas, *Scientific Method*, p. 179.

tions) brand carried. Also, we may make various contingency tests having to do with the likelihood that a member of one category is also a member of another category, but the usual statistical operations (calculations of means, standard deviations, etc.) are not empirically meaningful.

Ordinal scales are, as the name suggests, ranking scales. These scales require the ability to distinguish between elements according to a single attribute and direction. For example, a person may be able to rank a group of floor polish brands according to "cleaning ability." If we assign the number 1 to the highest ranking polish, number 2 to the second highest ranking polish, and so on, an ordinal scale results. Note, however, that the mere ranking of brands does not permit us to say anything about the _differences_ separating brands with regard to cleaning ability. We do not know if the difference in cleaning ability between the brand ranked 1 and the brand ranked 2 is larger, less than, or equal to the difference between the brand ranked 2 and the brand ranked 3. Thus, any series of numbers that preserves the ordering relationship (say 2, 4, 9, etc.) is as good as our original number assignment involving successive integers. Ordinal scales are thus unique up to a strictly increasing transformation (which is a function that preserves order).

An ordinal scale possesses all the information of a nominal scale in the sense that equivalent entities receive the same rank. Notice, however, that in dealing with ordinal scales, statistical description can employ positional measures such as the median, quartile, and percentile, or other summary statistics that deal with order among entities. The usual arithmetic averaging operations cannot be meaningfully interpreted with ranked data and the practice of calculating an overall index ranking (a weighted ranking of a set of brands according to several properties) is often suspect from an interpretative point of view. As an illustration, note the data summarized in Table 6-1.

From Table 6-1 we see that the brands A, B, and C are first ranked with respect to attribute X (cleaning ability) and then with respect to attribute

Table 6-1 Illustration of the misuse of ranked data

BRAND	Rank on Cleaning Ability, X	Rank on Ease of Application, Y	IMPORTANCE WEIGHTS $w(X)$	$w(Y)$	Weighted-Index Rank
A	1	2	0.2	0.8	1.8
B	2	3	0.2	0.8	2.8
C	3	1	0.2	0.8	1.4
A	2	11	0.2	0.8	9.2
B	20	100	0.2	0.8	84.0
C	50	10	0.2	0.8	18.0

Y (ease of application), where the number 3 denotes the highest ranked item. Numerical weights of 0.2 and 0.8 are then assigned to the attributes *X* and *Y*, respectively, to reflect the assumed relative importance of each attribute in contributing to overall evaluation. An overall index "rank" of each brand is then found. Notice, however, that by making two arbitrary order-preserving transformations in the lower half of the table, a different set of weighted indexes results, but, more importantly, this set does not have even the same *ordering* as the first set.

Interval scales approach the man-on-the-street's conception of measurement in that an interval scale does possess a constant unit of measurement. Interval scales permit one to make meaningful statements about the *differences* separating two objects. However, the zero point of this scale is arbitrary. Among the most common examples of interval scaling are the Fahrenheit and centigrade scales used to measure temperature.[4] While an arbitrary zero is assigned to each temperature scale, equal temperature differences are found by scaling equal volumes of expansion in the liquid used in the thermometer. Interval scales permit inferences to be made about the differences between the entities to be measured (say "warmness"), but we cannot meaningfully state that any value on a specific interval scale is a multiple of another.

An example should make this point clearer. It is not empirically correct to say that an object with a temperature of 50°F is "twice as hot" as one with a temperature of 25°F. Remembering the conversion formula from Fahrenheit to centigrade,

$$T_c = \tfrac{5}{9}(T_f - 32)$$

we can find that the corresponding temperatures on the centigrade scale are 10°C and -3.9°C, which are not in the ratio 2 : 1. We *can* say, however, that *differences between values* on different temperature scales are multiples of each other. That is, the difference 50°F $-$ 0°F is twice the difference 25°F $-$ 0°F. Corresponding differences on the centigrade scale are 10°C $-$ (-17.7°C) $= 27.7$°C and -3.9°C $-$ (-17.7°C) $= 13.8$°C, which, aside from rounding error, are in the same ratio of 2 : 1.

Interval scales are unique up to a transformation of the form $y = a + bx$; $b > 0$. This means that interval scales can be transformed from one to another by means of a positive linear transformation. It turns out that *differences* between interval-scale values can be expressed in terms of multiples of one another because, by taking differences, the constant in the above linear equation drops out in the computations.

[4]Various types of indexes, such as the Consumer Price Index, are typically interval scales. Also, the von Neumann–Morgenstern utility scale, described in Chapter 2, is an interval scale.

Most ordinary statistical measures to be discussed in later chapters (such as the arithmetic mean, standard deviation, and correlation coefficient) require only interval scales for their computation. For example, if we determine the average temperature in a certain city over a month and express it in either Fahrenheit or centigrade, those days of the month (if any) that are equal to the average will be the same days under each scale of measurement. (But some statistical measures, such as the geometric mean, would be empirically misleading if applied to interval-scaled data.)

Ratio scales represent the "elite" of scales, in that all arithmetic operations are permissible on ratio-scale measurements. These scales possess a unique zero point and are the scales usually found in the physical sciences (e.g., scales for measuring length and weight). As the name suggests, equal ratios among the scale values correspond to equal ratios among the entities being measured. Ratio scales are unique up to a positive proportionality transformation (of the form $y = cx$; $c > 0$).

As an illustration of ratio-scale properties, we can see that it is meaningful to talk about 3 yards being three times 1 yard. If transformed to feet, then we can say that 9 feet and 3 feet are in the same ratio, that is, $3:1$. We can move from one scale to another merely by applying an appropriate positive multiplicative constant; this is the practice that we follow when we go from grams to pounds or from feet to inches. As would be surmised, a ratio scale contains all the information (class, order, equality of differences) of lower-order scales and more besides. All types of statistical operations can be performed on ratio scales.

Relationships among Scales

To give the reader some idea of the relationships among nominal, ordinal, interval, and ratio scales, Table 6-2 has been reproduced from Stevens' excellent articles on the subject of scaling.[5] From the standpoint of the marketing researcher interested in analyzing data from sample surveys and the like, it is appropriate to note from the table that most commonly used descriptive statistics (arithmetic mean, standard deviation) and tests of significance (t test, F test) assume that the data are (at least) interval-scaled.

Some further interpretation of this statement is needed. From a purely mathematical point of view one can obviously do arithmetic with *any* appropriate set of numbers—integer ranks, numbers used to label classes, and so on. Certainly the *computation* of a t statistic is no different in principle, if the

[5]S. S. Stevens, "Mathematics, Measurement and Psychophysics," in *Handbook of Experimental Psychology*, ed. S. S. Stevens (New York: John Wiley & Sons, Inc., 1962), and S. S. Stevens, "Measurement, Psychophysics and Utility," in *Measurement: Definitions and Theories*, ed. C. W. Churchman and P. Ratoosh (New York: John Wiley & Sons, Inc., 1959).

Table 6-2 Scales of measurement

Scale	Mathematical Group Structure	Permissible Statistics	Typical Examples
Nominal	Permutation group $y = f(x)$ [$f(x)$ means any one-to-one correspondence]	Mode Contingency coefficient	Numbering of football players Assignment of type or model numbers to classes
Ordinal	Isotonic group $y = f(x)$ [$f(x)$ means any strictly increasing function]	Median Percentile Order correlation Sign test; run test	Hardness of minerals Quality of leather, lumber, wool, etc. Pleasantness of odors
Interval	General linear group $y = a + bx$ $b > 0$	Mean Average deviation Standard deviation Product-moment correlation t test F test	Temperature (Fahrenheit and centigrade) Energy Calendar dates
Ratio	Similarity group $y = cx$ $c > 0$	Geometric mean Harmonic mean Coefficient of variation	Length, weight, density, resistance Pitch scale Loudness scale

Source: Reproduced, with permission, from S. S. Stevens, "Mathematics and Psychophysics," in *Handbook of Experimental Psychology*, ed. S. S. Stevens (New York: John Wiley & Sons, Inc., 1962), p. 25, and S. S. Stevens, "Measurement, Psychophysics and Utility," in *Measurement: Definitions and Theories*, ed. C. W. Churchman and P. Ratoosh (New York: John Wiley & Sons, Inc., 1959), p. 27.

numbers are ranks as opposed to interval-scaled measurements. What is at issue here is the *interpretation* of the results—that is, our ability to make meaningful empirical statements. For example, a t statistic will vary if some arbitrary rank preserving transformation is made of the data, but this type of transformation is quite permissible with ordinal data.

SOME INTRODUCTORY REMARKS ON ATTITUDE MEASUREMENT

All attitude (and other psychological) measurement procedures are concerned with having people—consumers, purchasing agents, marketing managers, or whatever—respond to certain stimuli according to certain sets of instructions.

The stimuli may be alternative advertising copy themes, package designs, salespeople's presentations, and so on. The response may involve which copy theme is more pleasing than another, which package design is more appealing than another, which adjectives best describe each salesperson, and so on.

Other operations involving the application of some type of scaling model may then intervene before we finally get a scale along which the attitude is measured. Scaling procedures can be classified in terms of the measurement properties of the final scale (i.e., nominal, ordinal, interval, or ratio), the task that the subject is asked to perform, or in still other ways.

One important basis for classifying scaling methods is whether the emphasis is to be placed on subjects, stimuli, or both.[6] To illustrate, suppose that each member of a group of respondents has been asked independently to rate a set of dishwashing detergent brands (stimuli) with respect to "gentleness on the hands." Three types of scaling might be distinguished:

1. *Subject-centered approach*, in which the researcher examines systematic variation across respondents.
2. *Stimulus-centered approach*, in which the researcher investigates systematic variation across stimuli (the brands).
3. *Response approach*, in which the researcher examines *both* subject and stimulus variation.

In the subject-centered and stimulus-centered approaches, the experimenter chooses either stimuli or respondents whose variability is (at least roughly) controlled so as to emphasize variation in the other mode. For example, if one is interested in subject-centered variation, stimuli would be chosen so as to emphasize individual respondent differences. Similarly, in stimulus-centered cases a homogeneous group of subjects may be sought so as to reduce variation contributed by this source. In response methods, however, the researcher is interested in both sources of variability.

DATA COLLECTION METHODS

While we shall be emphasizing scaling methods that are stimulus-centered, it turns out that there is another (and independent) way to classify scaling techniques, and that is in terms of whether variability or quantitative-judgment procedures are used to *collect* the data. In *variability* methods it is assumed that the basic data are only ordinal-scaled. Some type of model is then applied to transform the ordinal data into an interval scale. In *quantita-*

---

[6]This classification method—and other descriptors used later in the chapter—is discussed in W. S. Torgerson, *Theory and Methods of Scaling* (New York: John Wiley & Sons, Inc., 1958). In this chapter we discuss only stimulus-centered and subject-centered approaches. Chapter 14 describes some techniques for scaling stimuli and subjects simultaneously.

tive-judgment methods, direct numerical judgments are made by the respondent and it is assumed that the original input data are either interval-scaled or ratio-scaled. In this method, use of a model is directed toward finding the scale values that are most consistent with the (errorful) input data. (Often the "model" will involve nothing more than a simple averaging of the original numerical responses.)

Variability Methods

Variability methods include paired comparison, ranking, ordered-category sorting, and rating techniques. We discuss each of these data collection procedures in turn.

Paired Comparisons

As the name suggests, *paired comparisons* require the respondent to choose one of a pair of stimuli that "has more of," "dominates," "precedes," "wins over," or "exceeds" the other with respect to some designated property of interest. If, for example, six dishwashing detergent brands are to be compared for "gentleness on the hands," a full set of paired comparisons (if order of presentation is not considered) would involve $(6 \cdot 5)/2$, or 15, paired comparisons.

The upper panel of Figure 6-1 shows illustratively how paired-compari-

Figure 6-1   Paired-comparison responses for a single subject*

		Brand						
		1	2	3	4	5	6	
Brand	1	x	0	1	1	1	1	
	2	1	x	1	1	1	1	
	3	0	0	x	0	0	0	(Original Data)
	4	0	0	1	x	0	0	
	5	0	0	1	1	x	1	
	6	0	0	1	1	0	x	

		Brand							
		2	1	5	6	4	3	Sum	
Brand	2	x	1	1	1	1	1	5	
	1	0	x	1	1	1	1	4	
	5	0	0	x	1	1	1	3	(Permuted Rows
	6	0	0	0	x	1	1	2	and Columns)
	4	0	0	0	0	x	1	1	
	3	0	0	0	0	0	x	0	

*A cell value of "1" implies that the row brand exceeds the column brand; "0," otherwise.

son responses may be recorded for a single subject. As noted from the figure, brand 2 dominates all of the other five brands. This is shown by the fact that all of its paired comparisons with the remaining stimuli involve 1's (arbitrarily letting row dominate column) in the table of original data. In the lower panel of Figure 6-1, rows and columns of the original table have been permuted to yield the stimulus rank order: 2, 1, 5, 6, 4, 3, from most gentle to least gentle. The total number of "votes" received by each brand appears in the last column.

These hypothetical data are characterized by the fact that the respondent was "transitive" in her judgments, leading (after row and column permutation) to the triangular response pattern of 1's shown in the lower panel of the figure.

But what does one do if the judgments are not transitive? For example, the respondent may say that brand 2 exceeds brand 1; brand 1 exceeds brand 5; and brand 5 exceeds brand 2, leading to what is called a *circular triad*. The presence of circular triads in a subject's data requires the researcher to examine two questions: (1) how serious are the subject's violations of transitivity, and (2) if not "too" serious, how can the data be made transitive with the fewest number of alterations in the original paired-comparisons table?

Kendall[7] has developed summary measures and statistical tests regarding the incidence of "tolerable" levels of intransitivity; one may compute his coefficient of consistency and test this measure against the null hypothesis that the respondent is responding randomly. Slater[8] and Phillips[9] have described ways of finding the "best" rank order (one that least disturbs the original paired-comparison judgments) in the presence of intransitive data. Of course, the motivation for using paired comparisons in the first place stems from the researcher's interest in the *consistency* of respondents' choices; otherwise, one might just as well have the respondent rank the six brands, thereby reducing labor (but *forcing* consistency within that set of choices).

Implicit in the preceding discussion has been the assumption that the respondent must force a choice between each pair of brands. Variations in the method of paired comparisons allow the subject to express indifference between members of the pair (i.e., to "tie" the stimuli with respect to the property level of interest) or, after having chosen between members of the pair, to indicate on an "intensity scale" *how much* the chosen member of the pair exceeds the other with regard to some designated property, such as "gentleness on the hands."

[7]M. G. Kendall, *Rank Correlation Methods* (New York: Hafner Publishing Company, 1962).

[8]Patrick Slater, "Inconsistencies in a Schedule of Paired Comparisons," *Biometrica*, 48 (1961), 303–12.

[9]J. P. N. Phillips, "A Procedure for Determining Slater's *i* and All Nearest Adjoining Orders," *British Journal of Mathematical and Statistical Psychology*, 20 (1967), 217–25.

Ranking Methods

Ranking procedures require the respondent to order stimuli with respect to some designated property of interest. For example, instead of using the paired-comparison technique for determining the perceived order of six dishwashing detergents with respect to "gentleness on the hands," each respondent might have been asked to *rank* the detergents with respect to that property.

There are a variety of ordering methods that may be used to order k items from a full set of n items. These procedures, denoted by Coombs[10] as "order k/n" (k out of n), expand the repertory of ordering methods quite markedly. At the extremes, "order 1/2" involves a paired comparison, while "order $(n - 1)/n$" involves a full rank order.

The various ordering methods may prespecify the value of k ("order the top three out of six brands with respect to gentleness on the hands") or allow k to be chosen by the respondent ("select those of the six brands that seem to exhibit the most gentleness on the hands, and rank them").

Variations on the paired-comparison procedure have been developed so as to effect a compromise between the greater time and effort associated with the "order 1/2" procedure versus the additional information it provides for checking on a subject's consistency. A number of statistical design methods are available.[11,12] Generally speaking, these designs reduce the number of comparisons per respondent but provide a type of balancing across stimulus pairs and subjects. To date most marketing researchers have not taken advantage of these special designs, but we suspect that the situation will change as information about them receives wider dissemination.

Ordered-Category Sorting

Various data collection procedures are available that have as their purpose the assignment of a set of stimuli to a set of _ordered categories_. For example, if 15 varieties of dishwashing detergents represented the stimulus set, the respondent might be asked to sort them into three ordered categories: (1) highly gentle on the hands, (2) moderately gentle, and (3) not gentle at all.

Sorting procedures vary with regard to:

1. The free versus forced assignment of so many stimuli to each category.

[10]C. H. Coombs, *A Theory of Data* (New York: John Wiley & Sons, Inc., 1964), Chap. 2, pp. 32–58.

[11]R. E. Kirk, *Experimental Design: Procedures for the Behavioral Sciences* (Belmont, Calif.: Wadsworth Publishing Company, Inc., 1968), Chap. 11, "Incomplete Block Designs."

[12]H. A. David, *The Method of Paired Comparisons* (New York: Hafner Publishing Company, 1963), p. 62.

2. The assumption of equal intervals between category boundaries versus the weaker assumption of category boundaries that are merely ordered with regard to the attribute of interest.

In variability methods one assumes only an *ordering* of category boundaries. (The assumption of equal intervals separating boundaries is part of the quantitative-judgment set of methods.) Ordered-category sorting appears especially useful when the researcher is dealing with a relatively large number of stimuli (e.g., over 15 or so) and it is believed that a subject's discrimination abilities do not justify a strict (no ties allowed) ranking of the stimulus objects.

If the equal-intervals assumption is not made, it then becomes the job of the researcher to scale these responses (by application of various models) to achieve "stronger" scales, if so desired.

Some data collection methods, most notably rating scales, are ambiguous. In some cases, the responses may be considered by the researcher to be only ordinal, while, in other cases, he may treat them as more strongly (interval or ratio) scaled. As such, rating procedures can be appropriate for *either* the variability or quantitative-judgment data collection methods.

Rating Methods

Rating methods, as used in both marketing research and the behavioral sciences, represent one of the most popular and easily applied data collection methods. Rating methods can take several forms: (1) numerical, (2) graphic, or (3) verbal. Often two or more of these formats appear together, as illustrated in Figure 6-2. As shown in Panel (a) of the figure, the respondent is given both a series of integers (1 through 7) and verbal descriptions of the degree of "gentleness–harshness." He would then be asked to circle the number associated with the descriptive statement that comes closest to how he feels about the gentleness–harshness of the brand(s) being rated. In Panel (b) of Figure 6-2 he need only check the category appropriate for expressing his feelings about some attitude statement regarding dishwashing detergents.

In Panel (c) of the figure a graduated thermometer scale with both numerical assignments and a (limited) set of descriptive statements illustrates another type of rating device. Panel (d) attempts to "anchor" the scale in comparison to "average-type" brands. Many other types of rating methods are in use, and in later chapters we shall encounter a number of these variations.

However, in many instances where rating scales are used, the researcher not only assumes that the items are capable of being ranked but also that the descriptive levels progress in *equal-interval* steps psychologically. That is, the numerical correspondences shown in panels (a) and (c) may be treated—

Figure 6-2 Examples of rating scales used in marketing research

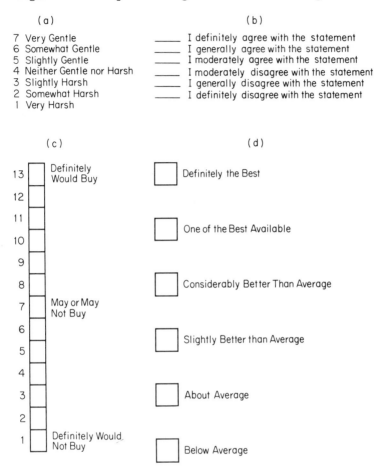

(a)

7 Very Gentle
6 Somewhat Gentle
5 Slightly Gentle
4 Neither Gentle nor Harsh
3 Slightly Harsh
2 Somewhat Harsh
1 Very Harsh

(b)

_____ I definitely agree with the statement
_____ I generally agree with the statement
_____ I moderately agree with the statement
_____ I moderately disagree with the statement
_____ I generally disagree with the statement
_____ I definitely disagree with the statement

(c)

13 Definitely Would Buy
12
11
10
9
8
7 May or May Not Buy
6
5
4
3
2
1 Definitely Would Not Buy

(d)

Definitely the Best

One of the Best Available

Considerably Better Than Average

Slightly Better than Average

About Average

Below Average

sometimes erroneously—as interval- or ratio-scaled data. Even in cases represented by Panels (b) and (d), it is not unusual to find that the researcher assigns successive integer values to the various category descriptions and subsequently works with the data as though the responses *were* interval-scaled.

Earlier in the chapter we illustrated some of the problems associated with treating ordinal data as interval- or ratio-scaled data. Although methods are available for scaling the stimuli under weaker assumptions about the intervals that separate category labels (as mentioned earlier under ordered-category sorting), in practice these methods are often cumbersome to use and, accordingly, may not justify the time and effort associated with their application. However, this should not negate the importance of being aware of the implicit assumptions that one makes about the scale properties of rating instruments when certain statistical techniques are used to summarize and interrelate the response data.

Volumes have been written on various aspects of rating scales. To illustrate:

1. Should negative numbers be used?
2. How many categories should be included?
3. What does one do about "halo" effects—that is, the tendency of raters to ascribe favorable property levels to all attributes of a stimulus object if they happen to like a particular object in general?
4. How does one examine raters' biases—for example, the tendency to use extreme values or, perhaps, only the middle range of the response scale?
5. How should descriptive adjectives for rating categories be selected?
6. How should anchoring phrases for the scale's origin be chosen?

Guilford,[13] among others, lists a large number of "do's and don't's" regarding rating scales, which the interested reader might examine.

In summary, rating methods—depending upon the assumptions of the researcher—can be considered to lead to ordinal-, interval-, or even ratio-scaled responses. The latter two scales are taken up next in the context of quantitative-judgment methods. We shall see that rating methods figure prominently in the development of quantitative-judgment scales.

Quantitative-Judgment Methods

Direct-judgment estimates, fractionation, constant sum—indeed, rating methods also, if the researcher wishes to assume more than ordinal properties about respondents' judgments—are all variants of *quantitative-judgment methods.*

Direct-Judgment Methods

In *direct-judgment methods* the respondent is asked to give a *numerical* rating to each stimulus with respect to some designated attribute. In the *unlimited-response category* subcase, the respondent is free to choose his own number or, in graphical methods, to lay off a tick mark along some line that reflects his judgment about the magnitude of the stimulus relative to some reference points. This is illustrated in Panel (a) of Figure 6-3 for the rating of brand A. The *limited-response category* subcase is illustrated by Panel (b)

[13] J. P. Guilford, *Psychometric Methods* (New York: McGraw-Hill Book Company, 1954).

Figure 6-3   Some illustrations of quantitative-judgment methods

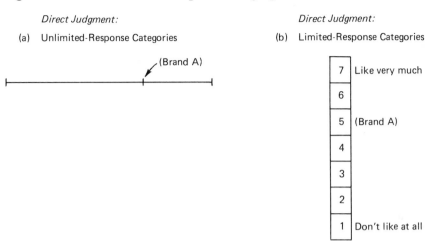

(c)   Fractionation

"Compare each brand to the standard: Brand A is assumed to be 1.0"

Relative degree of harshness compared to Brand A

Brand	Response
B	0.75
C	0.80
D	2.4
E	0.5

(d)   Constant Sum

"Assign 100 points across the five brands so as to reflect your relative degree of liking for them"

Brand	Response
A	20
B	25
C	10
D	5
E	40
	100

in Figure 6-3. Here the respondent is limited to choosing one of seven categories. We note that in this instance the direct-judgment method is nothing more than a straight rating procedure, with the important addition that the ratings are now treated as either interval- or ratio-scaled data (depending upon the application) rather than as simple rankings.

If the respondent has several items to rate, either the unlimited- or limited-response category procedures can also be employed. In the former case, the respondent arranges the stimuli (usually described on small cards) along some sort board, provided by the researcher, so that each appears approximately separated according to subjective distance relative to the others. In the latter case, one assigns cards to the designated category on the sort board that best matches one's evaluation of the stimulus.

Fractionation

Fractionation is a type of quantitative-judgment procedure in which the respondent is given two stimuli at a time (e.g., a standard dishwashing detergent and a test brand) and asked to give some *numerical* estimate of the ratio between them, with respect to some attribute, such as "harshness on the hands."

The respondent may answer that the test brand, in his judgment, is three-fourths as harsh as the standard. After this is done, a new test brand is compared to the same standard, and so on, until all test items are judged. Panel (c) in Figure 6-3 illustrates this procedure.

In other cases—where the test item can be more or less continuously varied by the respondent—the respondent is asked to vary the test item so that it represents some designated ratio of the standard. For example, if the attribute is sweetness of lemonade, the respondent may be asked to add more sweetener until the test item is "twice as sweet" as the standard.

Constant Sum

Constant-sum methods, primarily because of their simplicity and ease of instructions, have become quite popular in marketing research. In constant-sum methods the respondent is given some number of points—typically 10 or 100—and asked to distribute them over the alternatives in a way that reflects their relative magnitude regarding some attitudinal characteristic.

Panel (d) of Figure 6-3 shows an illustration of the constant-sum procedure. Constant sum forces the respondent to "allocate" his evaluations and has the effect of standardizing each scale across persons, since all scores must add to the same constant (e.g., 10 or 100). As such, the constant-sum procedure requires the respondent to make a comparative evaluation of the stimuli. Generally, it is assumed that a subjective ratio scale is obtained by this method.

Summary

Unlike variability methods, the major assumption underlying quantitative-judgment methods is that a unit of measurement can be constructed *directly* from respondents' estimates about scale values associated with a set of stimuli. The subject's report is taken at face value and any variation in repeated estimates (over test occasions within respondent or over respondents) is treated as error; repeated estimates are usually averaged over persons and/or occasions.[14]

---

[14]If interval-scale properties are assumed, an arithmetic mean is used. If ratio-scale properties are assumed, a geometric mean is often used in the averaging process.

Some of the problems associated with quantitative-judgment methods are:

1. Respondents' subjective scale units may differ across each other, across testing occasions, or both.
2. Respondents' subjective origins (zero points) may differ across each other, across occasions, or both.
3. Unit and origin may shift over stimulus items *within* a single occasion.

These problems should not be treated lightly, particularly when data for several subjects are being averaged.

In addition, researchers should be aware of the constraints placed on the subject's response format. For example, if the respondent is asked to rate dishwashing detergents on a 5-point scale, ranging from 1 ("gentlest"), to 3 ("neither harsh nor gentle"), to 5 ("harshest"), the task, in a sense, may not be capable of being carried out. That is, one's *subjective* distance between the harshest detergent and the neutral detergent(s) may not equal one's perception of the distance between the neutral detergent(s) and the gentlest detergent.

Most quantitative-judgment methods have the virtue of being easy to apply. Moreover, little additional work beyond averaging is required to obtain the unit of measurement directly. Indeed, if a unique origin can be established (e.g., a zero level of the property), then the researcher obtains both an "absolute" origin and a measurement unit. As such, a subjective ratio scale is obtained.

TECHNIQUES FOR SCALING STIMULI

Any of the data collection methods just described—whether of the variability class or the quantitative-judgment class—produce a set of raw-data responses. In the case of variability methods, the raw data, describing *ordinal-scaled* judgments, usually undergo a further transformation, via a *scaling model*, into a set of scale values that are *interval-scaled.*

Technically speaking, the raw data obtained from quantitative-judgment procedures also require an intervening model. However, in this case the "model" may be no more elaborate than averaging the raw data across respondents and/or response occasions.

Thurstone's Case V method is a popular model for dealing with ordinal data obtained from variability methods. Osgood's semantic differential is an illustration of a procedure for dealing with raw data obtained from quantitative-judgment procedures. We consider each of these techniques in turn.

Case V Scaling

Thurstone's Case V Scaling model permits the construction of a unidimensional interval scale using responses from variability data collection procedures, such as paired comparisons.[15] Several subcases of Thurstone's model have been developed. We shall first describe the general case and then concentrate our attention on Case V, a special version that is particularly amenable to application.

Essentially, Thurstone's procedure involves deriving an interval scale from comparative judgments of the type "A is fancier than B," "A is more prestigious than B," "A is preferred to B," and so on. Scale values may be estimated from data in which one individual makes many repeated judgments on each pair of a set of stimuli or from data obtained from a group of individuals with few or no replications per person.

The concept that underlies the model of comparative judgment on which Case V scaling is based is simple to describe. Suppose that we have a group of subjects, almost all of whom prefer A to B. Then the proportion of total comparisons (no ties allowed) in which A is preferred to B will be close to 100%. Suppose, however, that when B is compared to C, only 55% of the group prefers B to C. Intuitively, we might think that the difference between the scale values associated with A and B should be much larger than the difference between the scale values associated with B and C. Under certain assumptions Thurstone's model of comparative judgment provides a means for developing an interval scale from these stimulus-comparison proportions. The test of the theory is how well scale values can be used to work backward, that is, to predict the original proportions.

Thurstone calls the psychological process by which a person reacts to a stimulus his *discriminal process*. Since the same individual, on another occasion, may react differently to the same stimulus, Thurstone goes on to postulate a *modal* discriminal process that represents the sensory response that occurs most often when a particular stimulus is presented. The scale distance between the modal discriminal processes for any two stimuli represents the degree of separation assumed to be present on the individual's psychological scale and is called the *discriminal difference*. If each discriminal process is normally distributed—as assumed by Thurstone—the discriminal differences between pairs of stimuli are also normally distributed. Also, the mean of each discriminal process (as well as the median) will equal the mode. The same will be true of the discriminal differences.

Figure 6-4 illustrates this situation for a particular stimulus pair j and k. In the upper panel of the figure we note that each discriminal process is

---

[15] While illustrated here in the context of paired comparisons, Thurstone's model can be used to scale ranked data or ordered-category sorts. Thurstone's model is described in L .L. Thurstone, *The Measurement of Values* (Chicago: University of Chicago Press, 1959).

Figure 6-4 Illustration of response differences under Thurstone's model of comparative judgment

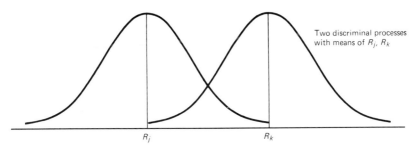

Two discriminal processes with means of R_j, R_k

R_j R_k

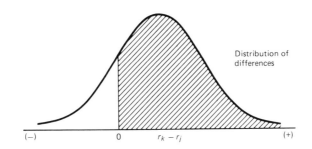

Distribution of differences

$(-)$ 0 $r_k - r_j$ $(+)$

assumed to be normally distributed with mode (and mean) R_j and R_k, respectively. If stimuli j and k are presented for comparison, the subject is figuratively assumed to draw some value from each of his (subjective) distributions of discriminal processes. Most of the time the value r_k will exceed r_j (see shaded area in the lower panel of the figure) and he will report that stimulus k exceeds stimulus j with respect to some predesignated attribute. However, some of the time (unshaded area) r_j will exceed r_k, and hence he will report the opposite.

The variability of the scale differences depends on both the intercorrelations between the discriminal processes and the possibility that their respective variances are unequal. We let R_j, R_k stand for mean values of the discriminal process j and k and σ_j^2, σ_k^2 stand for their variances; ρ_{jk} denotes their correlation coefficient.

What the researcher *observes*, however, is the proportion of times that stimulus j is preferred to stimulus k. His task is to *infer* scale values from the frequency data developed on each pair of stimuli.

Thurstone's most general model of comparative judgment is stated as

$$R_j - R_k = Z_{jk}\sqrt{\sigma_j^2 + \sigma_k^2 - 2\rho_{jk}\sigma_j\sigma_k}$$

where $R_j - R_k$ = linear distance (on the subject's psychological scale) between stimulus j and stimulus k

   Z_{jk} = standard (unit normal) variate associated with the observed proportion of cases in which stimulus j is preferred to stimulus k

   σ_j^2, σ_k^2 = discriminal dispersion (variance) of stimulus j and k, respectively

   ρ_{jk} = coefficient of correlation between the discriminal processes associated with stimulus j versus stimulus k judgments

A particularly simple form of Thurstone's model can be stated if one assumes that: (1) the discriminal dispersions are equal and (2) the correlation between each pair of discriminal processes is equal. By setting $\sigma_j^2 = \sigma_k^2$ for all j and k and letting ρ denote the *common* correlation across all pairs of discriminal processes, we obtain the following simplification, known as Case V, of Thurstone's model of comparative judgment:

$$R_j - R_k = Z_{jk}\sqrt{2\sigma^2(1 - \rho)}$$

However, it turns out that we can simplify things even more. This is because $\sqrt{2\sigma^2(1 - \rho)}$ is a *constant*. Since we plan to obtain an interval scale, we are free to choose the *unit of measurement* (and the origin or zero point as well). This being the case, we can set $\sqrt{2\sigma^2(1 - \rho)}$ equal to 1 and thus obtain the further simplification:

$$R_j - R_k = Z_{jk}$$

Thus, Z_{jk} equals the standard unit normal variate, Z.

An example should make the Case V procedure easier to follow. Assume that a group of 100 housewives was asked to compare five brands of canned tomato juice with respect to "overall goodness of flavor." Each housewife sipped a sample of each brand paired with a sample of every other brand (a total of ten pairs) from paper cups that were marked merely with identifying numbers. Table 6-3 shows the empirically observed proportion for each comparison.

Table 6-3   Observed proportions preferring brand X (top of table) to brand Y (side of table)

	PREFERRED BRAND				
BRAND	*A*	*B*	*C*	*D*	*E*
A	0.50	0.82	0.69	0.25	0.35
B	0.18	0.50	0.27	0.07	0.15
C	0.31	0.73	0.50	0.16	0.25
D	0.75	0.93	0.84	0.50	0.59
E	0.65	0.85	0.75	0.41	0.50

From this table we see, for example, that 82% of the respondents preferred juice B to juice A and the remainder, 18%, preferred juice A to juice B (if we arbitrarily let column dominate row).[16] From the data of this table we next prepare Table 6-4, which summarizes the Z values appropriate for each proportion. (These Z values were obtained from Table A-1 in Appendix A.) If the proportion is less than 0.5, the Z value carries a negative sign; if the proportion is greater than 0.5, the Z value carries a positive sign. The Z values are standard unit variates that are associated with a given propor-

Table 6-4 Z values related to preference proportions in Table 6-3

	BRAND				
BRAND	*A*	*B*	*C*	*D*	*E*
A	0	0.92	0.50	−0.67	−0.39
B	−0.92	0	−0.61	−1.48	−1.04
C	−0.50	0.61	0	−0.99	−0.67
D	0.67	1.48	0.99	0	0.23
E	0.39	1.04	0.67	−0.23	0
Total	−0.36	4.05	1.55	−3.37	−1.87
Mean ($\bar{Z}$)	−0.072	0.810	0.310	−0.674	−0.374
R^*	0.602	1.484	0.984	0	0.300

[16]It is customary to set self-comparisons (the main-diagonal entries of Table 6-3) to 0.5; this has no effect on the resulting scale values. See A. L. Edwards, *Techniques of Attitude Scale Construction* (New York: Appleton-Century-Crofts, 1957) for a discussion of this approach.

tion of total area under the normal curve. (We recall that the Thurstonian model assumes normally distributed scale differences.)

For example, from Table 6-3 we note that the proportion of respondents preferring juice B over juice A is 0.82. We wish to know the Z value appropriate thereto. This value (labeled Z in the standard unit normal table of Table A-1) is 0.92. That is, 82 % of the total area under the normal curve is between $Z = -\infty$ and $Z = 0.92$. All entries in Table 6-4 are obtained in a similar manner, a minus sign being prefixed to the Z value when the proportion is *less* than 0.5.

Column totals are next found for the entries in Table 6-4. In the Case V form of Thurstone's model illustrated here, scale values are obtained from the column sums by taking a simple average of each column's Z values. For example, from Table 6-4, we note that the sum of the Z's for the first column (juice A) is -0.36. The average $\bar{Z}_A$ is simply:

$$\bar{Z}_A = -\frac{0.36}{5} = -0.072$$

This scale value expresses brand A as a *deviation from the mean* of all five scale values. The mean of the five scale values, as computed from the full row of $\bar{Z}$'s, will always be zero under this procedure.

Similarly, we find the average Z value for each of the remaining four columns of Table 6-4. Next, since the zero point of an interval scale is arbitrary, we can let the scale value for juice D ($R_D = \bar{Z}_D = -0.674$) be the reference point (or origin) of zero. We then simply add 0.674 to each of the other $\bar{Z}$ values to obtain the Case V scale values of the other four brands. These are denoted by R^* and appear in the last row of Table 6-4 and in Figure 6-5.

The scale values of brands A through E indicate the preference ordering:

$$B > C > A > E > D$$

Moreover, assuming that an interval scale exists, we can say, for example, that the difference in "goodness of flavor" between brands B and A is 2.3 times the difference in "goodness of flavor" between brands C and A, since

$$1.484 - 0.602 = 2.3(0.984 - 0.602)$$
$$0.882 = 2.3(0.382)$$

(within rounding error).

One of the nice features of the Thurstonian Case V model is that we can find out how well this model fits the original proportions data. To do this, we simply work backward from the scale values shown in the last row of Table 6-4 to find the estimated proportions.

Figure 6-5 **Interval scale derived from Case V model for tomato juice illustration**

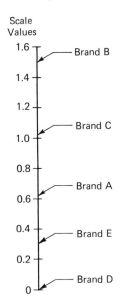

Scale
Values

For example, assume that we wanted to find the *predicted* proportion of respondents preferring brand A to brand B. We first find the scale difference:

$$R_A^* - R_B^* = 0.602 - 1.484$$
$$= -0.882$$

We then find from Table A-1 that the proportion of area under the standard unit normal curve corresponding to a Z of -0.882 (on an interpolated basis) is $1 - 0.81 = 0.19$. That is, the Case V model estimates that 19% of the respondents would prefer brand A to brand B.

Table 6-3 shows, in fact, that 18% of the respondents preferred A to B, a discrepancy of only 1 percentage point. Similarly, we can find predicted proportions for all the remaining pairs of brands and compare these to the actual proportions of Table 6-3.

Table 6-5 shows the results of this comparison. As noted from the table, the Case V model appears to fit the original proportions data quite well. For any specific brand, the highest mean absolute discrepancy is 0.025 (brand A). Moreover, the overall mean absolute discrepancy is only 0.0198.

Thus, even the simplest version (Case V) of the Thurstonian model leads to fairly accurate predictions. Now that the model has been illustrated,

Table 6-5   Actual proportions versus proportions predicted by the Case V model

ROW BRAND PREFERRED TO COLUMN BRAND	BRAND				
	A	B	C	D	E
A (actual)	—	0.18	0.31	0.75	0.65
A′ (predicted)	—	0.19	0.35	0.73	0.62
B	0.82	—	0.73	0.93	0.85
B′	0.81	—	0.69	0.93	0.88
C	0.69	0.27	—	0.84	0.75
C′	0.65	0.31	—	0.84	0.75
D	0.25	0.07	0.16	—	0.41
D′	0.27	0.07	0.16	—	0.38
E	0.35	0.15	0.25	0.59	—
E′	0.38	0.12	0.25	0.62	—
Mean absolute discrepancy	0.025	0.020	0.020	0.012	0.022
Overall mean absolute discrepancy					0.0198

we can examine the nature of the function that links the proportions data of Table 6-3 to the Z values of Table 6-4. Figure 6-6 shows this plot for the sample problem. As can be observed, the Z's (and, hence, the R^* scale values of the Case V model) follow a rank-preserving function of the original proportions data. As a matter of fact, over the proportions range of 0.15 to 0.85, the Case V function does not depart much from linearity. Only when the proportions are either very small or very large (e.g., less than 0.05 or more than 0.95) do we note a rapid change in the function.[17]

In summary, in this particularly simple version (Case V) of Thurstonian scaling, we assume that:

1. A given subject over trials or a group of "homogeneous" subjects display variability in their paired-comparisons judgments regarding any pair of stimuli j and k.

[17]Theoretically, Z goes to $-\infty$ or $+\infty$, respectively, for proportions that approach zero or one. In practice, zero proportions are often set equal to 0.025 and proportions of one are set equal to 0.975.

Figure 6-6   Plot of the Z values (Table 6-4) versus proportions (Table 6-3)

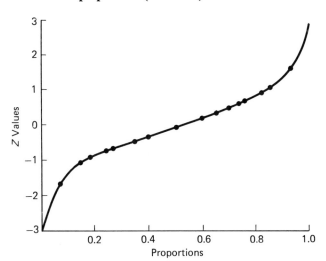

2. Each stimulus gives rise to a subjective (discriminal) process; this process is assumed to be normally distributed with particular modes (means) R_j, R_k, etc. The variances of the distributions are assumed to be equal and the correlations are assumed to be equal for all pairs of distributions.

3. The scale value R for stimulus j is obtained by summing its Z_{jk} values over all remaining stimuli and then finding the mean Z value for each column in Table 6-4.

4. Each scale value R is simply transformed to R^* by the addition of a constant that makes the least preferred item have a scale value of zero.

5. A "test" of the model is obtained by computing predicted portions and comparing these to the observed proportions. Although not demonstrated here, Mosteller has developed a chi-square test for determining if the predicted and observed proportions are in accord with each other—that is, if the model represents a satisfactory description of the data.[18]

As might be surmised, Case V scaling is easily programmed for the computer. In a subsequent chapter we apply one of these computer programs to some actual market survey data.

[18]F. Mosteller, "A Test of Significance for Paired Comparisons When Equal Standard Deviations and Equal Correlations are Assumed," *Psychometrika*, 16 (1959), 207–8.

The Semantic Differential

The *semantic differential* is a type of quantitative-judgment method that results in (assumed interval) scales that are often further analyzed by such techniques as factor analysis (see Chapter 13).[19] Unlike the Case V model, the semantic differential provides no way to test the adequacy of the scaling model itself. That is, it is *assumed* that the raw data are interval-scaled; the intent of the semantic differential is to obtain these raw data for later processing by various multivariate models.

Essentially, the semantic differential procedure enables the researcher to probe into *both the direction and the intensity* of respondents' attitudes toward such concepts as corporate image, advertising image, brand or service image, and so on. One way this is done is to ask the respondent to describe the company by means of ratings on a set of bipolar adjectives, as illustrated in Figure 6-7.

As shown in Figure 6-7, the respondent may be given a set of pairs of antonyms, the extremes of each pair being separated by seven, say, (assumed equal) intervals. For each pair of adjectives (e.g., powerful–weak) the respondent is asked to judge the corporation along the seven-point scale with descriptive phrases such as:

- Extremely powerful
- Very powerful
- Slightly powerful
- Neither powerful nor weak
- Slightly weak
- Very weak
- Extremely weak

In Figure 6-7, the subject scored the company as: (1) extremely powerful, (2) slightly reliable, (3) slightly modern, (4) slightly cold, and (5) very careful.

Figure 6-7   **Corporate profile obtained by means of the semantic differential**

```
Powerful  x  :_____:_____:_____:_____:_____:_____ Weak
Reliable  _____:_____: x :_____:_____:_____:_____ Unreliable
Modern    _____:_____: x :_____:_____:_____:_____ Old-fashioned
Warm      _____:_____:_____:_____: x :_____:_____ Cold
Careful   _____: x :_____:_____:_____:_____:_____ Careless
```

[19]C. E. Osgood, G. J. Suci, and P. H. Tannenbaum, *The Measurement of Meaning* (Urbana, Ill.: University of Illinois Press, 1957).

In practice, however, profiles would be built up for a large sample of respondents, with many more bipolar adjectives being used than given here.

By assigning integer values, such as $+3, +2, +1, 0, -1, -2, -3$, to the seven gradations of each bipolar scale in Figure 6-7, the responses can be quantified under the assumption of equal-appearing intervals. These scale values, in turn, can be averaged across respondents to develop semantic differential profiles. For example, Figure 6-8 shows the average-respondent profiles of two companies: X and Y. We note that company X is perceived as very weak, unreliable, old-fashioned, and careless, but rather warm. Company Y is perceived as powerful, reliable, and careful, but rather cold as well; it is almost neutral with respect to the modern–old-fashioned scale.

Figure 6-8   Average-respondent   profile   comparisons   of companies X and Y via the semantic differential

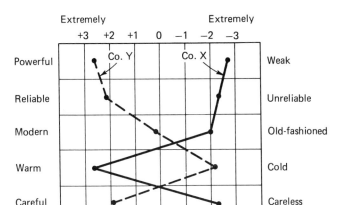

The same basic idea of direction–intensity scales that is utilized in the semantic differential has been extended to other aspects of attitude measurement. For example, Figure 6-9 shows an illustration where various scales were used to measure respondents' views about travel, vacations, and related activities. Note that the respondent checks both:

- Direction of agreement/disagreement with each statement
- Intensity level of agreement/disagreement

Moreover, attitude researchers have incorporated the semantic differential into various models of attitude. As an illustration, Martin Fishbein[20]

[20]See Martin Fishbein, "A Behavioral Theory Approach to the Relations between Beliefs about an Object and the Attitude toward the Object," in *Readings in Attitude Theory and Measurement*, ed. M. Fishbein (New York: John Wiley & Sons, Inc., 1967), pp. 389–400.

Figure 6-9   A direction-intensity scale for measuring attitudes toward travel and vacations

In this part of the questionnaire we are interested in your opinions about certain things. There are no right or wrong answers to any of these statements. What we would like you to do is simply read each statement as it appears. Then indicate the extent of your agreement or disagreement by circling the number that best describes your reaction to the statement: agree strongly (5), agree somewhat (4), neither agree nor disagree (3), disagree somewhat (2), disagree strongly (1).

Please circle the number that best describes your reaction

	Agree Strongly	Agree Somewhat	Neither Agree nor Disagree	Disagree Somewhat	Disagree Strongly
1. I would rather live in the city than in the suburbs.	5	4	3	2	1
2. When you take trips with the children you're not really on vacation.	5	4	3	2	1
3. When I visit a strange place for the first time, I prefer to be on a guided tour.	5	4	3	2	1
4. In the winter I need to go south to the sun.	5	4	3	2	1
5. I look for travel bargains	5	4	3	2	1
6. It is fun to spend money.	5	4	3	2	1
7. I love the fresh air and out-of-doors.	5	4	3	2	1
8. A good vacation shortens the year and makes life longer.	5	4	3	2	1
9. Every vacation should be educational.	5	4	3	2	1
10. I would feel lost if I were alone in a foreign country.	5	4	3	2	1

has proposed the following attitude model:

$$A_o = \sum_{i=1}^{n} B_i a_i$$

where A_o denotes a respondent's overall attitude toward some object, B_i denotes the respondent's strength of belief that the object is associated with some attribute x_i, and a_i denotes the respondent's evaluation of x_i.

For example, suppose that a researcher were measuring psychiatrists' attitudes toward five leading antidepressant drugs in terms of the attributes:

x_1: effective in controlling hallucinations and delusions
x_2: effective in controlling paranoid behavior
x_3: effective in treating withdrawn/apathetic patients
x_4: exhibits rapid onset of action
x_5: safe for use in long-term therapy

The semantic differential is frequently employed to measure both the strength of belief of object–attribute association:

- How strongly do you believe that drug _____ exhibits attribute x_i?

and the evaluation of the attribute:

- How desirable is it that a drug possess attribute x_i?

Each drug would be evaluated separately on each of the five attributes in terms of the physician's belief that it possesses each attribute and his rating of the attribute's desirability. His overall attitudinal score A_o is found (for each drug separately) by summing up the separate products of belief times value for each respective drug.[21]

Currently the semantic differential technique is being used in such applications as:

- Comparing corporate images, both among suppliers of particular products and against an "ideal" image of what respondents think a company *should* be.
- Comparing brands and services of competing suppliers.
- Determining the attitudinal characteristics of purchasers of particular product classes or brands within product class.
- Analyzing the effectiveness of advertising and other promotional stimuli toward changing attitudes.

The comparatively widespread use of the semantic differential by marketing researchers suggests that this method provides a convenient and reasonably reliable way for developing consumer attitudes on a wide variety of topics. The semantic differential has enjoyed a popularity in marketing research that is unmatched by any other psychological scaling procedure.

[21]The incorporation of bipolar scales entails a belief scale that often ranges from "definitely does not exhibit attribute x_i" to "definitely exhibits attribute x_i" (with "may or may not" in between). The desirability scale often ranges from "extremely undesirable" to "extremely desirable" (with the neutral point often being "neither undesirable nor desirable").

TECHNIQUES FOR SCALING RESPONDENTS

Thurstone's Case V model and Osgood's semantic differential are primarily designed for scaling stimuli—tomato juices, brands of toothpaste, corporate images, retailing services, and the like. Behavioral scientists have also proposed techniques whose primary purpose is to scale *respondents* along some attitude continuum of interest. Two of the better-known procedures for doing this are:

1. The summated scale.
2. The Q-sort technique.

Each of these is described in turn.

The Summated Scale

The *summated scale* was originally proposed by Rensis Likert, a psychologist.[22] To illustrate, assume that the researcher wishes to scale some characteristic, such as the public's attitude toward advertising. In applying the Likert summated-scale technique, the following steps are typically carried out:

1. The researcher assembles a large number (e.g., 75 to 100) of statements concerning the public's sentiments toward advertising.
2. Each of the test items is classified by the researcher as generally "favorable" or "unfavorable" with regard to the attitude under study. No attempt is made to scale the items; however, a pretest is conducted that involves the full set of statements and a limited sample of respondents.
3. In the pretest the respondent indicates approval (or not) with *every* item, checking one of the following direction–intensity descriptors:
   a. Strongly approve
   b. Approve
   c. Undecided
   d. Disapprove
   e. Strongly disapprove
4. Each response is given a numerical weight (e.g., $+2, +1, 0, -1, -2$).
5. The individual's *total-attitude score* is represented by the algebraic summation of weights associated with the items checked. In the scoring process, weights are assigned such that the direction of

---

[22] A complete discussion of this scale appears in F. N. Kerlinger, *Foundations of Behavioral Research*, 2d ed. (New York: Holt, Rinehart and Winston, Inc., 1973).

attitude—favorable to unfavorable—is consistent over items. For example, if a $+2$ were assigned to "strongly approve" for favorable items, a $+2$ should be assigned to "strongly disapprove" for unfavorable items.

6. After seeing the results of the pretest, the analyst selects only those items that appear to discriminate well between high and low *total* scorers. This may be done by first finding the highest and lowest quartiles of subjects on the basis of *total* score. Then, the mean differences on each *specific* item are compared between these high and low groups (excluding the middle 50% of subjects).

7. The 20 to 25 items finally selected are those that have discriminated "best" (i.e., exhibited the greatest differences in mean values) between high versus low total scorers in the pretest.

8. Steps 3 through 5 are then repeated in the main study.

Many users of the "final" Likert summated scale (the one developed after the pretest) assume only ordinal properties regarding the placement of respondents along the attitude continuum of interest. Nonetheless, two respondents could have the same total score even though their response patterns to individual items were quite different. That is, the process of obtaining a single (summated) score ignores the details of just which items were agreed with and which ones were not. Moreover, the total score is sensitive to how the respondent reacts to the descriptive intensity levels. (Some respondents tend to use the extreme ends of an intensity scale, while others tend to use the middle gradations.) For these (and other) reasons, the Likert summated scale should be used with more than the usual amount of attention to details. In particular, the classifying of items as favorable or unfavorable should be checked across several judges.

The Q-Sort Technique

The *Q-sort technique* was originally proposed by William Stephenson, a psychologist.[23] Q sort has aspects in common with the summated scale and proceeds as follows:

1. The respondent is given a large number (75 to 100) of attitude statements—usually described on individual cards—and asked to place them in 11 piles, ranging from "most highly agreed with" to "least highly agreed with."

[23]A discussion of this technique appears in F. N. Kerlinger, *Foundations of Behavioral Research*, Chap. 34. Also, see G. D. Hughes, *Attitude Measurement for Marketing Strategies* (Glenview, Ill.: Scott, Foresman and Company, 1971) for a general discussion of this and related techniques.

2. In Q sort the respondent is usually asked to place a *prespecified* number of items in each pile, usually set so as to result in an approximately normal distribution of items over the whole set.

3. Each pile is given a score, ranging from 1 to 11.

4. Each subject's responses are recorded as a column of scores based on the pile number in which each item is placed.

Unlike the Likert summated-scale procedure, however, in Q sort, interest centers not on the development of a total score for each respondent but rather on the extent to which each respondent's *pattern of scores is correlated with each other respondent's*. After all the sorts are completed, each subject's set of numerically coded responses is correlated with every other subject's. The objective is to classify respondents in terms of their *similarity* across the item sorts. Factor analysis and cluster-analysis techniques (see Chapter 13) are used for this purpose.

Q sort suffers from some of the same limitations as the summated scale. Questions arise regarding the use of successive integers to denote the subjective values of the 11 response categories and the forced choice of a specified number of items per pile. Problems can also arise concerning the respresentativeness of the respondent population and the statistical techniques (Q-type factor analysis) that are used to analyze the data after the sorts are completed.

Numerical Illustrations

To illustrate the similarities and differences of the summated scale and the Q sort, a simple, artificial example is presented. We shall use a limited case involving only seven items.

Suppose that a marketing researcher is interested in scaling consumer attitudes toward the advertising industry. Such statements as the following could be made up:

- *Item 1:* Advertising contributes very importantly to America's industrial prosperity.
- *Item 2:* Advertising merely inflates the prices I must pay for products without giving me any information.
- *Item 3:* Advertising does inform the public and is worth the cost.
- *Item 4:* The American public would be better off with no advertising at all.
- *Item 5:* Advertising old products is a waste of the consumers' dollar.
- *Item 6:* I wouldn't mind it if all advertising were stopped.
- *Item 7:* I wish there were more advertising than exists now.

Assume that 100 items such as these were prepared.

The Summated Scale

Assume now that each of the seven test items has been classified as "favorable" or "unfavorable"; items 1, 3, and 7 are considered favorable and items 2, 4, 5, and 6 unfavorable. In the summated-scale technique each item would appear as follows (illustrated for item 1):

Item 1: Advertising contributes very importantly to America's industrial prosperity.

Strongly				Strongly
Approve	Approve	Undecided	Disapprove	Disapprove

Each subject would be asked to underscore the description that most suits his feeling toward the statement. We may use the weights $+2$ for "strongly approve," $+1$ for "approve," 0 for "undecided," -1 for "disapprove," and -2 for "strongly disapprove." Since, by previous classification, items 1, 3, and 7 are "favorable" statements, we would use the preceding weights with no modification. On items 2, 4, 5, and 6 ("unfavorable" statements) we would reverse the order of the weights so as to maintain a consistent direction. Thus, in these items, $+2$ would stand for "strongly disapprove," and so on.

Suppose that a subject evaluated the seven items in the following way:

Item	*Response*	
1	Strongly approve	$+2$
2	Disapprove	$+1$
3	Approve	$+1$
4	Strongly disapprove	$+2$
5	Disapprove	$+1$
6	Strongly disapprove	$+2$
7	Strongly approve	$+2$

The subject would receive a total score of

$$+2 + 1 + 1 + 2 + 1 + 2 + 2 = 11$$

Suppose that another subject responded to the seven items with: (1) strongly disapprove, (2) undecided, (3) disapprove, (4) strongly approve, (5) strongly approve, (6) strongly approve, and (7) undecided. His score would be

$$-2 + 0 - 1 - 2 - 2 - 2 + 0 = -9$$

This listing indicates that the second subject would be ranked "lower" than the first—that is, as having a less favorable attitude regarding the advertising field. However, as indicated earlier, a given total score may have different meanings.

The Q-Sort Technique

In illustrating the Q-sort technique, assume that four subjects evaluate the test items. For purposes of illustration, only 3 (rather than 11) piles will be used. The subjects are asked to sort items into:

Most Approve (two items)	Neutral About (three items)	Least Approve (two items)
+1	0	−1

The numbers above the horizontal line represent the number of items that the subject must place into piles 1, 2, and 3, respectively. That is, he may first select the two items that he *most* approves; these go in pile 1. Next, he selects the two statements that he *least* approves; these go in pile 3. The remaining three items are placed in pile 2. The numbers below the line represent scale values. Suppose that the responses of the four subjects, A, B, C, and D, result in the following scale values:

	SUBJECT			
ITEM	A	B	C	D
1	+1	+1	−1	−1
2	0	0	0	0
3	+1	0	0	−1
4	−1	−1	+1	+1
5	0	0	0	0
6	−1	−1	+1	+1
7	0	+1	−1	−1

As can be noted, the subject pair A and B and the subject pair C and D seem "most alike" of the six distinct pairs that could be considered. We could, of course, actually correlate each subject's scores with every other subject and, similar to semantic differential applications, conduct factor or cluster analyses (see Chapter 13) on the resultant intercorrelations. Typically, these additional steps *are* undertaken in Q-sort studies.

VALIDITY AND RELIABILITY IN ATTITUDE SCALING

As the reader has probably gathered by now, the measurement of perceptions, preferences, motivations, and the like is fraught with difficulty. Such questions as:

1. Do the scales really measure what we are trying to measure?
2. Do subjects' responses remain stable over time?
3. If we have a variety of scaling procedures, are respondents consistent in their scoring over those scales that purport to be measuring the same thing?

are representative of the problems involved in establishing the validity and reliability of scaling techniques.

Validity

By *validity* the behavioral scientist means that the data must be unbiased and relevant to the characteristic being measured. We can thus view the validity of a scaling procedure (or measuring instrument, generally) in terms of its freedom from systematic error—that is, its ability to reflect "true" differences, either among individuals at a point in time or within a single individual over time. Systematic error may arise from the instrument itself, the user of the instrument, the subject, or the environment in which the scaling procedure is being administered. Since in practice we rarely know "true" scores, we usually have to judge a scaling procedure's validity by its relationship to *other* standards that are thought to be relevant. To a large extent this process is circular.

As can be surmised, validity of a measuring instrument hinges on the availability of some external *criterion* that is thought to be correct. Unfortunately the availability of such "outside" criteria is often low. What makes the problem even more difficult is that the researcher often is not interested in the scales themselves but in the underlying *theoretical* construct that the scale purports to measure. It is one thing to *define* IQ as a score on a set of tests; it is quite another to infer from test results that a certain construct, "intelligence," is being measured.

In "testing" the validity of a scale, the researcher might use any or all of the following: (1) content validity, (2) criterion validity, and (3) construct validity. The behavioral scientist ordinarily attempts to measure *content validity* by the personal judgments of experts in the field. That is, he may ask several content experts to judge whether the items being used in the instrument are "representative" of the field being investigated. The results of this procedure reflect the "informed" judgments of experts in the content field.

In pursuing the objective of *criterion validity*, the researcher attempts to develop or obtain an external criterion against which the scaling results can be matched. The outside criterion may, of course, be another scale. Criterion validity can be assessed by correlating the set of scaling results under study with some other set, developed from another instrument, that is administered at the same time. Alternatively, the correlation may be carried out with the results of another scaling procedure that is applied to a future testing occasion.

Construct Validation

In *construct validation* the researcher is interested not only in the question "Does it work?" (i.e., predict) but also in the development of criteria that permit answering theoretical questions of why it works and what deductions can be made concerning the theory underlying the instrument.

Construct validity involves three subcases: convergent, discriminant, and nomological validity. In *convergent validity* we are interested in the correspondence in results between attempts to measure the same construct by two or more independent methods. (These methods need not all be scaling techniques.) *Discriminant validation* refers to properties of scaling procedures that *do* differ when they are supposed to—that is, in cases where they are measuring different characteristics of stimuli and/or subjects. As Campbell and Fiske[24] indicate, since characteristics of the subject and the measuring instrument can each contribute variation to the scaling results, more than one instrument and more than one subject characteristic should be used in convergent–discriminant validation work.

Nomological validity comes closest to what is generally meant by "understanding" a concept (or construct). In nomological validity the researcher attempts to relate measurements to a *theoretical model that leads to further deductions, interpretations, and tests*, gradually building toward a nomological *net*, in which several constructs are systematically interrelated.

Ideally, the behavioral scientist would like to attain *construct* validity, thus achieving not only the ability to make predictive statements but understanding as well. Frequently he must settle for only *content* validity or at best *criterion* validity. It should be evident, however, that the quest for construct validity may be well justified, particularly if the instrument is to be used in new situations with new groups of individuals. That is, *generalization* of a

[24]D. T. Campbell and D. W. Fiske, "Convergent and Discriminant Validation by the Multi-trait–Multimethod Matrix," *Psychological Bulletin*, 56 (1959), 81–105.

scale's validity over groups, situations, and times is most readily accomplished by establishing construct validity.

Reliability

By *reliability* the behavioral scientist means the extent to which scaling results are free from experimental error. In this case we are concerned with the consistency of test results over groups of individuals or over the same individual at different times. It need hardly be added that a scaling procedure may be reliable but not valid. Reliability, however, establishes an upper bound on validity. An unreliable scale cannot be a valid one.

In measuring the reliability of a scale, our interest may sometimes center on the extent to which *repeated applications* of the instrument achieve consistent results, assuming that the relevant characteristics of the subject are stable over trials. On the other hand, the technique of *split-half reliability*, in which items are divided into equivalent groups (say, odd- versus even-numbered questions) and the item responses correlated is a common procedure for estimating reliability *within* single testing occasions.

We may also attempt to measure reliability by administering the instrument to a group of individuals (who are purportedly homogeneous with regard to the attribute under test) as well as by giving the instrument to a specific individual at different times.

The achievement of scale reliability is, of course, dependent upon how consistent the characteristic being measured is from individual to individual (homogeneity over individuals) and how stable the characteristic remains over time. Just how reliable a scaling procedure turns out to be will depend on the dispersion of the characteristic in the population, the length of the testing procedure and its internal consistency.

Although it is not our objective to pursue in detail the methods by which reliability or validity can be "tested," we hope that at least an appreciation of the difficulties encountered in designing and analyzing psychological measures has been conveyed to the reader. Unfortunately, scaling techniques in marketing research appear to have reached a stage of popularity that is not commensurate with our understanding of the measurements.[25] It is much easier to develop scales than to understand that which has been developed (i.e., the construct).

LIMITATIONS OF SCALING PROCEDURES

Although psychological measurement offers an interesting and potentially rewarding area of study by the marketing researcher, the reader should also

[25]A number of marketing applications of the techniques presented here appear in the Bibliography at the end of the book.

be made aware of the limitations of current scaling techniques from the standpoint of their applicability to marketing problems.[26]

First, it is apparent that more progress has been made in the construction of scales for measuring attitudes along a *single dimension* than in dealing with the more complex cases of *multidimensional* attitudes. A person's decision to purchase a particular brand, however, usually reflects a response to a variety of stimuli—for example, the brand's functional features, package design, advertising messages, corporate image, and so on. Much work still remains to be done on the development of scales to measure multidimensional stimuli. Accordingly, the nature of the progress that has been made in multidimensional scaling is a subject of later chapters, particularly Chapter 14.

Second, relatively little has been done on the development of anything like a general theory of individual buyer behavior that is *testable* in terms of empirical findings from psychological and sociological studies. In addition to consumer perception and preference studies, we still need to know much more about the influence of other persons (peers, superiors, subordinates) on the buyer decision process, consumer habit formation, and so on. The development of anything close to a general, operationally based, theory will require— at the least—validation of scaling techniques by behavioral-type measures under experimentally controlled conditions.

Finally, predictions from attitude scales, preference ratings, and the like still need to be transformed into measures (sales, market share) of more direct interest to the marketer. We still do not know, in many cases, how to translate verbalized product ratings, attitudes about corporations, and so on into the behavioral and financial measures required to evaluate the effectiveness of alternative marketing actions.

SUMMARY

In this chapter our major objective has been to discuss some of the fundamental concepts of operational defining, measurement, and psychological scaling and their relationship to the gathering and analysis of behavioral data.

We first described constitutive and operational definitions in research. We then discussed concepts of measurement and considered the primary scales (nominal, ordinal, interval, and ratio) used in measuring. This was followed by a discussion of variability and quantitative-judgment methods of data collection.

Scaling procedures were next commented upon within the framework of stimulus-centered and subject-centered methods. As examples of stimulus-centered techniques, Thurstone's Case V model and Osgood's semantic differ-

[26]For an excellent, general discussion of attitude scaling see R. M. Dawes, *Fundamentals of Attitude Measurement* (New York: John Wiley & Sons, Inc., 1972).

ential were described in a marketing research context. Subject-centered scaling techniques—the Likert summated scale and Stephenson's Q-sort technique— were also described and illustrated by numerical examples.

The chapter concluded with a discussion of some of the difficult problems associated with testing the validity and reliability of psychological scales.

ASSIGNMENT MATERIAL

1. Take an article from a current marketing journal and do the following:
   a. Define key terms from an operational standpoint.
   b. Examine the author's justification for the type of measurement scale(s) used.
   c. Criticize the article from the standpoint of its usefulness to marketing management.

2. Design and administer a short questionnaire on the topic of student attitudes toward the teaching competence of your university's faculty members. Include questions dealing with paired comparisons, agree–disagree responses, and rating-type scales.
   a. Apply Thurstone's Case V procedure to the paired-comparisons data.
   b. Summarize the rating-scale patterns in terms of a semantic differential profile.
   c. Evaluate the usefulness of these procedures in the context of your problem.

3. The Grandma's Own Soup Company was considering the possibility of changing the consistency of its famous tomato soup. Five test soups were prepared, ranging from "very light" to "very heavy" consistency. A consumer clinic was held in which 15 housewives ranked each soup (no ties allowed) from 1 (liked best) to 5 (liked least). The data for this test are as follows:

	SUBJECT														
SOUP	*1*	*2*	*3*	*4*	*5*	*6*	*7*	*8*	*9*	*10*	*11*	*12*	*13*	*14*	*15*
A	2	4	3	2	2	1	2	2	2	2	3	1	2	3	2
B	1	2	1	1	1	2	1	3	1	1	1	2	1	2	4
C	4	1	4	5	4	5	3	1	5	3	4	4	5	4	5
D	3	3	2	3	3	3	5	4	3	4	2	3	3	1	3
E	5	5	5	4	5	4	4	5	4	5	5	5	4	5	1

a. On the basis of a composite (sum of the ranks), what is the rank order of the soups—from best liked to least liked?

b. What, if anything, can be said about how much better soup B is than soup E?

c. By going across rows of the above table one can count the number of times one soup of each possible pair is ranked higher than the other soup in the pair. Prepare a table of paired comparisons as derived from the ranked data, express the table entries in terms of proportions, and construct an interval scale, using Thurstone's Case V scaling.

d. What major assumption are we making about the sample of subjects when we construct the interval scale above? Criticize this type of application of the Thurstone comparative judgment technique.

4. A method proposed by Guilford is the so-called method of choices. In this method we are concerned only with the frequency of *first* choices of subjects. For example, in the data of the preceding problem, soup B received nine first choices, soup A two first choices, and so on. The proportion of times that B is preferred to A, $p(B > A)$, is thus estimated to be

$$p(B > A) = \frac{f(B^*)}{f(B^*) + f(A^*)} = \frac{9}{11} = 0.82$$

where $f(B^*)$ = number of times B received first choice
  $f(A^*)$ = number of times A received first choice

a. Using the method above, construct an interval scale using Thurstone's Case V scaling.

b. Criticize the scale that you just derived from the standpoint of efficient use of ranked data.

5. Assume that two groups—a group of housewives and a group of small businessmen—are asked to rate the Mighty Electric Company on the basis of the bipolar adjective pairs:
   - Powerful—weak
   - Reliable—nonreliable
   - Modern—old-fashioned

The frequencies of each group of 100 respondents are shown below (numbers above the horizontal lines refer to housewives' responses; numbers below refer to businessmen's responses):

Powerful　　$\frac{20}{40} : \frac{42}{30} : \frac{10}{15} : \frac{5}{5} : \frac{4}{5} : \frac{12}{5} : \frac{7}{0}$　　Weak

Reliable $\quad \frac{52}{10} : \frac{12}{15} : \frac{8}{12} : \frac{10}{22} : \frac{8}{35} : \frac{5}{6} : \frac{5}{0} \quad$ Nonreliable

Modern $\quad \frac{5}{6} : \frac{14}{20} : \frac{21}{25} : \frac{25}{20} : \frac{20}{12} : \frac{10}{9} : \frac{5}{8} \quad$ Old-fashioned

a. Using a 7-point scale (where, for example, 7 = extremely power-ful and 1 = extremely weak), find a summary rating index for each group of raters for each set of adjective pairs.
b. What assumptions are made by using the integer weights 7, 6, . . . , 1?
c. In which adjective pairs are the rating indexes between the groups most similar; most dissimilar?
d. How would your answer to part (a) change if the weights $+3, +2, +1, 0, -1, -2$, and -3 were used instead of the weights 7, 6, . . . , 1? Would rank order between pairs of summary indexes (for each adjective pair) be affected and, if so, how?

Sampling Procedures in Marketing Research

7

INTRODUCTION

There are many questions that marketing researchers must answer when considering a project to collect additional information about some population of interest. Those that involve sampling are:

- Should we take a census (i.e., a complete canvas) or a sample?
- What kind of sample should be taken?
- What size should the sample be?

The answers to these questions depend upon the application of statistical inference. We first describe briefly the development of statistical reasoning up to its current formulation as the discipline of "making rational decisions in the face of uncertainty." We then consider the conditions under which a sample should be taken, the various kinds of samples, and the criteria to be used for selecting the right sample for a specific situation.

The final section of the chapter is concerned with the question of sample size. A brief review of the basic statistical models that underlie probability sampling—that is, the sampling distributions of the mean and proportion—is first given. We then describe the rationale and procedures for determining sample size using traditional inferential methods. Following a discussion of the limitations of these more commonly applied methods, we briefly describe the logic involved in determining sample size by means of the Bayesian approach.

THE DEVELOPMENT OF STATISTICAL REASONING—
A HISTORICAL NOTE

The development of statistics has passed through several reformulations, and even today nothing near universal agreement exists among statisticians regarding the discipline's foundations. Statistics as a scientific area of study is largely a twentieth-century development, marked by the contributions of the great names: Fisher, Neyman, Pearson, and Wald. Current emphasis on decision theory, however, represents a return to some of the concepts that existed as early as the eighteenth century.

In 1763 Bayes' theorem was published posthumously. As was described in Chapter 2, this theorem has been identified with the Bayesian approach to decision making under uncertainty. A key feature of the theorem is its use of prior probabilities assigned to alternative states of nature. Bayes' theorem *revises* these prior probabilities in the light of new information. The concept of prior probabilities—particularly the Laplace postulate to represent the case of total ignorance regarding the likelihood of various states of nature— eventually became a topic of heated controversy among statisticians.

Accordingly, the first statistical "revolution" was marked by most statisticians' rejection of the whole notion of prior probabilities. Attempts were then made to arrive at inferences on the basis of examining the probabilities associated with *sample evidence* alone.

R. A. Fisher[1] is to be credited with formulating rigorous statements regarding inferences to be drawn solely from sample observations. He defined the "null" hypothesis as an assertion about the real world whose validity was to be tested. The null hypothesis was to be rejected when sample observations would be "improbable" if the null hypothesis were true. That is, Fisher was interested only in the *conditional* probability of getting the sample observations he did get, given that the null hypothesis was true. If this probability turned out to be "low," the null hypothesis was to be rejected. Alternative hypotheses (states of nature) were *not* explicitly considered under Fisher's procedure.

Newman and Pearson[2] are credited with reintroducing alternative hypotheses (which had always been assumed in Bayesian analysis anyway) but *without recourse to prior probability assignments.* They reasoned that if the null hypothesis is rejected, another hypothesis must be accepted, leading to two types of error: (1) rejecting the null hypothesis when it is true (type I error), and (2) accepting the null hypothesis when it is false (type II error). They

[1] R. A. Fisher, *Statistical Methods for Research Workers* (Edinburgh: Oliver & Boyd Ltd., 1925).

[2] J. Neyman and E. S. Pearson, "On the Use and Interpretation of Certain Test Criteria for Purposes of Statistical Inference," *Biometrika*, 20A (1928), 175–240.

suggested holding the type I error probability constant and choosing a decision scheme that minimized the probability of making a type II error. Here again, however, their concern was with the *conditional* probabilities of making each type of error, given the hypotheses being tested. *Costs* of making type I or II errors entered only in the rather vague sense of influencing the *size* of the conditional probabilities of making the two types of errors. Prior probabilities did not enter at all.

The next major advance in statistics is credited to Abraham Wald.[3] Wald's contributions unified much of the earlier work in hypothesis testing. It was Wald who visualized statistics as a body of procedures for making wise decisions in the face of uncertainty, rather than merely as a means for drawing conclusions from sample data. His principal contributions involved:

1. The explicit use of the *economic consequences* of making errors.
2. The inclusion of an alternative involving *delay of decisions* (and, hence, further sampling on a sequential basis) until it would pay to stop sampling and make a terminal decision.
3. In addition to developing precise statements of the economic consequences of decisions (by means of payoff tables), Wald included the use of the maximin principle for choosing the course of action that leads to the maximum of the worst possible payoffs (see Chapter 1).

About all that was missing in Wald's treatment (versus the Bayesian approach) was the use of *prior probabilities* regarding the hypotheses under examination.

The notion of *personalistic* probability, meanwhile, had been gaining ground with several statisticians[4] and was summarized elegantly in a book by L. J. Savage.[5] Savage showed that personalistic probabilities could be developed under a set of "reasonable" assumptions regarding the meaning of a decision maker's *consistent* judgments about the occurrence of alternative states of nature. Robert Schlaifer[6] then combined the preceding developments into an elementary, yet highly significant, book that discussed the Bayesian approach in terms of practical business situations. Bayes' theorem (for revising prior probabilities in the light of new information) was revived and the notion of prior probabilities was now given a personalistic interpretation.

The difference between the traditional and Bayesian approaches can be

[3]A. Wald, *Sequential Analysis* (New York: John Wiley & Sons, Inc., 1947).

[4]For a review of these developments, see H. E. Kyburg, Jr., and H. E. Smokler, *Studies in Subjective Probability* (New York: John Wiley & Sons, Inc., 1964).

[5]L. J. Savage, *The Foundations of Statistics* (New York: John Wiley & Sons, Inc., 1954). Also, see F. P. Ramsey, *The Foundation of Mathematics and Other Logical Essays* (New York: Harcourt, Brace and Co., 1931).

[6]Robert Schlaifer, *Probability and Statistics for Business Decisions* (New York: McGraw-Hill Book Company, 1959).

perhaps most succinctly summarized by the remark that the former procedure utilizes decision rules that are determined by considering only the conditional probabilities of making wrong decisions. The setting up of these risks of error is supposed to be done *outside* the statistical model. On the other hand, the Bayesian approach, while also using the conditional probabilities of getting specific sample results, given a particular state of nature, further assumes that one can talk meaningfully about a probability distribution over the alternative states of nature themselves. The costs of wrong decisions are introduced *explicitly* into the Bayesian decision procedure and the alternative to be selected is that act which maximizes expected (monetary) value or, more generally, expected utility (see Chapter 2). As such, the modern Bayesian approach utilizes most of the concepts of the traditional approach, *plus* the contributions by Wald and the developers of personalistic probability.

THE DECISION CONCERNING WHETHER TO TAKE A CENSUS OR A SAMPLE

If the collection of all relevant information were always possible (and never costly) the marketing researcher would have no need for sampling techniques. Under these ideal conditions he would approach any problem with the potential for gaining full and accurate knowledge of the consequences associated with alternative courses of action by taking a *census*, or complete enumeration, of some characteristic(s) in the population of interest.

Obviously, such ideal conditions do not exist. A census may just not be feasible. Even if feasible, a sample may be preferable because of considerations of cost or of time. For example, even if possible, a census of *all* U.S. automobile owners regarding the type of wheels on their cars would hardly be economically practical for a manufacturer of magnesium wheels. In other instances a sample is necessary because of the *destructive nature of the measurement*, such as the testing of matches or paint. In still other cases a sample may be desirable for controlling *nonsampling errors*. The smaller-scale aspects of taking a sample may permit tighter control of the measuring operations (better interviewing, less nonresponse through more call-backs, and so forth) to a point where the total amount of sampling and nonsampling error is actually less for the sample than the nonsampling error alone would be for a census. Finally, a sample may be necessary to enable one to *concentrate attention on individual cases*. For example, studies in depth of why a product is bought and how it is consumed may not be feasible to carry out on other than a sample basis.

Under certain conditions, however, a census may be preferable to a sample. When *the population is small, the variance in the characteristic being measured high, the costs of error high, and/or the fixed costs of sampling high, sampling may not be useful.* If one were doing a study to determine the acceptability to U.S. original equipment manufacturers of a new drive mechanism for snowmobiles, one might be well advised to conduct a census of the seven manufacturers involved.

THE DECISION CONCERNING WHAT TYPE OF SAMPLE TO TAKE

Much of the sampling in marketing research is nonprobability in nature. That is, samples are selected on the basis of the judgment of the investigator, convenience, or by some other nonrandom process rather than by the use of a table of random numbers or some other randomizing device.

The advantages of probability sampling are that, if done properly, it provides a *bias-free method of selecting sample units and permits the measurement of sampling error.* Nonprobability samples offer neither of these features. In nonprobability sampling one must rely on the expertise of the person taking the sample, whereas in probability sampling the results are independent of the investigator.

One should not conclude that probability sampling always yields results that are superior to nonprobability sampling, nor that the samples obtained by nonprobability methods are necessarily less "representative" of the populations under study. For example, a marketing researcher working for a drug firm may develop an index of salespeople's performance by measuring such items as doctor calls completed per week, number of new drugs promoted during call, length of call, and so on. A particular item is included in the index because the marketing researcher feels that it is representative of something called "performance." And his nonprobability sampling may indeed be a better way to achieve a representation of the population than dropping a bunch of cards (on which are written possible characteristics of sales performance) in a hat and selecting five or six of the cards, blindfolded.

On the other hand, a cosmetics manufacturer may test consumer reactions to a new lipstick by giving samples of the product to the female members of his family and eliciting their responses a week or so later. In both cases, the samples are "biased" in the sense that they have been deliberately chosen to conform to the selector's idea of what the population does—or perhaps should—look like. In the first case we might argue that the marketing researcher's choice of characteristics is a reasonable one, in view of the purposes for which the index is being prepared. In the second case, assuming that the cosmetics manufacturer is attempting to infer "typical" consumer reaction to the lipstick, we might question the relevance of the reactions of his family members, independent of the fact that the sample size is small.

The choice between probability and nonprobability sampling ultimately turns on a judgment of the relative size of the sampling error of the probability sample versus the combined sampling error and selection bias of a nonprobability sample. For a given cost, one will normally be able to select a larger nonprobability sample than probability sample. This means that the sampling error should be lower in the nonprobability sample. However, a selection bias will have been introduced by the nonrandom process used for selecting the sample.

In this chapter we shall be primarily concerned with probability sampling. However, before discussing this topic it is useful to describe some of the procedures by which nonprobability samples are taken in marketing research.

NONPROBABILITY SAMPLING PROCEDURES

Quota Sampling

Perhaps the most commonly employed nonprobability sampling procedure in marketing research is the *quota sample*.[7] Roughly described, in quota sampling the sizes of various subclasses (or strata) in the population are first estimated from some outside source, such as from Bureau of the Census data. For example, one may use census data to find out the proportion of the adult population who fall into various age-by-sex-by-education classes.

Next, if an interviewer has a total number of, say, 100 interviews to obtain, the age–sex–education proportions in the population are applied to the 100 total interviews to determine the appropriate quotas. This could lead, for example, to 4 interviews of respondents who are between 18 and 30 years of age, female, with some college (or above) and 9 interviews of respondents who are over 30 years of age, male, with high school (or below) education.

So far, this approach to stratification is quite sound, statistically. Indeed, as will be discussed later, this same initial step is employed in proportionate stratified random sampling. However, in quota sampling the interviewer is *not* required to select the respondents necessary to fill each quota on a random basis. This is the major distinction between quota sampling and stratified random sampling.

Since the interviewer's judgment is relied upon to select actual respondents within each quota, many sources of selection bias are potentially present. For example, the interviewer may not bother to call back if the first call results in a not-at-home. Interviewers may go to selected areas where the

[7]Quota sampling is discussed rather extensively in F. J. Stephan and P. J. McCarthy, *Sampling Opinions* (New York: John Wiley & Sons, Inc., 1958). A critique of the method is offered by W. E. Deming, *Sample Designs in Business Research* (New York: John Wiley & Sons, Inc., 1960).

chances are good that a particular type of respondent is available. Certain houses may be skipped because the interviewer does not like the appearance of the property. Still other ways exist in which the habits and biases of interviewers can influence their selection of respondents within quota.

The advantages of quota sampling are, of course, the lower costs and greater convenience provided to the interviewer in selecting respondents to fill each quota. More recently, tighter controls have been established on the permissible travel patterns of interviewers, thus tending to reduce this potential source of selection bias.

Convenience Sampling

Convenience sampling is a generic term that covers a wide variety of ad hoc procedures for selecting respondents. For example, some cities, such as Fort Worth, Texas, and Syracuse, New York, are viewed as "typical" cities whose demographic makeups are close to the national average. In market tests of new products it is not unusual to select such cities to obtain consumer evaluations that are believed to reflect "national" tastes. As in any other nonprobability procedure, however, there is no sound basis for estimating statistical confidence intervals around the sample statistics of interest.

Other forms of convenience sampling are prevalent. Many firms conduct "intercept" interviews among shopping-mall customers or other areas where large numbers of consumers may congregate. Firms may also authorize samples to be taken from such intact groups as Parent–Teacher Associations, church groups, philanthropic organizations, and so on. Again, the purpose is to obtain a relatively large number of interviews quickly from a cooperating group of respondents. Usually the sponsoring organization receives a donation from the interviewing firm for the help and cooperation of the organization's members.

Surveys based on convenience sampling are also carried out by various magazines and newspapers (using subscriber lists), department stores (using charge account lists), or gasoline companies (using credit card lists). Again, many potential sources of selection bias are present, assuming that the population under study is larger than the members of the various lists.

Snowball Sampling

Snowball sampling is the rather colorful name given to a procedure in which initial respondents *are* selected randomly but where additional respondents are then obtained from referrals or by other information provided by the initial respondents. One major purpose of snowball sampling is to estimate various characteristics that are rare in the total population.

For example, in a study of international tourism, the researchers were required to interview respondents in the United Kingdom, France, and Germany who visited the United States during the Bicentennial year. As might be expected, in most areas of these three countries, the likelihood of finding a qualified adult respondent was less than 2%. Accordingly, stratified probability methods were used to select initial respondents. Then a referral procedure (up to two referrals per qualified respondent) was used to obtain a second group of qualified respondents. (However, subsequent referrals were *not* obtained from this second group of respondents, in this particular study.)

In other types of snowball sampling, referrals from referrals are obtained, and so on, thus leading to the term "snowballing." Even though some probability-based procedure may be used to select the initial group of respondents, the overall sample is a nonprobability sample. For example, referrals will tend to exhibit more similar demographic profiles to the persons referring them than would be expected by chance.

In general, the sampling of rare characteristics is often aided by the employment of short and inexpensive *screening interviews* (usually by telephone), whose major purpose is to locate the subpopulation of interest for a subsequent personal interview that is more extensive. Finally, it should be mentioned that, in the case of rare characteristics, it is not unusual to *over-sample* some of the subgroups so as to obtain a sample size that is adequate in terms of the actual number of respondents to produce reasonably stable estimates. That is, in sampling various rare characteristics, the allocation of interviews may *not* be in direct proportion to the relative size of the strata if this leads to too few respondents in the smaller strata.

PROBABILITY SAMPLING DESIGNS

The best-known type of probability sample is no doubt the simple random sample. However, in marketing research many occasions exist for more specialized sampling procedures than those that can be met by simple random-sampling methods. Statisticians have developed a variety of specialized probability-sampling designs that, although derived from simple random-sampling principles, can be used to gain lower sampling error for a given cost or equal sampling error for a lower cost. Designs of particular interest to the marketing researcher are systematic sampling, stratified sampling, cluster sampling, area sampling, and multistage sampling.

These techniques are discussed in turn, following a review of simple random sampling. Our purpose is to describe the major characteristics of each technique rather than to present a detailed mathematical exposition of these procedures.[8]

Simple Random Sampling

A *simple random sample* is one in which each sample element has a known and equal probability of selection, and each possible sample of *n* elements has a known and equal probability of being the sample actually selected. It is drawn by a random procedure from a sample *frame*, which is a list containing an exclusive and exhaustive enumeration of all sample elements.

Simple random samples are *not* widely used in marketing research, and especially so in consumer research, for two reasons. The first is that it is often difficult to obtain a sampling frame that will permit a simple random sample to be drawn. Consumer research usually requires that either *people, households, stores*, or *areas* be the basic sampling units. While a complete representation of areas is available through maps, there normally is no complete listing of persons (or the households in which they live) or of the stores available. When persons, households, or stores are to be sampled, therefore, some other sample design must be used.

However, in industrial marketing research, there is a greater opportunity for the application of simple random sampling. In this case, *people* (e.g., purchasing agents), *companies*, or *areas* are the usual sampling units. Since the population under study is often relatively small, one is in a better position to develop a complete respondent list or sample frame.

Industrial marketing research, however, provides a second reason for not using simple random sampling—that is, one may not want to have an *equal* probability of selection of all sample units. Most industries are characterized by a wide variation in the size of the firms that comprise them. One is likely to want to design the sample so that the larger firms have a considerably greater chance of being selected than the smaller firms.

Systematic Sampling

Systematic sampling involves only a slight variation from simple random sampling. A *systematic sample* is one in which each sample element has a known and equal probability of selection. The permissible samples of size *n*

---

[8]A brief review of the mathematical aspects of each of these sampling techniques is given in M. R. Frankel and L. R. Frankel, "Probability Sampling," in *Handbook of Marketing Research*, ed. R. Ferber (New York: McGraw-Hill Book Company, 1974), pp. 2–230–2–246. For a more extensive treatment see M. H. Hansen, W. N. Hurwitz, and W. G. Madow, *Sample Survey Methods and Theory*, Vols. 1 and 2 (New York: John Wiley & Sons, Inc., 1953).

that are possible to be drawn have a known and equal probability of selection, while the remaining samples of size n have a probability of zero of being selected.

The mechanics of taking a systematic sample are rather simple. If the population contains N ordered elements and a sample size n is desired, one merely finds the ratio of these two numbers N/n and rounds to the nearest integer to obtain the sampling interval. For example, if there are 600 members of the population and one desires a sample of 60, the sampling interval is 10. A random number is then selected between 1 and 10, inclusively; suppose the number turns out to be 4. The analyst then takes as his sample elements 4, 14, 24, and so on.

Essentially, systematic sampling assumes that the population elements are ordered in some fashion—names in a telephone directory, a card index file, or the like. Some types of ordering, such as an alphabetical listing, will usually be uncorrelated with the characteristic (say, income level) being investigated. In other instances, the ordering of the elements may be directly related to the characteristic under study as, for example, a customer list arranged in decreasing order of annual purchase volume.

If the arrangement of the elements of the sample is itself random with regard to the characteristic under study, systematic sampling will tend to give results close to those provided by simple random sampling. We say "close" for the reason that, in systematic sampling, all combinations of the characteristic do *not* have the same chance of being included. For example, it is clear that, in the preceding example, the fifth, sixth, and so on items have zero chance of being included in the *particular* sample chosen.

Systematic sampling may, however, *increase* the sample's representativeness when the items are ordered with regard to the characteristic of interest. For example, if the analyst is sampling a customer group by decreasing order of purchase volume, a systematic sample will be sure to contain some high-volume customers and some low-volume customers. On the other hand, the simple random sample may yield, say, only low-volume customers, and may thus be unrepresentative of the population being sampled if the characteristic of interest is related to purchase volume.

It is also possible that systematic sampling may *decrease* the representativeness of the sample in those instances where the items are ordered in such a way as to produce a cyclical pattern. For example, if a marketing researcher were to use systematic sampling of daily retail-store sales volume, and were to choose a sampling interval of seven days, his choice of day would result in a sample that would not reflect day-of-the-week variations in sales.

Although systematic sampling can lead to greater reliability (lower sampling error) than simple random sampling, the major difficulty with this technique is the problem of estimating the variance of the universe from the variance of the sample. For example, if in the preceding example we happened to sample all "Tuesdays," we would probably find that we have seriously underestimated the variance across all seven days in the week. If we have prior knowledge about the characteristics of the groups making up the population, however, we may be able to use this information to select our sample in such a way as to increase the reliability of the sample over that obtained by simple random-sampling methods.

Stratified Sampling

It is sometimes desirable to break the population into different strata based on one or more characteristics such as the frequency of purchase of a product, type of customer (e.g., credit card versus non-credit card), or the industry in which a company competes. In such cases a separate sample is then taken from each stratum. Technically, a *stratified random sample* is one in which a simple random sample is taken from each stratum of interest in the population. (In practice, however, systematic and other types of random samples are sometimes taken from each of the strata and the resulting design is still referred to as a stratified sample.)

Stratified samples have the following general characteristics:

- The entire population is first divided into an exclusive and exhaustive set of strata, using some external source, such as census data, to form the strata.
- Within each stratum a separate random sample is selected.
- From each separate sample, some statistic (e.g., a mean) is computed and properly weighted to form an overall estimated mean for the whole population.
- Sample variances are also computed within each separate stratum and appropriately weighted to yield a combined estimate for the whole population.

Two basic varieties of stratified samples are proportionate and disproportionate. In *proportionate stratified sampling*, the sample that is drawn from each stratum is made proportionate in size to the relative size of that stratum in the total population. In *disproportionate stratified sampling* one departs from the preceding type of proportionality by taking other circumstances, such as the relative size of stratum variances, into account.

The decision concerning whether to use proportionate or disproportionate stratified sampling among strata rests on whether or not the variances among the strata are (approximately) equal. Suppose that a marketing researcher is interested in estimating the average purchases of consumers of hot cereal. He may be willing to assume that, although average consumption would vary markedly by family size, the variances around the means of the strata would be more or less equal among family sizes. If so, he would make use of proportionate stratified sampling.

More generally, however, both means and variances will differ among strata. If this is the case, the researcher would make use of disproportionate stratified sampling. In this instance the number of families included in each stratum would be proportionate to (the product of) the relative size of the different family-sized strata in the population and the standard deviation of each family class. This requires, of course, that the researcher be able to estimate (from past studies) the within-group standard deviation around the average purchase quantity of each purchasing stratum.[9]

As intuition would suggest, the increased efficiency of stratified sampling over simple random sampling depends on how different the means (or some other statistic) really are among strata, relative to the within-stratum variability. What is desired are strata whose within-stratum variation is small but whose among-strata differences are large. That is, the greater the within-stratum *homogeneity* and the among-strata *heterogeneity*, the more efficient stratified sampling is relative to simple random sampling.

Cluster Sampling

Although the researcher will ordinarily be interested in the characteristics of some elementary element in the population (e.g., individual family attitudes toward a new product), he may wish to select primary sampling units on a larger than individual family basis. He may choose to sample city blocks and interview *all* the individual families residing therein. The *blocks*, not the individual families, would be selected at random. Each block consists of a cluster of respondents. Formally, a *cluster sample* is one in which a simple random or stratified random sample is selected of all primary sample units, each containing more than one sample element. Then, all elements within the selected primary units are sampled.

The main advantage of a cluster sample relative to simple random sampling is in lower interviewing costs rather than in greater reliability. One of the authors participated in a survey of salespeople's attitudes toward management policies of a large drug firm in which sales districts were the primary units that were sampled and all salespeople of the sampled districts were interviewed. As might be surmised, the attitudes of a given district's salespeople tended to be positively correlated among salespeople, resulting in greater sampling variance than would have been attained if random sampling (with the same sample size) had been performed at the individual salesperson level. On the other hand, the expense of transporting interviewers to various

[9]Formulas for computing sampling errors in stratified samples can be found in W. G. Cochran, *Sampling Techniques*, 2d ed. (New York: John Wiley & Sons, Inc., 1963).

parts of the firm's overall marketing territory would have added substantially to the costs of the study.

Area Sampling—Single Stage and Multistage

As the name suggests, *area sampling* pertains to primary sampling of geographical areas—for example, counties, townships, blocks, and other area descriptions. If only one level of sampling takes place (e.g., a sampling of blocks) before the basic elements are sampled (e.g., the households), it is a *single-stage area sample*. If one or more successive samples within the larger area are taken before settling on the final clusters, the resulting design is usually referred to as a *multistage area sample*.

An example of multistage sampling is the sample design used by the Gallup Organization, Inc., in taking a nationwide poll. A random sample of approximately 300 locations is drawn as the first stage of the sampling process. Blocks or geographic segments are then randomly sampled from each of these locations in a second stage, followed by a systematic sampling of households within the blocks or segments. A total of about 1,500 persons are usually interviewed in the typical Gallup poll.[10]

THE DECISION CONCERNING WHAT SIZE
SAMPLE TO TAKE

There are several ways to classify techniques for determining sample size. Two that are of primary importance here are whether the technique deals with fixed or sequential sampling and whether its logic is based on traditional or Bayesian inferential methods. Other than for the brief discussion of sequential sampling that follows, this section is concerned with the determination of a *fixed* sample size with emphasis on *traditional* (i.e., Neyman–Pearson) inference rather than Bayesian inference.

Fixed versus Sequential Sampling

As the name implies, in *fixed-size sampling* the number of items is decided upon in advance. The size of the sample is chosen in such a way as to achieve some type of balance between sample reliability and sample cost. In general, all observations are taken before the data are analyzed.

In *sequential sampling*, however, the number of items is not preselected. Rather, the analyst sets up in advance a decision rule that includes not only

[10]This description is contained in materials provided by the Gallup Organization, Inc.

the alternative of stopping the sampling process (and taking appropriate action, based on the sample evidence already in hand) but also the possibility of collecting more information before making a terminal decision. Observations may be taken either singly or in groups, the chief novelty being that the data are analyzed as they are assembled and sample size is not predetermined.

In general, sequential sampling will lead to smaller sample sizes, on the average, than those associated with fixed-size samples of a given reliability. The mathematics underlying sequential sampling are, however, more complex and time-consuming. In addition, the problem may be such that it is less expensive to select and analyze a sample of many items at one time than to draw items one at a time (or in small groups) and analyze each item before selecting the next.

Sampling Distributions and Standard Errors

Intuitively we might expect that when we increase the size of the sample, our estimate of the population parameter should "get closer" to the true value. Also, we might expect that the less dispersed the population's characteristics are, the closer our sample estimates should be to the "true" parameter. After all, the reason why we sample in the first place is to make some *inference* about the population. These inferences should be more reliable the larger the sample on which they are based and the less variable the items of the population are to begin with.

The reader will recall from elementary statistics the concept of a sampling distribution. A *sampling distribution* is the probability distribution of a specified sample statistic (e.g., the sample mean) for all possible random samples of a given size n drawn from the specified population. The *standard error* of the statistic is the standard deviation of the specified sampling distribution. We shall use the following symbols in our brief review of the elementary formulas for calculating the standard error of the mean and proportion (under simple random sampling):

μ = population mean
π = population proportion regarding some attribute
σ = standard deviation of the population
s = standard deviation of the sample, adjusted to serve
   as an estimate of the standard deviation of the population
$\bar{X}$ = arithmetic mean of a sample
p = sample proportion
n = number of items in the sample

As the reader will recall from elementary statistics, there are some important properties associated with sampling distributions:

1. The arithmetic mean of the sampling distribution of the mean ($\bar{X}$) or of the proportion (p) for any given size sample, equals the corresponding parameter value, μ and π, respectively.

2. The sampling distribution of the means of random samples will tend toward the *normal distribution* as sample size n increases, regardless of the original form of the population being sampled.

3. For large samples (e.g., $n \geq 100$ and for π fairly close to 0.5) the normal distribution also represents a reasonable approximation to the binomial distribution for dealing with sample proportions.

4. In the case of finite universes, where the sample size n is some appreciable fraction of the total number N of items in the universe, the standard error formulas should be adjusted by multiplication by the *finite multiplier*,

$$\sqrt{\frac{N-n}{N-1}}$$

For practical purposes, however, use of the finite multiplier is not required unless the sample contains an appreciable fraction, say 10% or more, of the population being sampled.

5. Probabilities of normally distributed variates depend only on the distance (expressed in multiples of the standard deviation) of the value of the variable from the distribution's mean. If we subtract a given population mean μ from a normally distributed variate X_i and divide this result by the original standard deviation σ, we get a *standardized* variate Z_i that is also normally distributed but with zero mean and unit standard deviation. In symbols,

$$Z_i = \frac{X_i - \mu}{\sigma}$$

Table A-1 in Appendix A presents the standardized normal distribution in tabular form. Note further that the original variate may be a sample mean, $\bar{X}$. If so, the denominator is the *standard error* (i.e., standard deviation of the sampling distribution). We can then define Z as some number of standard errors away from the mean of the sampling distribution

$$Z = \frac{\bar{X} - \mu}{\sigma_{\bar{x}}}$$

where $\sigma_{\bar{x}}$ denotes the standard error of the mean. (A similar idea is involved in the case of the standard error of the proportion.)

6. The formulas for the standard error of the mean and proportion of simple random samples are, respectively,

Mean	*Proportion*

$$\sigma_{\bar{x}} = \frac{\sigma}{\sqrt{n}} \qquad\qquad \sigma_{\bar{p}} = \sqrt{\frac{\pi(1 - \pi)}{n}}$$

7. If the population standard deviation σ is not known, which is often the case, we can *estimate* it from the sample observations by use of the formula

$$s = \sqrt{\frac{\sum_{i=1}^{n}(X_i - \bar{X})^2}{n - 1}}$$

We then consider s to be an *estimator* of the population standard deviation σ. In small samples (e.g., less than 30), the t distribution of Table A-2 in Appendix A is appropriate for finding probability points in this case. However, if the sample size exceeds 30 or so, the standardized normal distribution of Table A-1 is a good approximation to the t distribution.

In cases where σ is estimated by s, the standard error of the mean becomes

$$\text{est. } \sigma_{\bar{x}} = \frac{s}{\sqrt{n}}$$

where est. $\sigma_{\bar{x}}$ denotes the fact that σ is estimated from s, as defined above.

8. Analogously, in the case of the standard error of the proportion, we can use the sample proportion p as an estimator of π to obtain

$$\text{est. } \sigma_{\bar{p}} = \sqrt{\frac{p(1 - p)}{n}}$$

as an estimated standard error of the proportion.[11]

[11]Strictly speaking, $n - 1$ should appear in the denominator. However, if n exceeds about 100 (which is typical of the samples obtained in marketing research), this adjustment makes little difference in the results.

ESTIMATING SAMPLE SIZE BY TRADITIONAL METHODS

Two major classes of procedures are available for estimating sample sizes within the context of traditional (Neyman–Pearson) inference. The first, and better known, of these is based on the idea of constructing confidence intervals around sample means or proportions. This can be called the *confidence-interval approach.*

The second approach makes use of both type I (rejecting a true null hypothesis) and type II (accepting a false null hypothesis) error risks and can be called the *hypothesis-testing approach.* We discuss each of these approaches in turn.

The Confidence-Interval Approach

As will be recalled from introductory statistics, it is not unusual to construct a confidence interval around some sample-based mean or proportion. The standard error formulas are employed for this purpose. For example, a researcher may have taken a sample of 100 consumers and noted that their average per capita consumption of orange juice was 2.6 pints per week. Past studies indicate that the population standard deviation σ can be assumed to be 0.3 pint.

With this information, we can find a range around the sample mean level of 2.6 points for which some prespecified probability statement can be made about the *process underlying the construction of such confidence intervals.*

For example, suppose that we wished to set up a 95% confidence interval around the sample mean of 2.6 pints. We would proceed by first computing the standard error of the mean:

$$\sigma_{\bar{x}} = \frac{\sigma}{\sqrt{n}} = \frac{0.3}{\sqrt{100}} = 0.03$$

From Table A-1 in Appendix A we can find that the central 95% of the normal distribution lies within ± 1.96 Z variates (2.5% of the total area is in each tail of the normal curve).

With this information we can then set up the 95% confidence interval as

$$\bar{X} \pm 1.96\sigma_{\bar{x}} = 2.6 \pm 1.96(0.03)$$

and we note that the 95% confidence interval ranges from 2.54 to 2.66 pints.

Traditional statistics makes the following points with regard to confidence intervals:

1. The confidence limits (end points of the interval) are computed from samples and, hence, are also subject to sampling fluctuations.
2. In repeated samples, therefore, the confidence interval will vary from sample to sample.
3. The parameter being estimated, whatever it is, is assumed to be fixed.
4. If the analyst were to repeat the process of taking random samples of a given size and computing, via a prescribed way, a larger number of confidence intervals, any *single* interval would either include or not include the parameter.
5. Probability statements (i.e., levels of confidence) thus pertain to the *process* by which the intervals are computed.
6. The analyst can state: "If I were to take repeated random samples of a given size and compute (in a specified manner) confidence intervals, in the long run, $x\%$ of the intervals so computed would contain the population value. This $x\%$ is the confidence coefficient associated with the process of computing intervals."

Thus, the *preassigned* chance of finding the true population mean to be within 2.54 and 2.66 pints is 95%.

This basic idea can be adapted for finding the appropriate *sample size* that will lead to a certain desired confidence interval. To illustrate, let us now suppose that a researcher is interested in estimating annual per capita consumption of domestic wines for adults living in a particular area of the United States. He knows that he can take a random sample of respondents in the area and compute a sample mean. However, what he really wants to do is be able to state with, say, 95% confidence that the *population* mean falls within some *allowable* interval, computed about the sample mean. He wants to find a sample size that will permit this kind of statement.

The Case of the Sample Mean

Let us first assume that the allowable error is 0.5 gallon per capita and the level of confidence 95%. With this in mind, one goes through the following checklist:

1. *Specify the amount of error (E) that can be allowed.* This is the maximum allowable difference between the sample mean and the population mean. $\bar{X} \pm E$, therefore, defines the interval within which μ will lie with some prespecified level of confidence. In our example, the allowable error is set at $E = 0.5$ gallon per year.
2. *Specify the desired level of confidence.* In our illustrative problem

involving domestic wine consumption, the confidence level is set at
95%.

3. *Determine the number of standard errors (Z) associated with the
   confidence level.* This is accomplished by use of a table of probabilities for a normal distribution. For a 95% confidence level, reference
   to Table A-1 indicates that the Z value that allows a 0.025 probability
   that the population mean will fall outside *one* end of the interval is
   $Z = 1.96$. Since we can allow a *total* probability of 0.05 that the
   population mean will lie outside *either* end of the interval, $Z = 1.96$
   is the correct value for a 95% confidence level.

4. *Estimate the standard deviation of the population.* The standard
   deviation can be estimated by judgment, reference to other studies,
   or by the use of a pilot sample. Suppose that the standard deviation
   of the area's population for domestic wine consumption is assumed
   to be 4.0 gallons per capita per year.

5. *Calculate the sample size using the formula for the standard error of
   the mean.* One standard error of the mean is to be set equal to the
   allowable error $(E = 0.5)$ divided by the appropriate Z value of 1.96.

$$\sigma_{\bar{x}} = \frac{E}{Z} = \frac{0.5}{1.96} = 0.255$$

This will assure us that the interval to be computed around the
to-be-found sample mean will have a 95% preassigned chance of
being ± 0.5 gallon away from the population mean.

6. Neglecting the finite multiplier, we then solve for n in the formula

$$\sigma_{\bar{x}} = \frac{E}{Z} = \frac{\sigma}{\sqrt{n}}$$

or

$$\sigma_{\bar{x}} = 0.255 = \frac{4.0}{\sqrt{n}}$$

Hence,

$$n \cong 246 \quad \text{(rounded)}$$

7. In general, we can find n directly from the formula

$$n = \frac{\sigma^2 Z^2}{E^2} = \frac{16(1.96)^2}{(0.5)^2} \cong 246$$

A *nomograph* (Figure 7-1) has been developed which eliminates the
need for calculation of sample sizes in estimation problems involving means.

Figure 7-1 Nomograph for determining sample size for interval estimates of the mean using traditional methods of inference

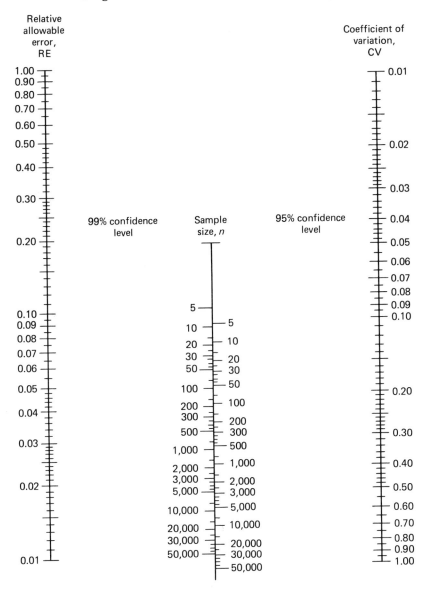

Source: *Nomograms for Marketing Research* (Audits and Surveys, Inc.), with permission.

To use the nomograph it is necessary to specify the allowable error as a fraction of the assumed population mean to give the *relative allowable error* (RE). It is also necessary to estimate the variability as a ratio of the standard deviation to the mean to give the *coefficient of variation* (CV).

As an example, let us return to the domestic wine problem. Now assume that the researcher believes that the population mean will be around 4 gallons per capita. If the allowable error is still 0.5 gallon, then the *relative* allowable error is RE = 0.5/4 = 0.125. The coefficient of variation CV is defined as

$$CV = \frac{\sigma}{\bar{X}} = \frac{4.0}{4} = 1$$

The resulting sample size can be read off from Figure 7-1, where a straightedge from RE = 0.125 to CV = 1 crosses the column marked sample size for a 95% confidence interval. The indicated sample size is approximately 250 respondents and, hence, in line with the more precise (computed) value of 246. (Note that Figure 7-1 also provides a scale for the 99% confidence case. In this illustration a sample size of slightly over 400 would be required.)

The reader should also note that the approximate sample size, as determined by the nomograph, is not dependent on the assumed mean. For example, if the assumed mean is 10, then RE = 0.5/10 = 0.05 and CV = 4/10 = 0.4. As noted from Figure 7-1, the approximate sample size is still 250 respondents. The sole purpose of using the assumed mean is to provide *relative* values so that single scales for RE and CV can be employed.

The Case of the Sample Proportion

Suppose that, in addition to estimating the mean number of gallons of domestic wine consumed per capita per year, the researcher is also concerned with estimating the proportion of respondents using one or more domestic wines in the past year. How should the sample size be determined in this case?

The procedures for determining sample size for interval estimates of proportions are very similar to those for interval estimates of means. In this case the following checklist would be followed:

1. *Specify the amount of error that can be allowed.* Suppose that the desired reliability is such that an allowable interval of $p - \pi = \pm 0.05$ is set; that is, the allowable error E is 0.05, or 5 percentage points.

2. *Specify the desired level of confidence.* Suppose that the level of confidence here, as in the preceding problem, is set at 95%.

3. *Determine the number of standard errors Z associated with the confidence level.* This will be the same as for the preceding estimation; $Z = 1.96$.

4. *Estimate the population proportion* (π). The population proportion can again be estimated by judgment, by reference to other studies, or by the results of a pilot sample. Suppose that π is assumed to be 0.4 in this case; that is, the researcher assumes that 40% of the population used one or more domestic wines last year.

5. *Calculate the sample size using the formula for the standard error of the proportion.* One standard error of the proportion is to be set equal to the allowable error ($E = 0.05$) divided by the appropriate Z value of 1.96.

$$\sigma_{\hat{p}} = \frac{E}{Z} = \frac{0.05}{1.96} = 0.0255$$

6. Neglecting the finite multiplier, we then solve for n in the formula

$$\sigma_{\hat{p}} = \frac{E}{Z} = \sqrt{\frac{\pi(1 - \pi)}{n}}$$

$$= 0.0255 = \sqrt{\frac{0.4(0.6)}{n}}$$

Hence,

$$n \cong 369 \quad \text{(rounded)}$$

7. In general, we can find n directly from the formula

$$n = \frac{\pi(1 - \pi)Z^2}{E^2} = \frac{0.4(1 - 0.4)(1.96)^2}{(0.05)^2} \cong 369$$

As was the case for the mean problem, a *nomograph* exists for determining sample size for proportions. One can determine the sample size directly from Figure 7-2 by placing a straightedge from $\pi = 0.4$ (40%) through an allowable error of $E = 5$ percent and reading the number on the sample-size column on the right. The indicated sample size is approximately 370 respondents, which agrees closely with the more precise (computed) value of 369.

Determining Sample Size When More Than One Interval Estimate Is to Be Made from the Same Sample

The usual case when collecting sample data for estimation of various parameters is that more than one estimate is to be made. The sample size for each of the estimates will usually be different. Since only one sample is to be chosen, what size should it be?

Figure 7-2   Nomograph for determining sample size
for interval estimates of a proportion
using traditional methods of inference

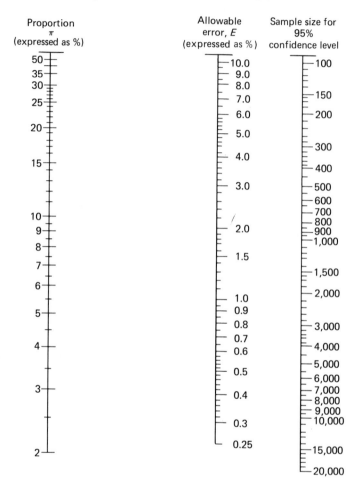

| Proportion
π
(expressed as %) | Allowable
error, E
(expressed as %) | Sample size for
95%
confidence level |

Source: *Nomograms for Marketing Research* (Audits and Surveys, Inc.), with permission.

A strict adherence to the allowable error and the confidence levels specified in the calculation of the sample sizes for the individual estimation problems leaves no choice but to take the *largest* sample size calculated. This will give more precision for the other estimates than was specified but will meet the specification for the estimate for which that size of sample was calculated.

In the domestic wine consumption problem, for example, the sample size would be 369 (the sample size calculated for estimating the proportion of users) rather than 246 (the sample size calculated for estimating the mean amount used).

In practice, the nomographs of Figures 7-1 and 7-2 usually provide sufficient accuracy to be quite helpful in rough-guide situations where the researcher is not all that sure of either allowable error levels or population standard deviations. Many marketing research firms use these kinds of nomographs on a routine basis.

The Hypothesis-Testing Approach

As indicated earlier, sample sizes can also be determined (within the apparatus of traditional statistical inference) by the hypothesis-testing approach. In this case the procedures are more elaborate. We shall need both an assumed probability of making a type I error—called the *alpha risk*—and an assumed probability of making a type II error—called the *beta risk*. These risks are, in turn, based on two hypotheses:

H_0: the null hypothesis
H_1: the alternate hypothesis

As recalled from basic statistics, in hypothesis testing the sample results sometimes lead us to reject H_0 when it is true. This is a type I error. On other occasions the sample findings may lead us to accept H_0 when it is false. This is a type II error. The nature of these errors is shown in Table 7-1.

Table 7-1 Types of error in making a wrong decision

Act	H_0 Is True	H_0 Is False
Accept H_0	No error	Type II error
Reject H_0	Type I error	No error

The symbol α (alpha) is used to denote the probability of making a type I error, while the symbol β (beta) is used to denote the probability of making a type II error. These background concepts are used in the hypothesis-testing approach to sample-size determination.

A numerical example should make this approach clearer. We first consider the case for means and then the case for proportions.

The Case Involving Means

As an illustrative example, let us assume that a store test of a new bleaching agent is to be conducted. It has been determined earlier that if the (population) sales per store average only 7 cases per week, the new product should not be marketed. On the other hand, a mean sales level of 10 cases per week would justify marketing the new product nationally. Using methods of traditional inference, how should the number of sample stores for the market test be determined?

The procedures are similar to those for interval estimation problems, but are somewhat more complicated. Specifically, we go through the following checklist:

1. *Specify the values for the null (H_0) and the alternate (H_1) hypotheses to be tested in terms of population means, μ_0 and μ_1, respectively.* (By convention, the null hypothesis is the one that would result in no change being made, if accepted.) In the bleach-market-introduction problem, the values are set at H_0: $\mu_0 = 7$ cases per week, and H_1: $\mu_1 = 10$ cases per week.
2. *Specify the allowable probabilities (α and β, respectively) of a type I and type II error.* The type I error is the error of rejecting a true

Figure 7-3   Alpha and beta risks in the hypothesis-testing approach

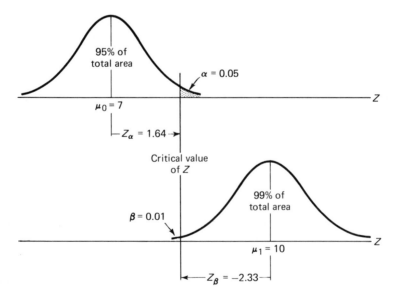

null hypothesis. The type II error is made when the alternate hypothesis is rejected when it is true. α and β are the allowable *probabilities* of making those two types of errors, respectively. They are shown graphically in Figure 7-3, where we assume that in the bleach-introduction problem the allowable probabilities of error are assigned as $\alpha = 0.05$ and $\beta = 0.01$.

3. *Determine the number of standard errors associated with each of the error probabilities α and β.* For a one-tailed test the Z values for the 0.05 and 0.01 risks, respectively, are found from Table A-1 in Appendix A to be $Z_\alpha = 1.64$ and $Z_\beta = 2.33$. These are shown in Figure 7-3. Note that in the figure we affix a *minus sign* to the value of Z_β since the critical value lies to the left of $\mu_1 = 10$.

4. *Estimate the population standard deviation σ.* In the case of the new bleach the standard deviation of cases sold per store per week is assumed to be 5 cases.

5. *Calculate the sample size that will meet the α and β error requirements.* Since *two* sampling distributions are involved, a simultaneous solution of two equations is required to determine the sample size and critical value that will satisfy both equations. These equations are:

$$\text{critical value} = \mu_0 + Z_\alpha \frac{\sigma}{\sqrt{n}}$$

$$\text{critical value} = \mu_1 - Z_\beta \frac{\sigma}{\sqrt{n}}$$

6. Setting the right-hand side of these two equations equal and solving for n gives

$$n = \frac{(Z_\alpha + Z_\beta)^2 \sigma^2}{(\mu_1 - \mu_0)^2}$$

In the bleach problem the desired sample size is

$$n = \frac{(1.64 + 2.33)^2 5^2}{(10 - 7)^2} \cong 44 \text{ stores} \quad \text{(rounded)}$$

Having solved for n, the sample size, we can then go on to solve for the critical value for the mean number of cases, by means of the substitution[12]

$$\text{critical value} = \mu_1 - Z_\beta \frac{\sigma}{\sqrt{n}}$$

$$= 10 - (2.33) \frac{5}{\sqrt{44}}$$

$$= 8.24 \text{ cases}$$

The decision rule then becomes: "Take a sample of 44 stores for the controlled store test. If the mean number of cases of the new bleach sold per week in the sample stores is less than or equal to 8.24 cases, do not introduce the product. If the mean number of cases of bleach sold per week is greater than 8.24 cases, introduce the product."

The Case Involving Proportions

For sample-size determination involving proportions, the following analogous steps are required:

1. *Specify the values of the null (H_0) and the alternate (H_1) hypotheses to be tested in terms of population proportions, π_0 and π_1, respectively.*
2. *Specify the allowable probabilities (α and β, respectively) of type I and type II errors.*
3. *Determine the number of standard errors associated with each of these error probabilities (Z_α and Z_β).*
4. *Calculate the desired sample size n from the formula:*

$$n = \left[\frac{Z_\alpha\sqrt{\pi_0(1 - \pi_0)} + Z_\beta\sqrt{\pi_1(1 - \pi_1)}}{\pi_1 - \pi_0} \right]^2$$

This formula is appropriate for relatively large samples ($n \geq 100$) where the normal distribution is a good approximation to the binomial. To illustrate its application, suppose that a researcher is interested in the true proportion of residents in a large city who would be willing to pay over $200 for a portable refrigerator–bar combination if it were commercialized.

Assume that the marketing researcher would recommend commercialization of the firm's refrigerator–bar combination if the true proportion of consumers who would pay over $200 for this class of goods is 70%. If the proportion is only 60%, he would not recommend commercialization. He

---

[12]Alternatively, we could find the critical value from the first of the two equations:

$$\text{critical value} = 7 + (1.64)\frac{5}{\sqrt{44}} = 8.24$$

then sets up the hypotheses:

$$H_0 : \pi_0 = 0.6$$
$$H_1 : \pi_1 = 0.7$$

The alpha risk associated with the null (status quo) hypothesis is selected by the researcher to be 0.05 *if* the true proportion π is equal to 0.6. Moreover, he is willing to assume a beta risk of 0.1 if the true proportion is equal to 0.7. With these assumptions it is possible to obtain the approximate sample size by using the formula above:

$$n = \left[\frac{Z_\alpha \sqrt{\pi_0(1 - \pi_0)} + Z_\beta \sqrt{\pi_1(1 - \pi_1)}}{\pi_1 - \pi_0} \right]^2$$

where $Z_\alpha = Z_{0.05} = 1.64$, $Z_\beta = Z_{0.1} = 1.28$, $\pi_0 = 0.6$, and $\pi_1 = 0.7$. The solution is

$$n = \left[\frac{1.64\sqrt{0.6(0.4)} + 1.28\sqrt{0.7(0.3)}}{0.7 - 0.6} \right]^2$$

$$\cong 193 \quad \text{(rounded)}$$

Accordingly, in this example the sample size to take is 193. The critical value can be found analogously as

$$\text{critical value} = \pi_1 - Z_\beta \sqrt{\frac{\pi_1(1 - \pi_1)}{n}}$$

$$= 0.7 - (1.28)\sqrt{\frac{0.7(0.3)}{193}}$$

$$= 0.658$$

In this case the decision rule is: "Take a sample of 193 residents. If the sample proportion who would pay over \$200 is less than or equal to 0.658, do not commercialize the refrigerator–bar combination. If the sample proportion exceeds 0.658, commercialize the product."

Determining Sample Size for Other Random-Sample Designs

Thus far we have discussed only the determination of *simple* random-sample sizes using the methods of traditional statistical inference. How are the sizes for other types of random-sample designs—systematic, stratified, cluster, area, and multistage—determined?

The answer to this question is that the same *general* procedures are used to determine the overall sample size but the formulas for the standard errors differ. The formulas become more complex and difficult to estimate as one considers stratified sampling, cluster sampling, or the other more elaborate designs. This is because the standard error for these designs is partially a function of the standard deviation (or proportion) of each stratum or cluster included in the design. For a multistage sample consisting of several strata in one stage followed by clusters in another and systematic sampling in a third, the standard error formula can become very complex indeed. And once the overall sample size is determined, it must be apportioned among the strata and clusters, which also adds to the complexity.

Appropriate formulas for estimating standard errors and sample sizes for other random-sample designs are available elsewhere.[13] In general, as compared with the size of simple-random samples, systematic samples may be the same (since, for purposes of calculating the standard error, the assumption is typically made that the systematic sample *is* a simple random sample). Stratified samples are usually smaller, and cluster samples will usually be larger in size to provide the same reliability as a simple random sample.

THE BAYESIAN APPROACH
TO SAMPLE-SIZE DETERMINATION

In the treatment of the traditional approach to sample-size determination the underlying concepts were discussed and formulas were then developed. Here we shall describe the concepts on which the Bayesian procedures are based but no attempt will be made to develop formulas. The reason for this is that calculating optimal sample sizes is much more difficult under the Bayesian approach.

Bayesian procedures are based on the central principle (first described in Chapter 2) that one should

> *select that sample size that results in the largest positive difference between the expected payoff of sample information and the estimated cost of sampling.*

The difference between the expected payoff of sample information and the estimated cost of sampling is frequently referred to as the *expected net gain from sampling.* An equivalent way of stating the principle above is that one should *select the sample size that leads to the largest expected net gain from sampling.*

[13]See, for example, Leslie Kish, *Survey Sampling* (New York: John Wiley & Sons, Inc., 1965).

In a decisional situation in which one of the primary objectives is to maximize payoff, this rule is a sound prescription. The general approach to applying it requires the decision maker to:

1. *Determine the expected value of sample information for a given sample size.*

2. *Estimate the sampling cost for that specific option.*

3. *Find the expected net gain from sampling under that option.*

4. *Search through other sample sizes to find the one that leads to the highest expected net gain from sampling.*

While logically sound and intuitively appealing in concept, the Bayesian approach is difficult to implement. The primary problem comes in operationalizing the first of the steps stated above. In order to determine the expected value of sample information for a given sample size, one must relate the sample size being considered to the *conditional probabilities of making errors*, including the effects of *nonsampling errors*. In realistic sampling situations, this can become very difficult to do. (The accurate estimation of nonsampling errors, in particular, is not an easy task.)

Once the conditional probabilities of making errors are determined, one goes through the procedures described in Chapter 2 for determining the expected value of the sample information. That is, estimates of the *conditional costs of errors* (the payoffs) and the *prior probabilities* of the decision maker are obtained, and the difference in the expected value, with and without the sample information, is calculated. This is the *expected value of sample information* for the size and design of the sample being considered (step 1 above).

It is then necessary to estimate the *cost of sampling* for that option (step 2).[14] Subtracting the estimated sampling cost from the expected value of sample information (step 3) gives the *expected net gain from sampling* (ENGS).

ENGS is computed for each of the potential sample sizes to find the one that provides the highest ENGS (step 4). The necessity to search through the entire range of potential sample sizes usually dictates the use of computer programs for problems of realistic size and complexity.[15] Owing to the general complexity of the technique, this section has provided only a brief overview of the Bayesian approach to sample-size determination. The reader interested

[14]For a discussion of estimating sampling costs see Seymour Sudman, *Applied Sampling* (New York: Academic Press, Inc., 1976), Chap. 5, and Kish, *Survey Sampling*, Chap. 8.

[15]See Robert Schlaifer, *Computer Programs for Elementary Decision Analysis* (Cambridge, Mass.: Division of Research, Graduate School of Business Administration, Harvard University, 1971).

in more detailed exposition of the underlying theory and of the specific procedures is advised to examine material by Sudman, Brown, and Mayer.[16]

EVALUATION OF THE TRADITIONAL AND BAYESIAN APPROACHES

If one were to devise the ideal method of determining sample size, as a minimum one would want it to meet the criteria of being: (1) logically complete, (2) adaptable to a wide range of sampling situations, and (3) simple to use. If the traditional (Neyman–Pearson) approach to sample-size determination were to be rated on these criteria the rating would be *low* for logical completeness and *high* for both adaptability and simplicity. By contrast, the Bayesian approach would rate *high* on logical completeness but *low* on adaptability and simplicity of use.

The traditional approach is logically *in*complete since sample size is specified as being a function only of the conditional probabilities of making errors. Consideration of the conditional costs of wrong decisions, prior probabilities, nonsampling errors, and the cost of sampling are not included in the model.[17]

The fact that these variables are excluded implies that somehow they must be taken into account *outside* the model. However, the only way that accommodation can be made is through adjustment of either the specified confidence level or the assigned alpha and beta risks.

Despite the fact that the Bayesian approach is a logically complete model for determining sample size in a decisional situation, its lack of adaptability and its complexity of use have resulted in only limited application. It is ironic that a methodology that is statistically sound and includes all the relevant variables also becomes so unwieldy that it is seldom used.

The traditional approach has been under development and use for more than 75 years. The (modern form of the) Bayesian model is much newer, having been developed in the late 1950s. With the advent of new computer programs and greater dissemination of the basic methodology, the Bayesian approach could become much more widely used in the future.

SUMMARY

In this chapter we have been concerned with the questions of whether to take a census or a sample and, when sampling, what type and size of sample to take.

---

[16]Sudman, *Applied Sampling*, Chap. 5; R. V. Brown, "Evaluation of Total Survey Error," *Journal of Marketing Research*, 4 (May, 1967), 117–27; Charles Mayer, "Assessing the Accuracy of Marketing Research," *Journal of Marketing Research*, 7 (August, 1970), 285–91.

[17]More advanced texts, however, do consider traditional sample-size determination by means of formulas that include the costs of sampling. For example, see Cochran, *Sampling Techniques*, Chap. 4.

Sampling by whatever method requires statistical reasoning. We first described briefly the development of statistical reasoning from the beginning of traditional methods of drawing statistical inferences through the more recent emergence of Bayesian inferential methods. We then considered the question of when a sample, rather than a census, should be taken, followed by a discussion of the various kinds of samples and the decisions concerning which kind to choose.

One of the most difficult problems in research design is the one concerned with the *size* of sample to take. We first discussed the determination of sample size from the standpoint of traditional inferential methods. A brief discussion of the rationale of sample-size determination from the Bayesian point of view was then given. We concluded the chapter with an evaluation of the two approaches to determining sample size.

ASSIGNMENT MATERIAL

1. Annual incomes of the 900 salespeople employed by the Lodish Hide Company are known to be approximately normally distributed. Last year the mean income of the group was $8,000 and the standard deviation of incomes was $1,000. Using Table A-1 in Appendix A:
   a. What per cent of salespeople were paid either more than $9,500 or between $7,500 and $8,500?
   b. What was the income level that was exceeded by 10% of the salespeople?
   c. This year (based on nine months' experience extrapolated to a one-year basis), a random sample of 49 of Lodish's salespeople was selected. What is the probability that the sample arithmetic mean would differ from last year's population mean by more than $150 (assuming no change in parameter values and neglecting the finite multiplier)?
   d. Now assume that the sample mean indicated $8,100 with a sample standard deviation (computed with $n - 1$ in the denominator) of $900. What is the probability of getting at least this large a sample mean given no change in last year's population mean of $8,000?
   e. If the company wants to be 95% "confident" that the true mean of this year's salespeople's income does not differ by more than 2% of last year's mean of $8,000, what size of sample would be required (assuming a population standard deviation of $1,000 and neglecting the finite multiplier)?
2. Past information about the proportion of shoppers in a large city who would be receptive to saving trading stamps indicates a figure of somewhere around 80%. Suppose that a supermarket chain would

adopt a trading stamp plan if the *true* proportion were 80%; if the true proportion were only 70%, it would not. The null and alternative hypotheses are as follows:

$$H_0: \pi_0 = 0.7$$
$$H_1: \pi_1 = 0.8$$

Assuming an alpha risk of 0.1 if $\pi_0 = 0.7$ and a beta risk of 0.2 if the true proportion were 0.8, what is the appropriate sample size (using traditional methods)?

3. The Wind Power and Light Company has recently launched a public relations campaign to persuade their subscribers to reduce the wasteful use of electricity. The firm's marketing research codirectors, Frank Carmine and Douglas Karrell, believe that about 40% of the subscribers are aware of the campaign. They wish to find out how large a sample would be needed to be 95% confident that the true proportion is within $\pm 3\%$ of the sample proportion.
   a. Solve the problem analytically via the confidence-interval approach.
   b. Solve the problem by recourse to the nomograph of Figure 7-2.
   c. If one sets up the hypotheses:

   $$H_0: \pi_0 = 0.4$$
   $$H_1: \pi_1 = 0.5$$

   with an alpha risk of 0.1 and a beta risk of 0.05 if $\pi_1 = 0.5$, what is the appropriate sample size under the hypothesis-testing approach?
   d. What is the implied decision rule?
4. If $n = 100$ and $N = 10,000$ and it is assumed that $\sigma = 2$, compute the standard error of the mean, first using the finite multiplier and then without. How large would the sample size n have to be (given $N = 10,000$) to make the standard error of the mean equal to 0.05?
5. Discuss how one might modify quota sampling to make it more closely approximate stratified random sampling.

Tabulation
of Survey Data

8

INTRODUCTION

With all the advances that have been made in the development of techniques for analyzing respondent data, the preparation of marginal (single-variable) and cross tabulations (two or more variables) continues to be the bread-and-butter business of the market survey analyst. It is easy to slight these procedures in favor of more esoteric methods; hence, this chapter has been prepared to illustrate their value in a piece of actual research.

This chapter departs somewhat from preceding ones in that it represents, in large part, a case application of survey research. After a brief introduction to some of the fundamentals of data tabulation, we describe an actual study (albeit one based on a small and nonrandomly selected sample) in which all data are real. Although other commercial studies—using larger and more representative samples—could have been chosen instead, the data would have required disguising in order to maintain sponsor confidentiality. (Here only the sponsor's name is withheld.)

While our discussion of this case is limited mainly to descriptive tools, we do focus on some of the broader substantive questions of problem formulation, questionnaire design, choice of variables for analysis, and so on. Indeed, the purpose here is partly integrative in nature, that is, to illustrate some of the principles discussed earlier in a type of case format that follows from study of a real problem.

The format of the chapter is arranged in two major sections. We first discuss some of the general characteristics of data coding and tabulation. The case study is then introduced and some of these general principles are applied to the basic data bank of the study.

GENERAL COMMENTS ON DATA TABULATION

Complete books could be written on various problems associated with data tabulation. Our discussion here will be comparatively brief. We consider basic aspects of the task: (1) the establishment of response categories, (2) editing and coding, and (3) tabulation. As simple as these steps are from a technical standpoint, they merit introductory discussion, prior to presenting the case study.

The Establishment of Categories

Analysis of any sizable array of data often requires that it be grouped into categories or classes. The early establishment of response categories has several advantages. It forces the analyst to consider alternative responses in more detail and often leads to improvements in the questionnaire or observation forms. It permits more detailed instruction of interviewers with a resulting higher consistency of interpretation and reduction in editing problems. Precoding of collection forms is often possible and has the advantage of reducing the amount of transcription required, with a decrease in both processing errors and costs.

As desirable as the early establishing of categories is, sometimes it can be done only after the data have been collected. This is usually the case when free-answer, or open-end, questions, unstructured interviews, and projective techniques are used. The varieties of responses to questions such as "Why do you prefer brand X cooking sherry?" have startled many a researcher. Some of the classes of responses to questions such as these are unlikely to be anticipated, even by the experienced analyst.

The selection of categories is controlled by both the purposes of the study and the nature of the responses. Useful classifications meet the following conditions:

1. *Similarity of responses within categories.* Each category should contain responses which, for purposes of the study, are sufficiently similar that they can be considered homogeneous.
2. *Differences of responses between categories.* Differences in category descriptions should be great enough to disclose any important distinctions in the characteristic being examined.
3. *Mutually exclusive categories.* There should be an unambiguous description of categories, defined so that any response can be placed in only one category.
4. *Categories should be exhaustive.* The partitioning should provide categories for all responses.

The employment of extensive open-end questions is a practice often associated with fledgling researchers. Open-end questions, of course, have their place in marketing research. However, the researcher should be aware of the difficulties that they can make for questionnaire coding and tabulation, not to mention their tendency to be more burdensome to the respondent. All of this is by way of saying that any open-end question should be carefully checked to see if a closed-end question (i.e., "check the appropriate box") can be substituted without doing violence to the intent of the question.

Editing and Coding

Editing

Editing is the process of reviewing the data to ensure maximum accuracy and unambiguity. Editing should be conducted as quickly as possible after the data have been collected. This applies to the editing of the collection forms used for pretesting as well as those for the full-scale project. Careful editing early in the collection process will often catch misunderstandings of instructions, errors in recording, and other problems at a stage when it is still possible to eliminate them from the later stages of the study. Early editing has the additional advantage of permitting the questioning of interviewers while the material is still relatively fresh in their minds.

Editing is normally centralized so as to ensure consistency and uniformity in treatment of the data. If the sample is not large, a single editor usually edits all the data to reduce variation in treatment. In those cases where the size of the project makes the use of more than one editor mandatory, it is usually best to assign each editor a different portion of the collection form to edit. In this way the same editor edits the same items on all forms, an arrangement that tends to improve both consistency and productivity.

Each collection form should be edited to ensure that the following requirements are fulfilled:

1. *Legibility of entries.* Obviously the data must be legible in order to be used. If an entry cannot be deciphered, and clarification of it cannot be obtained from the interviewer, it is sometimes possible to infer what it should be from other data on the form. In cases where any real doubt exists about the meaning of the entry, however, it should not be used.

2. *Completeness of entries.* On a fully structured collection form, the absence of an entry is ambiguous. It may mean that the interviewer failed to attempt to obtain the data, that the respondent could not or would not provide it, or that there was a failure to record collected data. If the omission was the result of the interviewer's not recording the data, prompt questioning of the interviewer may provide the

missing entry. If the omission was the result of either of the first two possible causes, it is still desirable to know which was the case.

3. *Consistency of entries*. As is the case with two watches that show different times, an entry that is inconsistent with another raises the question of which is correct. (If a respondent family is indicated as being a "nonuser" of cooking sherry, for example, and a later entry indicates that they purchased six bottles during the past month, an obvious question arises as to which is correct.) Again, such discrepancies should be cleared up by questioning of the interviewer, if it is possible to do so. When they cannot be resolved, discarding both entries is usually the wisest course of action.

4. *Accuracy of entries*. An editor should keep an eye out for any indications of inaccuracies of the data. Of particular importance is the detecting of any repetitive response patterns in the reports of individual interviewers. Such patterns may well be indicative of systematic interviewer bias or dishonesty.

Coding

Coding is the process by which responses are assigned to data categories and symbols (usually numbers) are assigned to identify them with the categories. *Precoding* results when codes are assigned to categories on structured questionnaires and observation forms *before* the data are collected. The interviewer, in effect, does the coding in this situation when he interprets the response and decides into which category it should be placed.

Postcoding, the assignment of codes to responses *after* the data are collected, is required for responses reported on unstructured forms. The assignment of codes to responses is normally done at the same time the data are edited. Careful interpretation and good judgment are required to ensure that the meaning of the response and the meaning of the category are consistently and uniformly matched.

An example of a simple and prevalent response that is often miscoded is the familiar "Don't Know" (DK). A respondent may give this reply for a variety of reasons; it may mean that he does not know the answer to the question. On the other hand, he may be undecided, he may be confused as to the meaning of the question, or he may use this reply to avoid giving an explicit answer. Good question construction and interviewing can do much to reduce the ambiguity of "Don't Know" answers. Careful coding can also assist in reducing this mismatching of response and category meaning.

Good coding requires training and supervision. The editor–coder should be provided with written instructions, including examples. He should be exposed to the interviewing or observing of respondents (whichever procedure is being used to collect the data) to acquaint him with the process and problems of collecting the data, and thus aid him in its interpretation. He should also be aware of the computer routines that are expected to be applied, insofar as they may require certain kinds of data formats.

Tabulation

Tabulating is the final step in the process. Tabulating is simply the counting of the number of responses in data categories.

The basic tabulation is the *simple tabulation*, often called the *marginal tabulation*, and familiar to all students of elementary statistics as the *frequency distribution*. A simple tabulation consists of a count of the number of responses that occur in each of the data categories that comprise a variable. An example is given in Table 8-1.

Table 8-1 Simple tabulation: cooking sherry purchased in past three months*

Number of Quarts	Number of Respondents
0	350
1	75
2	50
3 or more	25
Total	500

*Hypothetical data.

A *cross tabulation* is one of the more commonly employed and useful forms of tabulation for analytical purposes. *A cross tabulation involves the simultaneous counting of the number of observations that occur in each of the data categories of two or more variables.* An example is given in Table 8-2. We shall examine the use of cross tabulations in detail later in the chapter.

Tabulation can be done either by hand or by one of several mechanical methods. The choice of the method of tabulation to be used in a particular case is a function of the number of categories of data, the size of the sample, and the amount and kind of analyses to be performed. With few categories, a small sample, and limited analysis, hand tabulation is the fastest and least expensive method. As the number of categories, the size of the sample, and the amount and complexity of analysis required increase, a point is reached at which machine tabulation becomes more efficient. (In large-scale survey firms, programs for performing cross tabulation are a highly valued resource.)

Table 8-2   Cross tabulation: cooking sherry purchased
in past three months by income classes of respondents*

	NUMBER OF QUARTS PURCHASED				
				Three or	
INCOME CLASS	Zero	One	Two	More	Total
Less than $5,000	160	25	15	0	200
$5,000–$7,499	120	15	10	5	150
$7,500–$9,999	60	20	15	5	100
$10,000–$14,999	5	10	5	5	25
$15,000 and over	5	5	5	10	25
Total	350	75	50	25	500

*Hypothetical data.

Machine tabulation requires that the data be translated into machine language and transposed onto an input medium—punch cards, magnetic tape, paper tape, etc.—that the machine will accept. Preparation of the data is more expensive and time-consuming and must be carefully checked and rechecked at various stages to keep errors at a minimum. Once prepared, however, the tabulation and running of analytic calculations can be done quickly.

Although the use of machine tabulation provides added flexibility and ease of manipulation of data, these very features require that judgment and restraint be exercised in planning the tabulations to be made. There is a common tendency for the researcher to decide that, since cross tabulations (and correlations) are so easily obtained, large numbers of tabulations should be run. Not only is the way in which these tabulations are used frequently methodologically unsound, but it is costly in machine time and the time of the analyst as well. For 50 variables there are 1,225 different two-variable cross tabulations that can be made. Only a relatively few of these are potentially useful in a typical study.

We now turn to the case study.

A CASE STUDY: THE MANAGEMENT PROBLEM

The market for women's hair shampoos has become highly specialized and segmented. In recent years a large number of special-purpose shampoos have appeared on the market, each promising to provide various hair care benefits to the potential user. The sponsor of the study to be reported here is a diversified manufacturer of consumer packaged goods. At the time of the study the firm had no women's shampoo in its product line.

The firm's marketing research personnel met with one of the authors to discuss the possibility of a "live" class project—with findings to be considered nonconfidential—that might be undertaken in the Philadelphia area among young female adults living in the environs of the University of Pennsylvania.

The sponsor's representatives had established—through a series of recently completed interviews with small groups of women consumers—that "body" (apparently connoting hair thickness or fullness) in a hair shampoo was frequently mentioned as a desired characteristic. Armed with this still rather sketchy information concerning the desirability of "body" in a shampoo, the firm's laboratory personnel had set to work on developing some prototypical compounds that appeared potentially capable of delivering this characteristic to a greater extent than brands currently on the market.

During the initial conversations, the following managerial problems came to light:

1. Assuming that laboratory personnel could produce a woman's shampoo with superior "body," is the market for this product large enough to justify its commercialization?

2. What benefits in addition to "body" should be incorporated in the new shampoo?

3. What are the characteristics—product usage, hair type, demographics —of respondents who are particularly attracted to a shampoo with "body?" (Knowledge of these characteristics would be desirable in defining the target segment for the new product.)

4. How should the concept of "body" in shampoo be communicated; what does the *consumer* mean by "body" in shampoo? (Knowledge of the connotations of "body" would be valuable in the design of promotional messages and point-of-purchase materials.)

It is appropriate to note that the study's sponsors had relatively little to go on in the way of secondary sources of information because their firm had no entry in the field. While various market statistics could be obtained for existing brands, the firm was primarily interested in characteristics appropriate for a relatively new concept in the marketplace—a shampoo that emphasized "body."

Problem Structuring

Although formal statistical decision analysis was not applied in this case, it became apparent that the firm faced three primary courses of action:

1. Continue technical development of a new shampoo that delivers the consumer benefit: "body."
2. Terminate technical development related to this characteristic and switch effort to some other shampoo benefit.
3. Discontinue all effort in women's shampoo products.

Continuation of technical development on "body," in turn, is based on two considerations: (1) that the new product can be developed successfully from a technical standpoint, and (2) that the new product can be sold in sufficient quantities to justify future development outlays, start-up expense, ongoing production and marketing costs, plus earning an appropriate return on invested funds.

Informal analysis indicated a high probability of technical success during the ensuing 12 months with relatively modest additional outlays in technical resources. The major problem appeared to be one of market potential—more specifically, whether a target segment of sufficient size was available to warrant continued technical development and eventual commercialization.

Cost and Value of Marketing Research

Current uncertainties about potential demand for the new product suggested the desirability of conducting marketing research beyond the preliminary consumer group interviews that had recently been conducted by the firm. Crude estimates of the cost versus value of additonal information (including such aspects as the costs of continuing technical development and start up, the probability of technical and marketing "success," and the likelihood that survey results would correctly identify the appropriate state of nature) clearly indicated the advisability of further marketing research.

The problem was not whether more marketing research could be justified—the quickest and crudest estimates demonstrated its potential value—but, rather, what *kind of research* should be done that seemed most likely to answer management's questions. Indeed, the main purpose of the marketing personnel's visit was to discuss an exploratory study that could be helpful in designing the main study that was planned to be conducted on a national, probability-based sample. What should the main study cover? How could management's questions be translated into a research design? What additional research questions should be raised?

Parenthetically it is worth noting that most real studies start with only a single (and often vague) question or two. The dialogue that goes on between sponsor and researcher is frequently the most important part of the study. Often the sponsor has not thought very much about the research design.

However, he is in a good position to *react* to the researcher's questions about the people who should be interviewed, the variables that should be included, the desired reliability of results, and so on. While difficult to formalize, this dialogue, in effect, sets the framework, objectives, and constraints on the eventual research design.

THE RESEARCH DESIGN

Given the exploratory character of the research—and the sponsor's willingness to have it conducted as a graduate student project—questions of adequate sample size and representativeness were not of primary importance. What was germane to the pilot research was the need to translate management's questions into operational terms and, in the process, to develop additional questions of relevance to the design of the main piece of research, planned to be undertaken after the pilot results were analyzed.

The principal focus of the exploratory research was to be on shampoo benefits. In the course of conducting preliminary consumer group interviews the sponsor's marketing research personnel had assembled a list of approximately 30 benefits that had either been advertised or were thought by at least some consumers to be relevant in the choice of a hair shampoo. Not surprisingly, many of the benefit descriptions were redundant; hence, the first step was to trim down the list to a smaller set. Table 8-3 shows the 16 benefits that emerged from the culling process.

Table 8-3   List of 16 hair shampoo benefits used in questionnaire (white cards)

1. Hair Stays Clean a Long Time
2. Hair Stays Free of Dandruff or Flaking
3. Hair That Looks and Feels Natural
4. Hair That Has Body
5. Manageable Hair That Goes Where You Want It
6. Hair with Sheen or Luster
7. Hair with No Split Ends
8. Hair with Enough Protein
9. Hair That Doesn't Get Oily Fast
10. Hair That's Not Too Dry
11. Hair with Fullness
12. Hair That's Not Frizzy
13. Hair That Holds a Set
14. Hair with Texture
15. Hair That's Easy to Comb When It Dries
16. Hair That Looks Free and Casual

To check on the exhaustiveness of the final set, various shampoo advertisements were analyzed and some additional student interviews were made. This informal procedure suggested that the set in Table 8-3 was reasonably exhaustive of the things that women looked for in shampoos. And, in the process, it appeared as though the first 10 benefits were thought to be the more important of the 16. Indeed, the preliminary research suggested that the first 6 benefits probably constituted the "core set," i.e., those benefits of really primary importance to consumer choice.

A second matter of importance concerned the nature of respondents to be interviewed. The study's sponsor suggested a purposive sample of young female adults—aged 18 through 30—with an approximate 60–40 split between married and single. Only consumers who shampooed their hair at least twice a month, on the average, were to be interviewed. In brief, the sample was to be aimed at a specific age group of relatively active users of shampoo.

Key Research Questions

Given the emphasis placed on product benefit preferences, particularly the benefit of "body," a number of ancillary research questions were developed from the primary ones indicated by the sponsor:

1. How do consumers of hair shampoos perceive various benefits as commonly (or rarely) available in shampoos *currently* on the market?

2. Given freedom to make up her own"ideal" shampoo, what "bundles" of benefits do consumers want? Specifically, how often is "body" included in their ideal benefit bundles?

3. Assuming that a consumer desired and could get a shampoo that delivered "body," what *other* benefits are also desired in the same brand?

4. What is conjured up by the phrase "shampoo body" and its various connotations—that is, what words are elicited on a free-association basis?

5. How do preferences for "body" in shampoos relate to:
   a. Frequency of hair shampooing (i.e., heavy versus light users of shampoos)?
   b. Perceptions of its availability in current shampoos?
   c. Preference for other benefits in addition to "body"?
   d. Hair physiology and wearing style?
   e. Demographics (e.g, age, marital status, education, etc.)?

While other research questions could be and were raised, the foregoing ones set the stage for questionnaire development and data analysis.

Developing the Questionnaire

Once the major research questions had been thought through, development of the questionnaire and its pretest followed rather straightforwardly. Given the class project status of the study and the rather large number of questions to be raised—requiring the preparation of various interviewer "props"—the personal interview was selected as the mode of data collection.

The questionnaire is reproduced in Figure 8.1.[1] Note that the first two questions serve as screening criteria; in other words, to qualify for inclusion the respondent must: (1) shampoo her hair at home at least twice a month on the average and (2) be between 18 and 30 years of age.

Part A of the questionnaire first attempts to measure respondents' perceptions of the prevalence of each shampoo benefit in brands currently on the market. Then, respondents are allowed to choose from the total set of 16 benefits (see Table 8-3) those 4 benefits that they would most like to have in an "ideal" shampoo. Part B—using the first 10 benefits in Table 8-3—examines respondents' benefit preferences in a conditional sense, assuming that they could obtain a shampoo that delivered "body."

Part C deals with free-association data, whereas Part D requests information on hair style and hair problems. Part E is devoted to more or less standard questions dealing with demographic variables.

Administration

The questionnaire of Figure 8-1 was first administered on a pretest basis after class members reviewed its details and constructed the necessary interviewer props. Following this, the questionnaire was administered on a personal, in-the-home basis by class-member interviewers. Respondents were drawn from the University of Pennsylvania environs on a convenience basis. Interview time averaged about half an hour; all data were collected over the span of one week.

MARGINAL TABULATIONS

The first step in the analysis dealt with computing a series of marginal tabulations regarding the closed-end questions. These tabulations involved the total sample of 84 respondents.

---

[1]In order to simplify the subsequent analysis, the questionnaire of Figure 8-1 respresents an abridgement of the one actually used.

Figure 8-1   Questionnaire used in hair shampoo study

                    Time Interview Started_____
                                     Ended_____
Respondent Name_____   Respondent No._____
Address_____
City_____   State_____
Telephone No._____
Interviewer Name_____
Interview Date_____
Screening Questions (Part S)

   Hello, I'm_____of the Wharton School,
University of Pennsylvania. We're conducting a survey
on women's attitudes and opinions about hair care
products.
1. On the average, how often do you shampoo your hair
   at home?
        More than twice a week   _____
        Once or twice a week   _____
        Once or twice every two weeks _____
        Once or twice every three weeks _____
        Twice a month   _____
        Less than twice a month   _____
                                     IF LESS THAN TWICE A
                                     MONTH, TERMINATE
2. What is your age? _____
        (IF UNDER 18 OR OVER 30 TERMINATE)

PART A
   First I'm going to show you a set of 16 cards. Each
card contains the name of a benefit that a hair sham-
poo might provide. (PLACE SET OF WHITE CARDS ON TABLE
IN FRONT OF RESPONDENT.) Please take a few moments to
look over these benefits. (ALLOW TIME FOR RESPONDENT
TO STUDY THE CARDS.)
   Now, thinking about various brands of hair shampoo
that you have tried or heard about, pick out those
benefits that you think are most likely to be found
in almost any hair shampoo that one could buy today.
(RECORD CARD NUMBERS IN FIRST COLUMN OF RESPONSE FORM
A AND TURN SELECTED CARDS FACE DOWN.)
   Next, select all of those remaining benefits that
you think are available in at least some hair shampoo—but not necessarily all in a single brand—that's
currently on the market. (RECORD CARD NUMBERS IN

Figure 8-1   (cont.)

SECOND COLUMN OF RESPONSE FORM A. RECORD REMAINING
CARD NUMBERS IN THIRD COLUMN. THEN RETURN ALL CARDS
TO TABLE.

Next, imagine that you could make up an ideal type
of shampoo—one that might not be available on today's
market. Suppose, however, that you were restricted
to only four of the sixteen benefits shown on the
cards in front of you. Which four of the sixteen benefits would you most like to have? (RECORD CARD NUMBERS
IN FOURTH COLUMN OF RESPONSE FORM A.)

RESPONSE FORM A

(1)	(2)	(3)	(4)
Benefits Most Likely to be Found in Almost Any Hair Shampoo—Card Numbers	Benefits Available in Some Shampoo—Card Numbers	Remaining Benefits—Card Numbers	Four-Benefit Ideal Set—Card Numbers

PART B

Now, let's again return to some of the shampoo bene-
fits you have already dealt with. (SELECT WHITE CARD
NUMBERS 1 THROUGH 10; PULL OUT CARD 4 AND PLACE IT IN
FRONT OF RESPONDENT.)

Suppose a shampoo were on the market that primarily
stressed this benefit—"Produces Hair that Has Body."
If you could get a shampoo that made good on this
claim, which one of the remaining nine benefits would
you most like to have as well? (RECORD NUMBER IN
RESPONSE FORM B.) Which next most? (RECORD.) Please
continue until all of the 9 benefits have been ranked.

Figure 8-1 (cont.)

RESPONSE FORM B

(Enter Card Numbers 1 Through 10 Excluding Card #4)
( ) Most Like to Have   ( )
( ) Next Most   ( )
( )   ( )
( )   ( ) Least Most
( )

PART C

Now, I am going to read to you some short phrases about hair. Listen to each phrase carefully and then tell me what single words first come to your mind when you hear each phrase? (RECORD UP TO THE FIRST THREE "ASSOCIATIVE-TYPE" WORDS THE RESPONDENT SAYS AFTER EACH PHRASE IN RESPONSE FORM C.)

RESPONSE FORM C

(a) Hair that has body

_____   _____   _____

(b) Hair with fullness

_____   _____   _____

(c) Hair that holds a set

_____   _____   _____

(d) Bouncy hair

_____   _____   _____

(e) Hair that's not limp

_____   _____   _____

(f) Manageable hair

_____   _____   _____

(g) Zesty hair

_____   _____   _____

(h) Natural hair

_____   _____   _____

PART D

At this point I would like to ask you a few questions about your hair.

1. Does your hair have enough body?
                Yes_____   No_____

Figure 8-1 (cont.)

2. Do you have any special problems with your hair?
Yes_____   No_____
If yes, what types of problems?
_____

_____
_____

How would you describe your hair?
3. My hair type is:
Dry_____   Normal_____   Oily_____
4. The texture of my hair is:
Fine_____   Normal_____   Coarse_____
5. My hair style (the way I wear my hair) is:
Straight_____
Slightly wavy or curly_____
Very wavy or curly_____
6. The length of my hair is:
Short (to ear lobes)_____
Medium (ear lobes to shoulder)_____
Long (below shoulder)_____
7. How would you describe the thickness of your hair?
Thick_____   Medium_____   Thin_____

PART E
Now I would like to ask you a few background questions.
1. Are you working (at least twenty hours per week, for compensation)?
Yes_____   No_____
2. Are you married?
Yes_____   No_____
3. What is your level of education?
Some high school_____   Completed high
school_____   Some college_____
Completed college_____
4. (HAND RESPONDENT INCOME CARD.) Which letter on this card comes closest to describing your total annual family income before taxes? (CIRCLE APPROPRIATE LETTER.)

A. Under $3,000   E. $10,001-15,000
B. $3,000- 5,000   F. 15,001-20,000
C. 5,001- 7,000   G. Over $20,000
D. 7,001-10,000

(THANKS VERY MUCH FOR YOUR HELP)

Tabulations were first prepared for the "structured" parts of the questionnaire:

1. Frequency of the three categories of commonness–rareness in Part A, for each of the 16 benefits listed in Table 8-3.
2. Frequency with which each benefit appears in an ideal set (of 4), as also recorded in Part A of the questionnaire.
3. Frequency with which each of 9 benefits (first 10 listed in Table 8-3, excluding "body") is preferred to each of the other 8, as derived from the ranking of Part B.
4. Response frequencies associated with Parts D and E of the questionnaire (including the screening questions on hair washing frequency and respondent age).

The preparation of various marginal tabulations is a rather basic output of survey research and is often done at the outset in order that the researcher can get some quick, preliminary idea of the characteristics of his sample. Summary results appear in Table 8-4.[2]

Parts A and B of the questionnaire concern respondents' reactions to hair shampoo benefits. As can be noted from Part A of Table 8-4, benefit 4 ("body") is not viewed as a particularly rare shampoo benefit. Only 30% of the total sample view it as not currently available, a relative standing of eleventh out of 16. The rarest benefits are benefit 13 ("holds a set"), benefit 1 ("stays clean a long time"), benefit 11 ("hair with fullness"), and benefit 14 ("hair with texture").

"Body" is mentioned 34 out of 84 times (approximately 40%) as a member of the respondent's ideal set of 4. This represents a relative standing of seventh out of 16. The most popular benefits in the respondents' ideal sets are benefit 6 ("sheen or luster"), benefit 2 ("free of dandruff or flaking"), benefit 5 ("manageable hair"), and benefit 7 ("hair with no split ends"). Note that the rarest benefits, 13, 1, 11, and 14, do not correspond with those that receive the highest number of mentions as ideal-set members.

Part B shows that benefits 6 ("sheen or luster"), 2 ("free of dandruff or flaking"), and 1 ("stays clean a long time") receive highest preferences, given the presence of benefit 4 ("body"). Two of these—benefits 6 and 2— also appear with high frequency as members of respondents' ideal sets.

In summary, for the total sample, "body" is not highly distinguished from the standpoint of preference, nor is it thought to be extremely rare insofar as existing brands of shampoo are concerned. Benefits 6 ("sheen or

[2]Marginal tabulations for Parts D and E can be obtained from the cross tabulations, shown in Table 8-5.

luster") and 2 ("free of dandruff or flaking") are highly preferred—with or without "body"—but are not viewed as particularly rare. Finally, benefit 1 ("stays clean a long time") receives high preferences in Part B and is thought to be quite uncommon insofar as exising brands are concerned.

Table 8-4   Marginal tabulations—hair shampoo study
(sample size = 84)

Part A: Frequency and percentage with which each of three categories was checked regarding present availability of the 16 shampoo benefits of Table 8-3

Benefit	Found in Almost Any Shampoo	Per Cent	Available in Some Shampoo	Per Cent	Not Currently Available	Per Cent	Total Frequency	Per Cent
1	19	(23)	18	(21)	47	(56)	84	(100)
2	22	(26)	51	(61)	11	(13)	84	(100)
3	49	(59)	18	(21)	17	(20)	84	(100)
4	18	(21)	41	(49)	25	(30)	84	(100)
5	20	(24)	26	(31)	38	(45)	84	(100)
6	49	(59)	27	(32)	8	(9)	84	(100)
7	16	(19)	27	(32)	41	(49)	84	(100)
8	14	(17)	46	(55)	24	(28)	84	(100)
9	18	(22)	39	(46)	27	(32)	84	(100)
10	22	(26)	42	(50)	20	(24)	84	(100)
11	13	(15)	26	(31)	45	(54)	84	(100)
12	12	(14)	37	(44)	35	(42)	84	(100)
13	16	(19)	18	(22)	50	(59)	84	(100)
14	14	(17)	28	(33)	42	(50)	84	(100)
15	16	(19)	35	(42)	33	(39)	84	(100)
16	38	(45)	19	(23)	27	(32)	84	(100)

Part A: Frequency and percentage based on 84 respondents, with which each of 16 shampoo benefits of Table 8-3 appears in ideal set of 4

Benefit	Frequency	Per Cent	Benefit	Frequency	Per Cent
1	38	(45)	9	19	(23)
2	51	(61)	10	13	(15)
3	36	(43)	11	1	(1)
4	34	(40)	12	1	(1)
5	38	(45)	13	1	(1)
6	54	(64)	14	0	(0)
7	38	(45)	15	3	(4)
8	9	(11)	16	0	(0)

Table 8-4   (cont.)

Part B: Frequency with which each of 9 benefits (first 10 listed in Table 8-3, excluding "body") is preferred to each of the other 8

BENEFIT NUMBER	NUMBER OF TIMES COLUMN PREFERRED OVER ROW*								
	10	8	9	7	3	5	1	2	6
10	—	53	52	61	67	66	61	65	72
8	31	—	53	54	63	64	59	61	66
9	32	31	—	42	47	53	54	59	58
7	23	30	42	—	47	55	53	52	61
3	17	21	37	37	—	41	46	46	50
5	18	20	31	29	43	—	47	48	48
1	23	25	30	31	38	37	—	43	46
2	19	23	25	32	38	36	41	—	43
6	12	18	26	23	34	36	38	41	—
Column sum	175	221	296	309	377	388	399	415	444

*Columns and rows are permuted so that column sums progressively increase from left to right.

CROSS TABULATIONS

In any questionnaire of reasonable size the possibilities for cross tabulation of two or more variables become enormous. For example, if only ten questions were involved and we restricted ourselves to two-way comparisons, we could consider as many as 45 combinations (i.e., ten variables taken two at a time). Naturally, the total number of possibilities increases if we include three-way cross tabulations. Unless the sample size is very large, it is apparent that cell sizes for such higher-way cross tabulations will be quite small in many cases.[3] Consequently, the choice of key variables for cross tabulation with the remaining variables is usually based on strategic considerations.

In this study it seemed clear that one variable was of major importance —namely, whether the benefit "body" was included in the respondent's free choice of benefits appropriate for her four-element "ideal" shampoo (Part A).

As can be noted from Table 8-5, a total of 34 out of 84 respondents selected "body" as a member of their ideal set of 4 benefits. With this as a basic datum, we can cross-tabulate this partitioning of the sample with other variables in the questionnaire. These various cross tabulations also appear in Table 8.5.

[3]Given the small size (84 respondents) of our sample, all cross tabulations are restricted to the two-way case.

Few surprises are noted in Table 8-5. Insofar as Part A responses are concerned, we note that "body"-liking respondents tend to ascribe a lower subjective probability to the current availability of this benefit. Part B shows some difference between "body" likers and others insofar as conditional preferences are concerned. Those who include "body" in their ideal set most often mention "sheen or luster" as their first choice. Other first-choice mentions are rather dispersed over the remaining 8 benefits. Those respondents who do not include "body" in their ideal set most often mention "stays free of dandruff and flaking" and "stays clean a long time." The benefit "sheen or luster" ranks third in number of first-choice mentions for this group.

Part D shows (not surprisingly) that "body" likers tend to feel that their hair does not currently have enough "body" and report a higher incidence of special problems with their hair.[4] Moreover, their hair texture is felt to be

**Table 8-5   Cross tabulations of "body" as ideal-set member
with other responses (sample size = 84)**

Part A: Frequency with which "body" is viewed as presently available

	Found in Almost Any Shampoo	Found in Some Shampoos	Not Currently Available	Total
Body included in ideal set	9 (27)	13 (38)	12 (35)	34 (100)
Body excluded from ideal set	9 (28)	28 (56)	13 (26)	50 (100)
Total	18	41	25	84

Part B: Frequency of first-choice benefit, given the presence of "body"

	BENEFIT NUMBER*					OTHERS	
	1	*2*	*3*	*5*	*6*	*(7, 8, 9, or 10)*	*Total*
Body included in ideal set	4 (12)	5 (15)	3 (9)	5 (15)	10 (29)	7 (20)	34 (100)
Body excluded from ideal set	13 (26)	13 (26)	5 (10)	6 (12)	9 (18)	4 (8)	50 (100)
Total	17	18	8	11	19	11	84

*Benefit 4, "body," serves as the reference item and, hence, does not appear.

[4]Although not discussed here, the special problems associated with "body" likers not surprisingly centered on the lack of fullness and thickness. However, lack of luster was also mentioned rather frequently.

Table 8-5   (cont.)

Parts D and E: Frequencies of various hair style and background variables

D-1 Does your hair have enough body?

	No	Yes	Total
Body included in ideal set	26 (76)	8 (24)	34 (100)
Body excluded from ideal set	17 (34)	33 (66)	50 (100)
	43	41	84

D-2 Do you have special problems with your hair?

	No	Yes	Total
Body included in ideal set	9 (26)	25 (74)	34 (100)
Body excluded from ideal set	20 (40)	30 (60)	50 (100)
	29	55	84

D-3 My hair type is:

	Dry	Normal	Oily	Total
Body included in ideal set	5 (15)	20 (59)	9 (26)	34 (100)
Body excluded from ideal set	11 (22)	26 (52)	13 (26)	50 (100)
	16	46	22	84

D-4 The texture of my hair is:

	Fine	Normal	Coarse	Total
Body included in ideal set	21 (62)	10 (29)	3 (9)	34 (100)
Body excluded from ideal set	18 (36)	20 (40)	12 (24)	50 (100)
	39	30	15	84

E-1 Are you working (at least 20 hours per week for compensation)?

	Yes	No	Total
Body included in ideal set	24 (71)	10 (29)	34 (100)
Body excluded from ideal set	26 (52)	24 (48)	50 (100)
	50	34	84

Table 8-5 (cont.)

E-2 Are you married?

	Yes	No	Total
Body included in ideal set	21 (62)	13 (38)	34 (100)
Body excluded from ideal set	25 (50)	25 (50)	50 (100)
	46	38	84

E-3 What is your level of education?

	Some College or Less	Completed College	Total
Body included in ideal set	13 (38)	21 (62)	34 (100)
Body excluded from ideal set	16 (32)	34 (68)	50 (100)
Total	29	55	84

E-4 What is your total annual family income?

	Under $3,000 to $7,000	$7,001 to $10,000	$10,001 to $15,000	$15,001 and Over	Total
Body included in ideal set	9 (26)	8 (24)	8 (24)	9 (26)	34 (100)
Body excluded from ideal set	18 (36)	9 (18)	11 (22)	12 (24)	50 (100)
Total	27	17	19	21	84

on the fine side. Part E suggests that "body" likers tend to be working, married, and of somewhat higher income. The between-group differences are not striking, however.

In summary, Parts A through E suggest a profile of "body" likers (vs. nonlikers) that can be described as follows:

1. Belief that "body" is not as available in current shampoos.

2. Preference for sheen or luster, given the presence of body.

3. Hair that's fine and without body; a belief that hair does not have enough natural "body."

4. Working, married, with somewhat higher income.

ANALYSIS OF REMAINING RESPONSES

The questionnaire contained two sets of responses that we have commented upon only briefly so far:

1. Rankings of 9 shampoo benefits, conditional upon the availability of "body" (Part B).
2. Free-association data (Part C).

In this section of the chapter we discuss the analysis and results of these sections of the questionnaire.[5]

Thurstonian Case V Scaling

Thurstone's comparative-judgment model and scaling procedure (for Case V) were discussed in Chapter 6. Part B of the questionnaire provides a set of data sufficient for applying Case V scaling. For illustrative purposes, the total-sample frequencies with which each of the 9 benefits (column headings) is preferred to each of the other benefits (row headings) are shown under Part B in the "marginal" tabulations of Table 8-4. These frequencies are found by tabulating the pair comparisons implied by each respondent's rank ordering of the 9 shampoo benefits, conditional upon obtaining "body" in a shampoo.

As discussed in Chapter 6, these frequencies can then be converted into proportions. The proportions, in turn, are converted to Z values (Table A-1 in Appendix A), as shown in Table 8-6. (Note that the row and column permutations shown in Table 8-4 are maintained here.)

The Case V scaling program next computes column averages. Finally, the lowest scale value (that associated with benefit 10) is arbitrarily set at zero and other scale values are adjusted as differences from it.[6] As noted in Chapter 6, such operations are permissible because the scale is unique up to a linear transformation, that is, one involving choice of origin and unit.

Final scale values are shown in Table 8-6 and are plotted in Figure 8-2. We see that benefit 6, "sheen or luster," receives the highest scale value, followed by benefits 2, "stays free of dandruff and flaking," and 1, "stays clean a long time." Notice that these are also highly preferred benefits—in the sense of high frequency of inclusion in ideal sets—in responses to Part A of the questionnaire.

---

[5]Given the small size of the sample, Parts B and C are analyzed on only a total-sample basis.
[6]For example, the adjusted scale value for benefit 8 is $0.59 - 0.41 = 0.18$.

Table 8-6 *Z* **values associated with proportions (converted from frequencies) of paired comparisons involving 9 shampoo benefits**

	BENEFIT*								
BENEFIT	10	8	9	7	3	5	1	2	6
10	0.0	0.33	0.30	0.60	0.83	0.79	0.60	0.75	1.06
8	−0.33	0.0	0.33	0.36	0.67	0.71	0.53	0.60	0.79
9	−0.30	−0.33	0.0	0.0	0.14	0.33	0.36	0.53	0.49
7	−0.60	−0.36	0.0	0.0	0.14	0.39	0.33	0.30	0.60
3	−0.83	−0.67	−0.14	−0.14	0.0	−0.02	0.11	0.11	0.24
5	−0.79	−0.71	−0.33	−0.39	0.02	0.0	0.14	0.17	0.17
1	−0.60	−0.53	−0.36	−0.33	−0.11	−0.14	0.0	0.02	0.11
2	−0.75	−0.60	−0.53	−0.30	−0.11	−0.17	−0.02	0.0	0.02
6	−1.06	−0.79	−0.49	−0.60	−0.24	−0.17	−0.11	−0.02	0.0
Average	−0.59	−0.41	−0.14	−0.09	0.15	0.19	0.22	0.28	0.39
Final scale values	0	0.18	0.45	0.50	0.74	0.78	0.81	0.87	0.98

*Benefit 4, "body," has been excluded since it served as the reference item.

Figure 8-2 **Scale values of 9 shampoo benefits, as obtained from Thurstonian Case V analysis**

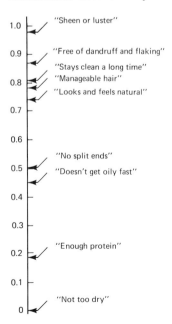

Free Association

Part C of the questionnaire (see Figure 8-1) consisted of free-association responses. The purpose of the free-association task was to examine what semantic associations were conjured up by various words or phrases that were thought to be related to the central benefit of "body." In particular, the sponsor was interested in whether the stimulus "body" tended to connote associations of "fullness" as opposed to associations of "manageability."

Respondent protocols were analyzed and frequency counts were made of various words or phrases that were evoked by each of the stimulus words of Part C. In total, some 50 word/phrases were evoked. Using the marginal frequencies (across all 8 stimulus words as a guide) the 19 most frequently evoked were summarized. The resulting tabulation appears in Table 8-7.

We see from Table 8-7 that the total frequency is 1,019. Note further that stimulus words, themselves, appear as evoked words. For example, when "body" serves as the evoking stimulus, "fullness" is evoked 44 times in terms of free association. This is probably not surprising, given the semantic closeness of the stimulus words to begin with and the fact that the respondent remembers some of the stimulus words used on previous trials. However, other stimulus words such as "not limp" and "zesty" (which are not commonly used words anyway) are seldom evoked (column frequencies of 3 and 4, respectively).

Nonstimulus words such as "clean," "sheen," and "curly" exhibit high evocations in general. Finally, it should be noted that the entries in the 8 × 8 subtable of Table 8-7 are not, in general, symmetrical. For example, "body" evokes "fullness" more frequently than "fullness" evokes "body."

Interpretation of the frequencies indicates that when "body" is a stimulus word the highest evocations are "fullness," "bouncy," and "manageable." That is, "body" appears primarily to connote texturelike aspects of hair and, secondarily, trainability or manageability aspects. "Body" as an evoked word is more frequently triggered by the stimulus words "not limp," "fullness," "holds set," and "manageable," again indicating the texturelike aspects, followed by the manageability aspects.

The frequency data of Table 8-7 can be portrayed in another way—by means of a set of techniques known as *cluster analysis*.[7] This topic is described in more detail in the latter half of Chapter 13. For the moment, however, we can describe the results of cluster analysis of the frequencies of Table 8-7. These appear in Figure 8-3.

Figure 8-3 shows these results in "treelike" form. Note that each of the 8 row stimuli is represented by two objects: one object refers to its role as an

---

[7]*Cluster analysis* refers to a set of techniques that take numerical indexes of interobject similarity and group objects into clusters so that each object is more like other objects in its own cluster than it is like objects outside its cluster.

Table 8-7 Word association frequencies involving eight stimulus phrases regarding shampoos (sample size = 84)

Stimulus Phrase	Body	Fullness	Holds Set	Bouncy	Not Limp	Manageable	Zesty	Natural	Clean	Sheen	Curly	Long	Grooming Aid	Soft	Nice	Combs Easily	Healthy	Alive	Pretty	Total
1. Body	—	44	5	23	1	19	1	3	6	9	8	3	4	6	1	1	3	4	2	143
2. Fullness	22	—	5	3	1	9	1	2	7	7	7	10	1	1	5	1	5	2	4	93
3. Holds set	17	21	—	5	0	17	0	5	4	2	17	2	14	3	5	2	0	1	6	121
4. Bouncy	15	12	3	—	1	5	0	14	12	14	22	9	4	3	4	2	1	9	5	135
5. Not limp	28	27	4	18	—	4	1	7	15	5	12	3	5	2	4	1	8	1	1	146
6. Manageable	17	13	11	2	0	—	0	3	15	7	3	0	8	8	5	18	0	0	1	111
7. Zesty	7	9	2	22	0	4	—	13	16	26	11	8	6	1	2	2	7	10	1	147
8. Natural	4	9	1	2	0	7	1	—	26	27	5	11	2	8	5	3	4	1	7	123
Total	110	135	31	75	3	65	4	47	101	97	85	46	44	32	31	30	28	28	27	1,019

Figure 8-3 Cluster analysis of word association data

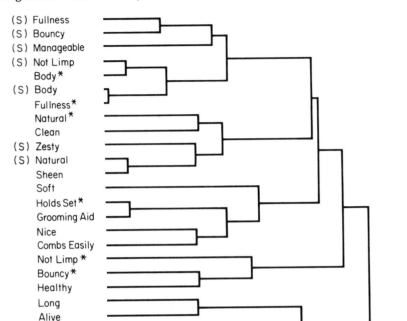

(S) Stimulus Word
  * Row Stimulus as Evoked Word

evoking stimulus, while the second refers to its role as an evoked word/phrase. In this way we try to preserve as much information in the original matrix of Table 8-7 as we can. Note further from Figure 8-3 that the objects (word/ phrases) start out as single "clusters." Then the most proximate pair is clustered first ("body" as a stimulus word with "fullness" as an evoked word). As one moves from *left to right* in the diagram, small clusters merge into larger clusters until at the extreme right of the tree diagram all objects are grouped into one cluster.

If we focus attention on "body" as a stimulus word, we see that after grouping with "fullness" this pair is joined by another pair—"body" as an evoked word and "not limp" as a stimulus word. This cluster of four word/ phrases is later joined by the cluster—"fullness" (stimulus), "bouncy" (stimulus), and "manageable" (stimulus). As can be noted from the tree diagram, then, the closest word associates of "body," as a stimulus word, involve texturelike aspects of hair, followed by manageability aspects.

Clustering techniques are covered more thoroughly in Part IV. At this point we need only state that they can serve to organize data in a graphical way that can be quickly grasped by the researcher.

RECAPITULATION

At this point we have presented descriptive findings, primarily utilizing the more or less traditional types of marginal and cross tabulations. Since a number of results have been reported, it seems useful to recapitulate the findings according to the managerial questions that preceded the development of the questionnaire.

Is the market for a shampoo with superior body large enough to justify commercialization?

The findings of the exploratory study indicated that 34 out of 84 respondents included "body" in their ideal set of four benefits. This is a target segment of appreciable (relative) size. However, "body" is not perceived as rare insofar as current brands are concerned. Of the 34 respondents in the "body"-inclusion group only 12 perceived this benefit as not being currently available in any shampoo.

What benefits in addition to "body" should be incorporated in the new shampoo?

The answer to this question depends on the target-group characteristics. For the "body"-inclusion group—the target group of interest—"sheen or luster" is the benefit to concentrate attention on. Hence, it would seem that a shampoo stressing *body–sheen* might represent a rather good combination of benefits (and perhaps even a brand name!)

What characteristics distinguish respondents who are particularly attracted to "body" versus those who are not?

The "body"-inclusion group (of 34 respondents) are respondents who tend to have hair without satisfactory "body" or thickness. Demographically, they show a greater incidence of working wives and somewhat higher income.

How should the concept of "body" in shampoo be communicated, or what does the consumer mean by "body" in a shampoo?

Analysis of the word-association data suggests that "body" usually connotes "fullness" or texturelike aspects followed by manageability aspects. Moreover, "fullness" also connotes "body." This might suggest promotional messages that first relate "fullness" to "body" and, secondarily, relate "manageability" to "body" and "fullness."

IMPLICATIONS OF STUDY

Given the exploratory character of the study, the small sample size and its nonrepresentativeness, this pilot work mainly provides general guidelines for the principal study that was planned to be undertaken in the future. However, a few implications could be gathered, even at this early stage. First, it would certainly appear that "body" is desired by a sizable segment of the market. None of the findings suggests that laboratory efforts should be dropped regarding the development of a shampoo that delivers superior "body." Second, initial investigatory effort might be made of the technical feasibility of incorporating "sheen or luster" with "body." Third, technical personnel should be apprised of the consumer's perception of "body" as comprising "fullness" first and "manageability" or "control" second.

More work would need to be done on the selection of a sample for the main study. Consideration might be given to interviewing respondents who, on the basis of a preliminary screening question, name "body" as a member of their ideal set of shampoo benefits. That is, an intensive study might be carried out with "body" likers as the *primary* respondent group (coupled with a relatively small, control-type sample).

Second, the present questionnaire should be modified in several respects. First, one might include questions on consumers' perceptions of, and preferences for, the long-lasting aspects of various shampoo benefits. The current favorable response to a shampoo that makes "hair stay clean a long time" suggests the possibility of finding out how consumers value the long-lasting aspects of *other* benefits—particularly "body" and "sheen."

In addition, the current battery of demographic variables should probably be augmented. Most of the demographic variables did not show marked differences between the "body" inclusion and the "body" exclusion groups. Although this may reflect the nonrepresentativeness of the sample, it may also be the case that other demographics, and hair care variables as well, may show greater differences if included in the larger study.

Other limitations are associated with the present pilot study. For example, the small (unrepresentative) sample suggests that the free-association data in the main study should be developed separately for high "body" likers and a control sample. Further investigation should be made of existing brand preferences of high "body" likers, both in shampoos and related hair care products.

Despite the limitations of the pilot study described here, it served several useful purposes for the sponsor. First, it indicated that the market for "body" seemed large enough to justify continued technical development. Second, it suggested that "sheen" might be a benefit to be coupled with "body." Third, it suggested that "body" elicits two types of associations, one emphasizing texture and the other emphasizing control. Fourth, it suggested various additional questions that might be included in the main study. Finally, it illustrated some ways in which data collected in the main study might be analyzed.

SUMMARY

Marginal and cross tabulations continue to represent major ways by which survey responses are summarized and analyzed. This chapter first discussed the topic from a general viewpoint. Introductory comments were made regarding category definition, editing, coding, and tabulation.

We then turned to a case example on the design and analysis of a miniature data bank comprising various responses regarding women's hair shampoos. The purpose of the case study was to integrate material presented in previous chapters as well as to illustrate the preparation of marginal and cross tabulations.

The pilot study indicated that the development of a shampoo with "body" might be an attractive business venture. Moreover, the pilot work, despite exhibiting a number of limitations, provided guidance for the design and analysis of the main piece of research that could be undertaken after the pilot results were reported.

ASSIGNMENT MATERIAL

1. Structure the shampoo-benefits problem in terms of a formal Bayesian prior analysis. Assume whatever probabilities and payoffs seem appropriate to you, given the study's description, and compute the expected value of each course of action.
   a. Which course of action would be chosen under a minimax regret approach?
   b. Under the Bayesian approach—using your assumed payoffs and probabilities—what is the expected value of perfect information?
2. Assume the role of research and development manager for the firm sponsoring the shampoo-benefits study.

a. How would you criticize the study in terms of its usefulness to you?

b. If you had the opportunity to design the pilot project from *your* viewpoint, what questions would you want to include in the questionnaire?

c. Considering the pilot project results, what questions would you now want to include in the main (national) study?

3. How would you approach the same (shampoo-benefits) problem if you were:

a. Developing a mail questionnaire?

b. Developing a telephone questionnaire?

4. Suppose that you wished to add a section to the questionnaire of Figure 8-1 that dealt with general attitudes toward hair and personal grooming.

a. Prepare a set of sample statements that ask for the respondent's degree of agreement/disagreement.

b. What other aspects of life-style might be worthwhile to include?

5. What kinds of questions should be added regarding:

a. Other types of hair-grooming products, such as rinses, setting gels, and the like?

b. Current brand usage and preference?

Analyzing
Associative Data

Analyzing Associative Data— Basic Concepts

9

INTRODUCTION

Our brief discussion of cross tabulations in Chapter 8 marks the beginning of a major topic of this book—the analysis of associative data. Although we shall continue to be interested in the study of variation in a single variable (or a composite of variables), a large part of the rest of the book will focus on methods for analyzing how this variation is associated with variation in *other* variables.

One of the most striking trends that has taken place in marketing research methodology over the past decade is the attention accorded to *multivariate* statistical procedures. Today an imposing array of such procedures—multiple regression, analysis of variance, discriminant analysis, cluster analysis, multidimensional scaling—is being used in the description and analysis of associative data. This chapter has been prepared as a bridge between the comparatively simple marginal and cross tabulations of Chapter 8 and the more sophisticated multivariate techniques that will command our attention in later chapters.

The computation of row or column percentages in the presentation of cross tabulations is taken up first. We then show how various insights can be obtained as one goes beyond two variables in a cross tabulation to three (or more) variables. In particular, examples are presented of how the introduction of a third variable can often refine or explain the observed association between the first two variables.

Chi-square analysis is the central technique for testing the *statistical significance* of association in cross-tabulated frequency data. This method is illustrated by means of several numerical examples. Related descriptive indexes for summarizing the *degree of agreement* between two categorical (nominal-scaled) variables are also described.

The concluding part of the chapter provides a brief overview of multivariate analysis. The central idea of a data matrix is introduced first. We then present a system for classifying multivariate techniques that is based on alternative ways of operating on the original data matrix. This classification system serves to organize the presentation of multivariate methods in subsequent chapters.

MORE ON CROSS TABULATION

Cross tabulation represents the simplest form of associative data analysis. At the minimum we can start out with only two variables, such as occupation and education, each of which is discretized into a set of exclusive and exhaustive categories. Such data are often called *qualitative* or *categorical*, since each variable is assumed to be only nominal-scaled.

If only two categories are involved, the variable is called *dichotomous*. If three or more categories are involved, the variable is called *polytomous*. It is not assumed that the classes or categories are orderable (even though they may well be).

The entities being cross-classified are often called *units of association*. Usually they will be people, objects, or events. The cross tabulation, at its simplest, consists of a simple count of the number of entities that fall into each of the possible categories of the cross classification.[1]

However, as noted in Table 8-5, we usually want to do more than show the raw frequency data. At the very least, row or column percentages (or both) are usually computed. Indeed, most computerized tabulation programs perform this step on a routine basis.

Percentages

The simple mechanics of calculating percentages are known to all readers. We are all also aware that the general purpose of percentages is to serve as a relative measure; that is, they are used to indicate more clearly the relative size of two or more numbers.

The ease and simplicity of calculation, the general understanding of its purpose, and the near universal applicability of the percent statistic has made

---

[1]Excellent discussions of ways to analyze cross tabulations can be found in J. A. Davis, *Elementary Survey Analysis* (Englewood Cliffs, N.J.: Prentice-Hall, Inc., 1971) and Hans Zeisel, *Say It with Figures*, 4th ed. (New York: Harper & Row, Publishers, 1957). This section of the chapter is based on the discussion of Zeisel.

it the most widely used statistical tool in marketing research. Yet its simplicity of calculation is sometimes deceptive, and the understanding of its purpose is frequently insufficient to ensure sound application and interpretation. The result is that the percent statistic is often the source of misrepresentations, either inadvertent or intentional.

Two problems in using percentages often crop up: (1) the direction in which percentages should be computed and (2) the interpretation of percentage change. Both these problems can be illustrated by a small numerical example.

Let us assume that an advertiser of salad dressings was interested in testing the effectiveness of spot TV ads in increasing consumer *awareness* of one of his brands—called *Gala*—that had been on the market for only four months. Two geographic areas were chosen for the test: (1) test area A and (2) control area B. The test area received a media weight of five 15-second television spots per week over an eight-week period, whereas the control area received no spot TV at all. (Other forms of advertising were equal between areas.)

Telephone interviews were conducted before and after the test in each of the areas. Respondents were asked to state all the brands of salad dressing they could think of, on an unprompted basis. If Gala was mentioned, it was assumed that this constituted consumer awareness of the brand. However, as it turned out, sample sizes differed across all four sets of interviews. (This common fact of survey life increases the value of computing percentages.)

Table 9-1 shows the original frequency tables that were compiled on a before-and-after-test basis. (All four samples were independent samples.) Interpretation of Table 9-1 is hampered because the data are expressed as raw frequencies and different bases are involved. Accordingly, Table 9-2 shows the data in percentages based on column totals while Table 9-3 shows percentages based on row totals. Which of these tables—Table 9-2 or Table 9-3—is the more useful for analytical purposes?

**Table 9-1   Aware of Gala salad dressing—
before and after spot TV**

	BEFORE SPOT TV			AFTER SPOT TV		
	Aware	*Not Aware*	*Total*	*Aware*	*Not Aware*	*Total*
Test area	250	350	600	330	170	500
Control area	160	240	400	160	220	380
Total	410	590	1,000	490	390	880

Table 9-2   Aware of Gala—test versus control,
percentages of column totals

	BEFORE SPOT TV			AFTER SPOT TV		
	Aware	*Not Aware*	*Total*	*Aware*	*Not Aware*	*Total*
Test area	61	59	60	67	44	57
Control area	39	41	40	33	56	43
Total	100	100	100	100	100	100

Table 9-3   Aware of Gala—test versus control,
percentages of row totals

	BEFORE SPOT TV			AFTER SPOT TV		
	Aware	*Not Aware*	*Total*	*Aware*	*Not Aware*	*Total*
Test area	42	58	100	66	34	100
Control area	40	60	100	42	58	100

Direction in Which to Compute Percentages

In examining the relationship between two variables, it is often clear from the context that one variable is more or less the independent or control variable while the other is the dependent or criterion variable. In cases where this distinction is clear the rule is to *compute percentages across the dependent variable.*

In the example of Table 9-1 we would expect that experimental area (test versus control) is the control variable and awareness the dependent variable. Accordingly, Table 9-3 is the preferred way to express the percentages. We note that, before the spot TV campaign, the percentage of respondents who are aware of Gala is almost the same between test and control areas: 42% and 40%, respectively.

However, after the campaign, the test-area awareness level moves up to 66%, while the control-area awareness (42%) stays almost the same. (Presumably the small increase of 2 percentage points reflects either sampling variability or the effect of other factors that might be serving to increase awareness of Gala in the control area.)

On the other hand, computing percentages across the independent variable in Table 9-2 makes little sense. We note that 61% of the aware group (before the spot TV campaign) originates from the test area; however, this is mainly a reflection of the differences in total sample sizes between test and control areas.

After the campaign we note that the percentage of aware respondents in the control area is only 33%, versus 39% before the campaign. This may be erroneously interpreted as indicating that spot TV beamed to the test area *depressed* awareness in the control area. But we know this to be false from our earlier examination of Table 9-3.

It is not always the case that one variable is clearly the independent or control variable while the other is the dependent or criterion variable. This should pose no particular problem as long as we agree, for analysis purposes, which variable is to be considered the control variable. Indeed, cases often arise in which each of the variables in turn serves as the "independent" and "dependent" variable.

As a case in point, in the cross tabulations of Table 8-5 we elected to consider the inclusion of "body" in the ideal set (or not) as the control variable. This was done to make it easier to compare percentage distributions across the rest of the variables, rather than because "body" was believed to be an independent or controlled variable in the research design.

A useful aid to thinking about which way to compute percentages is to consider the problem in *conditional probability* terms. In Table 9-3 we are appropriately interested in the estimated conditional probabilities:

	Before	*After*
$P(\text{aware} \mid \text{test})$	0.42	0.66
$P(\text{aware} \mid \text{control})$	0.40	0.42

On the other hand, it makes little sense to be interested in the estimated conditional probabilities:

$$P(\text{test} \mid \text{aware}) \quad \text{or} \quad P(\text{control} \mid \text{aware})$$

since respondents are assigned to test or control groups before (and independently of) their measurement on product awareness.

Interpretation of the Percentage Change

A second problem that arises in the use of percentages in cross tabulations is choosing the method to be used in measuring *differences* in percentages. Three principal ways for portraying percentage change are:

1. The absolute difference in percentages.

2. The relative difference in percentages.
3. The percentage of possible change in percentages.

The same example can be used to illustrate the three methods.

Table 9-4 shows the percentage of respondents who are aware of Gala before and after the spot TV campaign in the test and control areas. First, we note that the test-area respondents displayed a greater *absolute* increase in awareness. The increase for the test-area respondents is 24 percentage points, while that for the control-area respondents is only 2 percentage points.

Table 9-4   Aware of Gala—percentages before and after the spot TV campaign

	Before the Campaign	After the Campaign
Test area	42	66
Control area	40	42

The *relative* increase in percentage is $[(66 - 42)/42] \times 100 = 57\%$ and $[(42 - 40)/40] \times 100 = 5\%$, respectively, for test- and control-area respondents.

The *percentage of possible* increase for the test area is computed by first noting that the maximum percentage-point increase that could have occurred is $100 - 42 = 58$ points. The increase actually registered is 24 percentage points, or $100(24/58) = 41\%$ of the maximum possible. That of the control area is $100(2/60) = 3\%$ of the maximum possible.

In terms of the illustrative problem all three methods give consistent results in the sense that the awareness level in the test area undergoes greater change than that in the control area. However, in other situations conflicts among the measures may arise.

The *absolute difference* method is simple to use and requires only that the distinction between percentage and percentage points be understood. The *relative differences* method can be misleading, particularly if the base for computing the percentage change is small. The *percentage of possible difference* takes cognizance of the greater difficulty that is associated with obtaining increases in awareness as the difference between potential-level and realized-level decreases. In some studies all three measures are used, inasmuch as they emphasize different aspects of the relationship.

Introducing a Third Variable into the Analysis

Cross tabulation of marketing research data need not stop with two variables. Often much can be learned about the original two-variable association through the introduction of a third variable. As we shall illustrate, the third variable may refine or explain the original relationship. In some cases, it may show that the two variables are related even though no apparent relationship exists before the third variable is introduced. These ideas are most easily explained by numerical examples.

Consider the situation facing a marketing researcher who works for a company that specializes in telecommunications equipment for the residential market. The company had recently test-marketed a new device for the automatic recording of home telephone messages. Several months after introduction a telephone survey was taken in which respondents in the test area were asked whether they had adopted the innovation. The total number of respondents interviewed was 600.

One of the variables of major interest to the marketing researcher is the age of the respondent. Based on earlier studies of the residential market, it appeared that adopters of the firm's new products tended to be less than 35 years old. Accordingly, the marketing researcher decides to look at the current data by means of a cross tabulation between adoption and respondent age. Respondents are classified into the categories "under 35 years" (< 35) and "equal to or greater than 35 years" (≥ 35) and then cross-classified by adoption or not. Table 9-5 shows the cross tabulation. As noted from Table 9-5, the total sample of 600 is split evenly between those who are < 35 and those who are ≥ 35 years of age. Younger respondents display a higher percentage of adoption (37%) than older respondents (23%).

Table 9-5   Adoption of message recorder—percentage by respondent age

	<35 Years	*≥35 Years*
Adopters	37	23
Nonadopters	63	77
Total	100	100
Number of cases:	300	300

Example 1

The researcher wonders whether this finding would differ if he introduced a third variable, such as sex of the respondent, into the analysis. As it turned out, 400 respondents in the total sample were men while 200 were women. To simplify the three-way table, the researcher decides to show only the percentage of adopters, since 100 minus this percentage equals the percentage of nonadopters.

Table 9-6 shows the results of introducing sex as a third classificatory variable. In the case of men, 50% of the younger men adopt compared to only 30% of the older men. In the case of women, the percentages of adoption are much closer. Even here, however, younger women show a slightly higher percentage of adoption (11%) than older women (9%).

Table 9-6   Adoption—percentage by sex and age

	MEN		WOMEN	
	<35 Years	*≥35 Years*	*<35 Years*	*≥35 Years*
Adopters	50	30	11	9
Number of cases:	200	200	100	100

The effect of sex on the original association between adoption and age is to *refine* that association *without changing its basic character:* younger respondents show a higher incidence of adoption than older respondents. However, what can now be said is: if the respondent is a man, the *differential* effect of age on adoption is much more pronounced than if the respondent is a woman.

Figure 9-1 shows the same type of information graphically. The height of the bars within each rectangle represents the percentage of respondents who are adopters. The relative width of the bars denotes the relative size of the categories—men versus women—representing the third variable, sex.

Figure 9-1   Adoption—percentage by age and sex

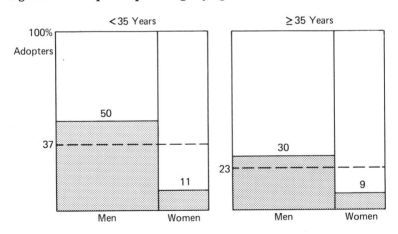

The shaded portions of the bars denote the percentage adopting by sex, while the dashed line represents the weighted average percentage *across* the sexes. It is easy to see from the figure that adoption differs by age group (37 versus 23%). Furthermore, the size of the difference depends on the sex of the respondent: men display a relatively higher rate of adoption, compared to women, in the *younger* age category.

Although not illustrated here, we could also have the cases where adoption is higher for men in the younger age group, while for women:

1. There is *no difference* in adoption by age group.
2. The adoption rate is *lower* for younger than for older women.

Any of these cases could be compatible with the general direction of the two-way summary in Table 9-5.

However, be that as it may, we do note from Table 9-5 that adoption and age are associated to begin with; that is, the rate of adoption *differs* between young and old respondents. Next, let us assume a case in which we first observe *no difference* between adoption and age.

Example 2

In this second example assume that the association between adoption and age is now shown by Table 9-7. As noted, it would appear that the percentage of adopters is not affected by age. In each case the percentage of adoption is the same, namely 50%.

Table 9-7   Adoption—percentage by respondent age

	<35 Years	*≥35 Years*
Adopters	50	50
Nonadopters	50	50
	100	100
Number of cases:	300	300

In this case let us assume that the effect of sex takes the form shown in Table 9-8 and Figure 9-2. As can be observed from either the table or the figure, the introduction of sex as a third variable shows that there is a strong association between adoption and age but that this association runs in *opposite directions* for men versus women. The overall effect is to suggest that adoption and age are *not* associated (when the effect of sex is not held constant).

Table 9-8 Adoption—percentage by sex and age

	MEN		WOMEN	
	<35 Years	≥35 Years	<35 Years	≥35 Years
Adopters	35	65	80	20
Number of cases:	200	200	100	100

Figure 9-2 Adoption—percentage by age and sex

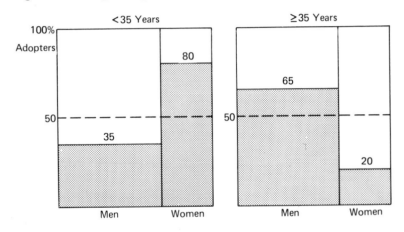

Example 2 is an illustration of what is often called a *suppressor* effect. That is, failure to control on sex differences suppresses the relationship between adoption and age to the point where there appears to be no association at all. However, once we hold the level of sex constant—by tabulating adoption by age *within* the level of sex—the association becomes evident.

Example 3

As an additional illustration of what might happen when a third variable (sex) is introduced, consider the situation of Table 9-9. In this example we see that the association between adoption and age is not affected at all by the introduction of sex.

In this case sex is *independent* of the association between adoption and age. Although a figure is not shown for this simple case, it should be clear that the bars for the two age groups—within the separate men and women classes—will look exactly the same. Furthermore, the total-sample adoption percentage will be 60%. Tabulation of adoption by sex (across the two age

Table 9-9 Adoption—percentage by sex and age

	MEN		WOMEN	
	<35 Years	*≥35 Years*	*<35 Years*	*≥35 Years*
Adopters	60	40	60	40
Number of cases:	200	200	100	100

categories) will show 50% adopters for both the men and women categories.

At this point, then, the various ways that the original relationship can be modified consist of: (1) refining the relationship when it already exists, (2) revealing a relationship that was earlier suppressed, or (3) finding no change at all in the original relationship. *In each of these cases we assumed that sex was not related to the initial independent variable, age.*

However, a fourth possibility exists in which the original relationship disappears upon the introduction of a third variable. Behavioral scientists often use the term *explanation* for this case. In order for the original association to vanish it is necessary that the third variable, sex, be *associated* with the original independent variable, age.

Example 4

To illustrate the idea of third-variable explanation, consider the new association between adoption and age that is shown in Table 9-10. Judging from this table it would appear to be the case that a higher percentage of adopters are drawn from the younger age group.

Table 9-10 Adoption—percentage by respondent age

	<35 Years	*≥35 Years*
Adopters	50	35
Nonadopters	50	65
	100	100
Number of cases:	300	300

However, let us now consider introducing sex as the third variable. Table 9-11 shows the cross classification within each level of the third variable, men versus women. As can be observed, within each separate category of sex, there is *no difference* in the percentage of adopters. The apparent relationship between adoption and sex is due solely to the *difference in the relative size of the subsamples of men versus women within the two age categories.*

Table 9-11   Adoption—percentage by sex and age

	MEN		WOMEN	
	<35 Years	*≥35 Years*	*<35 Years*	*≥35 Years*
Adopters	60	60	30	30
Number of cases:	200	50	100	250

Figure 9-3 shows this effect graphically. In the case of the < 35 age group there are 200 men and 100 women. However, in the ≥ 35 age group, there are 50 men and 250 women. These differences in subsample size affect the weighted-average percentages that are shown as dashed lines in the rectangles.

Figure 9-3   Adoption—percentage by age and sex

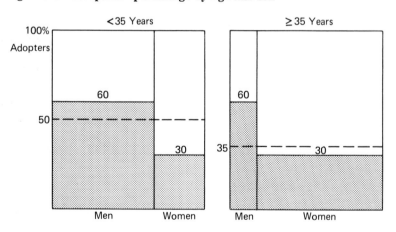

In the present case the sex variable is said to *explain* the (apparent) relationship between adoption and age. As observed from Table 9-11 and Figure 9-3, the percentage of adopters is *not* associated with age, once the data are examined separately for men and women.

Recapitulation

Representations of three-variable association can involve the following possibilities, as illustrated by the preceding adoption–age–sex example:

1. Adoption and age exhibit initial association; this association is still maintained in the aggregate but is *refined* by the introduction of the sex variable.
2. Adoption and age do not appear to be associated. However, controlling on the variable, sex, reveals *suppressed* association between the first two variables *within* the separate categories of men and women.
3. Adoption and age are not associated to begin with; furthermore, controlling on the *independent* variable, sex, does not change the situation.
4. Adoption and age exhibit initial association, which then disappears upon the introduction of the *explanatory* variable, sex.

Although the preceding examples were contrived to illustrate the concepts, none of these cases is all that unusual in practice. It goes almost without saying that the introduction of a third variable can often be useful in the interpretation of two-variable cross tabulations.

However, the reader should be aware of the fact that we have deliberately used the phrase *associated with*, not *caused by*. Association of two or more variables does *not* imply causation, and this statement is true regardless of our preceding efforts to refine some observed two-variable association through the introduction of a third variable.

In principle, of course, we could cross-tabulate four or even more variables with the possibility of obtaining further insight into lower-order (e.g., two-variable) associations. However, somewhere along the line, a problem arises in maintaining an adequate cell size for all categories. Unless sample sizes are extremely large in the aggregate and the number of categories per variable is relatively small, most cross tabulations rarely can deal with more than three variables at a time.[2] (Indeed, in practice most routine applications of cross tabulation involve only two variables at a time.)

As noted in Table 9-6, there are definite advantages associated with having a two-category criterion variable: adoption versus nonadoption. (In this case we can simplify the presentation by ignoring the complementary percentage of nonadoption.) In many applications, however, the criterion variable will have more than two categories. Cross tabulations can still be

---

[2] A further problem, independent of sample size, concerns the high degree of complexity of interpretation that is introduced by cross tabulations involving four or more variables.

prepared in the usual manner, although they become somewhat more tedious to examine.

Up to this point we have considered cross tabulations at only a descriptive, content-oriented level. It is now time to consider ways to test whether the association observed in various cross tabulations is *statistically significant*.

CHI-SQUARE TESTS

In addition to the substantive interpretation of cross-tabulation data, the marketing researcher is generally interested in two additional questions:

1. Is the observed association between the variables in the cross tabulation statistically significant?
2. How "strong" is this association?

Chi-square analysis is the technique that is typically used in answering the first question. The second question is answered by the computation of some type of *agreement index.*

Chi-square analysis can be used when the data consist of *counts or frequencies with which each category of a tabulation or cross tabulation appears.* Chi square is a useful technique for achieving the following objectives:

1. Determining the significance of sample deviations from assumed theoretical distributions; that is, finding out whether certain models fit the data. This is typically called a *goodness-of-fit test.*
2. Determining the significance of observed association in cross tabulations involving two or more variables. This is typically called a *test of independence.*

The procedure involved in chi-square analysis is basically quite simple. We compare the observed (frequency) data with another set of "data" based on a set of theoretical frequencies. These theoretical frequencies may result from application of some specific model of the phenomenon being investigated—objective 1 above. Or we might use the special model that the frequency of occurrence of two or more characteristics is mutually independent—objective 2 above. As an illustration of this second use, we may hypothesize that the presence of characteristic A (e.g., a consumer's purchase of a specific product) is unrelated to characteristic B (the consumer's occupational status).

In either case we compute a measure (chi square) of the variation between actual and theoretical frequencies, under the null hypothesis that the model fits the facts. If the measure of variation is "high," we reject the null hypothesis at some specified alpha risk. If the measure is "low," we accept the null hypothesis that the model's output is in agreement with the actual frequencies.

Single Classification

Suppose that we are interested in the frequency of selection of two test packages presented to a sample of respondents. Test package A contains an attached coupon involving so many cents off on a subsequent purchase of the brand by the respondent. Test package B is the same package but, rather than an attached coupon, it contains an attached premium (a ballpoint pen) that the respondent may keep. The packages are presented simultaneously to each of a sample of 100 respondents and each respondent is asked to choose one of the two packages.

The frequency of choice is presented in the first column (labeled "Observed") of Table 9-12. We see that 63 respondents out of 100 select package A. Suppose that the marketing researcher believes the "true" probability of selecting A versus B to be 50–50 and that the observed 63–37 split reflects sampling fluctuations. His model, then, would predict an estimated frequency of 50–50. Are the observed frequencies compatible with this theoretical prediction? In chi-square analysis we set up the null hypothesis that the observed (sample) frequencies are consistent with those expected under application of the model.

Table 9-12   Observed versus theoretical frequencies (test-package illustration)

Package	f_i Observed	F_i Predicted	$f_i - F_i$	$(f_i - F_i)^2/F_i$
A	63	50	13	$^{169}/_{50} = 3.38$
B	37	50	−13	$^{169}/_{50} = 3.38$
Total	100	100		6.76

We use the following notation. Assume that there are k categories and a random sample of n observations; each observation must fall into one and only one category. The observed frequencies are

$$f_i (i = 1, 2, \ldots, k); \quad \sum_{i=1}^{k} f_i = n$$

The theoretical frequencies are

$$F_i (i = 1, 2, \ldots, k); \quad \sum_{i=1}^{k} F_i = n$$

In the problem above,

$$f_1 = 63, f_2 = 37, F_1 = 50, F_2 = 50, n = 100$$

We next compute the chi-square statistic:

$$\chi^2 = \sum_{i=1}^{k} \frac{(f_i - F_i)^2}{F_i}$$

In the one-way classification of the problem the statistic above is approximately distributed as chi square with $k - 1$ degree of freedom. In our problem we have only two categories and, hence, 1 degree of freedom. Table A-3 in Appendix A shows the appropriate distribution.

In Table A-3 the tabular chi-square value for $\alpha = 0.05$ and $k - 1 = 1$ is 3.84. If the null hypothesis is true, the probability of getting a chi-square value greater than 3.84 is 0.05. Since our computed chi-square value is 6.76 (see Table 9-12), we *reject* the hypothesis that the output of the theoretical model corresponds with the observed frequencies. In using the chi-square table we note that only k, the number of categories, is pertinent, rather than the sample size n. (Sample size *is* important to the quality of the approximation and the power of the test.) A good rule of thumb, however, is that chi-square analysis should be used only when the *theoretical* frequencies in each cell exceed five; otherwise, the distribution in Table A-3 will not be a good approximation.

Two-Way Classification

In marketing research, observations may be cross-classified as, for example, when we are interested in testing whether occupational status is *associated* with brand loyalty. Suppose, for illustrative purposes, that a marketing researcher has assembled data on brand loyalty by consumers of a particular product class and also data on occupational status—white collar, blue collar, and unemployed/retired. The data for our hypothetical problem appear in Table 9-13. (Tables such as these are often called *contingency tables*.)

Our sample of 230 consumers suggests that *occupational status* may be associated with the characteristic *loyalty status*. But is the observed association a reflection of sampling variation? Expressed in probability terms, are the conditional probabilities of being highly loyal, moderately loyal, and brand switcher, given the type of occupational status, equal to their respective marginal probabilities?

In analyzing the problem by means of chi square, we make use of the

Table 9-13   Observed versus theoretical frequencies (brand-loyalty illustration)

Occupational Status	Highly Loyal	Moderately Loyal	Brand Switchers	Total
White-collar	30 (30.5)	42 (34.1)	18 (25.4)	90
Blue-collar	14 (22.1)	20 (24.5)	31 (18.4)	65
Unemployed/retired	34 (25.4)	25 (28.4)	16 (21.2)	75
Total	78	87	65	230

marginal totals (columns and rows) in computing theoretical frequencies, given (the hypothesized) independence between the attributes *loyalty status* and *occupational status*. For example, we note from Table 9-13 that 78 out of a total of 230 respondents are highly loyal. If possession of this characteristic is independent of occupational status, we would expect that 78/230 of the 90 respondents (i. e., 30.5) classified as white-collar workers would be highly loyal. Similarly, 87/230 of the 90 (34.1) would be moderately loyal, and 65/230 of the 90 (25.4) would be brand switchers. In a similar fashion we can compute theoretical frequencies for each cell on the null hypothesis that *loyalty status* is statistically independent of *occupational status*.

The theoretical frequencies (under the null hypothesis) are computed and appear in parentheses in Table 9-13. The chi-square statistic is then calculated as follows:

$$\chi^2 = \frac{(30 - 30.5)^2}{30.5} + \frac{(42 - 34.1)^2}{34.1} + \frac{(18 - 25.4)^2}{25.4}$$

$$+ \frac{(14 - 22.1)^2}{22.1} + \frac{(20 - 24.5)^2}{24.5} + \frac{(31 - 18.4)^2}{18.4}$$

$$+ \frac{(34 - 25.4)^2}{25.4} + \frac{(25 - 28.4)^2}{28.4} + \frac{(16 - 21.2)^2}{21.2}$$

$$= 21.1$$

The appropriate number of degrees of freedom to use in this example is 4. In general, if we have R rows and C columns, the degrees of freedom associated with the chi-square statistic are equal to the product

$$(R - 1)(C - 1)$$

If we use a significance level of 0.05, the tabular value of chi square (Table A-3) is 9.488. Hence, we reject the hypothesis of independence between the characteristics *loyalty status* and *occupational status*.

Chi-square analysis can be extended to deal with more classificatory variables than two. No new principles are involved. but the procedure naturally becomes more tedious. Two characteristics of the technique should be borne in mind, however. First, chi-square analysis deals with counts (frequencies) of data. If the data are expressed in percentage form, they should be converted to absolute frequencies. Second, the technique assumes that the observations are drawn independently.[3]

INDEXES OF AGREEMENT

Chi-square analysis is appropriate for making statistical tests of independence in cross tabulations. Usually, however, we are interested in the *strength* of association as well as the statistical significance of the association. Statisticians have devised a plethora of indexes—often called *indexes of argeement*—for measuring the strength of association between two variables in a cross tabulation.

The main descriptors for classifying the various indexes are:

1. Whether the table is 2 × 2 or larger, $R \times C$.
2. Whether one, both, or neither of the variables has categories that obey some natural order (e.g., age, income level, family size).
3. Whether association is to be treated symmetrically or whether we want to predict membership in one variable's categories from (assumed known) membership in the other variable's categories.

Space does not permit coverage of even an appreciable fraction of the dozens of agreement indexes that have been proposed. Rather, we shall illustrate one commonly used index for 2 × 2 tables and two indexes that deal with different aspects of the larger $R \times C$ (row-by-column) tables.

The 2 × 2 Case

The *phi correlation coefficient* is a useful agreement index for the special case of 2 × 2 tables in which both variables are dichotomous. Moreover, an added bonus is the fact that phi equals the product moment correlation—a cornerstone of multivariate methods—that one would obtain if he correlated the two variables expressed in coded 0–1 form.

To illustrate, consider the 2 × 2 cross tabulation in Table 9-14 (taken from one of the cross tabulations of Table 8-5). We wish to see if inclusion

---

[3]An elementary presentation of chi-square analysis, as applied to cross tabulations, can be found in A. E. Maxwell, *Analyzing Qualitative Data* (New York: John Wiley & Sons, Inc., 1961).

of the shampoo benefit of "body" in the respondent's ideal set is associated with the respondent's indication that her hair lacks natural "body". We first note from the table that high frequencies appear in the cells: (1) "body" included in ideal set and "no" to the question of whether her hair has enough (natural) body, and (2) "body" excluded from the ideal set and "yes" to the same question.

Table 9-14 Does hair have enough body versus body inclusion in ideal set (from Table 8-5)

	HAIR HAVE ENOUGH BODY?		
	No	*Yes*	*Total*
Body included in ideal set	26 (*A*)	8 (*B*)	34
Body excluded from ideal set	17 (*C*)	33 (*D*)	50
Total	43	41	84

Before computing the phi coefficient, first note the labels *A, B, C,* and *D* assigned to the four cells in Table 9-14. The phi coefficient is defined as

$$\Phi = \frac{AD - BC}{\sqrt{(A + B)(C + D)(A + C)(B + D)}}$$
$$= \frac{26(33) - 8(17)}{\sqrt{(26 + 8)(17 + 33)(26 + 17)(8 + 33)}}$$
$$= 0.417$$

The value 0.417 is also what would be found if an ordinary product-moment correlation, to be described in Chapter 10, is computed across the 84 pairs of numbers (the sample size in the shampoo study of Chapter 8), where the code values

- Body included in ideal set $\Rightarrow$ 1
- Body excluded from ideal set $\Rightarrow$ 0
- Hair have enough body? $\begin{cases} \text{No} \Rightarrow 1 \\ \text{Yes} \Rightarrow 0 \end{cases}$

are used to identify the responses.[4]

---

[4] This is a nice feature of phi in the sense that standard computer programs for calculating product-moment correlations can be used for dichotomous variables.

The phi coefficient can vary from -1 to 1 (just like the ordinary product-moment correlation). However, in any given problem the upper limit of phi depends on the relationships among the marginals. Specifically, a phi coefficient of -1 (perfect negative association) or 1 (perfect positive association) assumes that the marginal totals of the first variable are *identical* to those of the second.[5] The more different the marginals, the lower the upper limit that the (absolute) value of phi can assume.

The phi coefficient assumes the value of zero if the two variables are statistically independent (as would be shown by a chi-square value that is also zero). Indeed, the absolute value of phi is related to chi square by the expression

$$\Phi = \sqrt{\frac{\chi^2}{n}}$$

where n is the total frequency (sample size). This is a nice feature of phi, in the sense that it can be computed quite easily after chi square has been computed. Note, however, that phi, unlike chi square, is *not* affected by total sample size, since we have the divisor n in the above formula to adjust for differences in sample size.

Some statisticians do not restrict phi to the 2×2, or double-dichotomy, case. However, if phi is considered simply as a function of chi-square, its connection with the product moment correlation is lost. Here, we shall restrict our use of phi to the 2×2 table.

The R × C Case

One of the most popular agreement indexes for summarizing the degree of association between two variables in a cross tabulation of R rows and C columns is the *contingency coefficient*. This index is also related to chi square and is defined as

$$C = \sqrt{\frac{\chi^2}{\chi^2 + n}}$$

where n is again the total sample size. From Table 9-14 we can first determine that chi square is equal to 14.61, which, with 1 degree of freedom, is significant beyond the 0.01 level.

[5]Looking at the letters (A, B, C, D) of Table 9-14, assume that the row marginals equaled the column marginals; then, $\Phi = 1$ if $B = C = 0$; similarly, $\Phi = -1$ if $A = D = 0$.

We can then find the contingency coefficient C as:

$$C = \sqrt{\frac{14.61}{14.61 + 84}}$$

$$= 0.385$$

As may be surmised, the contingency coefficient lies between zero and 1, with zero reserved for the case of statistical independence (a chi-square value of zero). However, unlike the phi coefficient, the contingency coefficient can never attain a maximum value of unity. For example, in a 2×2 table,[6] C cannot exceed 0.707. In a 4×4 table its upper limit is 0.87. Therefore, contingency coefficients computed from different-sized tables are not easily comparable.

However, like phi, the contingency coefficient is easy to compute from chi square; moreover, like phi, its significance has already been tested in the course of running the chi-square test.

Both phi and the contingency coefficient are symmetric measures of association. Occasions often arise in the analysis of $R \times C$ tables (or the special case of 2×2 tables) where we desire to compute an *asymmetric* measure of the extent to which we can reduce errors in predicting categories of one variable from knowledge of the categories of some other variable. Goodman and Kruskal's *lambda-asymmetric coefficient* can be used for this purpose.[7]

To illustrate the lambda-asymmetric coefficient, let us return to the cross tabulation of Table 9-14. Suppose that we wished to predict what category— "no" versus "yes"—a randomly selected person would fall in when asked the question "Does your hair have enough body?" If we had no knowledge of the row variable (whether that person included "body" in her ideal set or not), we would have only the *column* marginal frequencies to rely on.

Our best bet, given no knowledge of the row variable, is always to predict "no," the *higher* of the column marginal frequencies. As a consequence we shall be wrong in 41 of the 84 cases, a probability of error of $41/84 = 0.49$.

---

[6]As might be noticed by the reader, there is an algebraic relationship between phi and the contingency coefficient (if the latter is applied to the 2×2 table):

$$\Phi^2 = \frac{C^2}{1 - C^2}$$

[7]See L. A. Goodman and W. H. Kruskal, "Measures of Association for Cross Classifications," *Journal of the American Statistical Association*, 49 (December, 1954), 732–64. However, the original development is contained in Louis Guttman, "An Outline of the Statistical Theory of Prediction," in *The Prediction of Personal Adjustment*, ed. Paul Horst, Social Science Research Council Bulletin 48 (New York, 1941).

Can we do better, in the sense of lower prediction errors, if we utilize information provided by the row variable?

If we know that "body" is included in the ideal set, we shall predict
"no" and be wrong in only 8 cases. If we know that "body" is not included
in the ideal set, we shall predict "yes" and be wrong in 17 cases. Therefore,
we have reduced our number of prediction errors from 41 to $8 + 17 = 25$,
a decrease of 16 errors. We can consider this error reduction *relatively*:

$$\lambda_{C|R} = \frac{(\text{number of errors in first case}) - (\text{number of errors in second case})}{\text{number of errors in first case}}$$

$$= \frac{41 - 25}{41} = 0.39$$

In other words, 39% of the errors in predicting the column variable are
eliminated by knowing the individual's row variable.

A less cumbersome (but also less transparent) formula for lambda-
asymmetric is

$$\lambda_{C|R} = \frac{\sum_{k=1}^{K} f_{kR}^* - F_C^*}{n - F_C^*} = \frac{(26 + 33) - 43}{84 - 43} = 0.39$$

where f_{kR}^* is the *maximum* frequency found within each subclass of the row
variable, F_C^* is the *maximum* frequency among the marginal totals of the
column variable, and n is the total number of cases.

Lambda-asymmetric varies between *zero*, indicating no ability at all to
eliminate errors in predicting the column variable on the basis of the row
variable, and 1, indicating an ability to eliminate all errors in the column
variable predictions, given knowledge of the row variable.

Not surprisingly, we could reverse the role of criterion and predictor
variables and find lambda-asymmetric for the row variable, given the column
variable. In the case of Table 9-14, this is

$$\lambda_{R|C} = \frac{\sum_{l=1}^{L} f_{lC}^* - F_R^*}{n - F_R^*} = \frac{(26 + 33) - 50}{84 - 50} = 0.26$$

Note that in this case we simply reverse the roles of row and column variables.

Finally, if desired, we could find a *lambda-symmetric* index via a weighted averaging of $\lambda_{C|R}$ and $\lambda_{R|C}$. In this case we have

$$
\begin{aligned}
\lambda &= \frac{\sum_{k=1}^{K} f^*_{kR} + \sum_{l=1}^{L} f^*_{lC} - (F^*_R + F^*_C)}{2n - (F^*_R + F^*_C)} \\
&= \frac{(26 + 33) + (26 + 33) - (50 + 43)}{2(84) - (50 + 43)} = 0.33
\end{aligned}
$$

However, in the authors' opinion, lambda-asymmetric is of particular usefulness to the analysis of cross tabulations since we often want to consider one variable as a predictor and the other as a criterion. Furthermore, lambda-asymmetric has a natural and useful interpretation as the percentage of total prediction errors that are eliminated in predicting one variable (e.g., the column variable) from another (e.g., the row variable).[8]

Computer Programs for Cross Tabulations

Virtually any computer installation has at least one program for constructing and analyzing cross tabulations from raw categorical input data. Indeed, all the cross tabulations shown in Chapter 8 were done by computer.

However, when it comes to computing agreement indexes, the biomedical program, BMD–PIF, has few equals.[9] This program can compute not only chi square, phi, the contingency coefficient, lambda-asymmetric, and lambda-symmetric, but some 20 other agreement indexes as well.

The BMD–PIF program is designed basically for the analysis of two-way contingency tables. However, a special feature of the program allows the user to single out various third variables of interest and tabulate two-way tables for each category of any third variable that is selected.

There are several options for reading in the data. The most common procedure is to read in each case as a profile where the specific category assignment of each unit of association appears for all of the classifying variables of interest. The program then makes up all two-way tables that are called for by the user. Outputs include:

1. Original frequencies in each two-way table.
2. Percent of total table frequency, percent of row totals, and percent of column totals.

---

[8]Significance tests and confidence intervals are also available for either lambda-asymmetric or lambda-symmetric. See L. A. Goodman and W. H. Kruskal, "Measures of Association for Cross Classification: Appropriate Sampling Theory," *Journal of the American Statistical Association*, 88 (June, 1963), 310–64.

[9]This program is described in W. J. Dixon, ed., *BMDP: Biomedical Computer Programs* (Berkeley, Calif.: University of California Press, 1975).

3. Expected cell frequency based on statistical independence, and the difference between observed and expected frequencies.

4. Chi-square-adjusted frequencies and other data-standardizing options.

In addition, a variety of indexes can be computed. A partial list of these is shown in Table 9-15.

Table 9-15   Agreement indexes obtained from the
BMD–PIF two-way contingency table program

For $R \times C$ tables with unordered categories
  chi square; contingency coefficient; Cramer's V; maximum-likelihood chi square; Goodman and Kruskal's lambda, lambda-asymmetric, and tau-asymmetric; uncertainty coefficient
Additional outputs if the table is 2×2
  phi; Yule's Q; Yule's Y; logarithm of the cross-product ratio; phi-max; C-max; Fisher's exact probability test
Additional measures if the rows and columns of $R \times C$
    table are ordered
  Spearman's rank correlation; Kendall's tau, Stuart's tau; Goodman and Kruskal's gamma, and gamma-asymmetric; Somer's d measure
Theoretical sources of indexes above:
  L. A. Goodman and W. H. Kruskal, "Measures of Association for Cross Classification," *Journal of the American Statistical Association*, 49 (1954), 732–64; 58 (1963), 310–64; 67 (1972), 415–21
  Y. M. M. Bishop, S. E. Feinberg, and P. W. Holland, *Discrete Multivariate Analysis: Theory and Practice* (Cambridge, Mass.: MIT Press, 1975), Chap. 11

As noted from the table, several different indexes can be computed for the general $R \times C$ case. However, if the table also happens to be 2×2, additional indexes that are specific to this case can also be computed. Finally, if the categories of each variable follow some natural order, such as age, income, or family size, various *rank-correlation measures* can be computed as well.

In short, the BMD–PIF program provides a complete approach to all of the topics considered in this chapter:

1. Computation of row and column percentages.

2. Introduction of a third variable in describing association between some other pair of variables.

3. Determining the statistical significance of the association observed in any cross tabulation of interest.

4. Measuring the strength of that association by means of some type of agreement index.

In practice, of course, the marketing researcher rarely needs to deal with more than one or two agreement indexes. Still it is comforting to know that this program provides the flexibility for examining almost any kind of two-way table that one could find in marketing research applications, including tables with *ordered* classes.[10]

AN OVERVIEW OF MULTIVARIATE PROCEDURES

Chi-square and the various agreement indexes discussed so far are typically used for analyzing association between two variables—what may be called *bivariate* data. In the remaining chapters of Part III and in Part IV, we shall be emphasizing *multivariate* data in which association among *three or more variables* is of primary interest. One of the first problems that crops up in analyzing association between variables concerns whether one variable *causes* another.

Association implies only that two or more variables tend to change together to a greater or lesser extent, depending upon the degree of the association involved. If we measure the amount of mutual change and find it to be persistent in both direction and degree, we may *not* conclude that there is a necessary *causal* relationship such that one variable is dependent (effect) and the other variable, or variables, are independent (deterministic or probabilistic causes). It should be understood, then, that *association does not imply causation.*[11] (However, if a set of variables are causally related, they will be associated in some way.)

The Data Matrix

The raw input to any analysis of associative data consists of the *data matrix*. This is a rectangular array of entries whose informational content is to be summarized and portrayed in some way. For example, the computation of the mean and standard deviation of a single column of numbers is often

[10] For agreement measures involving: (a) one nominal-scaled variable and one interval-scaled variable or (b) one nominal-scaled variable and one ordinal-scaled variable, the reader is referred to L. C. Freeman, *Elementary Applied Statistics* (New York: John Wiley & Sons, Inc., 1965).

[11] Recently the field of causal-path analysis has been developed to aid in examining possible causal relations in correlational data. For an introduction to this field, see H. M. Blalock, Jr., *Causal Inferences in Nonexperimental Research* (Chapel Hill, N.C.: University of North Carolina Press, 1961).

done simply because we are unable to comprehend the meaning of the entire column of values. In so doing we often (willingly) forgo the full information provided by the data in order to understand some of its basic characteristics, such as central tendency and dispersion.

In virtually all marketing research studies we are concerned with variation in some characteristic, be it per capita consumption of coffee or TV viewing frequency. (If there is no variation in the characteristic under study, there is little need for statistical methods.) Our objective now, however, is to concentrate on accounting for the variation in one variable or group of variables in terms of *covariation* with other variables. When we analyze associative data, we hope to "explain" variation according to one or more of the following points of view:

1. Determination of the overall strength of association between the *criterion* and *predictor* variables (often called "dependent" and "independent" variables, respectively).
2. Determination of a function or formula by which we can estimate values of the criterion variable(s) from values of the predictor variable(s).
3. Determination of the statistical "confidence" in either or both of the above.

In some cases of interest, however, we have no a priori basis for distinguishing between criterion and predictor variables. We may still be interested in their *interdependence* as a whole and the possibility of summarizing information provided by this interdependence in terms of other variables, often taken to be linear combinations of the original ones.

A Classification of Techniques for Analyzing Associative Data

The field of associative data analysis is vast; hence, it seems useful to enumerate various descriptors by which the field can be classified. The key notion underlying our classification is the data matrix. A conceptual illustration is shown in Table 9-16. We note that the table consists of a set of objects (the *n* rows) and a set of measurements on those objects (the *m* columns). The objects may be people, things, concepts, or events. The variables are characteristics of the objects. The cell values represent the state of object *i* with respect to variable *j*. Cell values may consist of nominal-, ordinal-, interval-, or ratio-scaled measurements or various combinations of these as we go across columns.

There are many descriptors by which we can characterize methods for

Table 9-16 Illustrative data matrix

	VARIABLE					
OBJECT	*1*	*2*	*3*	⋯	*j*	⋯ *m*
1	X_{11}	X_{12}	X_{13}	⋯	X_{1j}	⋯ X_{1m}
2	X_{21}	X_{22}	X_{23}	⋯	X_{2j}	⋯ X_{2m}
3	X_{31}	X_{32}	X_{33}	⋯	X_{3j}	⋯ X_{3m}
·	·	·	·		·	·
·	·	·	·		·	·
·	·	·	·		·	·
i	X_{i1}	X_{i2}	X_{i3}	⋯	X_{ij}	⋯ X_{im}
·	·	·	·		·	·
·	·	·	·		·	·
·	·	·	·		·	·
n	X_{n1}	X_{n2}	X_{n3}	⋯	X_{nj}	⋯ X_{nm}

analyzing associative data.[12] Although not exhaustive (nor exclusive), the following represent the more common bases by which this activity can be classified:

1. Purpose of the study and the types of assertions desired by the researcher: What kinds of statements—descriptive or inferential—does he wish to make?
2. Focus of research—emphasis on the objects (the whole profile or "bundle" of variables), the variables, or both.
3. Nature of his assumed *prior* judgments as to how the data matrix should be partitioned (subdivided) in terms of number of subsets of variables.
4. Number of variables in each of the partitioned subsets—the criterion versus predictor variables.
5. Type of association under study—linear, transformable to linear, or nonlinear.
6. Scales by which variables are measured—nominal, ordinal, interval, ratio, mixed.

All of these descriptors relate to certain decisions required of the researcher. Suppose that he is interested in studying descriptive interrelationships among variables. If so, he must make decisions about how he wants

[12]An excellent classification, based on a subset of the descriptors shown here, has been provided by M. M. Tatsuoka and D. V. Tiedeman, "Statistics as an Aspect of Scientific Method in Research on Teaching," in *Handbook of Research on Teaching*, ed. N. L. Gage (Skokie, Ill.: Rand McNally & Company, 1963), pp. 142–70.

to partition the set of columns (see Table 9-16) into subsets. He must also decide on the number of variables to include in each subset and on what type of relationship (linear, transformation to linear, nonlinear) he is asserting to hold among the variables.

Most decisions about associative data analysis are based on the researcher's private model of how the data are interrelated and what features are useful for study. His choice of various public models for analysis (multiple regression, discriminant analysis, etc.) is predicated on his prior knowledge of the characteristics of the statistical universe from which the data were obtained and his knowledge of the assumption structure and objectives of each candidate technique.

Fortunately, we can make a few simplifications of the preceding descriptors. First, insofar as types of scales, all the multivariate techniques of this book require no stronger measurement than interval scaling. Second, except for Chapter 14 (which deals with various types of ordinal-scaling methods), we shall assume that: (1) the variables are either nominal-scaled or interval-scaled, and (2) the functional form is linear in the parameters.[13] Even with these simplifying assumptions we shall be able to describe a wide variety of possible techniques.

The principal descriptors of interest are now:

1. Whether the matrix is partitioned into subsets or kept intact.
2. If partitioned into subsets of criterion and predictor variables, the number of variables in each subset.
3. Whether the variables are nominal-scaled or interval-scaled.

Analysis of Dependence

If we elect to partition the data matrix into criterion and predictor variables, the problem becomes one of analyzing *dependence structures*. This, in turn, can be broken down into two subcategories:

1. Single criterion/multiple predictor association.
2. Multiple criterion/multiple predictor association.

Multivariate techniques that deal with single criterion/multiple predictor association include such procedures as multiple regression, analysis of vari-

---

[13]While the original data may have been transformed by some nonlinear transformation (e.g., logarithmic), *linear in the parameters* means that all computed parameters *after* the transformation are of the first degree. For example, the function

$$Y = b_0 + b_1 X_1 + b_2 X_2 + \cdots + b_m X_m$$

is linear in the parameters. Note that b_0 is a constant, while the other parameters, $b_1, b_2, \ldots, b_m$ are all of the first degree. Moreover, none of the b_j's depends on the value of either its own X_j or any other X_k ($k \neq j$).

ance and covariance, two-group discriminant analysis, and automatic interaction detection.

Multivariate techniques that deal with multiple criterion/multiple predictor association include such procedures as canonical correlation, multivariate analysis of variance and covariance, and multiple discriminant analysis.

Analysis of Interdependence

In some cases we may not wish to partition the data matrix into criterion and predictor subsets. If so, we refer to this case as analyzing *interdependence structures*. Techniques such as factor analysis are used in this case if our focus of interest is on the *variables* of the (intact) data matrix. Cluster analysis is relevant if we wish to focus on the grouping of *objects* in the data matrix (as based on their profile similarities).

Table 9-17 shows where each of the multivariate techniques considered in later chapters is classified. (The chapter references provide a guided tour for the reader interested in particular methods.)

Table 9-17 Multivariate technique classification

DEPENDENCE STRUCTURES		INTERDEPENDENCE STRUCTURES	
Single Criterion/ Multiple Predictor Variables	*Multiple Criterion/ Multiple Predictor Variables*	*Emphasis on Variables*	*Emphasis on Objects*
• Multiple regression (Chapter 10)	• Multiple discriminant analysis (Chapter 12)	• Factor analysis (Chapter 13)	• Cluster analysis (Chapter 13)
• Analysis of variance and covariance (Chapter 11)	• Canonical correlation (Chapter 12)		
• Two-group discriminant analysis (Chapter 12)	• Multivariate analysis of variance and covariance (Chapter 12)		
• Automatic interaction detection (Chapter 12)			

Dummy Variables

Our discussion of this chapter has emphasized nominal-scaled (categorical) data. Moreover, we discussed methods for dealing with two types of nominal-scaled variables:

1. Dichotomies, where the variable consists of only two classes, such as male versus female.

2. Polytomies, where the variable is comprised of three or more (assumed *unordered*) classes, such as Protestant denomination: Episcopalian, Baptist, Methodist, all other Protestants.

A key concept in working with nominal-scaled variables in multivariate analysis is the *dummy variable*. If a nominal-scaled variable is a dichotomy, we can code one category (say, male) as 1 and the other category (female) as 0. The resulting variable is called a "dummy variable." From here on we can treat this variable as consisting simply of a string of 0's and 1's, depending on what sex each person in that column is.

The same idea holds for polytomies. However, in this case we are going to need more than a single dummy variable. If the polytomy consists of k classes, we shall need $k - 1$ dummy variables.

To illustrate, suppose that we had the nominal-scaled variable *occupation* expressed as a five-state polytomy. If so, we could set up four dummy variables, as follows:

OCCUPATIONAL CATEGORY	DUMMY VARIABLE			
	1	*2*	*3*	*4*
Professional	1	0	0	0
Clerical	0	1	0	0
Skilled laborer	0	0	1	0
Unskilled laborer	0	0	0	1
Other	0	0	0	0

As noted, if the person's occupation is Professional he receives a 1 on dummy variable 1 and zero on the other three dummies. The last category, Other, receives a zero on all four dummies. Notice that this is consistent with the dummy-variable coding of a dichotomy since in this case we have a single dummy variable for two states. Furthermore, since the dichotomy or polytomy is unordered to begin with, it does not matter which category receives which coding.

As we shall see in subsequent chapters, the concept of dummy variable provides a very useful and flexible way to introduce nominal-scaled variables in multivariate methodology. Furthermore, it links the discussion of cross tabulations, both here and in Chapter 8, with the material of multivariate analysis.

We shall return to the classification system of Table 9-17, as new techniques are introduced in subsequent chapters. Insofar as the present chapter is concerned we have been dealing with an analysis of dependence structures where both variables are nominal-scaled. Moreover, we have discussed both data description (via agreement indexes) and statistical testing, via chi-square analysis.

Although this chapter has emphasized bivariate association between nominal-scaled variables, it should be mentioned that more advanced techniques have extended chi-square analysis to multiway tables (involving 3 or more categorizations).[14]

In particular, there is increasing interest in the development of new models for analyzing multiway contingency tables in marketing research and in the behavioral sciences generally.[15]

SUMMARY

Analysis of associative data is the hallmark of modern marketing research. This chapter provides a bridge between the strictly descriptive treatment afforded by marginal and cross tabulations and the more highly sophisticated techniques of multivariate analysis.

We started the chapter with some introductory comments on the computation of percentages in cross tabulations. We then turned to a discussion of the interpretative value of introducing a third variable into the original two-variable cross tabulation.

The next main section of the chapter dealt with the analysis of contingency tables (cross tabulations of frequency data) via chi-square techniques. Agreement indexes for measuring the strength of association between two categorical variables were also illustrated. The BMD–PIF computer program was briefly described as an example of a program that offers high flexibility for analyzing cross-tabulation data.

The concluding section of the chapter dealt with introductory remarks on multivariate analysis, the principal topic of Parts III and IV. The data matrix is the grist of the multivariate analyst's mill. We described the various classes of multivariate techniques as consisting of:

1. Single criterion/multiple predictor association.

[14]See H. O. Lancaster, *The Chi Squared Distribution* (New York: John Wiley & Sons, Inc., 1969).

[15]As an example from marketing research, see P. E. Green, F. J. Carmone, and D. M. Wachspress, "On the Analysis of Qualitative Data in Marketing Research," *Journal of Marketing Research*, 14 (February, 1977), 52–59. An example from behavioral science is L. A. Goodman, "A General Model for the Analysis of Surveys," *American Journal of Sociology*, 77 (1971), 1035–86.

2. Multiple criterion/multiple predictor association.
3. The analysis of interdependence.

ASSIGNMENT MATERIAL

1. The marketing research department of a prominent advertising agency decides to measure the sales response to the magazine advertising of brand S hand soap. The product is to be advertised initially in the July 4 issue of Magazine M, a magazine issued every two weeks. The agency selects a simple random sample of 200 subscribing families to Magazine M and interviews each of these sample families on July 19. The interview is designed to determine: (1) whether the family shopper reads the soap advertisement, and (2) whether brand S soap was purchased within the period July 5 through July 18. The results are summarized in the accompanying table.

Reading of brand S advertisment in magazine M versus purchase of brand S during following two weeks

	Number Purchasing Brand S July 5–July 18	Number Not Purchasing Brand S July 5–July 18	Total
Subscribers who read the brand S advertisement in Magazine M issue of July 4	6	54	60
Subscribers who did *not* read the brand S advertisement in Magazine M issue of July 4	11	129	140
Total	17	183	200

a. Calculate the percentage of difference between those subscribers who read the advertisement and purchased and those who did not read the advertisement and purchased by each of the following methods:
   (1) Absolute difference in percentages.
   (2) Relative difference in percentages.
b. Which method(s) would you recommend that the agency use in preparing a report to the client?

2. A marketing researcher interested in the business-publication reading habits of purchasing agents has assembled the following data:

Business-publication preferences
(first-choice mentions)

Business Publication	Frequency of First Choice
W	35
X	30
Y	45
Z	55
Total	165

a. Test the null hypothesis ($\alpha = 0.05$) that there are no differences among frequencies of choice for publications W, X, Y, and Z.

b. Suppose that the researcher had aggregated responses for the publication pairs W–Y and X–Z. Test the null hypothesis ($\alpha = 0.05$) that there are no differences among frequencies of choice for the two publication pairs.

3. Assume next that the researcher was able to obtain information regarding whether each purchasing agent held a technical degree or not. The data are as follows:

BUSINESS PUBLICATION	FIRST-CHOICE MENTIONS		TOTAL
	Technical Degree	No Technical Degree	
W	20	15	35
X	15	15	30
Y	25	20	45
Z	30	25	55
Total	90	75	165

a. Is there association between business-publication choice and type of college degree ($\alpha = 0.1$)?

b. What is the appropriate null hypothesis for this illustration?

    c. Compute the contingency coefficient between business publication choice and types of college degree.

4. What are some marketing examples where we might be interested in:
    a. Single criterion/multiple predictor association?
    b. Multiple criterion/multiple predictor association?
    c. Cluster analysis of consumers into relatively homogeneous groups?
    d. Introducing a third variable into a cross tabulation involving choice of our brand (versus others) and respondent income?

Multiple   10
and Partial Regression

INTRODUCTION

The multiple regression model is the prototype of single criterion/multiple predictor association, as described in the concluding section of Chapter 9. This chapter presents an introductory discussion of the topic. The case of one criterion and one predictor variable (called simple or bivariate regression) is discussed first. We then introduce a second predictor variable and describe the principal concepts of multiple and partial regression.

Inasmuch as virtually all regression problems of realistic size are solved by the computer, we next turn to a discussion of two well-known programs: an all-variables regression program (BMD-03R) and a stepwise regression program (BMD-02R). The use of dummy-variable coding is also illustrated at this point.

The concluding section of the chapter deals with the important problem of multicollinearity in which some or all of the predictor variables are highly correlated. Ways are discussed for coping with this problem and caveats are presented regarding the interpretation of partial regression coefficients under these conditions.

SOME BASIC CONCEPTS

In the analysis of associative data the marketing researcher is almost always interested in *prediction* problems:

- Can we predict how much beer a consumer may purchase per week from that person's sex, age, income, and education level?

- Can we predict the dollar volume of purchase of our product by industrial purchasing agents as a function of our relative price, delivery schedules, product quality, and technical service?

The list of such problems is almost endless. Not surprisingly, the linear regression model—as applied in either the bivariate or multivariate form—is one of the most popular tools in the marketing researcher's kit.

Some Industry Examples

The regression model has been applied to problems ranging from estimating salespeople's quotas to predicting demand for new shopping centers.

As an illustration of an offbeat application, one of the leading ski resorts in northeastern Pennsylvania used a regression model to predict weekend attendance, based on such variables as:

- Turnpike driving conditions
- Average temperature in the three-day period preceding the weekend
- Local weather forecast for the weekend
- Amount of newspaper space devoted to the resort's advertisements in surrounding city newspapers
- A moving average of the three preceding weekends' attendance

The model's accuracy was within $\pm 6\%$ of actual attendance throughout the season.

One firm used a regression model to predict physicians' readership of various medical journals as related to physician ratings of each journal's:

- Writing style
- Quality of illustrations
- Informativeness of advertisements
- Relevance to physician needs
- Authoritativeness in the medical profession
- Frequency of issue

The model predicted actual readership in future time periods quite well. Moreover, it provided diagnostic information as to how various journals' editorial policy and advertising could be improved.

Many other kinds of applications of regression are described in the bibliography at the end of the book.

In all these problems the researcher wishing to use multiple regression (or its special case, bivariate regression) is interested in four main questions:

1. Can we find a linear composite of the predictor variables that will compactly express the relationship between a criterion variable and the set of predictors?
2. If we can, how strong is the relationship; that is, how well can we predict values of the criterion variable from values of the linear composite?
3. Is the overall relationship statistically significant?
4. Which predictors are most important in accounting for variation in the criterion variable; in particular, can the original model be reduced to fewer variables that still provide adequate prediction of the criterion?

The basic ideas of multiple regression are most easily explained by a numerical example. We proceed one step at a time by first discussing bivariate regression (involving a single criterion and a single predictor) and then on to multiple regression.

A Numerical Example of Simple Regression

Suppose that a marketing researcher is interested in consumers' attitudes toward nutritional additives in ready-to-eat cereals. Specifically, a set of written concept descriptions of a children's cereal are prepared in which two characteristics of the cereal are varied:

X_1: the amount of protein (in grams) per 2-ounce serving, and
X_2: the percentage of minimum daily requirements of vitamin D per 2-ounce serving.

In the nature of a pretest, the researcher obtains consumers' interval-scaled evaluations of the ten concept descriptions, on a preference rating scale, ranging from 1, dislike extremely, up to 9, like extremely well.

The (hypothetical) data appear in Table 10-1. For the moment let us confine our attention to columns 2, 3, 5, 6, and 7, which pertain to the criterion variable Y and the first predictor variable X_1. We wish to see if we can predict values of Y from values of X_1.

One of the first things that is usually done in examining two-variable relationships is to prepare a *scatter diagram* in which the ten values of Y are plotted against their X_1 counterparts. Figure 10-1 shows this plot. It appears that there is a direct relationship between Y and X_1. Moreover, it would seem that a linear or straight-line relationship might describe the functional form rather well.

Table 10-1 Consumer preference ratings of ten cereals varying in nutritional level

(1) Rater	(2) Preference rating, Y	(3) Protein, X_1	(4) Vitamin D, X_2	(5) Y^2	(6) X_1^2	(7) YX_1	(8) X_2^2	(9) YX_2	(10) X_1X_2
1	3	4	2	9	16	12	4	6	8
2	7	9	7	49	81	63	49	49	63
3	2	3	1	4	9	6	1	2	3
4	1	1	2	1	1	1	4	2	2
5	6	3	3	36	9	18	9	18	9
6	2	4	4	4	16	8	16	8	16
7	8	7	9	64	49	56	81	72	63
8	3	3	2	9	9	9	4	6	6
9	9	8	7	81	64	72	49	63	56
10	2	1	3	4	1	2	9	6	3
Total	43	43	40	261	255	247	226	232	229
Mean	4.3	4.3	4.0						
Standard deviation	2.908	2.791	2.708						

Figure 10-1   Scatter diagram and least-squares regression line—preference rating versus grams of protein

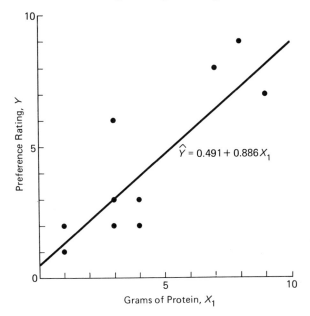

The linear model can be written

$$\hat{Y} = a + bX_1$$

where $\hat{Y}$ denotes values of the criterion that are predicted by the linear model; a denotes the intercept, or value of $\hat{Y}$ when X_1 is zero; and b denotes the slope of the line, or change in $\hat{Y}$ per unit change in X_1.

But how do we find the numerical values of a and b? The method used in this chapter is known as *least squares*. As the reader will recall from introductory statistics, the method of least squares finds that line whose sum of squared deviations of the observed values Y_i from their estimated counterparts $\hat{Y}_i$ (on the regression line) is a minimum.

Parameter Estimation

To compute the estimated parameters (a and b) of the linear model, we return to the data of Table 10-1. In the two-variable case the formulas are relatively simple:

$$b = \frac{\sum YX_1 - n\bar{Y}\bar{X}_1}{\sum X_1^2 - n\bar{X}_1^2}$$
$$= \frac{247 - 10(4.3)(4.3)}{255 - 10(4.3)^2}$$
$$= 0.886$$

where n is the sample size and $\bar{Y}$ and $\bar{X}_1$ denote the mean of Y and X_1, respectively. Having found the slope b, the intercept a is found from

$$a = \bar{Y} - b\bar{X}_1$$
$$= 4.3 - 0.886(4.3)$$
$$= 0.491$$

leading to the linear function

$$\hat{Y} = 0.491 + 0.886X_1$$

This function is plotted in Figure 10-1; it appears to fit the plotted points rather well.

Assumptions of the Model

Underlying least-squares computations is a set of assumptions. Although least-squares regression models do not need to assume normality in the (conditional) distributions of the criterion variable, we shall make this assumption for our subsequent discussion of significance testing. With this in mind the assumptions of the regression model are as follows:[1]

1. For each fixed value of X_1 we assume a normal distribution of Y from which our particular sample has been drawn independently.[2]
2. The means of all of these normal distributions of Y—as conditioned by X_1—lie on a straight line with slope β.

---

[1]Greek symbols α and β are used to denote universe counterparts of a and b.

[2]What is being described is the "classical" regression model. Modern versions of the model permit the predictors to be random variables, but their distribution is not allowed to depend upon the parameters of the regression equation.

3. The normal distributions of Y all have equal variances. This (common) variance does not depend on values assumed by the variable X_1.

Expressed algebraically, our model is

$$Y = \alpha + \beta X_1 + \epsilon$$

where α = mean of Y population when $X_1 = 0$

β = change in Y population mean per unit change in X_1

ϵ = error term drawn independently from a normally distributed universe with mean $\mu(\epsilon) = 0$ and variance $\sigma^2(\epsilon)$; the error term is independent of X_1

Figure 10-2 illustrates the nature of these assumptions. The reader should note that each value of X_1 has associated with it a normal curve for Y. The means of all these normal distributions lie on the straight line shown in the figure.

Figure 10-2   Two-variable regression model—theoretical

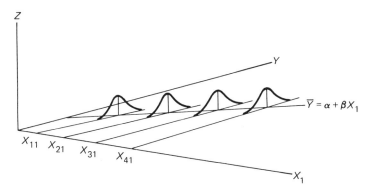

In constructing the estimating equation by least squares we have computed a *sample* regression line,

$$\hat{Y} = a + bX_1$$

where $\hat{Y}$ is the estimated mean of Y, given X_1, and a, b are the sample estimates of α and β in the theoretical model. As already noted, this line appears in Figure 10-1 for the specific bivariate problem of Table 10-1.

However, functional forms other than the linear may be suggested by the preliminary scatter plot. Figure 10-3 shows various types of scatter diagrams and regression lines for the two-variable case. Panel I shows the ideal case in which *all* the variation in Y is accounted for by variation in X_1. We note that the regression line passes through the mean of each variable and that the slope b happens to be positive. The intercept a represents the predicted value of $\hat{Y}$ when $X_1 = 0$. In Panel II we note that there is residual variation in Y, and, furthermore, that the slope b is negative. Panel III demonstrates the case in which no association between Y and X_1 is found. In this case the mean of Y is as good a predictor as the variable X_1 (the slope b is zero). Panel IV emphasizes that a linear model is being fitted. That is, no *linear* association is found ($b = 0$), even though a curvilinear relationship is apparent from the scatter diagram. Figure 10-3 illustrates the desirability

Figure 10-3   Illustrative scatter diagrams and regression lines

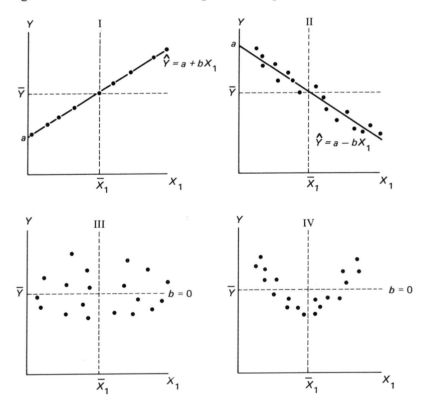

of plotting one's data *before* proceeding to formulate a specific regression model.

Strength of Association

It is one thing to find the regression equation (as shown in Figure 10-1), but at this point we still do not know how *strong* the association is. In other words, how well does X_1 predict Y?

The measure of strength of association in bivariate regression is denoted by r^2 and is called the *coefficient of determination*. This coefficient varies between 0 and 1 and represents the proportion of total variation in Y (as measured about its own mean $\bar{Y}$) that is accounted for by variation in X_1.

If we were to use $\bar{Y}$ to estimate each separate value of Y, then a measure of our *inability* to predict Y would be given by the sum of the squared deviations $\sum_{i=1}^{n} (Y_i - \bar{Y})^2$. On the other hand, if we tried to predict Y by employing a linear regression based on X_1, we could use each $\hat{Y}_i$ to predict its counterpart Y_i. In this case a measure of our *inability* to predict Y_i is given by $\sum_{i=1}^{n} (Y_i - \hat{Y}_i)^2$. We can define r^2 as a function of these two quantities:

$$r^2 = 1 - \frac{\sum_{i=1}^{n} (Y_i - \hat{Y}_i)^2}{\sum_{i=1}^{n} (Y_i - \bar{Y})^2}$$

If each $\hat{Y}_i$ predicts its counterpart Y_i perfectly, then $r^2 = 1$ since the numerator of the second term on the right is zero. However, if using the regression equation does no better than $\bar{Y}$ alone, then the second term on the right is 1 and $r^2 = 0$, indicating no ability to predict Y_i (beyond the use of $\bar{Y}$ itself).[3] What this formula says, in words, is

$$r^2 = 1 - \frac{\text{unaccounted-for variance}}{\text{total variance}} = \frac{\text{accounted-for variance}}{\text{total variance}}$$

Table 10-2 shows the residuals obtained after using the regression equation to predict each value of Y_i via its counterpart $\hat{Y}_i$. We then find $r^2_{yx_1}$ (where we now show the explicit subscripts) by computing from the table:

---

[3] The use of X_1 in a linear regression can do no worse than $\bar{Y}$. Even if b turns out to be zero, the predictions are $\hat{Y}_i = a = \bar{Y}$, which are the same as using the mean of the criterion values in the first place.

Table 10-2   Actual Y_i, predicted $\hat{Y}_i$, and residuals $Y_i - \hat{Y}_i$

Rater	Actual, Y_i	Predicted,* $\hat{Y}_i$	Residuals, $Y_i - \hat{Y}_i$
1	3	4.034	−1.034
2	7	8.464	−1.464
3	2	3.148	−1.148
4	1	1.377	−0.377
5	6	3.148	2.852
6	2	4.034	−2.034
7	8	6.692	1.308
8	3	3.148	−0.148
9	9	7.579	1.422
10	2	1.377	0.623
Mean	4.3	4.3	0

*From the equation $\hat{Y}_i = 0.491 + 0.886 X_{i1}$.

$$\sum_{i=1}^{n} (Y_i - \hat{Y}_i)^2 = (-1.034)^2 + (-1.464)^2 + \cdots + (0.623)^2$$
$$= 21.09$$

This is the sum of squared errors in predicting Y_i from $\hat{Y}_i$. Next, we find:

$$\sum_{i=1}^{n} (Y_i - \bar{Y})^2 = (3 - 4.3)^2 + (7 - 4.3)^2 + \cdots + (2 - 4.3)^2$$
$$= 76.10$$

This is the sum of squared errors in predicting Y_i from $\bar{Y}$.
Hence,

$$\boxed{\begin{aligned} r_{yx_1}^2 &= 1 - \frac{21.09}{76.10} \\ &= 0.723 \end{aligned}}$$

and we say that 72% *of the variation in Y has been accounted for by variation in X_1*. As might also be surmised, there is one more quantity of interest:

$$\sum_{i=1}^{n} (\hat{Y}_i - \bar{Y})^2 = (4.034 - 4.3)^2 + (8.464 - 4.3)^2 + \cdots + (1.377 - 4.3)^2$$
$$= 55.01$$

which is the accounted-for sum of squares due to the regression of Y on X_1.

Figure 10-4 puts all these quantities in perspective by first showing deviations of $Y_i - \bar{Y}$. As noted above, the sum of these squared deviations is 76.10. Panel II shows the counterpart deviations of Y_i from $\hat{Y}_i$; the sum of these squared deviations is 21.09. Panel III shows the deviations of $\hat{Y}_i$ from $\bar{Y}$; the sum of these squared deviations is 55.01. We note that the results are additive: $21.09 + 55.01 = 76.10$.

Figure 10-4   Breakdown of deviations $Y_i - \bar{Y}$ into two additive parts

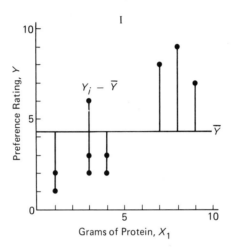

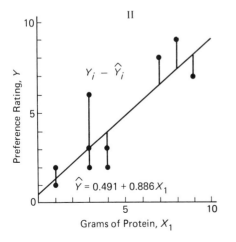

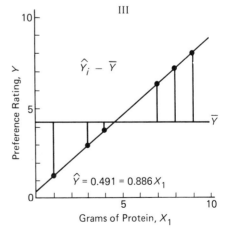

The Product-Moment Correlation

Another quantity of interest in bivariate regression is the well-known _product-moment correlation_. The correlation between Y and X_1, denoted r_{yx_1}, is defined most simply as the _average cross product:_

$$r_{yx_1} = \frac{1}{n} \sum_{i=1}^{n} Z_{y_i} Z_{x_{i1}}$$

when Z_{y_i} and $Z_{x_{i1}}$ are the standard unit variate forms of Y_i and X_{i1}, respectively. They are defined by

$$Z_{y_i} = \frac{Y_i - \bar{Y}}{s_y}; \qquad Z_{x_{i1}} = \frac{X_{i1} - \bar{X}_1}{s_{x_1}}$$

where s_y and s_{x_1} are the standard deviations of Y and X_1, respectively. Thus, each Z value has a zero mean and unit standard deviation. Computationally, however, we can also obtain r_{yx_1} from the regression coefficient b and the standard deviations of Y and X_1 (see Table 10-1 for the latter):

$$r_{yx_1} = b\frac{s_{x_1}}{s_y} = 0.886 \frac{2.791}{2.908}$$
$$= 0.850$$

The correlation coefficient r_{yx_1} varies between -1 for perfect negative correlation and 1 for perfect positive correlation. It is simply the regression of Y on X_1 when both are expressed in standard unit deviate form.[4] (In this case the intercept is zero, since the mean of both Y and X_1 is zero and the regression line will pass through their joint means.)

Finally, we note that the coefficient of determination, $r^2_{yx_1}$, computed earlier, is simply the _square_ of the product-moment correlation r_{yx_1}. That is, $0.723 = (0.85)^2$, even though each has been developed conceptually along somewhat different lines.

---

[4]If we were to reverse the process and regress X_1 on Y, we would find that the slope was 0.816 and

$$r_{yx_1} = 0.816\frac{2.908}{2.791} = 0.850$$

Either way, we get the same result. The product moment correlation is a _symmetric_ measure of association between Y and X_1.

MULTIPLE AND PARTIAL REGRESSION

It is time to introduce the second predictor variable X_2, as shown in Table 10-1. The theoretical model now becomes

$$Y = \alpha + \beta_1 X_1 + \beta_2 X_2 + \epsilon$$

with parameters estimated by

$$\hat{Y} = a + b_1 X_1 + b_2 X_2$$

All assumptions regarding the bivariate regression model continue to hold in the present case as well. However, it is important to remember that, in general, the current b_1—now called a *partial* regression coefficient with respect to X_1—will *not* equal its counterpart coefficient (b) obtained from the bivariate regression. This is because X_1 itself *will usually be correlated with* X_2. In the bivariate case X_2 was ignored and any of the variation in Y that was shared by X_1 *and* X_2 was credited solely to X_1. Such will no longer be the case.

In the case of only two predictors, X_1 and X_2, it is still possible to prepare a scatter plot. However, now the plot appears in terms of a *three-dimensional* space. In this case we fit a plane—that particular plane whose sum of squared deviations of the Y_i from their $\hat{Y}_i$ counterparts (on the plane) is a minimum. Figure 10-5 shows the original scatter and the fitted plane for the sample problem of Table 10-1. The estimated (least-squares) equation is

$$\hat{Y} = 0.247 + 0.493 X_1 + 0.484 X_2$$

The first slope coefficient of 0.493 denotes the change in $\hat{Y}$ per unit change in X_1 when X_2 is held constant; similarly, 0.484 denotes the change in $\hat{Y}$ per unit change in X_2 when X_1 is held constant. We note that $0.493 \neq 0.886$, the slope obtained earlier in the bivariate case. This is because X_1 and X_2 are, themselves, correlated and X_1 is now forced to share some of its Y-variable association with the second predictor X_2.

Parameter Estimation

Finding the partial regression coefficients $b_1 = 0.493$ and $b_2 = 0.484$ and the intercept $a = 0.247$ is considerably more complicated in the case of multiple regression. Table 10-1 provides the various sums of squares and

Figure 10-5   Scatter plot and fitted regression plane

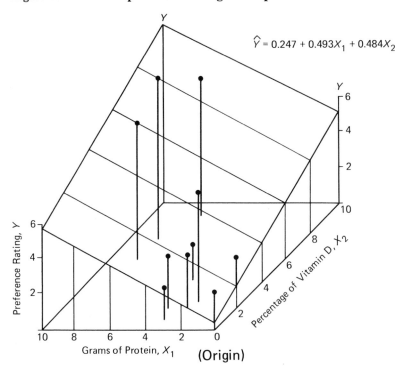

cross products that we need. Table 10-3 shows the results of solving the set of simultaneous equations to find b_1 and b_2. Following this, we compute the intercept value of $a = 0.247$ in the manner shown.

But what is the relationship of, say, $b_1 = 0.493$ to the case of simple regression? One way of thinking about the interpretation of b_1 is to imagine our first regressing X_1 on X_2 and then computing *residuals* $X_{i1} - \hat{X}_{i1}$ from this regression. If we then regress the original values of Y on the set of X_1 residuals, the "simple" regression coefficient in this situation turns out to be precisely the *partial regression coefficient*, $b_1 = 0.493$, that was obtained from Table 10-3.[5] Similar kinds of remarks pertain to b_2 but, in this case, it is X_2 whose linear association with X_1 is removed before regressing Y on the set of X_2 residuals.

The same general idea extends to three or more predictor variables. In the more general case, the appropriate residuals are found by regressing the particular X_j of interest on *all* the remaining predictors via a *multiple*

---

[5]Interestingly enough, we could also get b_1 by regressing Y residuals on X_1 residuals, where *both* are net of their linear association with X_2. (However, this extra step is not really needed to obtain the partial regression coefficient.)

Table 10-3   Computation of partial regression coefficients and the coefficient of multiple determination

---

From Table 10-1: mean corrected sums of squares and cross products:

$$\sum y^2 = \sum Y^2 - n\bar{Y}^2 \quad = 261 - 10(4.3)^2 \quad = 76.1$$
$$\sum x_1^2 = \sum X_1^2 - n\bar{X}_1^2 \quad = 255 - 10(4.3)^2 \quad = 70.1$$
$$\sum x_2^2 = \sum X_2^2 - n\bar{X}_2^2 \quad = 226 - 10(4.0)^2 \quad = 66.0$$
$$\sum yx_1 = \sum YX_1 - n\bar{Y}\bar{X}_1 \quad = 247 - 10(4.3)(4.3) = 62.1$$
$$\sum yx_2 = \sum YX_2 - n\bar{Y}\bar{X}_2 \quad = 232 - 10(4.3)(4.0) = 60.0$$
$$\sum x_1x_2 = \sum X_1X_2 - n\bar{X}_1\bar{X}_2 = 229 - 10(4.3)(4.0) = 57.0$$

Solving for the regression equation:

$$\sum yx_1 = \sum x_1^2 b_1 + \sum x_1x_2 b_2$$
$$\sum yx_2 = \sum x_1x_2 b_1 + \sum x_2^2 b_2$$
$$62.1 = 70.1b_1 + 57.0b_2$$
$$60.0 = 57.0b_1 + 66.0b_2$$
$$b_1 = 0.493; \quad b_2 = 0.484$$
$$a = \bar{Y} - b_1\bar{X}_1 - b_2\bar{X}_2$$
$$= 4.3 - 0.493(4.3) - 0.484(4.0)$$
$$= 0.247$$

Computing the coefficient of multiple determination:

$$R^2_{y\cdot x_1, x_2} = \frac{b_1 \sum yx_1 + b_2 \sum yx_2}{\sum y^2} = \frac{0.493(62.1) + 0.484(60.0)}{76.1} = 0.783$$

---

regression. Then, we would regress Y on the set of X_j residuals to get the b_j of interest. While this procedure would be going about the calculation of partial regression coefficients the hard way, it does serve to show their conceptual linkage to simple (bivariate) regression coefficients.

Coefficient of Multiple Determination

Finding the *coefficient of multiple determination* proceeds in just the same way as the bivariate case, although, as might be surmised, various computational shortcuts are available. Table 10-3 shows that application of a shortcut formula leads to

$$R^2_{y\cdot x_1, x_2} = 0.783$$

However, Table 10-4 shows that we can get the same thing through the more roundabout procedure of finding the predicted $\hat{Y}_i$ values from the *multiple* regression and then the residuals $Y_i - \hat{Y}_i$. This is the same approach as was followed in the bivariate case.

We note that the multiple regression equation does quite well at prediction, since 78% of the variation in Y is accounted for by variation in X_1 *and*

Table 10-4   Calculation of the coefficient of multiple determination from the regression residuals

Rater	Y_i	$\hat{Y}_i$	$Y_i - \hat{Y}_i$	Rater	Y_i	$\hat{Y}_i$	$Y_i - \hat{Y}_i$
1	3	3.185	−0.185	6	2	4.152	−2.152
2	7	8.066	−1.066	7	8	8.048	−0.048
3	2	2.209	−0.209	8	3	2.692	0.308
4	1	1.707	−0.707	9	9	7.574	1.426
5	6	3.176	2.824	10	2	2.191	−0.191

Coefficient of multiple determination:

$$R^2_{y \cdot x_1, x_2} = 1 - \frac{\sum_{i=1}^{n} (Y_i - \hat{Y}_i)^2}{\sum_{i=1}^{n} (Y_i - \bar{Y})^2}$$

$$= 1 - \left[\frac{(-0.185)^2 + (-1.066)^2 + \cdots + (-0.191)^2}{76.10} \right]$$

$$= 1 - \frac{16.49}{76.10} = 0.783; \qquad R_{y \cdot x_1, x_2} = 0.885$$

X_2. However, we recall that, if only X_1 is employed, the (simple) coefficient of determination is 72%. Apparently, X_2 and X_1 are so highly correlated—their simple correlation is 0.838—that once X_1 is in the multiple regression equation there is little need for X_2 as well.

What about the *square root* of $R^2_{y \cdot x_1, x_2}$? This is called the *coefficient of multiple correlation:*

$$R_{y \cdot x_1, x_2} = \sqrt{0.783} = 0.885$$

and is interpreted as the *simple correlation* (i.e., bivariate correlation) between Y_i and $\hat{Y}_i$ where, as we know, the $\hat{Y}_i$ are the *predicted* values obtained by the best linear composite of X_1 and X_2 in the least-squares sense; this composite is given by the multiple regression equation.

Other Coefficients of Interest

Computing the partial regression coefficients and the coefficient of multiple determination still does not exhaust the possible output coefficients in multiple regression. Marketing researchers frequently have interest in three other measures:

- The beta coefficients b_j^*
- The partial correlation coefficients $r_{yx_j \cdot x_k, x_p \ldots}$
- The part correlation coefficients $r_{yx_j (x_k, x_p \ldots)}$

As it turns out, these three measures are not difficult to understand, once they are defined conceptually:

1. The beta coefficients b_j^* are the partial regression coefficients (b_j) that one gets if all variables (Y, X_1, X_2) entering the analysis are each standardized to zero mean and unit standard deviation *before* the multiple regression equation is computed.

2. The partial correlation coefficients $r_{yx_j \cdot x_k, x_p, \ldots}$ are actually *simple* (two-variable) correlations between the *two sets of residuals* that remain after association of all other predictors is removed from Y and X_j separately.

3. The part correlation coefficients $r_{yx_j(x_k, x_p, \ldots)}$ are also simple correlations, this time between the *original* Y variable and the set of X_j residuals that remain after removing only X_j's linear association with all other predictors.

We do not delve into computational formulas for the beta coefficients, partial correlation coefficients, and part correlation coefficients, since, in practice, these measures are calculated by various regression programs.[6] Of these, the partial correlation coefficient is generally viewed as the most important; we consider its use in a later section.

Recapitulation

Once we get used to the idea of drawing parallels between multiple and simple regression we see that:

1. A partial regression coefficient is really a simple (bivariate) regression coefficient between the original Y and a set of X_j residuals that remain after X_j has been regressed on all the other predictors.

---

[6]However, a simple way to think about the (squared) *part* correlation is in terms of the change in R^2 before and after inclusion of, say, X_1. That is, the squared part correlation of Y with X_1 can be defined as

$$r_{yx_1(x_2, x_3, \ldots)}^2 = R_{y \cdot x_1, x_2, x_3, \ldots}^2 - R_{y \cdot x_2, x_3, \ldots}^2$$

Thus, the (squared) part correlation is simply the difference in R^2 between an equation that includes all predictors and one that omits the jth predictor of interest. Moreover, we can find the (squared) *partial* correlation of Y with X_1 from the *relative* measure:

$$r_{yx_1 \cdot x_2, x_3, \ldots}^2 = \frac{R_{y \cdot x_1, x_2, x_3, \ldots}^2 - R_{y \cdot x_2, x_3, \ldots}^2}{1 - R_{y \cdot x_2, x_3, \ldots}^2}$$

Similar remarks pertain to the (squared) partial correlation of Y with X_2 (or any other predictor X_j in the case of three or more predictors).

2. The multiple correlation coefficient is the simple correlation between the original criterion variable Y_i and $\hat{Y}_i$, where the latter is given by the least-squares multiple regression.

3. A partial correlation coefficient is the simple correlation between the set of Y residuals and the set of X_j residuals, where both are net of linear association with all other predictors.

4. The part correlation coefficient takes out the linear association of X_j (only) with the remaining predictors before finding its simple correlation with Y.

5. The beta coefficient is a partial regression coefficient that is obtained if all variables are previously expressed as standard unit variates before the multiple regression equation is computed.

At this point the reader should have some appreciation for the labor involved in computing multiple regression equations and related coefficients. Moreover, we still have not discussed questions of statistical significance and the possibility of finding regression models with fewer parameters than we begin with originally. These topics are best explored in the context of *computerized* regression procedures.

COMPUTERIZED REGRESSION

With the availability of a large variety of packaged programs, computation of multiple regressions is almost invariably carried out by the computer. (This is also the case for all the other multivariate techniques considered in this book.) For this reason, it is appropriate to describe the output that one obtains from such programs. Two programs of wide distribution—the BMD-03R all-variables regression and the BMD-02R stepwise regression—are discussed as prototypical cases.[7]

The BMD-03R Program

BMD-03R is an all-variables program in which the regression is computed across the full set of predictors, rather than on a one-at-a-time basis. Up to 49 predictors can be accommodated with a virtually unlimited number of cases. So as to show comparisons with our earlier computations, the same sample data of Table 10-1 were run through BMD-03R. Table 10-5 shows the output provided by this program. Most of the coefficients that were shown earlier appear here, along with some additional measures as well.

[7]W. J. Dixon, ed., *BMD: Biomedical Computer Programs* (Berkeley, Calif.: University of California Press, 1973).

Table 10-5 Summary output of BMD-03R regression analysis of sample data from Table 10-1

Sample R^2	0.783
Adjusted R^2	0.721
Sample R (unadjusted)	0.885
SS due to regression	59.61
SS of deviations from regression	16.49
Variance of estimate	2.356
Standard error of estimate	1.535
Intercept: $a = 0.247$	

ANALYSIS OF VARIANCE FOR THE FULL REGRESSION

Source of Variation	Degrees of Freedom	Sum of Squares	Mean Square	F Ratio
Due to regression	2	59.61	29.805	12.652
Deviations about regression	7	16.49	2.356	
Total	9	76.10		

ADDITIONAL STATISTICS

Variable Number	Mean	Standard Deviation	Regression Coefficient	Standard Error of Regression Coefficient	Computed t Value	Partial Correlation Coefficient	Sum of Squares Added	Proportion Total of Variation
X_1	4.3	2.791	0.493	0.336	1.466	0.485	55.013	0.723
X_2	4.0	2.708	0.484	0.346	1.397	0.467	4.597	0.060
Y	4.3	2.908					59.610	0.783

Starting at the top of the table we find the same coefficient of multiple determination that was computed in Table 10-3. However, we also note that an *adjusted* R^2 of 0.721 is printed out. This is computed from the sample R^2 as follows:

$$R^2 \text{ (adjusted)} = 1 - (1 - R^2)\frac{n-1}{n-m-1}$$

$$= 1 - \frac{0.217(9)}{7}$$

$$= 0.721$$

where m denotes the number of predictor variables. Adjusted R^2 is computed to reflect the fact that the sample R^2 capitalizes on chance variation in the *specific* data set under study. Adjusted R^2 provides a better estimate of the universe R^2 value.[8]

The quantities 59.61 (sum of squares due to regression), 16.49 (sum of squares of deviations from regression), and 76.10 (total sum of squares about the mean of Y) have all been discussed conceptually in Figure 10-4 (in the bivariate case) and numerically in Table 10-4.[9] What is new in Table 10-5, however, is the analysis of variance table in which the following (equivalent) hypotheses are tested:

$$R_p^2 = 0; \qquad \beta_1 = \beta_2 = 0$$

where R_p^2 denotes the population coefficient of multiple determination.

The F-Ratio Test

The F ratio is the appropriate test for these hypotheses.[10] We first obtain the mean squares, 29.805 and 2.356, by dividing the corresponding sums of

---

[8]More precisely, even if the null hypothesis H_0: $R_p^2 = 0$ is true, the expectation of R^2, denoted $E(R^2)$, does not equal zero. Rather, $E(R^2) = m/(n-1)$ so that as m approaches n, the sample size, $E(R^2)$ approaches 1. The adjusted R^2 can actually decrease if a new predictor enters the regression equation, since the increase in accounted-for sum of squares may be more than counterbalanced by the loss of a degree of freedom in the denominator $(n - m - 1)$. In contrast, unadjusted R^2 can never decrease as a new predictor is introduced into the regression equation.

[9]The quantity 2.356, called the *variance of the estimate*, is simply the sum of squared deviations from regression, 16.49, divided by 7, the associated degrees of freedom. It is analogous to the variance around a mean. Its square root is 1.535 and is called the *standard error of the estimate*. This later quantity is analogous to a standard deviation around a mean. The larger either of these two quantities is, the poorer the fit of the regression equation.

[10]This test is discussed in more detail in Chapter 11, in the context of analysis of variance. However, as recalled from basic statistics, the F distribution is the distribution followed by the ratio of two independent, unbiased estimates of the normal population variance σ^2. If R_p^2 is zero, then the sample R^2 reflects only sampling error and the F ratio will tend to be equal to unity.

squares by their respective degrees of freedom. Then we find the F ratio of 12.652. This value, with 2 degrees of freedom for numerator and 7 degrees of freedom for denominator, is compared to a tabular F (see Table A-4 in Appendix A) of 3.26 with an (illustrative) significance level of 0.1. We reject the preceding null hypotheses and conclude that the *overall regression equation is statistically significant.*

Having satisfied ourselves that at least one β coefficient is significant, there are two additional questions to raise:

1. Does each predictor separately account for statistically significant variation in Y?
2. What does each predictor contribute in terms of total accounted-for variation in Y?

We discuss these questions next, in the context of Table 10-5.

Standard Errors and *t* Tests

While the preceding analysis has indicated that the full regression is significant, it does not follow that *both* b_1 and b_2 contribute significantly to overall accounted-for variance. It may be the case that a simpler model involving only X_1 (or one involving only X_2) would be sufficient. The standard error of each individual regression coefficient is shown in Table 10-5. This is a dispersion measure that reflects two main things:

1. How highly correlated X_j is with the other predictor(s)
2. How much variance in Y is still to be accounted for

To illustrate, the standard error (SE) of b_1 is computed as follows:

$$
\begin{aligned}
\text{SE}(b_1) &= \frac{s_y}{s_{x_1}} \sqrt{\frac{1}{n-m-1} \cdot \frac{1 - R^2_{y \cdot x_1, x_2, x_3, \dots}}{1 - R^2_{x_1 \cdot x_2, x_3, \dots}}} \\
&= \frac{2.908}{2.791} \sqrt{\frac{1}{7} \cdot \frac{0.217}{0.298}} \\
&= 0.336
\end{aligned}
$$

where n is the sample size and m is the number of predictors. The standard error is a measure of dispersion about the average partial regression coefficient over repeated samplings of Y for a fixed set of values on each of the predictors. The larger the standard error is, the less reliable b_1 is across repeated samplings from the same universe. Thus, we would like to see intuitively how $\text{SE}(b_1)$ depends on the quantities to the right of the equals sign.

In particular, we note that $1 - R^2_{y \cdot x_1, x_2, x_3, \ldots}$ is the residual variance in Y after *all* predictors are considered; this is $1 - 0.783$, or 0.217. Other things equal, larger values of residual variance in Y (i.e., smaller R^2's) lead to higher standard errors.

Next, the value 0.298 in the denominator under the square-root sign is equal to the residual variance in X_1. The residual variance in X_1 is the variance of the X_1 residuals and, hence, that part of X_1 that cannot be predicted by the other predictor variables. Other things equal, *smaller* values of residual variance in X_1 lead to *higher* standard errors.

What this latter statement means conceptually is that the standard error of b_1 increases as X_1 becomes *more completely accounted for by the remaining predictor variables*. That is, as X_1 becomes increasingly redundant with the remaining predictors, its standard error increases.

The t value of 1.466 in Table 10-5 is simply the ratio of b_1 to its own standard error $SE(b_1)$. The test of significance of t_1 is carried out by finding the tabular value of the t distribution (Table A-2 in Appendix A) for 7 degrees of freedom. If we continue to use a significance level of 0.1, then the tabular value of t is 1.415 and b_1 is significant. However, b_2 (whose t value is 1.397) is *not* significant at the 0.1 level.

The t test for each individual partial regression coefficient tests whether the increment in R^2 produced by the predictor in question is significant when a model including the predictor (and all other predictors) is compared to a model including all predictors but the one being tested.

Contribution to Accounted-For Variation

The last column in the lower portion of Table 10-5, Proportion of Total Variation, still needs to be explained. First, we observe that the two contributory R^2's sum to the total sample R^2 of 0.783. However, the R^2 attributed to X_1 (0.723) is considerably greater than that (0.060) attributed to X_2.[11]

---

[11]By way of general interest, note that the squared partial correlation of Y with X_2 can be found from the formula stated earlier:

$$r^2_{yx_2 \cdot x_1} = \frac{R^2_{y \cdot x_1, x_2} - R^2_{y \cdot x_1}}{1 - R^2_{y \cdot x_1}}$$

$$= \frac{0.783 - 0.723}{1 - 0.723} = 0.217$$

We then find

$$r_{yx_2 \cdot x_1} = \sqrt{0.217} \cong 0.467$$

as shown in Table 10-5. To find the counterpart measure for X_1 we would need $R^2_{y \cdot x_2}$ or, in effect, the *simple* coefficient of determination of Y with X_2. While not computed in Table 10-5, this turns out to be 0.716 and $r^2_{yx_1 \cdot x_2}$ is then 0.236. Its square root, the partial correlation, is 0.485, and is shown in Table 10-5.

The reason is simple. This column of BMD-03R output assigns any shared variation between X_1 and X_2 to X_1, *the predictor appearing first in the input data*. $R^2 = 0.723$ is actually the *simple* coefficient of determination between Y and X_1, ignoring X_2. On the other hand, $R^2 = 0.06$ is the squared part correlation of Y with X_2 *after* the linear association of X_1 has been removed from X_2 only. This is the association between X_2 and Y which is independent of X_1.

Which Variable To Retain?

At this point we observe from the separate t tests that b_1 is significant at the 0.1 level but b_2 is not. Moreover, the introduction of X_2 *after* X_1 accounts for relatively little variation in Y (actually, an incremental R^2 of only 0.06). However, entering X_1 before X_2 is largely an arbitrary decision. We might now ask: Suppose that X_2, rather than X_1, had been entered first? If X_2 is entered first, followed by X_1, we would find that the only values that change in the whole set of output statistics in Table 10-5 are the last two columns. These become:

Variable Number	Sum of Squares Added	Proportion of Total Variance
X_1	5,065	0.067
X_2	54.545	0.716
	59.610	0.783

In practice, the question of which variables to retain is guided by substantive theory, assuming that the candidate predictors are statistically significant. Since the t value tests the *individual* significance of a partial regression coefficient (as though each variable being tested were the *last* to enter the regression), order does not matter in this case. Hence, we keep X_1 (at the 0.1 alpha level) and drop X_2, although the decision is a close one.

What *does* change by reversing the order of entry is the apportionment *between X_1 and X_2* of accounted-for variation. Accordingly, it is good practice in using BMD-03R to include those predictor variables of most theoretical interest to the researcher *in front of those variables of less interest*. This prior ordering has no effect on anything except the last two columns of the lower portion of Table 10-5. Here, however, any variable entered earlier will receive sole credit for variation shared with those entered after it.

In summary, Table 10-5 shows that BMD-03R provides the major output measures of interest in applied multiple regression studies:

1. The regression equation
2. R^2—both the sample-determined and the population-adjusted values
3. An F test for testing the significance of the overall regression (involving both X_1 and X_2)
4. Individual t tests and standard errors for testing each specific partial regression coefficient
5. Partial correlation coefficients
6. The accounted-for variance contributed by each predictor, where any shared variance of each predictor (beyond the first) is credited to the predictors that precede it, based on the researcher's order for including the predictor variables

In the sample problem R^2 was highly significant, but only the first variable X_1 was needed to account for most of the variance in Y. That is, the addition of X_2 accounted for an incremental variance of only 6 percentage points; moreover, the t test for b_2 was not significant at the 0.1 level. Therefore, in practice we would employ a *simple* regression of Y on X_1 alone. This has already been computed as $\hat{Y} = 0.491 + 0.886X_1$.

Some General Comments on R^2 and the b_j Values

Since multiple regression is the most often used technique of multivariate analysis, it is appropriate to add a few general comments regarding the key measures, R^2 and the b_j's. First, the coefficient of multiple determination R^2 cannot be lower than the highest simple r^2 with any single predictor variable. However, if all predictors correlate zero with the criterion variable, R^2 will also be zero.

When the predictors exhibit low intercorrelation among themselves, R^2 will tend to be larger; in the limit if all predictors are uncorrelated, R^2 equals the sum of the simple r^2 of each predictor, in turn, with the criterion variable. However, in the more usual case it is difficult to estimate R^2 from simple r^2's. Although rare, cases can exist where an r^2 with one predictor can be zero and yet R^2 can be substantially higher than the r^2 with the second variable; in this case the first predictor serves the function of a suppressor variable (a general concept that was described in Chapter 9 in the context of cross tabulations).

As additional predictor variables are added, R^2 cannot decrease, but usually diminishing returns set in, so that in most applications it is rare to find much increase in R^2 beyond the first several predictor variables. The upper limit of this measure is unity, and one often finds that the additional predictor variables are so highly correlated with ones already entered in the equation that little change is noted in total R^2 after their inclusion.

Finally, we should reiterate that R^2 is systematically biased upward; this was the reason for adjusting R^2 for degrees of freedom. However, when various computer programs using stepwise procedures (in which predictor variables are entered sequentially) are used to run multiple regressions, even adjusting R^2 for degrees of freedom in the final equation does not solve the "bias" problem. The reason is simple: with a large number of predictor variables it is quite easy in stepwise regression programs to take advantage of chance, not only by finding at least *some* variables that correlate highly with the criterion, but also because of the freedom such programs provide for selecting various *combinations* of predictor variables.

BMD-02R Stepwise Regression

The *BMD-02R stepwise regression program* is also widely distributed and represents an excellent prototype of stepwise procedures in general. By "stepwise" is meant that the predictor variables enter the regression equation one at a time. The purpose of this approach is to be able to screen through a large number of predictors to find some smaller subset that accounts for most of the variation in the criterion variable. BMD-02R will accommodate up to 79 predictors with a sample size that is virtually unlimited.[12]

In using BMD-02R certain control parameters need to be set. For example, the user is asked to state an F ratio for inclusion, an F ratio for deletion, and a tolerance level. (The tolerance level is defined as the value $1 - R^2$ for the jth predictor, when it is regressed on all predictors then in the equation. As such, it is a measure of the *lack* of redundancy of X_j with predictors already in the equation.) The program's default values for the preceding three control parameters are, respectively, 0.01, 0.005, and 0.001. These are "loose" values in the sense of tending to include and retain all predictors.

As preliminary output the program prints means, standard deviations, and the correlation matrix of all variables (including the criterion). Then the following features of the program are implemented:

1. The predictor with the highest (squared) simple r with the criterion (or, equivalently, the one with the highest F ratio) is entered, assuming that it passes the F-ratio control value to enter.[13]

---

[12]While BMD-02R is a highly flexible and useful program, we should warn the reader at the outset that stepwise procedures do not produce "optimal" regression equations. Because of correlatedness among the predictors (to be considered later), it is possible for an important variable never to get into the equation. Conversely, a less important variable may enter because of its particular correlation pattern with other predictors.

[13]We say "equivalently" in the sense that both measures give the same rank order of variables. The relationship between F and the square of the partial correlation coefficient is

$$F = \frac{r^2_{yx_j \cdot x_k}}{1 - r^2_{yx_j \cdot x_k}} (n - m - 1)$$

where $r^2_{yx_j \cdot x_k}$ denotes the (squared) partial correlation of Y with X_1, conditioned on the rest of the predictors (generically denoted by k in this case).

2. Any new predictor is added to the equation on the basis of its displaying the highest squared partial r (or, equivalently, the highest F value) with those predictors already in the equation, assuming that its F level and tolerance value exceed the control parameters.

3. A predictor can be deleted at any stage if its F value to remove drops below the control parameter. That is, at any given stage beyond the first, each predictor in the equation is tested as though it were the last to enter. If any F values are less than the F for retention, the one with the lowest F value is deleted at that stage.

4. At each stage in the accretion of predictors a regression equation is computed (including intercept), as well as a multiple R, and an ANOVA table for testing R^2. In addition, the standard error of each predictor in the equation is computed, as well as the F value associated with the predictor-retention test.

5. Also at each stage, the partial r's of all predictors not in the equation, their tolerance levels, and F values to enter are computed and displayed.

6. At the end of the process, a summary table with R, R^2, incremental R^2, and the F values to enter (associated with the full sequence of entered predictors) is printed.

7. The BMD-02R program also provides a capability for listing and plotting residuals $Y_i - \hat{Y}_i$ versus specified predictors and versus $\hat{Y}_i$ itself.

After the regression run has been made, the user is free to go back to that step in the sequence in which R^2 and all individual F values for retention are significant. Since the equation for that subset of variables is already available, the program does not need to be rerun.

Of course, considerations other than significance levels should direct which equation is chosen. Moreover, there is *no guarantee* that the particular subset of k ($< m$) predictors chosen by stepwise regression is the best possible subset of size k, in the sense of providing the largest (sample) R^2. One would have to compute all possible combinations of the predictors to see if this is so.

An Industry Application of BMD-02R

In a recent study conducted for a large manufacturer of steel-belted radial tires, interest centered on whether consumer interest in the firm's new radial tire brand—after exposure to a set of TV commercials, including the firm's and competitive brands—could be predicted from:

X_1: general interest in the product class of steel-belted radials;

X_2:   whether the firm's old brand was chosen on the respondent's last purchase of replacement tires;

X_3:   preexposure (before seeing the commercials) interest in the firm's new brand of steel-belted radials;

X_4:   age;

X_5:   family size;

X_6:   years of education;

X_7:   marital status;

$\left.\begin{array}{l}X_8: \\ X_9:\end{array}\right\}$ occupation; and

X_{10}:   income.

A sample of 252 male adults, all of whom were responsible for purchasing replacement tires in their respective households, provided the input data.

Dummy Variables

Of additional interest in the study was that five of the predictors were dummy variables. In particular, the following predictors were coded as dummies:

X_1:   Is the respondent interested in the product class of steel-belted radial tires? If yes, coded 1; if no, coded 0.

X_2:   Was the firm's old brand chosen as the last purchase by the respondent? If yes, coded 1; if no, coded 0.

X_7:   Is the respondent married? If yes, coded 1; if no, coded 0.

X_8:   Is the respondent's occupation professional or white-collar? If yes, coded 1; if no, coded 0.

X_9:   Is the respondent's occupation blue-collar? If yes, coded 1; if no, coded 0.

The dummy variables X_1, X_2, and X_7 are each dichotomies and present no special problems. On the other hand, the dummy variables X_8 and X_9 are developed from an originally polytomous classification:

	DUMMY VARIABLE	
OCCUPATION CATEGORY	X_8	X_9
Professional or white-collar	1	0
Blue-collar	0	1
Other (including unemployed)	0	0

Note, then, that the third category does *not appear explicitly* in the regression. Its contribution will be buried in the intercept term of the regression equation, while the contributions of X_8 and X_9 will be expressed as *differential* contributions relative to the third, or base, category. As recalled, the intercept term is obtained when all predictors (including X_8 and X_9) assume the value zero.

Generally, however, we are interested in only *relative effects* compared to some (often arbitrary) base category. Any of the three classes of occupation could serve as this base category without affecting the relative contribution of the remaining two categories, since *differential* effects are not influenced by which category serves as the reference class.

Stepwise Regression Results

The BMD-02R program produces a rather voluminous output, since summary statistics appear each time a new variable enters the regression equation. For this reason we show only two parts of the output:

1. The regression summary at step 3 of the analysis
2. Summary output at the end of the regression run[14]

Table 10-6 shows the step 3 results.

We note from Table 10-6 that the first three variables (of the ten candidate predictors) to enter are in the order X_3, X_1, and X_2. The overall regression equation is "significant." (The F ratio, with 3 degrees of freedom for numerator and 248 degrees of freedom for denominator, is significant well beyond the 0.001 level.) The multiple R is 0.58; hence, the three-predictor regression is accounting for about 34% of the variance in Y.

Judging from the last column of the table, predictor X_4 (with an F value of 1.534) will be the next variable to enter. Equivalently, its partial correlation of -0.079 is the highest in absolute value of those variables not yet in the equation.

The regression equation is

$$\hat{Y} = 2.957 + 0.585X_1 + 0.434X_2 + 1.209X_3$$

Based on these partial regression coefficients, postexposure interest in the firm's new brand increases with:

1. Interest in the product class of steel-belted radial tires
2. Purchase of the firm's old brand on the last purchase occasion
3. Preexposure interest in the firm's new brand

---

[14]This BMD-02R run was made with a rather loose criterion value of 0.3 each for the: (a) F value for inclusion, (b) F value for retention, and (c) tolerance level.

Table 10-6   Step 3 in the BMD-02R regression analysis of purchase interest in the firm's new tire brand

Step 3:

Variable entered	2
Multiple R	0.580
Standard error of estimate	2.419

ANALYSIS OF VARIANCE

	Degrees of Freedom	Sum of Squares	Mean Square	F Ratio
Due to regression	3	735.82	245.27	41.91
Residual	248	1,451.57	5.85	
Total	251			

VARIABLES IN EQUATION			VARIABLES NOT IN EQUATION			
ORDER OF ENTERING VARIABLES	Partial Regression Coefficient	Standard Error	Variable	Partial Correlation	Tolerance	F to Enter
3	1.209	0.317	4	−0.079	0.980	1.534
1	0.585	0.402	5	0.000	0.997	0.000
2	0.434	0.050	6	0.006	0.989	0.009
Intercept	(2.957)		7	−0.036	0.979	0.321
			8	0.030	0.961	0.222
			9	−0.028	0.979	0.187
			10	0.078	0.985	1.526

All three of these coefficients make sense from an interpretive point of view.

Judging from the small values of F to enter we would expect that not much is to be gained in going beyond three predictors. This hunch is borne out by the summary results appearing in Table 10-7.

We note from Table 10-7 that the program terminated after step 6, since the F values to enter (at step 7) were all less than 0.3.[15] Even with the three additional steps R^2 has only increased about 1 percentage point from that noted in step 3. We conclude that the demographic variables add little to accounted-for variation in Y. One may just as well stop with the three-predictor equation of Table 10-6. Although not shown here, it should be

---

[15] As it turned out, no predictors were deleted once they entered the regression; that is, their F values for deletion all exceeded the control value of 0.3.

Table 10-7   Summary output of BMD-02R stepwise regression of purchase interest in the firm's new tire brand

STEP NUMBER	VARIABLE Entered	Removed	MULTIPLE R	R^2	INCREASE IN R^2	F VALUE TO ENTER
1	3		0.539	0.291	—	102.51
2	1		0.575	0.331	0.040	14.85
3	2		0.580	0.336	0.005	2.12
4	4		0.584	0.341	0.005	1.53
5	10		0.588	0.346	0.005	1.94
6	5		0.589	0.347	0.001	0.41

reiterated that the same level of output illustrated in Table 10-6 is printed out at *each step* in the BMD-02R run.

The sponsor of this study decided to use the three-predictor equation of Table 10-6 in further studies of TV commercial effectiveness. Although the R^2 was not outstanding, enough variation in Y was accounted for (and the equation made sense from a content viewpoint) to justify its use in further studies of TV commercial effectiveness.

We close this section with a technical caveat concerning the use of polytomous predictors (recorded as dummy variables) in stepwise regression: arbitrariness of coding—in particular, assignment of one of the categories to be the kth class, consisting of all zeros in the $k - 1$ dummy-variable coding—can affect the results. This is because that kth class will *always* be in the regression (as part of the intercept value). Hence, if polytomies are used as predictors, it is advisable to make sure that *all* dummy-variable codes appear in the final regression equation. While variables X_8 and X_9 (the occupational dummies) never entered the regression, in other applications this problem may be encountered.[16]

MULTICOLLINEARITY AND RELATED PROBLEMS

Put rather simply, *multicollinearity* refers to an all-too-common problem in applied regression studies in which the *predictor variables exhibit excessively high correlation among themselves*. This problem has a bearing on two topics discussed earlier: (1) dummy-variable coding and (2) computing standard errors of the regression coefficients (as illustrated in Table 10-5).

[16]Fortunately, BMD-02R has a "forcing-variables" option by which the user can make sure that certain predictors enter and remain in the equation, regardless of the standard F-value criteria.

In our use of dummy-variable regression in BMD-02R, we made sure that the k-class polytomy was recoded into $k - 1$ dummy variables. Failure to have done this would have led to *perfect* multicollinearity—that is, the complete dependence of values in the kth class on values taken on by the other $k - 1$ dummies. If three classes and three dummies are involved, knowledge that no "1" appears in the first two dummies enables us to predict the appearance of a "1" in the third dummy variable with certainty. However, by choosing only two dummies and coding the third class (0,0), we guard against this type of redundancy.

Once one remembers to code k-class polytomies into $k - 1$ dummy variables, the potential problem of perfect multicollinearity in the case of polytomies disappears. However, the more subtle cases involve predictors that just happen to be highly (but not necessarily perfectly) correlated in the first place. As Johnston[17] points out, the *effects* of this more insidious problem may involve any of the following:

1. A reduction in the precision of estimating the coefficients of the regression equation and the difficulty, if not impossibility, of disentangling the separate effects of each predictor variable on the criterion variable.

2. Predictor variables may be dropped incorrectly (perhaps mechanically so in stepwise regression procedures) because of high standard errors.

3. Estimation of partial regression coefficients may become highly sensitive to the specific sample; addition or deletion of a few observations may produce marked differences in the values of the coefficients, including even changes in algebraic sign.

Unless one is dealing with experimental design data, it is almost always the case that predictor variables in multiple regression will be correlated to some degree. The question is: How much multicollinearity can be tolerated without seriously affecting the results? Unfortunately there is no simple answer to this question.

The study of multicollinearity in data analysis evolves around two major problems: (1) how can it be detected, and (2) what can be done about it? These problems are particularly relevant to marketing research, where one often faces the dilemma of needing a large number of variables to achieve accuracy of predictors yet finding that as more predictors *are* added to the model, their intercorrelations become larger.

As indicated above, what constitutes "serious" multicollinearity is ambiguous. Some researchers have adopted various rules of thumb: for

---

[17] J. Johnston, *Econometric Methods*, 2d ed. (New York: McGraw-Hill Book Company, 1972).

example, any pair of predictor variables must not correlate more than 0.9; if so, one of the predictors is discarded. While looking at simple correlations between pairs of predictors has merit, it can miss more subtle relationships involving three or more predictors.

The above rule can be extended, of course, to the examination of *multiple* correlations between each predictor and all other predictors. Usually one would want to guard against having any of these multiple correlations exceed the multiple correlation of the *criterion* variable with the predictor set.

Another test for multicollinearity provided in many regression programs involves examining the determinant[18] of the correlation matrix. As the value of the determinant approaches zero, extreme multicollinearity is the case; it approaches unity as the predictor variables become mutually uncorrelated. Unfortunately, it is not clear what a "reasonable" value of the determinant should be. However, research activity is being devoted to the development of more rigorous measures of multicollinearity and, in particular, to ways of pinpointing its presence in specific subsets of the predictor variables.

Procedures for Coping with Multicollinearity

Essentially there are three procedures for dealing with multicollinearity: (1) ignore it, (2) delete one or more of the offending predictors, and (3) transform the set of predictor variables into a new set of predictor-variable combinations that are mutually uncorrelated.

Ignoring multicollinearity need not be as cavalier as it might sound. First, one can have multicollinearity in the predictor variables and still have strong enough effects that the estimating coefficients remain reasonably stable. Second, multicollinearity may be prominent in only a subset of the predictors, a subset that may not contribute much to accounted-for variance anyway. A prudent procedure in checking one's predictor set for multicollinearity is to examine the standard errors of the regression coefficients (which will tend to be large in the case of high multicollinearity). Second, one may randomly drop some subset of the cases (perhaps 20% or so), rerun the regression, and then check to see if the signs and relative sizes of the regression coefficients are stable. Third, a number of recently developed regression routines incor-

---

[18]The determinant of a (square) matrix is a single number that represents the sum of alternately signed products of matrix elements. In the 2×2 case the determinant is computed as

$$|A| = \begin{vmatrix} a_{11} & a_{12} \\ a_{21} & a_{22} \end{vmatrix}$$

$$= a_{11}a_{22} - a_{12}a_{21}$$

If the determinant A is zero, the matrix is called *singular*; such would be the case under conditions of perfect multicollinearity.

porate checks for serious multicollinearity; if the program does not indicate this condition, the researcher can generally assume that the problem is not acute.

If multicollinearity is "severe," one rather simple procedure is to drop one or more predictor variables that represent the major offenders. Usually, because of their high intercorrelations with the retained predictors, the overall fit will not change markedly. (Pragmatically, if a particular pair of predictors are highly collinear, one would retain that member of the pair whose measurement reliability and/or theoretical importance is higher in the substantive problem under study.)

Methods also exist (e.g., principal components analysis) for transforming the original set of predictors to a mutually uncorrelated set of linear composites. If these components (linear composites) are interpretable in themselves, the researcher may use *these* in his regression analysis rather than the original variables. If *all* components are retained, the predictive accuracy will be precisely the same as that obtained from the original set of predictors. However, the problem here is that the components may *not* be interpretable in their own right. We discuss this approach in more detail in Chapter 13.

Cross Validation

Probably the safest procedure for coping with a variety of problems in multiple regression, including multicollinearity, is to use *cross validation*. We have frequently commented in this chapter on the tendency of regression models (and the same is true of other multivariate techniques as well) to capitalize on chance variation in the sample data. Since these techniques are optimizing methods, they find the best possible fit of the model to the *specific* data at hand. When the regression function is tried out on fresh data, one almost invariably finds a poorer fit.

Cross validation is a simple procedure for examining whether the regression equation holds up beyond the data on which its parameters are based. The researcher simply takes part of his data (perhaps a quarter to a third) and puts it aside. The regression equation is then computed from the remaining data. Following this, the researcher takes the held-out data and computes a set of $\hat{Y}_i$, using the earlier-computed regression equation and the predictor-variable values of the held-out sample. He then finds the simple coefficient of determination between the Y_i in the held-out sample and their predicted $\hat{Y}_i$ counterparts. This coefficient is compared to the R^2 obtained from the original analysis to see what the degree of "shrinkage" is.

An even better procedure is to *doubly cross-validate*. This is carried out by the following steps:

1. Split the cases randomly into halves.

2. Compute *separate* regression equations for each half.

3. Use the first-half equation to predict the second-half Y_i values.

4. Use the second-half equation to predict the first-half Y_i values.

5. Examine each partial regression coefficient across split halves to see if agreement is obtained in both directions (algebraic sign) and in magnitude.

6. Compute a regression equation for the entire sample, using only those variables that show stability in the preceding step.

Since high multicollinearity will make sample-to-sample regression coefficients unstable, double cross validation can help the researcher find out which coefficients exhibit stability across split halves.

Depending upon sample size, of course, one could split the sample into thirds, quarters, and so on. Usually, however, there are sufficient constraints on sample size, relative to the number of predictors, that split-half testing is about all that gets done. Even so, single or double cross validation is an extremely useful undertaking and, in the age of computer programs, not that difficult to implement.

Importance of Predictor Variables

In almost any applied regression problem there is an urge to use such measures as squared partial correlations or squared beta coefficients to rank predictors in order of importance in accounting for variation in the criterion. If the predictors are uncorrelated, this is a perfectly sensible thing to do.[19] If not, the urge should be tempered. This is simply because, in the case of correlated predictors, *there is no unambiguous measure of relative importance of predictor variables*.

The problem of relative importance of predictors is illustrated compactly in Figure 10-6, showing five cases of interest, as described by Gorsuch.[20] In Panel I, no problem arises; although X_1 and X_2 both contribute to variance in Y, their contributions are separate. This is the type of situation that arises in designed experiments and leads to an *unambiguous allocation* of criterion-variable variance across the predictors.

Panel II, however, is the more usual situation encountered in multiple regression and other instances in which the predictors exhibit multicollinearity. Here we note that X_1 and X_2 each contribute to accounted-for variance in Y but also share some of this accounted-for variance.

[19]If the predictors are uncorrelated, (squared) simple correlations, (squared) partial correlations, and (squared) betas will *all* be equal and, obviously, will rank the variables the same way. However, unless one is dealing with a designed experiment, such occasions are rare.

[20]Figure 10-6 has been adapted from R. L. Gorsuch, "Data Analysis of Correlated Independent Variables," *Multivariate Behavioral Research*, 8 (January, 1973), 89–107.

Figure 10-6 Procedures for dealing with overlapping variance

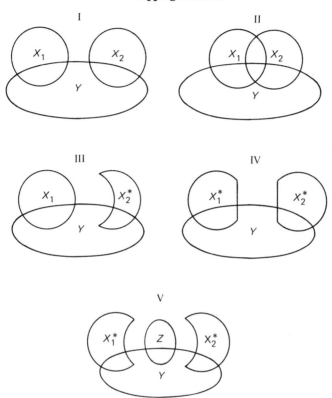

Panel III illustrates the case in which X_1 is credited not only with its unique variance but also with all that it shares with X_2. Panel IV splits, often in a rather arbitrary way, the shared variance between X_1 and X_2. Panel V shows the least common case (illustrated by Gorsuch) in which a new composite variable Z is created to represent shared variance in X_1 and X_2.

No firm recommendations can be made regarding which strategy to adopt in selecting an importance measure, since, obviously, the strategy will depend on the researcher's objective. It is worth repeating, however, that in BMD-02R—even though variables to be included are selected on the basis of highest incremental contribution to accounted-for variance—the contributions ascribed to new variables to be added are conditioned by predictors already in the equation.[21] (This is the situation of Panel III in Figure 10-6.)

[21] In BMD-03R the same idea holds except for the fact that a prior ordering of the variables is implicitly established by the researcher by the manner in which he enters the predictor variables.

SUMMARY

Our discussion of multiple and partial regression has been more detailed than will be the description of other multivariate techniques in subsequent chapters. This has been deliberate: multiple regression is not only the best known of these techniques but a grasp of its essentials markedly facilitates understanding of more advanced procedures.

We started the chapter with a discussion of simple (bivariate) regression and described such measures as regression coefficients, the coefficient of determination, and the product moment correlation. Graphical aids were employed wherever possible.

We next considered the multiple regression case and showed how its measures could be given interpretations in terms of counterpart simple coefficients.

Since nowadays almost all multiple regressions are carried out by computer, we discussed two programs, the BMD-03R all-variables program and the BMD-02R stepwise program, and illustrated their application numerically. Each aspect of their outputs was described conceptually and numerically.[22]

The concluding part of the chapter dealt with the interrelated problems of multicollinearity, cross validation, and the determination of the relative importance of predictor variables. As stressed throughout, in the case of correlated predictors relative importances are, at best, ambiguous and can be misleading. Only in designed experiments, involving uncorrelated predictors, do we find unequivocal measures of relative importance.

ASSIGNMENT MATERIAL

1. A sample survey of home swimming pool owners in southeast Pennsylvania has yielded the following information regarding pool costs versus annual income.
   a. Using least squares, compute a linear regression of Y on X. How do you interpret the formula?
   b. Compute the coefficient of determination and the variance of the estimate. Interpret these measures.
   c. What applications would you suggest for the regression formula if you were employed by a Pennsylvania swimming pool builder?

---

[22]More advanced material on multiple regression, including computer-based procedures, can be found in N. R. Draper and H. Smith, *Applied Regression Analysis* (New York: John Wiley & Sons, Inc., 1966) and J. Neter and W. Wasserman, *Applied Linear Statistical Models* (Homewood, Ill.: Richard D. Irwin, Inc., 1974).

Respondent	Pool Cost, Y (thousands of dollars)	Annual Income, X (thousands of dollars)
1	3.6	9.3
2	4.8	10.2
3	2.4	9.7
4	7.2	11.5
5	6.9	12.0
6	8.4	14.2
7	10.7	18.6
8	11.2	28.4
9	6.1	13.2
10	7.9	10.8
11	9.5	22.7
12	5.4	12.3

2. Assume next that the survey of swimming pool owners also yielded information on the total size of the pool owner's lot. The data (expressed in thousands of square feet) appear as follows:

Respondent	1	2	3	4	5	6	7	8	9	10	11	12
Lot size, Z	30.2	40.1	35.3	45.1	38.0	50.1	60.2	100.4	25.1	40.7	68.4	60.3

a. Using the data of the preceding problem, compute, by least squares, a linear multiple regression of Y on X and Z. How would you interpret this formula?

b. If you were told that a pool owner had an income of $12,500 annually and a lot size of 40,000 square feet, what pool cost would you predict?

c. Compute the coefficient of multiple determination R^2. What effect does knowledge of both annual income *and* lot size have on the "explanatory" power of the regression in contrast to knowledge only about annual income?

d. What are the assumptions underlying the least-squares regression model?

3. Apply a stepwise regression program (such as BMD-02R) to a data set of your choice.

a. Using the program's default values on variable inclusion and retention, run the analysis on the whole data set.

b. Next, split the data into halves by taking odd-numbered and even-numbered cases. Perform separate regressions. How do these split-half results compare with those obtained from the full sample?

4. Compare the advantages of partial regression coefficients versus partial correlation coefficients in representing the relative importance of predictor variables.

5. In what ways can multiple regression be used to forecast some industry's sales? A specific company's sales?

Experimental Data—   11
Analysis of
Variance and Covariance

INTRODUCTION

Field experimentation is receiving increased attention in marketing research. Marketing experiments have been conducted in such diverse activities as new-product evaluation, the selection of copy themes, determining the frequency of salespeople's calls, and so on. The purpose of this chapter is to acquaint the reader with the objectives of experimentation and to illustrate techniques for designing and analyzing marketing experiments.

We first describe the general nature of experimentation within the framework of a decision model, including such aspects as determining the value of the criterion variable in the model (the estimation and measurement problem), the functional form of the model, and the relevancy of the predictor variables to the decision problem.

Next we discuss some of the major designs used in experimentation, such as factorial designs, randomized blocks, latin squares, and switch-over designs. The apparatus (analysis of variance and covariance) for computing the statistical significance of various experimental "treatment" effects is described by numerical examples. Computer programs for analyzing experimental data are also illustrated.

In the last section of the chapter we discuss some of the difficulties encountered in designing field experiments in marketing. These difficulties involve lack of stability of the environment over time, the impact of uncontrolled variables on the response data at any given time, and the uncertainty of extrapolating experimental findings to the marketing population of interest.

THE NATURE OF EXPERIMENTATION

The term *experimentation* is used in a variety of ways and for a variety of objectives which, for our purposes, should be distinguished. Some marketing researchers use the term synonymously with market *measurement* and *estimation*. In this use of the term it is assumed that the analyst has already formulated a model of how the phenomenon under study behaves and is interested only in obtaining numerical values for some of the parameters of the model. Considered literally, "experimentation" in this context does *not* involve a possible rejection of the model itself.

In other cases, experiments may be conducted for the primary objective of determining the *functional form* that links some criterion variable to a set of input variables. For example, a marketing analyst may postulate that sales response to increasing amounts of advertising is either linear or quadratic over some range of interest. He may conduct an experiment to establish which functional form better fits the data.

In still other cases the experimenter may not even know what variables are relevant. An experiment may be conducted for the purpose of *identifying relevant variables* as well as the functional form of the model that links these variables with the criterion variable under study. In the discussion of this chapter we shall use the term "experimentation" in this third context, realizing that the term has been and will probably continue to be used in other ways as well. Perhaps the characteristic that best distinguishes experimentation from observational studies (which are also employed in measurement and estimation) is that the former term denotes some intervention and control over the factors affecting the response variable of interest to the researcher.

We have already discussed the nature of the term "cause" in Chapter 3. Experimentation permits the establishment of *causal relationships*. In contrast, correlation analysis (a useful technique in observational studies) permits the analyst to measure the degree to which changes in two or more variables are *associated* with each other.

Although we cannot infer causality from simple associations alone, correlation techniques are still useful. If association is found, we can use the results of this preliminary analysis to provide possible candidate variables for later experimentation.

As an illustration of tying in correlation analysis with experimentation, a major chemical firm was interested in the relationship of its antifreeze sales to changes in total expenditures for advertising. By using multiple regression analysis, the firm was able to establish an association between its sales and (regional) variations in advertising expenditures. Unfortunately, historical variations in past advertising expenditures by region had been too small to enable the firm to construct a sales-response function over a range of advertising sufficiently broad to be useful for policy purposes. Accordingly, a field experiment was designed that revealed the nature of the response function over a wide enough range to determine the "best" advertising expenditure level. Thus, the regression analysis first served to give insight into the variables that were affecting the sales-response function and later paved the way for direct manipulation of advertising expenditures.

Some Industry Examples

The use of experimental design principles and the analysis of variance and covariance are on the increase in marketing. To illustrate, a large Western petroleum refiner was recently interested in what type of merchandise catalog to send out to its credit card customers to induce them to purchase various kinds of gift merchandise.

An experiment was designed in which three test catalogs were prepared covering the same merchandise at the same prices. However, the catalogs differed in terms of layout and copy. A set of marketing regions were chosen as experimental "blocks" and an equal number of each of the three test catalogs were sent out to a random sample of credit card holders in each region. In addition to recording sales response to each test catalog, each merchandise order was analyzed to determine the credit card holder's extent of past purchases of the firm's catalog merchandise over the previous year.

A randomized block design (to be described later in the chapter) with past purchases serving as a covariate was used to analyze the data. After statistically adjusting for the effect of past purchases on current sales response, it turned out that one of the test catalogs resulted in 50% more purchases than the second and almost 80% more purchases than the third catalog. Needless to say, the company adopted the winning catalog for national distribution.

As a second example, a national producer of packaged candies was interested in children's preferences for various formulations of one of its well-known candy bars. Type of chocolate, quantity of peanuts, and amount of caramel were independently varied in a factorial design of 2 types of chocolate by 3 quantities of peanuts by 3 amounts of caramel.

Paired comparisons involving the 18 combinations were made up and evaluated by various school children between 8 and 12 years of age. Interestingly enough, the company found that preferences for type of chocolate varied with the amount of caramel. In addition, while children preferred more peanuts to fewer peanuts, the intermediate level of caramel was the most preferred. The company modified its formulation to match the most preferred test combination.

Many other experiments have been carried out involving taste testing, package design, advertising type and quality, and other marketing variables.

The bibliography at the end of the book lists a wide variety of applications of statistically designed experiments.

Classical versus Statistically Designed Experiments

We are all familiar with the stereotype of the laboratory scientist who carefully fixes all factors (or treatment variables) assumed to affect the outcome of his experiment except the one whose effect he is trying to measure. If several factors are under study, he then proceeds to fix all factors except the second one under study, and so on, until the effect of each factor is measured.

There are two things wrong with the "varying one factor at a time" approach. First, this procedure is inefficient in the sense that other experimental designs (to be described) yield more information per observation. Second, the procedure does not enable the researcher to measure *interactions* among the experimental factors. For example, suppose that a laboratory scientist (working in the field of electrolytic chemistry) is attempting to study the effect of temperature and reagent concentration on the amount of copper deposited (per unit of time) on a steel bar. If he holds temperature constant, we assume that so many additional milligrams of copper are deposited per each increase of five percentage points in the electrolytic concentration. Similarly, holding the concentration of the electrolytic solution constant while varying the temperature results in so many milligrams of copper desposited per unit of time. If, however, the milligrams deposited per unit change in temperature *differ* among levels of electrolytic concentration, the "varying one factor at a time" approach will *not* reveal this tendency. We define the term *interaction* to refer to the situation where *the response to changes in the levels of one treatment variable is dependent upon the level of some other treatment variable(s) in the experiment.*

Difficulty of Control

In any experiment, control over all possible variables affecting the response is rarely possible. Even in the laboratory it is not possible to control *all* variables that could conceivably affect the outcome. But compared to the laboratory situation, the researcher who is working in the marketplace has a really difficult control job on his hands. In real-world market experimentation, it is not possible to come even close to holding other factors constant. Rather the marketing researcher must try to design his experiment so that the effects of uncontrolled variables do not obscure and bias the nature of the response to the treatment variables that *are* being controlled.

An illustration should make this point clearer. Suppose that a marketing researcher is interested in conducting a series of taste-testing experiments for a new soft drink. Subjective interpretations of say, "sweetness" may well vary from subject to subject. If half the subjects were asked to taste only an established soft drink brand and the other half were asked to taste only the new brand, the average sweetness rating could reflect mainly the inherent perceptual differences between each group of subjects. A preferable procedure might be to have each subject taste each of two drinks on the assumption that intrasubject expressions of sweetness will affect each response approximately equally; that is, ratings will be expressed in terms of *differences* in sweetness over each subject. To avoid "ordering" effects on responses, the new and the control drink would be presented in randomized order. To reduce carryover tendencies, the subject would be asked to take a sip of water between tasting trials.

Such attempts to control *confounding*, or the tangling of effects of two or more treatment variables, are commonly used in experimentation. The fact remains, however, that confounding can *never* be entirely eliminated. Replicating (repeating) an experiment on a new test object or applying a second treatment to the same test object (after a "suitable" length of time) always leads to some confounding, since: (1) obviously no two test objects will ever be exactly alike, and (2) the conditions of the environment will usually be different over the time lapse required to apply the second treatment, even if one assumed that a "treated" object could return to its original state after the first treatment.

A major contribution that statisticians have made to experimental design is the development of statistical models that feature *randomization* over uncontrolled variables so as to reduce the effect of these variables on *comparative* measures of response to the variables that are under the experimenter's control. In general, the use of "matched groups" (where subjects possess similar characteristics), and "before and after" experiments (where measurements are made before and after the treatments are applied) is to reduce variation in response through variables that are not of direct interest to the experimenter. Randomization is a useful device for ensuring, at least *on the average*, that uncontrolled variables do not favor one treatment versus others.

Test-Object Differences

The experimenter must also contend with differences among the inherent properties of the test objects (people, stores, marketing regions, etc.). For example, if a researcher is interested in the effect of shelf height on the sales of a packaged consumer product, it is to be expected that stores will vary in their amount of shopping traffic, placement of gondolas, and the like. If the experimenter is interested in the effect of various shelf heights on product sales over a variety of store sizes, he will have to use several stores in his analysis.

If so, he may wish to use the technique of *covariance analysis*, in which responses to the controlled variables (shelf height) are adjusted for inherent differences in the test objects (stores) through measurement of these characteristics before (or during) the experiment. We shall discuss covariance analysis in a later section of the chapter.

In summary, the experimenter can use randomization, control groups, covariance analysis, and similar devices to reduce the impact of uncontrolled variations resulting from:

1. Other environmental variables affecting response
2. Inherent differences among the test objects receiving the treatments

so long as he is interested in *comparative* effects among the responses to variables under his control. In practice, however, he can never be sure that all uncontrolled sources of distortion have been guarded against or that even the very process of measurement does not distort the response of the test object being measured. The latter point is particularly true when the test object is a human being. It is not at all unusual to find distorted behavioral patterns when people know that they are participating in an experiment.

EXPERIMENTAL DESIGN
AND THE ANALYSIS OF VARIANCE

There are two principal aspects of experimental design: (1) the experimental layouts by which treatment levels are assigned to test objects, and (2) the techniques that are used to analyze the results of the experiment. However, it is more instructive to start with the latter. The generic name for these techniques is *analysis of variance and covariance*. Let us first consider the analysis of variance (abbreviated ANOVA).

At first glance, the phrase "analysis of variance" may give the impression that the technique is used to test for significant differences among the variances of two or more sample universes. Actually, however, the objective of ANOVA is to test the statistical significance of differences among *average responses* due to controlled variables, after allowance is made for influences on response due to uncontrolled variables. The label "analysis of variance" is appropriate because if the mean responses of the test objects are different *among* treatments, then the *variance of the combined groups will exceed the variances of the individual groups.*

An example should make this clear. Suppose that one universe of responses has, in fact, a mean of 4 and another universe of responses has a mean of 12, each with a variance of 1.

$$\mu_1 = 4, \qquad \sigma_1^2 = 1$$
$$\mu_2 = 12, \qquad \sigma_2^2 = 1$$

Suppose that we sampled from each universe and then *combined* these two samples and calculated a grand mean (based on an equal number of observations from each group). This mean would be approximately equal to 8, but the *variance* of the combined sample would be "close to" $(4 - 8)^2 = (12 - 8)^2 = 16$, which is much larger than the variances ($\sigma_1^2 = \sigma_2^2 = 1$) of the individual populations. This illustrates the danger of combining observations into a single sample, since such a procedure is strictly correct only *if the means and variances of the two universes being combined are equal.* In the analysis of variance we take advantage of the principle illustrated above by separating the total variance of all observations into two parts: variance due to the *within* variability of the universes and variance due to differences *among* the means of the universes from which the sample was taken. The latter variance will be larger than the former *if differences among means exist.*

In essence, then, the analysis of variance is used as a test of *means* among two or more universes. The null hypothesis is typically that all means are equal, although the experimenter (through appropriate technique refinements) may sometimes compare the means of specific individual universes. Analysis of variance thus involves making statistical inferences from samples to universes just as any sampling problem does.

From a formal standpoint, analysis of variance is a type of multiple regression with dummy-valued predictor variables.[1] The elegant apparatus of ANOVA is based on the *maintenance of independence among the treatment variables.* That is, by designing experiments in which the treatment variable is independently varied (and by ensuring an equal number of response observations for each combination of treatment variables), special analytical procedures can be employed to assess the effect of each predictor, unconfounded with other effects.

Among and Within Sums of Squares

In Chapter 10 we described how r^2, the coefficient of determination, utilized two sums of squares in its calculation:

- The sum of squared errors in predicting each Y_i from $\hat{Y}_i$ (the latter computed from the regression equation).
- The sum of squared errors in predicting each Y_i from $\bar{Y}_i$, the criterion-variable mean.

Furthermore, Figure 10-4 showed how the deviations of $Y_i - \bar{Y}$ could be

---

[1] We refer here to fixed-effects analysis of variance. While computations for the "random-effects" model are similar, interpretations of results differ. A comparison of these approaches is found in W. L. Hays and R. L. Winkler, *Statistics: Probability, Inference and Decision* (New York: Holt, Rinehart and Winston, Inc., 1971). Also, see William Mendenhall, *Introduction to Linear Models and the Design and Analysis of Experiments* (Belmont, Calif.: Wadsworth Publishing Company, Inc., 1968).

broken down into two additive parts—a deviation of Y_i from $\hat{Y}_i$ and a deviation of $\hat{Y}_i$ from $\bar{Y}$.

Similar ideas underlie analysis of variance. To illustrate, assume that we had responses to three treatment "levels," such as three magazine advertising copy themes: A, B, and C.

Replication	Theme A	Theme B	Theme C
1	6	8	0
2	4	11	2
3	3	5	1
4	3	4	1
$\bar{X}_j$	4	7	1
	Grand mean:	4	

For illustrative purposes the responses are assumed to be ratings on a 0–11 purchase-interest scale (0 denoting no interest and 11 denoting very high interest in purchasing the advertised brand). Each copy theme is evaluated by four randomly chosen persons and no person evaluates more than one copy theme.

The *sample* means show that theme B is highest on the average, followed by A and then C. Are the universe means significantly different? Before trying to answer the statistical question, let us calculate three sums of squares:

- The pooled within-samples sum of squares
- The among-samples sum of squares
- The total-samples sum of squares

The within-samples sum of squares is:

Theme

A: $(6 - 4)^2 + (4 - 4)^2 + (3 - 4)^2 + (3 - 4)^2 = 6$

B: $(8 - 7)^2 + (11 - 7)^2 + (5 - 7)^2 + (4 - 7)^2 = 30$

C: $(0 - 1)^2 + (2 - 1)^2 + (1 - 1)^2 + (1 - 1)^2 = \underline{2}$

$$38$$

The among-samples sum of squares is:

$$4(4 - 4)^2 + 4(7 - 4)^2 + 4(1 - 4)^2 = 72$$

The total-sample sum of squares is:

$$(6 - 4)^2 + (4 - 4)^2 + \cdots + (1 - 4)^2 + (1 - 4)^2 = 110$$

As shown, each within-sample sum of squares is computed around that specific sample's mean. The results are then added to obtain the pooled value of 38. In the case of the among-samples sum of squares, each sample mean is based on four observations; hence, if *each case* in a particular sample were represented by that sample's mean, the sum of squares around the total-sample mean would be 72, as shown. Finally, we note that the within-samples sum of squares plus the among-samples sum of squares equals the total-sample sum of squares of 110.

The basic idea of ANOVA is to compare the among-samples sum of squares (after adjustment by degrees of freedom to get a *mean square*) to the (similarly adjusted) within-samples value. This is the F ratio, described earlier in Chapter 10. The *larger the ratio of among to within,* the more we are inclined to reject the null hypothesis that the universe means μ_A, μ_B and μ_C, are equal.[2] Conversely, if the three sample means were very close to each other, the among-samples sum of squares would be close to zero and we would conclude that the universe means are not different, once we consider the variability of individual cases within each sample.

However, to make this comparison it is necessary to assume that the error-term distribution has constant variance over all observations. This is exactly the same assumption made in the regression model of Chapter 10.

Figure 11-1 represents the counterpart case of Figure 10-4. In Panel I of Figure 11-1 we show the deviations that would be obtained by trying to predict each individual observation by the total-sample mean. The sum of these squared errors is 110, as noted above. Panels II and III show how the errors break down into within and among portions.

Panel II shows the deviations obtained by trying to predict each case in a specific sample by that sample's mean (denoted by a small box in Panel II). The sum of these squared errors, added over the three samples, is 38, the within-samples sum of squares.

Panel III shows the deviations obtained by trying to predict each case—assuming it were equal to its respective sample's mean—by the total-sample mean. The sum of these squared errors is 72, the among-samples sum of squares. Thus, the analogy with regression is complete, once we get used to the idea that the predicted or $\hat{Y}_i$ values in ANOVA are the specific sample means (4, 7, or 1) for each of the four cases in that respective sample.

However, in the next section of the chapter we shall (1) use more efficient computational techniques, (2) consider the adjustment for degrees of freedom

---

[2] As may be recalled from elementary statistics, the Student *t* test, it turns out, is just a special case of the *F* test, when two samples are involved.

Figure 11-1   Breakdown of deviations $Y_i - \bar{Y}$ into two additive parts

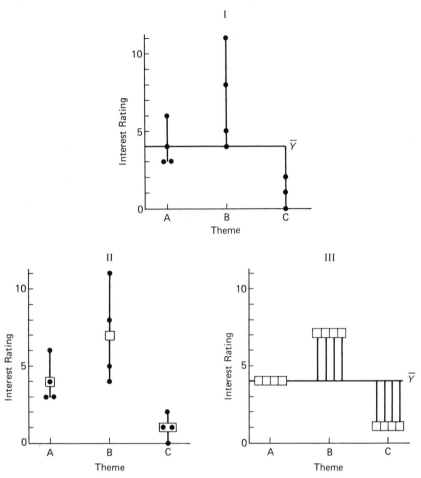

to obtain *mean* squares, and (3) show the case of the F ratio in testing signifi-
ance. Still, the foregoing remarks represent the basic ANOVA idea of comparing among- to within-samples variability.

Single-Factor Analysis of Variance

As an illustration of analysis of variance in its simplest (single-factor)
form, suppose that a marketer is interested in the effect of shelf height on
supermarket sales of canned dog food. He has been able to secure the cooperation of a store manager to run an experiment involving three levels of shelf
height ("knee" level, "waist" level, and "eye" level) on sales of a single brand
of dog food, which we shall call Arf. Assume further that our experiment

must be conducted in a single supermarket and that our response variable will be sales, in cans, of Arf dog food per some appropriate unit of time. But what shall we use for our unit of time? Sales of dog food in a single store may exhibit week-to-week variation, day-to-day variation, and even hour-to-hour variation. In addition, sales of this particular brand may be affected by the price or special promotions of competitive brands, the store management's knowledge that an experiment is going on, and other variables that we cannot control at all or would find too costly to control.

We shall address ourselves to some of these questions (and others) in a later section of this chapter, but for the time being, assume that we have agreed to change the shelf-height position of Arf three times per day and run the experiment over eight days. We shall fill the remaining sections of the particular gondola that houses our brand with a "filler" brand, which is not familiar to customers in the geographical area in which the test is being conducted. Furthermore, since our primary emphasis is on explaining the technique of analysis of variance in its simplest form (a single variable of classification), we shall assign the shelf heights at random over the three time periods per day and not deal explicitly with within-day and among-day differences. If so, our experimental results might look like those shown in Table 11-1. Here, we let X_{ij} denote the sales (in units) of Arf during the ith day under the jth treatment level. If we look at mean sales by each level of shelf height, it appears as though the waist-level treatment, the average response to which is $\bar{X}_2 = 90.9$, results in highest mean sales over the experimental period. However, we note that the last observation (93) under the eye-level treatment exceeds the waist-level treatment mean. Is this a fluke

Table 11-1 Sales of Arf dog food (in units) by level of shelf height

		SHELF HEIGHT				
Knee Level		*Waist Level*		*Eye Level*		GRAND TOTAL
X_{11}	77	X_{12}	88	X_{13}	85	
X_{21}	82	X_{22}	94	X_{23}	85	
X_{31}	86	X_{32}	93	X_{33}	87	
X_{41}	78	X_{42}	90	X_{43}	81	
X_{51}	81	X_{52}	91	X_{53}	80	
X_{61}	86	X_{62}	94	X_{63}	79	
X_{71}	77	X_{72}	90	X_{73}	87	
X_{81}	81	X_{82}	87	X_{83}	93	
$X_{T1} = 648$		$X_{T2} = 727$		$X_{T3} = 677$		$X_{TT} = 2{,}052$
$\bar{X}_1 = 81.0$		$\bar{X}_2 = 90.9$		$\bar{X}_3 = 84.6$		$\bar{X}_{TT} = 85.5$

observation? We know that these means are, after all, *sample* means, and our interest lies in whether the *universe* means are equal or not.

Now assume for the moment that we possess omniscience and can look into the *underlying process* that produced our experimental results. Assume that the universe means are *really different* and are as follows:

$$\mu_1 = 80; \qquad \mu_2 = 90; \qquad \mu_3 = 85$$

If we wish, however, we can represent the three means as deviations from a grand mean $\mu = 85$; then $\mu_1 = \mu - 5$; $\mu_2 = \mu + 5$; $\mu_3 = \mu + 0$. Let us also assume that the error term ϵ_{ij} of each universe is normally distributed with a zero mean and a (common) variance:

$$\sigma_1^2 = 16; \qquad \sigma_2^2 = 16; \qquad \sigma_3^2 = 16$$

With these assumptions we can run a "dummy" experiment by drawing random normal numbers from a common probability distribution that we shall call the ϵ (epsilon) distribution. Then *any* observation X_{ij} can be looked upon as the sum of three numbers:

$$X_{ij} = \mu + \tau_j + \epsilon_{ij}, \quad \sum \tau_j = 0; \quad i = 1, 2, \ldots, n_j, \quad j = 1, 2, 3$$
$$n = \sum n_j$$

where μ = grand mean over the three universes

τ_j = effect due to treatment j, $j = 1, 2, 3$

ϵ_{ij} = effect due to uncontrolled variation; this variable is assumed to be normally and independently distributed with $\mu(\epsilon) = 0$, and $\sigma^2(\epsilon) = 16$; $\sigma(\epsilon) = 4$

This is precisely what we have done in concocting the "data" of Table 11-1. To summarize, the parameter values are as follows:

$$\mu = 85$$
$$\tau_1 = -5, \quad \tau_2 = +5, \quad \tau_3 = 0$$
$$\mu(\epsilon) = 0; \qquad \sigma(\epsilon) = 4$$

For example, the first observation under the knee-level treatment column (77) was found by taking the random normal number -0.783 from a standard table[3] and multiplying this value by 4, the standard deviation of the error

---

[3]For an extensive list of random normal numbers, see Rand Corporation, *A Million Digits with 100,000 Normal Deviates* (New York: Free Press, 1955). For a short list of random normal numbers, see Table A-6 in Appendix A.

(epsilon) distribution, and rounding off the answer to the nearest integer. $4(-0.783) = -3.132 \cong -3$. Thus,

$$77 = 85 - 5 - 3$$

In a similar way, we developed the other entries of Table 11-1. Now we shall show what happens when one goes through typical analysis-of-variance computations for this problem. These calculations are shown in Table 11-2.

Table 11-2   Analysis of variance—Arf dog food experiment

Source of Variation	Degrees of Freedom	Sum of Squares	Mean Square	F Ratio
Among treatments	$t - 1 = 2$	399.3	199.7	14.6 ($p < 0.01$)
Within treatments	$n - t = 21$	288.7	13.7	
Total	$n - 1 = 23$	688.0		

Correction factor	$C = \dfrac{(X_{TT})^2}{n} = \dfrac{(2,052)^2}{24} = 175{,}446.0$
Total sum of squares	$\sum X_{ij}^2 - C = (77)^2 + (82)^2 + \cdots + (87)^2 + (93)^2 \\ \qquad\qquad\qquad\qquad\qquad - 175{,}446.0 = 688.0$
Treatment sum of squares	$\dfrac{\sum X_{Tj}^2}{n_j} - C = \dfrac{(648)^2 + (727)^2 + (677)^2}{8} \\ \qquad\qquad\qquad\qquad\qquad\qquad - 175{,}446.0 = 399.3$
Within treatment sum of squares	$\sum X_{ij}^2 - \dfrac{\sum X_{Tj}^2}{n_j} = (77)^2 + (82)^2 + \cdots + (87)^2 \\ \qquad\qquad\qquad\quad + (93)^2 - \dfrac{(648)^2 + (727)^2 + (677)^2}{8} \\ \qquad\qquad\qquad\quad = 288.7$

Table 11-2 shows the mechanics of developing the among-treatments, within-treatments, and total sums of squares, the mean squares, and the *F* ratio. Had the experimenter used an alpha risk of 0.01, he would have rejected the null hypothesis of no differences among treatment levels. (A table of *F* ratios is found in Table A-4, Appendix A.)

Note that Table 11-2 shows shortcut procedures for finding each sum of squares. For example, the total sum of squares is given by

$$\boxed{\;\sum X_{ij}^2 - \frac{(X_{TT})^2}{n} = 688.0\;}$$

This is the same quantity that would be obtained by subtracting the grand mean of 85.5 from each original observation, squaring the result, and adding up the 24 squared deviations. This mean-corrected sum of squares is equivalent to the type of formula used in Table 10-3. Note also that the mean squares are *universe estimates*, since we have divided each sum of squares by its degrees of freedom.

Our purpose in this exposition, however, is to look behind the preceding calculations and consider what we know about the distributions from which the data in the dummy experiment were derived. First, we know that the grand mean of all three universes μ is equal to 85. If we let $K^2 = (\sum \tau_j^2)$ $/(t - 1)$, the estimated "variance" among treatment ($t = 3$) means is

$$K^2 = \frac{(-5)^2 + (+5)^2 + (0)^2}{2} = \frac{50}{2} = 25$$

Also, note that each treatment effect is based on eight observations. The variance of the error distribution ϵ is, by design, equal to 16. The parameter that we have estimated by the among-treatments mean square is

$$\sigma^2(\epsilon) + 8K^2 = 16 + 8(25) = 16 + 200 = 216$$

The within-treatments mean square estimates just $\sigma^2(\epsilon) = 16$. Now, if the null hypothesis were true (which we know is *not* the case), then K^2 would be equal to zero, since the treatment effects τ_j *would all equal zero* and $\mu_1 = \mu_2$ $= \mu_3 = 85$. If so, the among-treatments mean square (i.e., variance) would be an estimate of *only* $\sigma^2(\epsilon) = 16$.

On the other hand, if the null hypothesis is *not* true and some of the μ_j's are unequal, then K^2 would be greater than zero and, *aside from sampling error*, we would expect the ratio of the among-treatments variance estimate to the within-treatments variance estimate to *exceed unity*. Thus, in Table 11-2 the mean square 199.7 estimates the number 216, and the mean square 13.7 estimates the number 16. Strictly speaking K^2 is a measure of the non-centrality of the treatment means—that is, the "spread" of these around the grand mean. It is *not* a variance in the usual sense of being a parameter of a probability distribution. However, the variance $\sigma^2(\epsilon)$ *is* a parameter of the error distribution ϵ.

Statistical Assumptions

Now that we have looked behind the computations involved in single-factor analysis of variance, it is well to summarize the statistical assumptions made in this model.

1. In the "fixed effects" model, which we have assumed in the preceding example, the treatment set τ represents the *entire* set of (three) treatments of interest, not just a sample of treatments from some larger group.

2. The error distribution ϵ is normally distributed with $\mu(\epsilon) = 0$ and $\sigma^2(\epsilon)$ constant over all observations. Moreover, ϵ does not depend on any of the treatment levels.

3. The effects of treatments are additive.

4. Observations represent independent "draws" from the error distribution ϵ.

In commenting upon assumption 1 we should note that other models (so-called *random-effects models*) exist for dealing with cases where the treatments represent some sample from a universe of treatments.[4] A *mixed effects*, or *composite, model* is also available for dealing with both fixed- and random-sample interpretations of the group of experimental treatments.

In commenting upon assumption 2 we may note that research has indicated that moderate departures from normality and equality of variances (homoscedasticity) do not seriously affect the validity of the tests. Moreover, mathematical transformations (logarithmic, square root, arc sine) are available to achieve equal variances and/or normality. Transformations are also available to satisfy assumption 3. For example, if the effects due to treatments are multiplicative, the experimenter may use logarithms of the data.

Departures from the conditions of assumption 4 can distort seriously the appropriate F ratios. The researcher should attempt to design his experiment to avoid dependency among observations or else should use other types of analytical techniques.

In addition to the assumptions noted above, the reader should observe that we have neglected mention of type II errors. Our null hypothesis of "no differences in mean response to treatments" used the standard F-ratio approach with an alpha risk of 0.01. Techniques are available for determining beta risks but, unfortunately, are seldom used in practice and are beyond the scope of this chapter.[5]

The important consideration to remember is that, aside from the statistical assumptions underlying the analysis of variance, the *variance of the error distribution* will influence markedly the significance of the results. That is, if this variance is *large* relative to differences among treatments, then the true effects may be swamped, leading to an acceptance of the null hypothesis when it is false. Chapter 7 has already indicated that increased sample size

[4]For an appropriate discussion, see G. W. Snedecor and W. G. Cochran, *Statistical Methods*, 6th ed. (Ames, Iowa: Iowa State University Press, 1967).

[5]For an appropriate discussion, see W. J. Dixon and F. J. Massey, *Introduction to Statistical Analysis* (New York: McGraw-Hill Book Company, 1952), pp. 256–59.

can reduce experimental error. In the next section we discuss more *specialized* experimental designs whose objective is to increase the efficiency of the experiment by reducing the error variance.

Finally, we should reiterate the connection between the analysis of variance carried out in Table 11-2 and the one conducted earlier in Table 10-6 (in the context of multiple regression). In both cases a *comparison of models* is involved where two independent sources of variance are compared to see whether the among-groups variation (analogous to variance due to regression) differs from within-groups variation (analogous to error variance after regression). The basic idea is the same.

MULTIPLE CLASSIFICATIONS

The preceding example dealt with the simplest of ANOVA designs—classification by a single factor. Suppose that our marketing researcher were interested in the effect of *other* point-of-purchase variables such as shelf "facings" (width of display) and shelf fullness on sales. Or, suppose that he would like to generalize the results of his experiment to other sizes of stores in other marketing regions. It may be preferable to "ask many rather than few questions of nature" if the researcher would like to establish the most general conditions under which his findings are expected to hold. That is, not only may single-factor manipulation be difficult to do in practice, but it may be inefficient as well. In this section we discuss somewhat more specialized experimental designs, all of which are characterized by *two or more variables of classification*.

Factorial Designs

A *factorial experiment* is one in which an equal number of observations is made of all combinations involving at least two levels of at least two variables. This type of experiment enables the researcher to study possible *interactions* among the variables of interest. Suppose we return to our canned dog food illustration but now assume that the researcher is interested in studying the effects of *two* variables of interest: shelf height (still at three levels) and shelf facings (at two levels—that is, at half the width of the gondola and at full width of the gondola). While his plan still is to use a single store for the experiment, the researcher intends to replicate each combination three times, leading to $3 \times 2 \times 3 = 18$ observations. Assume that his experiment results in the data shown in Table 11-3.

As noted in Table 11-3, for each combination of shelf height and shelf facing we have three observations. Again, we can set up a theoretical model for this experiment:

Table 11-3   Factorial display—Arf dog food experiment*

| | SHELF HEIGHT | | | |
FACINGS	*Knee Level*	*Waist Level*	*Eye Level*	TOTAL
Level 1	(70, 75, 79)	(85, 88, 93)	(77, 81, 78)	
(half width)	224	266	236	726
Level 2	(91, 90, 87)	(94, 97, 93)	(87, 90, 90)	
(full width)	268	284	267	819
Total	492	550	503	1,545

*Cell entries are sales in units.

$$X_{ijk} = \mu + \alpha_i + \beta_j + (\alpha\beta)_{ij} + \epsilon_{ijk}$$

where μ = mean of universe

α_i = true effect of shelf facings, $i = 1, \ldots, a; a = 2$

β_j = true effect of shelf height, $j = 1, \ldots, b; b = 3$

(the terms α_i and β_j are usually called *main effects*, since they refer to responses that are averaged over the other variable of interest)

$(\alpha\beta)_{ij}$ = true interaction effect of ith level of α and jth level of β

ϵ_{ijk} = random effect from uncontrolled variation with $\mu(\epsilon) = 0$

$\sigma^2(\epsilon)$ is = constant over all observations, $k = 1, 2, \ldots, m; m = 3$, and

$$\sum \alpha_i = \sum \beta_j = \sum (\alpha\beta)_i = \sum (\alpha\beta)_j = 0; \quad n = abm$$

In this model we are merely replacing the τ_j of our one-classification model with the symbols α_i and β_j standing for the effects of various levels of two factors.

As in Table 11-2 we need to compute the various sums of squares—in this case of treatments A, B, the A × B interaction, error, and total. (Computing formulas can be found in Snedecor and Cochran.[6]) Each mean square is compared, in turn, to the error mean square via the F ratio. The analysis-of-variance summary is shown in Table 11-4.

[6]See Snedecor and Cochran, *Statistical Methods*, Chap. 12.

Table 11-4   Analysis of Variance, factorial display—
Arf dog food experiment

Source of Variation	Degrees of Freedom	Sum of Squares	Mean Square	F Ratio
Treatments				
A (facings)	1	480.5	480.5	54.6 ($p < 0.01$)
B (height)	2	316.3	158.2	18.0 ($p < 0.01$)
$A \times B$	2	56.4	28.2	3.2 ($0.1 > p > 0.05$)
Error	12	105.3	8.8	
Total	17	958.5		

Looking at the F ratios of Table 11-4, we note that the AB interaction is insignificant at the 0.05 alpha level (but is significant at the 0.1 alpha level). Still, if the researcher were interested in the particular combination of shelf height and shelf facings that would produce highest sales, it would seem as though the combination full width, waist level is best (see Table 11-3).

One of the easiest ways to understand the nature of interaction is to plot the response variable against changes in one of the treatment variables at different levels of a second treatment variable. This is done for the averaged cell responses in Table 11-3 and the results are shown in Figure 11-2. The vertical axis of the chart shows average unit sales, whereas the horizontal axis shows levels of the shelf-height variable. Connecting lines between effects are shown strictly for visual purposes, since only discrete levels of A and B are involved.

For example, averaged unit sales when shelf height is at knee level and facings are at *half width* is 74.7 units, as shown on the chart. As can be seen, average sales increase (to 88.7) at waist level and then decline (to 78.7) at eye level. However, when we examine the average sales unit response to changes in shelf height when facings are *full width*, we see that the response *increments* differ; that is, the line segments are not parallel. That is, the response to changes in shelf height differs across the two levels of facings.

Another way of saying this is to note that the *differential effect* of moving from knee level to waist level depends on what the level of facings is. For facings at half width the difference is $88.7 - 74.7 = 14.0$. When facings are at full width, the difference is $94.7 - 89.3 = 5.4$; that is, the incremental effect is less pronounced. If the *observed* departures from parallelism in each of the line segment pairs cannot be ascribed to sampling fluctuations, then we say that a significant interaction exists.

Technically, what is shown here is an *ordinal* interaction. By this is meant that sales response to waist level is still higher than sales response to knee level, independent of facings level—it is the *incremental* difference that

Figure 11-2   Plot of the A × B (shelf height by facings) interaction

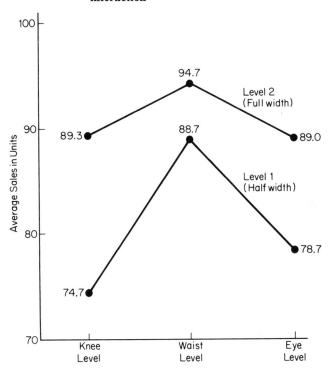

varies. Had average sales response to the combination of waist level and full-width facings been, say, only 72 units, then a *disordinal* interaction would be involved. The latter case is much more serious, since before we can specify what level of shelf height to consider from a marketing strategy standpoint, we must know what level of facings is involved. On the other hand, under ordinal interactions (assuming equal implementation costs for each alternative), waist level leads to highest sales at each level of facings.

In the case of quantitative factors, such as shelf height or facings, it is useful to distinguish between *interaction* and *nonlinearity*. For example, suppose we were to assume that the three levels of shelf height—knee level, waist level, and eye level—were equally spaced in inches. That is, waist level is halfway between knee level and eye level.

Figure 11-3 shows some hypothetical effects that might be obtained in an experiment of this type. As noted in Panel I, sales volume displays a linear relationship with shelf height (assuming that other experimental levels of shelf height would also lead to sales responses that fell on the same line connecting the three points). Moreover, the two lines are parallel for full-width

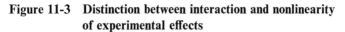

Figure 11-3   Distinction between interaction and nonlinearity of experimental effects

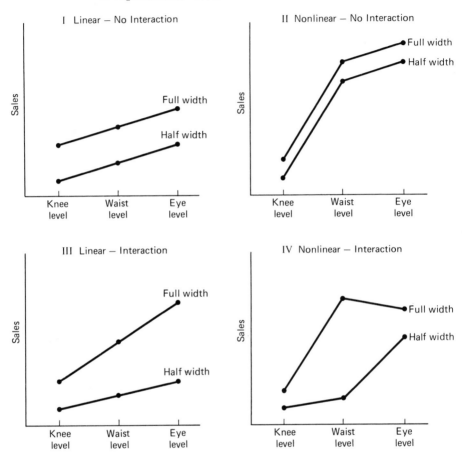

versus half-width facings, suggesting no interaction between this factor and shelf height.

Panel II shows the presence of a nonlinear relationship between sales and shelf height. In this case sales volume tapers off in its rate of increase as shelf height increases. However, the parallelism of the line segments suggests no interaction between shelf height and facings.

Panels III and IV show the remaining two cases, both involving interaction. In Panel III the slopes of the linear functions differ; hence, interaction exists. In Panel IV the data are characterized by *both* nonlinearity *and* interaction. (We assume, of course, the associated statistical tests support the graphical results; that is, the observed effects are statistically significant as well.)

Note that in the factorial experiment we can test for all main effects, and in this case, where we have replicated each combination, for the interaction of the variables as well. If the interaction term is significant, ordinarily the calculation of main effects is superfluous, since the experimenter will customarily be interested in the best *combination* of variables. In any event, we have included tests for main effects for the sake of illustration; as can be noted, both treatment effects *A* and *B* are significant at an alpha risk of 0.01.

In summary, factorial experimentation permits the researcher to study the effect on response of several variables in *combination*. Not only may main effects be estimated, but, more importantly, the researcher may study interaction effects as well. This latter advantage is particularly important in market experimentation where the researcher is typically interested in the *combination* of controlled variables which leads to the best payoff in terms of sales, cash flow, or some other measure of effectiveness. (We return to the topic of interaction later in the chapter.)

Other Multiple Classification Designs

Many specialized designs exist for dealing with multivariable classifications. Within the scope of this chapter we can only describe briefly the characteristics of some of these designs. The reader interested in exploring the subject further should see more specialized books in this area of interest.[7]

Latin-square designs are multivariable designs that are used to reduce the number of observations that would be required in a full factorial design. In using latin-square designs the researcher is usually assuming that interaction effects are negligible; in so doing, all main effects can be estimated by this procedure.

As an illustration of a latin-square design, suppose that the researcher were interested in *three* variables (each at four levels) on store sales. For example, in the dog food illustration the researcher may be interested in:

A: shelf height—four levels—knee level, waist level, eye level, reach level

B: shelf facings—four levels—25%, 50%, 75%, and 100% of total width of gondola

C: shelf fullness—four levels—25%, 50%, 75%, and 100% of total height of gondola section

[7]As illustrations, see O. L. Davies, *The Design and Analysis of Industrial Experiments*, 2nd ed. (New York: Hafner Publishing Co., 1956), and D. R. Cox, *Planning of Experiments* (New York: John Wiley & Sons, Inc., 1958).

If the researcher were to run a full factorial experiment, he would require, with one replication, $(4)^3 = 64$ observations. By using a latin-square design he can reduce the number of observations (with estimation of main effects only) to 16. Table 11-5 shows one possible latin-square design for this experiment.

Notice in Table 11-5 that each level of treatment C (shelf fullness) appears once in each row and each column. Also the number of levels (four) is the same for each treatment. The underlying model for analysis is

$$X_{ijk} = \mu + \alpha_i + \beta_j + \gamma_k + \epsilon_{ijk}$$

where $i, j, k = 1, \ldots, a$; $\mu(\epsilon) = 0$; $\sigma^2(\epsilon)$ is constant; and

$$\sum \alpha_i = \sum \beta_j = \sum \gamma_k = 0$$

Notice that *no interaction terms* appear in this model.[8]

**Table 11-5 Latin-square design—
Arf dog food experiment**

VARIABLE A— SHELF HEIGHT	VARIABLE B—SHELF FACINGS			
	B_1	B_2	B_3	B_4
A_1	C_1	C_2	C_3	C_4
A_2	C_4	C_1	C_2	C_3
A_3	C_3	C_4	C_1	C_2
A_4	C_2	C_3	C_4	C_1

Randomized-block designs represent a frequently used experimental framework for dealing with multivariable classifications. These designs are typically used when the experimenter desires to eliminate a possible source of uncontrolled variation from the error term in order that the effects due to treatments will not be masked by a larger-than-necessary error term. For example, suppose that our researcher were interested only in the effect of shelf height on sales of dog food but had designed his experiment so that more than a single store was used in the study. The effect of store type could influence sales, and the experimenter might wish to remove this effect from the error term by "blocking" on store types. That is, he would consider each

[8] An early marketing application of a latin-square design can be found in the article by R. J. Jessen, "A Switch-over Experimental Design to Measure Advertising Effect," *Journal of Advertising Research*, 1 (March, 1961), 15–22.

store as a test unit and test each level of shelf height in each store. To illustrate, if he were interested in examining three levels of shelf height in each of four stores, his results could be summarized in the form shown in Table 11-6. Table 11-6 indicates that we are dealing with a *two-variable* classification and can, accordingly, separate the block effect from the error term. Thus, if genuine treatment effects are present, this type of design will be more likely to detect them than a single-variable classification in which the block effect would become part of the error term. The general model for this design is

$$X_{ij} = \mu + \beta_i + \tau_j + \epsilon_{ij}$$

where β_i stands for the effect of block i ($i = 1, 2, \ldots, 4$) and the other factors are interpreted similarly to designs already discussed.

**Table 11-6   Randomized-block design—
Arf dog food experiment**

	TREATMENTS—SHELF HEIGHT		
BLOCKS—STORES	*Level 1*	*Level 2*	*Level 3*
1	X_{11}	X_{12}	X_{13}
2	X_{21}	X_{22}	X_{23}
3	X_{31}	X_{32}	X_{33}
4	X_{41}	X_{42}	X_{43}

Cross-over design is the name given to a type of design in which different treatments are applied to the *same* test unit in different time periods. Although use of this type of design can reduce the effect of variation among test units, the experimenter must consider another problem—the possibility that successive observations may not be independent. That is, the experimenter may have to contend with a *carry-over* effect. If the researcher can assume that no carry-over effect exists, then a latin-square design could be used, as shown in Table 11-7 In the case of Table 11-7, each test unit receives each treatment in "randomized" order over the three time periods, each treatment appearing once in each row and column.

In the case where carry-over effects *are* assumed to exist, the experimenter must make some assumptions about the nature of this carry-over effect. A particularly simple set of assumptions is that the effect obtained on a single test object in a specific time period is made up of:

1. A quantity reflecting only the test object–time period combination, plus
2. A quantity reflecting only the treatment applied in that time period, plus
3. A quantity reflecting only the treatment applied in the preceding period.

Table 11-7   Latin-square design— no carry-over effect

	TIME PERIOD		
TEST UNIT	*1*	*2*	*3*
1	*A*	*C*	*B*
2	*C*	*B*	*A*
3	*B*	*A*	*C*

In the case described above, the experimenter would design the experiment so that: (1) each treatment follows each other treatment the same number of times, and (2) each treatment occurs in each period and on each test unit. A design that meets these conditions is shown in Table 11-8. Notice that in Table 11-8 each treatment is followed by each treatment (except itself) the same number of times.

Covariance designs are appropriate in situations where some variable affects response but is *not subject to control* during the experiment. For example, if test units consist of human subjects and the response variable is the number of correct identifications of trademarks which are shown on a projection screen (where such factors as length of exposure and clarity of focus

Table 11-8   Latin-square design— carry-over effect

	TIME PERIOD		
TEST UNIT	*1*	*2*	*3*
1	*A*	*B*	*C*
2	*B*	*C*	*A*
3	*C*	*A*	*B*
4	*C*	*B*	*A*
5	*A*	*C*	*B*
6	*B*	*A*	*C*

are varied), it may be the case that response is affected by the general intelligence level of the viewing subject. Suppose that it is too costly to screen subjects, and select only those with approximately the same intelligence quotient. However, we shall assume that the researcher *is* able to measure each subject's IQ.

In this type of situation the researcher may use covariance analysis. Roughly speaking, the computational procedure is similar to a regression problem. The researcher, in effect, determines the effect on response resulting from differences (in IQ) among test units and removes this influence so that the effect of the controlled variables can be determined independently of the effect of test differences on response. (Covariance analysis is illustrated in the next section.)

Before we leave the subject of specialized experimental designs, some mention should be made of *experimental optimization techniques.* Briefly stated, experimental optimization techniques use an experimental framework for finding the combination of control variables that leads to an optimal response. This is usually done by a sequential design in which the response to a set of initial combinations is used to select the next set of combinations until an optimum is reached. *Evolutionary operations* techniques employ experimentation right along with production operations so that control settings can be optimally adjusted as environmental variables change. For details of these procedures the reader is referred to Myers' book.[9]

Recapitulation

As noted earlier, the study of experimental design is basically the study of two things: (1) various experimental layouts, such as single factor, factorial, latin-square, and randomized block designs; and (2) analysis-of-variance and covariance techniques for testing whether the various treatment effects are significant. Many other kinds of design layouts, including fractional factorial designs, balanced incomplete blocks, and partially balanced incomplete blocks, are available.[10] Excellent general discussions of these can be found in Davies and in Cox, as cited earlier.

COMPUTER ROUTINES FOR THE ANALYSIS
OF VARIANCE AND COVARIANCE

As the reader has no doubt surmised by now, the analysis of variance and covariance is typically carried out by means of computer programs. Three popular programs for doing this are:

[9]R. H. Myers, *Response Surface Methodology* (Boston: Allyn and Bacon, Inc., 1971).
[10]In the context of marketing research see P. E. Green, "On the Design of Choice Experiments Involving Multifactor Alternatives," *Journal of Consumer Research*, 1 (September, 1974), 61–68.

1. The BMD-01V program for single-factor analysis, of the type illustrated in Table 11-2

2. The BMD-02V program for factorial designs, of the type illustrated in Table 11-4

3. The BMD-03V program for the analysis of covariance

All three programs are part of the biomedical statistical package.[11]

The BMD-01V Program

The BMD-01V program concentrates on single-factor designs. Unequal sample sizes within the various levels of the single factor can be accommodated. The program has an extremely large problem capacity. Up to 5,000 different levels of the (single) factor and up to 20,000 cases within each level can be handled.

Among groups, within groups, and total sums of squares are computed. Mean squares, degrees of freedom, and F ratios are also calculated. Means and standard deviations of each group (level) are optional outputs.

The BMD-02V Program

The BMD-02V program will handle up to eight treatment variables with up to 999 levels for each (assuming a total number of combinations that is less than 18,000). In addition to the type of summary output illustrated in Table 11-4, BMD-02V provides various breakdowns of two-factor interactions and curvilinear effects, as well as cell and marginal means for each factor.

BMD-02V is designed for equal numbers of cases in each cell—that is, a *balanced* design in which all effects are uncorrelated. Missing data are not allowed.

The BMD-03V Program

The BMD-03V program is designed for covariance analysis in the context of either single-factor or factorial designs. This program handles up to six treatment variables with up to 999 levels for each (subject to an overall restriction of 1,500 combinations). Up to eight covariates can be accommodated. BMD-01V and BMD-02V have already been illustrated in Tables 11-2 and 11-4, respectively. However, we have not as yet shown an application of covariance analysis.

[11]W. J. Dixon, ed., *BMD: Biomedical Computer Programs* (Berkeley, Calif.: University of California Press, 1973).

An Illustration of Covariance Analysis

While space does not permit a detailed discussion of covariance, we can show the *results* of applying BMD-03V to the same type of data that were considered in Table 11-1. Let us now assume, however, that *traffic counts* of customers passing the dog food display can be made during the experiment. Although we cannot control this variable, we do suspect that store traffic affects dog food sales, and at least we are able to measure (if not control) its effect. Our primary interest still centers on the effect of shelf height on sales, but we would like to take into account the independent influence of store traffic on sales.

The covariance model for this experiment is very similar to the single-factor model described earlier:

$$Y_{ij} = \mu + \tau_j + \beta X_{ij} + \epsilon_{ij}$$
$$\sum \tau_j = 0; \quad \mu(\epsilon) = 0; \quad \text{variance} (\epsilon) = \sigma^2$$

First, since store traffic is going to be introduced as a covariate, we now let Y denote the response and X denote the covariate, similar to a regression model.

The principal novelty of the covariance model is the presence of a slope coefficient β denoting the (pooled) within-groups regression of Y on X, across all three groups. (Furthermore, for convenience we shall measure store traffic in terms of deviations from its own mean.) In brief covariance is a combination of regression and analysis of variance. We are not interested in the regression as such; rather we wish to "net out" the influence of X on Y so that the effect of the treatments can be made more precise. Without covariance adjustment the effect of X on Y would simply inflate the error term and reduce the sensitivity of the test.

Table 11-9 shows the input data for the covariance analysis. As shown, Y denotes the response variable and X denotes the covariate. Before carrying out the covariance analysis, Table 11-10 shows an ordinary analysis of variance that *ignores* the covariate. This analysis is just like that of Table 11-2 and was also carried out by BMD-01V, the single-factor program. We note that the F ratio is only 1.51 and is not significant at the $\alpha = 0.05$ level.

Table 11-11 shows what happens when BMD-03V is used to analyze the data of Table 11-9, *including* the covariate. In this case each sum of squares in the response variable is *adjusted for linear association with the covariate X*. As a result of introducing the covariate the *adjusted* sum of squares for Y decreases from a total of 1,621.83 (Table 11-10) to 853.15 (Table 11-11). Among- and within-treatment sums of squares decrease as well. The net effect is to produce an F ratio in Table 11-11 of 13.17 which, with 2 and 20 degrees

Table 11-9   Covariance problem—Arf dog food experiment

SHELF HEIGHT—KNEE LEVEL		SHELF HEIGHT—WAIST LEVEL		SHELF HEIGHT—EYE LEVEL	
Sales	Store Traffic	Sales	Store Traffic	Sales	Store Traffic
87	5	92	2	93	4
94	6	96	1	103	9
92	3	99	3	111	12
82	2	98	4	85	2
95	7	105	7	86	3
102	8	106	6	83	6
87	5	98	4	107	10
93	6	91	2	109	8
$Y_{T1} = 732,$	$X_{T1} = 42,$	$Y_{T2} = 785,$	$X_{T2} = 29,$	$Y_{T3} = 777,$	$X_{T3} = 54$
$\bar{Y}_1 = 91.50,$	$\bar{X}_1 = 5.25,$	$\bar{Y}_2 = 98.13,$	$\bar{X}_2 = 3.63,$	$\bar{Y}_3 = 97.13,$	$\bar{X}_3 = 6.75$
		Grand total	$Y_{TT} = 2{,}294,$	$X_{TT} = 125$	

Table 11-10   Preliminary calculations—Arf dog food experiment

Source of Variation	Degress of Freedom	Sum of Squares	Mean Square	F Ratio
Among treatments	$t - 1 = 2$	204.08	102.04	1.51 ($p > 0.05$)
Within treatments	$n - t = 21$	1,417.75	67.51	
	$n - 1 = 23$	1,621.83		

Table 11-11   Covariance analysis—Arf dog food experiment

	Adjusted Degrees of Freedom	Adjusted Sum of Squares	Mean Square	F Ratio*
Among treatments	2	484.97	242.49	13.17 ($p < 0.05$)
Within treatments	20	368.18	18.41	
Total	22	853.15		

*Tabular F (see Table A-4 in Appendix A) for 2 and 20 degrees of freedom is only 3.49 for $\alpha = 0.05$.

of freedom, is *highly significant at the 0.05 level.* (One degree of freedom is lost within treatments by computing the pooled within-treatments regression between response and covariate.)

The upshot of all of this is that introduction of the covariate has made the experiment much more sensitive and we now find that the treatments produce significant differences in response.

In summary, covariance analysis offers a partial substitute for control in cases where it is suspected that some variable(s) not under control is affecting the response variable. The effect of the covariate is removed separately (by regression) from both the among-groups and the within-groups sums of squares. In this way the *residuals* (following the regression part) are net of the covariate. The influence of the covariate is no longer buried in the error variance and the effect is to increase the sensitivity of the F test.

Ideally, covariance analysis should be employed in cases where the covariate is: (1) highly correlated with the response variable and (2) not correlated with the treatment variables. If correlation with the response variable is low, the sensitivity of the experiment is not appreciably increased. If the covariate is correlated with the treatment variables, removal of its effect also removes some of the variance that is shared with the treatment variable.

In this connection it should be noted that some researchers attempt to bypass the analysis of covariance entirely by performing a straight analysis of variance on a set of Y residuals found after regressing Y on X. This practice is not to be encouraged since, in general, it overestimates the among-groups sum of squares when the covariate is correlated with the treatment variable. This is because the covariance model employs a pooled within-groups regression, *not* a total-sample regression. If treatment-level means differ on the covariate, the two regression slopes will not be the same. (Moreover, degrees of freedom for the error variance differ between the two approaches.)

INTERPRETING EXPERIMENTAL RESULTS

Up to this point we have emphasized significance testing (via analysis of variance and covariance) and experimental layouts. Two other topics are central to the analysis of experimental data:

1. The varieties of interactions that may occur in experimental design work
2. Measuring the contribution of each experimental factor to accounted-for variance in the response variable, similar to the role that partial correlations play in multiple regression

We discuss each of these topics briefly.

Varieties of Interactions

Figures 11-2 and 11-3 have already shown how one can examine two-factor interactions graphically. As indicated earlier, interactions occur when response functions depart from parallelism (beyond what might be expected by chance). As also pointed out, interactions are of two basic kinds: *ordinal* and *disordinal*. In the former case the rank order of effects due to one treatment variable is not changed across levels of some second treatment variable. (More generally, the rank order is unaffected by the *joint levels* assumed by *all* other treatment variables.) In the case of disordinal interactions such is not the case.

Let us examine these concepts more closely. Assume that we have a two-variable factorial design with factor A at three levels and factor B at two levels. What are some of the ways that the response variable may be related to changes in factor A at each level of factor B?

Figure 11-4 shows some illustrative cases. Panel I illustrates the case of *no interaction* at all. All line segments are parallel and the joint effect of A

Figure 11-4   Alternative patterns of interaction

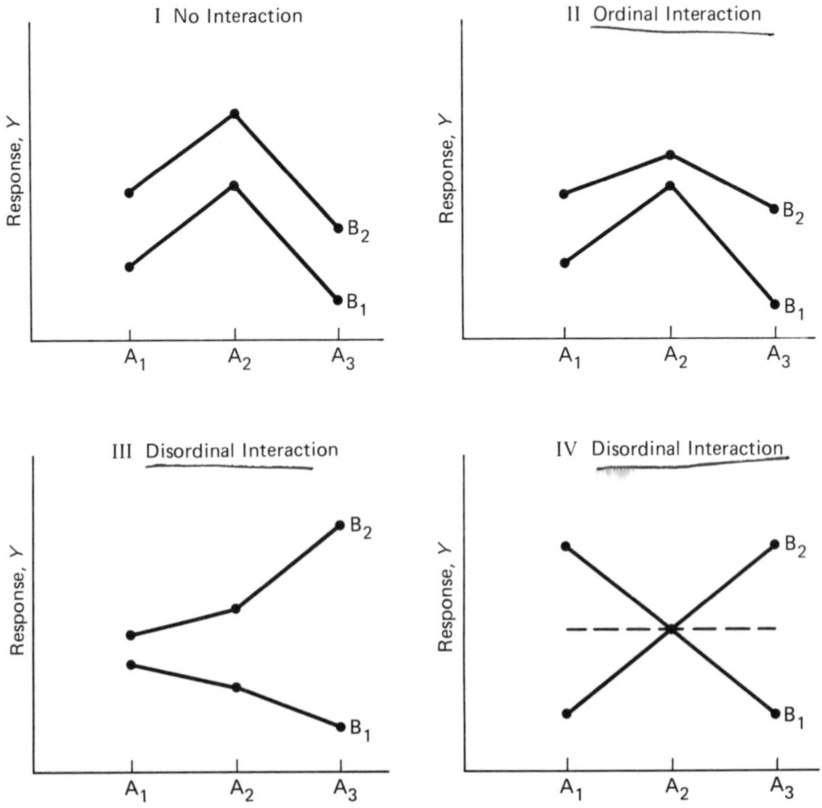

and B is given by the sum of their separate main effects. Note that the *increment* of B_2 over B_1 remains constant across the three levels of A.

Panel II shows a case of *ordinal interaction*. At level B_1 the effect of A is in the rank order A_2, A_1, and A_3, highest to lowest. At level B_2 the rank order of A effects is still A_2, A_1, and A_3. However, the line segments are not parallel. The difference in Y between B_2 and B_1 at level A_2 is much less than the difference noted at level A_3.

Panel III shows a case of *disordinal interaction*. Had only level B_1 been examined, we would have concluded that the Y effects are in the order A_1, A_2, and A_3, highest to lowest. Had only B_2 been examined, we would have concluded that the Y effects are in the opposite order, A_3, A_2, and A_1, highest to lowest.

Panel IV shows an even more stringent case of *disordinal interaction*. In this case the Y effect is *all* interaction. That is, if we average over levels of B, the dotted line, denoting the effect due to A, is horizontal. However, separating effects by each level of B shows how strong the differences really are.

From a decision-oriented viewpoint the presence of disordinal interaction is much more serious than the case of ordinal interaction. In disordinal interaction it is equivocal as to which level of, say, factor A is best unless we know the level of B as well. In the ordinal interaction case this ambiguity does not arise; even though the superiority of one level of A over another may depend on B, the best level of A still remains the best over both levels of B.

Hays' Omega-Square Measure

Marketing researchers are finding it increasingly useful to go beyond significance testing of various treatment variables in order to ascertain the relative importance of each factor in contributing to variation in some response variable Y. As a matter of fact, the balance that is achieved by employing an equal number of cases in each cell of a factorial design leads to *uncorrelatedness* among the treatment variables. This is all to the good, since one does not have the ambiguity that is associated with measuring the relative importance of predictor variables under correlated conditions (as is usually the case in multiple regression).

Hays has proposed a useful measure, called *omega square*, that can be readily computed for various kinds of experimental designs in the course of carrying out analysis of variance correlations.[12] The measure is defined as follows:

$$\hat{\omega}^2 = \frac{\text{SS among} - (\text{df among} \cdot \text{MS error})}{\text{SS total} + \text{MS error}}$$

[12]See W. L. Hays, *Statistics for Psychologists* (New York: Holt, Rinehart and Winston, Inc., 1963). Also see Hays and Winkler, *Statistics*.

where $\hat{\omega}^2$ denotes estimated (from the sample) omega square. The other quantities are obtained from the analysis-of-variance computations.

To illustrate, consider the analysis of the factorial design in Table 11-4. Suppose that we adopt an alpha risk of 0.1 so that all three effects are significant: A, B, and $A \times B$. If so, we can find the $\hat{\omega}^2$ for each contribution.

For example, let us take the case of factor A and substitute the appropriate quantities for SS (sum of squares) and MS (mean square) from Table 11-4:

$$\hat{\omega}_A^2 = \frac{480.5 - [1 \cdot (8.8)]}{958.5 + 8.8}$$

$$= 0.49$$

The quantity $\hat{\omega}_A^2$ bears a marked resemblance to R^2 in the context of multiple regression. Speaking *roughly*, the measure can be described in words as:

$$\hat{\omega}^2 = \frac{\text{accounted-for variation due to factor } A}{\text{total variation in the criterion variable}}$$

Similarly, we find the counterpart $\hat{\omega}^2$ measures for B and $A \times B$ to be 0.31 and 0.04, respectively. The three separate measures sum to 0.84. This last measure is analogous to R^2 in the context of multiple regression.

A theoretical rationale for omega square can be found in Hays' book. The application of omega square to marketing research is discussed by Green.[13] Omega square is not only simple to compute but it is also useful in showing which factors are the most important in accounting for variation in the response variable. (Ordinarily, omega square is computed only for those effects that are statistically significant.)

FIELD EXPERIMENTATION IN MARKETING

Now that some of the techniques for designing and analyzing experiments have been described, the reader may wonder if experimental methods are the wave of the future in the study of marketing phenomena. Unfortunately, the user of experimental procedures is beset by his own set of problems. When it comes to marketing, field experimentation may be:

1. Quite expensive
2. Subject to large amounts of uncontrolled variation

[13]P. E. Green, "On the Analysis of Interactions in Marketing Research Data," *Journal of Marketing Research*, 10 (November, 1973), 410–20.

3. Productive of results that are difficult to generalize to other products, market areas, or time periods

There is little question that field experimentation in marketing is a costly undertaking. Consider the case of a sales manager who wishes to determine the effects of varying amounts of sales effort on product sales of a nationally distributed brand. Sales in a given time period could be affected by point-of-purchase advertising, personal sales effort, broadcast promotion, competitors' selling efforts, relative prices, seasonal effects, past promotional expenditures, and so on. Suppose that the manager wished to consider only three levels each of his firm's point-of-purchase promotion, personal sales effort, and broadcast promotion. A full factorial experiment would require 27 market areas that, in turn, should be measured to account for differences in initial sales potential, competitive activity, and so on. Aside from the fact that regional managers may not like to see some of their market areas receive "low doses" of each of the variables, the administrative job of controlling the levels of the treatment variables, measuring response, adjusting response for different levels of various uncontrolled variables, and so on, is both time-consuming and expensive.

Suppose, however, that the initial cost of such an experiment could be justified and that the experiment yields a set of values for the three control variables which is deemed "optimal." Can the manager blithely assume that if this combination is introduced in *all* territories optimal profits will result? Not at all. First, some of the uncontrolled variables may be changing in some way different from that which existed at the time the experiment was conducted; that is, the environment may not be stable in terms of consumer tastes, consumer incomes, seasonal factors, and the like. Second, other producers may willfully change the competitive environment by changing the price or characteristics of their products. Third, the manager may find that he cannot implement the "best strategy," since promotional expenditures cannot be altered quickly enough to ensure that essentially the same environmental conditions prevailing during the experiment are still in effect.

Seymour Banks has pointed out that the test units of marketing experiments can be broadly classified as involving: (1) people, (2) stores, and (3) market areas.[14] Each class of units presents its own set of problems for the experimenter.

In cases where people are the test units (e.g., product usage, advertising copy themes, package tests), the researcher must contend with such things as interview bias, subject conditioning, subject drop-outs, and the like. In experiments in which the test units are stores (e.g., pricing, couponing, point-of-purchase displays) the researcher must contend with the possible reluctance

[14]See Seymour Banks, "Marketing Experiments," *Journal of Advertising Research*, 3 (March, 1963), 34–41.

of store managers to implement the design, competitors' activities, contamination of the data of control stores by test store influences, and so on. In experiments emphasizing market areas, the problems of measurement and control become the most difficult of all. Seldom can market territories be partitioned without sales-response overlap and stimulus (sales promotion, pricing) overlap as well. Furthermore, there is a danger that any experiment may be conducted for too short a period of time so that the carry-over effect of such treatments as advertising and sales promotion is not appropriately measured.

Although the preceding paragraphs suggest a rather bleak picture for the future of field experimentation in marketing, the fact remains that experimentation and measurement provide the *only sound basis for model validation in marketing and the establishment of causal relationships*. It is to be hoped that as our knowledge of techniques improves and superior means are developed for measuring sales (e.g., via consumer panels, store audits, home audits, etc.), market experimentation will provide a significant tool for the development of information for decision-making purposes.

The Cost versus Value of Market Experimentation

Market experimentation represents a cost-incurring activity, just as any other form of information gathering. The manager (and researcher) must weigh the potential value of the information against this cost. One point of interest, however, is that, given a reasonably *stable* marketing environment, a field experiment can yield information that is useful for a *series of future decisions*. If so, the value of the research should be appropriately estimated over a time horizon involving a series of future decision choices. This value will, of course, depend on how cleverly the researcher can design his experiment along lines that are expected to remain reasonably stable over time.

The desire for determining causal relationships of some generality suggests that the researcher may wish to include a fairly large number of variables in his field experiments so that he can gain pertinent information for making suitable transformations to other products, other markets, and other time periods. The problems involved in achieving this objective are hardly inconsequential, but the goal of developing *general* information that can be adjusted for specific situations appears more worthwhile than does a goal based on solving a "one-shot" problem.

The reader may wonder why our discussion of experimental designs centered on traditional rather than Bayesian statistical techniques. Experimental designs using Bayesian statistics have not been developed as yet to nearly the extent that traditional statistical designs have. At this point we can only say that experimentation represents another way of information gathering and should be approached in terms of its cost versus value (compared to other techniques) for decision-making purposes, both with regard to present and anticipated problems. Unfortunately it is much easier to state this objective than to design suitable techniques for implementing it.

SUMMARY

In this chapter our primary objectives were twofold: (1) to introduce the reader to the conceptual bases underlying marketing experimentation and (2) to develop the necessary statistical machinery (analysis of variance and covariance) to analyze experimental data.[15] The first section of the chapter dealt with the purposes of experimentation and a description of classical versus statistically designed experiments.

We next attempted to explain what goes on when one uses analysis of variance procedures. A simple numerical example was used to demonstrate the partitioning of variance into among- and within-components.

Some of the principal designs—single-factor analysis, factorial layouts, randomized blocks, latin squares, and covariance designs—were illustrated. The assumptions underlying the models were also pointed out, and a synthetic data experiment was analyzed to show how the models operate. The topics of interaction plotting and Hays' omega square were introduced to aid the researcher in interpreting the results of his analysis.

We concluded the chapter with a discussion of some of the problems involved in marketing experimentation and the relationship of this means of data collection to the cost and value of information.

ASSIGNMENT MATERIAL

1. The marketing research department of the Gamma Adhesive Company is attempting to find some attribute of their gummed labels that can be merchandised as being superior to competitive products. The manager of the department, Mr. Beckwith, feels that the strength of their adhesive represents a good promotional point. Accordingly, samples of the company's adhesive and three other brands are tested by an independent research company. The "strength indexes" of the four products are as follows:

---

[15]For more advanced discussions of experimental design, see B. J. Winer, *Statistical Principles in Experimental Design*, 2d ed. (New York: McGraw-Hill Book Company, 1962) and J. L. Myers, *Fundamentals of Experimental Design*, 2d ed. (Boston: Allyn and Bacon, Inc., 1972).

		COMPETITIVE ADHESIVE		
TRIAL	GAMMA ADHESIVE	X	Y	Z
1	35	32	22	24
2	11	29	18	19
3	28	17	23	26
4	26	24	17	19
5	32	15	19	22

Assume that trials are merely replications of the same experiment (that is, that a one-way classification is appropriate) and a common error variance exists for all four "treatments."

a. Test the null hypothesis that the means of all treatments are equal (use an alpha risk of 0.05).

b. Assume now that the trials can be treated as "blocks" and perform a two-way analysis of variance. Compare your answer with part (a).

c. What additional statistical assumptions (other than equality of variance) are you making in using analysis of variance procedures in this problem?

2. Referring to the latin-square problem in the chapter, assume that a researcher has carried out the suggested experiment (dealing with shelf height A_i, number of facings B_j, and shelf fullness C_k), using the particular design shown in the chapter. The data are as follows (table entries are unit sales):

	B_1	B_2	B_3	B_4
A_1	$C_1 = 13$	$C_2 = 16$	$C_3 = 16$	$C_4 = 14$
A_2	$C_4 = 9$	$C_1 = 17$	$C_2 = 20$	$C_3 = 20$
A_3	$C_3 = 14$	$C_4 = 19$	$C_1 = 17$	$C_2 = 21$
A_4	$C_2 = 15$	$C_3 = 17$	$C_4 = 18$	$C_1 = 19$

a. Test the hypothesis that no significant differences exist among sales responses due to shelf height, number of facings, and shelf fullness (use an alpha risk of 0.05).

b. Without carrying out statistical tests, do you notice any apparent trends in sales response for each treatment variable considered separately?

3. Consider the following factorial layout:

	PERSONAL SELLING EFFORT		
DIRECT MAIL	*Level 1*	*Level 2*	*Level 3*
Level 1	40; 33	49; 47	56; 60
Level 2	37; 40	47; 51	62; 56
Level 3	51; 47	51; 60	73; 76

As noted, two replications of personal selling effort and direct mail, each at three levels, are made. This leads to 18 observations of sales response.

a. Test the null hypothesis (alpha risk at 0.05) of no difference in sales due to personal selling effort versus direct mail.

b. Does a significant interaction exist (alpha risk at 0.05) between personal selling effort and direct-mail advertising?

c. If, as a researcher, you had to recommend one particular combination of personal selling effort and direct-mail advertising, what are the kinds of additional information that you would need before presenting your recommendation?

4. What are the major difficulties encountered in attempting to use field experimentation in marketing contexts?

Advanced Techniques in Analyzing Associative Data IV

Other Techniques for Analyzing Criterion–Predictor Association

12

INTRODUCTION

Multiple regression and the analysis of variance and covariance (Chapters 10 and 11, respectively) are both characterized by the fact that they deal with the analysis of *dependence* structures—in this instance a data structure that consists of a single criterion variable and multiple predictors.

Several other techniques are available for analyzing criterion–predictor association. In this chapter we describe the more important ones insofar as marketing research is concerned:

- Discriminant analysis: two-group and multiple-group
- Automatic interaction detection
- Canonical correlation
- Multivariate analysis of variance and covariance

These techniques are considerably more complex than those of Chapters 10 and 11. Accordingly, we do not delve deeply into technical details. Rather, our interest is applications oriented and our scope emphasizes the conceptual basis of each method.

Discriminant analysis is the most widely used of this group of techniques; hence, we start off the discussion with an introduction to two-group discriminant analysis. A sample problem is described and solved numerically. We then describe the assumption structure of the technique and a computer program for performing two-group discriminant analysis. The multiple (three or more groups) case is discussed next, including an illustrative application of a stepwise multiple discriminant program.

We then turn to automatic interaction detection (AID), a procedure for systematically splitting a large sample of multivariate data into smaller, more homogeneous groups whose criterion-variable means are widely separated. We show how AID can be used as a preliminary data-combing procedure prior to the application of parameterized models, such as multiple regression and two-group discriminant analysis.

The last techniques to be discussed in this chapter—and briefly at that—are canonical correlation and multivariate analysis of variance and covariance. Our presentation is kept at a descriptive level that emphasizes the objectives of each technique and its application to marketing research.

TWO-GROUP DISCRIMINANT ANALYSIS

As briefly described in Chapter 9, when dealing with associative data the marketing researcher may encounter cases where the criterion variable is categorical but where the predictor variables involve interval-scaled data. For example, he may wish to predict whether sales potential in a given marketing territory will be "good" or "bad," based on certain measurements regarding the territory's personal disposable income, population density, number of retail outlets, and the like.

Other potential applications also come to mind, such as:

- How do consumers who are loyal to my brand differ in their demographic profiles from those who are not loyal?
- How do respondents who show high interest in a new set of concept descriptions differ in their readership levels of certain magazines from those who show low interest?

The classification need not be limited to two groups. For example:

- Are significant demographic differences observed among purchasers of Sears, Goodyear, Goodrich, and Firestone tires?
- How do doctors, lawyers, and bankers differ in terms of their preference ratings of eight different luxury automobiles?

Still other such problems could be added to the list. However, each one has a common structure in which we assume that some test object (usually a person) falls into one of a set of categories. It is also assumed that we know that person's profile on a set of interval-scaled predictor variables, such as age, income, years of education, or other background variables.

The problem is to predict a person's category from some function of the predictor variables. Here we shall assume that the function is linear. If only two categories are involved, the problem is a *two-group* discriminant case; if three or more categories are involved, we are dealing with *multiple* (group) discriminant analysis. We first focus on the simpler, two-group case and then consider the multiple-group version.

Objectives of Two-Group Discriminant Analysis

Two-group discriminant analysis (and classification) involves four main objectives:

1. Finding linear composites of the predictor variables that enable the analyst to separate the groups by maximizing among-groups relative to within-groups variation.
2. Establishing procedures for assigning new individuals, whose profiles but not group identity are known, to one of the two groups.
3. Testing whether significant differences exist between the mean predictor-variable profiles of the two groups.
4. Determining which variables account most for intergroup differences in mean profiles.

Geometric Representation

If we have n persons measured on m variables, the profile of each person can be portrayed as a point in m dimensions. If we *also* know the group to which each person belongs, and the groups differ in terms of average profiles, often called *centroids*, we might expect to find different groups occupying different regions of the space. The less overlap noted among intergroup profiles in that space, the more likely it is that discriminant analysis can help us separate the groups.

One way to show what happens when a two-group discriminant function is computed is provided by the scatter diagram and projection in Figure 12-1. Suppose that we had two groups, A and B, and two measures, X_1 and X_2, on each member of the two groups. We could plot in the scatter diagram the association of variable X_2 with X_1 for each group, maintaining group identity by the use of filled-in dots or open circles. The resultant ellipses enclose some specified proportion of the points, say 95% in each group. If a straight line is drawn through the two points where the ellipses intersect and then projected to a new axis Z, we can say that the overlap between the *univariate* distributions A' and B' (represented by the shaded area) is smaller than would be obtained by any other line drawn through the ellipses representing the scatter plots.

The important thing to note about Figure 12-1 is that the Z axis expresses the two-variable profiles of groups A and B as *single* numbers. That

**Figure 12-1   Graphical illustration of two-group
discriminant analysis**

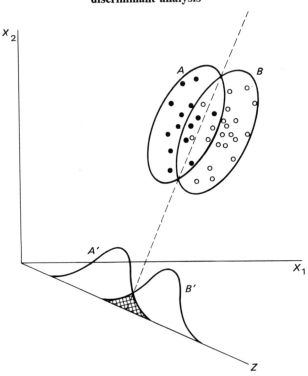

is, by finding a linear composite of the original profile scores we can portray each profile as a point on a line. Thus, the axis Z "condenses" the information about group separability (shown in the bivariate plot) into a set of points on a single axis. Z is the *discriminant* axis.

In most problems of realistic size, we have more than two predictor variables. If so, each predictor can represent a *separate* dimension (although we would be limited to three predictor variables if we wished to plot the data). In any case the basic objective is still to find one axis in the m-dimensional space that maximally separates the centroids of the two groups after the points are projected onto this new axis.

In our discussion of multiple regression analysis we noted that one finds a linear composite that maximizes the coefficient of multiple determination, R^2. Analogously, in two-group discriminant analysis we try to find a linear composite of the original variables that maximizes the *ratio* of among-to-within groups variability. It should be noted that if m, the number of predictor variables, is quite large, we shall be able to effect a great deal of parsimony by portraying among- to within-groups variation in many fewer dimensions (actually a *single dimension* in the two-group case) than found originally.

A Numerical Example

Let us return to the example involving ready-to-eat cereals that was first presented in Table 10-1 in the context of multiple regression. As recalled, we wished to see if amount of protein and vitamin D influenced consumers' evaluations of the cereals.

In the present case we shall assume that a different pretest has been run in which ten different test cereals are described. However, in the present case each of the ten consumer raters is simply asked to classify the cereal into one of two categories: *like* versus *dislike*. The (hypothetical) data appear in Table 12-1. The predictor variables are (again):

X_1: the amount of protein (in grams) per 2-ounce serving, and
X_2: the percentage of minimum daily requirements of vitamin D per 2-ounce serving.

Also shown in Table 12-1 are various sums of squares and cross products, the means on X_1 and X_2 of each group, and the total-sample mean. For example,

Table 12-1   Consumer evaluations (like versus dislike) of ten cereals varying in nutritional content

Person	Evaluation		Protein X_1	Vitamin D X_2		X_1^2	X_2^2	$X_1 X_2$
1	Dislike		2	4		4	16	8
2	Dislike		3	2		9	4	6
3	Dislike		4	5		16	25	20
4	Dislike		5	4		25	16	20
5	Dislike		6	7		36	49	42
		Mean	4	4.4	Sum	90	110	96
6	Like		7	6		49	36	42
7	Like		8	4		64	16	32
8	Like		9	7		81	49	63
9	Like		10	6		100	36	60
10	Like		11	9		121	81	99
		Mean	9	6.4	Sum	415	218	296
		Grand mean	6.5	5.4				
		Standard deviation	3.028	2.011				

the grand mean (i.e., grand centroid) is

$$\bar{X}_1 = 6.5; \qquad \bar{X}_2 = 5.4$$

We first note from the table that the two groups are much more widely separated on X_1 (protein) than they are on X_2 (vitamin D). If we were forced to choose just one of the axes, it would seem that X_1 is a better bet than X_2. However, there *is* information provided by the group separation on X_2, so we wonder if some linear composite of *both* X_1 and X_2 could do better than X_1 alone.

Figure 12-2 shows a scatter plot of the X_1 and X_2 data of Table 12-1. We note that perfect discrimination can be achieved with X_1 if we erected a line perpendicular to the horizontal axis between the scale values of 6 and 7. On the other hand, there is no way that the use of X_2 alone would enable us to separate the groups. Given this picture, we would not be surprised if the best linear composite turns out to favor X_1 with a considerably larger weight than X_2 receives.

Why not use X_1 alone, rather than a composite of X_1 and X_2? First, the data of Table 12-1 represent only a *sample*; it is quite possible that additional observations would show that X_1 alone would *not* effect perfect discrimination between the two groups. Second, we have not explicitly taken into consideration either the variability about X_1 versus X_2 or their correlation. One of the nice features of discriminant analysis is that all three aspects of the data—centroid, variance, and correlation—are considered in developing the linear composite that maximally separates the groups.

**Figure 12-2   Scatter plot of two-group
sample data of Table 12-1**

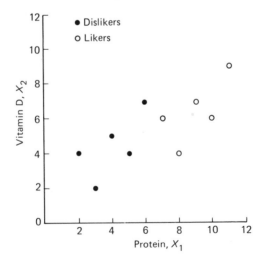

As noted earlier, the key problem of two-group discriminant analysis is to find a new axis so that projections of the points onto that axis exhibit the property of maximizing the separation between group means relative to their within-groups variability on the *composite*. This discriminant axis can be defined in terms of a set of weights—one for each predictor-variable axis— so that we have the following linear function:

$$Z = k_1 X_1 + k_2 X_2$$

where k_1 and k_2 are the weights that we seek.

But how shall we define variability? In discriminant analysis there are several ways to do this. However, the most straightforward way is to find the ratio of two sums of squares *after* the set of scores on the linear composite has been computed. One sum of squared deviations represents the variability of the two group means on the composite around their grand mean. The second sum of squared deviations represents the pooled variability of the individual cases around their respective group means—also on the linear composite. One can then find the ratio of the first sum of squares to the second. It is this ratio that is to be maximized through the appropriate choice of k_1 and k_2.

Finding the values of k_1 and k_2 in the first place also involves computing various sums of squares. However, in this case sums of cross products are required as well, since we have more than a single predictor variable. The reader should keep these two aspects straight. To find k_1 and k_2 we work with sums of squares *and* cross products. However, *after* k_1 and k_2 have been found and applied to X_1 and X_2, we have only a *single* variable, namely the linear composite. In this case we only need to talk about sums of squared deviations regarding various means on the linear composite, namely the grand mean or the separate group means.

Computing the Discriminant Weights

Solving for the *discriminant weights* (k_1 and k_2) that maximize the separation between the groups involves a procedure quite similar to that followed in Table 10-3 in the context of multiple regression. However, in the present case we shall want to find a set of sums of squares and cross products that relate to the variation *within* groups.[1]

[1] While the weights (k_1 and k_2) are developed here in the context of variation within groups, it should be mentioned that a proportional set of weights could be developed from variation across the *total* sample. Indeed, in the two-group discriminant case, multiple regression— in which the criterion variable is expressed as a 0–1 dummy variable—yields partial regression coefficients that are *proportional* to k_1 and k_2.

Table 12-2 shows the computations required to solve for k_1 and k_2. Note that we first find mean-corrected sums of squares and cross products within each group separately. These are then summed across the two groups to obtain the pooled quantities shown in the last column. Then, similar to solving for the partial regression coefficients in Table 10-3, we solve the set of simultaneous equations for k_1 and k_2. In the present case the right-hand side of each equation is the difference in means between likers and dislikers on each variable separately:

Protein: $\bar{X}_1$ (likers) $- \bar{X}_1$ (dislikers) $= 9 - 4 = 5$

Vitamin D: $\bar{X}_2$ (dislikers) $- \bar{X}_2$ (likers) $= 6.4 - 4.4 = 2$

Solving the two simultaneous equations leads to the desired discriminant function:

$$Z = 0.368X_1 - 0.147X_2$$

Having found the discriminant function, it is a straightforward procedure to apply it to each of the ten pairs of X_1, X_2 values in Table 12-1 to get the linear composite. For example, the discriminant score for the first case in the disliker group is

$$Z = 0.368(2) - 0.147(4)$$
$$= 0.148$$

Table 12-2   Solving for the discriminant weights

FROM TABLE 12-1: MEAN CORRECTED SUMS OF SQUARES AND CROSS PRODUCTS

	Dislikers	Likers	Total
$\sum x_1^2 = \sum X_1^2 - n\bar{X}_1^2$	$90 - 5(4)^2 = 10$	$415 - 5(9)^2 = 10$	20
$\sum x_2^2 = \sum X_2^2 - n\bar{X}_2^2$	$110 - 5(4.4)^2 = 13.2$	$218 - 5(6.4)^2 = 13.2$	26.4
$\sum x_1 x_2 = \sum X_1 X_2 - n\bar{X}_1\bar{X}_2$	$96 - 5(4)(4.4) = 8$	$296 - 5(9)(6.4) = 8$	16

Solving for the discriminant weights:
   To find k_1 and k_2, we solve the simultaneous equations:

$$\sum x_1^2 k_1 + \sum x_1 x_2 k_2 = \bar{X}_1 \text{ (likers)} - \bar{X}_1 \text{ (dislikers)}$$
$$\sum x_1 x_2 k_1 + \sum x_2^2 k_2 = \bar{X}_2 \text{ (likers)} - \bar{X}_2 \text{ (dislikers)}$$

We make the appropriate numerical substitutions and then solve for k_1 and k_2:

$$20k_1 + 16k_2 = 5$$
$$16k_1 + 26.4k_2 = 2$$
$$k_1 = 0.368; \qquad k_2 = -0.147$$

Discriminant function:

$$Z = 0.368X_1 - 0.147X_2$$

We can also find discriminant scores for the centroids of the two groups and the grand mean:

$$\bar{Z} \text{ (dislikers)} = 0.368(4) - 0.147(4.4) = 0.824$$
$$\bar{Z} \text{ (likers)} = 0.368(9) - 0.147(6.4) = 2.368$$
$$\bar{Z} \text{ (grand mean)} = 0.368(6.5) - 0.147(5.4) = 1.596$$

Plotting the Discriminant Function

The original scatter plot of the ten observations is reproduced in Figure 12-3. However, this time we also show the discriminant axis (linear composite) by passing a straight line through the point $(0.368, -0.147)$ and the intersection of the original axes.[2] The original points can then be projected onto this new axis.

Figure 12-3 Plot of the discriminant axis and point projections (see Figure 12-2)

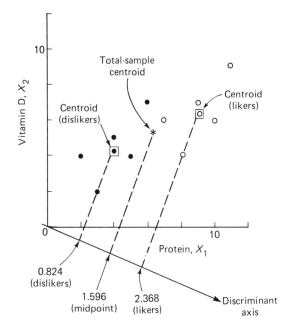

[2]Or one could use any point whose coordinates are proportional to $(0.368, -0.147)$. However, it should be noted that the *scale unit* on the discriminant axis in Figure 12-3 differs from the original unit in which X_1 and X_2 are expressed. To maintain the original unit, k_1 and k_2 would have to be normalized so that their sum of squares equals unity.

Illustratively, we show projections of the grand centroid and the centroids of the dislikers and likers, respectively. (Similarly, all of the ten original points could be projected onto the discriminant axis as well.) We note that the discriminant axis "favors" X_1 (as we guessed it would) by giving about 2.5 times the (absolute-value) weight ($k_1 = 0.368$ versus $k_2 = -0.147$) to X_1 as is given to X_2.

The discriminant scores of each person are shown in Table 12-3. As illustrated earlier for the first person in the disliker group, each score is computed by application of the discriminant function to the person's original X_1 and X_2 values. We can now examine the criterion being optimized in solving for the discriminant weights.

Table 12-3 **Scores on discriminant axis and values of the discriminant criterion**

	DISLIKERS		LIKERS	
Person	*Discriminant Score*	*Person*	*Discriminant Score*	
1	0.148	6	1.691	
2	0.809	7	2.353	
3	0.735	8	2.279	
4	1.250	9	2.794	
5	1.176	10	2.721	
Mean	0.824	Mean	2.368	
		Grand mean	1.596	

Between-groups variability:
$$5(0.824 - 1.596)^2 + 5(2.368 - 1.596)^2 = 5.96$$

Within-groups variability:

Dislikers: $(0.148-0.824)^2+(0.809-0.824)^2+\cdots+(1.176-0.824)^2 = 0.772$
Likers: $(1.691-2.368)^2+(2.353-2.368)^2+\cdots+(2.721-2.368)^2 = \underline{0.772}$
$$1.544$$

Discriminant criterion:
$$C = \frac{5.96}{1.544} = 3.86$$

The Discriminant Criterion

As stated earlier, the discriminant function represents a linear composite of the original data that maximizes the ratio of among-groups variability to within-groups variability. Table 12-3 shows what this means. First, we compute a measure of between-groups variability by finding the deviation of each of the two group means from the grand mean on the discriminant function. These deviations are squared, multiplied by the number of persons in each group, and summed. Table 12-3 details the calculations, and we note that the between-groups variability is 5.96.

The within-groups variability is found in a similar manner except for the fact that squared deviations are taken about each group's own mean. The two separate measures are then summed to give 1.544 as a pooled within-groups sum of squares. Finally, the discriminant criterion being maximized is the ratio of the between-groups to the within-groups sum of squares:

$$C = \frac{5.96}{1.544} = 3.86$$

We can now see whether using X_1, while ignoring X_2, can produce a higher discriminant ratio. All the input data needed for these comparison calculations appear in Tables 12-1 and 12-2. The between-groups variability (from Table 12-1) is calculated as

$$5(4 - 6.5)^2 + 5(9 - 6.5)^2 = 62.5$$

The pooled within-groups variability on X_1 (from Table 12-2) is calculated from

$$\sum x_1^2 \text{ (dislikers)} = 10$$
$$\sum x_1^2 \text{ (likers)} \quad = \underline{10}$$
$$20$$

and the discriminant criterion in this case is

$$C = \frac{62.5}{20} = 3.125$$

which, of course, is *less* than that obtained from the (best) linear composite. It is rather interesting that the optimal function,

$$Z = 0.368X_1 - 0.147X_2$$

is a *difference* function in which X_2 (vitamin D) receives a *negative* weight. However, as recalled, the two groups are *not* highly separated on X_2, even though the mean of the likers, 6.4, is somewhat higher than the mean of the dislikers, 4.4, on X_2.

More important is the fact that X_2 is *highly correlated* with X_1 and, hence, can account for some of the error variance in X_1. That is, X_2 serves as a *suppressor variable*. By giving X_2 a *negative* weight in the discriminant function in which X_1 has a positive weight, the predictability of the criterion is further enhanced. X_2 receives a negative weight because it does a better job of suppressing error variance in X_1 (through its high correlation with X_1) than it does in separating group means on its own account.

It is important to bring this point out because it is not unusual in various applied discriminant analyses to find evidence of suppressor effects. This is also true of applied regression analyses.

Classifying the Persons

It is all well and good to find the discriminant function, but the remaining three questions posed at the beginning of the chapter still remain to be answered:

1. How well does the function classify the ten cases?
2. Is the function statistically significant?
3. What is the relative importance of the predictor variables?

The classification problem, in turn, involves two additional questions: (1) how well does the function assign the known cases in the sample, and (2) how well does it assign new cases *not* used in computing the function in the first place?

These questions provide direct parallels to the topics of R^2 (strength of relationship) and cross validation in regression analysis. In the case of discriminant analysis we need an *assignment rule*. One rule that seems intuitively plausible is based on Figure 12-3. As can be seen from the figure, no misassignments will be made if we adopt the rule:

- Assign all cases with discriminant scores that are on the left of the midpoint (1.596) to the *disliker* group.
- Assign all cases with discriminant scores that are on the right of the midpoint (1.596) to the *liker* group.

That is, all true dislikers will be correctly classified as such and all true likers will be correctly classified. This can be shown by a 2×2 table:

TRUE STATE	ASSIGNED BY RULE		
	Disliker	*Liker*	TOTAL
Disliker	5	0	5
Liker	0	5	5
Total	5	5	10

We see that all entries fall along the main diagonal. For example, had any of the five true dislikers been called likers, the first row and second column would contain not a 0 but, rather, the number of such misassignments. Application of this rule can be stated in the equivalent terms:

- Substitute the centroid of each group in the discriminant function and find the respective group scores (in our case 0.824 for dislikers and 2.368 for likers).
- For any new case compute the discriminant score and assign the case to that group whose group score is closer.

This rule makes two specific assumptions: (1) the prior probability of a new case falling into each of the groups is equal across groups, and (2) the cost of misclassification is equal across groups.[3]

If a higher prior probability existed for likers, we could reduce the expected probability of misclassification by moving the cutting point of 1.596 to the left (closer to 0.824, the mean score for dislikers) so as to give a wider interval for the larger (likers) group. Similarly, if the cost of misclassifying a liker is higher than that for misclassifying a disliker, the cutting point would also be moved closer to 0.824. More advanced procedures are available for determining just what the new cutting point should be, given differences in prior probabilities or misclassification costs.[4]

A second point of interest concerns the tendency for assignment tables based on the calibration sample to show better results than would be found upon cross validation with new cases. That is, some capitalization on chance takes place in discriminant analysis and one needs a way to measure this bias, just as cross validation should be employed in multiple regression (as described in Chapter 10). Procedures are available to develop a truer summary of the degree of correct assignments that would be obtained from fresh data.[5]

Testing Statistical Significance

While the discriminant function does perfectly in classifying the ten cases of the calibration sample, we still have not tested whether the group

[3]There is a further assumption that is germane to linear discriminant functions: the predictors of each group must have equal variance-covariance matrices. These matrices are assumed to be based on multivariate normally distributed variables with known variances and covariances when the above rule is used for case assignments.

[4]See A. A. Afifi and S. P. Azer, *Statistical Analysis: A Computer Oriented Approach* (New York: Academic Press, Inc., 1972).

[5]For a general discussion of the topic, see P. A. Lachenbruch, *Discriminant Analysis* (New York: Hafner Press, 1975). Some specific procedures can be found in R. E. Frank, W. F. Massy, and D. G. Morrison, "Bias in Multiple Discriminant Analysis," *Journal of Marketing Research*, 2 (August, 1965), 250–58.

centroids differ significantly. This is analogous to testing for the significance of R^2 in multiple regression. Tests of the equality of group centroids also proceed on the basis of an F ratio that, in turn, is calculated from a variability measure known as *Mahalanobis squared distance.*

We do not delve into the technical details of Mahalanobis squared distance, other than to say that it is like ordinary (Euclidean) squared distance that is computed between two centroids in a space with correlated axes and different measurement units.[6] Fortunately, the F ratio for making the test is routinely computed by the computer program and we return to this test in discussing the computer run. We should reiterate, however, that with large sample sizes it is not difficult to get a significant F ratio, even though the classification accuracy is poor. If so, statistical significance is no substitute for operational significance; one should be guided by the classification accuracy.

Relative Importance of Predictor Variables

As recalled, the discriminant weights of the sample problem were

$$k_1 = 0.368; \qquad k_2 = -0.147$$

Since the original variables X_1 and X_2 were expressed in different units and display different standard deviations as well, the analyst generally *standardizes* the discriminant weights before assaying their relative importance.

Two standardization procedures are in vogue. One of these multiplies each discriminant weight by *total-sample standard deviation* of that variable. The other procedure multiplies the weight by the *pooled within-groups standard deviation* of that variable.

Method 1

From Table 12-1, the total-sample standard deviations are $s_{x_1} = 3.028$ and $s_{x_2} = 2.011$. The standardized discriminant weights are then:

$$
\begin{aligned}
k_1^{s(t)} &= 3.028(0.368) = 2.240 \\
k_2^{s(t)} &= 2.011(-0.147) = -0.296
\end{aligned}
$$

[6]See J. E. Overall and C. J. Klett, *Applied Multivariate Analysis* (New York: McGraw-Hill Book Company, 1972), for details. In the present problem Mahalanobis squared distance is equal to $8(1.544) = 12.353$, where 8 is the number of degrees of freedom and 1.544 is the pooled within-groups sum of squares from Table 12-3.

Method 2

From Table 12-2, we can find the pooled within-groups standard deviation of X_1 and X_2 from

$$s_{x_1}^{(w)} = \sqrt{\frac{\sum x_1^2}{8}} = \sqrt{\frac{20}{8}} = 1.581; \quad s_{x_2}^{(w)} = \sqrt{\frac{\sum x_2^2}{8}} = \sqrt{\frac{26.4}{8}} = 1.817$$

where $8 = n - 2$, the degrees of freedom for the pooled groups (where n denotes the total-sample size). The standardized weights are then

$$k_1^{s^{(w)}} = 1.581(\quad 0.368) = \quad 0.582$$
$$k_2^{s^{(w)}} = 1.817(-0.147) = -0.267$$

While the two methods yield different numerical values (and different ratios of standardized k_1 to standardized k_2), they *rank* the coefficients in the same way—and that ranking also agrees with the original ranking. That is, X_1 is "more important" than X_2.

It should be emphasized, however, that the same limitations regarding relative importance of predictor variables apply here as applied in the case of correlated predictors in multiple regression. Even *after* standardization a certain degree of ambiguity remains as long as the predictors are correlated (which certainly is the case here).

COMPUTERIZED TWO-GROUP ANALYSIS

Virtually all two-group discriminant analyses of any appreciable size are carried out by the computer. A particularly popular and useful program for two-group discriminant analysis is the BMD-04M program, drawn from the Biomedical program series.[7]

The BMD-04M program can handle up to 25 predictor variables and a sample size of up to 300 cases in each group. In addition to printing out the group means, the differences between group means and the discriminant weights, the program also computes a between-groups squared distance (Mahalanobis D-square) and associated F test for the difference in group means along the discriminant axis. Finally, the program prints out a group assignment of each individual case, ordered in terms of its values on the

---

[7]W. J. Dixon, ed., *BMD: Biomedical Computer Programs* (Berkeley, Calif.: University of California Press, 1973).

discriminant axis; cases misassigned by the function are easily spotted by this procedure.

For comparison purposes BMD-04M was applied to the sample data of Table 12-1. The results of the analysis appear in Table 12-4. The sections showing the group means, mean-corrected sums of squares and cross products, and the discriminant weights have been shown earlier.

The program computes the Mahalanobis D-square-distance measure[8] and converts it to the more familiar F ratio. The F ratio of 13.511, with 2 degrees of freedom for numerator and 7 degrees of freedom for denominator, is highly significant at the 0.01 level (Table A-4 in Appendix A shows a tabular F of only 9.55).

BMD-04M also computes summary statistics for the discriminant function Z. As noted earlier, the mean discriminant scores for likers and dislikers are 2.368 and 0.284, respectively. In this particular problem the within-groups variances happen to be the same for each group. From Table 12-3, we recall that the mean-corrected sum of squares within the likers and dislikers groups is 0.772.

The within-groups variance is 0.772 divided by degrees of freedom $5 - 1 = 4$, or 0.193 for each group. The standard deviation is the square root of 0.193, or 0.439.

One nice feature of the BMD-04M program is that it prints out individual discriminant scores that are ranked in size. In the sample problem the midpoint of the two group means is 1.596. Discriminant scores larger than this are assigned to the likers group; those that are lower are assigned to the dislikers group. As can be noted from Table 12-4, no misassignments are made. We see that person 4 in the likers group exhibits the highest discriminant score, while person 1 in the dislikers group displays the lowest score.

Concluding Comments on Two-Group Discriminant Analysis

Before moving on to a discussion of multiple discriminant analysis, it is appropriate to review the two-group model's assumptions:

1. If interest rests solely on finding *linear* functions that maximize between-groups to within-groups variability, then we must assume

---

[8]Mahalanobis D-square can also be computed from the expression: D-square $= 8[0.368(5.0) - 0.147(2.0)] = 12.353$, where 8 is the number of degrees of freedom for the pooled within-groups sum of squares. Each term inside the brackets is the product of the discriminant weight and the between-groups mean difference on each variable in turn.

Table 12-4   Summary output of BMD-04M two-group discriminant analysis

Predictor Variable Means by Group				Within-Groups Sum of Squares and Cross Products
Predictor	Means (Likers)	Means (Dislikers)	Difference	
				X_1 X_2
X_1	9.0	4.0	5.0	X_1 $\begin{bmatrix} 20 & 16 \\ 16 & 26.4 \end{bmatrix}$
X_2	6.4	4.4	2.0	X_2

Discriminant Function Weights

Predictor Variable	
1	2
0.368	−0.147

Mahalanobis D-square   12.353
F ratio (2, 7)   13.511   (significant beyond the 0.01 level)

Discriminant Score Statistics

Group	Sample Size	Mean Z	Variance of Z	Standard Deviation of Z
Likers	5	2.367	0.193	0.439
Dislikers	5	0.824	0.193	0.439

Rank	First Group Values (Likers)	Second Group Values (Dislikers)	First Group Item Number	Second Group Item Number
1	2.794		4	
2	2.721		5	
3	2.353		2	
4	2.279		3	
5	1.691		1	
6		1.250		4
7		1.176		5
8		0.809		2
9		0.735		3
10		0.148		1

that the within-groups sums of squares and cross products are equal (if unknown) across the groups.

2. If we are also concerned with statistical significance, then we add the assumption that the original profiles are multivariate normally distributed with unknown (but equal) sums of squares and cross products.

3. If we are further concerned with assigning cases to groups on the basis of which mean discriminant score is the closer, then the additional assumptions of: (a) equal prior probabilities, (b) equal costs of misclassification, and (c) *known* sums of squares and cross-product matrices must be made.

If the first assumption of equality of within-groups variability is not met, other functions, such as quadratic discriminants, may still be applicable. Moreover, tests are available for checking on the equality of within-groups variability before applying discriminant analysis programs, such as BMD-04M.[9]

MULTIPLE DISCRIMINANT ANALYSIS

All of the preceding discussion regarding objectives and assumption structure applies to multiple discriminant analysis, as well. Accordingly, discussion of this section will be comparatively brief. What primarily distinguishes *multiple discriminant analysis* from the two-group case is that *more than one* discriminant function may be computed.

For example, if we have three groups, we can compute, in general, *two* nonredundant discriminant functions (as long as we also have at least two predictor variables). In general, with G groups and m predictors we can find up to the lesser of $G - 1$, or m, discriminant functions. Some intuitive flavor of why we need no more than $G - 1$ functions for G groups is gotten by recalling that we can code any G-state polytomy into $G - 1$ dummy variables. Each dummy variable qualifies for a discriminant function. Note also that for two groups we get one function, as already described in the preceding section.

Not all the discriminants may be statistically significant, however. Moreover, it turns out to be a characteristic of multiple discriminant analysis that the *first* function accounts for the *highest* proportion of the among- to within-groups variability, the second function, the next highest, and so on.

[9]A discussion of quadratic discriminants and tests of the equality of within-groups sums of squares and cross products can be found in M. G. Kendall, *A Course in Multivariate Analysis*, 2d ed. (New York: Hafner Publishing Co., 1965).

Accordingly, we may want to consider only the first few functions, particularly when the input data are rather noisy or unreliable to begin with.

Multiple discriminant analysis is almost invariably carried out by means of computer programs. One of the most flexible and comprehensive programs for multiple discriminant analysis is BMD-07M, a stepwise procedure that is also part of the biomedical series.[10]

The BMD-07M Stepwise Program

In Chapter 10 we described BMD-02R, a stepwise multiple regression program. The BMD-07M program is analogous to BMD-02R in that predictor variables are entered sequentially in terms of their differential ability to effect discrimination among groups. Indeed, the stepwise feature of BMD-07M is just like that of BMD-02R.

BMD-07M can handle up to 80 groups and up to 80 predictor variables. As in BMD-02R, the user can set various control values for the inclusion or retention of predictor variables. The program routinely prints out the group means and standard deviations of each predictor variable as well as the within-groups correlation matrix. In the stepwise phase of the program the following computations are made:

1. At step 1 in the program separate F ratios are computed for each predictor. That is, a series of univariate analyses of variance across the groups are performed involving each predictor separately (analogous to simple correlations in the BMD-02R case).

2. The predictor variable with the largest F ratio is entered first (assuming that it meets certain significance and tolerance levels for inclusion) and discrimination is effected with respect to this variable only.

3. A second predictor is then added on the basis of the largest *adjusted* (or "partial") F ratio, conditioned by the predictor variable already entered.

4. Each variable entered is then tested for retention on the basis of its association with other predictors in the equation.

5. The process continues until all variables that pass significance levels for inclusion and retention are entered.

6. At each stage in the stepwise procedure tests are made of intergroup separation (considered across all group centroids) and pairwise group separation for all distinct pairs.

7. At selected stages discriminant functions are computed for the predictors included at that point. Also, classification matrices, com-

[10]W. J. Dixon, ed., *Biomedical Computer Programs* (Berkeley, Calif.: University of California Press, 1973).

paring actual group membership to group membership predicted by the model, are computed.

8. At the conclusion of the stepwise procedure a summary of predictors entered or removed, associated F values, intergroup significance, and the "posterior" probability of each case arising from each group is presented.[11]

Applying the Program

The output of BMD-07M is so voluminous that only a summary of some of its results is shown here for illustrative purposes. The data for this application were obtained from the same study (women's hair shampoo) that was described in Chapter 8. However, in the present case, data on group membership consisted of:

- High likers of "body"   ($n = 28$)
- Medium likers of "body"   ($n = 28$)
- Low likers of "body"   ($n = 28$)

while the predictor variables consisted of each respondent's rating of the following statements (not covered in Chapter 8) on a six-point agree–disagree scale:

1. I take exceptional interest in my personal appearance.
2. Compared to my friends I use relatively little makeup.
3. I have a lot more trouble keeping my hair healthy than do most of my friends.
4. Private or store brands are usually just as good as nationally advertised brands.
5. My friends consider me to be very conservative in hair style and dress.
6. Hippies and other "counterculture" groups are a drain on society's progress.

This three-group discriminant analysis problem (with six predictors) was analyzed by BMD-07M.

Table 12-5 shows a partial summary of the program's output. A (rather loose) F value of 1.0 was chosen for predictor-variable inclusion and retention. Even at that, only four of the predictors—variables 6, 5, 3, and 4—entered (in that order). All variables that entered were retained.

[11]BMD-07M also has the capability of dealing with user-supplied prior probabilities. Moreover, its P-series counterpart will perform a cross-validation step that obtains a more accurate estimate of the posterior classification probabilities.

Table 12-5   Partial summary of BMD-07M stepwise discriminant analysis

Group Mean Ratings: Agree Completely (1) to Disagree Completely (6)

Variable	Low "Body" Likers	Medium "Body" Likers	High "Body" Likers	Total-Sample Mean
1	2.429	2.036	1.929	2.131
2	2.857	2.857	3.250	2.988
3	5.036	4.607	4.393	4.679
4	3.821	3.179	3.321	3.440
5	4.464	3.857	3.357	3.893
6	5.143	5.036	4.143	4.774

Summary Table of Order in Which Predictors Entered

STEP NUMBER	VARIABLE Entered	VARIABLE Removed	F VALUE TO ENTER OR REMOVE
1	6		5.109
2	5		1.610
3	3		1.408
4	4		1.011

Classification Tables

First Two Predictors to Enter

ACTUAL	PREDICTED Low	PREDICTED Medium	PREDICTED High	TOTAL
Low	15	7	6	28
Medium	13	8	7	28
High	6	7	15	28
Total	34	22	28	84

All Four Predictors

ACTUAL	PREDICTED Low	PREDICTED Medium	PREDICTED High	TOTAL
Low	15	8	5	28
Medium	12	9	7	28
High	4	9	15	28
Total	31	26	27	84

Judging from the size of the F values, the process could have been stopped after predictor variable 6 (the first to enter). However, for comparison purposes we show the classification tables for the analysis based on the first two predictors versus that based on the four variables that eventually entered the analysis. In the former case, the "hit" ratio is $(15 + 8 + 15)/84$, or 45%. In the latter case, the ratio is $(15 + 9 + 15)/84$, or 46%. Since a chance assignment would involve 33%, little discrimination is effected by the psychographic variables.

If we confine our attention to only the first two variables to enter (predictors 6 and 5), we note that high likers of "body" in a shampoo tend to be conservative in cultural outlook (i.e., against hippies) and conservative in hair style and dress.

Multiple discriminant analysis is considerably more detailed than might be surmised by this brief review. Interested readers should consult more extensive and advanced discussions of the subject.[12]

AUTOMATIC INTERACTION DETECTION

One of the most interesting problems in associative analysis is the phenomenon of interaction in which the response to changes in the level of one predictor variable depends on the level of some other predictor (or predictors). When interaction effects exist, the simple additive property of individual predictor-variable contributions to changes in the criterion no longer holds.

The distinction between interaction effects and intercorrelated predictors is shown in Figure 12-4. Using an illustration drawn from public opinion research, assume that respondents are asked to rate the quality of some local municipality's bus service. Data are also collected on the respondent's extent of past usage of the service and whether he or she is working or not.

Suppose we wish to see if respondents' ratings of Y, the quality of the service (higher values indicating higher quality), are related to X_1, past usage of the service. However, we also suspect that the relationship between Y and X_1 might be dependent on whether the respondent is working or not (which can be denoted by a dummy variable X_2).

In Panel I we note the "classic" case of correlation between X_1 and X_2 but no interaction. We observe that Y is positively associated with changes in X_1 and that the slopes of the regression lines do not depend on the values of X_2 (working versus nonworking). Rather, it is the *intercept* that differs between the two cases, in the sense that respondents who are working report higher quality of service on the average than those who are not working. The correlation between X_1 and X_2 is indicated by the fact that average past usage by working respondents exceeds that of nonworking respondents.

[12]For example, see R. A. Eisenbeis and R. B. Avery, *Discriminant Analysis and Classification Procedures* (Lexington, Mass.: D. C. Heath and Company, 1972), and Chapters 9 and 10 of W. W. Cooley and P. R. Lohnes, *Multivariate Data Analysis* (New York: John Wiley & Sons, Inc., 1971).

Figure 12-4 Illustrations of correlation and interaction (hypothetical data)

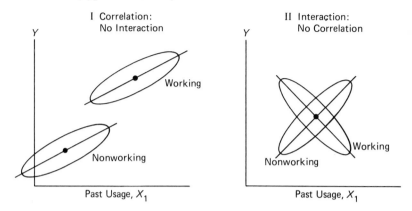

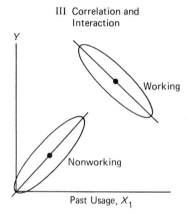

Panel II shows the case of interaction without correlation between X_1 and X_2. Here we see that across the *total sample* of working and nonworking respondents, Y does not depend on X_1 (i.e., the total-sample slope is horizontal). However, *within* the separate levels of X_2, Y increases with increases in X_1, given that the respondent is not working, while it decreases with increases in X_1, given that the respondent is working. The average past usage is the same for both working and nonworking respondents, showing no correlation between X_1 and X_2.

Panel III shows the combined case of correlation and interaction. Across the total sample Y is positively associated with X_1. However, within the separate levels of X_2 we see that Y increases with increases in X_1, given that the respondent is not working, but decreases with X_1, given that the respondent is working. The positive association between Y and X_1, at the total-sample level, results primarily from the fact that *average* past usage is considerably higher for working respondents than it is for nonworking respondents.

In the analysis of observational and survey data one often finds cases in which the predictors are interactive as well as correlated. Survey data is the type of data in which the analyst would ordinarily use multiple regression, which, as we know, is a type of additive model. If the researcher suspects interaction-type effects, it is a common procedure to add cross-product terms (of the type X_1X_2 or $X_1X_2X_3$) to the regression model. Unfortunately, cross-product terms express only one form of interaction (a multiplicative one) and, furthermore, the cross products will generally be highly correlated with the original predictors.

If only a few (multiplicative-type) interactions are believed to exist, the researcher could introduce cross-product terms for only those predictors. A major problem, however, is that in exploratory analyses of observational and survey data one does not ordinarily know *which* predictors are interactive (and how they are interactive). *Automatic interaction detection* (abbreviated AID) is a sequential search routine, developed by Sonquist and Morgan, in which one starts out with a criterion variable that is either interval-scaled or dichotomous.[13] While the predictor variables might orignally be: (1) nominal-, (2) ordinal-, or (3) interval-scaled, these predictors are *all* recoded into *nominal* variables in which:

1. Order across classes can be disregarded, or
2. Order across classes can be retained.

For example, if one of the original predictors is employment status (white-collar, blue-collar, unemployed) one may wish to treat this variable as an unordered polytomy. Some other variable such as age may be recoded into 18–20; 21–23; 24–26 years, etc. In this case one would probably wish to maintain order across classes. Each predictor variable can be designated by the researcher as unordered or ordered, independently of the rest.

Basic Concepts of AID

Now, given a criterion, say, average weekly consumption of beer for sample of individuals, the objective of AID is to perform a sequence of binary

---

[13] J. A. Sonquist, E. L. Baker, and J. N. Morgan, *Searching for Structure (Alias, AID-III)* (Ann Arbor, Mich.: Survey Research Center, University of Michigan, 1971). A related procedure designed to handle a polytomous criterion variable is described in R. Messenger and L. Mandell, "A Model Search Technique for Predictive Nominal Scale Multivariate Analysis," *Journal of the American Statistical Association*, 67 (December, 1972), 768–72. The original monograph on AID is J. A. Sonquist and J. N. Morgan, *The Detection of Interaction Effects*, Monograph No. 35 (Ann Arbor, Mich.: Survey Research Center, University of Michigan, 1964).

splits of the sample, choosing those splits (and predictor variables) that separate the sample into two subgroups that maximally account for criterion-variable variance at any given stage. For each candidate predictor variable, in turn, AID makes an exhaustive search of all allowable splits on that variable and chooses the split that maximizes between-groups variation associated with the two groups so split. It then chooses from all of these "best splits" (conditioned by predictor) the *specific* predictor variable and, hence, the split that leads to the maximum of these separate maxima.

To see this algebraically, assume that Y denotes the criterion variable. With no information about the predictor variables we would fall back on the mean of Y, that is, $\bar{Y}$, to estimate individual response. The "error" sum of squares would then be

$$\sum (Y_i - \bar{Y})^2 = \sum Y_i^2 - \frac{(\sum Y_i)^2}{n} = \sum Y_i^2 - n\bar{Y}^2$$

Now, however, assume that the total sample has been split into two groups of n_1 and n_2 persons with respective means, $\bar{Y}_1$ and $\bar{Y}_2$. If so, the error sum of squares is

$$(\sum Y_{i1}^2 - n_1\bar{Y}_1^2) + (\sum Y_{i2}^2 - n_2\bar{Y}_2^2) = \sum Y_i^2 - (n_1\bar{Y}_1^2 + n_2\bar{Y}_2^2)$$

The *reduction* in variation by splitting into two groups is simply

$$n_1\bar{Y}_1^2 + n_2\bar{Y}_2^2 - n\bar{Y}^2$$

This gain in error reduction assumes, of course, that the subgroup means are indeed different.

Basically, then, AID performs a series of one-way analysis of variance-type computations (similar in spirit to our discussion in Chapter 11). After splitting the initial sample on the basis of the "best" predictor, the process is repeated on each of the two subsamples, and so on. The main result of all of this is a tree structure that shows, at each stage:

1. The predictor variable leading to the best binary split and how that predictor *is* split
2. The number of persons assigned to each of the two subgroups
3. The criterion-variable mean on each of the two subgroups

While other summary statistics (e.g., error sums of squares) can also be shown, the above outputs represent the principal ones.

A few other key considerations, in the nature of restrictions, enter into the actual application of AID.

1. All partitionings of the sample may be subject to a requirement that the proportionate reduction in the criterion-variable sum of squares exceed some level (specified by the researcher). This is to guard against partitionings that do not appreciably reduce variation in the criterion variable.

2. To qualify for further splitting, a group must have a sum of squares greater than some level (specified by the researcher). This is to guard against splits that, pragmatically speaking, are not worth the effort, for example, where the group is already quite homogeneous.

3. In addition to the control parameters above, the researcher may place an upper limit on the total number of groups formed and/or the minimum number of persons (or objects) in each group.

A few caveats regarding the application of AID should be mentioned at this point. First, AID is generally designed for really large samples, on the order of 1,000 or more. Since many versions of AID will take as many as 30 to 35 predictors, the program has ample opportunity to capitalize on chance variation in the data. Moreover, no statistical inferential apparatus is associated with the approach. This suggests the value of cross-validating results on new data or, possibly, double cross-validating by applying AID to separate halves of the sample.

Second, AID, being a sequential search procedure, does *not* specify an explicit model in the way, for example, that ANOVA does. In this regard it is often useful to use AID as an initial "screening" device to find those predictors that appear to be most prominent in accounting for criterion variation. This can then be followed by the formulation of an *explicit* dummy-variable regression model that includes main effect and interaction terms of specific interest to the researcher. Sonquist,[14] in particular, recommends the *joint* use of AID and multiple classification analysis, the latter being a type of dummy-variable regression model with some useful features for exploratory data analysis.[15]

An Industry Example of AID

One of the nice characteristics of AID is its simplicity of output. The output takes the form of a tree diagram, in which one can follow the result

[14]J. A. Sonquist, *Multivariate Model Building: The Validation of a Search Strategy* (Ann Arbor, Mich.: Survey Research Center, University of Michigan, 1970).
[15]F. Andrews, J. N. Morgan, and J. A. Sonquist, *Multiple Classification Analysis* (Ann Arbor, Mich.: Survey Research Center, University of Michigan, 1967).

of each binary split as it takes place. This is illustrated in the brief case study that follows.

Rogers National Research is a Toledo-based consulting firm that specializes in marketing research for the automotive companies.[16] One of its annual studies involves a survey of various car troubles that new car buyers have experienced over the six months preceding the survey. Among other things, the respondents are asked to rate their car's overall quality of workmanship, and list the number and type of defects experienced during the past six months of ownership.

Of particular interest to Rogers' clients is the extent to which a respondent is "make-loyal." That is, when asked to consider his *next* car purchase, does he indicate that he plans to purchase another car of his current make (Chevrolet, Pontiac, Ford, Dodge, etc.) or some other make?

A large sample ($n = 4,364$) of respondents was available, involving their responses to 22 different questions regarding new-car workmanship, demographics, and so on. All respondents had recently purchased a compact car, either foreign or domestic. The criterion variable was whether the respondent indicated that he was make-loyal (coded 1) or not (coded 0) with respect to his next new car purchase.

AID was applied to this large data bank with the results shown in the tree diagram of Figure 12-5. At the top of the diagram we first note that the total-sample probability of being make-loyal is 0.27. That is, 1,178 out of the total of 4,364 respondents indicate that they are make-loyal. The first variable on which the total sample is split involves the respondent's rating of *overall quality* of workmanship of his present car. If rated good to excellent, the make-loyal probability in this subsample of 3,352 persons is 0.32; if rated fair to poor, the make-loyal probability for this subsample of 1,012 respondents is only 0.10. On the right-hand side of the tree, age is the next variable to enter, followed by number of defects, and then by a further split on quality of workmanship rating—this time between excellent versus good or very good. Finally, the name of the car manufacturer enters.

On the left-hand side of the tree diagram the only other predictor to enter involves the total number of reported defects. Notice, then, that this tree is *not* symmetrical and that different variables follow the initial split, based on quality of workmanship.

The upshot of all of this is that one can obtain a make-loyal probability as high as 0.68 if:

- The owner's current compact car is made by either General Motors or Ford
- Overall quality of workmanship is rated excellent

---

[16]The authors are indebted to Rogers National Research for permission to include this application of AID.

Figure 12-5   Automatic interaction detection—national car quality survey

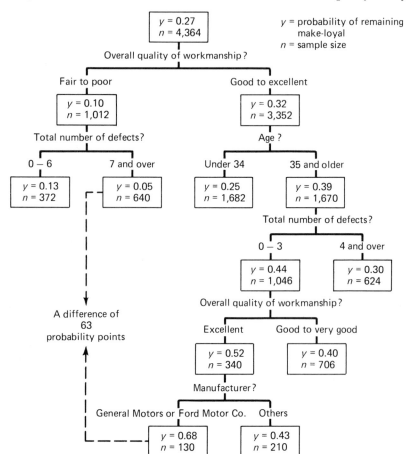

- 0–3 defects are reported
- The respondent is 35 years of age or older

On the other hand, one can find a make-loyal probability as low as 0.05 if:

- 7 or more defects are reported and
- Overall quality of workmanship is rated fair to poor.

In short, this type of information underscored the importance of certain types of quality control and led to a more detailed study of the kinds of defects that prompted the lowest incidence of make-loyal responses.

OTHER TECHNIQUES FOR CRITERION—PREDICTOR ASSOCIATION

Up to this point in the book, discussion of associative data analysis has emphasized the single criterion/multiple predictor techniques of:

- Multiple regression
- Analysis of variance and covariance
- Two-group discriminant analysis
- Automatic interaction detection

Only multiple discriminant analysis (briefly described earlier in the chapter) was of the multiple criterion/multiple predictor variety. We say "multiple criterion" because two dummy criterion variables were required to encode three groups and, in general, $G - 1$ dummies are required to encode G criterion groups.

There are two other techniques that are analogous to multiple discriminant analysis in that they are designed for *multiple* criteria as well as multiple predictors. Just as multiple discriminant analysis is a generalization of two-group discriminant analysis:

- Canonical correlation is a generalization of multiple correlation to two or more criterion variables.
- Multivariate analysis of variance and covariance is a generalization of analysis of variance and covariance to two or more criterion variables.

Canonical correlation and multivariate analysis of variance and covariance are considerably more complex than the techniques discussed so far. Moreover, their application to marketing research has been much less than the methods already discussed. For these reasons descriptions of them are brief and nontechnical.

Basic Concepts of Canonical Correlation

To illustrate the technique of *canonical correlation*, let us return to the radial tire study, described in our discussion in Chapter 10 of stepwise multiple regression. As will be recalled, the criterion variable was the respondent's postexposure interest rating—after watching a set of TV commercials—of the firm's new brand of steel-belted radial tires. The main predictor variables were:

X_1:   general interest in the product class of steel-belted radials;

X_2:   whether the firm's old brand was chosen as the respondent's last purchase of replacement tires; and

X_3:   preexposure (before seeing the commercials) interest in the firm's new brand of steel-belted radials.

Now, however, let us assume that *two* criterion variables are involved:

Y_1:   believability in the claims made in the firm's new TV commercial;

Y_2:   postexposure interest in the firm's new brand (as before).

What we would like to find out is how highly correlated the *battery* of two criterion variables is with the *battery* of three predictors. Moreover, we would like to find a linear composite of the Y-variable set and a (different) linear composite of the X-variable set that will produce a maximal correlation.

This is what canonical correlation is all about. In terms of the classification in Chapter 9, canonical correlation deals with: (1) both description and statistical inference of (2) a data matrix partitioned into at least two criteria and at least two predictors where (3) all variables are interval-scaled and (4) the relationships are assumed to be linear.

The mathematics of canonical correlation are sufficiently complex that computer programs are a necessity. The one illustrated here is the BMD-P6M canonical correlation program.[17] This program can handle up to a total of 90 variables and a virtually unlimited number of cases. In addition to finding the canonical correlations and linear composites it provides:

- Summary measures of means, standard deviations, etc.
- Input data correlations
- Tests of significance of the canonical correlations
- Canonical scores (analogous to discriminant function scores)
- Correlations of original variables with the linear composites (often called structure correlations)
- Bivariate plots for original variables versus their linear composites.

Only the highlights of the program are shown here.

Applying the BMD-P6M Program

Table 12-6 shows the results of applying BMD-P6M to the radial tire problem. In general with p criteria and q predictors one can obtain more than

---

[17]W. J. Dixon, ed., *BMDP: Biomedical Computer Programs* (Berkeley, Calif.: University of California Press, 1975).

a single pair of linear composites—up to a maximum of the smaller of p and q. Thus, in our case we could obtain two pairs of linear composites, uncorrelated across pairs, with the first pair exhibiting maximum correlation.[18] However, as it turned out, only the first pair of linear composites was statistically significant at the 0.05 alpha level; hence, only this pair of weights is shown.

Table 12-6 shows that the canonical correlation between the two batteries is 0.582. As is the case with multiple correlations, this measure varies between 0 (no correlation) and 1 (perfect correlation). Since *mutual* association between the pair of batteries is involved, we can say that the pair of linear composites account for $(0.582)^2$ or 34% of the shared variation between the two batteries.

The canonical weights for the criterion set show that Y_2 (postexposure interest) is the dominant variable in the criterion set; its canonical weight is 1.069. The dominant variable in the predictor set is X_3; its weight is 0.817.

Table 12-6   Results of BMD-P6M canonical correlation

	Canonical Weights	Structure Correlations
Criterion set		
Y_1	−0.110	0.594
Y_2	1.069	0.997
Predictor set		
X_1	0.346	0.539
X_2	0.141	0.382
X_3	0.817	0.930
Canonical correlation	0.582	

INPUT CORRELATIONS FOR CANONICAL ANALYSIS

	Y_1	Y_2	X_1	X_2	X_3
Y_1	1.000				
Y_2	0.659	1.000			
X_1	0.202	0.315	1.000		
X_2	0.097	0.218	0.086	1.000	
X_3	0.321	0.539	0.226	0.258	1.000

[18] In general, the canonical correlation of successive pairs decreases; that is, the first pair displays the highest correlation, the second pair the next highest, and so on. All composites are mutually uncorrelated *across* pairs.

Since all variables are standardized to zero mean and unit standard deviation *before* the analysis, the weights are already in standardized form.

What Table 12-6 really says is that if we formed a <u>linear composite of</u> the criterion variables using the canonical weights:

$$T_c = -0.110Y_{s1} + 1.069Y_{s2}$$

and another <u>linear composite of the predictors,</u> using the canonical weights:

$$T_p = 0.346X_{s1} + 0.141X_{s2} + 0.817X_{s3}$$

and took these two columns of numbers (the canonical scores) and correlated them, the result would be a *simple* correlation of 0.582 (the canonical correlation).

Also shown in Table 12-6 are the <u>structure correlations—the simple correlation of each original variable with the canonical scores of its own battery's linear composite.</u> Again we note that Y_2 is the most important variable (structure correlation of 0.997) in the criterion set and X_3 the most important variable (structure correlation of 0.930) in the predictor set. Indeed, as noted in the input correlation matrix, the *simple* correlation between Y_2 and X_3 is 0.539, almost as high as the correlation between full batteries.

As indicated earlier, canonical correlation has not received the kind of attention that the techniques covered earlier have. Part of this lack of application is based on its difficulty of interpretation, and part concerns its relative newness to marketing research. Accordingly, we refer the reader to other sources for further discussion of the procedure.[19]

Basic Concepts of Multivariate Analysis of Variance and Covariance

Like canonical correlation, multivariate analysis of variance and covariance has received little attention so far by marketing researchers. Our description of univariate analysis of variance (ANOVA) and covariance (ANCOVA) in Chapter 11 can provide the base for the present discussion. In recent years, statisticians have generalized these procedures to cases in which more than a single criterion variable is involved. For example, if a researcher were to set up a package-design experiment in which package shape, background color, and printing motif were the controllable variables,

---

[19]For more detailed discussion, see M. M. Tatsuoka, *Multivariate Analysis: Techniques for Educational and Psychological Research* (New York: John Wiley & Sons, Inc., 1971).

he might solicit subjects' responses on a variety of rating scales: (1) personal preferences, (2) judgments of the esthetic beauty of each package, (3) how well each package seemed to describe the product contents, and so on. If so, the subject's responses would consist of *more than a single criterion variable*. Moreover, in all likelihood the set of criterion (response) variables would, themselves, be correlated.

Multivariate analysis of variance and covariance is analogous to its univariate counterpart. Once again we are testing for differences between two or more group means—in this case centroids, since more than a single criterion is involved. Analogous to the assumption of common variance in the ANOVA model, we assume in multivariate analysis of variance and covariance that the within-groups sums of squares and cross products of deviations from their respective means are equal across the groups. Separate tests are available to see if this assumption of common within-groups variability is justified.[20]

Analogous to univariate ANOVA, we now assume that the set of criterion (response) variables is *multinormally* distributed. In ANOVA we recall than an *F* ratio was computed for testing the equality of treatment means. This *F* ratio involved a ratio of the among-groups mean square to the within-groups mean square. In the multivariate variety a similar type of ratio is involved; in this case, however, it consists of a generalization of the univariate *F* ratio to a function of the within-groups and total-groups sums of squares and cross products.

While the procedures for multivariate analysis of variance and covariance are considerably more complicated than their univariate counterparts, the motivation is *precisely the same:* to test for equality of group means (actually centroids in the multivariate case) where the groups have been formed on some prior basis—for example, as "treatment" groups in the format of an experimental design.

One computer program of rather wide applicability to multivariate analysis of variance and covariance is BMD-12V, also part of the biomedical series.[21] This program can perform *both* univariate and multivariate analyses of variance and covariance. Up to ten treatment variables can be handled; cell replications are easily accommodated as are full factorial and other types of designs, as long as an equal number of observations per cell are provided. More than a single covariate may be incorporated if desired.

Multivariate analyses of variance and covariance programs produce a rather voluminous output that includes a number of special-purpose measures whose description would exceed the scope of this text. Therefore, we

---

[20]See G. E. P. Box, "A General Distribution Theory for a Class of Likelihood Criteria," *Biometrika*, 36 (1949), 317–46.

[21]W. J. Dixon, ed., *Biomedical Computer Programs* (Berkeley, Calif.: University of California Press, 1973).

do not show a numerical illustration of this technique. The more technically trained reader is referred to books by Harris[22] and Green[23] on multivariate analysis per se.

SUMMARY

Chapters 10 and 11, as well as the current chapter, have all been concerned with various techniques for analyzing *between-set dependence*: regression, univariate analysis of variance and covariance, AID, two-group and multiple discriminant analysis, canonical analysis, and multivariate analysis of variance and covariance. At this point, it might appear that an almost bewildering array of techniques has been paraded before the reader.

Even at that, however, we have not discussed such extensions as canonical correlation of three or more sets of variables, tests for the equality of sums of squares and cross-products matrices, and so on. In addition, other related procedures, such as moderated regression, multiple-partial correlation, discriminant analysis with covariate adjustment, factorial discriminant analysis, to name a few, have been omitted from discussion.

What we have tried to do is to discuss the principal assumption structure of each technique, appropriate computer programs for applying it, and sufficient numerical applications to give the reader a feel for the kinds of output generated by each program.

Our coverage of so vast and complex a set of methods is limited in depth as well as breadth. The fact remains, however, that marketing researchers of the future will have to seek grounding in multivariate methodology, if current research trends are any indication. This grounding will probably embrace three facets: (1) theoretical understanding of the techniques; (2) knowledge of the details of appropriate computer algorithms for implementing the techniques; and (3) a grasp of the characteristics of substantive problems in marketing that are relevant for each of the methods.

Finally, we should reiterate the fact that all the preceding techniques display a penchant for capitalizing on chance variation in the data. One can hardly overemphasize the need to employ cross-validation procedures as well as the advisability of selecting criterion and predictor variables on the basis of conceptual relevance. Computer algorithms make it so easy to include as many variables as the researcher desires that one often develops a reluctance to think about *why* certain variables are included. Such temptations to "let the computer do the selection" are hard to resist but provide no substitute for hard thinking about the problem.

[22]See R. J. Harris, *A Primer of Multivariate Statistics* (New York: Academic Press, Inc., 1975), for further details on this test.

[23]See P. E. Green, *Analyzing Multivariate Data* (Hinsdale, Ill.: Dryden Press, 1978).

ASSIGNMENT MATERIAL

1. Assume that the Jain Pool Co., has assembled income and lot-size data on a group of pool and nonpool owners living in southeast Pennsylvania. In addition, data are available for each group on attitudes toward sun bathing, scaled from 0—"detest sun bathing," to 10—"extremely fond of sun bathing." The data are summarized below.

   a. Compute a two-group linear discriminant function using annual income, lot size, and attitude toward sun bathing as predictor variables.

Pool Owner	Annual Income (thousands of dollars)	Lot Size (thousands of square feet)	Attitudinal Measure
1	9.3	30.2	8
2	10.2	40.1	10
3	9.7	35.3	6
4	11.5	45.1	4
5	12.0	38.0	5
6	14.2	50.1	9
7	18.6	60.2	10
8	28.4	100.4	3
9	13.2	25.1	2
10	10.8	40.7	7
11	22.7	68.4	9
12	12.3	60.3	8

Nonpool Owner	Annual Income (thousands of dollars)	Lot Size (thousands of square feet)	Attitudinal Measure
1	8.2	30.2	2
2	7.8	40.2	0
3	11.4	44.8	1
4	16.3	50.6	4
5	12.4	42.5	8
6	11.5	60.3	0
7	6.8	39.7	6
8	10.4	35.4	4
9	14.2	42.6	3
10	11.6	38.4	2
11	8.4	30.2	4
12	9.1	25.7	5

   b. How might the pool builder use the results of the function computed in part (a)?

   c. Using the function computed in part (a), assign each of the 24 respondents to the class "pool owner" or "nonpool owner." Compare your answer to the known assignment. What is the percentage of correct classifications?

   d. The marketing researcher has received the following information about a new respondent not included in the original sample.

     (1) Annual income: $12,000.

     (2) Lot size: 42,000 square feet.

     (3) Attitude toward sun bathing: "8."

   Using the discriminant function, to which class would the respondent be assigned?

2. The credit firm of Maheshwari and Rao, Inc., has expressed interest in the possible use of discriminant analysis in the preliminary screening of credit applications. From past records the company has assembled information on three classes of married credit grantees: (a) poor risks, (b) equivocal risks, and (c) good risks. Additional information about a sample of credit grantees has also been obtained:

   a. Compute linear discriminant functions for a three-way analysis.

   b. Which variables appear to discriminate best among the three groups?

   c. Criticize the manner in which data were obtained for the three-way discriminant analysis.

   d. How might Bayesian procedures be used in the credit-screening problem?

Poor Risk	Annual Income (thousands of dollars)	Number of Credit Cards	Age	Number of Children
1	9.2	2	27	3
2	10.7	3	24	0
3	8.9	1	32	2
4	11.2	1	29	4
5	9.9	2	31	3
6	10.7	4	29	1
7	8.6	3	28	1
8	9.1	0	31	5
9	10.3	5	26	2
10	10.5	4	30	3

Equivocal Risk	Annual Income (thousands of dollars)	Number of Credit Cards	Age	Number of Children
1	14.4	4	34	4
2	14.7	7	33	2
3	13.6	3	41	1
4	10.3	1	37	1
5	14.9	6	39	0
6	15.8	5	37	3
7	16.0	4	36	5
8	11.2	2	35	3
9	12.6	8	36	2
10	14.7	3	29	4

Good Risk	Annual Income (thousands of dollars)	Number of Credit Cards	Age	Number of Children
1	18.6	7	42	3
2	17.4	6	47	5
3	22.6	4	41	1
4	24.3	5	39	0
5	19.4	1	43	2
6	14.2	12	46	3
7	12.7	8	42	4
8	21.6	7	48	2
9	26.4	5	37	3
10	19.4	9	51	1

3. Describe how a researcher might use automatic interaction detection to single out the best prospects for a firm specializing in selling classical records by mail.

   a. What criterion variable would you use?

   b. What predictor variables appear to be good candidates?

   c. How could the AID results be used as a preliminary approach to either multiple regression or two-group discriminant analysis?

4. Search the marketing research literature for an application of (1) canonical correlation and (2) multivariate analysis of variance and covariance.

   a. Why did the author use these techniques, as opposed to either multiple regression or univariate analysis of variance and covariance?

   b. Describe other ways that the problem could have been handled.

5. How could canonical correlation be used to analyze some of the shampoo data of Chapter 8? What criterion and predictor variables would you select?

Factor Analysis and Clustering Methods

13

INTRODUCTION

In this chapter we focus on the case in which the data matrix has *not* been partitioned in advance into subsets of criterion and predictor variables. Rather, the analyst is interested in the whole set of interdependent relationships. Interest can center on the variables in the sense that the analyst may wish to summarize them (columns of the data matrix) in terms of a smaller set of linear composites that preserve most of the information in the original set. Factor analysis represents a class of techniques for achieving this objective.

On the other hand, the researcher may wish to focus his interest on the objects themselves. That is, he may wish to partition the *rows* of the data matrix—where each row denotes an object—into homogeneous subsets of objects. In so doing he is allowing the data themselves to suggest groups of objects. Cluster analysis is an appropriate set of techniques for this objective.

We first discuss factor analysis at an intuitive level using numerical examples. The discussion leads to the portrayal of points (objects or persons) in variables space and rotations of that space that satisfy certain criteria. This viewpoint underlies subsequent discussion of *principal components* as a major factor-analytic technique for summarizing multivariate data.

Attention then turns to a discussion of special topics in factor analysis. We comment on such subjects as the rotation of principal components axes, other methods of factor analysis, the communality estimation problem, and statistical inference in factor analysis.

Clustering methods are introduced next. The fundamentals of cluster analysis are described in terms of questions concerning choice of proximity or similarity measure, clustering technique, and ways to define clusters.

Characteristics of various computer programs that have been proposed for grouping profiles are next described. This is followed by brief discussions of statistics for defining clusters and problems associated with statistical inference in this area. The chapter concludes with some empirical examples of cluster analysis.

BASIC CONCEPTS OF FACTOR ANALYSIS

Factor analysis is a generic name given to a class of techniques whose purpose often consists of data reduction and summarization. Factor analysis does *not* entail partitioning the data matrix into criterion and predictor subsets; rather, interest is centered on relationships involving the *whole* set of variables. In factor analysis:

1. The analyst is interested in examining the "strength" of the overall association among variables in the sense that he would like to account for this association in terms of a smaller set of linear composites of the original variables that preserve most of the information in the full data set. Often his interest will stress description of the data rather than statistical inference.
2. No attempt is made to divide the variables into criterion versus predictor sets.
3. The models are primarily based on linear relationships.
4. The models typically assume that the data are interval-scaled, although we shall briefly discuss the handling of nominal- and ordinal-scaled data as well.

The major *substantive* purpose of factor analysis is the search and (sometimes) test of constructs or "dimensions" assumed to underlie manifest variables. For example, a marketing researcher may collect a variety of consumer data on brand selection, store patronage, personality, and demographic variables. His main interest, however, might lie in the search for certain constructs, such as *private-brand proneness*. Proneness to purchase private brands may not represent an observable variable, but, rather, is to be *inferred* from (correlated) measures involving such observables as: (1) the proportion of total purchases devoted to private-label brands, (2) attitude test scores on "thriftiness," (3) family size, (4) average amount of time per week devoted to shopping, (5) store-switching behavior, and so on.

If studies should indicate that the observable variables are highly intercorrelated over repeated measurement occasions, we might attempt to develop a construct called private-brand proneness. This would entail the establishment of additional observable variables, subsequent testing, and so on. Much of the activity of the empirically oriented behavioral scientist is spent on just such pursuits in the domain of personality and cognitive theory. Factor analysis provides a means for the isolation of such constructs in addition to its "workhorse" role in data reduction.

An Industry Application

To help motivate later discussion, let us consider a recent industry application in which factor analysis was used to help a firm's marketing researchers determine the basic dimensions of their company's image. While previous research had accumulated a lot of information on customers' perceptions of the firm, the researchers wished to learn if noncustomers employed similar frames of reference in evaluating the firm. That is, even though the firm might be rated below other firms along some of the image dimensions, were the dimensions themselves pretty much the same for the noncustomers?

The company in question is a large firm in the Northeast that specializes in selling auto insurance policies by mail. Its growth had been rapid over the preceding decade; however, some recent tapering off in the rate of new-customer acquisition served to renew interest in ways to attract additional policyholders. Accordingly, a survey was designed in which a sample of 380 noncustomers (who nonetheless claimed some familiarity with the firm) were interviewed. Among other things, each respondent was asked to evaluate the company on the 12 image-type statements appearing in Table 13-1. (These same statements had been employed in previous studies with the firm's customers.)

A glance at Table 13-1 suggests intuitively that some statements may be more or less tapping the same general constructs. For example, we would not be surprised if statements 1, 8, and 9 led to similar responses, since all three statements deal with whether older people are looked after in terms of their special needs. By the same token, statements 2, 4, 6, 11, and 12 all suggest quite positive things about a firm's general attitudes toward the public, particularly a firm's humanistic qualities. Conversely, statements 3, 5, 7, and 10 are rather pejorative about a firm's interaction with its public.

Therefore, it would not be unusual to find that respondent answers to statements 1, 8, and 9 were highly correlated; similarly, we might expect relatively high correlations of responses *within* each of the other two sets as well. However, would we also find that the *across-set* correlations are low? Are the conjectured image dimensions:

- Relevance of policies for older people
- Humanistic and positive approach to its public
- Noncaring and negative approach to its public

Table 13-1   Statements used in image study of noncustomers

	Describes It Completely 1	2	3	4	5	Does Not Describe It At All 6
1. Will not cancel policy because of age or minor health problems.	1	2	3	4	5	6
2. Tries to handle claims equitably.	1	2	3	4	5	6
3. Difficult to do business with.	1	2	3	4	5	6
4. Provides excellent recommendations about what coverages should be purchased for individual needs.	1	2	3	4	5	6
5. Does not pay enough attention to its policyholders' problems.	1	2	3	4	5	6
6. Explains policies clearly and fully.	1	2	3	4	5	6
7. Tends to raise premiums without proper justification.	1	2	3	4	5	6
8. Its policies are better than others for older people.	1	2	3	4	5	6
9. Its coverage is generally renewable for life.	1	2	3	4	5	6
10. Takes a long time to settle claims.	1	2	3	4	5	6
11. Quick, reliable service— easily accessible.	1	2	3	4	5	6
12. A "good citizen" in the community.	1	2	3	4	5	6

more or less independent or are the second two "dimensions" really opposite ends of a single "desirable–undesirable" dimension?

Rather than trusting strictly to intuition, factor analysis systematically explores *which* variables exhibit high intraset correlations and low interset correlations, *how many* such sets there are (each set defining a dimension), and whether the dimensions can be considered as *uncorrelated* themselves.

Factor analysis has value only when correlations among subsets of the variables really exist. The higher these intraset correlations are, the better defined are the resulting factor dimensions. Moreover, as we shall see, each original variable will receive a weight on each factor dimension that describes how much that variable contributes toward defining the dimension.

In the next section we show (for a much simpler data set) how one technique for doing factor analysis works. Insofar as the present example is concerned, it turned out that only three image dimensions were needed to account for over 80% of the variation in the original data.

As anticipated, statements 1, 8, and 9 defined the first dimension. However, only statements 10 and 11 defined (opposite ends of) the third dimension. The remaining statements 2, 4, 6, and 12 versus 3, 5, and 7 defined opposite ends of the second (good–bad) dimension. Apparently, the speed with which the company handles its customer business is viewed differently from other evaluative aspects of its image.

The study also showed that the three image dimensions were common for customers *and* noncustomers, although the firm's *scores* on the variables defining the dimensions were generally better for customers. The most interesting result, however, was that the firm's scores on the first dimension (relevance of its policies for older people) were not appreciably different between customers and noncustomers; that is, the firm scored well with *both* groups.

This result prompted the company to design a special promotion to older insurance holders who were customers of *other* firms. The promotion outlined several new policies that were specially designed for senior citizens. The campaign was highly successful in attracting customers to the new policies and, in some cases, even switching policy holders completely away from their current companies.

Let us now turn to a simpler illustration that, nevertheless, covers the main concepts of factor analysis. This example deals with the performance characteristics of computer models. As such, all data are "hard," objective data on various aspects of computers' capabilities.

A Numerical Example

To illustrate the basic ideas of factor analysis it is much easier to work with a smaller data set. Table 13-2 shows a set of data involving only 15 rows and 6 columns (in contrast to the 380 rows and 12 columns that would be required to portray the image data based on Table 13-1).

In this case the units of association are all digital computer models. Each model was originally measured on six different performance characteristics:

1. Execution time for addition, in microseconds;
2. Execution time for multiplication, in microseconds;
3. Minimum number of words that can be put in storage;
4. Maximum number of words that can be put in storage;
5. Maximum total storage; and
6. Cycle time in microseconds.

Table 13-2 **Standardized data matrix used in factor analyses**

COMPUTER NUMBER	DESCRIPTION	CHARACTERISTIC NUMBER					
		1	*2*	*3*	*4*	*5*	*6*
1	Philco 2000/210	−0.28	−0.36	−0.49	−0.52	−0.48	−0.27
2	Recomp II	3.51	3.61	−0.55	−0.60	−0.87	3.74
3	Honeywell 800	−0.39	−0.34	−0.55	−0.53	−0.59	−0.27
4	GE 225	−0.06	−0.28	−0.55	−0.57	−0.83	−0.26
5	RPC 301/354, 355	0.38	−0.27	−0.46	−0.50	−0.88	−0.27
6	Burroughs B5500	−0.43	−0.38	−0.55	−0.52	−0.48	−0.27
7	IBM 7040	−0.26	0.37	−0.55	−0.52	−0.59	−0.27
8	Univac 1004-1	0.70	0.68	−0.60	−0.61	−0.92	−0.27
9	CDC 3400	−0.47	−0.39	−0.37	−0.52	−0.48	−0.27
10	RCA 3301/3303	−0.28	−0.23	−0.02	−0.14	−0.77	−0.27
11	GE 635	−0.49	−0.39	−0.13	0.16	1.71	−0.27
12	IBM 360/65	−0.50	−0.39	1.32	2.47	1.08	−0.27
13	Univac 1108	−0.51	−0.39	0.36	0.16	1.70	−0.27
14	IBM 360/75	−0.51	−0.39	3.26	2.47	1.08	−0.27
15	CDC 6800	−0.52	−0.12	−0.13	−0.23	1.33	−0.27

However, in Table 13-2 each of the six variables has been expressed as a *standardized* variate with zero mean and unit standard deviation. Intuitively, we would think that performance measures 1, 2, and 6 are indicants of *speed*. We would not be surprised if they exhibited high intercorrelation. Measures 3, 4, and 5 all seem to relate to computer *size or capacity* and may, in turn, be intercorrelated. However, this is all conjecture. Moreover, we do not know if speed and size can be considered as independent dimensions.

What *does* seem evident at the outset is the desirability of working with *standardized* data so that any differences in original measurement units—which are often arbitrarily chosen anyway—will not influence the analysis.

To simplify the problem even further, let us initially consider only the *first three columns* of the data matrix in Table 13-2. What we wish to do now is define some terms and then go on to factor-analyze the 15 × 3 data matrix obtained from the first three columns of the table.

Factor Scores

A *factor* of this 15 × 3 data matrix is simply a *linear combination* (or *linear composite*) *of the original scores*. For example, assume that we were to weight variable 1 by 0.5 and variables 2 and 3 by 0.1 each. Then a factor, F_1, could be written

$$F_1 = 0.5X_1 + 0.1X_2 + 0.1X_3$$

Each object has a *factor score*, where the weights are common for each object. For example, the factor score of the first computer is

$$F_{11} = 0.5(-0.28) + 0.1(-0.36) + 0.1(-0.49) = -0.225$$

In turn we could compute scores (using the same weights as above) for the other 14 computer models, giving us a new column of numbers, the factor scores. In general these factor scores will be different, because the original scores are different across computer models.

But there is nothing magical about the particular weights chosen above. Any set of weights, the same or different over each column, plus or minus, might suffice. As a matter of fact, it is the purpose of various factor-analytic procedures to select these weights according to certain criteria. *The various methods of factor analysis are differentiated in terms of the bases upon which the weights are selected.*

How do we choose the weights for the first linear combination? As will soon be shown, we choose them so that the first column of factor scores has *maximum variance*. Then, subject to the second set of factor scores being *uncorrelated* with the first, we choose a second set of weights so that the resulting second column of factor scores has maximum variance. This same principle will be invoked as we find additional linear combinations. In the present example, we shall be able to find three sets of factor scores; in general, with empirical data, we can find as many sets of (nonredundant) factor scores as there are columns to begin with (assuming that we have more objects than variables).

Factor Loadings

Suppose that we have gone ahead and found three factors (three sets of weights) and their associated factor scores. Assume that the linear combinations shown at the top of Table 13-3 were the ones actually used and that these, in turn, resulted in the three columns of (unstandardized) factor scores shown in the middle of the same table. We could then *correlate* each column of factor scores, in turn, with each of the three original variables in the data matrix, leading to the results shown in Table 13-4. A *factor loading* is defined simply as the correlation (across objects) of a set of factor scores with an original variable.

Let us examine this point more closely. The first set of weights in Table 13-3 are -0.68008, -0.67075, and 0.29596. (We discuss a bit later how these *particular* weights were obtained.) When these are applied to the three original variables, we obtain the first column of (unstandardized) factor scores shown in Table 13-3. For example, the first score of the first column is

$$0.28687 = -0.68008(-0.28) - 0.67075(-0.36) + 0.29596(-0.49)$$

Table 13-3 Three sets of weights (factors) and resulting factor scores

Variable	Factor 1 Weights	Factor 2 Weights	Factor 3 Weights
1	−0.68008	0.17393	0.71223
2	−0.67075	0.24455	−0.70019
3	0.29596	0.95391	0.04966

UNSTANDARDIZED FACTOR SCORES

COMPUTER	Factor 1	Factor 2	Factor 3
1	0.28687	−0.60415	0.02831
2	−4.97125	0.96866	−0.05505
3	0.33051	−0.67563	−0.06702
4	−0.01577	−0.58269	0.21147
5	−0.21347	−0.43873	0.43685
6	0.38454	−0.69237	−0.06750
7	0.26222	−0.66036	0.04657
8	−1.10974	−0.28430	−0.00736
9	0.47172	−0.53007	−0.08005
10	0.33877	−0.12402	−0.03938
11	0.55636	−0.30461	−0.08238
12	0.99230	1.07682	−0.01749
13	0.71498	0.15933	−0.07229
14	1.57326	2.92567	0.07174
15	0.39565	−0.24380	−0.29279

COMPUTER	STANDARDIZED FACTOR SCORES		
1	0.19900	−0.63728	0.18226
2	−3.44843	1.02177	−0.35447
3	0.22926	−0.71267	−0.43154
4	−0.01094	−0.61464	1.36161
5	−0.14808	−0.46279	2.81279
6	0.26675	−0.73033	−0.43464
7	0.18190	−0.69656	0.29988
8	−0.76980	−0.29989	−0.04740
9	0.32722	−0.55913	−0.51544
10	0.23500	−0.13082	−0.25353
11	0.38593	−0.32131	−0.53041
12	0.68833	1.13586	−0.11260
13	0.49596	0.16807	−0.46544
14	1.09133	3.08609	0.46190
15	0.27446	−0.25716	−1.88523

**Table 13-4   Correlations of factor scores (Table 13-3)
with first three performance variables of Table 13-2**

Performance Variable	Factor 1	Factor 2	Factor 3	Sum of Squared Correlations
1	−0.98009	0.16491	0.11057	1.000
2	−0.96665	0.23187	−0.10870	1.000
3	0.42652	0.90445	0.00771	1.000
Sum of squared correlations*	2.07692	0.89898	0.02410	3.000
Cumulative proportion of total variation in performance variables	0.69230	0.99196	1.00000	

*This row also denotes the variance of the factor scores.

Next, when we correlate this column, in turn, with each of the first three columns in Table 13-2, we obtain the first three rows of the first column shown in Table 13-4. We can then do the same thing with the other two sets of unstandardized factor scores shown in Table 13-3. Then we turn to Table 13-4 and note that performance variables 1 and 2 correlate highly (negatively) with factor 1, while variable 3 correlates highly with factor 2. None of the performance variables correlates very highly with factor 3.

These loadings (factor-variable correlations) in Table 13-4 are of interest in themselves. For example, variables 1 and 2 (execution time for addition and multiplication, respectively) are both indicants of "slowness." Since they both correlate highly (*negatively*) with the first factor, this suggests that the first factor is composed mainly of "speed." On the other hand, the fact that variable 3 (minimum number of words that can be put in storage) correlates highly with factor 2 suggests that the second factor is mostly a "capacity" dimension. Finally, the third factor appears to be mostly composed of error, since none of the original variables correlates highly with it.

However, things are not all this simple, particularly since variable 3 *is* correlated (0.296) with factor 1 and variables 1 and 2 *are* correlated (0.174 and 0.245) with factor 2. (We consider this point later in our discussion of rotating factor loadings to a "cleaner" structure.) Still, if we tried to account for the variance of the scores on factor 1 (scores appear in the first column in the middle portion of Table 13-3), which is 2.07692, we note from Table 13-4 that this also equals the sum of the squared correlations of each original variable, in turn, with factor 1. Thus, the contribution of each original variable to the variance of the scores on each factor is given by the *square of that variable's correlation (loading) with the factor*. In this way we can measure how important each variable is in defining each factor.

It is an interesting fact of the procedure that we can also turn the coin over and show how important each factor is in accounting for variance in each original variable. First, having found the three factors, can we use their scores to predict values on each of the original performance variables?

Recalling our discussion in Chapter 10 of beta weights in multiple regression, if *all* variables are in standardized form of zero mean and unit standard deviation *and* the predictor variables are uncorrelated, the least-squares estimate for say, object *i*, on variable 1 would be

$$Z_{1i} = r_{1F_1}F_{1i} + r_{1F_2}F_{2i} + r_{1F_3}F_{3i}$$

where *r* is a *simple correlation* between the variable and each factor in turn.

The first set of factor scores in Table 13-3 does *not* have unit standard deviation. The second set of scores *has* been standardized to unit standard deviation by dividing each of the entries of each column of the original set of factor scores by the square root of the column's variance (the mean of each column is already zero). The *variances*, incidentally, are 2.07692, 0.89898, and 0.02410, respectively, for factors 1, 2, and 3, as shown in Table 13-4. These are *also* the sum of the squared correlations between each factor and the performance variables.

Now, if we are interested in estimating the first computer model's original value (-0.28) on performance variable 1, our prediction formula is

$$Z_{11} = -0.98009(0.19900) + 0.16491(0.63728) + 0.11057(0.18226)$$
$$= -0.28$$

Moreover, if we examine Table 13-4 again, we can square each correlation of the first *row*:

$$(-0.98009)^2 = 0.96$$
$$(0.16491)^2 = 0.03$$
$$(0.11057)^2 = \underline{0.01}$$
$$1.00$$

and find the relative importance of each factor to the variation in each original variable. For example, in the case of variable 1 (execution time for addition) the first factor accounts for 96% of its variance.

In effect, then, we can account for factors in terms of variables or variables in terms of factors. At this point it might seem strange to find the factors first and, having done so, to use the factors to estimate the performance variables that were employed to find the factors in the first place. As it turns out, however, two benefits are derived from such a representation:

1. The factors can be chosen so that their factor scores, unlike the original variables' scores, are *uncorrelated.*

2. The factors can be chosen sequentially, so that the first one accounts for most of the variability in the original data set, the second accounts for most of the residual variability, and so on.

Recapitulation

At this point we have gone through a whole series of computational steps, which in their entirety may appear confusing. It would seem useful to recapitulate the procedure.

1. We first define a *factor* as a linear combination of the original variables. The weights used for the three factors "extracted" here are shown in the top portion of Table 13-3.

2. These weights are applied to the original data variables, yielding a set of three (unstandardized) factor scores for each object. These are shown in the middle portion of Table 13-3.

3. The factor scores are standardized to unit standard deviation by dividing each entry in each column by the square root of the column's variance. The variance of each column is shown in Table 13-4, while the standardized factor scores are shown in the bottom portion of Table 13-3.

4. Each column of factor scores (unstandardized or standardized—it makes no difference in this step) is then correlated with each of the columns of original variables, yielding the correlation matrix shown in Table 13-4.

5. When all scores are in standardized form and the factors have been chosen to be *mutually uncorrelated with each other*, the correlations of variables with factors—the factor loadings—can be viewed as regression coefficients to estimate the value of each computer model on each of the three performance characteristics. Generally speaking, the factors will diminish in importance in their estimating ability. That is, each set of factor scores accounts for a *diminishing proportion* of the variation in the original set of variables.

6. If we are willing to trade off some of the information in the original data matrix for a gain in data reduction, we would discard the last extracted factor first, the next to last second, and so on.

In the course of computing the various factor scores and factor loadings, we have been using a specific approach to factor analysis, called *principal components.* It is time to describe this procedure in more detail.

PRINCIPAL-COMPONENTS ANALYSIS

Principal-components analysis represents only one technique for extracting factors, or, in terms of this method, *components*.[1] This is the specific factoring technique that has been applied to the 15 × 3 matrix of Table 13-2 in order to find the factor scores of Table 13-3 and the factor loadings of Table 13-4.

Unlike some of the less structured factor-analytic procedures, principal-components analysis (in typical applications) leads to unique, reproducible results.[2] The objective is to portray a set of associated variables in terms of a set of orthogonal (mutually uncorrelated) linear combinations of those variables. The linear combinations are chosen so that each set of component scores accounts for a decreasing proportion of the total variance in the original variables, subject to being orthogonal with previously extracted components.

Let us consider the rationale underlying the method of principal components. Suppose that we return to the weights shown for each component at the top of Table 13-3. Of all of the infinitude of weights that *could* be chosen to make up to factor scores (shown in the middle portion of Table 13-3) these are the *unique* weights that are found by application of the principal-components procedure. *These particular sets of weights yield unstandardized component (i.e., factor) scores whose variance is maximal, subject to each set of component scores being uncorrelated with previously obtained component scores.*

That is, no other set of weights could lead to a column of component scores with higher variance (in this problem) than the set −0.68008, −0.67075, and 0.29596. In our illustration, the total variance in the data (sum of the variances of the three standardized performance variables) is equal to 3, hence, each variable accounts for 33% of the total variance. The sum of the variances of the three components (2.07692 + 0.89898 + 0.02410) is also equal to 3. Note, however, that the proportion of total variation accounted for by the first component alone is 69%, and the first two components together account for almost all (99%) of the variance in the original set of data. Quite often, the analyst desiring parsimony would simply omit

---

[1]Some factor analysts discuss principal components as a model that is distinct from "factor" models. In practice, however, the more generic term of *factor analysis* is increasingly being applied to cover the principal-components procedure as well.

[2]The method was first proposed by Karl Pearson in 1901. Its use in the analysis of associative data structures, however, is due to Harold Hotelling and is presented in the paper "Analysis of a Complex of Statistical Variables into Principal Components," *Journal of Educational Psychology*, 24 (1933), 417–44, 498–520. Inasmuch as iterative methods are used in principal-components analysis, the term "unique" is used somewhat advisedly. Such procedures stop short of an exact solution and are subject to round-off error.

the last component, preferring to portray the data set in terms of only two components. In this case little information would be lost.

Geometric Aspects of Principal Components

Figure 13-1 shows, in general form, the geometric rationale of principal-components analysis. If the original variables are correlated, as they are in the illustrative problem of Table 13-2, then the points will not be uniformly scattered throughout the space. Rather, in three dimensions (for example), they will tend to follow an ellipsoidal pattern, as illustrated in Panel I of Figure 13-1. Notice that this figure looks like a flattened cigar.

Figure 13-1   Geometrical aspects of principal-components factor analysis

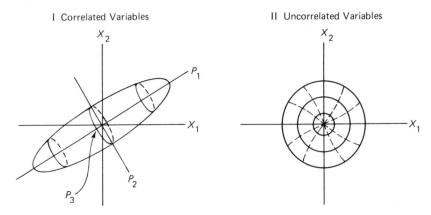

If we put an axis P_1 through the longest direction of the ellipse, another axis P_2 through the second longest, and P_3 through the shortest, it turns out that those three axes *are* the principal-component axes of the data matrix. Note that they *are* at right angles (orthogonal) to each other, and, further-more, the variance (which is proportional to squared length) of P_1 exceeds that of P_2, which, in turn, exceeds that of P_3.

Of course, in limited samples of data, the flattened cigar shape is only approximated (if the variables are correlated). In two dimensions the pattern looks like an ellipse. In four and higher dimensions the pattern is hyper-ellipsoidal. While we cannot graph the latter case, the same idea holds mathematically: principal-components axes correspond to axes of the hyperellipse.

Panel II of Figure 13-1 illustrates why principal-components analysis is *not* applicable to data that are uncorrelated. In this case (assuming stan-dardized variables), the points will trace out a spherelike figure. As we know, all directions through the center of a sphere lead to the same diameter and *no axis would display maximum variance*. Not surprisingly, no factoring method is relevant for this special case. However, this type of situation rarely arises insofar as empirical, nonexperimental data are concerned.

Geometrically speaking, it should be clear from Panel I that if we wish to discard any axis at all, the third axis P_3 is the best bet; little would be lost if the data were projected onto the plane formed by P_1 and P_2. Indeed, things could even be *improved* by projection if P_3 represented mostly an error dimension and the "intrinsic" dimensionality were only two dimensions.

We can now provide a geometric interpretation of the sets of weights that constitute the linear combinations of Table 13-3. For example, the first linear combination:

$$F_1 = -0.68008Z_1 - 0.67075Z_2 + 0.29596Z_3$$

constitutes a set of *direction cosines* that rotate the original three-dimensional space to the first principal-components axis; similarly, the second and third sets of weights are direction cosines for the second and third dimensions of the principal-components orientation.

COMPUTERIZED FACTOR ANALYSIS

In problems of realistic size the actual calculation of linear combinations, factor scores, and factor loadings is done by computer. One common strategy involves the following steps:

1. Compute the *full set* of principal components, including component loadings and scores.
2. Since the components will account for a decreasing proportion of the total variation in the data, keep only those component axes that cumulatively account for some appreciable percentage (e.g., 70 to 80 %) of the total variability in the original data.
3. Rotate the *retained* component solution to a more interpretable orientation. Recalculate factor loadings and scores in the rotated space.

As already shown, principal-components analysis orients the objects in variables space according to a definite set of criteria based on maximizing the variance of their projections on each axis, subject to maintaining orthogonality with previously "extracted" components. We now consider the possibility of rotating *this* orientation.

While principal-components analysis provides a useful tool from the standpoint of *data reduction*, it might *not* represent the best technique from an *interpretive* point of view. (Recall that one major purpose of factor analysis is the tentative identification of *constructs* underlying the manifest variables.) Interpretation is most often attempted at the *component-loading* level in which we are interested in the correlation of variables with components (see Table 13-4).

Easily interpreted component loadings are those in which each variable loads close to unity on one component and close to zero on all others. In this case the component whose variables show loadings close to unity can be interpreted in terms of whatever these particular variables appear to have in common.

Many criteria have been advocated for achieving interpretation of rotated components, and Thurstone[3] has been particularly active in this regard with his work on simple (or interpretable) structure. While the criteria of "interpretable" solutions differ among factor analysts, all seem to agree that it would be desirable to have *each variable load highly on one and only one factor*.

A variety of computer-based procedures have been advanced for rotating factor-loading matrices (as found initially by principal-components or some other factoring method). Generally these procedures can be divided into two groups—*orthogonal* versus *oblique* rotations. In orthogonal rotations the new axes must be mutually perpendicular and uncorrelated (just like the components were). Oblique rotations, as the name suggests, do not require the new axes to be uncorrelated; as such they are more precisely termed oblique "transformations" than "rotations."

Varimax Rotation

Varimax rotation of factor-loading matrices is an orthogonal procedure.[4] This procedure tends to produce some high loadings and some near-zero loadings on each factor. The Varimax technique leads to a new set of uncorrelated axes, keeping the *sum* of squared loadings for each row of the factor-loading matrix intact. Also the sum of cross products of loadings in any two rows of the rotated factor matrix equals the comparable quantity in the original factor-loading matrix. As such, the new axes account for (in total) just as much of the *common* variance as accounted for by the unrotated loading matrix. The Varimax rotation merely breaks up this variance in a different way.

When the original loading matrix has been obtained from a principal-components analysis, however, it is well to remember that successive "components" no longer account for maximum (residual) variance. That is, the

[3]L. L. Thurstone, *Multiple Factor Analysis* (Chicago: University of Chicago Press, 1947).
[4]H. F. Kaiser, "The Varimax Criterion for Analytic Rotation in Factor Analysis," *Psychometrika*, 23 (1958), 187–200.

variance-maximizing property of principal components, taken individually, is lost, although the retained components *as a group* account for the same proportion of total variance.

The BMD-08M Factor-Analysis Program

The BMD-08M program is another member of the biomedical series.[5] This program can factor-analyze large data matrices of up to 198 variables and a virtually unlimited number of cases. Both principal-components analysis and common factor analysis (to be described) can be carried out. Either Varimax rotation or various types of oblique transformations can be employed, as desired. Factor scores and loadings can be computed either in components or transformed factor space. Cross-products matrices other than the correlation matrix can be factored.

In order to show a more realistic example, we illustrate the application of BMD-08M (including subsequent Varimax rotation to a more interpretable solution) to the *full* 15 × 6 matrix of Table 13-2. Since BMD-08M provides a voluminous output, we restrict our attention to the component-loading matrix. This appears in Table 13-5.

Table 13-5 **Component-loading matrix—six performance variables, before rotation of first two components**

	COMPONENT					
VARIABLE	*1*	*2*	*3*	*4*	*5*	*6*
	Before Rotation					
1	−0.914	−0.379	−0.039	0.014	−0.110	0.078
2	−0.873	−0.468	0.063	−0.006	−0.062	−0.093
3	0.604	−0.727	−0.268	−0.181	−0.006	0.003
4	0.625	−0.726	−0.211	0.190	0.003	−0.005
5	0.637	−0.464	0.614	−0.011	−0.027	0.011
6	−0.830	−0.522	0.093	−0.006	0.164	0.019
	Variance of Component Scores					
	3.453	1.908	0.508	0.069	0.044	0.015
	Cumulative Proportion of Total Variance					
	0.575	0.893	0.978	0.990	0.997	1.000

[5] W. J. Dixon, ed., *BMD: Biomedical Computer Programs* (Berkeley, Calif.: University of California Press, 1973).

We note from Table 13-5 that the first component accounts for almost 58% of the total variance, while the first two components together account for over 89% of the total variance.[6] The variables' loadings on the first two components of Table 13-5 are plotted in Figure 13-2. We see that the absolute value of all six loadings is rather high on component 1, and substantial loadings also appear on component 2. We wonder if a rotation of the two-space plot shown in Figure 13-2 can be found that will tend to yield, for each variable, *a high loading on one of the new axes and a low loading on the other.*

Figure 13-2   Original and Varimax-rotated factor loadings

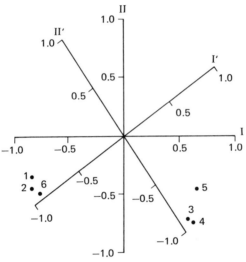

I, II — Original axes
I′, II′ — Rotated axes

Varimax rotation of these components accomplished this objective rather well. The new axes are also shown in Figure 13-2, and the table of rotated loadings is shown in Table 13-6. We note that performance variables 1, 2, and 6 load heavily (negatively) on axis I′, while variables 3, 4, and 5 load heavily (negatively) on axis II′. Moreover, we can interpret these axes quite easily as *speed* and *capacity* from our knowledge of the labels attached to the original variables.

[6]Another criterion that factor analysts often use involves retaining all components whose component score variance exceeds unity. In the case of Table 13-5 the first two components (with variances of 3.453 and 1.908, respectively) are the only ones that would be retained under this rule.

Table 13-6   Variables' loadings on first two
(Varimax-rotated) factors

Variable	Component 1	Component 2
1	−0.962	0.229
2	−0.982	0.133
3	0.062	−0.943
4	0.080	−0.955
5	0.243	−0.749
6	−0.979	0.064

Oblique transformations could also have been carried out on the load-ings of Table 13-5.[7] However, in marketing research applications it is almost always the case that the procedure outlined above is followed: principal com-ponents and subsequent Varimax rotation of the loadings to improve inter-pretability. There is a good reason for this, since interpretation of the (rotated) factor-loading matrix is easier under this option than under any of the oblique options.

OTHER TOPICS IN FACTOR ANALYSIS

Many other procedures are available for factoring data.[8] In particular, the *common-factor model* is sometimes used in marketing. We comment briefly on this model and then turn to other topics in factor analysis.

Communalities and the Common-Factor Model

Our selection of principal-components analysis as *the* factor-analytic technique to consider for detailed exposition was based on its value as a *reproducible* procedure in accounting for common variance in a set of associated variables.

Other factoring methods and, indeed, factoring theory, are often con-cerned *not* with accounting for common variance but with describing the *covariation* among the variables in terms of a small number of common

---

[7]As a matter of fact, one of the oblique transformation options of BMD-08M was applied for comparison purposes. Results were quite similar to those of Figure 13-2, although the resulting axes were slightly negatively correlated.

[8]A compendium of alternative methods can be found in H. Harman, *Modern Factor Analysis*, 2d ed. (Chicago: University of Chicago Press, 1960).

factors *plus* a term representing a *unique factor* for each variable. As was shown, principal components represent linear combinations of *actual* variables; *in extracting components from the correlation, matrix unities appear in the diagonal.*

In the common-factor model, numbers (i.e., the communalities) that are greater than zero but less than unity appear along the main diagonal of the correlation matrix to be factored. Each communality is initially estimated by the researcher and then the computer program adjusts these numbers so as to lead to the best fit of correlations estimated by the model to the actual (off-diagonal) correlations that one starts with.[9] The final communality estimates purport to be that part of the variance in each variable that is *held in common with the remaining variables.*

That is, the common factors account for only a portion of the variation in a single variable; the remainder of that variation is assumed to be ascribed to the variable *itself.*

Unlike the principal-components model the common-factor model does *not* produce exact factor scores. Rather, these factor scores also have to be estimated (usually by regression techniques), and there is no requirement that the estimated scores be uncorrelated across factors. In principal components, however, uncorrelated component scores are guaranteed by the model.

From a practical standpoint, the communality problem concerns *what values should be placed in the main diagonal of the original correlation matrix,* before factoring. Whether the common-factor model leads to a markedly different set of loadings than the principal-components model depends in large part on the *number* of variables. If the number exceeds 15 or so, both the components and common-factor models tend to produce similar results.

In marketing research applications it is not at all unusual to have at least 15 initial variables. Moreover, the components model is less susceptible to misinterpretation, since it entails linear combinations of *actual* variables. In the authors' view the components model has much to recommend it for the nonexpert in factor analysis.

Extensions of Basic Factor Models

A number of relatively new developments have taken place in factoring procedures. One particularly interesting methodology concerns what has

---

[9]The BMD-08M program provides the capability for applying the common factor model (with communality estimates). Usually the starting value of the communality estimates is provided by each variable's R^2 with the remaining variables; this serves as a lower limit while unity represents the upper limit of the final communalities.

become known as *confirmatory factor analysis.*[10] In confirmatory factor analysis one can test hypotheses about how well the data fit certain specified patterns of factor loadings. In some instances the researcher may specify the full pattern of loadings, while in other cases he may fix only a portion of the pattern and allow the technique to solve for estimates of the unspecified factor-loading parameters.

Congruence procedures are related techniques in which the researcher can match up two or more factor-loading solutions, either to a fixed-target pattern or to some compromise pattern formed from the original solutions themselves. This approach can be useful in running double cross validations of factor solutions, in which the original sample size has been split into halves and separate analyses carried out.[11]

Factor Analysis in Prediction Studies

Factor analysis can sometimes be useful in multiple regression and other analyses of dependence structures, where the predictors are both numerous and highly correlated. If the predictors are first factor-analyzed and the criterion variable is regressed on the *full* set of factor scores, R^2 will be identical to that obtained from the usual multiple regression analysis.

However, the advantages of a preliminary principal-components analysis do *not* stem from extracting all components. Suppose that we wished to use only the higher-variance components as predictors on the assumption that these components represent the *stable* part of the common variance shared by the set of predictor variables. In this case we would be regressing the criterion variable on fewer predictor "variables," *with fewer degrees of freedom being lost* than in the regression case using all predictor variables.

Still, one could encounter difficulty in interpreting the regression coefficients, since the predictors would then represent linear combinations of the original set. In some cases a more appropriate procedure would be to extract some relatively small set of components that account for most of the variance in the predictor set and then to select *actual* variables (with highest loadings on the components) as candidate predictors in the regression.

There is some danger associated with the above approach if one or more of the omitted variables just happens to be highly correlated with the

[10]For a good discussion of the differences between confirmatory and the usual (exploratory) factor analysis, see B. N. Mukherjee, "Analysis of Covariance Structures and Exploratory Factor Analysis," *British Journal of Mathematical and Statistical Psychology,* 26 (November, 1973), 125–54.

[11]Still another variant of factor analysis involves so-called higher-order methods. For example, see Yoram Wind, P. E. Green, and A. K. Jain, "Higher Order Factor Analysis in the Classification of Psychographic Variables," *Journal of the Market Research Society,* 15 (1973), 224–32.

criterion variable. The prudent analyst might do well to try out several regressions to see if R^2 changes very much as variables loading high on lesser components are dropped.

Empirically Derived Index Measures

A related use of principal-components analysis concerns the development of indexes for arraying various members of a data bank on some construct of interest. For example, in the shampoo study of Chapter 8 one might be interested in developing an index of "proneness" toward accepting a shampoo that promised "body" as a benefit, using such questionnaire items as: (1) "body" appears in respondent's ideal set, (2) fineness of hair, and (3) hair thickness.

The first principal component of a data matrix has the property of maximally separating individuals along its dimension. As an *internal* criterion it could be used to order individuals as well as provide interval-scaled weights that indicate the importance of each of the contributory variables to the "proneness" measure. Many cases arise in marketing research where one needs a *single composite measure* of some construct but where no prior basis exists for weighting the variables making up the composite. If an empirically derived index is satisfactory, the first principal component can provide both the weights (e.g., -0.68008, -0.67075, and 0.29596, at the top of Table 13-3) and the index values (i.e., factor scores).

Other Types of Scales

Factor analysis is typically applied to interval-scaled data, although some analysts have employed dichotomous variables or mixtures of interval-scaled and dichotomous variables. If all data are nominal-scaled, the researcher could consider a set of techniques—latent-structure analysis—that are specifically designed for this type of situation.[12]

Researchers have also expanded the technique base to provide algorithms for factor-analyzing ordinal-scaled data.[13] However, many of these methods are subject to their own sets of problems (considered in Chapter 14). Moreover, there is reason to believe that simple integer-rank transformations (that are later treated as intervally scaled data) can provide useful and robust approximations.[14]

[12]P. F. Lazarsfeld and N. W. Henry, *Latent Structure Analysis* (Boston: Houghton Mifflin Company, 1968).

[13]J. C. Lingoes and Louis Guttman, "Nonmetric Factor Analysis: A Rank Reducing Alternative to Linear Analysis," *Multivariate Behavioral Research*, 2 (1967), 485–505.

[14]An investigation of this type of transformation in a related context is found in P. E. Green, "On the Robustness of Multidimensional Scaling Techniques," *Journal of Marketing Research*, 12 (February, 1975), 73–81.

Finally, it should be mentioned that factor-analyzing *polytomous* variables that are coded into several dummy variables should generally be avoided (or at least used with caution). This is because their intraset correlations are bound to be negative, strictly as a consequence of the category coding. In some instances this artifact can lead to difficulties in the interpretation of both factor loadings and factor scores.

Statistical Inference in Factor Analysis

Throughout this chapter we have had relatively little to say about the statistical significance of such entities as factor scores, factor loadings, and the like. For example, the analyst using principal-components analysis would like to know *how many* components to extract—that is, those that are statistically significant. Wilks[15] and Bartlett[16] have provided approximate large-sample tests for this problem. Other tests are also available.

Despite the effort expended by mathematical statisticians to develop statistical tests related to factor analysis, it is fair to say that relatively little application has been made of these tests by applied researchers. Rather, use of various rules of thumb (have ten times as many objects as variables, extract only those components whose variances exceed unity, rotate one-third as many components as there are variables, etc.) appears to be more prevalent. While the authors do not advocate the inviolate use of such ad hoc rules, the fact remains that (current) statistical significance tests do not appear to be extremely helpful either.

There are two reasons for this. First, distribution theory in factor analysis is quite complex, and few of the significance tests are available in easily applied form. Second, with a large number of objects relative to the number of variables, the number of *statistically* significant factors tends to equal the number of variables if one uses, say, principal-components analysis. In such cases components that account for a very small portion of total variability might still turn out to be statistically significant, even though their *practical* significance from an interpretive standpoint might be nil.

At the current state of the art—and factor analysis seems to display a certain "artistic" flavor—the authors are more inclined to view factor-analytic procedures as *descriptive* summaries of data matrices rather than inferential devices. While this objective may seem quite limited, it appears to be realistic, considering the stringency of assumptions underlying the currently available statistical tests and the complexity of their implementation.

---

[15]S. S. Wilks, "The Large Sample Distribution of the Likelihood Ratio for Testing Composite Hypotheses," *Annals of Mathematical Statistics*, 9 (1938), 60–62.

[16]M. S. Bartlett, "Tests of Significance in Factor Analysis," *British Journal of Psychology*, 3 (1950), 77–85.

BASIC CONCEPTS OF CLUSTER ANALYSIS

Like factor analysis, clustering methods are applied to intact matrices. The usual objective of *cluster analysis* is to separate objects into groups such that each object is more like other objects in its group than like objects outside the group. Cluster analysis is thus concerned ultimately with classification, and its techniques are part of the field of numerical taxonomy.[17]

One of the major problems in marketing consists of the orderly classification of the myriad data that confront the researcher. The availability of household data from large consumer panels and the increasing detail with which corporate sales statistics are being recorded are illustrative of the growing need for a set of techniques that will automate, to some extent, the task of data reduction and classification.

The typical clustering procedure that we shall discuss assigns each object to one and only one class. Objects within a class are usually assumed to be indistinguishable from one another. Thus, we assume here that the underlying structure of the data involves an unordered set of discrete classes. In some cases we may also view these classes as hierarchical in nature, where some classes are divided into subclasses.

Primary Questions

Clustering procedures can be viewed as preclassificatory in the sense that the analyst has *not* used prior information to partition the objects (rows of the data matrix).[18] However, he *is* assuming that the data are "partially" heterogeneous—that is, that "clusters" exist. This type of presupposition is different from the case in discriminant analysis where a priori groups of objects have been formed on the basis of criteria *not* based on profile resemblance in the data matrix itself. Given no information on group definition in advance, the major problems of cluster analysis can be stated as:

1. What measure of interobject similarity is to be used, and how is each variable to be "weighted" in the construction of such a summary measure?

[17]For an elementary discussion of the field of numerical taxonomy, see R. R. Sokal and P. H. A. Sneath, *Principles of Numerical Taxonomy* (San Francisco: W. H. Freeman and Company, Publishers, 1963). More technical discussions may be found in Richard Stone, *Mathematics in the Social Sciences and Other Essays* (Cambridge, Mass.: MIT Press, 1966), Chap. 11; N. Jardine and R. Sibson, *Mathematical Taxonomy* (New York: John Wiley & Sons, Inc., 1971); and P. H. A. Sneath and R. R. Sokal, *Numerical Taxonomy* (San Francisco: W. H. Freeman and Company, Publishers, 1973).

[18]We note that partitioning is performed in terms of the objects rather than the variables; thus, cluster analysis deals with intact data (in terms of the variables). Moreover, the partitioning is not performed a priori but is based on the object similarities themselves.

2. After interobject similarities are obtained, how are the classes of objects to be formed?
3. After the classes have been formed, what summary measures of each cluster are appropriate in a descriptive sense—that is, how are the clusters to be defined?
4. Assuming that adequate descriptions of the clusters can be obtained, what inferences can be drawn regarding their statistical reliability?

These questions constitute the main points of our discussion in this section of the chapter.

Illustrative Profiles

Figure 13-3 portrays the performance profiles of three of the computers —models 1, 2, and 8 from the data of Table 13-2. If we were to try to cluster the models intuitively, we might say that models 1 and 8 exhibit fairly close

Figure 13-3   Performance profiles of computer models 1, 2, and 8 (from data of Table 13-2)

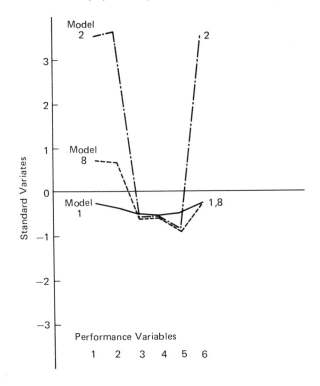

profiles, while model 2 is quite disparate. Still, we note that model 2 is quite close to model 8 on performance variables 3, 4, and 5; as a matter of fact, all three computers exhibit similar scores on these three variables.

While the profiles can be portrayed as shown in Figure 13-3, the reader can appreciate the problems encountered in plotting the profiles of all 15 computer models on the same grid. Imagine, then, the chaotic picture that would result if one wanted to cluster 100 computer models, each represented by 20 performance variables. The need for mechanistic clustering procedures becomes acute for problems of realistic size.

An alternative way to portray the data would be to consider the computer models as 15 points in six-dimensional space. While we cannot show this representation visually, we can still imagine each computer plotted in variables space. Natural measures of proximity, then, would be types of *distances* separating each pair of points. We discuss these various measures in a subsequent section of the chapter.

Choice of Proximity Measure

The choice of *proximity, similarity*, or *resemblance measure* (all three terms will be used synonomously here) is an interesting problem in cluster analysis. The concept of similarity always raises the question: similarity with respect to what? Proximity measures are viewed in relative terms—two objects are similar, relative to the group, if their profiles across variables are "close" or they share "many" aspects in common, relative to those which other pairs share in common.

Most clustering procedures use pairwise measures of proximity. The choice of which objects and variables to use in the first place is largely a matter for the researcher's judgment. While these (prior) choices are important ones, they are beyond our scope here. Even assuming that such choices have been made, however, the possible measures of pairwise proximity are many. Generally speaking, these measures fall into two classes: (1) distance-type measures and (2) matching-type measures. We discuss the characteristics of each in turn.

Distance Measures

A surprisingly large number of proximity measures can be viewed as distances in some type of metric space. We may recall from geometry the notion of Euclidean distance between two points in a space of r dimensions. The formula is

$$d_{ij} = \left[\sum_{k=1}^{r} (x_{ik} - x_{jk})^2 \right]^{1/2}$$

where x_{ik}, x_{jk} are the projections of points i and j on dimension k ($k = 1, 2, \ldots, r$).

Inasmuch as the variables in a data matrix are often measured in different units, the formula above is usually applied *after* each variable has been standardized to zero mean and unit standard deviation. Our subsequent discussion will assume that this preliminary step has been taken.

The Euclidean distance measure technically assumes that the space of (standardized) variables is orthogonal—that is, that the variables are uncorrelated. But in most data matrices the variables will be correlated. In cases where the original variables are highly correlated, some analysts follow a procedure of extracting the principal components of the matrix first and *then* finding the distance between pairs of points as referred to their scores on the (standardized) component axes:

$$d_{ij}^* = \left[\sum_{k=1}^{r} (y_{ik} - y_{jk})^2 \right]^{1/2}$$

where y_{ik} and y_{jk} denote *unit variance* component scores of profiles i and j on component axis k ($k \times 1, 2, \ldots, r$).

If we consider the square of each of these distance measures, the differences in the two approaches can be explained as follows:

1. Squared Euclidean distance in the original variables space has the effect of weighting each underlying principal component by that component's variance.

2. Squared Euclidean distance in the component space (where all components are first standardized to *unit* variance) has the effect of assigning *equal* weights to all components.

3. In terms of the geometry of the configuration, in the first case all points (computer models) are rotated to orthogonal axes with no change in their squared interpoint distance. The general effect is to portray the original configuration as a hyperellipsoid with principal-components axes serving as the axes of that figure. Equating all axes to equal length has the effect of transforming this hyperellipsoid into a hypersphere where all "axes" are of equal length.

However, if all of the (standardized) variables are also uncorrelated, both d_{ij} and d_{ij}^* will be equivalent.[19]

---

[19]An alternative procedure (in the case of the nonequivalence of d_{ij} and d_{ij}^*) is to perform a preliminary principal-components analysis and compute distances across the unit-variance dimensions involving only the larger-variance components. In this way the lesser components, which may be error variance, are *not* allowed to influence interpoint distance. This approach has much to recommend it.

Matching Measures

Quite often the analyst wishing to cluster profiles must contend with data that are only nominally scaled. The usual approach to this kind of situation employs attribute matching coefficients. Intuitively speaking, two profiles are viewed as similar *to the extent to which they share common attributes.*

As an illustration of this approach, consider the following two profiles:

			ATTRIBUTE			
OBJECT	*1*	*2*	*3*	*4*	*5*	*6*
1	1	0	0	1	1	0
2	0	1	0	1	0	1

Each of these objects is characterized by possession or nonpossession of each of six attributes, where a 1 denotes possession and a 0 nonpossession. Suppose we just count up the total number of matches—either 1, 1 or 0, 0—and divide by the total number of attributes. A simple matching measure can then be stated as

$$S_{12} = \frac{M}{N} = \frac{2}{6} = \frac{1}{3}$$

where M denotes the number of attributes held in common (matching 1's or 0's) and N denotes the total number of attributes. We notice that this measure varies between zero and one.

If weak matches (nonpossession of an attribute) are to be deemphasized, the measure above can be modified to

$$S'_{ij} = \frac{\text{number of attributes that are 1 for both object } i \text{ and } j}{\text{number of attributes that are 1 for either } i \text{ or } j \text{ or both}}$$

In this case $S'_{12} = 1/5$. A variety of such matching-type coefficients are described by Sokal and Sneath.[20]

Attributes need not be limited to dichotomies, however. In the case of polytomies, matching coefficients are often developed by means similar

[20]Sokal and Sneath, *Principles of Numerical Taxonomy*, pp. 128–41.

to the above by recoding the k-state variable into $k - 1$ dummy (0–1) variables. Naturally such coefficients will be sensitive to the variation in the number of states.

Finally, mention should be made of the case in which the variables consist of mixed scales—nominal, ordinal, and interval. Interval-scaled variables may be handled in terms of similarity coefficients by the simple device of computing the range of the variable R_k and finding

$$S_{ijk}^* = 1 - \frac{|x_{ik} - x_{jk}|}{R_k}$$

The measure S_{ijk}^* will then appropriately vary between 0 and 1, just like a similarity measure. This measure has been suggested by Gower[21] as a device to handle both nominal- and interval-scaled data in a single similarity coefficient.

Mixed scales that include ordinal-scaled variables present greater difficulties. If ordinal and interval scales occur, one can downgrade the interval data to ordinal scales and use a measure proposed by Kendall.[22] If all three scales—nominal, ordinal, and interval—appear, one is more or less forced to downgrade all data to nominal measures and use matching-type coefficients. An alternative approach would be to compute "distances" for each pair of objects according to each scale type separately, standardize the measures to zero mean and unit standard deviation, and then compute some type of weighted average. Such approaches are quite ad hoc however.

Clustering Programs

Once the analyst has settled on some pairwise measure of profile similarity, he must still use some type of computational routine for clustering the profiles. A large variety of such computer programs already exists, and more are being developed as interest in this field increases. Each clustering program tends to maintain a certain individuality, although some common characteristics can be drawn out. Ball and Hall[23] have made a rather extensive survey of clustering methods. The following categories are based, in part, on their classification:

[21]J. C. Gower, "A General Coefficient of Similarity and Some of Its Properties" (working paper, Rothamsted Experimental Station, England, 1968).

[22]See M. G. Kendall, "Discrimination and Classification," in *Multivariate Analysis*, ed. P. R. Krishnaiah (New York: Academic Press, Inc., 1966), pp. 165–85.

[23]G. H. Ball and D. J. Hall, "Background Information on Clustering Techniques" (working paper, Stanford Research Institute, Menlo Park, Calif., July, 1968).

1. *Dimensionalizing the association matrix.* These approaches use principal-components or other factor-analytic methods to find a dimensional representation of points from *interobject* association measures. Clusters are then developed visually or on the basis of grouping objects according to their pattern of component scores.

2. *Nonhierarchical methods.* These methods start right from the proximity matrix and can be characterized as follows:

   a. *Sequential threshold.* In this case a cluster center is selected and all objects within a prespecified threshold value are grouped. Then a new cluster center is selected and the process is repeated for the unclustered points, and so on. (Once points enter a cluster, they are removed from further processing.)

   b. *Parallel threshold.* This method is similar to the preceding method except that several cluster centers are selected simultaneously and points within threshold level are assigned to the nearest center; threshold levels can then be adjusted to admit fewer or more points to clusters.

   c. *Optimizing partitioning.* This method modifies categories (a) or (b) in that points can be later reassigned to clusters on the basis of optimizing some overall criterion measure, such as average within-cluster distance for a given number of clusters.

3. *Hierarchical methods.* These procedures are characterized by the construction of a hierarchy or treelike structure. In some methods each point starts out as a unit (single-point) cluster. At the next level the two closest points are placed in a cluster. At the following level a third point joins the first two, or else a second two-point cluster is formed, based on various criterion functions for assignment. Eventually all points are grouped into one large cluster. Variations on this procedure involve the development of a hierarchy from the top down. At the beginning the points are partitioned into two subsets based on some criterion measure related to average within-cluster distance. The subset with the highest average within-cluster distance is next partitioned into two subsets, and so on, until all points eventually become unit clusters.

While the above classes of programs are not exhaustive of the field, most of the more widely used clustering routines can be typed as falling into one (or a combination) of the above categories. Criteria for grouping include such measures as average within-cluster distance and threshold cutoff values. The fact remains, however, that even the "optimizing" approaches achieve only conditional optima, since an unsettled question in this field is *how many* clusters to form in the first place.

At this stage in the development of cluster analysis, the authors are of the opinion that clustering might best be approached in terms of a combination of dimensional representation of the points and techniques that group points in the reduced space (obtained from principal-components analysis or similar techniques). Alternatively, clusters based on the *original* distance measures may be embedded in the reduced space. This *dual* approach, if the dimensionality is small, enables the analyst to stay "close to his data" and possibly to augment the clustering results with visual inspection of the configuration.

Describing the Clusters

Once clusters are developed, the analyst still faces the task of describing them. One measure that is used frequently is the *centroid*—the average value of the objects contained in the cluster on each of the variables making up each object's profile. If the data are interval scaled and clustering is performed in original variables space, this measure appears quite natural as a summary description. If the space consists of principal-components dimensions, the axes cannot be described simply. Often in this case the analyst will want to go back to the original variables and compute average profile measures on these. He can then construct average cluster profiles similar to the graphical portrayal in Figure 13-3.

If matching-type coefficients are used, the analyst may describe a cluster in terms of the group's modal profile on each of the attributes.

In addition to central tendency, the researcher may compute some measure of the cluster's variability, such as average interpoint distance of all members of the cluster from their centroid or average interpoint distance between all pairs of points within the cluster.

Statistical Inference

Despite attempts made to construct various tests of the statistical reliability of clusters, no fully defensible procedures are currently available. The lack of appropriate tests stems from the difficulty of specifying realistic null hypotheses.[24] First, it is not clear just what the universe of content is. Quite often the researcher arbitrarily selects objects and variables and is interested in confining his attention to only that particular sample. Second, the analyst is usually assuming that "partial" heterogeneity exists in the first place; otherwise, why bother to cluster? Third, the clusters are formed *from the data*

[24]P. H. A. Sneath, "Some Statistical Problems in Numerical Taxonomy," *The Statistician*, 17 (1967), 1–8.

and not on the basis of outside criteria. Thus, one would be placed in the uncomfortable statistical position of "testing" the significance between groups formed on the basis of the data itself. Finally, the distributions of objects and variables are largely unknown, and it would be dangerous to assume that the variables conformed to some tractable model such as a set of multivariate normal distributions differing only in centroid locations.

Despite the formidable problems associated with statistical inference in cluster analysis, the analyst might try a few ad hoc procedures to provide rough checks on the clustering results. For example, he might apply two or more different clustering routines to the same data and compare results across algorithms. Or, he may wish to split the data randomly into halves, perform separate clusterings, and then examine the average profile values of each cluster across subsamples. Alternatively, he may delete various columns (variables) in the original profile data, compute dissimilarity measures across the remaining columns, and compare these results to the clusters found from using the full set of columns (variables).

Still other procedures are possible. One could construct random profile data by sampling from some common multivariate distribution and comparing the partitioning found by this procedure to the original partitioning. A variation of the multivariate distribution sampling procedure in which a null hypothesis can be specified involves the use of contingency tables. Here, the null hypothesis is that there is no significant difference between the location of the data points and a distribution of points generated independently from the marginal distributions of each variable. The data are partitioned into cells (regions of the space) and counts made to obtain the observed frequency in each. The expected frequencies are calculated from the marginal distributions of each of the variables. A chi-square analysis is then performed to test for the significance of difference between observed and expected frequencies.

We continue to believe, at least in the present state of cluster analysis, that this class of techniques should be viewed as *preclassification*, where the object is to *formulate* rather than test categorizations of data. After a classification has been developed and supported by *theoretical research* and subsequent reformulation of classes, other techniques such as discriminant analysis might prove useful in the assignment of new members to groups identified on grounds that are *not* solely restricted to the original cluster analysis.[25]

While the above caveats are not to be taken lightly, it seems to us that clustering techniques can still be useful—in ways comparable to the employment of factor analysis—as systematic procedures for the orderly preclassification of multivariate data. The results of using these approaches can be

[25]Discriminant analysis, as an ad hoc device, may be used to find "optimal" weights for variables *after* performing the cluster analysis. In this case, however, its use would be *strictly* descriptive rather than inferential.

helpful and meaningful (after the fact), as will be illustrated in the next section.

APPLICATIONS OF CLUSTER ANALYSIS

So many different clustering programs are available that even a cursory description of them would easily exceed our scope. What we can describe are three applications of varying degrees of difficulty:

- A synthetic data problem, made up of only 12 points in two dimensions;
- A product-positioning study involving sports car brands; and
- A performance-profile clustering of digital computers.

The BMD-P1M Hierarchical Program

Let us start out by illustrating one of the more popular clustering programs. Consider the standardized (artificial) data of Figure 13-4. In this case we have 12 points portrayed in two dimensions. Visually, it would seem that four clusters are present:

$$\{a, b\}$$
$$\{c, d, e, f, g\}$$
$$\{h, i, j, k\}$$
$$\{l\}$$

Figure 13-4   Initial configuration of points for BMD-P1M cluster analysis

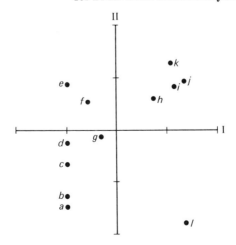

However, in most practical problems of interest, we cannot fall back on visual clustering. We could have hundreds of points in several dimensions (where each dimension is a variable). Nonetheless, let us examine how various clustering rules would group the 12 objects represented as points in Figure 13-4.

BMD-P1M is one of the P series of biomedical programs. This program can cluster up to 150 objects.[26] Various measures of resemblance, including Euclidean distance, can be accommodated. The program is a hierarchical algorithm that starts out with each point as its own unit cluster and eventually ends up with all points in one undifferentiated cluster. Three amalgamation rules for building up the clusters are available.

Single Linkage

The *single-linkage,* or *minimum-distance, rule* starts ouțby finding the two points with the shortest Euclidean distance. These are placed in the first cluster. At the next stage a third point joins the already formed cluster of two if its shortest distance to the members of the cluster is smaller than the two closest unclustered points. Otherwise, the two closest unclustered points are placed in a cluster.

The process continues until all points end up in one cluster. The distance between two clusters is defined as the *shortest* distance from a point in the first cluster to a point in the second.

Complete Linkage

The *complete-linkage option* starts out in just the same way by clustering the two closest points. However, the criterion for joining points to clusters or clusters to clusters involves maximum (rather than minimum) distance. In other words, the distance between two clusters is the *longest* distance from a point in the first cluster to a point in the second cluster.

Average Linkage

The *average-linkage option* starts out in the same way as the other two. However, in this case the distance between two clusters is the *average* distance from points in the first cluster to points in the second cluster.

Results

The three amalgamation rules showed similar, but not identical, clusterings. For example, at the four-cluster level there was a difference in the

[26]See W. J. Dixon, ed., *BMDP: Biomedical Computer Programs* (Berkeley, Calif.: University of California Press, 1975). While BMD-P1M is primarily designed to cluster variables, it is a simple procedure to reverse the role of variables and objects (as was done here).

placement of point c between the single- and average-linkage versus the complete-linkage rules:

Single Linkage	Complete Linkage	Average Linkage
$\{a, b, c\}$	$\{a, b\}$	$\{a, b, c\}$
$\{d, e, f, g\}$	$\{c, d, e, f, g\}$	$\{d, e, f, g\}$
$\{h, i, j, k\}$	$\{h, i, j, k\}$	$\{h, i, j, k\}$
$\{l\}$	$\{l\}$	$\{l\}$

Since the program provides the full clustering sequence, it is easy to prepare a tree diagram (called a *dendrogram*). Illustratively, Figure 13-5 shows the dendrogram for the complete-linkage rule.

We note that points a and b, the closest pair, first join at a distance of 0.23. The next pair to join are points i and j, and so on. The last two clusters to merge are $\{a, b, c, d, e, f, g\}$ and $\{h, i, j, k, l\}$ at a distance value of 3.5. We note that the dendrogram provides a succinct and convenient way to summarize the clustering sequence.

Figure 13-5   Dendrogram from complete-linkage clustering

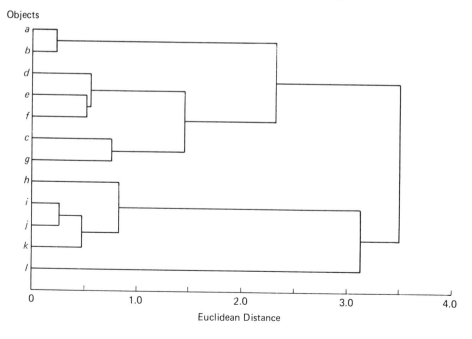

Objects

Euclidean Distance

Product-Positioning Application

Cluster analysis can be used in a variety of marketing research applications. For example, companies are often interested in determining how their products are positioned in terms of competitive offerings and consumers' views about the types of persons most likely to own the product.[27]

For illustrative purposes, Figure 13-6 shows the results of a pilot study in which interobject-distance data were developed for 7 sports cars, 6 types of stereotyped owners, and 13 attributes often used to describe cars. The distance data were based on respondents' degree-of-belief ratings about which

Figure 13-6   Complete-linkage analysis of product-positioning data

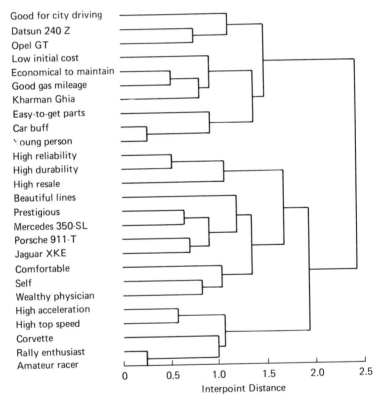

attributes and owners "described" which cars. In this case a complete-linkage algorithm was also used to cluster the objects.[28]

Looking first at the four large clusters, we note the *car* groupings:

- Datsun 240Z; Opel GT;
- Kharman Ghia;
- Mercedes 350-SL; Porsche 911-T; Jaguar XKE; and
- Corvette.

For example, the Corvette is seen as being in a class by itself with the attributes *high acceleration* and *high top speed*. Its perceived (stereotyped) owners are *rally enthusiast* and *amateur racer*.

Studies of this type can enable the marketing researcher to observe the interrelationships among several types of entities—cars, attributes, owners. The approach displays several advantages. For example, it can be applied to alternative advertisements, package designs, or other kinds of communications stimuli. That is, the respondent could be shown blocks of advertising copy (brand unidentified) and asked to provide degree-of-belief ratings that the brand described in the copy possesses each of the *n* features.

Similarly, in the case of consumer packaged goods, the respondent could be shown alternative package designs and asked for degree-of-belief ratings that the contents of the package possess various features. In either case one would be adding an additional set (or sets) of ratings to the response sets described earlier. Hence, four (or more) classes of items could be represented as points in the cluster analysis.

Performance Structure of the Computer Market

Computers, like many industrial products, such as electric motors, machine tools, and gas turbines, can be characterized by a set of performance characteristics. Assume that each computer model can be represented as a point in performance space. Some models will be "closer" to others in this performance space—that is, more competitive in terms of performance similarities.

Data for the cluster analysis reported here were obtained from published reports of first-time computer model installations made between 1964 and 1968. A sample of 47 models represented the objects for the grouping. Some 22 performance variables and features were used to develop the interobject similarity measures. These are shown in Table 13-7.

[28]S. C. Johnson, "Hierarchical Clustering Schemes," *Psychometrika*, 32 (September, 1967), 241–54.

The actual analysis was rather complex and involved a combination of reduced-space analysis and hierarchical clustering. The former technique indicated that four basic dimensions appeared to underlie the data:

- Capacity
- Speed
- Orientation (scientific versus business)
- Elaborateness of features

Table 13-7   Performance characteristics of 47 computer models

Measured Variables	*Features Data*
1. Word length in binary bits	13. Floating-point representation
2. Likely fixed-point execution time: $a + b$ in microseconds	14. Binary arithmetic
3. Likely fixed-point execution time: ab in microseconds	15. Checking of data transfers
4. Likely fixed-point execution time: a/b in microseconds	16. Program-interrupt facility
5. Maximum number of index registers	17. Indirect addressing
6. Maximum number of input–output channels	18. Special editing capabilities
7. Minimum number of words in storage	19. Boolean operations
8. Maximum number of words in storage	20. Table lookup
9. Maximum total storage in digits	21. Storage checking
10. Maximum total storage in characters	22. Storage protect
11. Cycle time in microseconds	
12. Effective transfer rate in characters per second	

Table 13-8 shows the eight-group clustering results from the hierarchical clustering. Various aspects of intermanufacturer competition are brought out. For example, cluster 5 shows rather clearly that segments of the IBM 360 computer series compete directly with segments of the RCA Spectra series (possibly a portent of RCA's eventual demise in the computer field). Cluster 3 brings out the competition among CDC, GE, Honeywell, IBM, and Univac. One notes, not surprisingly, that IBM has models in five out of the eight clusters. On the other hand, Honeywell has models in six of the eight clusters, an outcome that was not anticipated by the researchers.

The resulting clusters indicated which manufacturers competed with which other manufacturers in terms of similarity in the overall performance profiles of their machines. Moreover, the combination of reduced-space and cluster analysis provided a useful dual treatment of the data. The reduced-

Table 13-8   Cluster composition

Cluster 1	Cluster 5
Burroughs B2500	IBM 360/30
GE 415	IBM 360/40
GE 425	IBM 360/50
GE 435	IBM 360/65
Honeywell 1400	IBM 360/75
IBM 1130	IBM 360/44
	IBM 360/67
	RCA Spectra 70/35
	RCA Spectra 70/45
	RCA Spectra 70/55
	RCA 3301/3304

Cluster 2	Cluster 6
CDC 3100	GE 235
CDC 3200	Honeywell 200/120
CDC 3300	Honeywell 200/200
CDC 3400	IBM 360/20
Honeywell 1800	RCA Spectra 70/15
	RCA Spectra 70/25
	Univac 9200
	Univac 9300

Cluster 3	Cluster 7
CDC 6400	Honeywell 200/2200
CDC 6600	Honeywell 200/4200
CDC 6800	NCR 315 RMC
GE 625	
GE 635	
Honeywell 200/8200	
IBM 7092-II	
Univac 1108	

Cluster 4	Cluster 8
Burroughs B300	Burroughs B3500
GE 115	Honeywell 200/1200
IBM 1401-G	RCA 3301/3303

space phase provided help in summarizing the original variables in terms of a smaller number of dimensions, such as speed or capacity. The clustering phase permitted us to group machines according to their coordinates in the reduced, but still four-dimensional, space.

SUMMARY

This chapter has been concerned with two ways—factor analysis and clustering—to summarize associative information in interdependent data structures. Quite often reduced-space and cluster analysis can be usefully applied in tandem.

The factor-analytic method stressed here was principal-components analysis. This procedure has the property of selecting sets of weights for forming linear combinations of the original variables such that the variance of the obtained component scores is (sequentially) maximal, subject to each linear combination's being orthogonal to previously obtained ones. The principal-components model was illustrated on a small set of sample data. This was followed by a demonstration of Varimax rotation to improve interpretability of the component loadings. The concluding part of this section dealt with a miscellany of topics, such as communalities estimation, confirmatory factor analysis, factor analysis in prediction, index determination, and statistical inference.

Cluster analysis was described in terms of four general questions: (1) selecting a proximity measure, (2) algorithms for grouping objects, (3) describing the clusters, and (4) statistical inference. In addition, three applications of clustering were briefly described.

ASSIGNMENT MATERIAL

1. The marketing research firm of Brown and FitzRoy Ltd. is in the process of attempting to relate activity-interest test scores to "success" measures of applicants for retailing positions in a large Philadelphia department store. Activity-interest scores and success scores are available for a group of retailing personnel who have already been employed by the store. The activity-interest variables are: X_1—gregariousness, X_2—liking for outdoor sports, X_3—liking for music, and X_4—desire for travel. Higher values of the X_i or Y indicate higher interest or success, respectively.
   a. Conduct a principal-components analysis on the 14×4 matrix of activity-interest scores, utilizing the correlation matrix between variables as input.
   b. How would you interpret the first component?
   c. Rotate the component-loading matrix by means of the Varimax routine. How do you interpret the resulting loadings?

Person	X_1	X_2	X_3	X_4	Y^*
1	21	26	7	8	6.2
2	22	16	11	7	7.6
3	16	28	11	7	5.7
4	17	30	9	13	6.1
5	12	26	12	7	1.8
6	25	10	18	14	2.9
7	18	21	14	16	4.7
8	15	17	5	11	4.8
9	14	23	13	8	4.7
10	18	20	10	5	5.7
11	14	29	14	11	7.2
12	15	23	16	7	6.7
13	25	21	14	12	3.6
14	15	20	3	10	7.0

*Success measure.

2. Using the data of problem 1, compute component scores for each person on each of the (nonrotated) components.
   a. Assuming that you were required to arrive at a *single* index of activity-interest, how might you proceed? How would the 14 persons be arrayed in terms of this index?
   b. Conduct a multiple regression of the success measure Y versus the full set of component scores. Next, select the one variable that loads most highly on the first (unrotated) component and conduct a two-variable linear regression with Y as the criterion variable. Contrast the results of these findings in terms of accounted-for variance in Y.
   c. Conduct a multiple regression using scores on the first two (unrotated) components as predictors with Y as the criterion variable. Contrast the results of this step with those of the preceding analysis.

3. Discuss the similarities and differences among multiple regression, discriminant analysis, canonical correlation, and factor analysis in terms of (a) assumption structure and (b) objectives of the techniques.

4. The following data matrix was obtained from one of the computer runs utilizing the free-association data of Chapter 8 as input. This matrix portrays 19 shampoo benefits in three dimensions.
   a. Plot the coordinate values in three two-dimensional subspaces. What can be observed regarding benefit associations from these plots?

b. Using a clustering program of your choice, cluster the 19 points. (Your routine may require preliminary computation of a distance measure between pairs of points.) How would you interpret the clusters?

Matrix of reduced space coordinates

	COORDINATE		
BENEFIT	I	II	III
1. Body	−0.768	−0.274	−0.315
2. Fullness	−0.857	−0.240	−0.228
3. Holds Set	−0.116	−0.489	0.230
4. Bouncy	−0.113	−0.322	−0.769
5. Not Limp	−0.794	0.058	0.189
6. Manageable	−0.541	0.018	0.247
7. Zesty	0.651	−0.229	−0.425
8. Natural	0.088	0.782	−0.168
9. Clean	−0.006	0.381	0.045
10. Sheen	0.289	0.248	−0.312
11. Curly	0.257	−0.437	−0.178
12. Long	0.386	0.495	−0.433
13. Grooming Aid	0.480	−0.189	0.631
14. Soft	0.007	0.904	−0.216
15. Nice	0.317	−0.207	0.926
16. Combs Easily	−0.456	−0.229	0.504
17. Healthy	0.035	−0.344	0.349
18. Alive	0.707	−0.444	−0.129
19. Pretty	0.432	0.520	0.053

5. Examine the marketing literature for three applications of cluster analysis.
   a. What were the purposes of using cluster analysis by each of the authors?
   b. How would you critique the results of their analyses?
   c. What alternative multivariate methods can you propose for analyzing the data of these studies?

Multidimensional Scaling and Conjoint Analysis

14

INTRODUCTION

Up to this point our discussion of multivariate methods has not been tied into any particular content area; rather, we have emphasized the *versatility* of the techniques across a wide spectrum of marketing problems. In the current chapter, however, we wish to describe two sets of multivariate techniques, *multidimensional scaling* and *conjoint analysis*, that are particularly well suited (and were originally developed) for measuring human perceptions and preferences.

As such, this chapter is something of a continuation of the psychological scaling material of Chapter 6. In the present case we shall be emphasizing *multidimensional* scales and *multiattribute* tradeoffs that often, but not necessarily, make use of ordinal data. The methodology considered here is of comparatively recent origin and the field is still undergoing development and trial application.

Multidimensional scaling (MDS) of perceptions and preferences is discussed first. An intuitive introduction to the topic is provided by using a geographical example involving a set of intercity distances. In particular, we show how MDS takes a set of distance data and tries to find a spatial configuration or pattern of points in some number of dimensions whose distances best match the input data. Attention then turns to the MDS of *subjective* data regarding persons' judged similarities and preferences of various stimuli. Various models for portraying these judgments are described and illustrated geometrically.

We next discuss ways in which MDS has been (and can be) applied to marketing problems. Comments are also made on the limitations of the methodology and the types of future research that may be anticipated in this field.

We then turn to a related methodology—conjoint analysis. In conjoint analysis we are concerned with the measurement of utilities—how people make tradeoffs in choosing among multiattribute alternatives. As with MDS, the fundamentals of the methodology are first described, including some empirical illustrations. This is followed by brief descriptions of applications and also a discussion of some current limitations and future research prospects.

MDS FUNDAMENTALS

Let us start things off by taking a look at Panel I of Figure 14-1. Here we see a configuration of ten U.S. cities, whose locations have been taken from an airline map. By finding ruler distances between each city pair and converting these to miles, we could approximate the *numerical* interpoint distance entries of Panel II. (The distances were actually obtained from an airline atlas.) We recall from Chapter 13 that the Euclidean distance between a pair of points, i and j, in any number of r dimensions is given by

$$d_{ij} = \left[\sum_{k=1}^{r} (x_{ik} - x_{jk})^2 \right]^{1/2}$$

In the present case, $r = 2$, since only two dimensions are involved. For example, we could find the distance between Atlanta and Chicago by: (1) projecting their points on axis 1 (East–West), finding the difference and squaring it; (2) projecting their points on axis 2 (North–South) and doing the same; and then (3) taking the square root of the sum of the two squared differences.

In short, it is a relatively simple matter to go from the map in Panel I to the set of numerical distances in Panel II. However, the converse is *not* so easy. And that is what MDS is all about.

Suppose that we are shown Panel II of Figure 14-1 without the labels so that we do not even know if the objects are cities. The task is to work backward. That is, we wish to find, simultaneously, the:

- Number of dimensions and
- Configuration (or pattern) of points in that dimensionality

so that their computed interpoint distances most closely match the input data of Panel II. This is the problem of *metric* MDS.

Next, suppose that we were to take some order-preserving transformation of the 45 numbers in Panel II. For example, we could take the smallest

Figure 14-1   Nonmetric MDS of ten United States cities

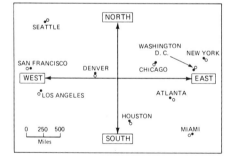

I   Geographic locations of ten U.S. cities

CITIES	ATLA.	CHIC.	DENV.	HOUS.	L. A.	MIAMI	N.Y.	S. F.	SEAT.	WASH. D. C.
ATLANTA		587	1212	701	1936	604	748	2139	2182	543
CHICAGO			920	940	1745	1188	713	1858	1737	597
DENVER				879	831	1726	1631	949	1021	1494
HOUSTON					1374	968	1420	1645	1891	1220
LOS ANGELES						2339	2451	347	959	2300
MIAMI							1092	2594	2734	923
NEW YORK								2571	2408	205
SAN FRANCISCO									678	2442
SEATTLE										2329
WASHINGTON, D. C.										

II   Airline distances between ten U.S. cities

III   Original (•) and recovered (o) city locations via nonmetric MDS

distance (205 miles between New York and Washington) and calls it 1. Then we could apply the same idea and rank-order the remaining 44 distances up to rank 45 for the distance (2,734 miles) between Miami and Seattle. We could then find the:

- Number of dimensions and
- Configuration of points in that dimensionality

so that the ranks of their computed interpoint distances most closely matched the ranks of the input data. This is the problem of *nonmetric* MDS.

In the error-free case (the situation considered here), it turns out that metric MDS methods can find, for all practical purposes, an exact solution. However, what is rather surprising is that, even after degrading the numerical data to ranks, nonmetric methods can achieve a virtually perfect recovery as well.

Panel III indicates that this is so by showing the results of applying a nonmetric algorithm to the ranks of the 45 numbers in Panel II.[1] As shown, even with only rank-order input information, the recovery of the original locations is almost perfect.

We should quickly add, however, that neither the metric nor nonmetric MDS procedures will necessarily line up the configuration of points in a North–South direction; all that the methods try to preserve are *relative* distances. The configuration can be arbitrarily rotated, translated, reflected, or uniformly stretched or shrunk so as to best match the target configuration of Panel I.[2] None of these operations will change the *relative* distances of the points.

Psychological versus Physical Distance

The virtues of MDS methods are not in the scaling of physical distances but rather in their scaling of *psychological "distances,"* often called *dissimilarities*. In MDS we assume that a person acts as though he has a type of "mental map," not necessarily visualized or explicated, so that he views pairs of entities that are near each other as similar and pairs of entities far from each other as dissimilar. Depending upon the relative distances among pairs of points, varying *degrees* of dissimilarity could be imagined.

We assume that the respondent is able to provide either numerical measures of his perceived degree of dissimilarity for all pairs of entities or, less stringently, ordinal measures of dissimilarity. If so, we can use the methodology of MDS to construct a *physical* map in one or more dimensions whose interpoint distances (or ranks of distances, as the case may be) are most consistent with the input data.

Not for a moment do we assume that this model *explains* perception. Quite the contrary: we only assume that it provides a useful *representation* of a set of subjective judgments about the extent to which a respondent views various pairs of entities as being dissimilar. Thus, MDS models are representations of data rather than theories of perceptual processes. That they can be interesting and useful is shown by the following example.

[1]See J. B. Kruskal, F. W. Young, and J. B. Seery, "How to Use KYST, A Very Flexible Program to Do Multidimensional Scaling and Unfolding" (working paper, Bell Laboratories, 1973).

[2]Techniques for doing this are called *configuration congruence* or *matching programs*. For example, see P. H. Schönemann and R. M. Carroll, "Fitting One Matrix to Another under Choice of a Central Dilation and a Rigid Motion," *Psychometrika*, 35 (June, 1970), 245–57.

A Bostonian's View of the United States

A few years ago, R. N. Shepard, one of the pioneers in the development of nonmetric scaling, was interested in persons' *subjective* judgments about the relative nearness of various U.S. states to each other. His experimental subjects were all long-term residents of Boston. Shepard obtained subjective data about how far each state was perceived to be from other states. Average subjective distances were then developed for all distinct pairs of the 48 continental states and the data were scaled by nonmetric MDS.

Figure 14-2 shows a Bostonian's view of the United States as reflected in Shepard's data. Notice that the eastern half of the United States is rather exaggerated compared to the western half. In particular, the northwestern portion looks rather pushed down. Still, it is remarkable that so much structure remains, considering the fact that the source of the input data was respondents' subjective judgments about relative distances. In short, percep-

Figure 14-2   "Map" of the United States based on subjective judgments

Source: Reproduced, with permission, from a research study of R. N. Shepard.

tual *distortion*, while operative, was not severe enough to obliterate the general character of the geographic relationships among the states. As noted, the respondents tended to exaggerate the size of areas nearer their home and attenuate those farther away (and presumably of lesser importance).

THE DEVELOPMENT OF MDS

As motivation for the ensuing discussion, assume that a respondent has been given the task of judging pairs of car names—the models shown in Figure 14-3—in terms of overall dissimilarity. To be specific, suppose that the respondent is shown a set of 55 cards. On each card appear the names of two of the car models; all possible distinct pairs (55) of 11 items appear once. The subject is first asked to place the cards into two classes, namely, pairs of cars that he feels are more or less similar, versus pairs of cars that are more or less different, according to criteria of his own choosing.

After this step the subject is asked to separate the "similar" pile into two subpiles—highly similar car pairs and somewhat similar car pairs. He is then asked to make two subpiles of the "different" pile—somewhat different pairs and highly different pairs of car models. Each subpile may contain about 12 to 15 cards.

The respondent is then asked to choose the most highly similar pair *within* the highly similar subpile, then the next most similar pair, until all cards in the first subpile are ranked. He then ranks the pairs in subpiles 2, 3, and 4. (Before settling on this final ranking he may shift cards from subpile to subpile if he so desires.) By means of this stepwise procedure a strict rank order of the 55 car pairs is eventually obtained; one such rank order is shown in Table 14-1.

Metric Methods

Now suppose, for a moment, that the 55 rank numbers ["1" (most similar) to "55" (least similar)] are more "strongly" scaled than just ranks; that is, let us assume that the data of Table 14-1 really represent *ratio-scaled distances*. This is the crucial assumption of metric methods.[3] Such methods use ratio-scaled distances to find a configuration whose distances are proportional to these.

As shown earlier, it is a simple matter to compute Euclidean distances between all pairs of points *if we know their coordinates*—that is, the configura-

---

[3] Metric methods can take interval-scaled data and determine an "additive constant" that makes the data ratio-scaled. In any event, the *final input data* are assumed to be (possibly errorful) ratio-scaled distances.

Table 14-1   **Rank order of dissimilarities between pairs of car models* (see Figure 14-3 for model descriptions)**

	STIMULUS										
STIMULUS	*1*	*2*	*3*	*4*	*5*	*6*	*7*	*8*	*9*	*10*	*11*
1	—	8	50	31	12	48	36	2	5	39	10
2		—	38	9	33	37	22	6	4	14	32
3			—	11	55	1	23	46	41	17	52
4				—	44	13	16	19	25	18	42
5					—	54	53	30	28	45	7
6						—	26	47	40	24	51
7							—	29	35	34	49
8								—	3	27	15
9									—	20	21
10										—	43
11											—

*The rank number "1" represents the most similar pair.

tion. The converse, however, is not so easy and represents the principal task of metric MDS methods—given a set of interpoint distances—to find the dimensionality and configuration of points whose distances most closely *match* the input values. In our usual appeal for parsimony, we would, of course, like to do this in the smallest possible number of dimensions.

Metric MDS goes back to 1938 and is based on a set of theorems proved by Young and Householder.[4] Computational methods for finding the desired configuration stem from factor analysis, as discussed in Chapter 13. Suffice it to say here that the techniques yield a configuration whose interpoint distances come as close as possible to reproducing the *numerical* values of Table 14-1. The earliest work in MDS utilized these methods, and they are still being used today.

Figure 14-3 shows the configuration resulting from the application of metric MDS to the data of Table 14-1. Metric methods assume that the input data are ratio-scaled distances. In turn, they yield metric output information, the configuration illustrated by Figure 14-3. If we were to compute the interpoint distances of all pairs of points in Figure 14-3—and if the configuration were a perfect fit to the data—the resulting numbers would be proportional to those of Table 14-1.

---

[4]G. Young and A. S. Householder, "Discussion of a Set of Points in Terms of Their Mutual Distances," *Psychometrika*, 3 (March, 1938), 19–22.

Figure 14-3   Metric-scaling solution based on data of Table 14-1

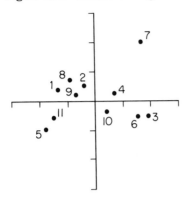

STIMULI—1968 CAR MODELS

1. Ford Mustang 6
2. Mercury Cougar V8
3. Lincoln Continental V8
4. Ford Thunderbird V8
5. Ford Falcon 6
6. Chrysler Imperial V8
7. Jaguar
8. AMC Javelin V8
9. Plymouth Barracuda V8
10. Buick Le Sabre V8
11. Chevrolet Corvair

In many kinds of marketing research studies it is difficult for respondents to make *numerical* judgments about the degree of relative dissimilarity among pairs of objects. However, they frequently experience no difficulty in making *ranking-type* judgments. If the input data consist of only a ranking, as is the case originally in Table 14-1, then we are dealing with nonmetric MDS.

Nonmetric MDS

The first operational computer program for carrying out nonmetric MDS was developed by R. N. Shepard.[5] Nonmetric MDS makes use of an ordered metric scale—a rank order of interpoint distances. Operations of the various computer programs that perform nonmetric MDS are quite complex, both mathematically and computationally, and are not described here.

However, the *conceptual* basis of nonmetric scaling is not difficult to grasp intuitively. Let us return to the rank-order data of Table 14-1. We note that the table is composed of rank numbers, ranging from the most similar pair, Continental and Imperial with rank 1, to the least similar pair, Continental and Falcon with rank 55. As the number of stimuli, n, increases, the number of rank-order constraints increases almost with the square of n—actually as $\frac{1}{2}[n(n-1)]$. However, to portray a set of points in r dimensions we need only rn numbers, namely, the coordinate of each point on each dimension. For example, if $r = 2$, we need only 22 numbers to fix the 11 points. In contrast, we have 55 nonmetric constraints from the relationships shown in Table 14-1.

[5]R. N. Shepard, "The Analysis of Proximities: Multidimensional Scaling with an Unknown Distance Function," Part I, *Psychometrika*, 27 (1962), 125–39.

As the number of inequalities increases relative to the number of *rn* numbers needed to specify a configuration, the inequalities serve to *restrict the movement* of the *n* points, so that with "enough" inequalities we obtain a unique configuration, asymptotically. In realistically sized problems the solution will be more or less unique. This means that we shall have relatively little freedom to move one or more points around without violating at least one of the inequalities. Remember that moving just one point changes its distances with the remaining $n - 1$ points.

Shepard demonstrated, via a series of synthetic-data analyses, that with as few as 8 points the correlation between the interpoint distances of a known two-dimensional configuration was 0.99, on the average, with the interpoint distances of a configuration constructed by his computer program from rank-order information alone.[6] For $n \geq 15$ the two configurations were virtually indistinguishable.

In general, as one increases the dimensionality of the space, the chances of finding such a configuration increase. (As a matter of fact, *any* set of rank orders on pairs of *n* points can be satisfied by a configuration in $n - 1$ dimensions.) The point at issue, however, is to find the *lowest* dimensionality for which the monotonicity constraint is "closely" met. That is, the analyst may wish to trade off achieving perfect fits for a solution of *lower dimensionality* whose distances are *almost* monotone with the original rank-order data.

In practice, nonmetric algorithms are applied by starting the computer run in a relatively high dimensionality, such as four dimensions or more, and then stepping down one dimension at a time until only a single dimension is examined. Each nonmetric MDS algorithm has a goodness-of-fit measure that tells the analyst how well the input data are reproduced by the solution in each dimensionality. One can then see how much improvement is gained by going from some lower to some higher dimensionality. So as to maintain visual contact with the results, most MDS applications typically emphasize three or fewer dimensions (although, in principle, higher dimensionalities could be selected).

Figure 14-4 shows the results of applying nonmetric MDS to the data—now considered *only as ranks*—of Table 14-1.[7] While the two solutions (Figures 14-3 and 14-4) are not identical, they are quite close. It is not unusual to find this high degree of correspondence in various applied studies, confirming the fact that metric solutions are often good approximations to nonmetric ones, even when the input data are only rankings.

One additional aspect of Figure 14-4 are the two labels, Luxurious and Sporty, that have been inserted to identify the axes. We hasten to add that

[6]R. N. Shepard, "Metric Structures in Ordinal Data," *Journal of Mathematical Psychology*, 3 (1966), 287–315.

[7]This particular solution was found by the TORSCA 8 program. See F. W. Young and W. S. Torgerson, "TORSCA, a FORTRAN IV Program for Shepard–Kruskal Multidimensional Scaling Analysis," *Behavioral Science*, 12 (1967), 498–99.

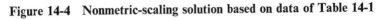

Figure 14-4   Nonmetric-scaling solution based on data of Table 14-1

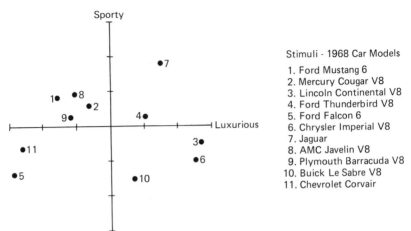

Stimuli - 1968 Car Models

1. Ford Mustang 6
2. Mercury Cougar V8
3. Lincoln Continental V8
4. Ford Thunderbird V8
5. Ford Falcon 6
6. Chrysler Imperial V8
7. Jaguar
8. AMC Javelin V8
9. Plymouth Barracuda V8
10. Buick Le Sabre V8
11. Chevrolet Corvair

these labels do *not* come from the computer program itself. Rather they are determined from either the analyst's judgment or various "property fitting" techniques in which candidate dimensions are examined via multiple regression procedures.[8]

Let us examine the labeled configuration of Figure 14-4. On the luxuriousness dimension we note that Continental and Imperial are perceived as the most luxurious cars while Falcon and Corvair are viewed as the least luxurious. The most sporty cars are Jaguar and Javelin, while the plainest car is the Le Sabre.

The degree of fit of the ranked distances in Figure 14-4 to the original ranking turned out to be quite good. In particular, note that Continental and Imperial (ranked as most similar in Table 14-1) are indeed located very close to each other while Continental and Falcon (ranked as most dissimilar in Table 14-1) are one of the most distant pairs of points. While the configuration of Figure 14-3 (based on the metric assumption) is not exactly the same, the interpretation would nevertheless be similar.

TYPES OF MDS MODELS

In most applications of MDS (metric or nonmetric) we are interested in scaling either dissimilarities data, as related to buyer perceptions, or dissimilarities *and* preference data. *Simple-space configurations* consist of only *one*

---

[8]For a discussion of these, see P. E. Green and V. R. Rao, *Applied Multidimensional Scaling: A Comparison of Approaches and Algorithms* (New York: Holt, Rinehart and Winston, Inc., 1972).

set of points, usually the stimuli, such as the 11 automobile models, shown in Figures 14-3 and 14-4. If based on subjective dissimilarities, they are often called *perceptual maps*.

Joint-space solutions consist of at least two sets of entities—usually stimulus and person entities. They are often called *perceptual-preference maps*. To illustrate, let us return to the automobile dissimilarities data of Table 14-1. Suppose that two respondents, *I* and *J*, gave virtually the same rank order of judged dissimilarities shown in the table. As such, their perceptual maps of the 11 car models would each look like the configuration of Figure 14-4.

Next, assume that respondents *I* and *J* were also asked to rank the 11 car models *in order of preference*. As it turned out, respondent *I* most liked the Thunderbird, liked the Cougar second best, and least liked the Falcon. On the other hand, respondent *J* most liked the Corvair, liked the Falcon second best, and least liked the Jaguar.

Ideal-Point Models

How can these disparate preferences be accommodated? Figure 14-5 shows that they can also be modeled by the simple device of developing a new type of entity, called an *ideal point*. By "ideal" point is meant a *hypothetical* car model possessing just that combination of perceived luxuriousness and sportiness represented by its projections on each dimension of the map. Respondent *I*'s ideal is near the Thunderbird, his first choice, while respondent *J*'s ideal point is near the Corvair, his first choice. However, the *full* rank order determines the actual position of the ideal point of each respondent.

Ideal-point fitting attempts to find a point in the original simple space (of stimuli only) so that a respondent's preference ranking—from most to

Figure 14-5   Illustration of joint space of ideal points and stimuli

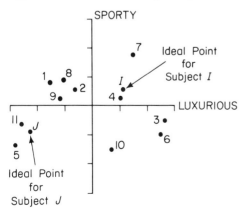

STIMULI—1968 CAR MODELS

1. Ford Mustang 6
2. Mercury Cougar V8
3. Lincoln Continental V8
4. Ford Thunderbird V8
5. Ford Falcon 6
6. Chrysler Imperial V8
7. Jaguar
8. AMC Javelin V8
9. Plymouth Barracuda V8
10. Buick Le Sabre V8
11. Chevrolet Corvair

least liked—is represented by an increasing distance of car models to ideal point, as preference decreases. Thus, car models near the ideal point are preferred to those farther away.

Figure 14-6 shows conceptually what an ideal point is. If we imagine a third dimension in Figure 14-5, representing a utility or value dimension, respondent *I* is assumed to have a most preferred combination of luxuriousness and sportiness at the ideal point. Utility declines monotonically (and symmetrically in all directions) as one moves farther from the point of maximum utility. This is represented by the dome-shaped surface.

J. D. Carroll has developed a procedure that fits ideal points via a type of nonmetric quadratic regression procedure.[9] Input data consist of the respondent's perceptual map (Figure 14-4) and the same respondent's preference ranking. If two or more respondents have more or less similar perceptions, one can fit a specific point for each in the same stimulus space, as illustrated in Figure 14-5.

Figure 14-6   Illustrative utility function leading to ideal point fitting

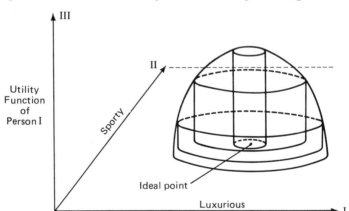

Vector Models

Some respondents, when asked to evaluate car models in terms of preferences, may feel that you can't get too much of either luxuriousness or sportiness. Conversely, for some other subjects, the plainer the car the better. In either case, the ideal point lies *outside the range of the stimuli* and, in principle, extends to infinity. Along each dimension, utility is assumed to

[9]J. D. Carroll, "Individual Differences and Multidimensional Scaling," in *Multidimensional Scaling: Theory and Application in the Behavioral Sciences*, ed. R. N. Shepard, A. K. Romney, and S. Nerlove, Vol. 1 (New York: Seminar Press, 1972).

increase without limit, depending upon direction. The cosine of the angle that the vector makes with the attribute dimensions represents the tradeoffs that the respondent makes among changes along the attribute dimensions.

Figure 14-7 illustrates this case for two other respondents, *L* and *M*, each of whom follows a vector model. In the case of respondent *L*, we note that his tradeoffs highly favor luxury versus sportiness. The Continental projects highest on his utility vector, while the Falcon projects lowest. In contrast, respondent *M* weights about equally changes in luxury and non-sportiness. In this case the plainer Imperial projects most highly on *M*'s vector, while the (less plain) Continental comes in second. Ford Mustang comes in last in preference. The dashed lines from the point denoting Con-

Figure 14-7   Illustration of joint space involving vector model

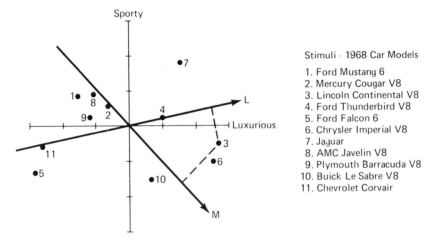

Stimuli - 1968 Car Models

1. Ford Mustang 6
2. Mercury Cougar V8
3. Lincoln Continental V8
4. Ford Thunderbird V8
5. Ford Falcon 6
6. Chrysler Imperial V8
7. Jaguar
8. AMC Javelin V8
9. Plymouth Barracuda V8
10. Buick Le Sabre V8
11. Chevrolet Corvair

tinental show that this model is most preferred for *L* but only second in preference for *M*.

Carroll's algorithm can fit vector models as well as ideal-point models (and still other preference models that allow *weighted* dimensions in the context of ideal points). Moreover, statistical tests are provided as a rough basis for deciding upon the type of model needed to portray a specific subject's data.

A wide variety of other MDS techniques are available for similar tasks, although even brief coverage would exceed our scope.[10] What can be said is

[10]R. M. Johnson, "Market Segmentation: A Strategic Tool," *Journal of Marketing Research*, 9 (February, 1971), 13–18, describes the application of multiple discriminant analysis to MDS. J. D. Carroll and J. J. Chang, "Analysis of Individual Differences in Multidimensional Scaling via an N-Way Generalization of Eckart–Young Decomposition," *Psychometrika*, 35 (1970), 283–319, describe a particularly powerful model, called INDSCAL, for portraying individual differences in perceptual mapping.

that the methodology of MDS, if anything, has outstripped its applications. Accordingly, we briefly discuss some recent applications and then turn to comments about areas for potential application of MDS.

MARKETING APPLICATIONS OF MDS

To date, most MDS studies have been of a pilot-type or diagnostic nature, used to help marketing managers get some feel for how their brand is positioned in the minds of consumers, vis-à-vis competing brands. Some capsule illustrations follow.

Soft Drink Slogans

A prominent producer of soft drinks wished to consider the adoption of a new slogan—one that would connote the distinct features of the brand. The firm's advertising department had prepared 15 candidate slogans and the problem was: which one to choose?

A study of consumers' perceptions of these slogans and their association with various brands of soft drinks was undertaken. The study indicated that 11 of the 15 slogans were perceived as more closely associated with the images of one or more competitive brands than the firm's own brand. Had no comparison of brand–slogan congruence been attempted, it is conceivable that a slogan might have been chosen that would be more closely associated with a competitor's brand than with the company's own brand.

Computer-Firm Images

A large producer of electronic computers was concerned with the relationship between the physical characteristics of its hardware and data processors' perceptions.[11] Computer models—the firm's and its competitors' —were first positioned geometrically in performance space (e.g., how long it would take the computer to perform a multiplication, size of core, etc.). Perceptual judgments of computer-model similarity were also obtained from the firm's sales personnel, its customers, and its noncustomers.

Of the three respondent groups, the sales personnel's perceptions agreed most closely with the objective (performance) positioning of the computer models. However, the firm's customers' perceptions of its computers disagreed with objective performance along a few of the key dimensions, suggesting that the salespeople were not emphasizing certain characteristics of the company's line that would enhance customer satisfaction. Perceptions of the firm's

---

[11]This application is discussed in more detail in Chapter 16.

noncustomers had relatively little correspondence with the true performance characteristics of its computers. Quite the contrary: noncustomers perceived the firm's computer line as more or less undifferentiated from those of other firms.

The firm's noncustomers, to a large extent, evoked criteria other than physical performance in evaluating competitive models. Noncustomers were chiefly concerned with the prominence of the computer firm, the size of its technical support staff, and the various marketing services it could offer. Not surprisingly, the firm's noncustomers tended to be less technically sophisticated data processors—ones who would be attracted to a large, well-established (albeit higher-priced) computer supplier.

High-Nutrition Cereals

A marketer of a high-nutrition brand of cereal was becoming increasingly concerned over the relevance of his advertising toward promoting a cereal that both tasted good and had high nutritional value. Discussions with advertising agency personnel led to a new campaign that humorously stressed qualities of "good tasting" and high nutrition. The firm's marketing personnel wondered if this new message was getting across to the consumer.

A study of housewife perceptions of the firm's brand vis-à-vis other cereals was undertaken. The study indicated that the advertising goals *were* being achieved: while perceived as a high nutrition cereal, the firm's brand plotted closer in "perceptual space" to good-tasting cereals than did any of the other high nutrition brands. That is, consumers *were* perceiving the hybrid advertising appeal in ways desired by the company. In this case perceptions were measured for the purpose of *monitoring the results* of a basic change in advertising appeal.

Magazine Positioning

A large publisher of medical magazines was interested in the positioning of one of his journals.[12] A sample of physician readers of his and other medical magazines were asked to rank each of ten popular magazines on a series of criteria, such as:

- Information useful for daily practice
- Best to read when in a hurry
- Greatest breadth of appeal

[12]This study (undertaken by P. E. Green) appears in Yoram Wind and P. J. Robinson, "Product Positioning: An Application of Multidimensional Scaling," in *Attitude Research in Transition*, ed. R. I. Haley (Chicago: American Marketing Association, 1972).

Figure 14-8   Joint-space configuration of medical journals and criterion vectors

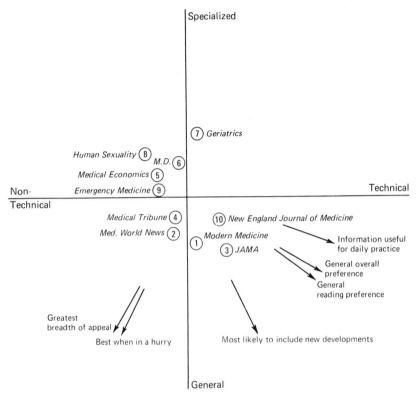

and so on. Figure 14-8 shows a joint-space map of the ten journals and the six vectors representing the criteria. As noted, the dimensions were labeled technical–nontechnical, and specialized–general. Contrary to expectations, the publisher found that his journal was evaluated as less technical and less general than originally believed. Along with corroborating information this finding led to changes in editorial content and advertising solicitations.

POTENTIAL APPLICATIONS

MDS methods have still to become a routinely applied tool in the marketing researcher's kit and much of their potential is yet to be realized. As illustrations of other applications, we can consider two areas: (1) market segmentation and (2) large-scale new-product development models.[13]

---

[13]Pilot studies of MDS in product-performance studies have also been made. As an example, see P. E. Green and F. J. Carmone, "The Performance Structure of the Computer Market: A Multivariate Approach," *The Economic and Business Bulletin*, 20 (Fall, 1968), 1–11.

Market Segmentation

One class of potential applications for MDS involves market segmentation. Suppose that one could characterize a product class and its buyers as points in a joint space whose dimensions are perceived product characteristics. Each brand could be represented as a stimulus point and each buyer as an ideal point in the same attribute space. Actually, however, this would be a "superspace" in the sense that different buyers could perceive the same stimuli differently as well as occupy different positions in the space that is perceived.

Conceptually, then, a market segment might be viewed as a subspace in which all members of the subspace perceive the stimuli similarly and occupy approximately the same ideal-point position. We could, logically, have the other three cases where (1) the stimuli are perceived differently but common ideal points exist,[14] (2) individuals exhibit similar perceptions but possess different ideal-point positions, and (3) neither stimulus perception nor ideal-point position is common over individuals. Further, we might be interested in the relationship of perception and/or ideal-point position to other characteristics of the buyer, such as the usual socioeconomic, personality, and demographic variables.

Partitioning the superspace of ideal points and stimuli into reasonably homogeneous subspaces—and identifying the characteristics of consumers who exhibit commonality of perception and preference—appears to be in the spirit of market-segmentation strategy. Perhaps such analysis would show "empty regions" where a high concentration of ideal points, but no "close" brands, are found. At the very least, the analysis should point out the competitive position of a firm's brand with other brands as viewed *perceptually* by different market segments, regardless of the brand's similarity with respect to physical and/or chemical characteristics.

From the manufacturer's point of view, the task is to modify his product, package, advertising, or whatever for the purposes of either (1) moving his brand toward some region in the space that has a high "concentration" of ideal points, or (2) attempting to move the ideal points themselves toward his brand. We might also conceive of the possibility of changing the relative importance of the dimensions or even the number of dimensions, as might be the case in truly "innovative" brands. Or the manufacturer might try to move consumers (through "identification-with-reference-group" advertising) from an unfavorable market segment to a favorable one. Inasmuch as other brands also appear in the attribute space, the problem of estimating share of choices must be contended with as well.

While this approach is still speculative, pilot-type applications have already been carried out. Such spatial configurations have even been traced

---

[14]This case is "inadmissible," since we assume here that the arguments of the preference function are the perceived dimensions.

through time—a perceptual and preference characterization analogous to a Nielsen-type audit of goods movement.

Allied with this approach is the potential use of MDS in intracorporate research. Do the advertising department, field sales, product development staff, and the firm's distributors have *congruent* images of the company's product or service? If so, do these perceptions agree with that of the ultimate buyer's? If not, what are the implications of such inconsistency for the effectiveness of interrelated policy decisions regarding pricing, advertising theme, product design, and distribution practice?

Large-Scale New-Product Models

Some of the earliest applications of MDS have been in new-product development.[15] Recently, several researchers have proposed large-scale, integrated procedures for new-product development and testing that are primarily based on MDS.[16] Although developed independently, the models are quite similar in several aspects:

1. Emphasis on developing perceptual maps by the use of consumer ratings on prespecified attribute scales.
2. The general assumption of homogeneity of perceptions across consumers.
3. Fitting of preference data into previously constructed perceptual maps via external (regression-type) methods involving ideal-point and/or vector representations of preferences.
4. Incorporation of some function for relating probability of choice to distance from ideal point.

In short, the models are designed to make *predictions* as to how new products positioned in the perceptual space will fare insofar as share of choices is concerned.

---

[15]D. H. Doehlert, "Similarity and Preference Mapping: A Color Example," in *Proceedings of the Denver Conference of the American Marketing Association*, ed. R. L. King (Chicago: American Marketing Association, 1968), p. 258; V. J. Stefflre, "Market Structure Studies: New Products for Old Markets and New Markets (Foreign) for Old Products," in *Application of the Sciences in Marketing*, ed. F. M. Bass, C. W. King, and E. A. Pessemier (New York: John Wiley & Sons, Inc., 1969), pp. 251–68; N. Morgan and J. M. Purnell, "Isolating Openings for New Products in a Multidimensional Space," *Journal of the Market Research Society*, 11 (July, 1969), 245–66.

[16]E. A. Pessemier and H. P. Root, "The Dimensions of New Product Planning," *Journal of Marketing*, 37 (January, 1973), 10–18; A. D. Shocker and V. Srinivasan, "A Consumer-Based Methodology for the Identification of New Product Ideas," *Management Science*, 20 (February, 1974), 921–37; G. L. Urban, "PERCEPTOR: A Model for Product Design" (working paper 689–73, Massachusetts Institute of Technology, December, 1973).

The jury is still out on whether the models will indeed make good on their promise. What is less controversial, however, is the fact that many researchers in marketing have long passed the curiosity stage regarding MDS and are experimenting with various ways in which it may be applied.[17]

Limitations and Future Prospects

MDS methods still suffer from a number of limitations. For example, in the case of nonmetric methods all the methods are subject to the possibility of local optima and "degenerate" solutions where the answer is meaningless, even though the goodness-of-fit criterion has been satisfied. Fortunately, researchers are starting to learn that the older (metric) methods often provide good (and inexpensively run) approximations to the nonmetric versions. Simulation studies on the robustness of metric MDS methods have indicated that they generally produce good approximations in all but highly unusual circumstances.[18]

The content side of MDS—dimension interpretation, relating physical changes in products to psychological changes in perceptual maps—poses by far the most difficult problems for future research. However, two trends appear in the offing.

First, methodologists are developing MDS models that provide more flexibility than a straight dimensional interpretation. For example, recent models have coupled the ideas of cluster analysis and MDS into hybrid models of categorical-dimensional structure. Second, conjoint analysis, to be discussed next, offers high promise for relating changes in the physical (or otherwise controlled) aspects of products to changes in their psychological imagery and evaluation.

FUNDAMENTALS OF CONJOINT ANALYSIS

Conjoint analysis, like MDS, is concerned with the measurement of psychological judgments, such as consumer preferences. However, one of the main distinctions between the two sets of methods is that in conjoint analysis the *stimuli are designed beforehand* according to some type of factorial structure.[19]

In conjoint analysis the objective is to decompose a set of overall responses to factorially designed stimuli so that the utility of each stimulus

---

[17]For a review of these developments, see P. E. Green, "Marketing Applications of MDS: Assessment and Outlook," *Journal of Marketing*, 39 (January, 1975), 24–31.

[18]P. E. Green, "On the Robustness of Multidimensional Scaling Techniques," *Journal of Marketing Research*, 12 (February, 1975), 73–81.

[19]Typically, conjoint analysis deals with preference (and other dominance-type) judgments rather than similarities. However, more recent research has extended the methodology to similarities judgments.

component can be inferred from the respondent's *overall evaluations* of the stimuli.

The solution technique involves a type of analysis of variance in which the respondent's overall preferences serve as a criterion variable and the predictor variables are represented by the various factorial levels making up each stimulus. (Equivalently, design variables can be viewed as a set of dummy-valued predictors in the context of multiple regression.) The major difference is that in (the nonmetric version of) conjoint analysis, the criterion variable is only *ordinally scaled.* A second difference is that in problems of realistic size the researcher often employs *fractional* (rather than full) factorials in conjoint analysis.

Two principal methods for collecting conjoint-analysis data are in use. We illustrate each of these procedures first and then turn to a discussion of how conjoint data are analyzed.

Two-Factor Evaluations

Perhaps the simplest way to obtain tradeoff information for conjoint analysis involves a *two-at-a-time* procedure, as illustrated in Figure 14-9. This exhibit is drawn from an actual mail questionnaire, used in a survey that was undertaken in the early 1970s, right after the first wave of major gasoline price increases.[20] In particular, interest centered on the relative importance of miles per gallon in the respondent's purchase of his next new car.

Six factors, each described at three "levels," were under study:

- Miles per gallon;
- Price;
- Maximum speed;
- Length;
- Roominess; and
- Country of manufacture.

As can be observed from the sample instructions, the respondent is asked to rank the nine combinations of price and warranty (the latter being used only for illustrative purposes) from most to least preferred. We note the (hypothetical) respondent's decision to pay $3,200 for the car, rather than give up a year of warranty. This implies that, for him, the utility decrease associated with a price change from $3,000 to $3,200 is less than the utility decrease associated with a change in warranty from three to two years.

---

[20]The study was conducted by Rogers National Research, Toledo, Ohio. The exhibit in Figure 14-9 is reproduced with their permission.

Figure 14-9   Two-factor-at-a-time evaluations

What is more important to you?	There are times when we have to give up one thing to get something else. And, since different people have different desires and priorities, the automotive industry wants to know what things are most important to you.	We have a scale that will make it possible for you to tell us your preference in certain circumstances — for example, gas mileage vs. speed. Please read the example below which explains how the scale works — and then	tell us the order of your preference by writing in the numbers from 1 to 9 for each of the six questions that follow the example.

| Example: Warranty vs. price of the car | Procedure: Simply write the number 1 in the combination that represents your first choice. In one of the remaining blank squares, write | the number 2 for your second choice. Then write the number 3 for your third choice, and so on, from 1 to 9. | |

Years of warranty

Price of Car	3	2	1
$3,000	1		
$3,200			
$3,400			

Years of warranty

Price of Car	3	2	1
$3,000	1		
$3,200	2		
$3,400			

Years of warranty

Price of Car	3	2	1
$3,000	1	3	
$3,200	2		
$3,400			

Years of warranty

Price of Car	3	2	1
$3,000 -	1	3	6
$3,200	2	5	8
$3,400	4	7	9

Step 1 (Explanation)

You would rather pay the least ($3,000) and get the most (3 years). Your first choice (1) is in the box as shown.

For each of the following questions, please write in the numbers from 1 to 9 to show your order of preference for your next new car.

Step 2

Your second choice is that you would rather pay $3,200 and have a 3-year warranty than pay $3,000 and get a 2-year warranty.

Step 3

Your third choice is that you would rather pay $3,000 and have a 2-year warranty than pay $3,400 and get a 3-year warranty.

Sample:

This shows a sample order of preference for all possible combinations. Of course, your preferences could be different.

Miles per gallon

Price of Car	22	18	14
$3,000			
$3,200			
$3,400			

Miles per gallon

Maximum speed	22	18	14
80 mph			
70 mph			
60 mph			

Miles per gallon

Length	22	18	14
12 feet			
14 feet			
16 feet			

Miles per gallon

Roominess	22	18	14
6 passenger			
5 passenger			
4 passenger			

Miles per gallon

Made in	22	18	14
Germany			
U.S.			
Japan			

Price of car

Made in	$3,000	$3,200	$3,400
Germany			
U.S.			
Japan			

If all pairs of tradeoffs are collected, the respondent must go through $6(5)/2 = 15$ such 3×3 tables. The problem, then, is to find a set of utility numbers—three numbers each for the six factors of Figure 14-9. These utility numbers are often called *part-worths*.

Having found the part-worths, we could then construct a *predicted* set of utilities for the 15 possible two-way tables, by adding the separate part-worths to find the total utility of any two-factor combination. The entries in each of the 15 prediction tables could then be ranked (1 to 9) so as to provide a counterpart set of tables. The objective is to find the separate utility numbers so that the correspondence between actual and predicted rankings is highest, when considered across all 15 pairs (actual versus predicted) of tables.

Multiple-Factor Evaluations

While the two-factor-at-a-time approach makes few cognitive demands on the respondent and is simple to follow, it is both time-consuming and tedious. Moreover, it is conducive to respondents' losing their place in the table or developing some stylized pattern, just to get the job done. Most importantly, however, the task is unrealistic; real alternatives do not present themselves for evaluation on a two-factor-at-a-time basis.

The *multiple-factor approach* is illustrated by the two sample cards of Figure 14-10. Eighteen cards, in all, are made up according to a special type of factorial design (to be discussed later). The respondent is then asked to group the 18 cards into three piles (with no need to place an equal number in each pile) that are described as:

- Definitely like
- Neither definitely like nor dislike
- Definitely dislike

Following this, the respondent takes the first pile and ranks the cards in it from most to least liked, and similarly so for the second and third piles. By means of this two-step procedure, the full set of 18 cards is eventually ranked from most liked to least liked.

Figure 14-10   Multiple-factor evaluations (sample profiles)

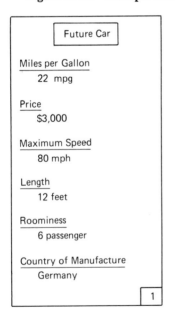
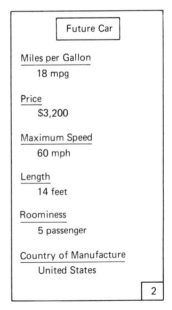

Again, the analytical objective is to find a set of part-worths for the separate factor levels so that, when these are appropriately added, one can find a total utility for each combination. The part-worths are chosen so as to produce the highest possible correspondence between the derived ranking and the original ranking of the 18 cards.

As may be surmised, the multiple-factor evaluative approach makes greater cognitive demands on the respondent since the full set of factors appears each time. In practice, if more than six or seven factors are involved, this approach is modified to handle specific *subsets* of interlinked factors across two or more evaluation tasks.

ANALYZING THE DATA

Since both the two-factor and multiple-factor approaches utilize similar computational procedures, let us illustrate the solution technique with the multiple-factor version. The reader should note the following features of this approach:

1. The respondent is presented with a set of stimulus profiles, constructed along factorial design principles.
2. The respondent ranks the stimuli according to some overall criterion, such as preference.
3. The problem is to find a set of part-worths for the factor levels such that the sum of each specific combination of part-worths equals the total utility of any given profile.
4. The goodness-of-fit criterion relates to how closely the derived ranking of stimulus profiles matches the original ranking.

The MONANOVA Program

The principal computational procedure of conjoint analysis involves what is known as *monotonic analysis of variance* (MONANOVA).

While we shall not delve into the mathematical details of the algorithm, we can sketch out their conceptual nature in terms of a sample problem. To illustrate, consider the 18 stimuli shown in Figure 14-11. Each of these stimuli involves a combination of five factors that could be used to describe a spot remover for upholstery and carpets.[21]

Eighteen cards are made up in which the information in each row of Figure 14-11 appears on a separate card. Using the two-step procedure just

[21] This example and the preceding car example are both drawn from P. E. Green and Yoram Wind, "New Way to Measure Consumers' Judgments," *Harvard Business Review*, 53 (July–August, 1975), 107–17.

Figure 14-11 Experimental design used in spot-remover product evaluation

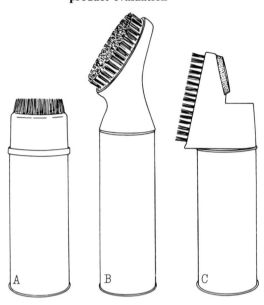

Stimulus Combinations

Card	Package design	Brand name	Price	Good Housekeeping seal?	Money-back guarantee?	Respondent's evaluation (rank number)
1	A	K2R	$1.19	No	No	13
2	A	Glory	1.39	No	Yes	11
3	A	Bissell	1.59	Yes	No	17
4	B	K2R	1.39	Yes	Yes	2
5	B	Glory	1.59	No	No	14
6	B	Bissell	1.19	No	No	3
7	C	K2R	1.59	No	Yes	12
8	C	Glory	1.19	Yes	No	7
9	C	Bissell	1.39	No	No	9
10	A	K2R	1.59	Yes	No	18
11	A	Glory	1.19	No	Yes	8
12	A	Bissell	1.39	No	No	15
13	B	K2R	1.19	No	No	4
14	B	Glory	1.39	Yes	No	6
15	B	Bissell	1.59	No	Yes	5
16	C	K2R	1.39	No	No	10
17	C	Glory	1.59	No	No	16
18	C	Bissell	1.19	Yes	Yes	1*

*Highest ranked

described, the respondent provides the rank order of preferences shown in the last column of the figure. Notice that a full factorial design would have entailed $3 \times 3 \times 3 \times 2 \times 2 = 108$ combinations; only 18 of these appear in Figure 14-11.

For analytical purposes each of the factorial combinations could be coded into a set of dummy variables. For example, package type could be coded

$$\text{package } A \Longrightarrow 10$$
$$\text{package } B \Longrightarrow 01$$
$$\text{package } C \Longrightarrow 00$$

Similarly, each of the other k-state factors could also be coded into $k - 1$ dummies per factor, yielding a full dummy-variable profile of $2 + 2 + 2 + 1 + 1 = 8$ predictor variables.

MONANOVA is a popular conjoint analysis program for analyzing data of this type.[22] Moreover, it does all of the above encoding automatically. MONANOVA then performs what is tantamount to an iterative set of dummy-variable regressions of the criterion variable (the respondent's set of 18 rank numbers) on the dummy predictors. Each successive analysis of variance, however, has its criterion values adjusted so as to retain the *original rank order*. The program then finds that set of parameter values (the part-worths) so that their appropriate sums correlate maximally with a monotonic function of the original ranks (also found by the program). Since each successive analysis of variance maintains the original rank order constraints, the procedure is called *monotonic* analysis of variance.

Results of the Analysis

Figure 14-12 shows the MONANOVA results for the rank-order data of Table 14-11.[23] Each of the five charts denotes one set of part-worths. These functions can be used to obtain a total utility for each of the 18 combinations in Figure 14-11. For example, to find the utility for the first combination in Figure 14-11, we can read off the part-worths of each factor level in the five charts of Figure 14-12 that correspond to the factor levels of the first combination:

$$U(A) = 0.1, \qquad U(\text{No}) = 0.2$$
$$U(\text{K2R}) = 0.3, \qquad U(\text{No}) = 0.2$$
$$U(\$1.19) = 1.0$$

[22]J. B. Kruskal, "Analysis of Factorial Experiments by Estimating Monotone Transformations of the Data," *Journal of the Royal Statistical Society*, Ser. B, 27 (1965), 251–63.
[23]The program's fit measure (called *stress*) indicated an essentially perfect fit of model to data.

The total of these part-worths is 1.8, the utility for the first combination.[24]

On the other hand, the utility of combination 18 is $0.6 + 0.5 + 1.0 + 0.3 + 0.7 = 3.1$, which is the respondent's *highest* evaluation of all 18 combinations listed. However, as can be easily seen from Figure 14-12, if combination 18 is modified to include package design B (in place of C), its utility is even higher. As a matter of fact, it then represents the highest possible utility, even though this specific combination *did not appear among the original 18*.

What can be done for the 18 test stimuli can also be carried out for the 90 combinations that were *not* used in the experimental design. That is, the part-worths of Figure 14-12 can be used to construct predicted utilities for all of the remaining 90 profiles. As such, the model is truly a predictive one.

**Figure 14-12   Results of MONANOVA
(analysis of Figure 14-11 data)**

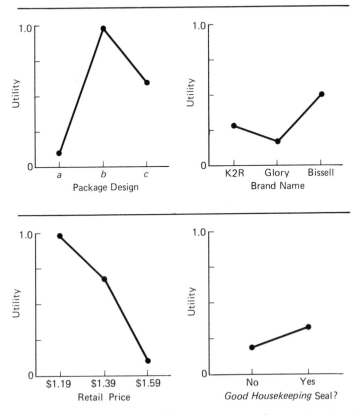

[24]The scale unit in MONANOVA is arbitrary; moreover, each separate part-worth scale has an arbitrary origin. The important point is that all of the separate (interval) scales are measured in terms of a *common* unit. This condition is required in order to be able to meaningfully sum the various part-worths to obtain a total stimulus utility.

Figure 14-12 (continued)

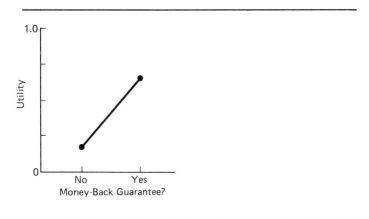

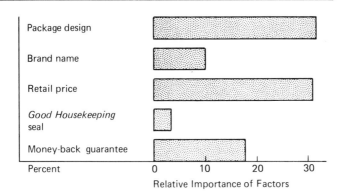

Relative Importance of Factors

Computing Factor Importances

The main analysis also yields a useful by-product, namely, the *relative importance* of each of the five factors. Perhaps the simplest way to measure relative importance in this context is to find the five utility ranges from Figure 14-12:

Highest — Lowest

- Package design $\qquad$ $1.0 - 0.1 = 0.9$
- Brand name $\qquad$ $0.5 - 0.2 = 0.3$
- Price $\qquad$ $1.0 - 0.1 = 0.9$
- *Good Housekeeping* seal $\quad$ $0.3 - 0.2 = 0.1$
- Money-back guarantee $\quad$ $0.7 - 0.2 = \underline{0.5}$

Total $\qquad$ $\overline{2.7}$

For example, the highest utility in the case of package designs is $U(B) = 1.0$, while the lowest is $U(A) = 0.1$; therefore, the range is 0.9.

As shown in the lower portion of Figure 14-12, a simple bar chart can be constructed to show the *relative* sizes of the utility ranges. Hence, we note that package design and price each represent about a third of the total utility range of 2.7 utility units.

It should be remembered, of course, that relative importance will depend upon the experimental design to begin with. For example, had the original levels of price ranged from $1.19 to $1.79, this factor could have turned out to have been "more important" than package design. This dependence of utility on factor levels underscores the need to choose realistic ranges for each of the factors under study.

Reliability and Validity Checks

In carrying out a conjoint analysis it is useful to include the following ancillary analyses: (1) test–retest reliability, (2) a comparison of actual utilities with those of random respondents, and (3) an internal validity check on model-based utilities.

The test–retest reliability can be conducted by including a few replicate judgments (drawn from the original set of 18) at a later stage in the interview. The purpose here is to see if the judgments are highly enough correlated, on a test–retest basis, to justify the analysis of his data.

Random-respondent utilities are obtained by running a sample of pseudo-subjects through MONANOVA. The pseudo-subjects' input data consist of random rank orders. As the sample size increases we would expect, on average, *equal utilities* within each set of factor levels. However, any specific pseudo-subject would depart from this expected value through sampling variability alone. By analyzing a sample of 100 or so pseudo-subjects, the researcher can develop a crude type of confidence interval around each set of averaged part-worths with which to compare real respondents' results.

The internal-validity check can be carried out by collecting a few new evaluations (drawn randomly from the 90 stimulus combinations not utilized in Figure 14-11). These constitute a hold-out sample. Their rank order is to be predicted by the part-worths developed from the calibration sample of 18 combinations.

OTHER ASPECTS OF CONJOINT ANALYSIS

The theoretical development of conjoint analysis in the behavioral sciences is of very recent origin.[25] Its application to marketing is only a few years old.[26]

[25]R. D. Luce and J. W. Tukey, "Simultaneous Conjoint Measurement: A New Type of Fundamental Measurement," *Journal of Mathematical Psychology*, 1 (February, 1964), 1–27.

[26]P. E. Green and V. R. Rao, "Conjoint Measurement for Quantifying Judgmental Data," *Journal of Marketing Research*, 8 (August, 1971), 355–63.

Even so, interest in the topic has grown rather dramatically. Some marketing research firms have developed considerable expertise in the field.[27] Commercial applications of conjoint analysis have entailed additional features of interest, some of which are briefly covered here.

Experimental Design

As mentioned earlier, if multiple-factor evaluations are used, highly fractionated factorial designs are pretty much a necessity if the researcher wishes to keep the stimulus set down to some reasonable number. *Orthogonal arrays* represent a special type of fractional factorial design that allows orthogonal estimation of all main effects (the type of model assumed in additive utility formulations) with the smallest possible number of combinations.

Orthogonal arrays are available for virtually any number of factors and levels within factor that the marketing researcher might need. As long as two-factor and higher-order interactions can be assumed to be negligible, orthogonal arrays represent the most efficient class of fractional factorial design that is available. Introduction to orthogonal arrays, and to other useful designs in the context of conjoint analysis, can be found elsewhere.[28]

Use of Visual Aids

Another problem in the application of conjoint measurement is the pragmatic one of getting across to the respondent what may be fairly complex concepts. Verbal descriptions of the type covered in Figure 14-9 are not only difficult for the respondent to assimilate but permit unwanted perceptual differences to intrude. For example, two respondents may have quite different perceptions of the car-length and car-roominess verbalizations.

Wherever possible, *visual props* can help in transmitting complex information more easily and uniformly than verbal description. (The sketches of the three package designs in Figure 14-11 represent a case in point.) As an illustration of the value of visual props, mention can be made of a recent study involving styling designs for future compact cars. In the course of preparing the questionnaire, rather complex experimental factors such as:

- Overall size and interior layout
- Trunk size and fuel-tank capacity
- Exterior/interior width
- Interior spaciousness/visibility

[27]R. M. Johnson, "Tradeoff Analysis of Consumer Values," *Journal of Marketing Research*, 11 (May, 1974), 121–27.

[28]P. E. Green, "On the Design of Choice Experiments Involving Multifactor Alternatives," *Journal of Consumer Research*, 1 (September, 1974), 61–68.

had to be considered. To provide quick and uniform treatment of these style factors, visual props were prepared, as illustrated for two of the factors in Figure 14-13. (These can be projected on screens in full view of the respondents during the interview or made part of the questionnaire itself.)

Visual props work particularly well for the multiple-factor approach,

Figure 14-13   Illustrations of visual props used in conjoint analysis

OVERALL SIZE/INTERIOR LAYOUT

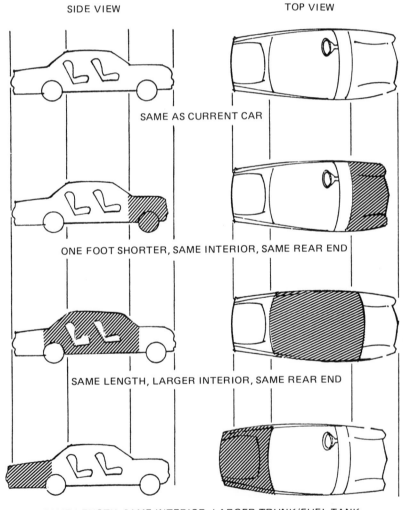

SIDE VIEW   TOP VIEW

SAME AS CURRENT CAR

ONE FOOT SHORTER, SAME INTERIOR, SAME REAR END

SAME LENGTH, LARGER INTERIOR, SAME REAR END

SAME LENGTH, SAME INTERIOR, LARGER TRUNK/FUEL TANK

Figure 14-13 (continued)

EXTERIOR/INTERIOR WIDTH

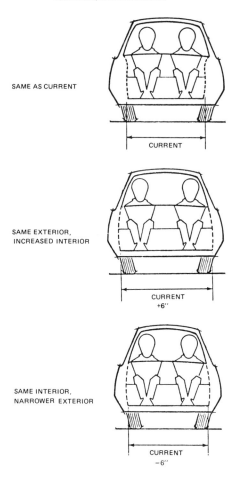

since a relatively large amount of information can be communicated realistically and quickly by this means.

Other Models

So far our discussion has centered on the most widely applied conjoint model—an ordinal-criterion main-effects model. Other models, dealing with different types of data collection, criterion variables, or composition rules, are available.

For example, cases can arise in which the respondent is asked to rate each stimulus on, say, a 9-point scale of desirability. Alternatively, the respondent may compare each stimulus, in turn, to a standard one and indicate whether the test stimulus is liked better (or worse) than the standard. Following this, the respondent is asked to indicate his *intensity* of, say, liking, on a 4-point scale: like very much more, like much more, like somewhat more, like slightly more.

In either case, if the researcher wishes to treat the responses as *interval-scaled*, the conjoint analysis model turns into an ordinary analysis of variance application. At the other extreme the respondent may simply be asked to group the stimuli into a set of unordered classes: the product is appropriate for adult men, appropriate for adult women, appropriate for teenagers, and so on. In this case a special type of conjoint analysis, categorical conjoint measurement, can be called upon.[29]

Composition models that permit some or all two-factor interactions to be measured (as well as all main effects) have also been developed. These models again make use of various types of fractional factorial designs; specialized computer programs have been designed to implement them.[30] In short, the user of conjoint analysis currently has a highly flexible set of models and data collection procedures at his disposal.

Strategic Aspects

The output of conjoint analysis is frequently employed in additional analyses. Since most studies collect full sets of data at the individual respondent level, *individual utility functions and importance weights* can be computed. This fosters two additional types of analyses: (1) market segmentation and (2) strategic simulation of new factor-level combinations. Frequently, both kinds of analyses are carried out in the same study.

In segmentation studies, the respondents are usually clustered in terms of either their commonality of utility functions or their commonality of importance weights. Having formed the segments in one of these ways, the analyst can then determine how the segments differ with regard to other background data—product-class usage, brand-selection behavior, demographics, and so on.

Strategic simulations are also relatively easy to construct from conjoint-analysis data by the simple device of including each individual respondent's utility function in a computerized choice model. Various combinations of factor levels can then be tried out to see what their share of choices would be under different assumptions regarding competitive offerings and total-market demand.

[29] J. D. Carroll, "Categorical Conjoint Measurement," in *Multiattribute Decisions in Marketing*, P. E. Green and Yoram Wind (Hinsdale, Ill.: Dryden Press, 1973), pp. 339–48.

[30] P. E. Green, J. D. Carroll, and F. J. Carmone, "A Stagewise Approach to Estimating Interactions in Conjoint Analysis" (working paper, University of Pennsylvania, June 1976),

The simulators can employ a variety of consumer-choice procedures, ranging from having each consumer simply select the alternative with the highest utility to more elaborate probability-of-choice rules where probability is related to utility differences in the set of alternatives under evaluation.

APPLICATIONS OF CONJOINT ANALYSIS

Despite its recent development, conjoint analysis has already been applied to a wide variety of problems in product design, price elasticity of demand, transportation service design, and the like. Table 14-2 shows a representative list of applications. As can be noted, areas of application cover the gamut—products and services, consumer, industrial, and institutional markets.

Perhaps the applications areas most conducive to conjoint analysis are those in which the product or service involves a relatively high resource

Table 14-2　Sample list of conjoint measurement applications

Consumer nondurables	*Other products*
1. Bar soaps	1. Automotive styling
2. Hair shampoos	2. Automobile and truck tires
3. Carpet cleaners	3. Car batteries
4. Synthetic-fiber garments	4. Ethical drugs
5. Gasoline pricing	5. Toaster/ovens
6. Panty hose	6. Cameras
7. Lawn chemicals	7. Apartment design
Financial services	*Other services*
1. Branch bank services	1. Car rental agencies
2. Auto insurance policies	2. Telephone services and pricing
3. Health insurance policies	3. Employment agencies
4. Credit card features	4. Information-retrieval services
5. Consumer discount cards	5. Medical laboratories
Industrial goods	*Transportation*
1. Copying machines	1. Domestic airlines
2. Printing equipment	2. Transcontinental airlines
3. Facsimile transmission	3. Passenger train operations
4. Data transmission	4. Freight train operations
5. Portable computer terminals	5. International Air Transportation Association

commitment and tends to be "analyzable" by the purchaser (e.g., banking or insurance services, industrial products). Some idea of the range of possibilities may be gained from the capsule applications that follow.

Designing Bar Soaps

In one recent study researchers related the psychological imagery of physical characteristics of actual bars of soap to end-use appropriateness; this study was conducted for the laboratory and marketing personnel of a diversified soap manufacturer.

Although the designing of a bar of soap—by varying weight, size, shape, color, fragrance type and intensity, surface feel, and so on—may seem like a mundane exercise, the fact remains that a cleverly positioned bar soap (for example, Irish Spring) can rapidly become a multimillion-dollar enterprise. Still, the extent of knowledge about the importance of such imagery is woefully meager.

The researchers formulated actual bars of soap in which color, type of fragrance, and intensity of fragrance were constructed according to a factorial design. All the other characteristics of the soap were held constant.

Respondents examined the soaps and assigned each bar to the end use that they felt best matched its characteristics: moisturizing facial soap, deep-cleaning soap for oily skin, woman's deodorant soap, or man's deodorant soap. The data were then analyzed by conjoint analysis, leading to a set of psychophysical functions for each of the characteristics.

The study showed that type of fragrance was the most important physical variable contributing to end-use appropriateness. Rather surprisingly, the type of fragrance (medicinal) and color (blue) that appeared best suited for a man's deodorant soap were also found to be best for the deep-cleaning soap, even though deep-cleaning soap had been previously classed for marketing purposes as a facial soap in which floral fragrances predominated. On the other hand, fragrance intensity played a relatively minor role as a consumer cue for distinguishing among different end uses.

In brief, this study illustrated the feasibility of translating changes in various physical variables into changes in psychological variables. Eventually, more detailed knowledge of these psychological transformations could enable a laboratory technician to *synthesize color, fragrance, shape, and so forth to obtain soaps that conjure up almost any desired imagery.* Moreover, in such other product classes as beers, coffees, and soft drinks it appears possible to develop a psychophysics of taste in which such elusive verbal descriptions as "full-bodied" and "robust" are given operational meaning in terms of variations in physical or chemical characteristics.

New Concept Descriptions

In many product classes, such as automobiles, houses, office machines, and computers, the possible design factors are myriad and expensive to vary physically for evaluation by the buying public. In cases such as these, the researcher usually resorts to verbalized descriptions of the principal factors of interest.

In the Rogers study (see Figure 14-9) it was found that consumer evaluations of attributes were highly associated with the type of car currently owned and the type of car desired in the future. Not surprisingly, gas mileage and country of manufacture were highly important factors in respondent evaluations of car profiles. Somewhat surprising, however, was the fact that even large-car owners (and those contemplating the purchase of a large car) were more concerned with gas economy than owners of that type of car had been historically. Thus, while they fully expected to get fewer miles per gallon than they would in compact cars, they felt quite strongly that the car should be economical compared to others in its size class.

Airline Services

One of the most interesting application areas for conjoint analysis is in the transportation industry, particularly airlines and other forms of passenger travel, where the service aspect is important to consumer choice.

As a case in point, a large-scale study of consumer evaluations of airline services was conducted in which consumer utilities were developed for some 25 different service factors such as on-ground services, in-flight services, decor of cabins and seats, scheduling, routing, and price. Moreover, each utility function was developed on a route (city-pair) and purpose-of-trip basis.

As might be expected, the utility function for each of the various types of airline service differed according to the length and purpose of the flight. However, in addition to obtaining consumers' evaluations of service profiles, the researchers also obtained information concerning their *perceptions* of each airline (that is, for the ones that they were familiar with) on each of the service factors for which the consumers were given a choice.

These two major pieces of information provided the principal basis for developing a simulation of airline services over all major traffic routes. The purpose of the simulation was to estimate the effect on share of choices that a change in the service configuration of the sponsor's services would have, route by route, if competitors did not follow suit. Later, the sponsor used the simulator to examine the effect of assumed retaliatory actions by its competitors. A procedure was also designed to update the model's parameters periodically by the collection of new field data.

Each new service configuration was evaluated against a base-period configuration. In addition, the simulator showed which competing airlines would lose business and which ones would gain business under various changes in perceived service levels. Thus, in addition to single, ad hoc studies, conjoint measurement can be used in the ongoing monitoring (via simulation) of consumer imagery and evaluations over time.

Future Developments

Conjoint analysis, like MDS, has a number of limitations. For example, the approach assumes that the important attributes of a product or service can all be identified and that consumers behave as though tradeoffs are being considered. In some products, where imagery is quite important, consumers may not evaluate a product analytically, or, even if they do, the tradeoff model may be only a gross approximation to the actual decision rules that are employed.

Studies are needed on such questions as how many different factors can be allowed to vary in the multiple-factor data collection procedure and how this number depends on the way in which the information is communicated. Other studies are needed on the statistical robustness of the nonmetric models to errorful data as well as studies of how closely metric (ANOVA) models can approximate the more expensive nonmetric models.

In short, conjoint analysis is still maturing and much remains to be done. In this regard it is of interest to point out that a new approach to market segmentation, called *componential segmentation*, has been developed. Interestingly enough, conjoint analysis plays a central role in this approach. The model develops *consumer parameters* (utility saliences) as well as product utilities from quite small, but efficiently designed, stratified samples.[31]

SUMMARY

This chapter has been devoted to two multivariate techniques that are special-purpose in nature: (1) MDS and (2) conjoint analysis. Both methods deal with the measurement of human judgments and both are capable of handling data that are only of rank-order quality.

MDS methods are designed for portraying subjective similarities or preferences as points (or vectors) in some multidimensional space. Psycholog-

[31]For a description of componential segmentation, see P. E. Green, J. D. Carroll, and F. J. Carmone, "Design Considerations in Attitude Measurement," in *Attitude Research Moves Ahead*, ed. Yoram Wind and M. G. Greenberg, (Chicago: American Marketing Association, 1977).

ical distance is given a physical distance representation. In this part of the chapter we discussed metric and nonmetric MDS methods and ideal-point and vector preference models. A variety of applications were described to give the reader some idea of the scope of the methodology.

Conjoint analysis was described along similar lines. We first discussed the primary ways of collecting tradeoff data and then showed how such data are analyzed via a kind of monotonic analysis of variance. The importance of fractional factorial designs was discussed, as well as other practical problems in the implementation of conjoint analysis.

We next turned to some illustrative applications of conjoint analysis, including the design of new products and services. The chapter concluded with a brief description of future developments that could serve to increase the flexibility of the methodology.

ASSIGNMENT MATERIAL

1. The following half matrix of dissimilarities was developed for eight of the shampoo benefits described in Chapter 8:

	BENEFIT							
BENEFIT	*1*	*2*	*3*	*4*	*5*	*6*	*7*	*8*
1. Body	0.0	5.54	6.64	6.32	5.71	6.61	7.29	8.45
2. Fullness		0.0	5.70	4.86	4.80	6.13	6.26	6.03
3. Holds Set			0.0	6.12	6.83	5.65	8.31	8.19
4. Bouncy				0.0	5.80	7.25	5.06	5.90
5. Not Limp					0.0	6.93	6.35	7.41
6. Manageable						0.0	8.21	7.17
7. Zesty							0.0	6.87
8. Natural								0.0

a. What can you say about the association among benefits from examining the table of dissimilarities?
b. Enter the above dissimilarities data in a MDS program and compute solutions in three, two, and one dimensions. How does goodness-of-fit behave with respect to dimensionality?
c. Obtain dissimilarities regarding the above eight benefits from class members and repeat the analysis. How do the results compare?

2. Collect similarities data from class members regarding a stimulus set of your choice—for example, desserts, political candidates, toothpaste brands, automobiles, and so on.
   a. Using an MDS program of your choice, scale the group data.
   b. Randomly divide your sample of respondents in half and scale the two subgroups' data separately. How do these subgroup scalings compare with the total group?
   c. Cluster-analyze the respondents by treating the similarities as profile data. Then separately scale the cluster averages. How do your configurations compare across clusters?

3. Describe three problems in marketing research (not mentioned in the chapter) that you feel might be amenable to MDS.

4. What types of consumer products do you think would *not* be amenable to conjoint analysis?

5. Suppose that you were asked to develop a set of factors for a prospective conjoint analysis of general credit cards. What factors (and levels within factor) can you suggest?

Selected
Activities
in Marketing Research

V

Forecasting Procedures in Marketing Research 15

INTRODUCTION

As we have stressed throughout this book, the most pervasive characteristic of decision making is that it must take place under imperfect knowledge of the future; every decision is based on a forecast, whether or not formal techniques are used. The purpose of this chapter is to discuss the more formal nature of forecasting and its relationship to decision making under uncertainty. In doing so, we shall describe the classes of forecasting problems with which the market researcher must cope, the techniques that are available to assist him in this effort, and the evaluation of alternative forecasting techniques in terms of their value versus cost.

We first discuss the place of forecasting in decision making, what to forecast, and the role that marketing research plays in the gathering of information about the likelihood of alternative future events.

We then describe some of the more formal techniques of forecasting market potential, sales and costs. The techniques discussed include persistence models, barometric forecasting, time-series decomposition, exponential smoothing, correlation models, econometric models, and polling. Although it is not our intent to provide a complete cataloging of available procedures, the reader should get from the discussion some flavor of the variety of techniques that are available for forecasting purposes.

We conclude the chapter with a discussion of the cost versus value of alternative forecasting procedures. We shall show that the solution to many business problems is not highly sensitive to forecast errors and, hence, that the value of the effort required to achieve greater forecast accuracy may not be justified by its cost.

THE NATURE OF FORECASTING

Why Forecasts Are Made

Any purposive activity in which there are uncertainties associated with future outcomes involves forecasting. The designation of one problem as being "more important" than another or the choice of one alternative as being "better" than another implies that forecasts have been made. The question is not *whether* we are to forecast but rather *what* we should forecast and *how* we are to do it.

There are two major reasons why forecasts are necessary:

1. Forecasts are made to help *identify* problems.
2. Forecasts are made to help *solve* problems.

The responsibility for forecasting sales for the firm typically rests with the marketing department. The purpose of the forecasts is often one of problem identification. Sales forecasts are usually made for each product and product line as well as for total company sales. They are frequently broken down by geographic area and type of customer as well. A sales forecast of this type is a form of performance measurement. It serves to identify products and/or sales areas that will not be performing at the level expected unless corrective steps are taken.

Sales forecasts are also used in setting performance standards. A forecast is implicit in any overall sales target or quota for a salesperson or a territory. Sales performance standards are usually established on the basis of a formal sales forecast. If later measurements indicate that the desired performance level has not been maintained, a problem is identified.

Forecasts are also made to help solve problems. The evaluation of alternative courses of action proposed as potential solutions to a problem always requires forecasts. Such evaluations usually involve forecasts of financial outlays as well as of sales. Should a new product be added to a product line that is not performing as well as it should? If it were added, what profit and discounted cash flow increments could be expected?

The Assumption of Stability

It is clear that any attempt to forecast the future assumes that past information is relevant and that the phenomenon under study possesses some regularity over space and time. By *stability*, however, is *not* meant that the phenomenon is necessarily constant through time or space, but only that the *rules* (or super-rules) for making the appropriate transformation are stable.

What to Forecast?

As was indicated earlier, one of the usual responsibilities of the marketing research department is to provide the factual data for the setting of marketing-related performance standards. Some of the more widely used standards in marketing include the following:

- *Profit* as a percentage of overall company sales, by product line, by product, by geographic area, by distribution channel, and by type of customer.
- *Sales and/or market share targets* for the company as a whole, by product line, by product, by distribution channel, by type of customer, and by individual customer.
- *Sales quotas* by geographic territory and by salesperson.
- *Budgets* by type of marketing effort, by product line, and by geographic area.

It is also the responsibility of the marketing research department to analyze and to make recommendations concerning prospective changes in the marketing-mix configuration, such as potential new products, changes in promotional budgets and/or media, increases or decreases in prices, and changes in the distribution system.

A unifying concept by which the courses of actions of a profit-seeking firm can be evaluated is the cash-flow model (discussed in Chapter 2). This model requires that both revenues and financial outlays be forecasted over time. As such, consideration must be given to alternative uses of funds and the determinants of revenue and outlay flows.

Uncertainty in Forecasts

Decision makers may view the future in a variety of ways, depending upon how sensitive the decision is to the unknown events of interest and how willing the manager is to "absorb uncertainty." For example, if a particular action is assumed to be superior to all other possible actions, irrespective of the course of future events, no forecast of these events is required. In other instances the consequences of a wrong decision may be quite sensitive to the unknown event(s) of interest and, hence, may justify the effort spent on reducing the manager's uncertainty. We can enumerate some of the major ways in which managers may treat uncertainty and their implications for marketing research activity.

At one extreme the manager may wish to view the future in *certainty-equivalent* terms. That is, he may be willing to assume only one possible outcome associated with a particular course of action, or, in somewhat more subtle terms, he may be willing to replace a whole distribution of possible events by a single number (e.g., the mean of the distribution). If he desires to act in this fashion, he might request only a single estimate from the marketing researcher. Probably all practicing marketing researchers have been exposed to the phrase "Don't confuse me with ranges and probability numbers; all I want is your best single guess of what sales volume will be next year." This would be loosely akin to a "point" estimate.

In other cases the manager may wish to have the forecast expressed in terms of a *range of possibilities* with some statement about the likelihood that the "true" value will fall somewhere within the range. In still other cases the manager may only desire an expression of the chances that some outcome, say sales volume, will exceed a specified level.

In terms of the Bayesian approach outlined in earlier chapters, both of the above illustrations can be viewed as special cases of treating the class of unknown events in terms of a probability distribution. This distribution may be based on "relative frequency" notions or may reflect a more personalistic interpretation of the problem. The point to remember, however, is that *all* forecasts of future events are, in a sense, "acts of faith" that perceived past regularities will persist into the future. Creativity in model building often is displayed in the *level* of rules (or super-rules) at which stability is assumed. The comment "our business is changing too fast to model it" is rather naive. The challenge is to *upscale the level of abstraction* at which stability must necessarily be assumed.

Fortunately, many decisions do not require high accuracy in the prediction of future events or long time horizons over which events must be predicted. We have already seen in earlier chapters that the costs of wrong decisions may not be highly sensitive to changes in the unknown values of the parameters affecting the outcome. We have also seen that the process of sequential commitment frequently allows the decision maker more or less to "feel his way" by choosing courses of action that can be modified in the light of additional information. We shall amplify these remarks in later sections.

APPROACHES TO FORECASTING SALES

Two general approaches are available for forecasting sales of a firm. The first is a *derived forecast* that is made by first estimating market potential and then applying a forecasted market share for the firm. The result is a forecast of company sales for the period involved. The second approach is to forecast company sales directly without becoming involved in estimating market potential. This is known as a *direct forecast* of sales.

The term *market potential* has two different and commonly used meanings. It is sometimes understood to mean the amount of a product service that *could* be absorbed by the market during a specified period under *optimum* conditions of market development. It is also frequently used to mean the estimated amount of a product or service that *will* be absorbed by the market during a specified period.

The first of these definitions is the appropriate one to use in market planning. If a product is viewed as having considerably more potential than is currently being realized, an opportunity exists. With the proper changes in the marketing mix, sales may be increased.

The second usage of the term is synonymous with an industry sales forecast. That is, in forecasting the amount of a product or service that *will* be absorbed by the market in a specified period of time one is making a forecast of industry sales.

Our later discussion of sales forecasting techniques applies both to industry and to individual firm sales forecasts. It should be understood, therefore, that the terms "market potential" and "industry sales forecast" will have the same meaning unless otherwise specified. The term "sales forecast" will be understood to apply to the forecast for an individual firm.

Standard Industrial Classification

One of the primary tools used in market-potential estimation, and therefore commonly used in derived forecasting methods, is the *Standard Industrial Classification (SIC) system*.[1] The SIC system is particularly well suited to determining market potential for industrial products. It represents a uniform numerical coding procedure for classifying U.S. establishments by type of activity. For industrial marketers the system is highly useful for relating company activities to data produced by the federal and state governments, trade associations, publishing firms, and the like.

The SIC system divides U.S. firms into nine key divisions: (1) agriculture; (2) mining; (3) contract construction; (4) manufacturing; (5) transportation, communications, electric, gas, and sanitary services; (6) wholesale and retail trade; (7) finance, insurance, and real estate; (8) services; and (9) government. These divisions, in turn, are divided into major groups (two-digit codes), groups (three-digit codes), industries (four-digit codes), and so on, in a hierarchical fashion, to six-digit codes in some cases.

Figure 15-1 shows an illustration in the area of metalworking. As can be noted, the classification proceeds from major groups to groups to industries. The reporting of data by SIC code provides the industrial marketer with uniform statistics for estimating market potential and related tasks. Moreover, several business publications, such as *Iron Age*, regularly publish statistics utilizing the same codes. A number of market-survey firms, such as

---

[1]Standard Industrial Classification Manual (Washington, D.C.: Government Printing Office, 1967).

Figure 15-1   How SIC classifies metalworking

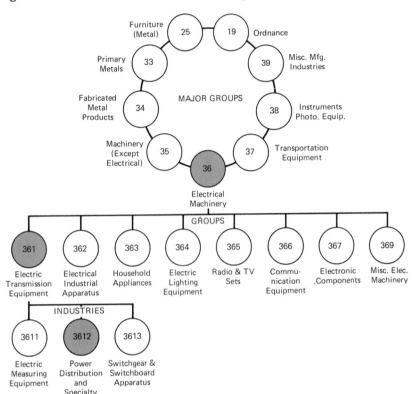

Source: From P. J. Robinson, C. L. Hinkle, and Edward Bloom, "Standard Industrial Classification for Effective Marketing Analysis," p. 21, Marketing Science Institute, November, 1967, by permission.

the Chilton Company, Philadelphia, and Dun and Bradstreet, New York, provide plant lists, coded by SIC, that can be used in preparing mail questionnaires. Moreover, *County Business Patterns*, published annually by the U.S. Department of Commerce, contains statistics at the county level for use in preparing market-potential figures by sales territory.

The SIC classification is also quite useful in conjunction with input–output tables, a topic discussed later in the chapter. In brief, the SIC codes (and accompanying statistics) are useful for a variety of market-potential estimation and forecasting tasks, including the measurement of market share, development of sales prospect lists, planning sales calls, and the like. The interested reader is referred to the Robinson, Hinkle, and Bloom publication.[2]

FORECASTING TECHNIQUES

The marketing researcher is concerned with forecasts of both sales and costs. We will accordingly be concerned with the forecasting of both. The techniques used in forecasting market potential, sales, and costs share a common classification. The forecasting techniques used in forecasting these variables for existing products are those of *extrapolation, correlation, econometric models,* and *polling.*

1. *Extrapolation techniques.* These procedures utilize past changes in only the *variable of interest* as a basis for future projection of that variable; as such, the only "independent" variable is time. Illustrations of extrapolation techniques are various types of naive models, time-series decomposition, and exponential smoothing.

2. *Correlation techniques.* These procedures utilize past relationships between the variable to be forecasted and *other* variables (e.g., disposable income, customer inventory levels) that are thought to be related to the variable being forecasted. The forecast problem thus involves two major tasks: (a) quantifying the past relationship between the dependent variable and the predictor variables, and (b) forecasting values of the predictor variables as a necessary step before making a forecast of the dependent variable. In lead-lag models, the forecaster may be able to identify a fairly long and stable leading series early enough to forecast the lagged variable (without first forecasting the leading variable). If so, uncertainty still surrounds the stability of the functional relationship that links the two variables together.

3. *Econometric techniques.* These procedures are usually expressed as being "less empirical" than correlative models in the sense that they are based upon some *underlying theory* about the relationships that exist among a set of economic variables. A set of equations may be stated that reflects how the phenomena should be interrelated (if the theory holds), and parameters of the models are estimated by statistical analysis of past data.

4. *Polling techniques.* Although all forecasting involves judgment, polling techniques are probably the least "formal" of the procedures enumerated above. As the name suggests, salespeople and executives

[2]See P. J. Robinson, C. L. Hinkle, and Edward Bloom, "Standard Industrial Classification for Effective Marketing Analysis," Marketing Science Institute, November, 1967.

may be polled with regard to the sales outlook and executives may be polled with respect to profit in the case of a new venture. These opinions may be "averaged" or combined in some manner as to reflect the opinions of company personnel closest to the market situation. Although this procedure is looked upon as less "scientific" than other techniques, it might more fairly be called *less explicit* in the sense that the process by which people make judgments from a variety of source data and experience is not understood. These procedures, however, may lead to fairly accurate forecasts and can serve as an independent check on the reasonableness of forecasts derived from more explicit models.

Since new products have no sales history, extrapolation as a method of sales forecasting is not possible. Correlation, econometric models, and polling techniques are applicable, however, as are *experimental techniques* and the use of *historical analogy*.

5. *Experimental techniques.* Test markets and controlled store tests (discussed in Chapter 11) are types of field experiments that are widely used to help forecast sales of new products. Laboratory experiments involving "purchases" in a simulated-purchase situation have also been used for this purpose.

6. *Historical analogy.* The sales experience of an earlier, similar product is sometimes used as the basis for forecasting sales of a new product. A necessary assumption in using this approach is that the economic and market environment of the two products are either similar or that the effects of differences can be adequately reflected by adjustments to the sales data of the earlier product. An example of the application of historical analogy for forecasting the sales of a new product is the use of sales of black and white television sets for the first few years after their introduction to forecast sales of color television sets for a similar period.

Forecasting techniques, like any model, are difficult to test in the real world. Some analysts will attempt to test more formal models retrospectively. For example, they may divide the time series roughly into halves, calculate values for the parameters in the model by using the first half of the time series, and then use these values in forecasting the second half of the time series. Other researchers will employ two or more forecasting techniques and see if they arrive at forecasts that are more or less in agreement. The fact remains, however, that the observance of past regularities in the data provides no guarantee that these regularities will persist or that some other technique might not be more efficient in terms of lower total cost (forecast preparation cost plus the cost of forecast error).

Experimental techniques have been described elsewhere and historical analogy needs no further discussion. The first four of the techniques shown above do require additional discussion, however, and we now turn to that task.

Extrapolation Techniques

Market Potential/Sales Forecasting by Extrapolation

Extrapolation of past sales or market-share data can take a variety of forms. At one extreme are *persistence*, or *naive*, models, which merely use the value for the most recent period as a forecast for the next period. For short-range forecasts of sales data that are changing rather slowly over time, this simple and inexpensive procedure can provide reasonably accurate forecasts. Slight variations in the procedure involve extrapolating a trend for two or more periods. For example, if the most recent period's sales were 100 units and the next to the most recent period's sales were 80 units, sales forecasted for the next period would be $(100/80)(100) = 125$ units.

Persistence models are often used as a basis for evaluating other forecasting techniques. For example, Parker and Segura[3] used a five-year linear extrapolation to forecast sales for a home furnishings company and compared the results with those obtained from a regression model. For an 18-year forecasting period (1952–1970) the coefficient of determination for the extrapolation forecasts was 0.86 whereas that for the regression forecasts was 0.95.

Time-series decomposition techniques (trend and cyclical and seasonal analysis) and the fitting of various *growth curves* (logistic, Gompertz, modified exponential) are not far different in principle from the simple procedures enumerated above. The former set of procedures can be used for making short-range (less than one year) projections, intermediate-range (one- to five-year) projections, or longer-range (over five-year) projections. Growth curves are usually reserved for long-range projections where the trend of the series is deemed to be the sole component of interest for planning purposes.

The rationale underlying time-series decomposition is based on the assumption that the original data of a series are composed of a trend, cyclical component, seasonal component, and an "irregular" component. A common functional form is to assume that these variables are multiplicative. Hence, the original data can be expressed as follows:

$$O = T \times C \times S \times I$$

[3]G. G. C. Parker and E. L. Segura, "How to Get a Better Forecast," *Harvard Business Review*, 49 (March–April, 1971), 99–109.

where $O =$ original data; $T =$ trend component; $C =$ cyclical component; $S =$ seasonal component; and $I =$ irregular component. Other functional forms (e.g., additive) can be used as well, and rather elaborate procedures (many of which are computerized) are available for isolating the assumed components. Of the available computer programs, one of the more comprehensive is the X-11 program developed by the Bureau of the Census.[4]

Growth curve forms of the traditional S-shaped variety are typically reserved for extrapolation of annual data for several years ahead on the assumption that these functional forms generally describe long-term behavior of many time series. Other variations of trend fitting use logarithms of the original data in a variety of functional forms: straight line, quadratic, and so on.

The mechanics underlying all the above procedures are reasonably simple, once a mathematical model to describe the past behavior of the series has been selected. The rub, of course, rests on *which* model (of a large variety of possible models) is to be selected. This choice must rest largely on empirical grounds and the use of limited retrospective tests of "goodness of fit."

For short-range forecasting, increasing attention in recent years is being given to an extrapolation technique known as *exponential smoothing.*[5] Exponential smoothing is an extrapolation technique that "smooths" the time series in a manner not unlike a moving average. Originally applied to inventory control problems, exponential-smoothing procedures combine the virtues of simplicity of computation and flexibility (associated with moving averages) with advantages that make their utilization particularly applicable to computer storage and computation. When hundreds of items have to be forecasted, as, for example, in inventory control systems, there are decided advantages in being able to update historical data rapidly.

Briefly stated, exponential smoothing is a type of moving average that represents a weighted sum of all past numbers in the time series with the heaviest weight placed on the most recent information. A fraction called a "smoothing constant" (and usually designated by the symbol α) is used to smooth the data. To see how this procedure is related to the conventional moving average (M_t), we first define this latter term as follows:

$$M_t = \frac{X_t + X_{t-1} + \cdots + X_{t-N+1}}{N}$$

[4]U.S. Department of Commerce, Bureau of the Census, "X-11 Information for the User," *Papers Prepared for the Seminar on Seasonal Adjustments of the National Association of Business Economists*, March 10, 1969.

[5]The primary references are R. G. Brown, *Statistical Forecasting for Inventory Control* (New York: McGraw-Hill Book Company, 1959), and R. G. Brown, *Smoothing, Forecasting and Prediction* (Englewood Cliffs, N.J.: Prentice-Hall, Inc., 1963).

The moving average for the next period $(t + 1)$ is found by adding X_{t+1} to the numerator series and dropping X_{t-N+1}. For example, assume that N, the number of periods in the average, is 7. The moving average for the tenth period is thus

$$M_{10} = \frac{X_{10} + X_9 + \cdots + X_4}{7}$$

The moving average for the next period (M_{11}) is then

$$M_{11} = \frac{X_{11} + X_{10} + \cdots + X_5}{7}$$
$$= M_{10} + \frac{X_{11} - X_4}{7}$$

If X_4 were not available for some reason, since we know that M_{10} was computed from a series of values containing X_4, we could substitute M_{10} for X_4 as a "best estimate" of this (now) missing value:

$$\overset{*}{M}_{11} = M_{10} + \frac{X_{11} - M_{10}}{7}$$
$$= \frac{X_{11}}{7} + \left(1 - \frac{1}{7}\right)M_{10}$$

where $\overset{*}{M}_{11}$ is used an an estimate of M_{11}. The simplest exponential model is merely a reflection of the above process and can be represented symbolically by

$$\overset{*}{S}_t = \alpha X_t + (1 - \alpha)\overset{*}{S}_{t-1}$$

where $\alpha(0 \leq \alpha \leq 1)$ takes the place of the ratio $\frac{1}{7}$ described above.

The determination of the correct numerical value to assign to α is, of course, the principal problem in using this technique. If the time series changes very slowly, we would like the value of α to be small so as to keep in the effect of earlier observations. If the series changes rapidly, we would like the value of α to be large so that the forecasts may be responsive to these changes. In practice, the value of α is often estimated by trying several values and making retrospective tests of the associated forecast error.[6] The value of α leading to the "smallest" forecast error is then chosen for future smoothing.

More elaborate formulations of the basic exponential smoothing model enable the analyst to incorporate explicitly trends and seasonal elements of the time series. In special cases, the technique permits the use of statistical control procedures for signaling when the basic parameters of the model have changed.

The *Box–Jenkins model* is a computerized technique for trying various extrapolation models to see which one best fits the data.[7] If the process that generates the sales data is a reasonably stable one, the use of the Box–Jenkins program will indicate which extrapolative technique gives the best forecast.

Cost Forecasts by Extrapolation

Most manufactured products are produced by processes that have cost elements that are partially time-dependent. The price of materials, labor time per unit, labor rates, and overhead rates are examples. The same is true of salaries, travel, and media costs in marketing.

Extrapolations can be made of each of these cost elements using the same techniques as used for making extrapolations of sales data.[8] Such extrapolations are of use to the marketing researcher primarily in evaluating "no change" versus one or more "change" alternatives in a specific problem situation.

Correlation Techniques

Market Potential/Sales Forecasting by Correlation

The distinguishing feature of correlation techniques as applied to forecasting is that past changes in the variable to be predicted are related to other variables on the assumption that these historical associations will continue into the future. That is, the analyst is interested in examining *serial* correlation between the variable to be forecasted (say, company sales) and various "independent" variables (personal disposable income, distributor inventory levels, etc.) that might be expected to bear some plausible relationship to the

[6]In special cases (stable autocorrelation functions), specific techniques are available for computing an "optimal" value of α (see Brown, *Smoothing, Forecasting and Prediction*, pp. 72–80). Of course, in economic series such stable autocorrelative functions are extremely rare.

[7]G. E. P. Box and G. M. Jenkins, *Time Series Analysis, Forecasting and Control* (San Francisco: Holden-Day, Inc., 1970).

[8]Cost extrapolation techniques are discussed in Nicholas Dopuch and J. G. Bunting, *Cost Accounting* (New York: Harcourt, Brace and World, Inc., 1969), Chap. 3.

variable to be forecasted. Illustrations are so-called lead-lag indicators and barometric indexes.

The essence of serial correlation techniques is that *if* a relationship is found to exist in the past and *if* this relationship can be expected to persist in the future, the series to be forecasted might be more accurately predicted by first predicting the levels of the predictor variables and then applying the historical functional relationship to predict the level of the dependent variable.

As previously indicated, Parker and Segura[9] forecasted the sales of a home furnishings company using a regression model. Housing starts of the previous year (H_{t-1}), sales of the previous year (S_{t-1}), disposable income of the present year (I_t), and time (T) were used as predictor variables. The resulting equation was $S_t = 33.51 + 0.033H_{t-1} + 0.373S_{t-1} + 0.672I_t - 11.03T$; $R^2 = 0.95$ for a 22-year period.

The assumption behind this approach is that more accurate forecasts can be obtained by forecasting national income (and using the lagged values of the other predictor variables) than by forecasting the sales of the company directly. One of the dangers involved in using correlation techniques, however, is that the high autocorrelation in each series may give the appearance of high serial correlation (that is, one may be, in effect, correlating the trends of each series) when the other components of each series, say cyclical or seasonal, are not highly correlated. For long-range forecasting, where emphasis *is* on the trend component, good results can sometimes be obtained by serial correlation procedures, but, for shorter-range projections, reliance on high-correlation coefficients may be misleading because of the reason just mentioned. The central problem, of course, is to be able to forecast the predictor variables accurately.

The quest for "leading" series is one of the chief preoccupations of some professional forecasters. *Barometric*, or *indicator*, *forecasting* is the name applied to the use of such a series. If a "true" leading series can be found, for example, the analyst might be fortunate enough to have the actual (not forecasted) value of the predictor variable from which he could derive from a regression equation the predicted value of the criterion variable. Such occasions, where leading series consistently "lead," say, a firm's sales volume, by a sufficiently long period to be useful, are extremely rare.

Nevertheless, quite a bit of empirical work has been done on examining the relationships among various United States time series. The National Bureau of Economic Research has analyzed some 800 monthly and quarterly time series for consistent lead, coincidental, or lag relationships.[10]

[9]Parker and Segura, *Harvard Business Review*, 49, p. 107.
[10]See G. H. Moore, *Statistical Indicators of Cyclical Revivals and Recessions*, National Bureau of Economic Research Occasional Paper 31 (New York).

Finally, mention should be made of the use of various demographic series for long-range forecasting of total industry demand for such goods and services as geriatric care, baby food, new housing, applicances, and the like. Despite some much-publicized errors, long-range forecasts of the total, sex, and age distribution of the population can provide interesting background material for long-range planning. That these time series could provide much help for forecasting *individual* company sales is obviously open to more question.

Cost Forecasting by Correlation

Forecasts of costs using correlation techniques are relatively common. The study cited earlier by Parker and Segura provides an example of regression analysis used for cost forecasting as well as for sales forecasting. They developed regression equations for "raw material costs," "wages and salaries," "other costs," "depreciation," "interest," "sales taxes," and "income taxes." Knowledge of such relationships is useful to the researcher when evaluating potential new products similar to the ones currently produced and marketed by the firm.

Econometric Techniques

Market Potential/Sales Forecasting by Econometric Models

Econometric techniques essentially entail explicit models about how the economy or a specific segment of the economy behaves. The usual econometric model involves a series of equations that have their origins in economic theory. Most of the models described in the literature deal with the macro-economy and are used for forecasting GNP and its components.

The input–output model of the economy, alluded to earlier and developed by Leontieff,[11] is econometric in nature but assumes a somewhat different form. It is a way of organizing the national accounts in which the flow of goods and services between industries is shown. A matrix of industries as rows (87 industries in one version and 370 in another) and the same industries as columns has been prepared. Interindustry transactions have been determined empirically for each cell in the matrix. The value of the transaction shown in a single cell represents both an output of one industry—the industry of that row—and an input for an industry—the industry of that column. If one is interested in a particular industry, say Industry 43, Engines and Turbines (87 industry version), he can find the distribution of outputs for that industry by examining the row on which it is located and the distribution of inputs by examining the column.

[11]W. W. Leontieff, *Structure of the American Economy*, 1919–1929 (New York: Oxford University Press, Inc., 1951).

The table is also provided in other forms to facilitate research use. A direct-requirements table has been prepared in which each cell entry is a coefficient obtained by dividing the dollar amount for that cell by the total of the column in which it is located. The result is an input coefficient. One can obtain the distribution of input coefficients for an industry by examining the column for that industry. A third form is a total-requirements table that shows the indirect as well as the direct requirements of each industry listed. The requirements are shown in coefficient form. This table permits the calculation of the total effect on all industries of a change in final demand on any one of them.

These forms of the input–output table permit forecasts of sales at the industry level to be made from GNP forecasts and forecasts of the effects of changes in final demand faced by a customer industry. An example of the forecasting of sales for an industrial product is given by Ranard.[12] For a GNP increase of 5% per year, sales for the motor vehicle industry were forecasted as increasing 3.9% per year. A 10% increase in demand for automobiles was estimated to require a 2.1% increase in steel output to meet direct and indirect requirements.

Given the reluctance of private firms to publicize the use of forecasting techniques that they find useful, it is difficult to estimate to what extent input–output and other econometric models have been used in practice. It is probably fair to say, however, that the individual firm's use of econometric models for forecasting sales is still relatively limited. However, the available evidence on the accuracy of econometric model forecasts compared to that of forecasts by other methods, indicates that the econometric forecasts are more accurate, particularly as the length of the forecast period increases.[13] So long as this conclusion continues to be supported by the experience of companies using econometric models one can expect that their use in sales forecasting will experience substantial growth.

Cost Forecasting Using Econometric Models

Much empirical work has been done by econometricians to determine whether the relationships of costs to output postulated in theory exist in fact.[14]

---

[12]E. D. Ranard, "Use of Input/Output Concepts in Sales Forecasting," *Journal of Marketing Research*, 9 (February, 1972), 53–58.

[13]See J. S. Armstrong and M. G. Grohman, "A Comparative Study of Methods of Long-Range Market Forecasting," *Management Science*, 19 (October, 1972), 211–21; R. F. Kosobud, "Forecasting Accuracy and Uses of an Econometric Model," *Applied Econometrics*, 2 (1970), 253–63; and V. Zarnowitz, *An Appraisal of Short-Term Economic Forecasts*, National Bureau of Economic Research Occasional Paper 104 (New York, 1967) for comparisons of the accuracies of different methods of forecasting.

[14]A definitive work in this area is J. Johnston, *Statistical Cost Analysis* (New York: McGraw-Hill Book Company, 1960).

The methodology of statistical cost analysis has been developed to a considerable extent as a result and has carried over into practice.

A problem that always arises in evaluating new product ventures is estimating production costs. Such estimates are usually required early in the evaluation in order to permit tentative prices to be set and conditional sales forecasts to be made.

A model that is widely used for this purpose in the electronic, appliance, aircraft, and shipbuilding industries is the *learning curve* model, sometimes called the *manufacturing progress function*. Empirical investigations of the labor hours required to produce successive units of new products have indicated that there is an exponential relationship between the hours required to produce the present unit, the hours required to produce the first unit, and the number of units that have already been produced. More specifically, the functional form of the relationship is

$$Y_i = Y_1 i^{-b}$$

where Y_i = labor hours required for the ith unit to be produced

$\quad\quad Y_1$ = labor hours required for the first unit

$\quad\quad i$ = number of units produced thus far (including the ith unit); $i > 1$

$\quad -b$ = rate at which the labor hours decline as the number of units produced increases

This equation may be expressed in logarithmic form as

$$\log Y_i = \log Y_1 - b \log i$$

In this form it is apparent that the function plots as a straight line.

The usual finding is that every time the number of units to be produced is doubled, the number of hours required to produce the last unit is reduced to a constant percentage of its former value. Thus, the term "80% curve" means that each time output is doubled, the number of hours required to produce the last unit is only 80% of the amount required before the doubling. If the amount required for unit 1 were 1 hour, for example, the amount required for unit 2 would be 0.80 hour, for unit 4, 0.64 hour, and so on.

The estimate of labor hours required to produce the ith unit therefore requires a determination of the slope of the curve and an estimate, or a measurement, of the time required to produce the first unit (or some unit before the ith one). Tables have been prepared of unit labor costs (and average cumulative total labor costs as well) for a wide range of learning curves.[15] If tables are not available, a graph of the curve at the learning rate desired can be prepared by making calculations for two values, plotting them on log-log paper, and drawing a straight line through them over the range of output of interest.

The values of the slope of the curves vary between industries and between companies within an industry. The Ford Motor Company experienced an 85% curve in producing the Model T from 1909 through 1923.[16] A study involving a number of industries reports values ranging from 67 to 86%.[17] This range of learning rates is wide enough to indicate that an investigation of rates in one's own company should be made before this cost forecasting model is used.

The labor hours per unit of product is, of course, only one element of the total product cost in a new product venture. However, the other classes of production costs, material, and overhead are usually much easier to estimate. Material costs are relatively constant over wide ranges of output, and manufacturing overhead costs are typically allocated on a direct labor-hour base. The estimate of labor hours thus provides a basis for estimating overhead.

Polling Techniques

Market Potential/Sales Forecasting Using Polls

The job of forecasting individual company sales is fraught with so much uncertainty that it is not surprising that opinion polling is used by many firms, whether or not the procedure is formalized. In one sense, the personalistic forecasts obtained by polling can reflect any or all of the models discussed under the previous classifications. That is, it is possible that a business executive may be basing his opinion on some underlying model that involves extrapolation, correlation, or some type of personalistic econometric theory about how his firm's sales are affected by various economic variables. Although less *explicit*, it does not necessarily follow that forecasts obtained by polling techniques are less accurate than more formalistic techniques. As a matter of fact, serious study is being given to the so-called predictive expert in forecasting events for which no satisfactory alternative procedures are even available, let alone superior.

Some polling procedures are used to forecast *general* economic series, such as the McGraw-Hill survey of expenditures for plant and equipment

---

[15]See R. W. Conway and Andrew Schultz, Jr., "The Manufacturing Progress Function," *The Journal of Industrial Engineering*, 10 (January–February 1959), 53, for an example of such a table.

[16]W. J. Abernathy and K. Wayne, "Limits of the Learning Curve," *Harvard Business Review*, 52 (September–October, 1974), p. 111.

[17]R. W. Conway and Andrew Schultz, Jr., *The Journal of Industrial Engineering*, 10, p. 54.

and the Survey Research Center of the University of Michigan, which prepares surveys of consumer anticipations regarding the purchase of consumer durables. From the standpoint of individual firm planning, however, our concern is more with polling procedures of company executives, sales personnel, distributors, and the firm's consumers.

Executive polling procedures are used quite frequently in the development of long-range forecasts for the firm. Product managers and end-use experts may be asked to estimate sales levels for their particular product or market specialization, subject to a set of overall assumptions regarding various economic activities and competitors' behavior. One of the authors elicited sales executives' opinions regarding the implications of various pricing strategies on: (1) competitors' retaliation, (2) market penetration, and (3) industry capacity changes. These opinions were expressed in terms of subjective probabilities. Although each group of executives was questioned independently, the agreement between groups was quite high. Although such consistency does not imply accuracy, it does suggest that personnel familiar with the marketing characteristics of a product do form similar judgments about the environments in which the firm operates. Furthermore, in this particular problem no alternative procedure existed for developing some of the inputs needed in the evaluation of pricing alternatives.

The polling of salespeople is a commonly used procedure to develop sales forecasts. Salespeople's estimates of sales for their particular districts may be next reviewed by the district manager, regional manager, and so on, and finally subjected to review by the firm's market analyst for consistency and correspondence with other sources of information.

Forecasts may also be developed by using "trade experts" drawn from the firm's distribution channels or directly from samples of customer groups. This procedure is used quite frequently in developing sales estimates for new products. In these cases no historical data are available for forecasting purposes, other than sales experience with broadly similar products or information about sales of the products with which the new product candidate will compete.

One type of polling procedure, the Delphi method,[18] has achieved increasing application in recent years. The idea behind Delphi is simple: a group of experts are polled regarding their judgments about when each of some set of specified events falling within their area of expertise might happen. They may also be asked to state their degree of confidence in each judgment and the implications for present policies if the event were to occur. Typically, each participant "votes" in closed ballot and the results are tabulated and displayed in group form so that the participant can see what others

---

[18]See, for example, Olaf Helmer, *Social Technology* (New York: Basic Books, Inc., Publishers, 1966).

(not identified) have forecasted. Successive rounds of voting, augmented by each participant's explication, in written but anonymous form, of assumptions underlying his judgments (for perusal by other participants) take place until results more or less stabilize in terms of a common understanding of the events being forecasted.

Cost Forecasting Using Polls

The use of polling in forecasting costs is less frequent than the other techniques that have been discussed. It is largely restricted to the polling of suppliers to obtain estimates of prices and of price changes for materials. By way of summary, polling procedures can be used effectively or can end up in a "pick a number" game, depending upon the care with which opinions are assembled and the thoroughness with which checks for internal consistency and crosschecking with other information sources are carried out. Relying on the "objectivity" of more formal forecasting techniques can, however, result in as many pitfalls as naive treatment of more personalistic forecasts. The prudent marketing analyst may be well advised to consult several sources of information, whether or not some of this information may be based on intuition or hunch.

FORECASTING MARKET SHARE

Market share is the percentage of industry sales made by the company over some stated time period. As described earlier, a derived forecast of company sales requires a forecast of industry sales and a market-share estimate.

Industry sales data are often, but not always, available on a historical basis from such sources as trade associations and government reports. When they are not available from these sources, they may be developed by the marketing research staff or, in some cases, purchased as part of the data supplied by a syndicated service (Neilsen, MRCA, and others).

In general, forecasts of market share may be made using the same techniques as described for market potential and sales forecasts. Data on market share over time comprise a time series that is susceptible, in principle, to the same kinds of treatment as a time series of sales. That is, one may extrapolate market-share data for forecasting purposes using the same persistence models (naive models, time-series decomposition, exponential smoothing, and others) as described for sales data. Correlation models appear to be at least as widely used for market-share forecasting as for sales forecasting. Econometric models and polling procedures can also be employed for this purpose.

PROBABILITY FORECASTING AND COST
VERSUS VALUE OF INFORMATION

In this section we discuss two questions that can be classified under the general heading of "probability forecasting":

1. In "few action–few state" problems, how precise must be the probabilities associated with the occurrence of alternative states of nature?
2. In "many action–many state" problems, how is the best action chosen when the values assigned to alternative states of nature are subject to continuous variation?

We shall see that both questions are illustrative of "probability forecasting" in which the forecaster prepares not a single point estimate but a *probability* distribution (discrete or continuous) of possible values that the unknown parameter(s) of interest can assume.

Few Action–Few State Problems

As an example of the first class of problems, suppose that a new product planner is interested in marketing a food supplement, called Lottadyne, for baked goods. The product is made by a batch process that through equipment indivisibilities is restricted to the following annual capacities:

$$A_1: \text{1 million pounds}$$
$$A_2: \text{2 million pounds}$$
$$A_3: \text{5 million pounds}$$

The conditional opportunity losses under S_1 ("high" sales) and S_2 ("low" sales) are shown in Table 15-1. As noted from the table, in this simplified example if S_1 obtains, act A_3 is the best course of action and is accordingly assigned a conditional opportunity loss of zero. If S_2 obtains, however, act

Table 15-1   Conditional opportunity losses
(millions of dollars)—
food-supplement problem

	STATE OF NATURE	
ACT	S_1	S_2
A_1	6	0
A_2	3	3
A_3	0	8

A_1 becomes the best course of action. Act A_2 is a kind of "hedging" act in the sense that the conditional opportunity losses associated with it are not extreme under either S_1 or S_2.

The problem facing the product planner is to estimate the probabilities of occurrence of S_1 and S_2, respectively. More appropriately, how precise must these estimates be? Suppose that $P(S_1)$ can vary over the interval 0 to 1. Then $P(S_2)$ is equal to $1 - P(S_1)$. If $P(S_1)$ were equal to 0.1, then the expected opportunity losses of the three acts would be:

$$EOL(A_1) = 0.1(6) + 0.9(0) = \$0.6 \text{ million}$$
$$EOL(A_2) = 0.1(3) + 0.9(3) = \$3.0 \text{ million}$$
$$EOL(A_3) = 0.1(0) + 0.9(8) = \$7.2 \text{ million}$$

Clearly, under these conditions act A_1 (the low-capacity facility) would be preferable to the other courses of action. By assuming various values that $P(S_1)$ *could* have, we can construct the chart of expected opportunity losses shown in Figure 15-2.

We see from Figure 15-2 that if $P(S_1)$ is less than 0.5, then act A_1 is best, whereas if $P(S_1)$ is between 0.5 and 0.625, act A_2 is best. If $P(S_1)$ should exceed 0.625, then act A_3 is best. If $P(S_1)$ is exactly 0.625, either A_2 or A_3 could be chosen. These "indifference" points are determined by finding th points on the abscissa where the lines of expected opportunity loss intersect, that is, where

$$\boxed{EOL(A_1) = EOL(A_2)}$$

Letting $P(S_1) = P$, we have

$$6P + 0(1 - P) = 3$$
$$P = 0.5$$

The implication of these oversimplified calculations is that the product planner does *not* need to know the precise value of $P(S_1)$ but only that it falls in specific ranges. In terms of the assumptions of this problem, the same act (act A_1) would be chosen if $P(S_1)$ were, say 0.1, as would be chosen if $P(S_1)$ were, say 0.4. Although the illustration is simple, it does serve to demonstrate that in some marketing problems forecasts do *not* need to be made with high precision.

Many Action–Many State Problems

In more realistic cases, of course, a greater number of states of nature and courses of action are possible. For example, in inventory-control prob-

**Figure 15-2 Expected opportunity losses (millions of dollars)—
food-supplement problem**

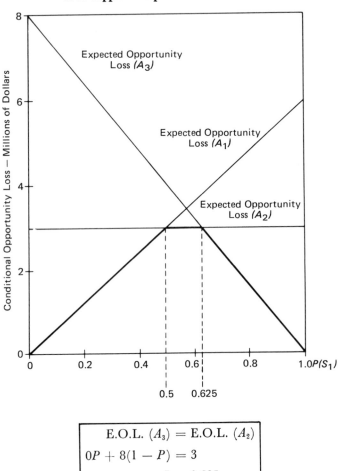

$$E.O.L. \ (A_3) = E.O.L. \ (A_2)$$
$$0P + 8(1 - P) = 3$$
$$P = 0.625$$

lems some "best" level of inventory may exist for each possible sales level. In production-planning problems the quantity of product produced may vary more or less continuously within a certain range.

To make the "many act–many state" case more specifie, suppose that a promotion planner in the ethical drug field is interested in determining the "best" number of samples to produce for distribution to physicians by the firm's detailing salesmen. If physicians' requests for samples exceed the quantity produced, ill will incurred is assumed to be associated with unfilled requests as a function of the level of demand. If the number of samples produced exceeds the requests, there will be costs associated with excess production and inventory. For purposes of illustration, suppose that the imputed "cost" for each *unfilled* physician's request (for one sample) is $1.20 and suppose that the cost associated with each sample produced *in excess* of requests is $0.30. The promotion planner is interested in recommending some best level of sample production that minimizes expected cost under an uncertain demand for samples of the new product.

Assume that the upper panel of Figure 15-3 shows the promotion planner's probability distribution (expressed in histogram form) of the possible demand levels for samples of the new product. The planner is willing to believe that demand for the new drug samples will exceed 20,000 units and will be no higher than 80,000 units. His most "probable estimate" of demand (highest bar of the histogram) is that demand will be between 30,000 and 40,000 units.

The lower panel of Figure 15-3 shows the cumulative probability distribution derived from the histogram in the upper panel of the chart. The smooth curve in the lower panel of the chart is used to approximate cumulative probabilities *within* the histogram intervals. For example, the estimated probability of physician demand being less than 35,000 units is 0.45, as read from this curve.

To determine the best number of drug samples to produce, the promotion planner would like to find the appropriate balance point where the expected cost of underproducing just equals the expected cost of overproducing.[19] We already know that both these costs are proportional to the difference between the amount produced and the amount requested. Fortunately, however, we do not have to construct a payoff table for *each* possible act and demand level. Instead, we may follow the principle "Keep increasing the production quantity until highest level *n* is reached for which the expected incremental cost of adding the *n*th unit is still less than the expected incremental cost of not adding the *n*th unit to the production level."

If we let D = demand level, C_o = $0.30 = cost per unit of overproduction, and C_u = $1.20 = cost per unit of underproduction relative to demand, we have, by application of the principle above,

$$C_o P(D < n) < C_u[1 - P(D < n)]$$

$$[P(D < n)](C_o + C_u) < C_u$$

$$P(D < n) < \frac{C_u}{C_o + C_u}$$

$$P(D < n) < \frac{\$1.20}{\$1.20 + \$0.30}$$

$$P(D < n) < 0.80$$

---

[19] For an extensive discussion of this problem, see Robert Schlaifer, *Probability and Statistics for Business Decisions* (New York: McGraw-Hill Book Company, 1959).

**Figure 15-3   Probability distribution—demand for
samples of new drug product (thousands of units)**

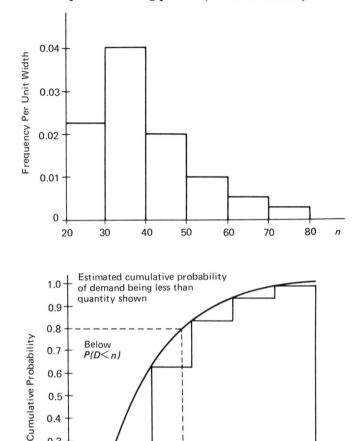

Returning to the lower panel of Figure 15-3, we note that the largest n for which $P(D < n) < 0.80$ is approximately 48,000 units. This represents the graphical solution to the problem. Had the promotion planner *not* considered the *asymmetry in the costs of over- versus underproduction*, he might have planned for either (1) a production level equal to the midpoint of the highest bar in the histogram (i.e., 35,000 units) or (2) a production level equal to the median or 0.5 cumulative probability level of the distribution (i.e., 36,000 units). In either case he would have "underproduced" relative to the solution that takes into consideration the conditional costs of over- versus under-production.

The essence of this problem is that forecasts should, in some cases, be *biased* to reflect the possible asymmetry of costs. In the present illustration we can see that *neither* the "most probable" (modal) forecast nor the median forecast necessarily represents the best level to plan for. As a matter of fact, in this illustration even the mean of the original probability distribution (39,300 units) would have provided too low a production level for mini-mizing expected total cost.

The preceding illustrations have demonstrated, first, that forecasts do not necessarily have to be precise to be useful and, second, that "best" single estimates of the unknown parameter do not necessarily lead to the best decision.

We can view the selection of forecasting procedures in the same general fashion as any other decision problem under uncertainty. Frequently, to achieve greater forecasting accuracy, the marketing researcher will have to employ more expensive forecasting procedures. The value of this increased accuracy for decision-making purposes should be balanced against the increased cost. The marketing researcher must continually ask: what would management do *differently* if a forecasting procedure yielding greater accuracy could be employed? Even if increased accuracy *can* be obtained, it is rarely obvious that the additional cost entailed is justified.

SUMMARY

The central theme of this chapter has been the treatment of forecasting activ-ity within the framework of cost and value of information. We first discussed the general nature of forecasting and some of the problems associated with it.

Some of the major mechanistic techniques—exponential smoothing, correlation, trend analysis, and econometric models—were next briefly described. The role of less formal procedures—polling techniques—was also pointed out, and it was suggested that these techniques, though less formal, should not be summarily dismissed as being ineffective.

We concluded the chapter with a discussion of forecasting in the framework of decision theory. It was shown that: (1) forecasts need not necessarily be highly accurate in order to support good decisions, and (2) depending upon the nature of the forecast error, a "biased" estimate may lead to better results than "unbiased" estimating procedures.

ASSIGNMENT MATERIAL

1. The McKeon Company is a firm selling industrial supplies. Its marketing manager desires to find whether a useful forecasting formula can be developed by correlating its monthly sales with the ratio of unfilled orders to production for its major customers two months in advance. Data obtained for the preceding 12 months are as follows:

Month	Y, McKeon Sales in Time $t - 2$	Month	X, Ratio of Unfilled Orders to Production in Time t
Jan.	$1.2 million	Mar.	1.15
Feb.	1.3	Apr.	1.20
Mar.	1.1	May	0.90
Apr.	1.0	June	0.80
May	0.8	July	0.75
June	1.2	Aug.	1.00
July	1.5	Sept.	1.35
Aug.	1.7	Oct.	1.40
Sept.	1.6	Nov.	1.65
Oct.	1.9	Dec.	1.80
Nov.	1.4	Jan.	1.45
Dec.	1.2	Feb.	1.20

   a. Prepare a scatter diagram for these data.
   b. Compute a linear regression equation.
   c. Assuming that the value of X in the next time period is 1.3, what is your estimate (using the regression equation) of McKeon's sales?
   d. What assumptions are you making in preparing the forecast in part (c)?

2. The Bird Company is interested in using exponential smoothing for short-range forecasting purposes for inventory control. Monthly sales data (in millions of dollars) are shown below for a two-year historical period:

	1963				1964		
Jan.	3.4	July	4.2	Jan.	4.4	July	5.8
Feb.	3.6	Aug.	3.9	Feb.	4.7	Aug.	6.0
Mar.	3.7	Sept.	3.8	Mar.	4.9	Sept.	5.7
Apr.	3.9	Oct.	4.1	Apr.	5.2	Oct.	6.2
May	4.2	Nov.	3.9	May	5.3	Nov.	6.4
June	4.7	Dec.	3.7	June	5.6	Dec.	6.7

a. Using smoothing constants of 0.1 and 0.2, respectively, prepare two exponential smoothings of these data. (Use the mean of the first three months, in each case, as a starting value for $\overset{*}{S}_{t-1}$. Then start the smoothing process in the fourth period.)

b. Compute the mean absolute deviation under each smoothing procedure for the period April, 1963, through December, 1964, according to the formula

$$\text{MAD} = \frac{1}{21} \sum_{t=4}^{21} | \overset{*}{S}_t - X_t |$$

where $\overset{*}{S}_t$ is the smoothed value and X_t the actual value for period t.

c. Compute the mean absolute deviation under each smoothing procedure for one-period-ahead forecasts according to the formula

$$\text{MAD} = \frac{1}{20} \sum_{t=4}^{23} | \overset{*}{S}_t - X_{t+1} |$$

Which value of the smoothing constant leads to the lower mean absolute deviation over the time series?

3. The marketing researcher for a breakfast food manufacturer is interested in determining the best number of premiums (a small toy) to order in conjunction with a forthcoming couponing campaign. If the number of requests for the premium should exceed its stock, the firm's policy is that the toy must be purchased on the open market to fill any demand excess. The opportunity cost per unit of demand unfilled by initial stock is $0.45. On the other hand, if too large a stock is ordered, the cost per unit of excess stock is $0.20. The marketing researcher's estimate of the demand distribution for the premium is as follows:

Demand Less Than or Equal to (Units)	Cumulative Probability
50,000	0.00
60,000	0.10
70,000	0.35
80,000	0.60
90,000	0.85
100,000	0.95
110,000	1.00

a. Compute an estimated mean demand for the premium.
b. Determine the best level of stock to order.
c. In this problem, is the midpoint of the model demand interval a better or worse forecast than the estimated mean?

4. If it requires 75 minutes to assemble the first unit of a new appliance, what is the estimated time required for the 1,000th unit, given an 80% learning curve?

5. Given the following opportunity-loss table:

ACT	STATE OF NATURE S_1	S_2
A_1	9	0
A_2	4	5
A_3	0	7

a. Construct a chart of expected opportunity losses as a function of the probability $P(S_1)$.
b. If $P(S_1)$ is 0.6, which act leads to the lowest expected opportunity loss?
c. Multiply all entries of the original table by 3. Does this change your answer to part (b)?

Brand Positioning 16
and Market Segmentation

INTRODUCTION

The basic question underlying many specialized procedures used in marketing research is simply: what makes people buy what brands or services? Depending upon the resolution of this question are various decisions regarding changes in marketing mix variables—product, promotion, pricing, personal selling, packaging, distribution, after-the-sale service, and the like.

Over the years marketing researchers have developed a number of specialized procedures for dealing with such problems as advertising-copy testing, market segmentation, and new-product concept generation and testing, to name a few. These procedures have demonstrated their usefulness in helping marketers understand at least some of the reasons why people buy. This chapter (and Chapter 17 as well) is concerned with describing some of these methods in order to give the reader a flavor of the kinds of things that a marketing researcher may be called upon to do.

Both chapters offer more of a survey-type treatment than the material in Parts III and IV. For the most part, we do *not* delve deeply into the mechanics of the techniques but rather attempt to provide illustrations of their application and rationales for their development.

Brand positioning and market segmentation appear to be the hallmarks of today's marketing research. *Brand* (or *service*) *positioning* deals with measuring the perceptions that buyers hold about alternative marketplace offerings. *Market segmentation* deals with those situations in which perceptions, preferences, or other aspects of consumer choice differ across buyer groups.

In either case we are interested in designing strategies that will enhance the firm's offerings in terms of market share and earnings. Accordingly, the first part of the chapter describes a framework for examining prospective marketing strategies—market penetration, market development, product development, and diversification.

We then discuss a brand-positioning study that was undertaken by a large manufacturer of digital computers. We examine the congruence of the firm's product image across various groups—its salespeople, customers, and noncustomers.

Market segmentation is discussed next. We first describe the major methodological approaches to segmentation and then comment on the myriad bases or criteria that have been suggested for defining segments. Following this, two industry studies are discussed. The first study is a combined application of brand positioning and segmentation, undertaken for a midwest brewery facing a severe loss in market share in one of its historically best trading areas. The second example is drawn from the auto insurance field and illustrates an application involving various consumer types that are identified in terms of perceptions, psychographics, and demographics.

In brief, the chapter tries to weave in some theoretical and methodological material with actual industrial examples that have been part of the authors' consulting experiences.

MARKET STRATEGY FORMULATION

Brand positioning and market segmentation—indeed, any of the tools that are discussed in this and the succeeding chapter—ultimately are concerned with *strategy* formulation. *Marketing strategy* involves a simultaneous consideration of the firm's offerings and the market's wants and needs.

Ansoff's 2 × 2 Strategy Classification

In his 1965 book on corporate strategy, Ansoff[1] developed a 2 × 2 table in which he considered four basic strategies in marketing:

- Market penetration
- Market development
- Product development
- Diversification

These four strategies were based on whether present versus new products were made available to present versus new markets.

Table 16-1 shows this schema. As noted, maintaining the same product line and the same markets (i.e., *market penetration*) suggests tactics that

[1]I. Ansoff, *Corporate Strategy* (New York: McGraw-Hill Book Company, 1965).

Table 16-1   Ansoff's 2 × 2 classification of marketing strategies

	Present Markets	*New Markets*
Present products	Market penetration	Market development
New products	Product development	Diversification

attempt to increase the intensity of usage among present customers by: (1) promoting new end uses for the product, (2) increasing its disposability, (3) making it more price competitive with substitutes, and so on.

In *market development*, new classes of buyers (e.g., those from different geographic locations or different demographic backgrounds) are sought in an effort to broaden demand for the present product line. In *product development*, new items or modifications of the present ones are sought to increase the line's breadth of usage among present customers. Finally, in *diversification*, changes in products and markets are pursued simultaneously.

An Expanded Version

The 2 × 2 schema of Ansoff can be easily expanded by the simple idea of splitting products and markets into two subcategories: (1) *structural* and (2) *functional* characteristics. Table 16-2 shows the resulting 4 × 4 schema. (The term *offering* is used in Table 16-2 to cover both products and services.)

Structural characteristics of products include physical- and chemical-attribute levels, packaging, distribution, and price. "Structural" characteristics of persons refer to their demographic and socioeconomic characteristics. Although the latter characteristics are expected to change over time, they may be treated as fixed for relatively short time intervals. Moreover, it is reasonable to assume that demographic and socioeconomic variables moderate peoples' choices among offerings but, in turn, are pretty much independent of the firm's marketing strategies.

Functional characteristics of offerings pertain to the uses or purposes to which the products are to be put. (Included here are the symbolic values that offerings may display in a sociopsychological context.) Stretching the analogy a bit, functional characteristics of people pertain to one's style of living and one's perceptions and values in the marketplace.

Two different structural offerings (e.g., a candle and a table lighter) may serve the single function of lighting one's cigarette. Conversely, a single

Table 16-2 Expanded (4 × 4) version of the Ansoff schema

		Present Segments		New Segments	
		Structural Characteristics	*Functional–Expressive Behavior*	*Structural Characteristics*	*Functional–Expressive Behavior*
Present Offerings	Structural Characteristics Functional–Symbolic Appeals	MARKET PENETRATION		MARKET DEVELOPMENT	
New Offerings	Structural Characteristics Functional–Symbolic Appeals	PRODUCT DEVELOPMENT		DIVERSIFICATION	

offering (e.g., a lemon–lime soft drink) may serve two or more functions, such as a midafternoon refreshment or a mixer with one's favorite bourbon at bedtime. The functions that an offering purports to fill are part of its array of promotional appeals, claims, and symbolic characteristics.

By the same token, two different demographic structures could display (within limits) a similar life-style, benefit-seeking pattern, or brand-preference profile. Conversely, a single type of demographic structure could manifest different goal-seeking and expressive behaviors.

The original Ansoff schema did not distinguish between structural and functional characteristics of offerings and markets. From the standpoint of strategy formulation, a more detailed classification might be preferred. For example, in the field of auto insurance one might want to distinguish between structural product development in which the actual policy's characteristics are altered (e.g., increased benefits, extended coverage, increased premium) and functional product development in which different appeals for selling the original policy are implemented. In turn, these appeals could be targeted to specific demographic groups, selected life-style segments, or different life-styles within a demographic group.

Depending upon the empirical context, the interconnections between structure and function may be loosely or tightly coupled. For example, lowering an insurance policy's premium and offering the policy by mail may markedly change the offering's functional–symbolic character. Conversely, including a new restriction on claims (as part of the policy's fine print) may exert no effect whatsoever on the policy's image. Whatever may be the case, a general problem in strategy formulation is to achieve *congruence* between structure and functional–symbolic appeals. In particular, one may wish to find a specific structure that allows for a variety of believable functional–symbolic appeals, each one being attractive to a different market segment.

The value of the schema of Figures 14-1 and 14-2 is the guidance it provides for designing a brand-positioning or segmentation study in the first place. For example, consider the problem of a telephone company wishing to increase revenues for long-distance usage. Clearly, little can be gained by attempting to increase installed sets; the market is already saturated. Similarly, little opportunity (except for the exploitation of picture phones) exists for dramatically changing the physical structure of telephones.

What *can* be done involves such strategic aspects as:

- Increasing the variety of appeals related to why people call long distance
- Changing the pricing or discount structure for further load leveling and increased overall demand
- Appealing to special demographic groups—senior citizens, college students, military service personnel—via special rates or gift certificates

- Appealing to special life-styles—the highly mobile, gregarious, and involved person—via special appeals or channels, such as direct mail

The reader can probably think of other illustrations where the permissible courses of action shape the kind of positioning or segmentation study that should be implemented. As basic as this point is, many research studies are launched and the data analyzed *before* the central idea of formulating strategy alternatives even comes up. Accordingly, in each of the studies that follow we shall devote attention to the kinds of strategies that motivated the study design in the first place.

BRAND AND SERVICE POSITIONING

At any point in time the firm has some array of brands or services competing with other brands or service suppliers in the market place. A number of questions are associated with one's interest in the *status quo*:

1. How are our brands positioned in the minds of consumers and the trade vis-à-vis competing brands?
2. What kinds of people prefer our brands and how do these people compare with noncustomers in terms of brand perceptions and preferences, benefits sought, life-style, and demographics?
3. What appears to be happening to brand position from a more or less dynamic standpoint; that is, from what brands are we gaining customers and to what brands are we losing customers?

The three questions above are rather pervasive in any assay of the current (and short-range future) market position of the firm. Not surprisingly, a number of specialized procedures have been developed to help provide answers to these questions. We first take up the topic of brand and service positioning.

One of the major activities pursued by contemporary marketing researchers is *brand* or *service positioning*. One approach to this problem is concerned with the development of perceptual and preference "maps" (as described in Chapter 14) of how consumers or industrial users "see" various brands as being similar or different and what combination of attribute levels they most prefer in their personal (or possibly household or organizational) choice of a product or service.

To illustrate the idea of brand/service positioning, we draw on a study undertaken for a large computer firm concerned with industrial users' evaluations of its offerings compared to other major competitors in the market.

A Computer Company Example

As is well known, the computer field is dominated by a few large-scale producers. International Business Machines, in particular, has enjoyed a commanding share of this market. As described in Chapter 14, computers are highly complex from a technological point of view and their marketing requires sizable expenditures in providing the customer with technical backup, maintenance, and software capabilities. Computer users' views of alternative suppliers might be expected to include a variety of image characteristics that are not restricted to the performance features of competing computers.

One of the firms in this field was concerned with its positioning in the minds of computer users vis-à-vis competitive manufacturers.[2] In particular, the firm's management wished to know how its evaluation on a large number of attributes might compare with other firms in the field. In addition, the firm wished to learn how important each attribute might be in various users' (e.g., government, financial institutions, utilities) selection of computers and, in particular, whether these attribute "importances" might vary among present customers, noncustomers, and the company's own sales employees.[3]

For purposes of these (and related) questions a sample of 310 computer users was drawn up in terms of:

1. Current customers—130 respondents, half of whom held positions directly involved with data processing and half of whom were other customer-firm employees who played some role in equipment selection.
2. Noncustomers (i.e., users of other firms' computers)—130 respondents, half data-processors, and half other employees with a stake in equipment selection.
3. Sponsoring company's sales employees—50 respondents.

In addition, the consumer group was stratified by end-use industry—fabrication, processing, utilities–communications, and so on.

A list of 15 attributes (including *overall* preference) was developed in cooperation with the sponsor's internal marketing research group. These appear in Table 16-3. Also shown in Table 16-3 are the eight firms that were to be evaluated with respect to each of the attributes.

---

[2] We are indebted to Robinson Associates, Inc., for permission to reproduce some of these materials.

[3] A large number of other research questions were associated with this study that are not covered here (in view of space limitations).

**Table 16-3   List of attributes and computer firms used
in supplier-positioning study**

Attributes

---

1. Favorableness of Performance/Cost Ratio
2. Provision for Utilizing a Large Number of Programming Languages
3. Reliability of Hardware
4. Extensiveness of Software Packages
5. Ease of Changeover from Other Systems
6. Quality of Education/Training
7. Quality of Technical Backup Services
8. Quality of Sales Presentations
9. Most Effective Use of Virtual Memory
10. High Acceptance by Systems Personnel
11. Innovativeness
12. Thoroughness and Speed of Service after the Sale
13. Flexibility regarding Price Negotiation
14. Suitability for Time Sharing
15. Your Overall Preference

Computer Firms Being Ranked

---

1. Burroughs
2. Control Data Corporation (CDC)
3. Honeywell
4. International Business Machines (IBM)
5. National Cash Register (NCR)
6. Radio Corporation of America (RCA)
7. Univac
8. Xerox (XDS)

Computer Manufacturer Evaluation

Each respondent, data processor, equipment specifier, or sponsoring firm employee, was then asked to rank the eight computer firms with respect to each attribute, in turn,[4] in accord with the following instructions:

> In this part of the questionnaire we are going to show you a set of cards—each card has the name of a computer firm. (HAND RESPONDENT THE SET OF 8 WHITE CARDS.)
>
> Now we're going to mention various characteristics regarding computer manufacturers. For each such characteristic we'd like you to *rank* the various manufacturers in terms of how they stand relatively on each attribute, or characteristic.

[4]Instructions were modified in the case of sponsoring firm's employees.

For example, let's take the characteristic "performance/cost ratio." In your judgment, which of the computer manufacturers, in general, seems to offer the most favorable performance/cost ratio? Which next most? And so on. Don't be concerned if your knowledge of the various firms is limited. We're interested in your impressions, however vague they may seem to you. (HAVE RESPONDENT RANK THE 8 WHITE CARDS, IN TURN, FOR THE CHARACTERISTICS LISTED.)

In analyzing the rankings data obtained from this part of the questionnaire, we employed multidimensional scaling techniques of the type discussed in Chapter 14. For summary purposes, Figure 16-1 shows the total-sample results of respondent evaluations of the eight manufacturers in terms of

Figure 16-1 Total-sample perceptions of computer manufacturers and attribute directions

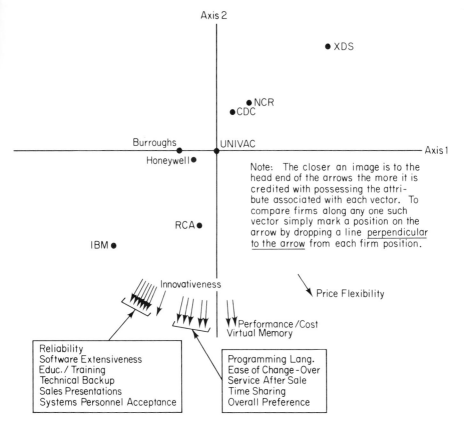

a two-dimensional plot. The 15 attributes are represented by vectors in the same space. The scaling algorithm finds these point locations and the attributes' vector directions simultaneously so that the total-sample's rankings of the eight computer firms on each attribute can be estimated by merely dropping perpendiculars from each of the eight points onto each vector, in turn.

To illustrate, we consider the attribute "reliability of hardware," abbreviated as "reliability" in Figure 16-1. If we project each of the eight points onto this vector we obtain the scale-value ordering: IBM (first); RCA; Honeywell; Burroughs; Univac; CDC; NCR; and XDS (last). Although not described here, it turns out that each derived scale approaches interval-scale properties (where scale separations are meaningful) from input data that are only rank-ordered originally.

In terms of the problem at hand, the dominance of IBM is clearly indicated. On every attribute except "price flexibility," IBM ranks first insofar as the total sample is concerned. Interestingly enough, RCA ranks first on "price flexibility" and second on the remaining attributes.[5] Burroughs, Honeywell, and Univac are somewhat clustered as are CDC and NCR. The Xerox Corporation's computers (XDS) represent a rather isolated point, quite possibly a result of their relative newness in the market and the resultant lack of respondent familiarity regarding their features.[6]

It is also of interest to point out that all 15 attributes are highly correlated, suggesting a type of "halo" effect. That is, if a respondent really has high regard for a firm he tends to rank the firm highly on *all* attributes. Only the attribute "price flexibility" appears to be highly distinguished from the others.

Attribute Importance

An additional question of interest to the firm concerned the relative importance that respondents would give to the attributes themselves in selecting a computer supplier. In particular, the sponsor wished to know if attribute importance varied by end-use industry—government, utilities–communications, educational–medical, financial, fabrication, process, transportation–retail—and by customer versus noncustomer, versus its own sales employees.

Accordingly, 14 of the 15 preceding attributes (excluding overall preference) were submitted for respondent evaluation in the following manner:

Now we are going to show you 14 cards, each card bearing the name of a characteristic of computer manufacturers. (HAND RESPONDENT THE SET OF 14 GREEN CARDS SHOWING

---

[5]This study, which includes RCA, was undertaken *before* this company announced plans to discontinue its computer operations.

[6]Subsequent to this study, however, Xerox also dropped its XDS product line.

ATTRIBUTES.) What we would like you to do is group the cards into four piles, with approximately 3 cards per pile. The first pile should include those characteristics that you feel are *crucial* in your choice of a supplier.

The second pile should contain those characteristics that are *highly important* to your choice of a supplier. The third pile should contain those characteristics that are *fairly important*. The fourth pile should contain those cards that are *not particularly important* to your evaluation of competing suppliers. (RECORD CARD NUMBERS OF SORTINGS IN RESPONSE FORM.)

The ratings obtained by the above procedure, with the wording modified in the case of the sponsor's sales employees, were also analyzed via multi-dimensional scaling. In this case, however, the sample was partitioned twice, first by end-use industry (excluding the firm's employees' responses) and then on a customer versus noncustomer versus sales employee basis. In the latter case customer and noncustomer respondents were further subdivided into data processors (technically oriented, data-processing respondents, designated as the A group) and other equipment specifiers (e.g., controllers, engineers and other management personnel not directly involved in data processing, designated as the B group).

Figure 16-2 shows the results of this analysis, using the same type of analysis and diagram described earlier. In this case, however, attributes are represented as points (the things being rated) and respondent groups as vectors (the "things" performing the ratings).

As can be observed from Figure 16-2, the 14 attribute points reflect an underlying evaluative dimension that is almost unidimensional; that is, the attribute points lie very close to the horizontal axis of the figure.

The scale values of the 14 attribute points indicate that reliability of hardware is evaluated as the most important characteristic, followed by quality of technical backup services and extensiveness of software packages. Quality of sales presentations is viewed as least important. Note that the vector labeled "grand average" is almost coincident with the horizontal axis; this vector was developed from input data for the total sample.

Insofar as end-user industry differences are concerned, we first examine the initial partitioning by industry class. Respondents in the government sector exhibit evaluations that are most highly separated from those in the transportation–retailing field. Even so, the rankings are virtually the same (e.g., for both groups reliability of hardware is viewed as most important), a reflection of the fact that little scatter of the points is found about the horizontal axis, although scale separations differ between the two groups.

When one examines the second basis for partitioning—users (groups A and B) versus nonusers (groups A and B), versus the sponsoring firm's sales

**Figure 16-2   Importance of computer manufacturer attribute
by type of respondent**

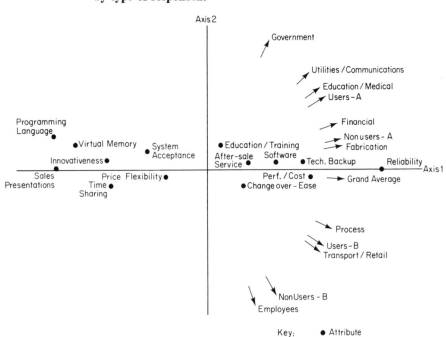

Key: ● Attribute
           ◄────── Respondent Type

employees—it seems that the main characteristic on which the groups'
evaluations are separated is in terms of data-processing jobs versus other
kinds of jobs. That is, both customers and noncustomers evaluate the attributes approximately the same, given the fact that they are respondents directly
involved in data processing. However, their evaluations differ from those of
respondents (group B) who are *not* directly involved in data processing.
Interestingly enough, the sponsor's sales employees exhibit attribute evaluations that are close to those of the *non-data-processor respondents.*[7]

In brief, the sponsor firm's customers evaluated the attributes about the
same as noncustomers if one holds constant on type of job held by the
respondent; attribute importance appears to be more a function of respondent job than it is of customer versus noncustomer status.

---

[7]Although not discussed in detail here, the cosine of the angular separation between any
pair of vectors represents a direct measure of the correlation between respondent group
ratings. Thus, the vector denoting users-A is more highly correlated with the vector denoting
nonusers-A than it is with users-B.

Implications

The material abstracted here represented only a small part of the study. Based on other information collected in the study, the sponsoring firm's perceived position in the market was found to be considerably different from that based on the *objective* characteristics of its hardware vis-à-vis its competitors'. Moreover, from a total-sample standpoint, the sponsor firm tended to be rated highly on the *less important* attributes underlying supplier choice. And, those respondents who rated the firm most highly tended to be: (1) highly technically trained data processors, (2) interested in performance/cost, (3) former IBM customers, and (4) data processors with high-level authority for choosing suppliers.

Unfortunately the sponsor's sales employees were: (1) emphasizing the *less important* features of the product line; (2) failing to get across the story of the firm's superiority in specific aspects of performance/cost; and (3) catering more to the less sophisticated, nondata processor (group B respondents), who, in turn, were less likely to switch from the full-service features provided by IBM.

This example illustrates how market positioning can be used to examine the relationship between "objective" and "subjective" performance characteristics, on the one hand, and image contrasts among customers, noncustomers, and sales employees, on the other. In this case it appeared that the sponsor's salespeople were failing to capitalize on the firm's strengths with respect to the more sophisticated type of computer user. Instead, they were employing a sales strategy that was incompatible with the firm's image as a technical, performance/cost-oriented supplier that did *not* presume to provide the full service features of the industry giant IBM.

MARKET SEGMENTATION

To some extent the preceding example of supplier positioning involved market segmentation in the sense that different types of respondents were found to view computer manufacturers differently. Product-service positioning and segmentation studies often will proceed hand-in-hand because we are usually interested in how products or services are perceived and evaluated by *different* groups of consumers.

The topic of market segmentation is a vast one and an interesting one for the marketing researcher.[8] No attempt will be made here to cover this

---

[8]W. R. Smith, "Product Differentiation and Market Segmentation as Alternative Marketing Strategies," *Journal of Marketing*, 21 (July, 1956), 3–8. For prescriptive theory on the topic, see H. J. Claycamp and W. F. Massy, "A Theory of Market Segmentation," *Journal of Marketing Research*, 5 (November, 1968), 388–94.

field in depth; rather we shall merely illustrate how one might go about doing a particular type of segmentation study.

Briefly stated, *market segmentation* is concerned with individual or intergroup differences in response to market-mix variables. The managerial presumption is that if these response differences exist, can be identified, are reasonably stable over time, and the segments can be efficiently reached, the the firm may increase its sales and profits beyond those obtained by assuming market homogeneity.

Methods for Forming Segments

There are two major problems that come up in any market-segmentation study:

1. What method is to be used in carrying out the segmentation?
2. What base or criterion is to be used for defining the segments?

As it turns out, options for dealing with the first problem are quite limited; those for dealing with the second are quite varied.

Insofar as methods for forming segments are concerned, there are, basically, two:

1. *A priori segmentation,* in which the researcher chooses some cluster-defining descriptor in advance, such as respondent's favorite brand. Respondents are then classified into favorite-brand segments and further examined regarding their differences on other characteristics, such as demographics or product benefits being sought.
2. *Post hoc segmentation,* in which respondents are clustered according to the similarity of their multivariate profiles regarding such characteristics as purchasing behavior or attitudes. Following this, the segments may then be examined for differences in other characteristics, not used in the original profile definition. In post hoc segmentation one does not know the number of clusters or their relative size until the cluster analysis has been completed.

As an example of a priori segmentation, one might classify all respondents according to their stated favorite brand of beer. Having done this, some technique such as multiple discriminant analysis might be used to determine if the groups differ in terms of average demographic profiles or life-style variables.

In post hoc segmentation, we prespecify only the set of variables on which consumers are to be clustered—benefits sought, problems encountered with the product, or whatever. One then takes the consumers' response profiles on the whole *battery* of selected variables and clusters the respondents. Having done this, a technique such as multiple discriminant analysis (or simple cross classification, for that matter) can be employed to see if the various clusters differ with regard to demographics, product usage, and so on. In the preceding beer example, respondents could first be clustered on the basis of the commonality of their benefit-seeking profiles. One could then see if the various clusters differed significantly with regard to such things as weekly consumption of beer, favorite brand, respondent age, and so on.

In some studies a hybrid of the two approaches is used. For example, respondents could first be grouped according to favorite brand and then a clustering procedure employed to see if segments evincing common benefit-seeking profiles appear *within* each of the brand-favorite segments that were found via the a priori approach.

Figure 16-3 shows, in stylized form, hypothetical examples of each approach. To illustrate, assume that we have *n* consumers' consumption data (in cases, over some base period) of three brands of beer: A, B, and C. Under a priori segmentation we may elect to group people on the basis of the brand that enjoys the highest consumption rate. The second matrix is a simple transformation of the first in which an X appears under the brand for which consumption is highest for each respondent. (We note, for example, that the first two respondents are assigned to segment C.)

In post hoc segmentation, an extra step—computation of a matrix of interperson dissimilarity measures—is involved. Then, the actual grouping process is carried out by some type of clustering algorithm. To illustrate, assume that each of the *n* consumers responds to a set of needs-type attitude statements regarding beer consumption, on a 7-point agree–disagree scale. The first matrix shows the original response profiles. This matrix is transformed into an $n \times n$ symmetric matrix of dissimilarity measures in which each cell entry measures how dissimilar each pair of consumers is across the whole set of needs-type statements. This matrix is then submitted to a cluster analysis, yielding, in this illustrative case, four segments.

Hybrid segmentation starts out with both data sets. Respondents are first clustered by favorite brand. Following this, separate and independent dissimilarity-measure computations and cluster analyses are carried out *within* each favorite-brand segment. As seen in Figure 16-3, different numbers of clusters may emerge and, in general, the needs-type subgroups found by the hybrid approach differ from those found by the post hoc approach. (It should be mentioned that the order of this two-step process could be reversed.)

As can be noted from the preceding example, segmentation is an *aggregative* process insofar as matrices of individual data are concerned. Whether a single variable is selected for respondent assignment or whether a clustering is performed over a general measure of interperson dissimilarity, the net effect is to reduce the *n* original respondents to a more manageable

Figure 16-3   Alternative ways to form segments

A Priori Segmentation

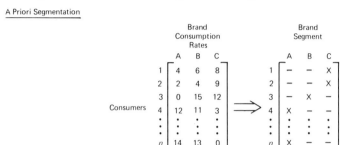

Post Hoc Segmentation

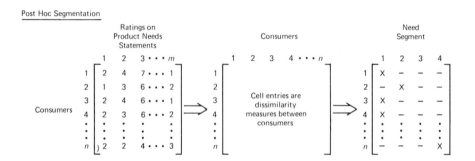

Hybrid Segmentation

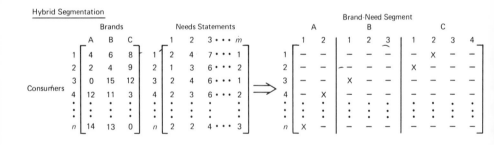

number of groups. In the process of doing this, information about detailed consumption of brands or detailed responses to needs-type statements is (willingly) discarded.

Two other points are worth making. First, in Figure 16-3, only persons were grouped into segments. While this is generally the way market segmentation proceeds, it is quite possible to take the obverse point of view and to cluster offerings. For example, in the case of a large number of brands, one could just as easily develop a dissimilarity measure for pairs of brands across persons' consumption profiles and cluster those brands that exhibit a relatively high commonality of usage. Just this kind of approach is frequently undertaken in the implementation of *positioning* studies. While this may not always be a useful thing to do, the point to be made is that one can cluster offerings just as readily as clustering people.

Second, the choice entities need not be products or services in the more narrow sense. They could be political candidates, legislative actions, charitable appeals, home site locations, or whatever.

Bases for Defining Segments

In contrast to the small number of segment-forming methods, the researcher has almost a surfeit of alternatives to serve as *bases for defining segments*. Some of the more popular bases are shown in Table 16-4. As can be observed, the bases run the gamut from highly brand-specific criteria to quite general and person-related criteria.

An illustration of a priori based segmentation would involve splitting the market for, say, toothpastes into favorite brands such as Crest users, Colgate users, and the like. One could then see if the groups differed in terms

Table 16-4 Illustrative bases for defining segments

Product-class behavior	*Brand-selection behavior*
Usage rate	Favorite brand
Number of different brands used regularly	Acceptable brand
Knowledge and experience with product class	Disliked brand
Brand-loyal versus brand switcher	Store versus nationally advertised brand
Product-class-related attitudes	*Brand-related attitudes*
Benefits sought	Brand perceptions
Problems enountered in using product	Brand preferences
Attribute tradeoff functions	
Person-dominant attitudes	*Other bases*
Personality	Stage in life cyle
Psychographics	Social class
Life-style	Ethnic origin
Self-concept	Other demographics
	Region and city size
	Geographic mobility

of various background characteristics, such as sex, age, personality profile, and so on.

Alternatively, a post hoc segmentation could be carried out by clustering people on the basis of benefits sought and needs fulfilled. This would proceed by first preparing a large number (50 to 60) of statements, such as:

- I'm more concerned than most of my friends about having an attractive smile.
- I often have problems of bad breath.
- To me, the most important thing in toothpastes is their ability to prevent cavities.
- I have had a long history of problems with my teeth.
- I use a mouthwash almost every morning.

Respondents are asked to indicate their degree of agreement or disagreement with each statement on some, say, 7-point rating scale, ranging from *highly agree* to *highly disagree*.

The matrix of n persons' responses on the m statements is then transformed into an $n \times n$ dissimilarity matrix (see Figure 16-3 and Chapter 13), and respondent clusters are formed. The clusters are identified in terms of benefits sought and then cross-classified with other respondent background data. As R. I. Haley describes it, "the benefits which people are seeking in consuming a given product are the basic reasons for the existence of true market segments."[9] Haley provides an example of this viewpoint in the context of toothpaste brand choices; his classification is reproduced in Table 16-5.

As can be observed from the table, Haley describes four segments, denoted as: The Sensory Segment, The Sociables, The Worriers, and The Independent Segment. The principal benefit sought is used to provide the *primary* basis for describing the market. Haley also looks at other characteristics of the resulting segments: demographics, special behavioral characteristics, brand favorites, personality characteristics, and life-style. From each composite description he then develops a shorthand label (e.g., "The Sensory Segment") for convenience of identification and discussion.

This example is a good illustration of how one primary basis, in this case the *principal benefit sought*, is used to define the market, and then other characteristics (e.g., brand preferences, life-style, etc.) are employed to describe the segments in ways that are potentially useful for copy design, media selection, package modification, and the like.[10]

[9]R. I. Haley, "Benefit Segmentation: A Decision-Oriented Research Tool," *Journal of Marketing,* 32 (July, 1968), 30–35.

[10]A more recent approach to the problem replaces the principal benefit sought with preferences for benefit bundles. See P. E. Green, Yoram Wind, and A. K. Jain, "Benefit Bundle Analysis," *Journal of Advertising Research*, 12 (April, 1972), 31–36.

Table 16-5   Toothpaste market segment description

Segment Name:	The Sensory Segment	The Sociables	The Worriers	The Independent Segment
Principal benefit sought:	Flavor, product appearance	Brightness of teeth	Decay prevention	Price
Demographic strengths:	Children	Teens, young people	Large families	Men
Special behavioral characteristics:	Users of spearmint flavored toothpaste	Smokers	Heavy users	Heavy users
Brands dispro-portionately favored:	Colgate, Stripe	Macleans, Plus White, Ultra Brite	Crest	Brands on sale
Personality characteristics:	High self-involvement	High sociability	High hypo-chondriasis	High autonomy
Life-style characteristics:	Hedonistic	Active	Conservative	Value-oriented

Reproduced, with permission, from R. I. Haley, "Benefit Segmentation: A Decision-Oriented Research Tool," *Journal of Marketing*, 32 (July, 1968), 30–35.

POSITIONING AND SEGMENTATION COMBINATIONS— A BEER COMPANY EXAMPLE

Many marketing research studies (as illustrated by the preceding computer image survey) are concerned with *both* product-service positioning and market segmentation. The first of these provides competitive information—which brands are seen as substitutible for which others—while the second empha-sizes intergroup differences in perceptions or preferences. Accordingly, we now describe a second study in which both aspects were important to the firm's strategy.

A prominent midwestern beer producer was becoming increasingly concerned with the decline underway in share of market in one of its histor-ically best sales areas. A new radio and spot television promotional campaign had been recently launched in an attempt to combat the situation but, for unknown reasons, it was seemingly ineffective in stemming the decline.

The sponsor wished to know several things about his product, including its market position, the segments attracted toward his firm's beer, and the brand-switching tendencies of consumers in the market area that was declin-ing in share. In particular, should the current promotional campaign be continued? Expanded in intensity? Changed in theme? Should the product formulation be changed? A new product developed?

A representative sample of male beer drinkers was drawn from the marketing area of interest and personal in-home interviews were conducted. Data were obtained on:

1. Judged dissimilarities of 12 popular beers sold in the market area.
2. Semantic differential ratings of the beers on a series of bipolar scales.
3. Preference rankings of the 12 beers.
4. Brand substitution, that is, other brands that the respondent would consider purchasing if his favorite were unavailable.
5. Life-style and demographic data.

The highlights of this study are illustrated next.

Brand Perceptions

For summary purposes, the data on judged brand dissimilarities for the total sample were scaled multidimensionally (see Chapter 14), resulting in the configuration shown in Figure 16-4. The 12 brands are represented by

Figure 16-4   Perceptual-vector spaces of brand positioning

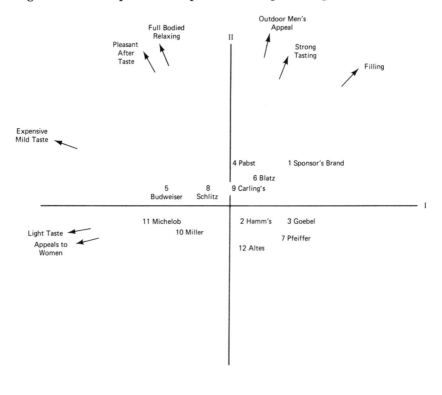

points and the various semantic differential (averaged) ratings are then fitted into the space via multiple regression, as an aid in interpreting the configuration. The horizontal axis of Figure 16-4 appears to be a type of premium-popular dimension with extremes represented, on the one hand, by Michelob, Budweiser, and Miller versus the sponsor's brand, Goebel, and Pfeiffer. The vertical axis appears to be a strength dimension. From the vector directions shown in the chart the sponsor's brand is perceived as strong and appealing to outdoor men. It is also perceived as the most filling of all the 12 brands.

Preference rankings of the 12 brands were transformed to paired comparisons and analyzed by Thurstonian Case V scaling (see Chapter 6). Prior to applying the scaling procedure, each respondent was classified, on the basis of length of time he had been drinking his stated regular brand, as:

1. Sponsor brand-loyal—had been drinking the sponsor's brand regularly for at least a year.
2. Other brand-loyal—had been drinking a particular (competitive) brand regularly for at least one year.
3. Switcher—others not meeting either of the above conditions.

Thurstonian scales of preferences were then developed for each of the preceding segments and appear in Figure 16-5.

As can be noted from the figure, the sponsor's brand-loyal segment is *really* loyal in the sense that the second-place brand (Pabst) is positioned far below the favorite and, as a matter of fact, all 11 of the other brands are rather bunched at the low-end of the scale.

Insofar as the remaining two segments are concerned, we note that Budweiser and Pabst appear as favorites in both cases. Moreover, the sponsor's brand fares rather poorly—third from last in the case of other brand-loyals and switchers. Hence, it became rather evident that the sponsor's brand exhibited little attraction potential from either other brand-loyals or switchers.

Segment Definition

The life-style and demographic information provided further background information for describing the three segments defined above. Multiple discriminant analysis (see Chapter 12) led to the following capsule descriptions of the segments:

Sponsor Brand-Loyal. A heavier beer drinker than average; one who is fairly optimistic regarding future income increases; higher than average in self-confidence; generally perceives beer drinking as refreshing and rewarding rather than as escape or as a means of loosening up; moderate to conservative

Figure 16-5   Thurstonian scales by beer-drinker class (overall preferences)

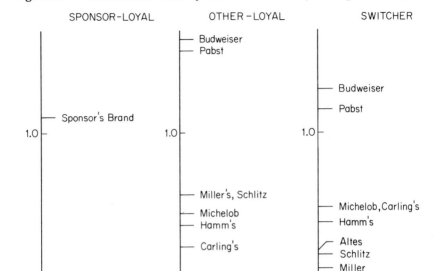

politically; higher proportion married and of foreign extraction; displays low interest in alcoholic beverages other than beer; working-class people, for the most part.

Other Brand-Loyal.   Moderate beer drinker in terms of glasses consumed per week; feels somewhat rushed and in a hurry; somewhat opportunistic; enjoys beer most in a social setting; drinks other alcoholic beverages (rye and bourbon) as well as beer; drinks beer to enjoy parties more; higher-than-average income; likes to gamble; predominantly white-collar.

Switcher. Lower-than-average beer drinker in terms of glasses consumed per week; feels that life is too routine; does not enjoy planned activities; likes to try new things; enjoys beer drinking with others; most of his friends prefer liquor to beer; has not accomplished life's goals as yet; younger in age; below-average income; does not expect large income increases; fewer years in current job; tends to drink other alcoholic beverages (particularly vodka); both white-collar and blue-collar representation.

From the preceding capsule descriptions we get some idea of the sponsor brand-loyal type as a steady, generally optimistic but settled individual who views beer as a way of refreshing and rewarding himself—one who is primarily a beer drinker and desires the stronger taste that the sponsor's beer exhibits.

Brand-Switching Tendencies

Data were also developed from the study on the question of what *other* brands the respondent would consider if, for some reason, his favorite brand were unavailable. The data represent the extent to which other brands are seen as *substitutes* if the respondent is unable to obtain his favorite. Analysis of this type of data can be useful from a diagnostic standpoint.

Table 16-6 shows the total-sample findings where row denotes current favorite brand and column denotes brands considered as substitutes if one's favorite brand cannot be obtained. For example, if the sponsor's brand is unavailable, respondents indicate that the major substitutes are Pabst, Hamm's, Carling's, and Budweiser (as might be inferred from Figure 16-4).

More important are the entries involving brands other than the sponsor's. In these cases the sponsor's brand receives highest frequency as an acceptable substitute only in the case of Budweiser drinkers (first column of Table 16-6). When one examines the *stability* of substitution—that is, the column frequency divided by the row frequency, shown only for the cases in which both frequencies are at least 15—the implications for the sponsor's brand are not favorable.

The sponsor's ratio of 0.3 (column total divided by row total) is the lowest of the group. The only other brand whose frequency of mentions as substitutes is less than the frequency of other acceptable brands is Schlitz (a ratio of 0.7). The other major brands, Hamm's, Pabst, Budweiser, and Carling's, all exhibit ratios of at least 1.0. Thus, drinkers of the sponsor's brand appear to exhibit a reasonably wide latitude regarding acceptable substitute brands, but regular drinkers of competing brands do *not* generally consider the sponsor's brand as an acceptable substitute.

Table 16-6   Brand-substitution frequencies—conditioned upon favorite brand

BRAND	\multicolumn{13}{c}{BRANDS CONSIDERED AS SUBSTITUTES}	
	1	*2*	*3*	*4*	*5*	*6*	*7*	*8*	*9*	*10*	*11*	*12*	*13*	*Total*
1. Sponsor's brand	—	20	5	22	15	1	4	7	20	3	—	—	—	97
2. Hamm's	1	—	—	9	1	1	—	—	—	5	1	—	—	18
3. Goebel	—	—	—	—	—	—	3	—	3	—	—	—	—	6
4. Pabst	6	3	—	—	15	6	—	1	4	3	1	1	1	41
5. Budweiser	8	5	—	5	—	1	—	2	2	4	4	3	—	34
6. Blatz	—	—	—	3	—	—	—	—	—	—	3	—	6	6
7. Pfeiffer	—	—	—	—	—	—	—	—	—	—	—	—	2	2
8. Schlitz	3	2	—	10	—	—	—	—	—	5	—	—	1	21
9. Carling's	3	1	—	15	5	2	1	1	—	2	—	3	4	37
10. Miller's	2	—	—	—	—	—	—	—	1	—	—	—	3	6
11. Michelob	—	3	—	—	3	—	—	—	—	—	—	—	—	6
12. Altes	2	3	—	6	7	—	—	1	3	—	1	—	—	23
13. Other	—	—	—	—	—	—	—	3	3	—	—	—	—	6
	25	37	5	70	46	11	8	15	36	22	7	10	11	303
Ratio*	0.3	2.1	—	1.7	1.4	—	—	0.7	1.0	—	—	—	—	

*Column frequency/row frequency.

Note that this type of information can be supplementary to preference data in that one can highly prefer a brand yet *still consider a variety of other brands as acceptable* if for some reason one's favorite is unavailable. While the sample size underlying this particular table is small, the qualitative indication is that the sponsor's brand is *not* seen as an acceptable substitute by drinkers of many competitive brands.

Implications

Other findings of the study reinforced the observation already noted: the sponsor's brand attraction potential from other brands was not high. While a loyal segment existed—one composed of heavier, predominantly blue-collar drinkers—it was of interest to examine this profile against the type of promotional campaign recently introduced by the firm's advertising agency.

The promotional campaign, rather surprisingly, was addressed to the more affluent, sophisticated beer drinker and emphasized a folk-rock musical jingle with humorous, clever sales appeals. It did not seem to the research team that this type of advertising was at all congruent with either the beer's strong, masculine image or the life-style and demographic characteristics of its consumers. Moreover, although the campaign had been running for six months prior to the study, there was little indication that it was winning away customers of competitive brands. Thus, it seemed to be antithetical to current sponsor brand-loyals and ineffective in attracting new customers. Accordingly, the research team recommended that examination be made of alternative promotional campaigns that might have greater potential for the retention of sponsor brand-loyals. In addition, recommendations (based on evidence not reported here) were made for product development aimed at new brands that might be attractive to two new segments: (1) nonwhites and (2) younger beer drinkers.

However, insofar as the purpose of this chapter is concerned, the preceding study shows how the questions of product positioning, market segmentation, and consumer switching propensities can all be interrelated (and frequently are) in a single study.

SEGMENT-CONGRUENCE ANALYSIS

Our last topic for discussion in this chapter concerns a relatively new approach to market segmentation, called *segment-congruence analysis*.[11] In carrying out segmentation studies it is not always clear what set of variables (e.g., brand favorite, benefits sought, psychographics, demographics) should constitute *the* base for defining segments, on either an a priori or post hoc basis. That is, one often finds an embarrassment of riches insofar as choice of a "distinguished" variable or set of (segment-defining) variables is concerned.

Segment-congruence analysis—which turns out to be simple in concept, if somewhat complex methodologically—is motivated by three principal problems:

1. In cases where it is not clear which variables should constitute the distinguished base, are the segments obtained from alternative bases mutually associated?

2. If so, which one of the bases makes the highest contribution to their mutual association?

3. In cases where one has preselected a distinguished base, how does the probability of a respondent's being a member of each of the segments formed from the distinguished base depend on membership in segments formed from the other bases?

[11]P. E. Green and F. J. Carmone, "Segment Congruence Analysis: A Method for Analyzing Association among Alternative Bases for Market Segmentation," *Journal of Consumer Research*, 3 (March, 1977), 217–22.

We illustrate the approach with an example drawn from the auto insurance industry.

An Insurance Company Example

The sponsor of this study is a prominent northeastern insurance company, specializing in the selling of auto insurance by mail. The motivation for this study stemmed from the sponsor's interest in the types of people choosing its offerings versus those who did not. Various possible bases were proposed for defining the segments:

- Whether or not the respondent was a customer of the firm
- Commonality of respondents' images of their supplier
- Commonality of respondents' psychographic profiles
- Commonality of respondents' demographic profiles.

In the first case, the segmentation could be based on a priori grounds, while in the latter three cases, post hoc methods would have to be used to develop the segments.

A survey was conducted among 534 respondents, each of whom had some type of auto insurance. Of the total sample, 155 were customers of the firm and 379 were noncustomers. The set of variables on which supplier-image segments were developed involved 13 attitude statements. Psychographic profiles were developed from 19 statements, while demographic profiles were based on 9 variables. Table 16-7 shows illustrations of the image and psychographic statements (as evaluated on a 6-point agree–disagree rating scale). Also shown are the 9 demographic variables.

Preliminary Data Processing

The first segmentation—the customer versus noncustomer grouping—required no additional processing since information was already available on segment membership. In the latter three cases, involving 13, 19, and 9 variables, respectively, a uniform segmentation procedure was followed:

- Each response battery of interest was factor-analyzed by principal components. Components whose variances exceeded unity were Varimax-rotated and unit-variance factor scores were obtained (see Chapter 13).
- The factor scores were then submitted to a hierarchical clustering program, and two-group through five-group clusterings were sought (see Chapter 13).

Table 16-7 Input data for alternative segmentations

Illustrative image statements (13 in total)

1. Settles claims fairly.
2. Inefficient and hard to deal with.
3. Provides good advice about types and amount of coverage to buy.
4. Too big to care about individual policyholders.
5. Policies are especially good for retired persons.

Illustrative psychographic statements (19 in total)

1. For specific medical problems I usually go to a specialist rather than a general practitioner.
2. I usually look for the lowest possible prices when I shop.
3. I like to try new and different things.
4. My friends or neighbors often come to me for advice.
5. Most people don't realize the extent to which their lives are controlled by accidental happenings.

Demographics

1. Sex
2. Marital status
3. Education
4. Age
5. Employment status— retired versus working
6. Current (or previous) occupation—professional or management versus all other
7. Number of persons at current address
8. Number of years at current address
9. Family income

The analysis was carried out for the case in which all clusterings were maintained at the two-group level. This yielded a $2 \times 2 \times 2 \times 2$ contingency table of 16 cells. Table 16-8 shows the frequencies with which the 534 respondents were distributed across the 16 cells.

Table 16-8 also summarizes the principal differentiating characteristics of the separately obtained segmentations. In the case of insurance supplier, segment 1 members are customers of the sponsoring firm. The image segments consist of those who believe that their insurance supplier caters to older people (segment 2) versus those who do not make this distinction. The psychographic segments consist of those who are more or less risk takers and willing to try new things (segment 2) versus those who perceive themselves as more conservative and old-fashioned. The demographic segments are made up of those who are primarily older widows living alone (segment 2) versus those who are principally married couples, younger, and with larger household sizes.

**Table 16-8   Distribution of frequencies within
the multidimensional contingency table**

Insurance-Supplier Segments	Image Segments	Psycho-graphic Segments	Demographic Segments	Frequency
1	1	1	1	5
2	1	1	1	52
1	2	1	1	12
2	2	1	1	22
1	1	2	1	11
2	1	2	1	46
1	2	2	1	9
2	2	2	1	16
1	1	1	2	18
2	1	1	2	59
1	2	1	2	29
2	2	1	2	42
1	1	2	2	34
2	1	2	2	111
1	2	2	2	37
2	2	2	2	31
				534

Insurance-supplier segments

1: Sponsor's customers
2: Other firms' customers

Psychographic segments

1: Controlled; conservative; old-fashioned
2: Risk taker; somewhat fatalistic; willing to try new things

Image segments

1: No specialization by age of insured
2: Caters especially to older people

Demographic segments

1: Primarily married couples; younger in age; larger number of household members
2: Greater incidence of widows and other single females; older in age; smaller number of household members

Mutual Association across All Four Segmentations

Tests of mutual association across the four separate bases of segmentation were carried out by means of a generalized approach to chi-square analysis (see Chapter 9). The following hypotheses were tested by generalized chi square:

- All four clusterings are mutually independent
- Insurance supplier is independent of the other three segmentations
- Image is independent of the other three segmentations
- Psychographics are independent of the other three segmentations
- Demographics are independent of the other three segmentations

As it turned out, all four segmentations exhibited *mutual* association. Moreover, if one had to select the most representative base of the four it would be the one developed from the *supplier-image* data. At this point, then, it appeared that all four independently carried out segmentations exhibited association and, hence, could serve as useful predictor variables if the sponsor desired to select one of them as a distinguished base.

Analysis of the Distinguished Base

After reviewing the tests of mutual association the sponsor decided to choose the first base—sponsor's customers versus noncustomers—as the distinguished base. The problem then became one of developing a model for predicting the probability of membership in the segment representing the sponsoring firm's customers, given knowledge of the respondent's membership in the segments formed from the other three bases: image, psychographics, and demographics.

A relatively new approach, using what is known as a logit model, was employed to find the necessary parameters.[12] First, it turned out that image-segment membership was the primary variable for predicting whether the respondent was a customer or noncustomer of the sponsoring firm. Demographics were next in importance, followed by psychographics.

The results of the analysis can be interpreted by looking at the segments that are listed in Table 16-8. As recalled, two segments appear under each of the four bases of segmentation. As it turned out, the model's parameters indicated that *higher probabilities of being a sponsoring firm's customer* are associated with:

- Being a member of image segment 2—caters especially to older people
- Being a member of psychographic segment 2—higher risk taker; somewhat fatalistic
- Being a member of demographic segment 3—female, widowed, older, small household size

[12]P. E. Green, F. J. Carmone, and D. P. Wachspress, "On the Analysis of Qualitative Data in Marketing Research," *Journal of Marketing Research*, 14 (February, 1977), 52–59.

In brief, a rather interesting profile emerges of the type of respondent most attracted to the sponsoring firm's auto insurance policies.

Table 16-9 shows the actual proportions that are customers of the firm versus those predicted by the model. Column (4) of Table 16-9 is derived from Table 16-8. For example, the first entry of column (4) is simply the ratio

$$\frac{5}{5+52} = 0.088$$

as obtained from the segment 1 of each of the predictor bases in Table 16-8. However, the model predicted a proportion of 0.125, leading to a residual of $0.088 - 0.125 = -0.037$.

As noted from column (6), the model performs reasonably well; its mean absolute deviation is about 3 percentage points.

Table 16-9 **Results of analysis in which sponsoring firm's customer is the criterion variable**

(1)	(2)	(3)	(4)	(5)	(6)
OTHER	SEGMENTATION BASES		SPONSOR'S	PROPORTION	
	Psycho-	*Demo-*	CUSTOMERS	PREDICTED	RESIDUALS
Image	*graphics*	*graphics*	(PROPORTION)	BY MODEL	[(4) − (5)]
1	1	1	0.088	0.125	−0.037
2	1	1	0.353	0.315	0.038
1	2	1	0.193	0.165	0.028
2	2	1	0.360	0.390	−0.030
1	1	2	0.234	0.195	0.039
2	1	2	0.408	0.439	−0.031
1	2	2	0.234	0.251	−0.017
2	2	2	0.544	0.520	0.024
				Mean absolute deviation	0.031

Implications

The implications of the study suggested that the type of customer drawn to the sponsor's offerings tended to be older than average, and in many cases widowed as well. Moreover, there was some tendency for customers to be greater risk takers, suggesting that they might be less concerned about the reliability and stability of firms that offer insurance by mail.

On the other hand, the results indicated that a way to attract *noncustomers* might be to emphasize the personalistic touch, perhaps by the availability of local personal contacts or company representatives that could be reached, on demand, by toll-free telephone numbers. In short, the company was provided with a useful target profile of *potential* customers that was described demographically and psychographically.

SUMMARY

This chapter has emphasized two major types of marketing research studies: brand-service positioning and market segmentation. We started off the chapter by describing various classes of marketing strategies: market penetration, market development, product development, and diversification. The detailed aspects of these strategies should influence the types of positioning studies that are undertaken by the firm.

Product positioning was illustrated by the digital computer study. In this case we were interested in how the sponsor's products were perceived vis-à-vis those of competitors. Moreover, we were also interested in the correspondence of these images across industry groups and across customers, noncustomers, and company sales personnel. The study showed that the company's salespeople were not emphasizing the firm's selective performance advantages and, moreover, were utilizing sales appeals that were attractive to those noncustomers who were *least* likely to switch computer suppliers.

The next section dealt with ways to form segments—the a priori, post hoc, and hybrid methods—and bases by which segments could be defined. A combination positioning–segmentation study, carried out for a midwestern brewery, was discussed as an example of how both approaches can be used to advantage. The study indicated that the firm's current promotional theme was out of step with the brand's loyal-customer base and also unattractive to new customers.

We concluded the chapter with a brief description of a recent approach to segmentation, called *segment-congruence analysis*. In this approach we examined the mutual association among alternative bases for defining segments and showed the results of a model for predicting the probability of membership in various classes of a specified segmentation base, given the respondent's membership in various background segments.

ASSIGNMENT MATERIAL

1. Describe how you would go about developing a brand-positioning study for the toothpaste market.
   a. What are the major attributes by which toothpaste brands can be characterized?

    b. What procedures (see Chapter 14) might be used to develop brand-positioning maps?

    c. How might multiple discriminant analysis (see Chapter 12) be used to accomplish this purpose?

2. Make a search of the current journal literature and record the bases that researchers have used to segment markets.

    a. What are the respective advantages and disadvantages of these bases?

    b. How would you design a segmentation study for the marketing of bar soaps?

    c. How might respondents' reported brand substitutions (see Table 16-6 as an example) be utilized in this study?

3. Some researchers assert that benefits segmentation only plays back what advertisers have instilled in the respondents' minds. These critics believe that *problems-oriented* research, involving: (1) problems experienced in using the products, (2) judged seriousness of each problem, and (3) the best brand for solving the problem, should be used instead of benefits-oriented research. Discuss the pros and cons of each method.

4. What kind of market-segmentation strategy does Datsun appear to be following in the United States? If you were a local dealer for this product line, how would you go about designing your own positioning and segmentation study?

5. How would you describe the positioning that Schweppes, Canada Dry, 7-Up, and Dr. Pepper are attempting to achieve in the marketplace?

Evaluating   **17**
New Marketing Strategies

INTRODUCTION

Brand positioning and market-segmentation activities, the main topics of the preceding chapter, are primarily concerned with measuring the firm's *current status*. A companion area of interest to the marketing researcher involves the evaluation of proposed *changes* to the present marketing program, such as new-product introductions, changes in promotion, pricing, packaging, or brand name. Within this class of activities are found procedures for new-concept generation and testing, advertising tests, package evaluations, and so on. Emphasis is on changing the status quo, either the structural characteristics of the firm's offerings or their functional–symbolic characteristics. A number of tools have been developed to assist the researcher in the design and evaluation of new marketing strategies. We consider some of them here.

The chapter starts off with a discussion of new-product-planning evaluation. Such tools as the repertory and consumption grids are illustrated as devices for developing perceptual and use-occasion frameworks that consumers employ in dealing with various products or services. The frameworks, in turn, are useful in both new-product idea generation and promotional-theme planning.

Concept screening and testing are described next. By means of an industry example, we show how surveys can be set up for evaluating verbalized descriptions of new products rather quickly and economically. We conclude the section with a brief discussion of market testing, including test-market simulators.

The next principal topic includes procedures for testing various marketing-mix components—promotion, package, price, and so on. These research activities are also illustrated by industry examples.

The chapter concludes with a discussion of large-scale market planning models. An industry example of one such market simulator is presented, and we comment more briefly on other kinds of computer-based marketing models.

NEW-PRODUCT DEVELOPMENT AND TESTING

The procedures described in the preceding chapter—brand or supplier positioning and market segmentation—are primarily concerned with quantifying the *current* situation in the marketplace (i.e., what brands are competing with what others, what kinds of people favor what brands, and the patterns of brand substitution). Concomitant with the monitoring of current brand performance are various behind-the-scene activities aimed at changing the firm's status via new products, packages, promotional campaigns—in short, the generation and pretesting of *alternatives* to the present marketing mix.

New-product activities, including idea generation, concept testing, prototype testing, and test-market introductions, comprise a sizable undertaking on the part of many business firms. Not surprisingly, marketing research plays a key role in these product-centered activities.

New-product development (including modifications of existing products) is usually an expensive and time-consuming process. As Pessemier and Root indicate in their article on new-product planning,[1] billions of dollars are spent annually for new-product research and development. While product-development procedures may vary considerably by company, many programs of this type involve formalized procedures for: (1) idea generation, (2) concept screening and testing, (3) prototype construction and evaluation, (4) marketing-mix formulation (including packaging, promotion, and pricing), and (5) market testing.

In this section of the chapter we briefly describe three classes of procedures utilized in the idea-generation and concept-evaluation stages:

1. The repertory and consumption grids, as used in the development of constructs and use occasions by which consumers describe various products or services.
2. Concept screening and testing procedures.
3. Test marketing.

[1]E. A. Pessemier and H. P. Root, "The Dimensions of New Product Planning," *Journal of Marketing*, 37 (January, 1973), 10–18.

Repertory and Consumption Grids

Both the repertory and consumption grids are aimed at developing consumers' perceptual encoding schemes. In the former case we are interested in the verbal constructs that consumers use to describe similarities and differences among brands or schemes. In the latter case we are interested in: (1) their perceived occasions of use, (2) their perceptions of interproduct substitution, and (3) their views about the types of users for whom the products may have particular appeal.

The *repertory grid* is based on Kelly's personal-construct theory in which man is assumed to develop over time a set of personalized constructs or "dimensions" with which he views entities or events.[2] From a marketing point of view, these constructs are typically product attributes. As a case in point, a major producer of frozen foods was recently interested in introducing a new type of toaster item that could be made up to taste like a variety of freshly baked products: blueberry muffins, Danish pastries, coffee cakes, and so on. The firm's marketing research director was particularly interested in the attributes of bakery items that consumers use to talk about and distinguish one product from another.

In this case, a series of focus-group interviews were set up and, in the course of these interviews, a repertory grid was developed. The typical procedure for developing a repertory grid of constructs is quite simple and involves the following steps:

1. The stimuli of interest—in this case the 20 bakery-type items shown in Table 17-1—are printed on a set of numbered cards.[3]
2. The respondent is asked to sort through the cards and remove any items with which he is completely unfamiliar.
3. Triples of cards are then selected (according to a prespecified sequence), and the respondent is asked to think of any way in which any two of the three items are similar to each other but different from the third.
4. The task is repeated for a new triple, and the respondent is asked for some new way in which any two of the stimuli are similar to each other and different from the third.

[2]See G. A. Kelly, *Psychology of Personal Constructs* (New York: W. W. Norton & Company, Inc., 1955). Also, see W. A. K. Frost and R. L. Braine, "The Application of the Repertory Grid Technique to Problems in Market Research," *Commentary*, 9 (July, 1967), 161–75.

[3]The illustration is drawn from P. E. Green and F. J. Carmone, "The Effect of Task on Intra-Individual Differences in Similarities Judgments," *Multivariate Behavioral Research*, 6 (October, 1971), 433–50.

**Table 17-1   List of food-item stimuli used
in repertory-grid study**

Stimulus	Stimulus
1. Toast pop-up	11. Cinnamon bun
2. Buttered toast (white)	12. Danish pastry
3. English muffin and margarine	13. Buttered toast (rye)
4. Jelly donut	14. Chocolate chip cookie
5. Cinnamon toast	15. Glazed donut
6. Blueberry muffin and margarine	16. Coffee cake
7. Hard rolls and butter	17. Apple strudel
8. Toast and marmalade	18. Toasted pound cake
9. Buttered toast and jelly	19. Corn muffin and butter
10. Toast and margarine (white)	20. Bagel and cream cheese

5. Constructs are recorded until the respondent fails to elicit any new ones as new triples are presented.

The construct sets of several individual respondents can be pooled (as was done in arriving at the 22 constructs shown as bipolar scales in Table 17-2) or maintained separately for each respondent. In either case the resulting stimuli and constructs can be set up in a grid or tabular fashion and respondents then asked to rate each stimulus (e.g., bakery item) on each construct.

The *consumption grid* also starts out with a set of stimuli, but in this case the respondent is presented with a *single stimulus* each time. For example, he may be shown the first stimulus, "toast pop-up," and asked to *list all occasions in which this item would be appropriate for his consumption*. For example, he may say: "with coffee at breakfast." For each occasion elicited he is then asked what *other products* might be appropriate for the same occasion, again elicited on a free-response basis. For the items thus elicited he may be asked for new occasions, and so on.

The consumption grid thus involves free-response data for both use occasions and new items. One can start out with a small core set of items and expand both the item set and the occasion set via sequentially obtained free responses. As a final step one can then present the *whole set of items and occasions* in grid fashion and have the respondent check off those occasions for which each item is appropriate. The net result of all of this is an items-by-occasions table in which each entry is coded 1 (denoting appropriateness) or 0 (denoting inappropriateness). Recent developments in scaling and clustering (see Chapter 14) permit this type of data to be portrayed as hierarchical clusters, at either the aggregate sample or subgroup levels.

Variations on the above procedure can be obtained via changes in instructions, for example: Who in the family would be most likely to con-

Table 17-2 List of 22 bipolar scales found from repertory grid

1. Nonfruity flavor	1	2	3	4	5	6	7	Fruity flavor
2. Easy to prepare	1	2	3	4	5	6	7	Hard to prepare
3. Low crispness	1	2	3	4	5	6	7	High crispness
4. Natural flavor	1	2	3	4	5	6	7	Artificial flavor
5. Dry texture	1	2	3	4	5	6	7	Moist texture
6. Complex flavor	1	2	3	4	5	6	7	Simple flavor
7. Complex shape	1	2	3	4	5	6	7	Simple shape
8. Not very filling	1	2	3	4	5	6	7	Highly filling
9. Appeals mainly to kids	1	2	3	4	5	6	7	Appeals mainly to adults
10. Served formally	1	2	3	4	5	6	7	Served informally
11. Primarily breakfast item	1	2	3	4	5	6	7	Primarily non-breakfast item
12. Soft texture	1	2	3	4	5	6	7	Hard texture
13. High perishability	1	2	3	4	5	6	7	Low perishability
14. Mostly eaten at home	1	2	3	4	5	6	7	Mostly eaten away from home
15. High calories	1	2	3	4	5	6	7	Low calories
16. Highly nutritious	1	2	3	4	5	6	7	Low in nutrition
17. Drab appearance	1	2	3	4	5	6	7	Colorful appearance
18. Usually eaten alone	1	2	3	4	5	6	7	Usually eaten with other foods
19. Low general familiarity	1	2	3	4	5	6	7	High general familiarity
20. Highly liked by men	1	2	3	4	5	6	7	Highly disliked by men
21. Ordinary-occasion food	1	2	3	4	5	6	7	Special-occasion food
22. Expensive	1	2	3	4	5	6	7	Inexpensive

sume this particular item? What other items would go well with this item? and so on.

The main purpose of the repertory and consumption grids is to find consumers' perceptual frameworks regarding brands or product substitutability or complementarity in terms of other facets (e.g., product attributes, use occasions, or user characteristics). The grids are often used in the generation of new-product concepts in the following manner:

1. Ideas for new products might be obtained by searching for new combinations of construct levels (so-called gap analysis[4]) from the repertory-grid analysis (e.g., a blueberry-flavored bagel).
2. Ideas might be suggested by the substitution of existing attributes (e.g., a vanilla-chip cookie or a mocha- (nonfruit) flavored strudel).

[4]N. Morgan and J. M. Purnell, "Isolating Openings for New Products in a Multidimensional Space," *Journal of the Market Research Society*, 11 (July, 1969), 245–66.

3. The consumption grid may be used as a preliminary device to search for ways in which two nominally different products (e.g., chewing gum and soft drinks), used on similar occasions, might be made morphologically more similar—developing a chewing gum with a a "carbonated" taste.

4. Ideas might be suggested by modifying products to encompass currently inappropriate use occasions—a cold-soup substitute for use occasions in which soft drinks are typically consumed.

5. Ideas might be suggested by complementarity motivations (e.g., a peanut-flavored pretzel as a cocktail party snack).

The above procedures are hardly exhaustive of how repertory- and consumption-grid data can be used in idea generation. Possibilities for changing product form, mode of application, range of application, function, type of consumer to whom the product will appeal, and the like are illustrative of the uses of these procedures in concept generation.

Indeed, whole families of new concepts might be generated by a type of "cross-pollination" in which one imagines that foods can be (metaphorically) designed to serve the functions of music or visual art, that pet foods are designed like human foods, that clothing is designed to appeal to all five senses, and so on. While many of these metaphorical studies are carried out with executives (in "brain-storming" sessions) rather than with consumers, there is no compelling reason why consumers could not be used.

Concept Screening and Testing

New-product ideas (however obtained) are often subjected to consumer evaluation by means of procedures known as *concept screening or concept testing*.[5] The usual objective is to check for market acceptability of the ideas, usually expressed in verbal or pictorial form, *before* costly developments are undertaken to build actual prototypes. Concept testing is often undertaken in parallel (or subsequent to) internal studies of technical feasibility.

Most concept-evaluation procedures exhibit the following characteristics:

1. A sample of potential buyers is presented with verbal or pictorial descriptions of the product—what its characteristics are, what functions it is designed to serve, its unique features compared to existing products. Control concepts (describing existing, but unidentified, products) are often included as well.

[5]Concept screening usually entails a rather crude consumer evaluation of a relatively large number of ideas while concept testing involves fewer concepts that are articulated in more detail; the latter procedure usually follows the preliminary application of concept screening. For illustrations of new developments in concept evaluation, see Yoram Wind, "A New Procedure for Concept Evaluation," *Journal of Marketing*, 37 (October, 1973), pp. 2–11.

2. Respondents are asked to rate each concept on various scales—degree of interest, intentions-to-buy, willingness to obtain the product versus an "equivalent" amount of cash.

3. Ratings may also be obtained on various prespecified attributes of the concept and respondents may be asked to list particular likes and dislikes about the concept, additional information that would be desirable to have about the concept, and so on.

From data obtained from tasks similar to the above, concepts are arrayed in terms of consumer interest. Often, normative data are also assembled over time on the relationship between various test scores from previous concept evaluations and the success rate of past product introductions (or between test and control concepts where market-share data are available for the latter).

Whatever the specific details of the procedure, the data are used as part of the basis on which the decision to undertake prototype development is made.

An Illustration of Concept Evaluation

To illustrate the principles of concept evaluation, we describe a study conducted by a large producer of chemically based consumer items. The sponsor of this study had been engaged in a series of product-development and diversification efforts. The company's development department, assisted by outside sources, had come up with a set of 31 product concepts that were technically feasible to manufacture.

The problem at this point was to obtain rather gross consumer evaluations of the concepts—a type of concept screening—for later refinement and subsequent testing of the most attractive concepts from the consumer's point of view. A verbal description and artist sketch were prepared for each concept. Illustrations of four of these are shown in Figure 17-1.

A mail questionnaire was designed and sent to members of a national panel. The respondents consisted of men and women (one person per household) from demographically matched households. A total of 986 returns were received from women and 774 from men.

Each respondent was asked first to group the 31 concepts into those that were personally "interesting" versus those that were "not interesting." For each of the "interesting" ones the respondent was asked a series of questions, as shown in Figure 17-2. Following this, she (or he) was asked to imagine that she was given an extra $100 and had to select at least one of the items (but could select more than one) and keep the change. She was then asked to select the item(s) she would choose.

Results of the study indicated that 5 of the 31 concepts received high evaluations from both men and women in terms of both single evaluation

Figure 17-1 Illustrative product-concept descriptions

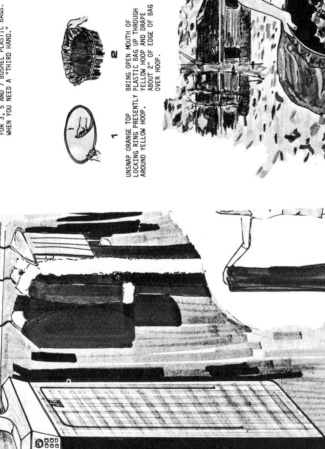

WRINKLE RIDDER PRODUCT NO. 64

WRINKLE RIDDER ... HAVE THAT FRESHLY PRESSED LOOK EVERY DAY, WITH A COMBINATION OF WARM MOIST AIR AND GENTLE VIBRATING ACTION, WRINKLE RIDDER TAKES THE WRINKLES OUT OF CLOTHES.

PLACE THE DRESS OR SUIT ON THE HANGER AND PRESS THE START BUTTON, THAT'S ALL! AFTER THE WRINKLES HAVE BEEN REMOVED, A DEODORIZER IS AUTOMATICALLY SPRAYED ON THE CLOTHES. THE DEODORIZER HAS NO FRAGRANCE OF ITS OWN, BUT REMOVES THE SMELL OF TOBACCO AND OTHER UNPLEASANT ODORS.

$24.95

THIRD HAND PRODUCT NO. 58

THIRD HAND PLASTIC BAG OPENER. EASY PLASTIC BAG FILLING EVERY TIME. FOR 3, 5 AND 7 BUSHEL PLASTIC BAGS. REUSABLE. FOR THOSE TIMES WHEN YOU NEED A "THIRD HAND." $ .99

1
UNSNAP ORANGE TOP LOCKING RING PRESENTLY AROUND YELLOW HOOP.

2
BRING OPEN MOUTH OF PLASTIC BAG UP THROUGH YELLOW HOOP AND DRAPE ABOUT 2" OF EDGE OF BAG OVER HOOP.

3

4
REPLACE ORANGE TOP LOCKING RING AROUND INSIDE OF BAG AND YELLOW RING, AS ORIGINALLY ON RING.

READY TO USE.
YOUR THIRD HAND.

READY WASH.....THE WINDOW WASHER THAT KEEPS ON CLEANING PRODUCT NO. 71

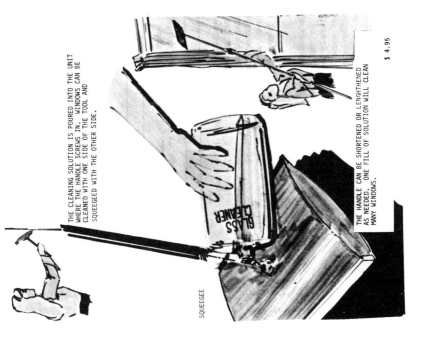

THE CLEANING SOLUTION IS POURED INTO THE UNIT WHERE THE HANDLE SCREWS IN. WINDOWS CAN BE CLEANED WITH ONE SIDE OF THE TOOL AND SQUEEGED WITH THE OTHER SIDE.

THE HANDLE CAN BE SHORTENED OR LENGTHENED AS NEEDED. ONE FILL OF SOLUTION WILL CLEAN MANY WINDOWS..

SQUEEGEE

$ 4.95

TRASH PACK PRODUCT NO. 74

THE ECONOMICAL WAY TO REDUCE THE VOLUME OF HOUSEHOLD TRASH. TRASH PACK SQUEEZES DOWN TIN CANS, CARDBOARD BOXES AND OTHER REFUSE. THE VOLUME IS REDUCED BY 70%. THE ONLY TYPE OF CONTAINER THAT TRASH PACK WON'T HANDLE IS GLASS.

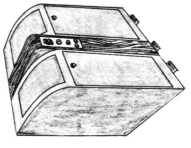

TRASH PACK IS LIKE AN ELECTRIC WASTE BASKET.

NO EXPENSIVE INSTALLATION COST!

$39.95

Figure 17-2   Response form used for each product-concept description

1. From what you have seen and read, which word or phrase best describes your reaction to this product?

    Excellent   ( )5   Good( )2
    Extremely good( )4   Fair( )1
    Very good   ( )3   Poor( )0

2. What, if anything, do you think you might like about this product?

    _____

    _____

3. What, if anything, do you think you might dislike about this product?

    _____

    _____

4. If you were thinking of buying this product, what other information would you like to have about the product?

    _____

    _____

5. Where would you shop to buy this product?

    Grocery or   Variety store   ( )16
       supermarket   ( )11   Door-to-door, or
    Hardware store   ( )12   in-home sales person ( )17
    Department store ( )13   Mail-order
    Discount store   ( )14   catalog   ( )18
    Drugstore   ( )15   Trading
                                        Stamp store   ( )19
                                        Other   ( )20

6. If this product were available at a local store, how likely do you think you would be to buy it?

    Absolutely sure I would buy it   ( )6
    Almost sure I would buy it   ( )5
    Probably would buy it   ( )4
    Might or might not buy it   ( )3
    Probably would not buy it   ( )2
    Almost sure I would not buy it   ( )1
    Absolutely sure I would not buy it   ( )0

7. Would this product make a good gift?

                                    YES( ) NO( )

scores and inclusion in the set of products that the respondent would consider if $100 were available for spending.

Two of these five "winners" are shown in Figure 17-1, the "Wrinkle Ridder" and the "Third Hand." For purposes of contrast, the other two concepts—"Trash Pack" and "Ready Wash"—received scores (for both men and women) around the middle of the array of 31 items. These were not recommended for further testing.

The five "winners" and three (control) items were recommended for further testing, involving price experimentation and more articulated descriptions, as developed from an analysis of the open-ended responses (to questions shown in Figure 17-2 on likes, dislikes, and further information desired). Hence, concept evaluation can often involve a recycling of the research as the concepts undergo revision and further articulation, based on the results of earlier surveys.

Prototype Evaluation and Market Testing

Concept screening, concept testing, prototype design, in-home use tests, and market tests can be viewed as a sequence of research steps in which the output of previous stages enters as input to subsequent ones. Of course, the possibility exists that a given stage may be recycled.

In concept screening and testing, one typically deals with verbalized or pictorial material only. In prototype and in-home testing one deals with the physical object, perhaps constructed in alternative forms, that can be tried out and compared to current products. A *prototype test* is any kind of evaluation that involves the physical product. *In-home tests* involve consumption of the prototype. As one moves from concept screening to prototype tests, the "stimuli" become more realistic, but the research costs mount.

The costs are particularly high in the *test-marketing* phase, where actual supplies of the product are placed on sale and alternative pricing, packaging, and promotional programs may be under test. (In general, the flexibility for program modification decreases as one moves through the sequence, although the similarity of the study to real marketing conditions increases.)

Another problem associated with full-scale market tests is the difficulty of controlling and monitoring the progress of the test. This problem is particularly acute in those cases in which marketing mixes are experimentally varied so that the researcher obtains information beyond that required for a "go, no go" decision.

A third problem concerns the fact that market tests can tip off one's competitors about the new-product candidate. Not only does this give them more lead time for developing strategies to combat the new entrant, but cases are known in which competitors have actually tried to thwart the market test itself by running special price promotions or other disruptive activities.

Finally, the amount of time required to assemble data on the results of the test market is substantial—often 12 to 18 months or more before a go, no-go decision is reached. Bearing in mind that additional lead time is then required for copy development and product placement, the total elapsed time can be significant. Recently, more efficient ways have been sought to: (1) test marketing-mix alternatives at the same time that one is testing new-product acceptance and (2) reduce measurement costs, risks of competitive exposure, and the time lapse associated with test marketing.

Insofar as the first point is concerned, new services have been introduced to deal with comparative promotional mix evaluation. For example, Adtel, a Chicago research firm, offers a variety of test-market services, including dual-cable TV, where alternative copy experiments can be run at the time a new product is test-marketed. Other firms provide a series of in-home use tests where the respondent can "purchase" additional quantities of the product after their initial supply has been exhausted.

One of the latest trends in test marketing is to *simulate* the whole activity. A number of consulting firms are offering test-market simulators that attempt to predict the time path of market share and sales, if the new product is introduced nationally under specified marketing-mix conditions. Typical inputs to these models include:

- An estimate of initial trial probability;
- An estimate of first repeat-purchase probability;
- Empirical functions relating second and later repeat purchases to first repeat purchase; and
- Functions relating model parameters to the firm's advertising and promotion, price, and distribution coverage.

Initial trial probability is usually estimated from simulated market-choice tests, such as laboratory shopping experiments. Repeat purchasing is usually estimated from in-home use tests involving test and control products.

A test-market simulation costs but a fraction of the typical full-scale test-market study. However, to date, relatively little is known about the simulators' accuracy in predicting market share and sales for new products and services that have been introduced by this means. As experience accumulates on their application, a more accurate evaluation of test-market simulators' benefits versus costs should be forthcoming.

TESTING COMPONENTS OF THE MARKETING MIX

Marketing researchers are frequently called upon to design and analyze tests of advertisements, package alternatives, and so on. These tests may be made in the context of either new products or existing products. The specialized procedures for carrying out this type of activity are myriad and no attempt will be made to catalog them. Rather, we provide a few illustrations of how such tests are designed and analyzed. The procedures described here are believed to be reasonably typical of the many kinds of techniques that are used in practice.

Promotion Testing

Many firms, almost as a matter of routine, conduct tests of new TV commercials, radio spots, or print ads. These tests are often but not necessarily made in the context of new-product introductions. An illustration of the type of questionnaire used in these tests is shown in Figure 17-3. In this case the context involved changes in promotional theme for an existing product.

The purpose underlying this study was to examine consumer reaction to three new (test) commercials for auto batteries. A sample of 400 men—all between 18 and 65 years of age and all responsible for maintaining a car that was two years old or older—were selected and interviewed in central location facilities. Each respondent of the test group viewed one of the three test commercials (on a special type of color–sound projector) and three competitive commercials. A control group viewed a current commercial of the sponsor and the three competitive commercials. Hence, each set of test or control data was based on 100 respondents and all four were evaluated in the context of the same three competitive commercials.

Figure 17-3 shows portions of the questionnaire containing questions dealing with reactions to each commercial (order rotated across respondents). Also shown is the set of preliminary questions related to product-class familiarity, brand predispositions, product-attribute importance, and perceived-attribute uniqueness. (Not shown are the sections of the questionnaire dealing with life-style, previous auto battery purchases, demographics, etc.)

Part A is included to obtain information on brand awareness and interest, for comparison with test results. Part B is designed to record main idea playback, general impressions, believability, evaluation of product attributes, and buying interest for the brand advertised in each commercial, as reacted to separately. Part C is designed for direct comparison of all four commercials (each of which involved Part B-type responses). Here the respondent is placed in a position of having to compare the brands involved in all four commercials—one sponsor and three competitive—in terms of choosing among the four products being advertised. Hence, comparison data are available on a before-exposure basis (Part A), separate-exposure basis (Part B), and comparison basis after all four exposures (Part C). Responses include global-type, single-stimulus evaluations (e.g., degree of interest in the product), global-type comparison evaluations (e.g., which of the four batteries would you buy?), and attribute-type responses.

In this particular study only one of the three test commercials significantly outrated the sponsor's control commercial (as well as outrating the

Figure 17-3 Portions of response form used in TV commercial testing: Part A—Awareness and interest

1. You indicated that you had an automobile that was more than two years old. What is the exact make, model and year of this auto? (REPEAT FOR EACH AUTO OVER TWO YEARS OLD.) Did you buy this auto new or used?

Car	Make		Model		Year		New	Used
(a)	13-22		23-32		33-34		35	
(b)	36-45		46-55		56-57		58	
(c)	59-68		69-78		79-80		8	

Subj. No.   1-4
Card No.2 5-6

2. Now I would like you to think about the different companies that make automobile batteries, or places where you can buy automobile batteries that you know of. Please tell me all the ones you know of. (PROBE WITH: What others?) (DO NOT READ LIST.)

A. Amoco _____ 9
B. Atlas _____ 10
C. Delco _____ 11
D. Exide _____ 12
E. Firestone Supreme _____ 13
F. Ford (not specified) _____ 14
   Motor Craft _____ 15
   Autolite _____ 16
G. Goodyear Power House _____ 17
H. Montgomery Ward's
   Riverside _____ 18

I. J.C. Penney's (not
            specified) _____ 19
   Survivor _____ 20
   Foremost _____ 21
J. Sears (not specified) _____ 22
   Die Hard _____ 23
   Allstate _____ 24
K. Shell Superlife _____ 25
L. Western Auto's Wizard _____ 26
M. Willard _____ 27
N. Willard-Exide _____ 28
   Other (SPECIFY)_____ 29

(HAND RESPONDENT CARD A.)

3. Imagine you were going to buy an automobile battery today. Please tell me which number on this card best describes how interested you think you would be in buying a _____(INSERT NAME) battery.

(REPEAT FOR EACH BRAND MENTIONED IN Q.2, AND FOR THE STARRED BRANDS, WHETHER OR NOT THEY WERE MENTIONED.)

	Not at all interested										Extremely Interested	
	0	10	20	30	40	50	60	70	80	90	100	
A. Amoco												30-32
B. Atlas												33-35
C. Delco												36-38
D. Exide												39-41
E.*Firestone Supreme												42-44
F. Ford (not specified)												45-47
*Ford-Motor Craft												48-50
Autolite												51-53
G.*Goodyear Power House												54-56
H. Montg. Ward's Riverside												57-59
I. J.C. Penney's (not spec.)												60-62
J.C. Penney's-Survivor												63-65
Foremost												66-68
J. Sears (not specified)												69-71
*Sears-Die Hard												72-74
Allstate												75-77
K. Shell Superlife												78-80
L. Western Auto's Wizard												8-10
M. Willard												11-13
N. Willard-Exide												14-16

Figure 17-3 (continued)
Part B—Single commercial test

Commercial-- "Ford Motor Craft"

Show respondent Commercial--"Ford Motor Craft." When he finishes say...

1. What was the one main thing the advertiser was trying to tell you about this product? (PROBE WITH: What was the one main thing about this product they were trying to get across to you?) (PROBE FOR CLARIFICATION.)

_____

_____

_____

2. What impressed you most about this product? (PROBE)

_____

_____

_____

3. (HAND CARD B TO RESPONDENT.)
   Please look at this card and tell me which number on it best indicates how believable the things they say about this product are to you.

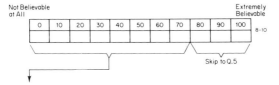

4. What are some of the things about this product you find hard to believe? (PROBE)

_____

_____

5. (HAND CARD C TO RESPONDENT.)
   I am going to read some statements that might be used to describe auto batteries. When I read each please look at this card and tell me to what extent you agree the statement describes the battery discussed in the commercial. Pick the big "yes"— if you agree completely. Pick the big "no" if you disagree completely. Or, you can pick any other size "yes" or "no" that best indicates how you feel.

   There are no right or wrong answers. We just want your opinions.

   Let's start. To what extent do you agree or disagree that the auto battery discussed in this commercial (READ FIRST STATEMENT)? Just read me the number corresponding to your opinion. (REPEAT FOR EACH STATEMENT.)

	STATEMENTS	YES	YES	YES	NO	NO	NO	
A	Starts car even in the coldest weather	6	5	4	3	2	1	11
B	Won't wear down even when your engine is hard to start	6	5	4	3	2	1	12
C	Has bigger plates and more acid	6	5	4	3	2	1	13
D	Starts your car when other batteries won't	6	5	4	3	2	1	14
E	Starts car even in the hottest weather	6	5	4	3	2	1	15
F	Has a very strong battery case	6	5	4	3	2	1	16
G	Guaranteed to be replaced free of cost	6	5	4	3	2	1	17
H	Has twice as much power as new car batteries	6	5	4	3	2	1	18
I	Has more power than you need until it's necessary	6	5	4	3	2	1	19
J	Keeps your car away from the tow truck	6	5	4	3	2	1	20
K	Has extra reserve power	6	5	4	3	2	1	21
L	Is thoroughly tested to withstand punishment	6	5	4	3	2	1	22
M	Has an easy-to-check water level	6	5	4	3	2	1	23
N	Is guaranteed to hold a charge under normal use for as long as you own that car	6	5	4	3	2	1	24

Figure 17-3 (continued)
Part B (continued)

6. (HAND CARD A TO RESPONDENT.)

Please look at this card and tell me which number on it best describes how interested you think you would be in buying the product described in the commercial.

Not at All   Extremely
Interested   Interested

0	10	20	30	40	50	60	70	80	90	100

25-27

7. Imagine you were going to buy the product exactly as it is described in the commercial. How much do you think it would cost? _____ 28-31

Part C—Comparison of commercials

Subj. No.   1-4
Card No. _13_ 5-6

1. (a) If you were going to buy a car battery, which of the four auto batteries you saw would you buy?

None	_____	8
Sears Die Hard	_____	9
Ford Motor Craft	_____	10
Goodyear Power House	_____	11
Firestone Supreme	_____	12

  (b) Why would you select that one?

_____

_____

  (c) Why wouldn't you select any one?

_____

_____

_____

2. (a) Which of the batteries you saw in the commercials has the best starting power?

Sears Die Hard	_____	13
Ford Motor Craft	_____	14
Goodyear Power House	_____	15
Firestone Supreme	_____	16

  (b) Why do you think this battery has the best starting power?

_____

3. (a) Which of the batteries you saw in the commercials has the best reserve power?

Sears Die Hard	_____	17
Ford Motor Craft	_____	18
Goodyear Power House	_____	19
Firestone Supreme	_____	20

  (b) Why do you think this battery has the best reserve power?

_____

_____

three competitive commercials). This particular test commercial scored well on recall of the main copy points, believability of claims, and product interest (Part B). Moreover, its share of choices in the comparison test of Part C was significantly higher than those of the other test commercials and control.

Interestingly enough, the winning test commercial emphasized reserve battery power and the ability to start the car under adverse weather conditions (in which other batteries might fail). Average price perceptions of the battery were also higher than those associated with commercials of competitive batteries, even though its average market price was about the same. Even allowing for the fact that the product had disproportionately high consumer awareness and interest (Part A responses), the winning test commercial displayed significantly higher brand scores. Finally, its comparative performance remained high over various demographic subgroups, suggesting an appeal of general interest to virtually all classes of respondents.

It would take us too far afield to describe the techniques used in the analysis of the responses obtained in this study. Suffice it to say that testing procedures can be rather elaborate (as illustrated here), even for such a seemingly simple task as TV commercial evaluation.

Packaging and Price Testing

The testing of alternative packages and prices often utilizes many of the same devices described earlier. To illustrate, a prominent manufacturer of carpet cleaning agents had developed a new type of foam cleaner, called *Lift Away*, made especially for spot cleaning. The cleaner was to be sprayed onto the carpet, worked in with an attached applicator, and left to dry. When dry, the same applicator would be used to brush away the dried foam (and the spot along with it).

The study summarized here was designed to test four alternative aersol packages and two alternative prices for the new cleaner. A sample of 220 housewives (drawn from five cities) who had used a rug shampoo in the last 60 days was drawn. Color photographs of the four package designs were shown to the respondent (first with no accompanying price information), and the respondent was asked to rank the four packages in terms of personal preference. Figure 17-4 shows sketches of the four package designs and frequencies of choice.[6] As clearly indicated, the third alternative receives the highest frequency of first choices.

The sample was then split and each respondent was shown a set of 11 alternatives and her own brand—as determined from an earlier question—if not one of the stimulus brands. Group A received the lower-price informa-

---

[6]Three of these packages (cans 2 through 4) were later used in a conjoint analysis, highlights of which are described in Chapter 14.

Figure 17-4   Frequencies of preference for new package designs

		Can 1	Can 2	Can 3	Can 4	Total Frequency
Preference Without Price	Most Prefer	8	6	124	82	220
	2nd Most Prefer	13	16	75	116	220
	3rd Most Prefer	47	152	9	12	220
	Least Prefer	152	46	12	10	220

tion for the four test packages, whereas group B received the higher-price information.

In each group the respondent was asked to check:

1. Those items she would consider purchasing on her next buying occasion (including her present brand, if desired).
2. Her most preferred item for future purchase.
3. Her second most preferred item if she could not obtain her first choice.

Prices of all existing brands were actual prices determined at the time of the study.

Table 17-3 shows the results of this part of the study. Of the four test designs, the third alternative continues to receive the highest percentage of: (1) considered purchases and (2) first-choice mentions, independent of price assignment. Not surprisingly, the percentage favoring alternative 3 declines from 25% (group A price conditions) to 14% (group B price conditions).

Table 17-3   Consumer reactions to various Lift Away packages
at different prices

		PERCENTAGE OF RESPONDENTS WHO:		
GROUP A LOWER PRICES FOR LIFT AWAY	PRICE	*Would Consider*	*Chose as Most Preferred*	*Chose as Second Most Preferred*
Lift Away 1	$ .88	65	2	6
Lift Away 2	$1.29	62	2	4
Lift Away 3	$1.41	83	25	17
Lift Away 4	$1.39	76	6	17
K2R	$1.59	72	17	21
Glory Spot	$ .77	68	9	13
Bissell Aerosol Rug Shampoo	$1.49	68	7	11
Dog Gone Carpet Kit	$3.98	7	1	2
Stain-Ex	$ .99	19	0	2
Out Carpet Spot Remover	$1.49	11	0	0
Abra-Cadabra	$0.79	10	0	0
Subject's brand		93	31	7
Total			100	100
GROUP B HIGHER PRICES FOR LIFT AWAY				
Lift Away 1	$1.19	61	2	8
Lift Away 2	$1.59	60	1	3
Lift Away 3	$1.98	79	14	18
Lift Away 4	$1.79	77	8	15
K2R	$1.59	69	14	14
Glory Spot	$ .77	70	13	19
Bissell Aerosol Rug Shampoo	$1.49	75	12	11
Dog Gone Carpet Kit	$3.98	13	1	3
Stain-Ex	$ .99	21	1	3
Out Carpet Spot Remover	$1.49	12	0	0
Abra-Cadabra	$0.79	12	1	0
Subject's brand		95	33	6
Total			100	100

However, an examination of cost and volume considerations indicated
that the higher price ($1.98) was justified, at least initially, from a profit
standpoint. From other information obtained in the survey, an initial target
group for promotion of the new product was found to involve:

1. Relatively high social classes, living primarily in the Midwest and
West.

2. Higher-than-average education, socially oriented, and active in the acquisition of new products.

3. Higher proportion owning pets.

The packaging alternative and pricing strategy found from this study were used in the subsequent national introduction of the product that took place after market testing.

LARGE-SCALE MARKET SIMULATORS

Over the past few years, increasing attention has been given to the development of large-scale market simulators in which various strategies involving new or redesigned products or services are evaluated. One of the main applications of *conjoint analysis* (see Chapter 14) has been its use in developing input parameters to market simulators. This type of application is illustrated in the context of a study involving airline services.

An Airline Company Example

The selection of an airline for domestic or transcontinental flights depends on a large number of service elements: departure time, number of stops en route, on-time reliability, type of aircraft, on-board amenities, friendliness of the airline personnel, and so on. A few years ago, a prominent airline, specializing in domestic flights, was interested in finding out which of its services were most important to passenger choice and how it was perceived, vis-à-vis competing airlines, on each of several service dimensions.[7]

Since evaluations of airline services (and perceptions of them as well) could be expected to vary by type of traveler, business versus nonbusiness, and by length of route, all data were collected according to a specific route–purpose combination, based on the trip last flown by the respondent.

Conjoint Analysis

Data were collected at central facility locations from respondents who had traveled by air during the past three months on one of the routes served by the study's sponsor. The total sample size was 680. The sponsor's identity was kept confidential during all interviews.

After collecting details of his last flight, the respondent was shown sets of pictures, each set describing one aspect of a hypothetical flight: ground services, in-flight services, physical decor of plane, and scheduling informa-

[7]The actual study is considerably abridged for purposes of this chapter.

tion. Wherever possible, visual props were used to illustrate the specific conditions. For example, Figure 17-5 shows two levels of one in-flight factor involving the placement and grooming of cabin attendants. Each set of sketches was prepared according to a fractional factorial design (see Chapter 14).[8]

Using the methodology of conjoint analysis, utility functions were prepared for each respondent. Some 15 different service factors were involved, as illustrated in Table 17-4. The "levels," or varieties, of each service factor ranged from two to five.

Illustratively, Figure 17-6 shows the utility functions obtained from business travelers on one of the longer hauls (two-hour flight time) for the four in-flight services listed in Table 17-4. As can be observed from the utility ranges, cabin attendants (placement and grooming) and type of food and beverages are the more important factors within this group of four.

Insofar as inputs to the market simulator are concerned, all utility functions were developed at the individual level, and each individual was classified by route and purpose of trip.

Figure 17-5 Illustrative levels for factor involving cabin attendants

I Two Attendants Up Front, Well-Groomed II One Attendant Up Front, Well-Groomed
One Attendant in Galley, Badly Groomed

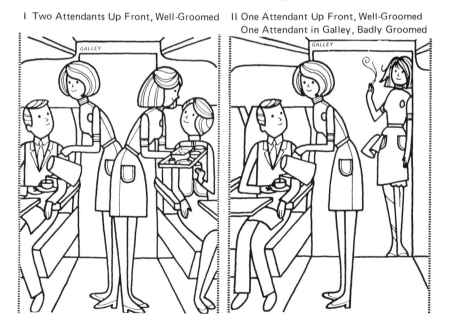

[8]Typically, in each scene there were four to six factors varying independently. Factors were interlinked over evaluations so that comparable utilities could be obtained for all components of the hypothetical flight.

Table 17-4   Airline service factors for
which utility functions were developed

Ground services	Physical decor
1. Quality of telephone service information	1. Amount of leg room
2. Courtesy and efficiency of check-in personnel	2. Seat width and comfort
3. Length of waiting line for check-in	3. Type of baggage racks
	4. Type and number of lavatory facilities
In-flight service	*Scheduling and other*
1. Cabin attendants (placement and grooming)	1. On-time arrival reliability
2. Type of reading material	2. Number of stops en route
3. Type of food and beverages	3. Departure relative to ideal time
4. Type of entertainment	4. Type of aircraft: regular versus wide body

Airline Perception Data

Following the flight evaluation task all respondents were shown the names of airlines serving the particular route to which they had been assigned. They were then asked to check off all of those airlines with which they had travel experience over the route in question.

Following this they were shown, for each of the 15 factors, the set of levels appropriate for that factor. Then, for the airlines with which they had claimed familiarity they were asked to select the factor level that most closely matched their perception of the airline's service level on that factor.

Since few respondents claimed familiarity with all airlines serving their route, the perception data were rather sparse (in addition to being crudely obtained). To increase the stability of the analysis these data were aggregated within route–purpose so that empirical probability functions were constructed across the levels of each factor. Each function represented the empirically estimated probability that the factor would display each level of service, under each specific airline. In this way, a perceptual service-level profile—actually a probability distribution of such profiles—was developed for each airline–route combination.

Constructing the Simulator

The individual utility functions, classified by trip purpose and route, and the probability distribution of airline service profiles, classified by route, constituted the primary input data for the simulator. The simulator was

Figure 17-6 Average business traveler utility functions for route involving two-hour flight

Utilities

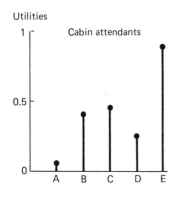

Cabin attendants

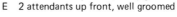

Legend

Cabin attendants
A 2 attendants in galley; badly groomed
B 2 attendants in galley; well groomed
C 1 front attendant, well groomed
   1 galley attendant, badly groomed
D 2 attendants up front, badly groomed
E 2 attendants up front, well groomed

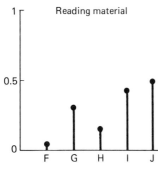

Reading material
F No reading material
G Assorted magazines
H Magazines only, buy newspapers at airport stand
I Magazines and free newspaper on board
J Magazines, newspaper, cassettes, dictating equipment

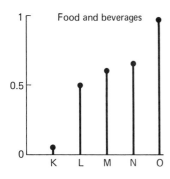

Food and beverages
K None
L Free coffee, tea, milk, soft drink
M Bar service; (free) coffee, tea, milk, soft drink
N Bar service; coffee, tea, milk, soft drink; snack
O Bar service; coffee, tea, milk, soft drink; meal

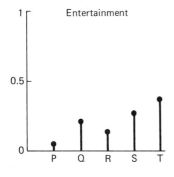

Entertainment
P None
Q Music only
R Games only
S Music and games
T Music, games, movie featurette

constructed so that the following aspects of the problem could be examined:

- Effect on sponsor's share of airline choices (compared to the base case from survey) if various levels of his service are changed, while all competitors' probability distributions remain the same.
- Effect on sponsor's share (compared to base) if his service levels and selected competitors' levels are simultaneously changed.
- Effect on sponsor's share (compared to base) if his service levels, competitors' service levels, and some of the utility functions themselves are simultaneously changed.

While the simulator incorporated all three levels of capability, in practice most of the simulator's runs were carried out at the first level of analysis. The first-level simulation operated along the following lines:

- The user reads in the base-case service-level distributions.
- Random numbers are chosen and a particular service profile is selected for each airline's probability distribution by route.
- Each member of that route applies his specific utility function to all airlines on which familiarity had been claimed by that individual.
- The consumer chooses the airline with the highest utility (according to his specific utility function).
- The test case is next introduced (with its new probability distributions for the sponsor firm), while all competitive profiles remain as before.
- A choice is made under the test case, also on the basis of highest utility.
- Share of choices going to each airline are then compared, base versus test case, for each route–purpose and in-total.
- Tables and charts are provided by the simulator on the comparative performance of all test cases versus the base case (and versus each other, as well). It should be mentioned, however, that this simulator was quite crude by present standards.

Second-generation simulators of considerably greater sophistication have been proposed. For example, Frank J. Carmone, Drexel University, has developed a simulator called PRODSIM that has all the capabilities of the above and, in addition:

- Incorporates several different choice functions, including probability-of-choice mechanisms.

- Allows the user complete freedom in specifying individual probability distributions over any service or product profile.
- Provides brand-switching information regarding where new products or services will attract their business.
- Can handle up to 30 different product or service factors with up to six levels per factor.
- Provides interpolation possibilities for continuous factors.
- Allows the user to systematically search for "optimal" service and product regions to aid in designing alternatives with high choice potential.

In short, this program (and others like it) can be used on a more or less continuous market-planning basis. As new perceptual and utility data are collected, the simulator's parameters can be updated for future testing of competitive strategies.

In the airline example the sponsor of the study tried out a wide variety of possible strategies and explored their implications on a cost–benefits basis. One decision involved the hiring of additional terminal check-in personnel to reduce customer waiting time. On the other hand, some (costly) services that had originally been planned for some routes were not implemented after the simulator indicated that their impact on increased demand would not justify their cost.

Other Computer-based Models

A number of researchers have specialized in the construction of large-scale market-strategy models. Presently, models exist for advertising-budget determination, marketing-mix decisions, new-product forecasting and sales-call planning, to name a few.

These *second-generation* models are distinguished from earlier models by five important characteristics:

1. The models do not attempt to "optimize" in the traditional sense but rather try to search intelligently for good decisions, based on a realistic data-based, predictive model.
2. The models make liberal use of the manager's judgments in key areas when objective data are unavailable or too costly to obtain.
3. The models are user-oriented, allowing the manager to learn simplified versions of the model before complex ones—a type of evolutionary approach toward understanding the model.
4. The models are set up on time-share systems in which the manager has ready access to the algorithm via portable terminals and can

communicate with the model by means of simple English commands.[9]

5. The models are easily adapted for changes in assumptions while providing rapid feedback on the consequences of changes in parameter values that the manager might wish to consider.

These modifications in the philosophy (as well as practice) of model building make a great deal of sense to the present authors and they augur well for continued progress in this area.

In addition to the above models, whose descriptions have been published, a number of other models have been developed on an intracompany or intraconsulting firm basis. In particular, a number of firms are currently experimenting with approaches to test market simulation, although details of these activities are not generally available.

Insofar as the motivation underlying this book is concerned, we note that the more recently developed models allow directly for the input of managerial judgments (frequently in the form of prior probabilities), a characteristic that is fully in accord with this book's presentation. Second, the models emphasize the need for data banks and systematic updating of parameter values. Clearly, the models are on the side of the marketing researcher: his future role may well be even more important than his current contributions to marketing decision making.

SUMMARY

By dealing with specialized procedures for the design and evaluation of marketing strategies, we have tried to provide a broad sampling of the types of studies in which marketing researchers participate. While the examples are drawn mainly from the authors' own consulting experience, it is felt that they are representative of current efforts on the part of the more technically trained researcher. However, no attempt has been made to present all of the implications of each study.

We discussed a variety of procedures, such as new-product generation, concept evaluation, ad testing, packaging, and pricing studies, aimed at examining proposed changes to the status quo. Capsule studies were used to illustrate the procedures in the form of actual marketing analyses. In cases where specialized techniques (multidimensional scaling, conjoint analysis, etc.) were used, the reader was referred to appropriate chapters for details.

[9]L. M. Lodish, "Decision Models for Marketing Management," *Wharton Quarterly*, 7 (Fall, 1972), 53–56.

We concluded the chapter with a discussion of large-scale marketing models, their characteristics, future potential, and relationship to the data input and analytical functions of the marketing researcher.

ASSIGNMENT MATERIAL

1. Design and carry out a small repertory-grid study in which the stimuli are brands of beer.
   a. What are some of the ways in which the resulting grid can be analyzed?
   b. How would you proceed to conduct a consumption-grid study using the same stimuli as used in the repertory grid?
   c. How would you go about developing a free-association grid for the brands of beer used above? (See Chapter 8.)

2. Describe how you would set up a field experiment that considers simultaneously changes in brand name, packaging features, and pricing for a new cereal product (see Chapter 14).
   a. What factor levels would you use?
   b. How would you prepare the stimuli?
   c. What response measure would you select and what techniques for analysis seem appropriate?

3. Select from the literature some large-scale marketing model.
   a. Critique the model from the standpoint of managerial usefulness.
   b. How would you proceed to construct a model that simulated market testing in which you wish to obtain: (1) first trial rate and (2) first repeat-purchase rate?

4. How would you go about trying to improve the (crude) simulator described in the airline study?
   a. How would you change the respondent-choice rule?
   b. How would you go about incorporating an explicit time path of share of choices?
   c. How would you plan to "test" the simulator's output?

5. Describe how you would go about using conjoint analysis to construct a simulator of network program selection in prime-time television viewing. What types of data would you collect? What are the control variables of interest?

APPENDIX A

Statistical Tables

Table A-1 Cumulative normal distribution—values of probability

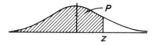

Values of P corresponding to Z for the normal curve. Z is the standard normal variable. The value of P for $-Z$ equals 1 minus the value of P for $+Z$, e.g., the P for -1.62 equals $1 - .9474 = .0526$.

Z = standard normal variate

Z	.00	.01	.02	.03	.04	.05	.06	.07	.08	.09
.0	.5000	.5040	.5080	.5120	.5160	.5199	.5239	.5279	.5319	.5359
.1	.5398	.5438	.5478	.5517	.5557	.5596	.5636	.5675	.5714	.5753
.2	.5793	.5832	.5871	.5910	.5948	.5987	.6026	.6064	.6103	.6141
.3	.6179	.6217	.6255	.6293	.6331	.6368	.6406	.6443	.6480	.6517
.4	.6554	.6591	.6628	.6664	.6700	.6736	.6772	.6808	.6844	.6879
.5	.6915	.6950	.6985	.7019	.7054	.7088	.7123	.7157	.7190	.7224
.6	.7257	.7291	.7324	.7357	.7389	.7422	.7454	.7486	.7517	.7549
.7	.7580	.7611	.7642	.7673	.7704	.7734	.7764	.7794	.7823	.7852
.8	.7881	.7910	.7939	.7967	.7995	.8023	.8051	.8078	.8106	.8133
.9	.8159	.8186	.8212	.8238	.8264	.8289	.8315	.8340	.8365	.8389
1.0	.8413	.8438	.8461	.8485	.8508	.8531	.8554	.8577	.8599	.8621
1.1	.8643	.8665	.8686	.8708	.8729	.8749	.8770	.8790	.8810	.8830
1.2	.8849	.8869	.8888	.8907	.8925	.8944	.8962	.8980	.8997	.9015
1.3	.9032	.9049	.9066	.9082	.9099	.9115	.9131	.9147	.9162	.9177
1.4	.9192	.9207	.9222	.9236	.9251	.9265	.9279	.9292	.9306	.9319
1.5	.9332	.9345	.9357	.9370	.9382	.9394	.9406	.9418	.9429	.9441
1.6	.9452	.9463	.9474	.9484	.9495	.9505	.9515	.9525	.9535	.9545
1.7	.9554	.9564	.9573	.9582	.9591	.9599	.9608	.9616	.9625	.9633
1.8	.9641	.9649	.9656	.9664	.9671	.9678	.9686	.9693	.9699	.9706
1.9	.9713	.9719	.9726	.9732	.9738	.9744	.9750	.9756	.9761	.9767
2.0	.9772	.9778	.9783	.9788	.9793	.9798	.9803	.9808	.9812	.9817
2.1	.9821	.9826	.9830	.9834	.9838	.9842	.9846	.9850	.9854	.9857
2.2	.9861	.9864	.9868	.9871	.9875	.9878	.9881	.9884	.9887	.9890
2.3	.9893	.9896	.9898	.9901	.9904	.9906	.9909	.9911	.9913	.9916
2.4	.9918	.9920	.9922	.9925	.9927	.9929	.9931	.9932	.9934	.9936
2.5	.9938	.9940	.9941	.9943	.9945	.9946	.9948	.9949	.9951	.9952
2.6	.9953	.9955	.9956	.9957	.9959	.9960	.9961	.9962	.9963	.9964
2.7	.9965	.9966	.9967	.9968	.9969	.9970	.9971	.9972	.9973	.9974
2.8	.9974	.9975	.9976	.9977	.9977	.9978	.9979	.9979	.9980	.9981
2.9	.9981	.9982	.9982	.9983	.9984	.9984	.9985	.9985	.9986	.9986
3.0	.9987	.9987	.9987	.9988	.9988	.9989	.9989	.9989	.9990	.9990
3.1	.9990	.9991	.9991	.9991	.9992	.9992	.9992	.9992	.9993	.9993
3.2	.9993	.9993	.9994	.9994	.9994	.9994	.9994	.9995	.9995	.9995
3.3	.9995	.9995	.9995	.9996	.9996	.9996	.9996	.9996	.9996	.9997
3.4	.9997	.9997	.9997	.9997	.9997	.9997	.9997	.9997	.9997	.9998

Table A-2   Upper percentiles of the *t* distribution

$1-\alpha$ df	.75	.90	.95	.975	.99	.995	.9995
1	1.000	3.078	6.314	12.706	31.821	63.657	636.619
2	.816	1.886	2.920	4.303	6.965	9.925	31.598
3	.765	1.638	2.353	3.182	4.541	5.841	12.941
4	.741	1.533	2.132	2.776	3.747	4.604	8.610
5	.727	1.476	2.015	2.571	3.365	4.032	6.859
6	.718	1.440	1.943	2.447	3.143	3.707	5.959
7	.711	1.415	1.895	2.365	2.998	3.499	5.405
8	.706	1.397	1.860	2.306	2.896	3.355	5.041
9	.703	1.383	1.833	2.262	2.821	3.250	4.781
10	.700	1.372	1.812	2.228	2.764	3.169	4.587
11	.697	1.363	1.796	2.201	2.718	3.106	4.437
12	.695	1.356	1.782	2.179	2.681	3.055	4.318
13	.694	1.350	1.771	2.160	2.650	3.012	4.221
14	.692	1.345	1.761	2.145	2.624	2.977	4.140
15	.691	1.341	1.753	2.131	2.602	2.947	4.073
16	.690	1.337	1.746	2.120	2.583	2.921	4.015
17	.689	1.333	1.740	2.110	2.567	2.898	3.965
18	.688	1.330	1.734	2.101	2.552	2.878	3.922
19	.688	1.328	1.729	2.093	2.339	2.861	3.883
20	.687	1.325	1.725	2.086	2.528	2.845	3.850
21	.686	1.323	1.721	2.080	2.518	2.831	3.819
22	.686	1.321	1.717	2.074	2.508	2.819	3.792
23	.685	1.319	1.714	2.069	2.500	2.807	3.767
24	.685	1.318	1.711	2.064	2.492	2.797	3.745
25	.684	1.316	1.708	2.060	2.485	2.787	3.725
26	.684	1.315	1.706	2.056	2.479	2.779	3.707
27	.684	1.314	1.703	2.052	2.473	2.771	3.690
28	.683	1.313	1.701	2.048	2.467	2.763	3.674
29	.683	1.311	1.699	2.045	2.462	2.756	3.659
30	.683	1.310	1.697	2.042	2.457	2.750	3.646
40	.681	1.303	1.684	2.021	2.423	2.704	3.551
60	.679	1.296	1.671	2.000	2.390	2.660	3.460
120	.677	1.289	1.658	1.980	2.358	2.617	3.373
∞	.674	1.282	1.645	1.960	2.326	2.576	3.291

df = degrees of freedom

Source: From Table III of R. A. Fisher and F. Yates, *Statistical Tables for Biological, Agricultural, and Medical Research,* published by Oliver & Boyd Ltd., Edinburgh, by permission of the authors and publishers.

Table A-3 Percentiles of the χ^2 distribution

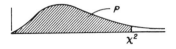

Values of χ^2 corresponding to P

df	$\chi^2_{.005}$	$\chi^2_{.01}$	$\chi^2_{.025}$	$\chi^2_{.05}$	$\chi^2_{.10}$	$\chi^2_{.90}$	$\chi^2_{.95}$	$\chi^2_{.975}$	$\chi^2_{.99}$	$\chi^2_{.995}$
1	.000039	.00016	.00098	.0039	.0158	2.71	3.84	5.02	6.63	7.88
2	.0100	.0201	.0506	.1026	.2107	4.61	5.99	7.38	9.21	10.60
3	.0717	.115	.216	.352	.584	6.25	7.81	9.35	11.34	12.84
4	.207	.297	.484	.711	1.064	7.78	9.49	11.14	13.28	14.86
5	.412	.554	.831	1.15	1.61	9.24	11.07	12.83	15.09	16.75
6	.676	.872	1.24	1.64	2.20	10.64	12.59	14.45	16.81	18.55
7	.989	1.24	1.69	2.17	2.83	12.02	14.07	16.01	18.48	20.28
8	1.34	1.65	2.18	2.73	3.49	13.36	15.51	17.53	20.09	21.96
9	1.73	2.09	2.70	3.33	4.17	14.68	16.92	19.02	21.67	23.59
10	2.16	2.56	3.25	3.94	4.87	15.99	18.31	20.48	23.21	25.19
11	2.60	3.05	3.82	4.57	5.58	17.28	19.68	21.92	24.73	26.76
12	3.07	3.57	4.40	5.23	6.30	18.55	21.03	23.34	26.22	28.30
13	3.57	4.11	5.01	5.89	7.04	19.81	22.36	24.74	27.69	29.82
14	4.07	4.66	5.63	6.57	7.79	21.06	23.68	26.12	29.14	31.32
15	4.60	5.23	6.26	7.26	8.55	22.31	25.00	27.49	30.58	32.80
16	5.14	5.81	6.91	7.96	9.31	23.54	26.30	28.85	32.00	34.27
18	6.26	7.01	8.23	9.39	10.86	25.99	28.87	31.53	34.81	37.16
20	7.43	8.26	9.59	10.85	12.44	28.41	31.41	34.17	37.57	40.00
24	9.89	10.86	12.40	13.85	15.66	33.20	36.42	39.36	42.98	45.56
30	13.79	14.95	16.79	18.49	20.60	40.26	43.77	46.98	50.89	53.67
40	20.71	22.16	24.43	26.51	29.05	51.81	55.76	59.34	63.69	66.77
60	35.53	37.48	40.48	43.19	46.46	74.40	79.08	83.30	88.38	91.95
120	83.85	86.92	91.58	95.70	100.62	140.23	146.57	152.21	158.95	163.64

df = degrees of freedom

Source: Adapted with permission from *Introduction to Statistical Analysis*, 2d ed., by W. J. Dixon and F. J. Massey, Jr., Copyright 1957, McGraw-Hill Book Company.

Table A-4 Percentiles of the F distribution

n_1 = degrees of freedom for numerator

$F_{0.90}(n_1, n_2)$ $\alpha = 0.1$

$n_2 \backslash n_1$	1	2	3	4	5	6	7	8	9	10	12	15	20	24	30	40	60	120	∞
1	39.86	49.50	53.59	55.83	57.24	58.20	58.91	59.44	59.86	60.19	60.71	61.22	61.74	62.00	62.26	62.53	62.79	63.06	63.33
2	8.53	9.00	9.16	9.24	9.29	9.33	9.35	9.37	9.38	9.39	9.41	9.42	9.44	9.45	9.46	9.47	9.47	9.48	9.49
3	5.54	5.46	5.39	5.34	5.31	5.28	5.27	5.25	5.24	5.23	5.22	5.20	5.18	5.18	5.17	5.16	5.15	5.14	5.13
4	4.54	4.32	4.19	4.11	4.05	4.01	3.98	3.95	3.94	3.92	3.90	3.87	3.84	3.83	3.82	3.80	3.79	3.78	3.76
5	4.06	3.78	3.62	3.52	3.45	3.40	3.37	3.34	3.32	3.30	3.27	3.24	3.21	3.19	3.17	3.16	3.14	3.12	3.10
6	3.78	3.46	3.29	3.18	3.11	3.05	3.01	2.98	2.96	2.94	2.90	2.87	2.84	2.82	2.80	2.78	2.76	2.74	2.72
7	3.59	3.26	3.07	2.96	2.88	2.83	2.78	2.75	2.72	2.70	2.67	2.63	2.59	2.58	2.56	2.54	2.51	2.49	2.47
8	3.46	3.11	2.92	2.81	2.73	2.67	2.62	2.59	2.56	2.50	2.50	2.46	2.42	2.40	2.38	2.36	2.34	2.32	2.29
9	3.36	3.01	2.81	2.69	2.61	2.55	2.51	2.47	2.44	2.42	2.38	2.34	2.30	2.28	2.25	2.23	2.21	2.18	2.16
10	3.29	2.92	2.73	2.61	2.52	2.46	2.41	2.38	2.35	2.32	2.28	2.24	2.20	2.18	2.16	2.13	2.11	2.08	2.06
11	3.23	2.86	2.66	2.54	2.45	2.39	2.34	2.30	2.27	2.25	2.21	2.17	2.12	2.10	2.08	2.05	2.03	2.00	1.97
12	3.18	2.81	2.61	2.48	2.39	2.33	2.28	2.24	2.21	2.19	2.15	2.10	2.06	2.04	2.01	1.99	1.96	1.93	1.90
13	3.14	2.76	2.56	2.43	2.35	2.28	2.23	2.20	2.16	2.14	2.10	2.05	2.01	1.98	1.96	1.93	1.90	1.88	1.85
14	3.10	2.73	2.52	2.39	2.31	2.24	2.19	2.15	2.12	2.10	2.05	2.01	1.96	1.94	1.91	1.89	1.86	1.83	1.80
15	3.07	2.70	2.49	2.36	2.27	2.21	2.16	2.12	2.09	2.06	2.02	1.97	1.92	1.90	1.87	1.85	1.82	1.79	1.76
16	3.05	2.67	2.46	2.33	2.24	2.18	2.13	2.09	2.06	2.03	1.99	1.94	1.89	1.87	1.84	1.81	1.78	1.75	1.72
17	3.03	2.64	2.44	2.31	2.22	2.15	2.10	2.06	2.03	2.00	1.96	1.91	1.86	1.84	1.81	1.78	1.75	1.72	1.69
18	3.01	2.62	2.42	2.29	2.20	2.13	2.08	2.04	2.00	1.98	1.93	1.89	1.84	1.81	1.78	1.75	1.72	1.69	1.66
19	2.99	2.61	2.40	2.27	2.18	2.11	2.06	2.02	1.98	1.96	1.91	1.86	1.81	1.79	1.76	1.73	1.70	1.67	1.63
20	2.97	2.59	2.38	2.25	2.16	2.09	2.04	2.00	1.96	1.94	1.89	1.84	1.79	1.77	1.74	1.71	1.68	1.64	1.61
21	2.96	2.57	2.36	2.23	2.14	2.08	2.02	1.98	1.95	1.92	1.87	1.83	1.78	1.75	1.72	1.69	1.66	1.62	1.59
22	2.95	2.56	2.35	2.22	2.13	2.06	2.01	1.97	1.93	1.90	1.86	1.81	1.76	1.73	1.70	1.67	1.64	1.60	1.57
23	2.94	2.55	2.34	2.21	2.11	2.05	1.99	1.95	1.92	1.89	1.84	1.80	1.74	1.72	1.69	1.66	1.62	1.59	1.55
24	2.93	2.54	2.33	2.19	2.10	2.04	1.98	1.94	1.91	1.88	1.83	1.78	1.73	1.70	1.67	1.64	1.61	1.57	1.53
25	2.92	2.53	2.32	2.18	2.09	2.02	1.97	1.93	1.89	1.87	1.82	1.77	1.72	1.69	1.66	1.63	1.59	1.56	1.52
26	2.91	2.52	2.31	2.17	2.08	2.01	1.96	1.92	1.88	1.86	1.81	1.76	1.71	1.68	1.65	1.61	1.58	1.54	1.50
27	2.90	2.51	2.30	2.17	2.07	2.00	1.95	1.91	1.87	1.85	1.80	1.75	1.70	1.67	1.64	1.60	1.57	1.53	1.49
28	2.89	2.50	2.29	2.16	2.06	2.00	1.94	1.90	1.87	1.84	1.79	1.74	1.69	1.66	1.63	1.59	1.56	1.52	1.48
29	2.89	2.50	2.28	2.15	2.06	1.99	1.93	1.89	1.86	1.83	1.78	1.73	1.68	1.65	1.62	1.58	1.55	1.51	1.47
30	2.88	2.49	2.28	2.14	2.05	1.98	1.93	1.88	1.85	1.82	1.77	1.72	1.67	1.64	1.61	1.57	1.54	1.50	1.46
40	2.84	2.44	2.23	2.09	2.00	1.93	1.87	1.83	1.79	1.76	1.71	1.66	1.61	1.57	1.54	1.51	1.47	1.42	1.38
60	2.79	2.39	2.18	2.04	1.95	1.87	1.82	1.77	1.74	1.71	1.66	1.60	1.54	1.51	1.48	1.44	1.40	1.35	1.29
120	2.75	2.35	2.13	1.99	1.90	1.82	1.77	1.72	1.68	1.65	1.60	1.55	1.48	1.45	1.41	1.37	1.32	1.26	1.19
∞	2.71	2.30	2.08	1.94	1.85	1.77	1.72	1.67	1.63	1.60	1.55	1.49	1.42	1.38	1.34	1.30	1.24	1.17	1.00

n_2 = degrees of freedom for denominator

Source: Adapted with permission from *Biometrika Tables for Statisticians*, Vol. I, 2nd ed., edited by E. S. Pearson and H. O. Hartley, Copyright 1958, Cambridge University Press.

591

Table A-4 (continued)

$$F_{.95}(n_1, n_2) \qquad \alpha = 0.05$$

n_1 = degrees of freedom for numerator

n_2 = degrees of freedom for denominator

n_2 \ n_1	1	2	3	4	5	6	7	8	9	10	12	15	20	24	30	40	60	120	∞
1	161.4	199.5	215.7	224.6	230.2	234.0	236.8	238.9	240.5	241.9	243.9	245.9	248.0	249.1	250.1	251.1	252.2	253.3	254.3
2	18.51	19.00	19.16	19.25	19.30	19.33	19.35	19.37	19.38	19.40	19.41	19.43	19.45	19.45	19.46	19.47	19.48	19.49	19.50
3	10.13	9.55	9.28	9.12	9.01	8.94	8.89	8.85	8.81	8.79	8.74	8.70	8.66	8.64	8.62	8.59	8.57	8.55	8.53
4	7.71	6.94	6.59	6.39	6.26	6.16	6.09	6.04	6.00	5.96	5.91	5.86	5.80	5.77	5.75	5.72	5.69	5.66	5.63
5	6.61	5.79	5.41	5.19	5.05	4.95	4.88	4.82	4.77	4.74	4.68	4.62	4.56	4.53	4.50	4.46	4.43	4.40	4.36
6	5.99	5.14	4.76	4.53	4.39	4.28	4.21	4.15	4.10	4.06	4.00	3.94	3.87	3.84	3.81	3.77	3.74	3.70	3.67
7	5.59	4.74	4.35	4.12	3.97	3.87	3.79	3.73	3.68	3.64	3.57	3.51	3.44	3.41	3.38	3.34	3.30	3.27	3.23
8	5.32	4.46	4.07	3.84	3.69	3.58	3.50	3.44	3.39	3.35	3.28	3.22	3.15	3.12	3.08	3.04	3.01	2.97	2.93
9	5.12	4.26	3.86	3.63	3.48	3.37	3.29	3.23	3.18	3.14	3.07	3.01	2.94	2.90	2.86	2.83	2.79	2.75	2.71
10	4.96	4.10	3.71	3.48	3.33	3.22	3.14	3.07	3.02	2.98	2.91	2.85	2.77	2.74	2.70	2.66	2.62	2.58	2.54
11	4.84	3.98	3.59	3.36	3.20	3.09	3.01	2.95	2.90	2.85	2.79	2.72	2.65	2.61	2.57	2.53	2.49	2.45	2.40
12	4.75	3.89	3.49	3.26	3.11	3.00	2.91	2.85	2.80	2.75	2.69	2.62	2.54	2.51	2.47	2.43	2.38	2.34	2.30
13	4.67	3.81	3.41	3.18	3.03	2.92	2.83	2.77	2.71	2.67	2.60	2.53	2.46	2.42	2.38	2.34	2.30	2.25	2.21
14	4.60	3.74	3.34	3.11	2.96	2.85	2.76	2.70	2.65	2.60	2.53	2.46	2.39	2.35	2.31	2.27	2.22	2.18	2.13
15	4.54	3.68	3.29	3.06	2.90	2.79	2.71	2.64	2.59	2.54	2.48	2.40	2.33	2.29	2.25	2.20	2.16	2.11	2.07
16	4.49	3.63	3.24	3.01	2.85	2.74	2.66	2.59	2.54	2.49	2.42	2.35	2.28	2.24	2.19	2.15	2.11	2.06	2.01
17	4.45	3.59	3.20	2.96	2.81	2.70	2.61	2.55	2.49	2.45	2.38	2.31	2.23	2.19	2.15	2.10	2.06	2.01	1.96
18	4.41	3.55	3.16	2.93	2.77	2.66	2.58	2.51	2.46	2.41	2.34	2.27	2.19	2.15	2.11	2.06	2.02	1.97	1.92
19	4.38	3.52	3.13	2.90	2.74	2.63	2.54	2.48	2.42	2.38	2.31	2.23	2.16	2.11	2.07	2.03	1.98	1.93	1.88
20	4.35	3.49	3.10	2.87	2.71	2.60	2.51	2.45	2.39	2.35	2.28	2.20	2.12	2.08	2.04	1.99	1.95	1.90	1.84
21	4.32	3.47	3.07	2.84	2.68	2.57	2.49	2.42	2.37	2.32	2.25	2.18	2.10	2.05	2.01	1.96	1.92	1.87	1.81
22	4.30	3.44	3.05	2.82	2.66	2.55	2.46	2.40	2.34	2.30	2.23	2.15	2.07	2.03	1.98	1.94	1.89	1.84	1.78
23	4.28	3.42	3.03	2.80	2.64	2.53	2.44	2.37	2.32	2.27	2.20	2.13	2.05	2.01	1.96	1.91	1.86	1.81	1.76
24	4.26	3.40	3.01	2.78	2.62	2.51	2.42	2.36	2.30	2.25	2.18	2.11	2.03	1.98	1.94	1.89	1.84	1.79	1.73
25	4.24	3.39	2.99	2.76	2.60	2.49	2.40	2.34	2.28	2.24	2.16	2.09	2.01	1.96	1.92	1.87	1.82	1.77	1.71
26	4.23	3.37	2.98	2.74	2.59	2.47	2.39	2.32	2.27	2.22	2.15	2.07	1.99	1.95	1.90	1.85	1.80	1.75	1.69
27	4.21	3.35	2.96	2.73	2.57	2.46	2.37	2.31	2.25	2.20	2.13	2.06	1.97	1.93	1.88	1.84	1.79	1.73	1.67
28	4.20	3.34	2.95	2.71	2.56	2.45	2.36	2.29	2.24	2.19	2.12	2.04	1.96	1.91	1.87	1.82	1.77	1.71	1.65
29	4.18	3.33	2.93	2.70	2.55	2.43	2.35	2.28	2.22	2.18	2.10	2.03	1.94	1.90	1.85	1.81	1.75	1.70	1.64
30	4.17	3.32	2.92	2.69	2.53	2.42	2.33	2.27	2.21	2.16	2.09	2.01	1.93	1.89	1.84	1.79	1.74	1.68	1.62
40	4.08	3.23	2.84	2.61	2.45	2.34	2.25	2.18	2.12	2.08	2.00	1.92	1.84	1.79	1.74	1.69	1.64	1.58	1.51
60	4.00	3.15	2.76	2.53	2.37	2.25	2.17	2.10	2.04	1.99	1.92	1.84	1.75	1.70	1.65	1.59	1.53	1.47	1.39
120	3.92	3.07	2.68	2.45	2.29	2.17	2.09	2.02	1.96	1.91	1.83	1.75	1.66	1.61	1.55	1.50	1.43	1.35	1.25
∞	3.84	3.00	2.60	2.37	2.21	2.10	2.01	1.94	1.88	1.83	1.75	1.67	1.57	1.52	1.46	1.39	1.32	1.22	1.00

Table A-4 (continued)

$$F_{.99}(n_1, n_2) \qquad \alpha = 0.01$$

n_1 = degrees of freedom for numerator

n_2 = degrees of freedom for denominator

n_2 \ n_1	1	2	3	4	5	6	7	8	9	10	12	15	20	24	30	40	60	120	∞
1	4052	4999.5	5403	5625	5764	5859	5928	5982	6022	6056	6106	6157	6209	6235	6261	6287	6313	6339	6366
2	98.50	99.00	99.17	99.25	99.30	99.33	99.36	99.37	99.39	99.40	99.42	99.43	99.45	99.46	99.47	99.47	99.48	99.49	99.50
3	34.12	30.82	29.46	28.71	28.24	27.91	27.67	27.49	27.35	27.23	27.05	26.87	26.69	26.60	26.50	26.41	26.32	26.22	26.13
4	21.20	18.00	16.69	15.98	15.52	15.21	14.98	14.80	14.66	14.55	14.37	14.20	14.02	13.93	13.84	13.75	13.65	13.56	13.46
5	16.26	13.27	12.06	11.39	10.97	10.67	10.46	10.29	10.16	10.05	9.89	9.72	9.55	9.47	9.38	9.29	9.20	9.11	9.02
6	13.75	10.92	9.78	9.15	8.75	8.47	8.26	8.10	7.98	7.87	7.72	7.56	7.40	7.31	7.23	7.14	7.06	6.97	6.88
7	12.25	9.55	8.45	7.85	7.46	7.19	6.99	6.84	6.72	6.62	6.47	6.31	6.16	6.07	5.99	5.91	5.82	5.74	5.65
8	11.26	8.65	7.59	7.01	6.63	6.37	6.18	6.03	5.91	5.81	5.67	5.52	5.36	5.28	5.20	5.12	5.03	4.95	4.86
9	10.56	8.02	6.99	6.42	6.06	5.80	5.61	5.47	5.35	5.26	5.11	4.96	4.81	4.73	4.65	4.57	4.48	4.40	4.31
10	10.04	7.56	6.55	5.99	5.64	5.39	5.20	5.06	4.94	4.85	4.71	4.56	4.41	4.33	4.25	4.17	4.08	4.00	3.91
11	9.65	7.21	6.22	5.67	5.32	5.07	4.89	4.74	4.63	4.54	4.40	4.25	4.10	4.02	3.94	3.86	3.78	3.69	3.60
12	9.33	6.93	5.95	5.41	5.06	4.82	4.64	4.50	4.39	4.30	4.16	4.01	3.86	3.78	3.70	3.62	3.54	3.45	3.36
13	9.07	6.70	5.74	5.21	4.86	4.62	4.44	4.30	4.19	4.10	3.96	3.82	3.66	3.59	3.51	3.43	3.34	3.25	3.17
14	8.86	6.51	5.56	5.04	4.69	4.46	4.28	4.14	4.03	3.94	3.80	3.66	3.51	3.43	3.35	3.27	3.18	3.09	3.00
15	8.68	6.36	5.42	4.89	4.56	4.32	4.14	4.00	3.89	3.80	3.67	3.52	3.37	3.29	3.21	3.13	3.05	2.96	2.87
16	8.53	6.23	5.29	4.77	4.44	4.20	4.03	3.89	3.78	3.69	3.55	3.41	3.26	3.18	3.10	3.02	2.93	2.84	2.75
17	8.40	6.11	5.18	4.67	4.34	4.10	3.93	3.79	3.68	3.59	3.46	3.31	3.16	3.08	3.00	2.92	2.83	2.75	2.65
18	8.29	6.01	5.09	4.58	4.25	4.01	3.84	3.71	3.60	3.51	3.37	3.23	3.08	3.00	2.92	2.84	2.75	2.66	2.57
19	8.18	5.93	5.01	4.50	4.17	3.94	3.77	3.63	3.52	3.43	3.30	3.15	3.00	2.92	2.84	2.76	2.67	2.58	2.49
20	8.10	5.85	4.94	4.43	4.10	3.87	3.70	3.56	3.46	3.37	3.23	3.09	2.94	2.86	2.78	2.69	2.61	2.52	2.42
21	8.02	5.78	4.87	4.37	4.04	3.81	3.64	3.51	3.40	3.31	3.17	3.03	2.88	2.80	2.72	2.64	2.55	2.46	2.36
22	7.95	5.72	4.82	4.31	3.99	3.76	3.59	3.45	3.35	3.26	3.12	2.98	2.83	2.75	2.67	2.58	2.50	2.40	2.31
23	7.88	5.66	4.76	4.26	3.94	3.71	3.54	3.41	3.30	3.21	3.07	2.93	2.78	2.70	2.62	2.54	2.45	2.35	2.26
24	7.82	5.61	4.72	4.22	3.90	3.67	3.50	3.36	3.26	3.17	3.03	2.89	2.74	2.66	2.58	2.49	2.40	2.31	2.21
25	7.77	5.57	4.68	4.18	3.85	3.63	3.46	3.32	3.22	3.13	2.99	2.85	2.70	2.62	2.54	2.45	2.36	2.27	2.17
26	7.72	5.53	4.64	4.14	3.82	3.59	3.42	3.29	3.18	3.09	2.96	2.81	2.66	2.58	2.50	2.42	2.33	2.23	2.13
27	7.68	5.49	4.60	4.11	3.78	3.56	3.39	3.26	3.15	3.06	2.93	2.78	2.63	2.55	2.47	2.38	2.29	2.20	2.10
28	7.64	5.45	4.57	4.07	3.75	3.53	3.36	3.23	3.12	3.03	2.90	2.75	2.60	2.52	2.44	2.35	2.26	2.17	2.06
29	7.60	5.42	4.54	4.04	3.73	3.50	3.33	3.20	3.09	3.00	2.87	2.73	2.57	2.49	2.41	2.33	2.23	2.14	2.03
30	7.56	5.39	4.51	4.02	3.70	3.47	3.30	3.17	3.07	2.98	2.84	2.70	2.55	2.47	2.39	2.30	2.21	2.11	2.01
40	7.31	5.18	4.31	3.83	3.51	3.29	3.12	2.99	2.89	2.80	2.66	2.52	2.37	2.29	2.20	2.11	2.02	1.92	1.80
60	7.08	4.98	4.13	3.65	3.34	3.12	2.95	2.82	2.72	2.63	2.50	2.35	2.20	2.12	2.03	1.94	1.84	1.73	1.60
120	6.85	4.79	3.95	3.48	3.17	2.96	2.79	2.66	2.56	2.47	2.34	2.19	2.03	1.95	1.86	1.76	1.66	1.53	1.38
∞	6.63	4.61	3.78	3.32	3.02	2.80	2.64	2.51	2.41	2.32	2.18	2.04	1.88	1.79	1.70	1.59	1.47	1.32	1.00

Table A-5   Short table of random numbers

46	96	85	77	27	92	86	26	45	21	89	91	71	42	64	64	58	22	75	81	74	91	48	46	18
44	19	15	32	63	55	87	77	33	29	45	00	31	34	84	05	72	90	44	27	78	22	07	62	17
34	39	80	62	24	33	81	67	28	11	34	79	26	35	34	23	09	94	00	80	55	31	63	27	91
74	97	80	30	65	07	71	30	01	84	47	45	89	70	74	13	04	90	51	27	61	34	63	87	44
22	14	61	60	86	38	33	71	13	33	72	08	16	13	50	56	48	51	29	48	30	93	45	66	29
40	03	96	40	03	47	24	60	09	21	21	18	00	05	86	52	85	40	73	73	57	68	36	33	91
52	33	76	44	56	15	47	75	78	73	78	19	87	06	98	47	48	02	62	03	42	05	32	55	02
37	59	20	40	93	17	82	24	19	90	80	87	32	74	59	84	24	49	79	17	23	75	83	42	00
11	02	55	57	48	84	74	36	22	67	19	20	15	92	53	37	13	75	54	89	56	73	23	39	07
10	33	79	26	34	54	71	33	89	74	68	48	23	17	49	18	81	05	52	85	70	05	73	11	17
67	59	28	25	47	89	11	65	65	20	42	23	96	41	64	20	30	89	87	64	37	93	36	96	35
93	50	75	20	09	18	54	34	68	02	54	87	23	05	43	36	98	29	97	93	87	08	30	92	98
24	43	23	72	80	64	34	27	23	46	15	36	10	63	21	59	69	76	02	62	31	62	47	60	34
39	91	63	18	38	27	10	78	88	84	42	32	00	97	92	00	04	94	50	05	75	82	70	80	35
74	62	19	67	54	18	28	92	33	69	98	96	74	35	72	11	68	25	08	95	31	79	11	79	54
91	03	35	60	81	16	61	97	25	14	78	21	22	05	25	47	26	37	80	39	19	06	41	02	00
42	57	66	76	72	91	03	63	48	46	44	01	33	53	62	28	80	59	55	05	02	16	13	17	54
06	36	63	06	15	03	72	38	01	58	25	37	66	48	56	19	56	41	29	28	76	49	74	39	50
92	70	96	70	89	80	87	14	25	49	25	94	62	78	26	15	41	39	48	75	64	69	61	06	38
91	08	88	53	52	13	04	82	23	00	26	36	47	44	04	08	84	80	07	44	76	51	52	41	59
68	85	97	74	47	53	90	05	90	84	87	48	25	01	11	05	45	11	43	15	60	40	31	84	59
59	54	13	09	13	80	42	29	63	03	24	64	12	43	28	10	01	65	62	07	79	83	05	59	61
39	18	32	69	33	46	58	19	34	03	59	28	97	31	02	65	47	47	70	39	74	17	30	22	65
67	43	31	09	12	60	19	57	63	78	11	80	10	97	15	70	04	89	81	78	54	84	87	83	42
61	75	37	19	56	90	75	39	03	56	49	92	72	95	27	52	87	47	12	52	54	62	43	23	13
78	10	91	11	00	63	19	63	74	58	69	03	51	38	60	36	53	56	77	06	69	03	89	91	24
93	23	71	58	09	78	08	03	07	71	79	32	25	19	61	04	40	33	12	06	78	91	97	88	95
37	55	48	82	63	89	92	59	14	72	19	17	22	51	90	20	03	64	96	60	48	01	95	44	84
62	13	11	71	17	23	29	25	13	85	33	35	07	69	25	68	57	92	57	11	84	44	01	33	66
29	89	97	47	03	13	20	86	22	45	59	98	64	53	89	64	94	81	55	87	73	81	58	46	42
16	94	85	82	89	07	17	30	29	89	89	80	98	36	25	36	53	02	49	14	34	03	52	09	20
04	93	10	59	75	12	98	84	60	93	68	16	87	60	11	50	46	56	58	45	88	72	50	46	11
95	71	43	68	97	18	85	17	13	08	00	50	77	50	46	92	45	26	97	21	48	22	23	08	32
86	05	39	14	35	48	68	18	36	57	09	62	40	28	87	08	74	79	91	08	27	12	43	32	03
59	30	60	10	41	31	00	69	63	77	01	89	94	60	19	02	70	88	72	33	38	88	20	60	86
05	45	35	40	54	03	98	96	76	27	77	84	80	08	64	60	44	34	54	24	85	20	85	77	32
71	85	17	74	66	27	85	19	55	56	51	36	48	92	32	44	40	47	10	38	22	52	42	29	90
80	20	32	80	98	00	40	92	57	51	52	83	14	55	31	99	73	23	40	07	64	54	44	99	21
13	50	78	02	73	39	66	82	01	28	67	51	75	66	33	97	47	58	42	44	88	09	28	58	00
67	92	65	41	45	36	77	96	46	21	14	39	56	36	70	15	74	43	62	69	82	30	77	28	7
72	56	73	44	26	04	62	81	15	35	79	26	99	57	28	22	25	94	80	62	95	48	98	23	8
28	86	85	64	94	11	58	78	45	36	34	45	91	38	51	10	68	36	87	81	16	77	30	19	3
69	57	40	80	44	94	60	82	94	93	98	01	48	50	57	69	60	77	69	60	74	22	05	77	1
71	20	03	30	79	25	74	17	78	34	54	45	04	77	42	59	75	78	64	99	37	03	18	03	3
89	98	55	98	22	45	12	49	82	71	57	33	28	69	50	59	15	09	25	79	39	42	84	18	7
58	74	82	81	14	02	01	05	77	94	65	57	70	39	42	48	56	84	31	59	18	70	41	74	6
50	54	73	81	91	07	81	26	25	45	49	61	22	88	41	20	00	15	59	93	51	60	65	65	6
49	33	72	90	10	20	65	28	44	63	95	86	75	78	69	24	41	65	86	10	34	10	32	00	9
11	85	01	43	65	02	85	69	56	88	34	29	64	35	48	15	70	11	77	83	01	34	82	91	0
34	22	46	41	84	74	27	02	57	77	47	93	72	02	95	63	75	74	69	69	61	34	31	92	1

Source: Adapted with permission from *A Million Random Digits* by The Rand Corporation, Copyright 1955, The Free Press.

Table A-6 Short table of random normal deviates

				$\mu = 0, \sigma = 1$					
−0.670	0.518	0.387	0.523	0.641	1.243	0.322	−2.607	−1.097	−0.012
−2.912	1.448	1.343	−0.122	0.726	−0.617	0.609	2.319	−0.450	−1.197
−0.028	−0.790	0.057	1.425	1.940	1.161	−0.878	−0.716	−0.244	−1.151
−1.257	0.774	0.003	0.388	1.060	1.028	−0.236	1.172	0.442	−0.157
2.372	−1.376	−1.318	1.236	0.738	0.337	−0.534	0.090	0.886	0.676
−0.970	0.438	−0.672	−0.180	0.667	1.370	−0.481	0.329	0.842	0.449
−1.228	0.129	−0.426	−0.165	0.028	2.696	1.201	−1.351	0.724	−1.017
−0.369	0.310	0.432	0.237	0.884	−1.224	0.539	0.852	0.497	−0.283
1.161	1.219	1.615	0.336	1.100	−0.528	0.161	0.278	0.675	−1.143
−0.284	2.609	0.792	1.825	−0.249	1.654	0.621	0.979	−1.472	−1.173
−0.578	−0.789	0.106	0.832	−0.597	0.496	−0.561	−1.033	−0.578	−0.378
0.074	0.261	−0.766	−1.046	0.361	−0.043	−1.927	1.527	0.605	1.475
0.230	0.046	0.978	−1.901	1.162	−0.545	0.697	1.151	2.033	0.080
2.162	−0.562	1.190	0.925	−1.057	0.015	−1.371	1.067	−1.080	−1.129
−1.020	−1.130	−0.315	0.628	−0.140	2.050	−0.030	−0.629	0.128	−1.221
1.323	−0.836	−0.284	−0.249	−0.768	1.242	−1.879	−0.417	0.013	−0.502
2.329	1.884	0.033	0.598	−0.217	0.260	0.431	−1.914	0.205	1.155
2.761	1.800	−0.562	0.714	−0.407	0.009	−0.724	−1.168	0.247	1.166
−0.232	0.605	−0.023	−0.531	0.542	−0.155	0.697	1.037	−0.316	−0.003
−0.742	0.210	−0.741	−1.099	0.158	2.112	−0.765	−0.319	−0.247	0.345
−1.410	0.413	0.705	1.444	1.057	−0.843	0.043	−0.571	−0.001	0.203
2.272	−0.719	0.679	2.007	−0.180	0.698	−1.137	0.688	−0.571	−0.100
2.832	0.925	−1.350	1.529	−0.260	−1.007	−2.350	−1.501	0.289	1.522
−1.086	−0.558	−0.973	−1.285	−0.021	0.077	0.915	−0.241	−0.249	−0.529
0.134	1.815	0.313	1.571	−0.216	2.261	0.696	−0.130	0.393	0.017
0.783	0.600	−0.745	1.127	−0.684	−0.519	0.125	−0.499	1.543	−0.082
0.174	−0.897	0.575	−0.751	0.694	−2.959	0.529	1.587	0.339	−0.813
−1.319	0.556	2.963	1.218	1.199	−1.746	1.611	0.467	−0.490	0.202
1.298	−0.940	−1.143	−1.136	−1.516	0.548	0.629	0.250	−1.087	0.322
−0.676	−1.107	−1.483	0.278	0.493	−0.442	1.078	−0.336	−0.177	−0.057
−1.287	0.775	−1.095	1.161	−1.877	1.874	1.703	−1.619	−0.725	−1.407
0.260	−0.028	−1.982	0.811	0.999	1.662	0.908	1.476	−1.137	−0.945
0.481	1.060	1.441	0.163	0.720	1.490	−0.026	−0.502	0.427	−0.351
0.794	0.725	1.971	0.384	−0.579	−1.079	−1.440	−0.859	−0.346	0.077
0.584	−0.554	1.460	0.791	−0.426	−0.682	0.430	1.922	−2.099	0.221
−0.114	0.379	−0.698	1.570	−0.511	−0.725	0.680	−0.591	−1.091	0.357
−1.128	−1.707	0.921	−0.859	−1.566	1.523	−0.900	−0.988	0.264	0.282
0.691	0.153	0.076	1.691	0.553	0.457	−1.107	0.322	0.633	0.007
1.115	0.777	−0.738	0.868	1.484	−1.792	0.950	−0.842	−0.192	0.620
−0.389	0.559	0.670	−0.315	1.234	0.475	1.117	1.286	−0.649	−1.880
0.330	0.750	−0.642	0.148	−0.608	0.866	−1.720	0.653	−0.210	−0.959
−0.333	−0.084	1.239	−0.049	−0.095	−0.197	−0.213	−1.420	−0.491	0.102
1.718	1.111	−0.548	−0.653	1.534	−0.456	−0.395	1.614	−0.531	−0.785
−0.182	0.620	1.178	−1.071	0.444	−0.072	−1.001	1.325	−0.302	−1.119
1.260	−1.192	0.182	−0.397	−0.705	−1.085	−1.492	1.642	0.673	−0.707
−1.204	−1.725	1.695	1.473	0.665	−0.489	0.020	0.267	1.230	0.865
−0.619	0.307	−0.226	−0.096	0.987	−1.195	−1.412	0.433	2.052	0.022
−0.272	−0.096	0.137	−0.361	0.653	−0.156	1.309	−0.480	−0.397	1.302
0.245	−0.690	0.493	−1.123	1.465	0.132	0.582	−0.429	0.225	0.125
0.101	−0.855	0.782	−1.040	2.113	−1.423	−1.010	0.158	0.106	−1.232

Marketing
Research Cases

Twenty-one situations involving actual or potential marketing research projects are described in this section. The descriptions are intentionally brief so that attention can be focused on those aspects of the problem that relate to marketing research.

CASE STUDY 1

Prior Executive Opinion and
Marketing Research Results

The statement "Marketing executives make correct decisions about 58 % of the time" has circulated in the marketing field for a number of years. This statement has its origin in the findings of a study conducted by a large, private marketing research firm.

The study was initiated as the result of an incident that occurred during a conference between representatives of the research organization and executives of a prospective client who manufactured and distributed a line of drug products. The client had experienced a persistent decline in sales of one of its products. During the meeting with the representatives of the research organization, the possible causes of the sales decline and the alternative actions that could be taken to remedy it were discussed.

It quickly became apparent that there were strong differences of opinion among the company executives as to the cause or causes of the loss in sales. Some of them thought that the product formula needed to be changed; some believed that the price was too high; others believed that the amount of advertising to consumers should be increased; and still others were of the opinion that the retail distribution coverage in terms of the number and types of retail outlets handling it was inadequate.

Since such diverse and strong opinions were held, no consensus was reached during the conference. The research firm was retained to conduct a comprehensive market study. The study was performed, and, a few months later, the findings and recommendations were presented to the same group of executives. The presentation was made by the president of the research firm who had also been present at the initial meeting.

The president of the research firm was pleased, if surprised, to note that there was virtually complete agreement with the findings and recommendations of the study, even among those executives whose expressed opinions at the first meeting had been completely at variance with the results of the study. The general reception of the results was that they simply served to confirm the opinions that the company executives already held.

The president of the research firm drew the tentative conclusion from this experience that, at some time or another during the period that sales had been declining, each of the executives had held the opinion that the findings of the study substantiated. He knew from his prior experience in working with marketing executives that, in situations where adequate factual data are not available, opinions tend to be swayed by recent bits of information or rumor. For example, if there have recently been several reports by sales personnel that the price is too high, a product manager may conclude that this is the case. If the following week a number of reports are received that the product formula is inferior to that of a competitive product, he may change this opinion concerning price and conclude that the formula is the basic problem.

The president of the research firm therefore concluded that it was entirely possible that each of the executives had been basically honest in asserting that the survey findings agreed with his opinion, even though, in most cases, the findings were at variance with executive opinions at the time the study was authorized.

At a subsequent meeting with another prospective client the president described this experience and suggested that it would be to the interest of the client to determine if the prior opinions of their marketing executives were usually substantially correct. If so, the client would be well advised *not* to spend money on research. If not, they could hardly afford to be without the assistance provided by marketing research in making sound marketing decisions.

As a means of getting information about the "correctness" of executive opinion, the president of the research firm proposed that a list of the major questions to be studied in the research project be prepared. Then, at the time the study was authorized, each of the executives would write down his opinion with respect to each of the questions. All the answers would then be sealed in an envelope and kept in the safe of the client company. Upon completion of the study, these prior opinions would be compared with the findings of the study.

This procedure was followed in virtually every marketing research study performed by the research firm for a number of years. When what was believed to be an adequate sample had been collected, a composite analysis was made and the conclusion drawn that "marketing executives make correct decisions about 58% of the time."

Was this conclusion warranted? Why or why not?

CASE STUDY 2

The Baystat Chemical Company

Recently the Baystat Chemical Company developed a new dye compound for noncellulosic–natural fiber blended fabrics. The dyestuff, trademarked Hue-Lock, was then produced in only pilot plant quantities. Baystat personnel felt that the product had superior properties, but did not consider them sufficiently superior to establish a price premium over competitive dyes. Also, Baystat personnel believed that established channels would have to be used in marketing the product, and that little flexibility existed in regard to the magnitude of promotional efforts.

Baystat faced two principal decisions: Should the product be made on a commercial scale? And if so, how large should the initial facilities be? Both decisions hinged on unknown events or states of nature—that is, future sales of Hue-Lock.

The marketing management of the company believed that because of the nature of the product and the time required for full market penetration, a planning period of five years should be used as a basis of evaluating the attractiveness of the proposed venture. Consultation with process engineers indicated that two plant sizes—10 and 5 million pounds per year—represented the range of feasible capacities. Although economies of scale were associated with the higher capacity plant, investment costs and break-even costs were likewise higher. If sales were high, payoffs obviously would favor the larger plant, but if sales were low, the smaller plant would be more profitable. If, however, the smaller capacity were chosen, and sales turned out to be high, lead time and high costs of plant conversion would be too high to make capacity additions within the five-year period feasible. After five years capacity could be enlarged, but such possibilities were assumed too tenuous for consideration in the present evaluation.

Baystat's process group assembled production cost estimates as a function of unit sales volume. If introduced, the product was to be priced at the current market level of $1 per pound over the five-year planning period. Management agreed to consider net present value (net cash flow discounted at a rate of 6% annually) as the relevant payoff measure. The major unknown was, of course, yearly sales.

Marketing was asked to prepare a forecast of sales over the five-year period. From experience in launching similar products, the conclusion was reached that Hue-Lock's ultimate market share would be realized by the end of the third year. Further, they felt that modest sales gains during the following two years would reflect increases in total market demand only, and that sales during the first two years would represent 60 and 85%, respectively, of the third-year sales.

Third-year sales volume thus became the key variable to be forecast. While Baystat personnel knew that sales during the third year could fall at any point within a wide range, they believed that some sales levels were more likely to occur than others and that subjective probabilities could be attached to different values of third-year sales.

As shown in Table B-1, marketing personnel believed that third-year sales would fall between 1 and 11 million pounds, with the greatest probability (0.40) falling between 3.0 and 4.9 million pounds. Yet sales could amount to only 1.0 to 2.9 million pounds (0.20 probability) or as much as 9.0 to 11.0 million pounds (0.10 probability).

Table B-1   Third-year sales probabilities

Sales Volumes (millions of pounds)	Prior Probability
1.0–2.9	0.20
3.0–4.9	0.40
5.0–6.9	0.20
7.0–8.9	0.10
9.0–11.0	0.10

With these and the earlier estimates it was possible to prepare a conditional-payoff table. A conditional payoff was estimated for each act being considered for each level of demand for Hue-Lock in the third year. The estimates are shown in Table B-2.

After reviewing the conditional-payoff table, Baystat management decided to have a customer survey conducted. For a total cost of $20,000,

Table B-2 Conditional payoff table for Hue-Lock commercialization—demand in third year (millions of pounds)

Act	9.0–11.0 (S_1)		7.0–8.9 (S_2)		5.0–6.9 (S_3)		3.0–4.9 (S_4)		1.0–2.9 (S_5)	
	$P(S_1)$	Payoff (millions of dollars)	$P(S_2)$	Payoff (millions of dollars)	$P(S_3)$	Payoff (millions of dollars)	$P(S_4)$	Payoff (millions of dollars)	$P(S_5)$	Payoff (millions of dollars)
A_1: build 10 million-pound plant	0.10	4.55	0.10	2.23	0.20	(0.59)	0.40	(3.40)	0.20	(6.23)
A_2: build 5 million-pound plant	0.10	2.50	0.10	2.35	0.20	1.96	0.40	0.36	0.20	(3.05)
A_3: do not commercialize	0.10	0	0.10	0	0.20	0	0.40	0	0.20	0

a random sample of 100 potential customers out of a total customer population of 1,200 was presented with test fabrics that had been dyed with the new material. Survey response indicated that the average third-year sales would be 2,100 pounds with a standard deviation of 7,000 pounds. Thus, based on the total customer population (1,200), total third-year sales would amount to 5.52 million pounds (1,200 × 2,100).

1. If no additional information had been obtained, what decision should have been made about the commercialization of Hue-Lock?
2. Should the management of Baystat have authorized the survey?
3. Given that the survey was to be taken, was this the proper size sample to take?
4. Given the results of the actual survey, what decision should have been made about the commercialization of Hue-Lock?

CASE STUDY 3

Hanson Foods, Inc.: Preliminary Research and Decision Concerning Market Testing of Product H-2[1]

Product H-2 is a variation of a common canned food item that is used regularly in over 80% of the households in the United States. The product can be used as a cooking ingredient or eaten by itself. The normal retail price is between $0.70 and $0.75.

The category of products into which product H-2 falls is dominated by three major brands. These three manufacturers share over 70% of the market with the remainder split among many small canners and private-label brands. The total retail value of all brands sold in the product category is over $825 million per year. This is considerably greater than the retail value of such categories as peanut butter, jams and jellies, canned beans, canned peas, or packaged deserts.

Hanson Foods is one of the fastest growing, most aggressive companies in the industry. In the past year, sales of its regular item in this category (product H-1) had been growing at a rate three times faster than either of its competitors, but the brand was still third in market share. Brand K had been the historical market leader and was regarded by most consumers as the best quality item in the product category. The retail price for brand K had been 0.75 per can for many years. This was normally 8 to 15 cents higher than

[1] Product H-2 is not identified in the case because to do so would have almost certainly identified the company that developed it. The company preferred to remain anonymous. A fictitious company name has also been used.

either brand V or brand H-1. A large part of the total volume of brand H-1 was sold at specially reduced prices.

The popularity of brand K varied considerably in different regions of the country (Table B-3). In many eastern areas, its market share was over 50%, while, in the West and South, the brand dropped to third position.

Table B-3   Share of market

	Brand K (%)	Brand V (%)	Brand H-1 (%)	All Others (%)
New England	37.0	10.1	12.5	40.4
New York	42.6	14.2	27.7	15.5
Middle Atlantic	37.6	11.7	13.6	37.1
East Central	27.2	17.4	17.3	38.1
West Central	25.6	24.7	14.6	35.1
Southeast	13.0	22.1	22.7	42.2
Southwest	11.6	35.4	25.6	27.4
Pacific	19.8	27.7	29.4	23.1
Total	25.3	21.4	20.1	33.2

The development of product H-2 may be described as the result of an attempt to differentiate an existing product. Two years earlier, the management of Hanson and its advertising agency were faced with a problem common to many companies in the food industry. They were attempting to develop an advertising campaign that would differentiate brand H-1 from its competition, but the three major brands had essentially the same formulation. It was decided that product differentiation was needed, and, in order to accomplish this, the research and development people within the company were instructed to reformulate the product to incorporate some new and exotic spices. The copy strategy would emphasize the taste difference resulting from the new spices.

In the course of this development work, some interesting things began to happen. As various new spices were added to product H-1 and different flavor-intensity levels were evaluated by employee taste panels, it became apparent that some of these changes were perceived as completely new products.

It was quickly recognized that the introduction of a new product such as this could expand Hanson's shares of the market considerably and increase sales for the whole product category. The possibility of cannibalization existed because a new product might derive a major part of its sales from Hanson's current brand. But this strategy of fragmentation had been utilized in the soap industry with great success. New products were continually introduced for specialized uses, with resulting volume increases for the whole category. There was another danger that was not generally recognized by the company management. This new-product idea had originated in the research and development laboratories rather than having evolved from a discovered consumer need. This is a common cause of failure of many new consumer products by many manufacturers.

Further work by the research and development department resulted in three variations of product H-1, with distinctly different tastes resulting from different spices used. These products were retested by the employee taste panels, and the most popular formulation of the three was packed in limited quantities for consumer and market tests.

The next step was to find out if the idea made any sense to consumers. A small pilot study was conducted in which 24 respondents were asked for their reaction to the product idea. They were then given a sample can to use and the interviewer returned a week later to question them. The concept of product H-2 appeared to be well received by over three-fourths of the consumers contacted. The product seemed to live up to their prior expectations and there were no appreciable complaints about the flavor. The participants in the test were given a three-months' supply of the product and a further interview was conducted after eight weeks had elapsed. At this time, 64 % of the respondents said, "If this were available, I would go out and buy some right away."

Further research was then conducted on a national basis to determine consumer acceptance of the concept and formulation. Depth interviews were used to probe top-of-mind meanings and associations generated by the concept. Then the respondent was given a can of the product and the interviewer returned a week later to measure the response to the product itself. Approximately 450 interviews were conducted in Los Angeles, Minneapolis, Atlanta, Philadelphia, Tacoma, Topeka, Columbus, and Bridgeport. The reaction to the product in this study is summarized in Table B-4.

With this apparent consumer satisfaction with the product concept and formulation, the next step was to determine whether or not they would *purchase* the product with satisfactory regularity over a period of time. In order to measure this without going into an actual test market, an extended in-home usage test was conducted. Consumers in four cities, Sacramento,

Table B-4   Respondent study results

	Respondents (%)
Would use	34
Probably would use	15
Might use	6
Probably would not use	15
Would not use	30

Baltimore, Milwaukee, and Jacksonville, were given the product to try for two weeks. If they had an interest in participating in the study, all competitive products were removed from their homes, and from then on they purchased their requirements from survey representatives. They were allowed to purchase product H-2 or any of the three major brands K, V, or H-1, as well as the strongest local brand in the area. Each family was contacted once a week for orders. The product was delivered to the participants' homes and a 10% discount on the normal retail price was given for all items purchased.

The response to product H-2 in this test was much better than had been anticipated, and the demand for it did not diminish appreciably in a 16-week test period. The management of Hanson had not previously been exposed to tests of this type, but representatives from the advertising agency who had observed the experience of other products in such tests were surprised to find a very high level of product usage and a negligible dropoff in demand.

On the basis of their previous experience with this type of extended use testing of new grocery products, the advertising agency projected first-year sales and market-share estimates for product H-2. The forecasts were based on different levels of distribution that might be achieved by the product in its first year:

- At 35% distribution, sales were estimated at 847,000 cases, or 8% of the market.
- At 45% distribution, sales were estimated at 1,220,000 cases, or 12% of the market.
- At 55% distribution, sales were estimated at 1,500,000 cases, or 15% of the market.

Distribution of 35% would mean that the product would be available for sale in stores doing 35% of the total grocery business in the United States. The agency believed that a distribution level of 45% was the most likely of the three if the product were introduced. Hanson management concurred in this judgment.

The Finance Department at Hanson was asked to make projections of profit (or loss) for the first three years after H-2's introduction, conditional on the distribution level achieved. Assuming that the distribution level achieved in the first year would be maintained over the full three-year period, their estimates were as follows:

	Year 1	Year 2	Year 3
35% distribution	($1,800,000)	($700,000)	($700,000)
45% distribution	($ 700,000)	$950,000	$1,200,000
55% distribution	($ 200,000)	$1,650,000	$2,000,000

These estimates were discussed by Hanson's management with the account executive from the agency. He recommended that they run a market test for H-2. He thought that the test should be conducted in four or five cities for a period long enough to determine trial and repeat-purchase rates. He estimated that such a test would cost $400,000 to $450,000.

1. Evaluate the concept and use tests conducted on the product.
2. What action should the Hanson management have taken?

CASE STUDY 4

Jason and Townsend Ltd.

In July, 1976, Jason and Townsend Ltd., a British firm, requested a marketing research firm in New York to collect some information on the soft drink market in the United States. They asked the firm to collect readily available secondary information and to report back their findings in one week.

The research firm reported the following:

1. Wholesale sales of soft drinks in the United States in 1974 totaled $7.83 billion, up from $6.22 billion in 1973. Wholesale sales for the three previous years were $5.68 billion in 1972, $5.35 billion in 1971, and $4.80 billion in 1970.

2. Per capita consumption of soft drinks had risen accordingly, from 27.0 gallons in 1970 to 33.3 in 1974. This is an annual growth rate of approximately 5% and represents a slight slowing in the growth rate from that experienced during the 1960s. The annual rate of increase then was about 6%. The rate of increase is expected to slow even more during the next five years. Because of a declining birth rate, the under-17 age group, which accounts for 37% of all soft drink consumption in the United States, will shrink in size from now through 1980.

3. Soft drink companies have not only diversified into the use of varied containers for their products but have added lines normally sold by other industries. Pepsico, for example, now has more than one-half of its sales (53%) from products such as wines (Monsieur Henri), snack foods (Frito-Lay), sporting goods (Wilson's Sporting Goods), and from several leasing, moving, and truck-rental operations.

4. The market shares of the leading soft drink companies in the United States for 1974 were as follows:

Type	Market Share (%)
Coca-Cola (Coke, Fresca, Tab, Sprite)	32.7
Pepsi (Pepsi and Diet Pepsi)	18.9
Royal Crown (R.C. Cola and Diet-Rite)	4.7
7-Up	7.0
All others	36.7
Total	100.0

5. Diet drinks had a 9% share of the total soft drink market in 1974.

6. The market share by flavors for 1974 was as follows:

Flavor	Market Share (%)
Cola	60
Lemon–lime	18
Orange	3
Root beer	3
Ginger ale	2
Grape	2
All others	2
Total	100

7. The seasonal pattern of soft drinks in 1974 was as follows:

Season	Sales (%)
July–September	28
April–June	27
October–December	23
January–March	22
1974 total	100

8. The percentage of sales of packaged soft drinks accounted for by each of the major outlets in 1973 and 1974 was as follows:

Outlet	Sales in 1973 (%)	Sales in 1974 (%)
Food stores	52	53
Other retail stores	21	19
Vending machines	19	16
All other outlets	8	12
Total	100	100

9. The total number of soft drink bottles in the United States has declined from about 2,450 in 1974 to 2,200 in mid-1976. This has been the result of economies of scale from the development of high-speed bottling equipment and the need for more equipment as the number of different-sized cans and bottles have proliferated.

10. Advertising expenditures by each of the major producers of soft drinks by medium in 1974 were as follows:

MEDIUM	COCA COLA CO. $ (millions)	%	PEPSICO $ (millions)	%	7-UP CO. $ (millions)	%
Magazine	0.6	1.4	1.5	4.0	—	—
Newspaper supplements	1.0	2.4	—		—	—
Network TV	17.3	41.6	19.7	52.4	1.7	13.2
Sports TV	21.7	52.2	15.6	41.5	9.9	76.7
Network radio	—	—	0.5	1.3	0.1	0.8
Outdoor	1.0	2.4	0.3	0.8	1.2	9.3
Total	41.6	100.0	37.6	100.0	12.9	100.0

Indicate the potential sources for each of these items of secondary information.

CASE STUDY 5

Graves Upright Piano

The question of why an upright piano sounds tinny or wooden when compared with a grand piano first interested Howard Graves as an engineering student at MIT. When he asked piano makers why this was the case, all they could tell him was, "If you lay the sounding board flat, it will sound better."

Graves, an independent consulting engineer, spent more than $90,000 of his own funds and several years in designing an upright piano with improved performance. His efforts have resulted in a prototype upright with bass tones that can play one octave lower than the conventional upright and with high tones that have a reasonant, bell-like quality that compares favorably with grand pianos.

He expects that his design will compete in the higher-priced end of the market with such pianos as Steinway and Baldwin. There has been a continuing high demand for quality pianos; Steinway and Sons, for instance, has maintained a two-year backlog of orders for several years. Graves believes that there may be a sizable market for a quality upright piano that the grand piano cannot tap. This is the market comprised of people who have always wanted the quality that a grand piano provides but have not had the space in their living room or family room that it requires.

Manufacturers of pianos typically have averaged only a 2 to 3% margin above their costs. Pianos have traditionally been built by highly skilled craftsmen with methods that have changed little over the years. Graves has designed his piano to be built by more modern methods such that, with volume production, he estimates that his piano could be priced competitively and still return a 15 to 17% pretax margin.

He plans to produce and market the piano with his own company rather than sell the design to an existing piano manufacturer. To do this it will be necessary to raise the required capital from outside investors.

For a prospectus that is to be prepared for potential investors:

1. Gather the secondary data concerning the market for pianos that should be included.
2. Design a study to obtain the information concerning buyer reaction to the Graves' design that would be of interest.

3. What aspects of the market would you consider in developing an appropriate price for the new piano?

CASE STUDY 6

Hewlett-Packard Company

The Hewlett-Packard Company manufactures hand-held calculators that are at the more expensive end of the product line. Some of them are programmable and have other sophisticated features such that they qualify to be considered as minicomputers.

The calculators are sold primarily through book and department stores. The salespersons who sell them typically have no training in the finer points of calculator features of operation and so are often unable to answer customer questions. As a result, sales of Hewlett-Packard calculators are believed to be lower than they would be if customer queries could be competently and quickly answered.

The national sales manager of Hewlett-Packard believes that a workable solution may be to provide wide-area-telephone-service (WATS) lines from retail stores to the plant in California and to encourage prospective customers to call and talk with a calculator specialist. He would like to market-test this idea by installing the WATS lines in sales booths at a sample of stores carrying the calculators.

1. How can the sales manager be sure that the inability of sales clerks to answer customer questions actually results in lost sales?
2. Should a marketing research project, designed to establish if this is the case, be conducted prior to a market test?
3. Assuming that a lack of competence on the part of the sales clerks has resulted in lost sales, what other approaches might the national sales manager consider for solving this problem?
4. Should marketing research projects be conducted on any of these potential solutions?
5. Design a market test for the use of WATS lines. As a part of your design, specify:
   a. The number of stores and how they should be chosen.
   b. How the measurement(s) of the effect of the WATS line service is (are) to be made.

CASE STUDY 7

Chrysler Corporation: Consumer Testing
of Turbine-Powered Car

The Chrysler Corporation, in pioneering the development of the turbine-powered car, had an obvious interest in obtaining consumer evaluations and reactions before making the final decision to introduce it. There were substantial uncertainties as to how the consumer would react to the different operating characteristics and the product image associated with a turbine engine. These uncertainties, when coupled with the sizable outlays required for production tooling and the introduction of the car, made it highly desirable to obtain information from consumers who had actually used the car under conditions approximating normal car usage. The question was how should such information be obtained?

Conventional market testing, such as that used in grocery products and drug sundries, has never been practical for use with new automobiles. It is far too costly to tool up for the quantity of cars required, there are serious morale problems in dealer selection, and the cars tend to be bought by customers who are not representative of the prospective market. Such market tests have been used only in testing the market for an existing model car in a foreign market.

It was evident that some sort of consumer use test would have to be conducted, however. The method decided upon to obtain the desired information was to place the turbine-powered car with selected users under a no-charge user agreement. Each selected user was to drive the car for a period of three months and agreed to furnish Chrysler with the information required for the market evaluation program.

It was decided that 50 prototype cars would be built and placed with users at a rate of one per week beginning in late October. The test was to be continued until evaluations had been received from a total of 200 users.

A news release of the program was made in midyear. Over a period of a few weeks Chrysler received some 20,000 unsolicited requests to participate in the evaluation program. It was decided that participants would be selected from among these 20,000 persons. Eligibility for participation would be limited to those candidates who owned a car (or were a member of a household in which a car was owned by the head of the household) and who had a valid driver's license. He also had to be a resident of a major population center in one of the 48 continental United States. This stipulation was made to assure a high degree of market exposure to the car and to test it under a variety of weather and terrain conditions. The users were then selected randomly from among the remaining candidates who had been grouped according to the make, price category, and age of the new and used cars owned. The intent was to select users whose car ownership pattern was representative of the population car-ownership pattern at that time.

Each candidate was asked to complete the questionnaire reproduced below. The completed questionnaire, along with the original correspondence, was forwarded to the public accounting firm of Touche, Ross, Bailey, and Smart, who made the final selection of users.

1. Evaluate the questionnaire in terms of:
   a. The information requested versus that needed for selection of users.
   b. The types and degree of potential errors in the information obtained.
2. From the information given, would you conclude that a random sample of the population of prospective buyers of the turbine-powered car was taken? Why or why not?

QUESTIONNAIRE

Thank you for your request to test the Chrysler Corporation turbine car. Since we first announced our turbine evaluation program, we have been complimented with thousands of such requests which demonstrate the enthusiasm for this new automotive power concept. As you know from information already published, the program was successfully launched on October 29 of this year with the assignment of the first turbine car to a Chicago user for a three-month trial period. We expect to continue placing turbine cars with users at the rate of about one a week, until the 50 cars we are building have provided us with a sample of 200 turbine users.

A brochure explaining the selection process is enclosed. This was previously sent to those who are presently part of the active inquiry file. In addition, we have also included an interesting booklet about the turbine car.

The questionnaire included with this letter asks for certain information which would be helpful to us. Naturally, its return in no way obligates you and, likewise, our request for this information does not mean that you will be selected as a turbine car user.

Your interest is appreciated, and we hope that you will forward the filled-in questionnaire to us within the next two weeks if convenient. When we receive it, we will send your original correspondence and the questionnaire to the independent accounting firm of Touche, Ross, Bailey, and Smart. They have been engaged by us to select the participants in this program. It will not be necessary for you to supply us with any further data except, of course, a change of address, if it occurs.

1. In all, how many miles do you travel a year for both business and pleasure?
   _____ miles per year

2. How much of this traveling is by automobile?
   _____ miles per year

3. How large an area do you normally cover in your routine driving?
   _____ 50 mile radius _____300 mile radius _____1000 mile radius
   _____100 mile radius _____400 mile radius _____if more, specify
   _____200 mile radius _____500 mile radius _____

4. In routine driving do you normally travel alone or with someone else?
   _____alone   _____with someone else
   If not alone, how many others usually?_____

5. What portion of your driving is done:
   _____% at low speeds (under 50 m.p.h.)
   _____% at highway speeds (over 50 m.p.h.)

6. What make of car(s) do you own?
   1. _____ Year _____ Body Style _____
   2. _____ Year _____ Body Style _____
   3. _____ Year _____ Body Style _____

7. May we know your age? _____
   Education:
   _____Grade school   _____Completed high school
   _____Some high school   _____Some college
   _____ College graduate
   Marital status: _____ Married
   _____ Single
   Children: How many? _____

8. Do you have any hobbies? If so, would you please tell us what they are?

_____

9. How are you employed?
   _____self employed   _____employee of a
                                         company
   If self employed:
   What is the name of your business and the business address?

   _____

   What is the nature of your business? (For instance what do you manufacture, sell, or what service do you provide?)

   _____

   How long have you been in business for yourself?
   _____yrs.
   If an employee of a company:
   What is the name of the company, and the business address where you are located?

   _____

   In what capacity are you employed?_____
   How long have you been employed by this company?
   _____yrs.
10. Additional comments:

   _____

   _____

CASE STUDY 8

Zenith Sales Company

The Zenith Sales Company, a division of Zenith Radio Corporation, decided to conduct a study on the attitudes and experience of independent television servicepeople with regard to the repair and ownership of color television sets. The specific objectives of the study involved a determination of the brand of television set that service personnel: (1) believed needed the fewest repairs, (2) believed was the easiest to repair, and (3) would prefer to buy for themselves.

The study was conducted for Zenith by the Gallup Organization, Inc. The study design called for telephone interviews to be held with a nationwide probability sample of approximately 800 independent servicepeople during a 10-day period in April.

To obtain the sample of servicepeople a random sample of 200 areas was initially drawn. These areas were drawn with a probability proportionate to size and were prestratified by city size within regions.

The most current telephone directories were obtained for these areas and a count of the independent TV service shops listed in the yellow pages was made. In total, close to half of all the TV service shops in the country (as indicated by Bureau of the Census data) were listed in the yellow pages of the directories for the 200 areas. A comparison of the distribution of TV service shops to population was made, and it showed a close comformity to the distribution of population.

In each telephone directory, a systematic sample of four TV service shops was drawn for interviewing purposes (four alternate shops were also drawn in case interviews could not be completed with the initial four shops).

The name and telephone numbers of the selected TV repair shops were sent to resident Gallup interviewers in each of the areas. The interviewers were instructed to make up to six calls to complete an interview and the questionnaire was structured to screen out service shops which did *not* service more than one brand of TV. All interviews were conducted with TV service-people themselves and not with others working in the shops.

In total, 1,215 TV service shops were contacted. A total of 722 completed and usable interviews resulted, with another 75 interviews that were completed but could not be used because only one brand of TV was serviced. The persons contacted at a total of 64 shops refused to be interviewed, and 359 could not be reached after repeated attempts to contact them were made.

The primary findings were as follows:

Question: *In general, of the brands you are familiar with, which* one
would you say requires the fewest repairs?

Zenith	30%*
RCA	11
Motorola	9
All other brands	43
About equal	21
Don't know	11

Question: *In general, of the brands you are familiar with which* one
would you say is easiest to repair?

Zenith	35%*
RCA	25
Motorola	11
All other brands	19
None easier/about equal	18
Don't know	1

Question: *If you were buying a new color TV set for yourself today,
which brand would you buy?*

Zenith	35%*
RCA	21
Motorola	12
All other brands	31
Don't know	6

1. What kind of a sample was taken?
2. What biases are potentially present in the sample?
3. What nonsampling errors are potentially present?
4. How do you assess the effects of these errors on the findings of the survey?
5. Contrast traditional and Bayesian points of view in the context of sample selection.
6. What kinds of additional research are suggested by this study's findings?

CASE STUDY 9

No-Fault Insurance Company

The No-Fault Insurance Company, a relatively small company specializing in insuring automobiles, was interested in learning in what proportion of automobile accidents, in which the police were not called, an insuree was involved who had been driving under the influence of alcohol or some form of drugs.

A member of the company's marketing research department took a simple random sample of 100 accidents by their insurees over the past 12 months in which there was no police investigation. (If the insuree had had more than one such accident during the year, only the last accident was included in the sample.) The insuree was interviewed personally and, after a suitable introduction, handed a card with the following instructions printed on it:

*Total adds to more than 100% because some respondents named more than one brand.

PLEASE READ THIS CARD ALL THE WAY THROUGH
BEFORE DOING ANY OF THE THINGS REQUESTED

1. The interviewer will hand you a penny after you have finished reading the card and have asked any questions you may have.

   Please flip the penny and determine whether it came up HEADS or TAILS without letting the interviewer know which it was.

2. The side of the coin that came up will determine which of the two questions given below you will answer. Please answer the question with a "YES" or a "NO" only and do not say anything else as we do not want the interviewer to know which question you answer.

3. If the penny came up HEADS, answer "YES" or "NO" (*only*) to the question:

   "Was your mother born in August?"

4. If the penny came up TAILS, answer "YES" or "NO" (*only*) to the question:

   "Before your last automobile accident had you been drinking alcohol or taken any drugs (including tranquilizers) that *might* have caused you to be unable to drive as well as you usually do?"

5. If you have any questions about any of these instructions please ask the interviewer for an explanation before you flip the penny. If the instructions are followed properly ONLY YOU SHOULD KNOW WHICH QUESTION YOU ANSWERED.

Responses were obtained from 91 persons (4 had died or otherwise could not be contacted and 5 refused to answer). Twenty–four (24) of the respondents answered "Yes."*

1. What is the estimated proportion of respondents who answered "Yes" to the question concerning driving after drinking alcohol or taking drugs?

2. What are the nonsampling errors that are actually or potentially present in this estimate?

3. Should these nonsampling errors be reflected in the estimate? If so, how?

*These data are contrived.

CASE STUDY 10

Saturday Review

The management of the *Saturday Review* decided to obtain current information about the magazine's subscribers to provide to present and prospective advertisers. Information of special interest was subscriber readership and attitudes toward the publication, personal and household characteristics and activities at work and leisure.

The survey was conducted by a well-known research firm in New York City. In accordance with their specifications, a systematic sample of 2,000 names was selected by *Saturday Review*. An eight-page questionnaire was mailed with a covering letter on *Saturday Review* stationery. The mailing included a one-dollar bill as an incentive.

An advance postcard was mailed on July 18, followed by the questionnaire on July 22. After one followup mailing the survey was closed on September 8. The Post Office returned 40 questionnaires as "undeliverable," leaving a net mailing of 1,960. By the closing date, 1,375 completed questionnaires, or 70% of the net mailing, had been received.

Table B-5 shows the geographical distribution of the 1,375 returns as compared with the distribution of subscribers to *Saturday Review* shown in their Audit Bureau of Circulation statement for the six months ending on the preceding June 30.

The research firm reported that it opened all replies, tabulated the answers, and prepared the tables for the report in accordance with accepted

Table B-5 Comparative Geographical Distributions

	Survey Returns (%)	*Circulation per ABC Statement* (%)
New England	8	8
Middle Atlantic	21	20
East North Central	19	19
West North Central	7	8
South Atlantic	14	13
East South Central	3	3
West South Central	6	6
Mountain	5	5
Pacific	17	18
Total	100	100

marketing research procedure. They stated in the report that "the controlled conditions under which this survey was made and the high response rate assure the reliability of the survey."

1. The findings for the question "*On the average, how many people other than yourself read or look through your copy of* Saturday Review? (*Please answer in terms of a typical issue.*) were as follows:

Number of Persons	%
1	45.6
2	10.5
3	4.4
4	1.5
5	0.8
None, not stated	37.2
	100.0
Average number of readers	0.9
Base—all 1,375 respondents	

Prepare an interval estimate of the average number of readers with a 95.4% level of confidence.

2. What is the probable effect of the 40 undeliverable questionnaires and the 586 nonresponses on:
   a. The mean number of people reading a typical issue?
   b. The width that an interval estimate of the average number of readers with a 95.4% level of confidence should have, compared with the one calculated in question 1?

3. What steps might have been taken by the research firm to:
   a. Increase the response rate?
   b. Estimate the effect of the 586 nonresponses?

CASE STUDY 11

MBA Magazine Poll

Each year *MBA Magazine* conducts a poll to obtain rankings of M.B.A. degree programs. A poll of readers is conducted by asking them to respond to a questionnaire printed in the magazine. The deans of the member schools of the American Association of Collegiate Schools of Business and the recruiters of a sample of major corporations are also surveyed to obtain their rankings. The results are tabulated and reported in a later issue of the magazine.

The questionnaire for the poll of readers for a recent year is reproduced below. The actual questionnaire is printed on heavy paper with the reverse side printed as a self-addressed, business-reply card with a first-class postage permit. The paper is perforated around the questionnaire so that it can be torn out easily for mailing.

How Would You Rank the Schools?

We will publish our third annual survey of opinion this December ranking the nation's business schools. We would like you to participate. In addition to our survey of the readership, we are asking—under separate cover—for the opinions of the deans of the 123 AACSB-accredited business schools. A third group, the M.B.A. recruiters of nearly 80 major corporations, will be queried for the first time.

We ask three questions this year. Write in the five schools that best excel in each of the three categories. There will be two published rankings in December: the first by frequency of mention; the second by order of entry.

The first two questions—about academic excellence and job value—refer only to the school's *master's* degree program. The third question, new this year, asks the value of each school's *nondegree* management programs for *working* executives, in other words, the school's continuing education program.

Please clip your responses below and mail in by *October 1.*

We look forward to hearing from you.

Thomas J. Goff
Editor

QUESTIONNAIRE
A. In academic terms, what M.B.A. programs are best overall?

1. _____

2. _____

3. _____

4. _____

5. _____

B. What M.B.A. degrees bring the best salaries in the job market?

1. _____

2. _____

3. _____

4. _____

5. _____

C. What nondegree executive education programs are most useful to working managers?

1. _____

2. _____

3. _____

4. _____

5. _____

We need to know where and when you received your M.B.A.:

M.B.A. School _____ Year _____

---

1. What biases, if any, would you expect to be present in the rankings of M.B.A. programs with respect to academic quality (question A in the questionnaire) as measured by the responses from:
   a. The readers?
   b. The deans of AACSB member schools?
   c. The sample of recruiters?

2. What biases, if any, would you expect to be present in the rankings of M.B.A. programs with respect to salaries received (question B in the questionnaire) as measured by the responses from:
   a. The readers?
   b. The deans of the AACSB member schools?
   c. The sample of recruiters?
3. What biases, if any, would you expect to be present in the rankings of nondegree executive programs (question C in the questionnaire) as measured by the responses from:
   a. The readers?
   b. The deans of the AACSB member schools?
   c. The sample of recruiters?
4. Overall, how helpful do you think the results of such a poll would be to you if you were deciding to which universities you should apply for work toward an M.B.A. degree?

CASE STUDY 12

Senatorial Questionnaire

A United States senator recently sent the questionnaire reproduced below to a mailing list of his constituents. Comment on the questionnaire indicating:

1. Your evaluation of each question.
2. Your appraisal of the questionnaire as a device for informing the senator of his constituents' opinions.

QUESTIONNAIRE

1. Under present law, families who run small businesses and farms are often forced to sell their holdings rather than pass them on to the next generation owing to the burden of estate taxes. Would you favor legislation to ease this burden?   yes___   no___
2. Of the following areas of federal spending choose *one* in which you would prefer to make a budget cut:
   a. Public welfare payments   ___
   b. Public works projects   ___
   c. Defense spending   ___
   d. Foreign assistance programs   ___

    e. Food stamps   ___

    f. Education   ___

    g. Other _____   ___

3. Do you believe that charitable organizations such as churches and nonprofit hospitals should remain tax-exempt?   yes___   no___

4. Which *one* of the following would you choose as the most important in solving the energy shortage over the next 20 years?

    a. Solar/geothermal power development   ___

    b. Nuclear power development   ___

    c. Conservation of present sources of energy   ___

    d. Expansion of domestic oil reserves   ___

    e. Increased use of coal   ___

5. Which *one* of the following would you say is the most important effort Congress could make to prevent crime?

    a. Enact harsher penalties to deter crimes   ___

    b. Reenact the death penalty for certain crimes   ___

    c. Enact restrictions on violence on television   ___

    d. Increase funding for the courts   ___

    e. Increase funding for law enforcement agencies   ___

    f. Reform the country's prison system   ___

6. Most of the economic indicators for the nation show positive signs of a recovery. Unemployment is down to 7.6%, personal incomes are up, and the prime lending rate is down.

    a. Do you feel that we are in a recovery?   yes___   no___

    b. Do you feel that the economy has stabilized?   yes___   no___

    c. Do you expect inflation to increase?   yes___   no___

    d. Do you believe that unemployment will increase?   yes___   no___

    e. Should Congress finance more jobs producing programs with tax revenues?   yes___   no___

7. In each of the following areas do you feel that Congress's efforts should be *increased*?

    a. Energy research and development   yes___   no___

    b. Health care and insurance   yes___   no___

    c. Crime control   yes___   no___

    d. Tax reform   yes___   no___

    e. Preservation of the environment   yes___   no___

    f. Other _____   yes___   no___

CASE STUDY 13

American Airlines

American Airlines conducts a periodic in-flight passenger survey, using questionnaires similar to the one below. About 50,000 such questionnaires are completed and analyzed each year. The Director of Market Research and Development is responsible for preparing the questionnaires, making the necessary arrangements for administering them, and analyzing the responses.

American views these questionnaires as providing information relevant to two major areas. First, it provides trend data on attitudes toward passenger services. Information on the passengers' attitudes toward the general services provided by American is requested in questions 8 through 15 and on food services in questions 17 through 29. Second, it provides trend information on the characteristics of American Airlines passengers—sex, age, frequency of air travel, purpose of the trip, and similar information.

The results are used by both the Passenger Sales and the Service Departments to identify problem areas that require management attention. If the trend of the passengers' appraisal of reservations accuracy is slipping downward, for example, an investigation can be made to pinpoint the cause of the dissatisfaction so that corrective action can be taken.

```
          May We Have One Minute of Your Time?*

As part of our planning to give you the best in airline
travel, we occasionally need to ask your help.
If you are 14 years of age or over, will you please
answer the few questions in this questionnaire?
It is very important that we get a questionnaire back
from you even if you are traveling with someone else.
If you have already filled out a questionnaire like
this within the last two weeks, please fill this one
out anyway.
This is a completely confidential questionnaire—please
do not give your name.
Please seal your questionnaire in the envelope pro-
vided. It will be picked up shortly.
```

*Reproduced with the permission and through the courtesy of American Airlines.

PASSENGER SURVEY

1. Please indicate the city where you boarded this flight and where you will get off:
   Boarded at:_____ Will get off at:_____

2. Which class of service are you using today? (Please mark your answer with an "X")
   1( ) FIRST CLASS   2( ) COACH

3. Flight number:_____   4. Date:_____

5. What is the main purpose of your trip today?
   1( ) BUSINESS 2( ) VACATION 3( ) VISITING RELA-TIVES OR FRIENDS 4( ) PERSONAL AFFAIRS

6. Before this trip today, about how many airline trips have you made in all in the last 12 months? (Include trips on all domestic airlines you have used, and count a round trip as one trip.)
   ( ) NONE BEFORE THIS TRIP

( )1	( )4	( )7	( )10-19	( )40-49
( )2	( )5	( )8	( )20-29	( )50 OR MORE
( )3	( )6	( )9	( )30-39	

7. If you checked "None before this trip" on question 6, is this the first airline trip you have ever taken?
   1( )YES   2( )NO

We'd like to get your frank opinions about some items of service connected with your flight today. Will you please give us your ratings on each of the following items?

(Please mark one "X" on each line.)

	Poor	Fair	Good	Excel-lent
8. The accuracy of your reservation	1( )	2( )	3( )	4( )
9. Checking in at the airport	1( )	2( )	3( )	4( )
10. Getting information at the airport on when your flight would leave	1( )	2( )	3( )	4( )
11. Courtesy and treatment by employees at offices and airports	1( )	2( )	3( )	4( )
12. Your flight leaving on time	1( )	2( )	3( )	4( )
13. Courtesy and treatment by the stewardess	1( )	2( )	3( )	4( )

14. Announcements during
    the flight   1( ) 2( ) 3( ) 4( )
15. Your meal   1( ) 2( ) 3( ) 4( )
16. What meal were you served on this flight?
1( )Lunch ⌉   Please   3( )Breakfast⌉   Please
2( )Dinner⌋ ─→ Continue 4( )No meal,   │─→ skip to
                             or snack   │   question
                             only   ⌋   30.

Here are a few more questions about your meal on
this flight. Will you please rate your meal on the
following items? If you didn't have an item, please
check the last column:

(Please mark
one "X"   Excel-   Didn't
on each line.) Poor Fair Good lent Have This

17. The appetizer   1( ) 2( ) 3( ) 4( )   5( )
18. The meat (or sea-
    food) part of
    the main course 1( ) 2( ) 3( ) 4( )   5( )
19. The vegetable   1( ) 2( ) 3( ) 4( )   5( )
20. The salad   1( ) 2( ) 3( ) 4( )   5( )
21. The dessert   1( ) 2( ) 3( ) 4( )   5( )
22. The coffee   1( ) 2( ) 3( ) 4( )   5( )
23. Appetizing
    appearance of
    the meal   1( ) 2( ) 3( ) 4( )   5( )
24. Attractive
    appearance of
    the dishes,
    glassware, and
    silver   1( ) 2( ) 3( ) 4( )   5( )
25. Promptness in
    serving the meal
    and removing the
    dishes   1( ) 2( ) 3( ) 4( )   5( )
26. Meal served in a
    gracious manner 1( ) 2( ) 3( ) 4( )   5( )
27. What meat or seafood were you served for your
    main course on your flight today?
MAIN COURSE_____
28. Did you have a highball or cocktail before your
    meal on this flight?
    1( )YES   2( )NO

29. Do you have any comments or suggestions for improving American's meals or meal service?

_____

30. Within the last 12 months, have any airline salesmen or sales representatives called on you?
   1( )YES   2( )NO

31. If you checked "Yes" on question 30, what airline or airlines did they represent?
   1( )AMERICAN   5( )EASTERN   9( )TWA
   2( )BRANIFF   6( )NATIONAL   0( )UNITED
   3( )CONTINENTAL   7( )NORTHEAST X( )WESTERN
   4( )DELTA   8( )NORTHWEST X( )OTHER:_____

32. Where do you live?
   City or town:_____County:_____
   State:_____

33. If you live outside the United States, how and through whom did you select American Airlines for your flight today?

_____

34. In what city did you make your reservation for this flight?
   1( )BALTIMORE   5( )FORT WORTH   9( )SAN FRANCISCO
   2( )BOSTON   6( )LOS ANGELES 0( )WASHINGTON
   3( )CHICAGO   7( )NEWARK   X( )OTHER (PLEASE
   4( )DALLAS   8( )NEW YORK   SPECIFY):_____

35. Including the day of your outbound flight and the day of your return flight, what is the total length of time you will be away from home on this trip?
   1( )1-2 DAYS   4( )7-8 DAYS   7( )13-14 DAYS
   2( )3-4 DAYS   5( )9-10 DAYS   8( )15 DAYS OR MORE
   3( )5-6 DAYS   6( )11-12 DAYS 9( )NOT A ROUND
                                      TRIP BY AIR

36. Your age:
   1( )14-17 YEARS   5( )40-49 YEARS
   2( )18-21 YEARS   6( )50-59 YEARS
   3( )22-29 YEARS   7( )60 YEARS OR OVER
   4( )30-39 YEARS

37. Please check: 1( )MAN   2( )WOMAN

THANK YOU

1. Evaluate this approach to obtaining information in terms of the purposes stated.

2. Evaluate this questionnaire in terms of the purposes stated.

3. What type of scale is implied by questions 8 through 15 and 17 through 26?

4. Describe how you would go about analyzing the responses to these questions.

CASE STUDY 14

National Observer: Mail Questionnaire

In 1975 the *National Observer*, a respected weekly published by Dow Jones and Co., commissioned a marketing research firm to conduct a study of its readers. The study was authorized to obtain information on the demographic and purchasing characteristics of the paper's readers. This information was to be provided to present and potential *Observer* advertisers.

The research firm selected a random sample of subscribers and sent each a questionnaire it had prepared. The questionnaire was stamped "CONFIDENTIAL" and did not ask for the respondent's name or address. One of the recipients was a professor of optics at the University of Wisconsin. He happened to have the questionnaire with him in his laboratory one evening and, out of curiosity, exposed it to ultraviolet light. Somewhat to his surprise, he found a four-digit identification number stamped in the upper left-hand corner of the first page in ink, visible only in ultraviolet light.

The professor wrote the publisher of the *Observer*, Henry Gemmill, asking for a public explanation of such a procedure. Gemmill, who knew the study was being conducted but knew nothing about the secret coding, was surprised and angered by what he considered to be a piece of trickery by the research firm, and a violation of the assurance of confidentiality.

One of the principals of the research firm pointed out that some method is needed for identifying the respondents who return mail questionnaires to prevent sending followup questionnaires to respondents as well as to nonrespondents. If the name and address of the respondent is requested on the questionnaire, he said, the response rate will be significantly reduced. He stated that some keying device is used on most mail questionnaires. Some that are commonly used are: (1) printing a serial "form number" at the end of the questionnaire, (2) printing the code number under the stamp or the flap of the return envelope, and (3) cutting the questionnaire paper in a special way, as well as the use of invisible ink. He defended the use of an invisible ink code by his own firm by noting that the confidentiality of the information that was promised was strictly adhered to. Anonymity of the responses was not promised, he said, and so there was no violation of ethics involved.

1. Was there a violation of an implied assurance of anonymity to the respondent?
2. Should researchers using mail questionnaires avoid the use of secret coding devices?

CASE STUDY 15

Oerlikon Synchromatic Watch

The Oerlikon Watch Company recently introduced a new type of wrist watch. Named the "Synchromatic," it operates on the principle of establishing a constant frequency in a tuning fork that is actuated by a small battery in the watch. The tuning fork vibrates at a frequency of 360 cycles per second and produces a slight humming sound instead of the ordinary ticking. The watch has very few moving parts and is highly accurate. It is shockproof, waterproof, and antimagnetic. The battery has a life expectancy of approximately one year.

Before the watch was introduced, a consumer use test was held in which a judgment sample of 25 men was selected to wear the watch. These men collectively represented a wide range of occupational and age groups. They each agreed to wear the watch at all times and under the same conditions they would normally wear a wrist watch. They also agreed to being interviewed at the end of a three-month period.

Two of the questions that each man was asked during the interview after having worn the watch were: "What did you find that you liked about the watch?" and "What did you find that you disliked about the watch?" The responses to these questions for each of the 25 respondents are given below.

Question: "What did you find that you liked about the watch?"

Respondent Number	Response
1.	"Most accurate watch I have ever worn."
	"Everyone at the plant was impressed."
2.	"I didn't have to wind it once."

Respondent Number	Response
3.	"Kept very good time." "I could see the dial at night."
4.	"I never had to worry about whether my watch was off and I would be late for an appointment."
5.	"I didn't miss a single train to work because my watch was wrong."
6.	"I work with a group of engineers, and they were all impressed with the watch."
7.	"I always forget to wind my watch, and, since I am on the road driving a lot, this causes me a lot of trouble. I like this one because I didn't have to wind it."
8.	"I like to try new things. I don't understand how this watch works but I was talking to my doctor about it, and he said he would like to get one too."
9.	"I always like to know how things work. I got so interested in how a tuning fork could be used to keep time that I read all the company literature they would send me. I think the design is very clever."
10.	"I work around a lot of equipment that generates electrical fields. I found that the watch kept perfect time while my present watch, which is supposed to be antimagnetic, is pretty erratic."
11.	"I like a watch with a little heft to it that you don't have to worry about banging it up. This one I dropped at least three times on a hardwood floor, and it didn't affect it at all."
12.	"I don't know whether you have other doctors trying the watch or not, but we need watches that are accurate and dependable. I found this watch to be both highly accurate and always running." "Since I have to wash my hands a lot, I have to have a watch that is waterproof. This one seemed completely waterproof." "I need a watch that has a clean design that will not catch and hold dust and dirt. I like the design of this one since it doesn't have a stem."
13.	"All my friends never heard of a watch like this before. The other guys kept asking me who I knew to get to wear a watch like this. This is the kind of a watch a man can be proud of."

Respondent Number	*Response*
14.	"This is the most accurate watch I have ever worn. It is even better than my pocket watch and I thought it was good."
15.	"Everything is electronic these days. An electronic watch is something that not very many people have, however."
16.	"We get time signals from the Naval Observatory at the radio station at which I work. I didn't believe that you could get a watch that was this accurate until I had tried it."
17.	"I skin-dive a lot and need a watch I can depend on so that I will know how long I have been down. This one worked well. I also need a watch that has a large luminous dial that I can read under water. I could read the time easily with this watch."
18.	"I sometimes have trouble getting to sleep and always wear my watch. The ticking often annoys me on my watch. I like the low hum of this one."
19.	"All the guys in the fraternity were pretty impressed. Even my physics prof thought it was a good watch. We checked out the frequency one day in class on a scope."
20.	"Riding in a cab over a diesel engine all day I get a lot of vibration. If this watch continues to keep as good time for the next year as it has for the last three months I would say you have a good product on your hands."
21.	"I always take off my watch at work and leave it on my desk. The self-winding watch I now have sometimes stops. I didn't have any trouble with this one."
22.	"I never placed much stock in this 'taste-maker' concept you read about, but I found that I enjoyed showing and telling people about this watch."
23.	"This is a watch that I would like to give my son for graduation, as I think he would be proud to own one." "I found I became more time-conscious as a result of wearing such an accurate watch."
24.	"The boss heard about me wearing this new kind of watch and called me in one day. We must have spent half an hour talking about it. It was the first time I ever knew he knew I even worked for him."
25.	"When are you going to start selling this watch? Everybody I talked with about it seemed very impressed."

Question: "What did you find that you disliked about the watch?"

Respondent Number	Response
1.	"The watch is too big. My sleeve is always getting hung on it."
2.	"The humming bothered me at night. When I put my arm under the pillow, it seemed to come right through."
3.	"I was annoyed that it tended to fray the cuff of the left sleeve on my shirts. You ought to do something about the sharp edges on the case."
4.	"I would imagine this is going to be a high-priced watch. I didn't like the styling at all. It looked like an inexpensive watch."
5.	"The watch is far too large."
6.	"I think the watch is too thick and big around even for a man's watch. I don't see how you ever sell a watch of this size to women."
7.	"It's a funny thing, but the humming bothered me when I was trying to get to sleep. I never noticed the ticking on my regular watch, but the humming noise kept me awake. I don't understand it, as I couldn't even hear the humming during the day."
8.	"It wore out the cuff on my sleeve."
9.	"I think you ought to make it look more expensive." "Something ought to be done about making it smaller. I suppose you have problems with the battery and all, but the watch is too big in my opinion."
10.	"I am a physicist and I noticed that the headboard of my bed tended to act as a sounding board for the humming. However, since I don't suppose many people tend to wear their watches at night, this wouldn't pose much of a problem generally."
11.	"I don't like the styling of the watch."
12.	"I prefer a thin case on a watch and one that has a contemporary design. This one looks like the old Ingersoll dollar pocket watch to me." "I had a problem with this watch wearing the cuff on my shirt sleeve. I always wear starched cuffs and the watch tended to catch and pull threads in the cuff."

Respondent Number	Response
13.	"You should reduce the size of the watch."
14.	"This watch doesn't look like one an executive should be wearing."
15.	"I was bothered somewhat by the humming of the watch while I was trying to get to sleep."
16.	"The dial is apparently made out of plastic which scratches easily. This gives a very poor appearance to the watch."
17.	"I recognize some of the problems of miniaturizing a watch of this kind, but I think you are going to have to get it down to the size of a conventional watch before it will sell very well."
18.	"I don't know whether I happened to get a lemon or not, but it kept stopping on me. I notified the people you told me to and they adjusted it several times but it never did work right."
19.	"It got to the point where I began to roll back my shirt cuff at work because the edge of the case was wearing it out."
20.	"This watch isn't styled very well in my opinion. It looks like it was designed for installation in the instrument panel of a locomotive."
21.	"This watch is definitely too large." "I don't like the styling at all. It looks cheap."
22.	"The crystal scratches awfully easily." "I think you could improve on the way the watch looks."
23.	"You ought to do something about the crystal. It got so scratched that sometimes when the light was from a certain angle I couldn't see the hands."
24.	"The styling is old-fashioned." "The watch did a pretty good job on my shirt cuffs. It seemed as if every time I pulled the cuff up to see what time it was it would catch on the watch."
25.	"I didn't find anything I disliked about the watch."

1. a. Establish categories and tabulate the responses to the question "What did you find that you liked about the watch?"
   b. Prepare a table that presents the results.

c. What conclusions could be drawn from the responses about the features that appealed to the wearers? Sould these features be the ones that should have been used in the appeals and copy of an introductory advertising campaign?

2. a. Establish categories and tabulate the reponses to the question "What did you find that you disliked about the watch?"

b. Prepare a table that presents the results.

c. What conclusions could be drawn from the responses about the features or attributes of the watch that were undesirable? Which of these, in your judgment, should have been changed before the product was introduced?

CASE STUDY 16

Federal Adding Machine

In 1919 the Federal Adding Machine Company brought out the Standard Federal "A" Adding and Listing Machine. Federal distributed its machines through salespeople calling directly on industrial and financial accounts. They had experienced high selling costs and the sales manager was looking for a method of distribution that was more economical but that would still provide the volume they required.

The sales manager proposed to the president of the company that they send a direct mail piece to all prospective accounts east of the Mississippi. He planned to offer the machine at a price of $225.50 if bought by mail versus $300.00 if sold through a personal call by a salesperson. An inventory of 1,000 machines was to be established for quick shipment of orders received through the proposed direct-mail campaign. If the results were favorable, the sales manager was of the opinion that Federal should adopt direct mail as their method of distribution.

The president agreed to the proposal and the mailing pieces were prepared and sent. An advertisement explaining the program was also prepared and run in the *Literary Digest* and other leading magazines (see the accompanying figure).

1. What was the purpose(s) of the program proposed by the sales manager?

2. Do you believe that the proposed program was well designed to serve this purpose (these purposes)?

3. Would you consider this program to be an "experiment"? Explain.

4. Had you been involved in this program, what design changes, if any, would you have suggested? Why?

A National Experiment to
Reduce Sales Expense ~
In Which <u>You</u> May Participate

Do YOU realize that it has been costing you up to 45% of the price of every adding machine you buy, just to be induced to buy it?

For years the established price of a 9-column adding and listing machine has been $300 or more. Nearly half of this represents selling expense, but the Federal Adding Machine Company is seeking to determine by means of a national economic experiment, whether this price cannot be greatly *reduced.*

We believe a great number of business men are convinced that adding machines are a necessity and are now ready to *buy* without having adding machines *sold* to them by expensive sales organizations—and thus greatly reduce that expense.

Every business and financial house east of the Mississippi will receive through the mails within the next two weeks, an announcement of the Federal experimental selling plan — *an offer of 1000 standard $300 Federal Adding Machines at $222.50.*

We are doing this in order to determine the actual selling cost, and to establish the future selling policy of this company.

The "serve-self" idea is gaining recognition in all lines of business. That is, the wise economy of cutting out all expensive "frills" in getting merchandise into the consumer's hands.

By being your own salesman, you can save in selling cost. When that cost in the past has run as high as 45% it means a *real* saving to you. This is the idea behind this experiment, that we believe meets the new conditions and business needs of the present time.

We would have no trouble marketing the Federal along the old sales lines for $300. It is the "last word" in adding machines, designed by the veteran adding machine designer and builder, Charles Wales, as the crowning result of his genius and experience. It is backed by a well-financed corporation, and is manufactured by one of the finest mechanical and engineering organizations in the country—Colt's Patent Fire Arms Mfg. Co., Hartford, Conn.

But we know that right now American business men are demanding that needless waste be eliminated in merchandising methods just as truly as in factory methods.

Are we right? You, who use and need adding machines—would you rather BUY one for $222.50 or BE SOLD one for $300?

FEDERAL ADDING MACHINE CORP'N
251 Fourth Avenue   New York

In constant use for five years by some of the largest corporations in the east, including the Federal Government. Exacting tasks have proved its merit finally.

The Standard Federal "A" Adding and Listing Machine has nine-column capacity, eighty-one keys; 13-inch carriage; roll paper holder; flexible keyboard; easy handle pull, (motor equipment if desired). Only half as many parts in the Federal as in other standard machines. Stronger construction, standardized interchangeable parts. Every item visible. Adding machine service guaranteed. Write for sixteen-page illustrated booklet.

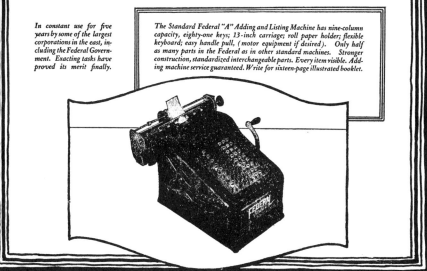

CASE STUDY 17

Exxon U.S.A.: Test of Cash Discount

Users of credit cards not only benefit from the convenience of their use but can delay payment from the time of purchase through the billing and payment dates. If the customer is not charged for the use of the credit card, the seller must finance the purchase until payment is made. Such costs inevitably get reflected in prices, and so the customer who pays cash actually pays a part of the cost of financing credit card purchases as well. Recognizing that this was the case, Congress passed an amendment to the Robinson–Patman Act in 1976 which gave retailers permission to set cash discounts of up to 5%.

Exxon decided to test the effects of a 5% discount on cash and credit gasoline sales by conducting a market test. The test was to be conducted at Exxon stations in Abilene, Texas, and Charleston, South Carolina. It was planned to run the test for six months, after which a survey of dealers and customers would be conducted and the sales results analyzed. If the results were favorable, the cash discounts were to be introduced nationwide.

1. Was this an appropriate research design to test the use of the cash discount? Explain.
2. In your judgment, what would constitute sufficiently favorable results from the test using this design to warrant use of the cash discount at all Exxon stations?

CASE STUDY 18

Florida Citrus Mutual

The Florida Citrus Mutual has as its members a large proportion of the orange growers in Florida. Shortly after Mutual was formed, the members established two primary objectives for the marketing program. They were to help create stability in the market for oranges and to set prices that would assure them a "fair" return.

The setting of prices for oranges is a difficult problem. The better grades of oranges are sold as fresh fruit, while the lower grades are sold to juice processors. The middle grades of oranges can be sold in either market. Since oranges originally sold in the fresh and the juice markets are rarely resold in the other market, and production costs are the same regardless of grade, Mutual could set prices in each of the two market segments based on the relative levels of demand. The problem was that little was known about the elasticities of demand over the relevant range of prices in the two market segments.

Economists at the Agricultural Experiment Station at Gainesville were interested in the general problem of determining demand elasticities, not only as it applied to oranges, but to other citrus products as well. As a first step toward its solution they decided to undertake a small scale pricing experiment for fresh oranges. The stated purposes of the experiment were to (1) determine the characteristics of the demand for fresh oranges in a comparatively small segment of society and (2) to investigate the feasibility of using experimental techniques to establish demand relationships for citrus products.

An experiment was designed to determine the sales response to different retail prices per dozen oranges. Seven price levels were tested which consisted of the then-established actual price per dozen and the three negative and three positive variations at intervals of 5 cents per dozen. The range over which the prices varied was therefore 30 cents per dozen.

A national supermarket chain agreed to let the test be conducted in a sample of their stores. A judgment sample of seven of their stores in central Kentucky was selected, and arrangements were made to conduct the experiment during the seven-week period from late April to mid-June. Each of the price levels was to be tested once in each store during one of the weeks of the test. The assignments by price levels by stores and weeks were done randomly and are shown in Table B-6.

Efforts were made to maintain consistency in the quality of the fruit, the nature of the displays, and prices of competing fruits both among stores and over time. To allow for differences in patronage levels of the stores, counts of sales on cash register tapes in each of the stores were made each

Table B-6   Deviations of experimental prices from
the established market price per dozen oranges
in seven supermarkets in central Kentucky,
April 28 through June 16

WEEK BEGINNING	STORE NUMBER						
	I	*II*	*III*	*IV*	*V*	*VI*	*VII*
April 28	− 5	+15	+10	0	−10	+ 5	−15
May 5	+15	+10	0	−10	+ 5	−15	− 5
May 12	+10	0	−10	+ 5	−15	− 5	+15
May 19	0	−10	+ 5	−15	− 5	+15	+10
May 26	−10	+ 5	−15	− 5	+15	+10	0
June 2	+ 5	−15	− 5	+15	+10	0	−10
June 9	−15	− 5	+15	+10	0	−10	+ 5

week and sales of oranges per 100 customers were computed. Sales of oranges per 100 customers at each price level for each week were as shown in Table B-7.

Table B-7   **Weekly purchases of dozens of oranges per 100 customers at varying premiums and discounts from the established market price in seven supermarkets in central Kentucky, April 28 through June 16**

PRICE DIFFERENTIAL PER DOZEN (cents)	WEEK BEGINNING								
	April 28	May 5	May 12	May 19	May 26	June 2	June 9	Total	Mean
−15	17.59	10.58	12.55	26.86	17.86	9.32	13.59	108.35	15.48
−10	14.20	17.00	15.68	8.74	9.00	10.00	3.70	78.32	11.19
− 5	7.67	9.11	5.64	8.65	10.95	8.72	5.90	56.64	8.09
0	14.58	14.92	8.10	6.86	66.30	3.81	3.92	58.49	8.36
+ 5	5.33	8.55	9.66	11.74	5.90	5.52	3.25	49.95	7.14
+10	11.88	5.96	5.69	5.25	3.86	5.50	6.03	44.17	6.31
+15	5.62	5.04	4.35	3.44	5.55	5.61	4.99	34.60	4.94
Total	76.87	71.16	61.67	71.54	59.42	48.48	41.38	43.52	61.50
Mean	10.98	10.17	8.82	10.22	8.48	6.93	5.91	61.50	8.79

1. How appropriate was the research design for the nature of the problem?
2. What kind of experimental design was used?
3. How should the data be analyzed?
4. What are the results of your analysis?

CASE STUDY 19

Student Union Tavern

After many years of trying, the Associated Students of the University of Oregon (ASUO) obtained permission from the University administration to operate a tavern in the Student Union. The tavern was planned to be located on the first floor of the Union adjacent to a snack bar already being operated by the ASUO. Food service in the tavern was therefore to be minimal. Beer and wine would be served, but the serving of hard liquors was not to be permitted. The tavern would cover approximately 3,000 square feet of floor space.

A local consulting firm was retained by the ASUO to do a feasibility study for the proposed tavern. The study was to provide estimates of the initial investment and a projection of beer and wine revenues and of operating costs for the first year of operation.

Two methods of forecasting beer and wine revenues were considered by the consultants. The first was to obtain data on the revenues from this source for the previous year from taverns operated on other university campuses. By obtaining data on student enrollments at the same universities, estimates of dollars of beer and wine revenues per student per year could be developed. Multiplying the average revenues per student per year by the number of students enrolled at the University of Oregon would then provide a projection of beer and wine revenues for the proposed tavern for the first year.

This approach was abandoned primarily for reasons of time and the fact that the second method was believed to provide a better forecast. A survey was made of the four taverns (Arno's, Kilroy's, The Sudser, and The Kamikaze) within a four-block walking distance of the campus. The manager of each tavern was interviewed and asked for information on the percentage of sales represented by draft beer, bottled beer, and wine; the volume of each of these sold in an average month (kegs of draft beer, cases of bottled beer, and gallons of wine); and the prices per unit of each. The volume sold of each of the products was obtained only for Arno's and The Kamikaze, however. The problem of the missing data was solved by obtaining estimates of the average number of kegs of beer sold per month by Kilroy's and The Sudser from the beer wholesaler who supplied them. The volume of bottled beer and wine was estimated from the product-mix-revenue percentages already supplied by the manager of each tavern. Calculation of the estimated annual beer and wine revenue for each tavern was then made using known unit prices. The resulting revenue estimates are shown in Table B-8.

Table B-8 Dollar revenues and serving area

Tavern	Estimated Annual Beer and Wine Revenues ($)	Estimated Serving Area (square feet)
Arno's	351,588	3,367
Kilroy's	313,764	2,385
The Sudser	177,732	1,230
The Kamikaze	149,484	600
Total	992,568	7,582

It was hypothesized that, other things being equal, dollar revenues should be a function of the serving area of the tavern. It is a generally accepted rule of thumb that the serving area in a tavern will occupy about two-thirds of the total tavern floor space. Total floor space for each of the taverns was obtained from the county Real Property Appraisal Division and multiplied by 0.67 to obtain estimates of the serving areas. The estimates that resulted are also shown in Table B-8.

A univariate regression was run with beer and wine revenues as the criterion variable and serving area as the predictor variable. The regression equation, standard error of the estimate, and coefficient of correlation were as follows:

$$\hat{y} = \$97,791 + \$79.32x$$

$$SE = \$24,714$$

$$r = 0.979$$

The consultant was pleased with the high coefficient of correlation. He concluded that this meant that over 95% of the variance in revenues was explained ($r^2 = 0.958$) and that the use of the regression equation should therefore provide a reliable forecast of revenue for the proposed tavern. Since the Student Union tavern was planned to have a floor space of 3,000 square feet, the serving area was estimated to occupy two-thirds of that, or 2,000 square feet. The point forecast of annual revenues from beer and wine was then arrived at by substituting the square footage figure in the regression equation and solving to get

$$\hat{y} = \$97,791 + 79.32(2,000) = \$256,431$$

The consultant recognized, of course, that there are many factors that affect revenues other than serving area. The location and atmosphere of the tavern, the quality of the products sold and of the service provided, and the pricing policies are each important. He allowed two standard errors of estimate for these factors and for sampling variation and obtained an interval estimate of beer and wine revenues for the first year of

$$\$256,431 \pm (2)\$24,714 = \$207,003 \text{ to } \$305,859$$

1. Comment on the procedures used to obtain the point and interval forecasts of beer and wine revenues.
2. In your judgment, should the officers of the ASUO have accepted the interval forecast as a basis for their planning for the proposed tavern? Explain.

CASE STUDY 20

U.S. Postal Service

The Postal Reorganization Act of 1970 stipulates that the postal service is to be financially self-sustaining. The Act established a Postal Rate Commission, whose function it is to recommend rate schedules that will allow the service to pay its own way, and a Postal Service Board of Governors, which has the final authority for determining rates.

The U.S. Postal Service has segmented the market for its services by establishing four classes of mail. In addition, it has differentiated the services it provides by making airmail, special handling, special delivery, registered mail, COD mail, and certified mail services available. The types of mail handled as first-, second-, third-, and fourth-class mail and the rate schedules in 1976 for each are shown in Table B-9.

Table B-9 Description of kinds of mail included and rate schedule for first-, second-, third-, and fourth-class mail, 1976

FIRST CLASS

Kind of Mail	Rate
first-class mail weighing 13 ounces or less xcept postal and post cards.	13c for the first ounce or fraction; 11c for each additional ounce or fraction.
r 13 ounces	Priority mail (heavy pieces) rates apply.
le postal cards sold by the post office	9c each.
ble postal cards sold by the post office	18c (9c each half).
le post cards_____	9c each.
ble post cards (reply half of double post rd does not have to bear postage when riginally mailed).	18c (9c each half).
sort rate	Consult Postmaster
ness reply mail	Consult Postmaster

SECOND CLASS

spapers and periodical publications with second-class mail vileges).	
es mailed by public.	10c for first 2 ounces; 4c each additional ounce or fraction thereof, or the fourth-class rate, whichever is lower.

THIRD CLASS

Circulars, books, catalogs, and other printed matter; merchandise, seeds, cuttings, bulbs, roots, scions, and plants, weighing less than 16 ounces.

SINGLE PIECE RATE*

0 to 2 ozs. ------------------- 14c	Over 8 to 10 ozs.-------------- 61c
Over 2 to 4 ozs.--------------- 28c	Over 10 to 12 ozs.------------- 72c
Over 4 to 6 ozs.--------------- 39c	Over 12 to 14 ozs.------------- 83c
Over 6 to 8 ozs.--------------- 50c	Over 14 to 15.99 ozs.--------- 94c

BULK RATE
CONSULT POSTMASTER

Over 12 ounces, use the 4th class zone rate if lower.

FOURTH CLASS
(PARCEL POST) ZONE RATES

Weight 1 pound and not exceeding (pounds)	ZONES							
	Local	1 and 2	3	4	5	6	7	8
2_____	$0.77	$0.90	$0.93	$1.04	$1.15	$1.28	$1.40	$1.48
3_____	.82	.97	1.02	1.15	1.29	1.46	1.62	1.74
4_____	.86	1.04	1.10	1.25	1.42	1.63	1.84	2.00
5_____	.91	1.11	1.19	1.36	1.56	1.81	2.06	2.26
6_____	.95	1.18	1.27	1.46	1.69	1.98	2.28	2.52
7_____	1.00	1.25	1.36	1.57	1.83	2.16	2.50	2.78
8_____	1.04	1.32	1.44	1.67	1.96	2.33	2.72	3.04
9_____	1.09	1.39	1.53	1.78	2.10	2.51	2.94	3.30
10____	1.13	1.46	1.61	1.88	2.23	2.68	3.16	3.56

(Rates are set by pound by zone up to a maximum of 70 pounds.)

There has been considerable question (and controversy) within the postal service in recent years concerning the equity of the rate structure. It has been argued by some, for example, that first-class rates have been so high that first-class mailers have been subsidizing mailers in the other classes. The proponents of this view have recommended reducing first-class rates and imposing substantial increases—as much as 122% in one proposal—for non-first-class mail. The opponents of this view have argued that such a move might well reduce postal service volume and revenues and thus eventually force first-class rates to rise even higher than they now are.

1. What other bases for segmentation might be used by the postal service?
2. How should a study to investigate the desirability of using alternative segments be designed and conducted?
3. How should a study be designed and conducted to obtain information on the probable change in revenues for different rate schedules for second-, third-, and fourth-class mail (as these classes are presently defined)?

CASE STUDY 21

Mount Rushmore Insurance Company

The management of the Mount Rushmore Insurance Company, a company specializing in automobile insurance, asked the marketing research manager to conduct a survey to determine consumer interest in a new auto insurance concept then under consideration. The concept involved coverage for costs incurred as a result of a car breaking down while on a trip.

The marketing research manager designed and conducted a small telephone survey involving a sample of 60 respondents. Half the sample was drawn randomly from the company's present customer list, and half was drawn by means of random-digit dialing. In each interview the following statement describing the proposed insurance coverage was read to the respondent over the telephone:

> An insurance company is considering providing a policy that would pay toward expenses incurred when your car breaks down while you are driving more than 150 miles from home. It pays up to $500 toward such items as towing, repair costs, other transportation, rooms, and meals. Payments are subject to a $50 deductible amount. The policy will cost $15 a year.

Following the reading of this statement, the respondent was asked to state his or her degree of interest in the policy on a 5-point scale ranging from 1 (definitely not interested) to 5 (very much interested).

The respondent was then asked to supply a small amount of background data regarding:

- Age
- Marital status
- Number of cars owned
- Average age of car(s)
- Number of trips taken by automobile (for any purpose whatsoever) over the past year that exceeded 300 miles on a round-trip basis

The data obtained from the survey are shown in Table B-10.

Table B-10   Telephone survey data*

Respondent	Concept Rating	Current Insurance Supplier	Age	Marital Status	Number of Cars	Average Age of Car(s)	Number of Trips
1	4	Rushmore	42	M	1	0.5	3
2	3	R	39	M	1	1.5	1
3	5	R	47	M	1	1	4
4	2	R	24	S	3	1	2
5	4	R	43	M	2	1.5	4
6	5	R	62	M	1	0.5	6
7	1	R	27	M	1	2	3
8	5	R	55	M	2	0.5	4
9	4	R	42	S	1	2	2
10	3	R	36	M	2	2.5	1
11	4	R	39	M	3	1.5	5
12	2	R	24	S	4	2	0
13	5	R	58	M	1	2	6
14	4	R	43	M	1	0.4	2
15	1	R	23	S	2	2.5	0
16	5	R	59	M	1	0.5	7
17	4	R	43	M	3	1.5	3
18	3	R	36	S	1	2	0
19	3	R	47	M	1	2	1
20	4	R	42	M	1	1.5	4
21	4	R	47	M	4	1.5	4
22	4	R	38	M	2	1	3
23	5	R	37	M	2	0.8	8
24	3	R	39	S	1	2	0
25	4	R	51	M	1	1	2
26	4	R	47	M	2	1.5	1

Table B-10   (continued)

Respondent	Concept Rating	Current Insurance Supplier	Age	Marital Status	Number of Cars	Average Age of Car(s)	Number of Trips
27	5	R	51	M	1	2	6
28	1	R	30	S	1	2	0
29	1	R	28	S	2	4.5	2
30	3	R	42	M	2	3.5	1
31	2	Other	32	M	3	3	0
32	4	O	29	M	1	2	3
33	2	O	32	M	1	1	0
34	1	O	37	M	1	1	0
35	3	O	24	S	4	2.5	1
36	2	O	41	M	1	2	3
37	3	O	23	M	1	2	0
38	1	O	34	M	5	3	1
39	2	O	38	M	2	2	0
40	4	O	47	M	2	1	5
41	5	O	24	M	1	0.5	9
42	3	O	32	M	1	1.5	0
43	1	O	22	S	1	3	1
44	2	O	27	S	1	2.5	0
45	2	O	29	M	3	2.5	0
46	4	O	43	M	2	1	2
47	5	O	48	S	1	0.5	3
48	3	O	36	M	1	1.5	0
49	4	O	42	M	3	1.5	2
50	2	O	26	S	2	2	2
51	2	O	29	S	1	2.5	1
52	1	O	23	S	1	3	0
53	3	O	34	M	1	1.5	0
54	4	O	37	S	1	1.5	2
55	2	O	24	S	2	3	0
56	3	O	32	M	2	2	1
57	5	O	44	M	1	0.5	7
58	1	O	28	M	1	2.5	0
59	1	O	22	S	2	3	1
60	2	O	26	S	1	2	1

*These data are contrived.

1. Based on a *visual* examination of the data, how does degree of interest in the new concept appear to be related to:
   a. Whether the respondent is a current Rushmore customer or not?
   b. Respondent age?
   c. Number of automobile trips?

2. Divide the sample into two groups:
   a. Those showing high interest—"4" or "5" ratings.
   b. Those showing lower interest—"1," "2," or "3" ratings.
   Cross-tabulate high versus low interest in Rushmore customers versus customers of other companies. What do you note from this result: is the association statistically significant at the 0.05 level?

3. What happens to the association observed in the preceding cross tabulation when older (40 years and over) versus younger respondents are introduced as a third two-category variable?

4. We can consider the concept rating as a criterion variable and the remaining six variables as predictor variables in a multiple regression. In the case of current insurance supplier, we can use the dummy-variable coding:

$$\text{If Rushmore customer} \implies 1$$
$$\text{If other company customer} \implies 0$$

Similarly, in the case of marital status, we can use the dummy-variable coding:

$$\text{If single} \implies 1$$
$$\text{If married} \implies 0$$

Having done this, regress the column of concept ratings (criterion variable) on the six predictor variables:
   a. Interpret the regression equation.
   b. What is the value of R^2?
   c. Is each separate predictor statistically significant at the 0.05 level?
   d. Can a simpler model (involving fewer predictor variables) be developed?
   e. How do the predictors enter under a stepwise regression procedure?

5. Divide the sample into four groups: Rushmore, single; Rushmore, married; other company, single; and other company, married.
   a. If we consider these four groups in a single-factor analysis of variance with the concept rating serving as a criterion variable, do we accept the null hypothesis that the four mean concept ratings are equal (at the 0.05 level)?
   b. What are the assumptions about the error term in the single-factor ANOVA model?

6. Divide the sample into two groups: those rating the concept "4" or "5" versus those rating it "1," "2," or "3."

    a. Run a two-group discriminant analysis with the predictor variables of respondent age, number of cars owned, and number of trips.

    b. Interpret the discriminant function.

    c. How well does the function classify the known membership of the sample?

7. Factor-analyze the full 60 × 7 data matrix by principal components followed by Varimax rotation on those factors whose variance accounted-for values exceed unity.

    a. How would you interpret each set of rotated factor loadings?

    b. What other variables are associated with that factor showing high loadings for the concept-rating variable?

    c. Cluster-analyze the Varimax-rotated factor scores (after first finding interpoint distances in rotated factor space). Find three clusters of respondents.

    d. How would you interpret these clusters with regard to average concept ratings and Rushmore versus other company customers?

8. Having completed the various analyses, what should the marketing research manager recommend regarding:

    a. The wisdom of offering the policy?

    b. Its target market?

    c. Merchandising strategy?

    d. Future research to take before actual introduction of the policy?

APPENDIX C

Bibliography

MARKETING APPLICATIONS OF SCALING AND MULTIVARIATE TECHNIQUES

Over the past 15 years, marketing applications of various scaling and multivariate statistical techniques have increased enormously. No attempt is made here to provide anything approaching an exhaustive listing. Rather we focus on a selected (and hoped-for representative) subset of marketing applications that have been published relatively recently. For other applications, the reader can examine the following journal sources:

- *Journal of Marketing Research*
- *Journal of Marketing*
- *Journal of the Market Research Society* (British)
- *Journal of Consumer Research*
- *Management Science*
- *Journal of Advertising Research*
- *Journal of Business*
- *Decision Sciences*

GENERAL REFERENCES

Case applications and conceptual discussions of selected scaling and multivariate techniques are available in various marketing research texts, as illustrated by the following:

BOYD, H. W., JR., RALPH WESTFALL, and S. F. STASCH, *Marketing Research: Text and Cases* (4th ed.). Homewood, Ill.: Richard D. Irwin, Inc., 1977.

CHURCHILL, G. H., JR., *Marketing Research: Methodological Foundations*. Hinsdale, Ill.: Dryden Press, 1976.

COX, K. K., and B. M. ENIS, *The Marketing Research Process*. Pacific Palisades, Calif.: Goodyear Publishing Co., Inc., 1972.

FERBER, ROBERT, ed., *Handbook of Marketing Research*. New York: McGraw-Hill Book Company, 1974.

SCHONER, BERTRAM, and K. P. UHL, *Marketing Research: Information Systems and Decision Making* (2nd ed.). New York: John Wiley & Sons, Inc., 1975.

TULL, D. S., and D. I. HAWKINS, *Marketing Research: Meaning, Measurements and Method*. New York: Macmillan Publishing Co., Inc., 1976.

WENTZ, W. B., *Cases in Marketing Research*. New York: Harper & Row, Publishers, 1975.

ZALTMAN, GERALD, and P. S. BERGER, *Marketing Research: Fundamentals and Dynamics*. Hinsdale, Ill.: Dryden Press, 1975.

SCALING METHODS

Scaling methods involving unidimensional techniques were discussed in Chapter 6. Multidimensional methods and conjoint analysis were discussed in Chapter 14. Chapters 16 and 17 also described various industry applications in which scaling methods were used. References to these chapters are organized under the headings: General Sources; Unidimensional Scaling Techniques and Attitude Models; Multidimensional Scaling Techniques; and Conjoint Analysis and Related Methods.

General Sources

ANDERSON, B. B., *Advances in Consumer Research*, Vol. 3. Cincinnati, Ohio: Association for Consumer Research, 1976.

GREEN, P. E., and F. J. CARMONE, *Multidimensional Scaling and Related Techniques in Marketing Analysis*. Boston: Allyn and Bacon, Inc., 1970.

GREEN, P. E., and V. R. RAO, *Applied Multidimensional Scaling: A Comparison of Approaches and Algorithms*. New York: Holt, Rinehart and Winston, Inc., 1972.

GREEN, P. E., and YORAM WIND, *Multiattribute Decisions in Marketing: A Measurement Approach*. Hinsdale, Ill.: Dryden Press, 1973.

HALEY, R. I., ed., *Attitude Research in Transition*. Chicago: American Marketing Association, 1972.

HUGHES, G. D., *Attitude Measurement for Marketing Strategies*. Glenview, Ill.: Scott, Foresman and Company, 1971.

KING, C. W., and D. J. TIGERT, eds., *Attitude Research Reaches New Heights*. Chicago: American Marketing Association, 1970.

LEVINE, PHILIP, ed., *Attitude Research Bridges the Atlantic.* Chicago: American Marketing Association, 1973.

MYERS, J. G., *Consumer Image and Attitude.* Berkeley, Calif.: Institute of Business and Economic Research, University of California at Berkeley, 1968.

SCHLINGER, M. J., ed., *Advances in Consumer Research*, Vol. 2. University of Illinois at Chicago Circle: Association for Consumer Research, 1975.

WARD, SCOTT, and PETER WRIGHT, eds., *Advances in Consumer Research*, Vol. 1. Urbana, Ill.: Association for Consumer Research, 1974.

WIND, YORAM, and M. G. GREENBERG, eds., *Moving Ahead with Attitude Research.* Chicago: American Marketing Association, 1977.

Unidimensional Scaling Techniques and Attitude Models

ALPERT, M. I., "Identification of Determinant Attitudes: A Comparison of Methods," *Journal of Marketing Research*, 8 (May, 1971), 184–91.

AXELROD, J. N., "Attitude Measures That Predict Purchase," *Journal of Advertising Research*, 8 (March, 1968), 3–17.

BETTMAN, J. R., "Information Processing Models of Consumer Behavior," *Journal of Marketing Research*, 7 (August, 1970), 370–76.

BROWN, GORDON, TONY COPELAND, and MAURICE MILLWARD, "Monadic Testing of New Products—An Old Problem and Some Partial Solutions," *Journal of the Market Research Society*, 15 (April, 1973), 112–31.

CLANCY, K. J., and R. GARSEN, "Why Some Scales Predict Better," *Journal of Advertising Research*, 10 (October, 1970), 33–38.

CRANE, L. E., "How Product, Appeal, and Program Affect Attitudes toward Commercials," *Journal of Advertising Research*, 4 (March, 1964), 15–18.

DANIELS, PETER, and JOHN LAWFORD, "The Effect of Order in the Presentation of Samples in Paired Comparison Product Tests," *Journal of the Market Research Society*, 16 (April, 1974), 127–32.

DOLICH, I. J., "Congruence Relationships between Self Image and Product Brands," *Journal of Marketing Research*, 6 (February, 1969), 80–84.

EASTLACK, J. O., "Consumer Flavor Preference Factors in Food Product Design," *Journal of Marketing Research*, 1 (February, 1964), 38–42.

HAWKINS, D. I., GERALD ALBAUM, and ROGER BEST, "Stapel Scale or Semantic Differential in Marketing Research?" *Journal of Marketing Research*, 11 (August, 1974), 318–22.

HOLMES, CLIFF, "A Statistical Evaluation of Rating Scales," *Journal of the Market Research Society*, 16 (April, 1974), 87–107.

HUGHES, G. D., "A New Tool for Sales Managers," *Journal of Marketing Research*, 1 (May, 1964), 32–38.

HUGHES, G. D., "Upgrading the Semantic Differential," *Journal of the Market Research Society*, 17 (January, 1975), 41–44.

HUGHES, G. D., and P. A. NAERT, "A Computer-Controlled Experiment in Consumer Behavior," *Journal of Business*, 43 (July, 1970), 354–72.

HYETT, G. P., and J. R. McKENZIE, "Discrimination Tests and Repeated Paired Comparison Tests," *Journal of the Market Research Society*, 18 (January, 1976), 24–31.

LUNDSTROM, W. J., and L. M. LAMONT, "The Development of a Scale to Measure Consumer Discontent," *Journal of Marketing Research*, 13 (November, 1976), 373–81.

LUSK, E. J., "A Bipolar Adjective Screening Methodology," *Journal of Marketing Research*, 10 (May, 1973), 202–3.

RICHARDS, E. A., "A Commercial Application of Guttman Attitude Scaling Techniques," *Journal of Marketing*, 22 (October, 1957), 166–73.

RILEY, STUART, and JOHN PALMER, "Of Attitudes and Latitudes: A Repertory Grid Study of Perceptions," *Journal of the Market Research Society*, 17 (April, 1975), 74–89.

SAMPSON, PETER, "Using the Repertory Grid Test," *Journal of Marketing Research*, 9 (February, 1972), 78–81.

SHARPE, L. K., and W. T. ANDERSON, JR., "Concept-Scale Interaction in the Semantic Differential," *Journal of Marketing Research*, 9 (November, 1972), 432–34.

WILKIE, W. L., and E. A. PESSEMIER, "Issues in Marketing's Use of Multiattribute Attitude Models," *Journal of Marketing Research*, 10 (November, 1973), 428–41.

WORCESTER, R. M., and T. R. BURNS, "A Statistical Examination of the Relative Precision of Verbal Scales," *Journal of the Market Research Society*, 17 (July, 1975), 181–97.

Multidimensional Scaling Techniques

BEST, R. J., "The Predictive Aspects of a Joint-Space Theory of Stochastic Choice," *Journal of Marketing Research*, 13 (May, 1976), 198–204.

DAY, G. S., "Evaluating Models of Attitude Structure," *Journal of Marketing Research*, 9 (August, 1972), 279–86.

DAY, G. S., TERRY DEUTSCHER, and A. B. RYANS, "Data Quality, Level of Aggregation and Non-metric Multidimensional Scaling Solutions," *Journal of Marketing Research*, 13 (February, 1976), 92–97.

DOYLE, PETER, and JOHN MCGEE, "Perceptions of, and Preferences for, Alternative Convenience Goods," *Journal of the Market Research Society*, 15 (January, 1973), 24–34.

GREEN, P. E., "Marketing Applications of MDS: Assessment and Outlook," *Journal of Marketing*, 38 (January, 1975), 24–31.

GREEN, P. E., "On the Robustness of Multidimensional Scaling Techniques," *Journal of Marketing Research*, 12 (February, 1975), 73–81.

GREEN, P. E., and F. J. CARMONE, "Multidimensional Scaling: An Introduction and Comparison of Nonmetric Unfolding Techniques," *Journal of Marketing Research*, 6 (August, 1969), 330–41.

GREEN, P. E., and V. R. RAO, "Configuration Synthesis in Multidimensional Scaling," *Journal of Marketing Research*, 9 (February, 1972), 65–68.

GREEN, P. E., ARUN MAHESHWARI, and V. R. RAO, "Self-Concept and Brand Preference: An Empirical Application of Multidimensional Scaling," *Journal of the Market Research Society*, 11 (1969), 343–60.

GREEN, P. E., YORAM WIND, and H. J. CLAYCAMP, "Brand Features Congruence Mapping," *Journal of Marketing Research*, 12 (August, 1975), 306–13.

GREEN, P. E., YORAM WIND, and A. K. JAIN, "Analyzing Free-Response Data in Marketing Research," *Journal of Marketing Research*, 10 (February, 1973), 45–52.

GREEN, P. E., YORAM WIND, and A. K. JAIN, "Benefit Bundle Analysis," *Journal of Advertising Research*, 12 (April, 1972), 31–36.

GREEN, P. E., YORAM WIND, and A. K. JAIN, "A Note on Measurement of Social-Psychological Belief Systems," *Journal of Marketing Research*, 9 (May, 1972), 204–8.

GREEN, P. E., YORAM WIND, and A. K. JAIN, "Preference Measurement of Item Collections," *Journal of Marketing Research*, 9 (November, 1972), 371–77.

HENRY, W. A., and R. V. STUMPF, "Time and Accuracy Measures for Alternative Multidimensional Scaling Data Collection," *Journal of Marketing Research*, 12 (May, 1975), 165–70.

HUBER, JOEL, "Bootstrapping of Data and Decisions," *Journal of Consumer Research*, 2 (December, 1975), 229–34.

HUBER, JOEL, "Predicting Preference on Experimental Bundles of Attributes: A Comparison of Models," *Journal of Marketing Research*, 12 (August, 1975), 290–97.

JAIN, A. K., "A Method for Investigating and Representing an Implicit Theory of Social Class," *Journal of Consumer Research*, 2 (June, 1975), 53–59.

JOHNSON, R. M., "Market Segmentation: A Strategic Management Tool," *Journal of Marketing Research*, 9 (February, 1971), 13–18.

KINNEAR, T. C., and J. R. TAYLOR, "The Effect of Ecological Concern on Brand Perceptions," *Journal of Marketing Research*, 10 (May, 1973), 191–97.

KLAHR, DAVID, "Decision Making in a Complex Environment: The Use of Similarity Judgments to Predict Preferences," *Management Science*, 15 (1969), 595–618.

LEHMANN, D. R., "Judged Similarity and Brand-switching Data as Similarity Measures," *Journal of Marketing Research*, 9 (August, 1972), 331–34.

MACKAY, D. B., and R. W. OLSHAVSKY, "Cognitive Maps on Retail Locations: An Investigation of Some Basic Issues," *Journal of Consumer Research*, 2 (December, 1975), 197–205.

MOINPOUR, REZA, J. M. MCCULLOUGH, and DOUGLAS MACLACHLAN, "Time Changes in Perception: A Longitudinal Application of Multidimensional Scaling," *Journal of Marketing Research*, 13 (August, 1976), 245–53.

MORGAN, N., and J. PURNELL, "Isolating Openings for New Products in a Multi-dimensional Space," *Journal of the Market Research Society*, 11 (July, 1969), 245–66.

MYERS, J. H., "Benefit Structure Analysis: A New Tool for Product Planning," *Journal of Marketing*, 40 (October, 1976), 23–32.

NEIDELL, L. A., "Procedures for Obtaining Similarities Data," *Journal of Marketing Research*, 9 (August, 1972), 335–37.

NEIDELL, L. A., "The Use of Nonmetric Multidimensional Scaling in Marketing Analysis," *Journal of Marketing*, 33 (1968), 37–43.

PERCY, LARRY, "How Market Segmentation Guides Advertising Strategy," *Journal of Advertising Research*, 16 (October, 1976), 11–26.

PESSEMIER, E. A., and H. P. ROOT, "The Dimensions of New Product Planning," *Journal of Marketing*, 37 (January, 1973), 10–18.

RAO, V. R., "Changes in Explicit Information and Brand Perceptions," *Journal of Marketing Research*, 9 (May, 1972), 209–13.

RITCHIE, J. R. B., "Structuring the Leisure Market—A Multivariate Analysis," *Decision Sciences*, 7 (July, 1976), 547–61.

Conjoint Analysis and Related Methods

GREEN, P. E., "Multivariate Procedures in the Study of Attitudes and Status Impressions," *Social Science Research*, 2 (December, 1973), 353–69.

GREEN, P. E., "On the Design of Choice Experiments Involving Multifactor Alternatives," *Journal of Consumer Research*, 1 (September, 1974), 61–68.

GREEN, P. E., and F. J. CARMONE, "Evaluation of Multiattribute Alternatives: Additive versus Configural Utility Measurement," *Decision Sciences*, 5 (April, 1974), 164–81.

GREEN, P. E., and V. R. RAO, "Conjoint Measurement for Quantifying Judgmental Data," *Journal of Marketing Research*, 8 (August, 1971), 355–63.

GREEN, P. E., and YORAM WIND, "New Way to Measure Consumers' Judgments," *Harvard Business Review*, 53 (July–August, 1975), 107–17.

GREEN, P. E., YORAM WIND, and A. K. JAIN, "Preference Measurement of Item Collections," *Journal of Marketing Research*, 9 (November, 1972), 371–77.

HAUSER, J. R., and G. L. URBAN, "A Normative Methodology for Modeling Consumer Response to Innovation," *Operations Research*, in press.

JOHNSON, R. M., "Tradeoff Analysis of Consumer Values," *Journal of Marketing Research*, 11 (May, 1974), 121–27.

SCOTT, J. E., and PETER WRIGHT, "Modeling An Organizational Buyer's Product Evaluation Strategy: Validity and Procedural Considerations," *Journal of Marketing Research*, 13 (August, 1976), 211–24.

WESTWOOD, DICK, TONY LUNN, and DAVID BEAZLEY, "The Tradeoff Model and Its Extensions," *Journal of the Market Research Society*, 16 (July, 1974), 227–41.

MULTIVARIATE METHODS

Multivariate techniques were discussed in Chapters 9 through 13. In addition, Chapters 16 and 17 dealt with a number of industry applications that involved various kinds of multivariate analysis. References to these chapters are organized under the headings: General Sources; Regression Analysis; Experimental Designs, Including the Analysis of Variance and Covariance; Other Methods for Analyzing Dependence Structures; and Factor Analysis and Clustering Methods.

General Sources

AAKER, D. A., *Multivariate Analysis in Marketing: Theory and Application*. Belmont, Calif.: Wadsworth Publishing Company, Inc., 1971.

DAY, R. L., and L. J. PARSONS, *Marketing Models: Quantitative Applications.* Scranton, Pa.: Intext Educational Publishers, 1971.

EHRENBERG, A. S. C., *Data Reduction.* London: John Wiley & Sons, Inc., 1975.

FITZROY, P. T., *Analytical Methods for Marketing Management.* Maidenhead, England: McGraw-Hill Book Co. Ltd., 1976.

GREEN, P. E., with contributions by J. D. Carroll, *Analyzing Multivariate Data.* Hinsdale, Ill.: Dryden Press, 1978.

GREEN, P. E., with contributions by J. D. CARROLL, *Mathematical Tools for Applied Multivariate Analysis.* New York: Academic Press, Inc., 1976.

KOTLER, PHILIP, *Marketing Decision Making: A Model Building Approach.* New York: Holt, Rinehart and Winston, Inc., 1971.

MASSY, W. F., D. B. MONTGOMERY, and D. G. MORRISON, *Stochastic Models of Buying Behavior.* Cambridge, Mass.: MIT Press, 1970.

MYERS, J. H., and JONATHAN GUTMAN, "How to Analyze Consumer Behavior," *Journal of Advertising Research*, 15 (December, 1975), 19–26.

PARSONS, L. J., and R. L. SCHULTZ, *Marketing Models and Econometric Research.* New York: North-Holland Publishing Company, 1976.

SHETH, J. N., "Multivariate Analysis in Marketing," *Journal of Advertising Research*, 10 (February, 1970), 29–39.

WILSON, E. J., "Computational Segmentation in the Context of Multivariate Statistics and Survey Analysis," *Journal of the Market Research Society*, 16 (April, 1974), 108–26.

Regression Analysis

AAKER, D. A., and G. S. DAY, "A Recursive Model of Communication Processes," in D. A. Aaker, ed., *Multivariate Analysis in Marketing: Theory and Application.* Belmont, Calif.: Wadsworth Publishing Company, Inc., 1971.

BASS, F. M., "A Simultaneous Equation Regression Study of Advertising and Sales of Cigarettes," *Journal of Marketing Research*, 6 (August, 1969), 291–300.

BASS, F. M., and L. J. PARSONS, "Simultaneous Equation Regression Analyses of Sales and Advertising," *Applied Economics*, 1 (April, 1969), 103–24.

BASS, F. M., and D. R. WITTINK, "Pooling Issues and Methods in Regression Analysis with Examples in Marketing Research," *Journal of Marketing Research*, 12 (November, 1975), 414–25.

BECKWITH, N. E., and M. W. SASIENI, "Criteria for Market Segmentation Studies," *Management Science*, 22 (April, 1976), 892–903.

CLAYCAMP, H. J., and L. E. LIDDY, "Prediction of New Product Performance: An Analytical Approach," *Journal of Marketing Research*, 6 (November, 1969), 414–20.

ESKIN, G. J., "A Case for Test Market Experiments," *Journal of Advertising Research*, 15 (April, 1975), 27–34.

GINTER, J. L., "An Experimental Investigation of Attitude Change and Choice of a New Brand," *Journal of Marketing Research*, 11 (February, 1974), 30–40.

LUCAS, H. C., C. D. WEINBERG, and K. W. CLOWES, "Sales Response as a Function of Territorial Potential and Sales Representative Workload," *Journal of Marketing Research*, 12 (August, 1975), 298–305.

MORRISON, D. G., "Regression with Discrete Dependent Variables: The Effect on R^2," *Journal of Marketing Research*, 19 (August, 1972), 338–40.

MORRISON, D. G., "Reliability of Tests: A Technique Using the 'Regression to the Mean' Fallacy," *Journal of Marketing Research*, 10 (February, 1973), 91–93.

NYSTROM, HARRY, HANS TAMSONS, and ROBERT THAMS, "An Experiment in Price Generalization and Discrimination," *Journal of Marketing Research*, 12 (May, 1975), 177–81.

PASOLD, P. W., "The Effectiveness of Various Modes of Sales Behavior in Different Markets," *Journal of Marketing Research*, 12 (May, 1975), 171–76.

PETERSON, R. A., "Trade Area Analysis Using Trend Surface Mapping," *Journal of Marketing Research*, 11 (August, 1974), 338–42.

PRASAD, V. K., and L. W. RING, "Measuring Sales Effects of Some Marketing Mix Variables and Their Interactions," *Journal of Marketing Research*, 13 (November, 1976), 391–96.

STOBAUGH, R. B., and P. L. TOWNSEND, "Price Forecasting and Strategic Planning: The Case of Petrochemicals," *Journal of Marketing Research*, 12 (February, 1975), 19–29.

TURNER, R. E., and J. C. WIGINTON, "Advertising Expenditure Trajectories: An Empirical Study for Filter Cigarettes 1953–1965," *Decision Sciences*, 7 (July, 1976), 496–509.

WILDT, A. R., "Multi-firm Analysis of Competitive Decision Variables," *Journal of Marketing Research*, 11 (February, 1974), 50–62.

WILDT, A. R., "On Evaluation: Market Segmentation Studies and the Properties of R^2," *Management Science*, 22 (April, 1976), 904–8.

WINTER, F. W., "A Laboratory Experiment of Individual Attitude Response to Advertising Exposure," *Journal of Marketing Research*, 10 (May, 1973), 130–40.

Experimental Design, Including the Analysis of Variance and Covariance

ANDERSON, E. E., "The Effectiveness of Retail Price Reductions: A Comparison of Alternative Expressions of Price," *Journal of Marketing Research*, 11 (August, 1974), 327–30.

BANKS, SEYMOUR, *Experimentation in Marketing* (New York: McGraw-Hill Book Company, 1965).

BARROW, L. C., JR., "On Methods: New Uses of Covariance Analysis," *Journal of Advertising Research*, 7 (December, 1967), 49–54.

BETTMAN, J., NOEL CAPON, and R. J. LUTZ, "Cognitive Algebra in Multi-Attribute Attitude Models," *Journal of Marketing Research*, 12 (May, 1975), 151–64.

BUSCH, PAUL, and D. T. WILSON, "An Experimental Analysis of a Salesman's Expert and Referent Bases of Social Power in the Buyer–Seller Dyad," *Journal of Marketing Research*, 13 (February, 1976), 3–11.

CAPON, NOEL, and J. U. FARLEY, "The Impact of Message on Direct Mail Response," *Journal of Advertising Research*, 16 (October, 1976), 69–75.

CHEVALIER, MICHEL, "Increase in Sales Due to In-Store Display," *Journal of Marketing Research*, 12 (November, 1975), 426–31.

Cox, K. K., and B. M. Enis, *Experimentation for Marketing Decisions* (Scranton, Pa.: International Textbook Company, 1969).

Craig, C. S., Brian Sternthal, and Clark Leavitt, "Advertising Wearout: An Experimental Analysis," *Journal of Marketing Research*, 13 (November, 1976), 365–72.

Curhan, R. C., "The Effects of Merchandising and Temporary Promotional Activities on the Sales of Fresh Fruits and Vegetables in Supermarkets," *Journal of Marketing Research*, 11 (August, 1974), 286–94.

Doyle, Peter, and Ian Fenwick, "Planning and Estimation in Advertising," *Journal of Marketing Research*, 12 (February, 1975), 1–6.

Ford, N. M., "Questionnaire Appearance and Response Rates in Mail Surveys," *Journal of Advertising Research*, 8 (September, 1968), 43–45.

Green, P. E., "On the Analysis of Interactions in Marketing Research Data," *Journal of Marketing Research*, 10 (November, 1973), 410–20.

Gross, Irwin, "How Many Ads Does It Pay to Pretest?" *Tenth Meeting of the ARF Operations Research Discussion Group* (New York: Advertising Research Foundation, March 10, 1964), pp. 1–18.

Holland, C. W., and D. W. Cravens, "Fractional Factorial Experimental Designs in Marketing Research," *Journal of Marketing Research*, 10 (August, 1973), 270–76.

Jessen, R. J., "A Switch-over Experimental Design to Measure Advertising Effect," *Journal of Advertising Research*, 1 (March, 1961), 15–22.

Kilbourne, W. E., "A Factorial Experiment on the Impact of Unit Pricing on Low-Income Consumers," *Journal of Marketing Research*, 11 (November, 1974), 453–55.

Lipstein, Benjamin, "The Design of Test Marketing Experiments," *Journal of Advertising Research*, 5 (December, 1965), 2–7.

Mazis, M. B., R. B. Settle, and D. C. Leslie, "Elimination of Phosphate Detergents and Psychological Reactance," *Journal of Marketing Research*, 10 (November, 1973), 390–95.

Nevin, J. R., "Laboratory Experiments for Estimating Consumer Demand: A Validation Study," *Journal of Marketing Research*, 11 (August, 1974), 261–68.

Olshavsky, R. W., and J. A. Miller, "Consumer Expectations, Product Performance, and Perceived Product Quality," *Journal of Marketing Research*, 9 (February, 1972), 19–21.

Winter, F. W., "The Effect of Purchase Characteristics on Postdecision Product Reevaluation," *Journal of Marketing Research*, 11 (May, 1974), 164–71.

Other Methods for Analyzing Dependence Structures

Automatic Interaction Detection and Related Methods

Assael, Henry, and A. M. Roscoe, Jr., "Approaches to Market Segmentation Analysis," *Journal of Marketing*, 40 (October, 1976), 67–76.

Doyle, Peter, and Ian Fenwick, "The Pitfalls of AID Analysis," *Journal of Marketing Research*, 12 (November, 1975), 408–13.

Farley, J. U., and L. W. Ring, "Empirical Specification of a Buyer Behavior Model," *Journal of Marketing Research*, 11 (February, 1974), 89–96.

GENSCH, D. H., and RICHARD STAELIN, "The Appeal of Buying Black," *Journal of Marketing Research*, 9 (May, 1972), 141–48.

GREEN, P. E., and F. J. CARMONE, "Segment Congruence Analysis: A Method for Analyzing Association among Alternative Bases of Market Segmentation," *Journal of Consumer Research*, 3 (March, 1977), 217–22.

GREEN, P. E., F. J. CARMONE, and D. P. WACHSPRESS, "On the Analysis of Qualitative Data in Marketing Research," *Journal of Marketing Research*, 14 (February, 1977), 52–59.

HENRY, W. A., "Cultural Values Do Correlate with Consumer Behavior," *Journal of Marketing Research*, 13 (May, 1976), 121–27.

NEWMAN, J. W., and R. A. WERBEL, "Multivariate Analysis of Brand Loyalty for Major Household Appliances," *Journal of Marketing Research*, 10 (November, 1973), 404–09.

Discriminant Analysis

ALBAUM, GERALD, and KENNETH BAKER, "The Sampling Problem in Validation of Multiple Discriminant Analysis," *Journal of the Market Research Society*, 18 (July, 1976), 158–61.

ANDERSON, W. T., and WILLIAM CUNNINGHAM, "Gauging Foreign Product Promotion," *Journal of Advertising Research*, 12 (February, 1972), 29–34.

BASS, F. M., and W. W. TALARZYK, "An Attitude Model for the Study of Brand Preference," *Journal of Marketing Research*, 9 (February, 1972), 93–96.

BUCKLIN, L. P., "Trade Area Boundaries: Some Issues in Theory and Methodology," *Journal of Marketing Research*, 8 (February, 1971), 30–37.

CRASK, M. R., and W. D. PERREAULT, JR., "Validation of Discriminant Analysis in Marketing Research," *Journal of Marketing Research*, 14 (February, 1977), 60–68.

DARDEN, WILLIAM, and W. D. PERREAULT, JR., "A Multivariate Analysis of Media Exposure and Vacation Behavior with Life Style Covariates," *Journal of Consumer Research*, 2 (September, 1975), 93–103.

DARDEN, WILLIAM, and FRED REYNOLDS, "Backward Profiling of Male Innovators," *Journal of Marketing Research*, 11 (February, 1974), 79–85.

ETGAR, MICHAEL, "The Effects of Administrative Control on Efficiency of Vertical Marketing Systems," *Journal of Marketing Research*, 13 (February, 1976), 12–24.

HUSTAD, THOMAS, and E. A. PESSEMIER, "Will the Real Consumer Activist Please Stand Up: An Examination of Consumers' Opinions about Marketing Practices," *Journal of Marketing Research*, 10 (August, 1973), 319–24.

JONES, F. L., "Cluster Analysis and Market Segmentation: A Note on Other Techniques with An Illustration from Urban Sociology," *Journal of the Market Research Society*, 14 (April, 1972), 124–26.

LESSIG, V. P., and JOHN TOLLEFSON, "Market Segmentation through Numerical Taxonomy," *Journal of Marketing Research*, 8 (November, 1971), 480–87.

MASSY, W. F., "On Methods: Discriminant Analysis of Audience Characteristics," *Journal of Advertising Research*, 5 (March, 1965), 39–48.

MONTGOMERY, D. B., "New Product Distribution: An Analysis of Supermarket Buyer Decisions," *Journal of Marketing Research*, 12 (August, 1975), 255–64.

MORRISON, D. G., "On the Interpretation of Discriminant Analysis," *Journal of Marketing Research*, 6 (May, 1969), 156–63.

OSTLUND, L. E., "Identifying Early Buyers," *Journal of Advertising Research*, 12 (April, 1972), 25–30.

OSTLUND, L. E., "Perceived Innovation Attributes as Predictors of Innovativeness," *Journal of Consumer Research*, 1 (September, 1974), 23–29.

PETERSON, R. A., and VIJAY MAHAJAN, "Practical Significance and Partitioning Variance in Discriminant Analysis," *Decision Sciences*, 7 (October, 1976), 649–58.

ROBERTSON, T. S., and JOHN ROSSITER, "Children and Commercial Persuasion: An Attribution Theory Analysis," *Journal of Consumer Research*, 1 (June, 1974), 13–20.

SHUCHMAN, ABE, and P. C. RIESZ, "Correlates of Persuasibility: The Crest Case," *Journal of Marketing Research*, 12 (February, 1975), 7–11.

STANTON, JOHN, and JEFFREY LOWENHAR, "A Congruence Model of Brand Preference: A Theoretical and Empirical Study," *Journal of Marketing Research*, 11 (November, 1974), 427–33.

UHL, KENNETH, ROMAN ANDRUS, and LANCE POULSEN, "How Are Laggards Different? An Empirical Inquiry," *Journal of Marketing Research*, 7 (February, 1970), 51–54.

WOODSIDE, A. G., and JAMES CLOKEY, "Multi-attribute/Multi-brand Models," *Journal of Advertising Research*, 14 (October, 1974), 33–40.

Canonical Correlation and Multivariate Analysis of Variance and Covariance

ALPERT, M. I., "Personality and the Determinants of Product Choice," *Journal of Marketing Research*, 9 (February, 1972), 89–92.

ALPERT, M. I., and ROBERT PETERSON, "On the Interpretation of Canonical Analysis," *Journal of Marketing Research*, 9 (May, 1972), 187–92.

DARDEN, WILLIAM, and FRED REYNOLDS, "Shopping Orientation and Product Usage Rates," *Journal of Marketing Research*, 8 (November, 1971), 505–8.

ETGAR, MICHAEL, "Channel Domination and Countervailing Power in Distributive Channels," *Journal of Marketing Research*, 13 (August, 1976), 254–62.

FARLEY, J. U., and L. W. RING, "Empirical Specification of a Buyer Behavior Model," *Journal of Marketing Research*, 11 (February, 1974), 89–96.

FRANK, R. E., "Predicting New Product Segments," *Journal of Advertising Research*, 12 (June, 1972), 9–13.

FUTRELL, C. M., JOHN SWAN, and JOHN TODD, "Job Performance Related to Management Control Systems for Pharmaceutical Salesmen," *Journal of Marketing Research*, 13 (February, 1976), 25–33.

GREEN, P. E., M. H. HALBERT, and P. J. ROBINSON, "Canonical Analysis: An Exposition and Illustrative Application," *Journal of Marketing Research*, 3 (February, 1966), 32–39.

LAMBERT, Z. V., and R. M. DURAND, "Some Precautions in Using Canonical Analysis," *Journal of Marketing Research*, 12 (November, 1975), 468–75.

PERREAULT, W. D., JR., and W. R. DARDEN, "Unequal Cell Sizes in Marketing Experiments: Use of General Linear Hypothesis," *Journal of Marketing Research*, 12 (August, 1975), 333–42.

PRUDEN, H. O., and ROBERT PETERSON, "Personality and Performance Satisfaction of Industrial Salesmen," *Journal of Marketing Research*, 8 (November, 1971), 501–4.

SPARKS, D. L., and W. T. TUCKER, "A Multivariate Analysis of Personality and Product Use," *Journal of Marketing Research*, 8 (February, 1971), 67–70.

WIND, YORAM, and JOSEPH DENNY, "Multivariate Analysis of Variance in Research on the Effectiveness of TV Commercials," *Journal of Marketing Research*, 11 (May, 1974), 136–42.

Factor Analysis and Clustering Methods

Factor Analysis and Related Methods

BELK, RUSSELL, "An Exploratory Assessment of Situational Effects in Buyer Behavior," *Journal of Marketing Research*, 11 (May, 1974), 156–63.

BRUNO, A. V., "The Network Factor in TV Viewing," *Journal of Advertising Research*, 13 (October, 1973), 33–39.

BURGER, PHILIP, and BARBARA SCHOTT, "Can Private Brand Buyers Be Identified?" *Journal of Marketing Research*, 9 (May 1972), 219–22.

CHURCHILL, GILBERT, NEIL FORD, and ORVILLE WALKER, "Measuring the Job Satisfaction of Industrial Salesmen," *Journal of Advertising Research*, 11 (August, 1974), 254–60.

CUNNINGHAM, W. H., and WILLIAM CRISSY, "Market Segmentation by Motivation and Attitude," *Journal of Marketing Research*, 9 (February, 1972), 100–2.

DARDEN, WILLIAM, and WILLIAM PERREAULT, JR., "Identifying Interurban Shoppers: Multiproduct Purchase Patterns and Segmentation Profiles," *Journal of Marketing Research*, 13 (February, 1976), 51–60.

EHRENBERG, A. S. C., "On Methods: The Factor Analytic Search for Types," *Journal of Advertising Research*, 8 (March, 1968), 55–63.

EKELBLAD, F. A., and S. F. STASCH, "On Methods: Criteria in Factor Analysis," *Journal of Advertising Research*, 7 (September, 1967), 48–57.

FRANK, R. E., JAMES BECKNELL, and JAMES CLOKEY, "Television Program Types," *Journal of Marketing Research*, 8 (May, 1971), 204–11.

GATTY, RONALD, "Multivariate Analysis for Marketing Research," *Applied Statistics*, 15 (1966), 157–72.

GENSCH, DENNIS, and THOMAS GOLOB, "Testing the Consistency of Attribute Meaning in Empirical Concept Testing," *Journal of Marketing Research*, 12 (August, 1975), 348–54.

GENSCH, DENNIS, and B. RANGANATHAN, "Evaluation of Television Program Content for the Purpose of Promotional Segmentation," *Journal of Marketing Research*, 11 (November, 1974), 390–98.

HEELER, R. M., T. W. WHIPPLE, and T. P. HUSTAD, "Maximum Likelihood Factor Analysis of Attitude Data," *Journal of Marketing Research*, 14 (February, 1977), 42–51.

HUGHES, G. D., and J. L. GUERRERO, "Automobile Self-Congruity Models Re-examined," *Journal of Marketing Research*, 8 (February, 1971), 125–27.

McEWEN, W. J., and CLARK LEAVITT, "A Way to Describe TV Commercials," *Journal of Advertising Research*, 16 (December, 1976), 35–42.

MURPHY, J. R., "Responses to Parts of TV Commercials," *Journal of Advertising Research*, 11 (April, 1971), 34–38.

OLSHAVSKY, R. W., and JOHN SUMMERS, "A Study of the Role of Beliefs and Intentions in Consistency Restoration," *Journal of Consumer Research*, 1 (June, 1974), 63–70.

PETER, J. P., and LAWRENCE TARPEY, "A Comparative Analysis of Three Consumer Strategies," *Journal of Consumer Research*, 2 (June, 1975), 29–37.

PETERSON, R. A., and IVAN ROSS, "How to Name New Brands," *Journal of Advertisting Research*, 12 (December, 1972), 29–34.

PLUMMER, J. T., "Evaluating TV Commercial Tests," *Journal of Advertising Research*, 12 (October, 1972), 21–27.

RAO, V. R., "Taxonomy of Television Programs Based on Viewing Behavior," *Journal of Marketing Research*, 12 (August, 1975), 355–58.

SCHLINGER, M. J., "Cues on Q-Technique," *Journal of Advertising Research*, 9 (September, 1969), 53–60.

VAVRA, T. G., "Factor Analysis of Perceptual Change," *Journal of Marketing Research*, 9 (May, 1972), 193–99.

VILLANI, K. E., and YORAM WIND, "On the Usage of 'Modified' Personality Trait Measures in Consumer Research," *Journal of Consumer Research*, 2 (December, 1975), 223–28.

WIND, YORAM, P. E. GREEN, and A. K. JAIN, "Higher Order Factor Analysis in the Classification of Psychographic Variables," *Journal of the Market Research Society*, 15 (1973), 224–32.

ZIFF, RUTH, "Psychographics for Market Segmentation," *Journal of Advertising Research*, 11 (April, 1971), 3–9.

Cluster Analysis

CLAXTON, J. D., J. N. FRY, and BERNARD PORTIS, "A Taxonomy of Prepurchase Information Gathering Patterns," *Journal of Consumer Research*, 1 (December, 1974), 35–42.

DAY, G. S., and R. M. HEELER, "Using Cluster Analysis to Improve Marketing Experiments," *Journal of Marketing Research*, 8 (August, 1971), 340–47.

FORD, G. T., "Patterns of Competition in the Computer Industry: A Cluster Analytic Approach." Unpublished Ph.D. dissertation, State University of New York at Buffalo, 1973.

FRANK, R. E., and P. E. GREEN, "Numerical Taxonomy in Marketing Analysis: A Review Article," *Journal of Marketing Research*, 5 (February, 1968), 83–94.

GREEN, P. E., and F. J. CARMONE, "The Performance Structure of the Computer Market: A Multivariate Approach," *The Economic and Business Bulletin*, 20 (Fall, 1968), 1–11.

GREEN, P. E., F. J. CARMONE, and D. P. WACHSPRESS, "Consumer Segmentation via Latent Class Analysis," *Journal of Consumer Research*, 3 (December, 1976), 170–74.

GREEN, P. E., R. E. FRANK, and P. J. ROBINSON, "Cluster Analysis in Test Market Selection," *Management Science*, 13 (April, 1967), B-387–400.

GREENO, D. W., MONTROSE SOMMERS, and JEROME KERNAN, "Personality and Implicit Behavior Patterns," *Journal of Marketing Research*, 10 (February, 1973), 63–69.

JOYCE, TIMOTHY, and C. CHARRON, "Classifying Market Survey Respondents," *Applied Statistics*, 15 (November, 1966), 191–215.

KAMEN, J. M., "Quick Clustering," *Journal of Marketing Research*, 7 (May, 1970), 199–204.

KERNAN, J. B., "Choice Criteria, Decision Behavior and Personality," *Journal of Marketing Research*, 5 (May, 1968), 155–64.

KERNAN, J. B., and GRADY BRUCE, "The Socioeconomic Structure for an Urban Area," *Journal of Marketing Research*, 9 (February, 1972), 15–18.

LANDON, E. L., "Self Concept, Ideal Self Concept, and Consumer Purchase Intentions," *Journal of Consumer Research*, 1 (September, 1974), 44–51.

LEHMANN, DONALD, "Some Alternatives to Linear Factor Analysis for Variable Grouping Applied to Buyer Behavior Variables," *Journal of Marketing Research*, 11 (May, 1974), 206–13.

LESSIG, V. P., and JOHN TOLLEFSON, "Market Segmentation through Numerical Taxonomy," *Journal of Marketing Research*, 8 (November, 1971), 480–87.

MONTGOMERY, D. B., and ALVIN SILK, "Clusters of Consumer Interests and Opinion Leaders' Spheres of Influence," *Journal of Marketing Research*, 8 (August, 1971), 317–21.

MORRISON, B. J., and R. C. SHERMAN, "Who Responds to Sex in Advertising?" *Journal of Advertising Research*, 12 (April, 1972), 15–19.

MORRISON, D. G., "Measurement Problems in Cluster Analysis," *Management Science*, 13 (August, 1967), B-775–80.

MYERS, J. G., and F. M. NICOSIA, "New Empirical Directions on Market Segmentation." Paper presented at the American Marketing Association Annual Meeting, Washington, D.C., 1967.

MYERS, J. G., and F. M. NICOSIA, "On the Study of Consumer Typologies," *Journal of Marketing Research*, 5 (May, 1968), 182–93.

NICOSIA, F. M., and J. G. MYERS, "Cognitive Structures, Latent Class Models and the Leverage Index." Paper presented at the American Association of Public Opinion Research National Conference, Santa Barbara, California, May, 1968.

SETHI, S. P., "Comparative Cluster Analysis for World Markets," *Journal of Marketing Research*, 8 (August, 1971), 348–54.

SEXTON, D. E., JR., "A Cluster Analytic Approach to Market Response Functions," *Journal of Marketing Research*, 11 (February, 1974), 109–14.

Indexes

SUBJECT INDEX